# The Electronic Media

# The Electronic Media

## An Introduction to the Profession

❑

### Peter B. Orlik
CENTRAL MICHIGAN UNIVERSITY

## Allyn and Bacon
Boston London Toronto Sydney Tokyo Singapore

To my media colleagues

who inspired this project;

and to

My loving wife, who inspires me.

Series Editor:                      Stephen P. Hull
Series Editorial Assistant:         Amy Capute
Production Administrator:           Marjorie Payne
Editorial-Production Service:       Grace Sheldrick,
                                      Wordsworth Associates
Cover Administrator:                Linda Dickinson
Composition Buyer:                  Linda Cox
Manufacturing Buyer:                Louise Richardson
Text Designer:                      David Kelley Design

**Library of Congress Cataloging-in-Publication Data**
Orlik, Peter B.
    The electronic media : an introduction to the profession  /  Peter
B. Orlik.
      p.   cm.
    Includes bibliographical references and index.
    ISBN 0-205-13032-1
    1. Mass media.  I. Title.
P90.074  1992
302.23—dc20                                              91-27748
                                                          CIP

Printed in the United States of America
10  9  8  7  6  5  4  3  2  1     97  96  95  94  93  92

*Photographs, graphics, and scripts provided courtesy of:*
p. 1: © Bob Daemmrich/The Image Works; p. 4: Thomas G. Tofty and Shari Wolk, the American Medical Association; p. 9: *Broadcasting* Magazine; p. 12: John I. Taylor, Zenith Electronics Corporation; p. 18: J. B. Fohr, FMR Associates, Inc., Tucson, Arizona. EARS is a trademark of FMR Associates, Inc.; p. 19: Per Mar Research, Davenport, Iowa; p. 21: © Susan Van Etten/Photo Edit; p. 31: John Stevens, VOA; p. 35: ROHN Photo; p. 39: Lisa O'Hara, Conifer Telecommunications Products; p. 40: Radiation Systems, Inc., SatCom Technologies Division Model 280K; p. 42: Hughes Communications, Inc.; p. 46: ©Tony Freeman/Photo Edit; p. 51: VIDEOpal® is a registered trademark of General Instrument Corporation; p. 55: John I. Taylor, Zenith Electronics Corporation; p. 57: C-SPAN, photo by Paul Potera; p. 62: VideoCipher® is a registered trademark of General Instrument Corporation; p. 64: Blockbuster Video; p. 68: Neil J. Kirby; p. 79: Farm

*Photo credits continue on p. 491, which should be considered a continuation of the copyright page.*

# BRIEF CONTENTS

List of Professional Profiles   xi

List of Illustrations   xii

Preface   xvii

### SECTION ONE • The Big Picture   1

1. Bringing Mass Media into Focus   1
2. Subdividing the Electronic Landscape   21
3. Industry Dichotomies   46
4. Associated Enterprises   68

### SECTION TWO • Chronicles   99

5. Technological Maturation   99
6. Legal Legacies   127
• Benchmarks   162
7. Radio Operational History   169
8. Television Operational History   201
• Benchmarks   237
9. Noncommercial and International Adventures   241
• Benchmarks   272

### SECTION THREE • Professional Perspectives   277

10. Creative and Performance Functions   277
11. Facilitative Functions   317
12. Directive Functions   357
13. Evaluative and Analytical Functions   400

### SECTION FOUR • Sneak Preview   441

14. Toward the New Millennium   441
15. Cueing Up Your Career   463

Appendix   468

Endnotes   471

Index   481

# Contents

List of Professional Profiles                  xi

List of Illustrations                          xii

Preface                                        xvii

SECTION ONE

## The Big Picture   1

**1. Bringing Mass Media into Focus**          1
  Clarifying the Communication Task       1
  Communications as Communication
    Extender                          5
  Achieving Mass Communication            6
  Comparing Delivery Systems              10
  Key Nonmass Media                       13
  Tuning in the Electronic Mass Media     14
  Facing One-Way Realities                16
  Chapter Flashback                       19
  Review Probes                           20
  Suggested Background Explorations       20

**2. Subdividing the Electronic**
  **Landscape**                               21
  Hanging in There: AM Radio               21
  Today's Audio Mainstream:
    FM Radio                          24
  Shortwaves and All Waves                 25
  Comparing Frequencies and
    Wavelengths                       29
  Television's Dual Spectrum               31
  Cable and Microwave Systems              33
  Associated Video Vehicles                36
  Keeping Technology in Perspective        41

  Chapter Flashback                       42
  Review Probes                           45
  Suggested Background Explorations       45

**3. Industry Dichotomies**                    46
  Broadcast/Nonbroadcast                  46
  Free/Pay                                49
  Commercial/Noncommercial                53
  Private/Publicly Held                   57
  Local/Network                           60
  Scrambled/Unscrambled                   62
  Home Delivery/Take-Out                  64
  The Dichotomy Dynamic                   65
  Chapter Flashback                       65
  Review Probes                           66
  Suggested Background Explorations       66

**4. Associated Enterprises**                  68
  Advertising Agencies                    68
  Public Relations Firms                  71
  Audio Recording Companies               77
  Television and Film Producers           82
  News Services                           85
  Audience Measurement Services           87
  Telephone Companies                     91

Electronics Manufacturers 94
Chapter Flashback 96

Review Probes 97
Suggested Background Explorations 97

S E C T I O N   T W O

# Chronicles 99

**5. Technological Maturation** **99**
The Roots of Radio 100
Radio Telephony Blossoms into
   Radio 104
Radio Comes of Age 109
The Video Venture Begins 113
Television Becomes a Mass Medium 118
The Cable Option 122
Chapter Flashback 124
Review Probes 126
Suggested Background Explorations 126

**6. Legal Legacies** **127**
Early Precedents 127
The Rules of the Game Solidify 133
Wars of Many Kinds 137
Postwar Scrutiny 141
Midcentury Corrections 145
More Issues, More Media 150
The Dynamics of Deregulation 156
Chapter Flashback 160
Review Probes 160
Suggested Background Explorations 161
**Benchmarks** **162**

**7. Radio Operational History** **169**
Stumbling on a Moneymaker 169
Radio's Glory Years 177
Postwar Perplexities 185
(Mostly) Profitable Fragmentation 191
Chapter Flashback 199
Review Probes 200
Suggested Background
   Explorations 200

**8. Television Operational History** **201**
Big Excitement from Small Pictures 201
Mixed Metaphor: The Freeze Heats
   Up an Industry 205
Regroupings 210
TV's Young Adulthood 214
More Expansion and Tougher
   Choices 222
Competition Unlimited 230
Chapter Flashback 234
Review Probes 235
Suggested Background
   Explorations 236
**Benchmarks** **237**

**9. Noncommercial and International**
**Adventures** **241**
Orienting Definitions 241
The Postponed Promise 242
New Support, New Missions 247
Raised to Chase Dollars 253
External Ventures—Private
   Shortwave 255
Voice of America Development 258
Surrogate Services 263
Armed Forces Radio Television
   Services Expeditions 266
Satellites and the Global Village 266
Chapter Flashback 269
Review Probes 271
Suggested Background
   Explorations 271
**Benchmarks** **272**

# Professional Perspectives   277

**10. Creative and Performance**
    **Functions**                                277
    Disc and Video Jockeys                       277
    Talk Show Hosts                              281
    Newspersons                                  284
    Copywriters                                  289
    Art Directors and Designers                  295
    Feature Writers and Personalities            300
    Industrial Performers and
        Scripters                                308
    Music Suppliers                              312
    Chapter Flashback                            313
    Review Probes                                316
    Suggested Background
        Explorations                             316

**11. Facilitative Functions**                  317
    Audio and Video Engineers                    317
    Lighting Directors                           322
    Camera Operators, Videographers,
        and Cinematographers                     323
    Film and Tape Editors                        329
    Directors: Technical, Assistant,
        and Main                                 332
    Station/System Salespersons                  338
    Station Representatives                      343
    Program Salespersons (Syndicators)           347
    Promotions People                            350
    Production House Marketers                   352
    Chapter Flashback                            355
    Review Probes                                356
    Suggested Background
        Explorations                             356

**12. Directive Functions**                     357
    Program Directors                            357
    Sales Managers                               365
    General Managers                             368
    News Directors                               371
    Entertainment Producers                      378
    Creative Directors                           381
    Account Executives and Managers              385
    Media Services Executives                    388
    Owners                                       390
    Chapter Flashback                            397
    Review Probes                                398
    Suggested Background
        Explorations                             399

**13. Evaluative and Analytical**
    **Functions**                                400
    Regulators                                   400
    Communications Attorneys                     406
    Lobbyists and Other Influence
        Wielders                                 408
    Political and Public Relations
        Communicators                            411
    Critics and Commentators                     414
    Brokers and Financial Analysts               416
    Business Development Executives              421
    Consultants and Standards
        Officials                                425
    Librarians and Teachers                      430
    Chapter Flashback                            438
    Review Probes                                439
    Suggested Background
        Explorations                             439

# Sneak Preview   441

**14. Toward the New Millennium**               441
    Video Thrusts                                441
    Audio Thrusts                                450
    Pending Legal Issues                         453

x

Operational Outlooks 457
Our Global Profession 459
Chapter Flashback 460
Review Probes 461
Suggested Background
  Explorations 462

**15. Cueing Up Your Career** 463
"Back to the Basics,"
by Frederick Jacobs 463

**Appendix** 468
Important Electronic Media
  Associations 468
Major Unions Active
  in the Electronic Media 470

**Endnotes** 471

**Index** 481

# LIST OF PROFESSIONAL
## PROFILES

John Kompas, President, Kompas/Biel & Associates, Inc.  37

Ron Herman, Vice-President, Marketing and Development, General Television Network  43

Wayne Hindmarsh, Sales Manager, Continental Cablevision Advertising  54

Gary Stevens, President, Gary Stevens & Company Media Brokerage  59

Gerald Downey, Creative Director, Visual Services, Inc.  70

Robert Bradsell, Political Media Consultant  74

David Salzman, President, Lorimar Television  83

John Dimling, Executive Vice-President, Nielsen Media Research  88

Denise Gallant, Advanced Systems Planner, The Chyron Group  95

Alan Campbell, Attorney and Partner, Dow, Lohnes & Albertson  155

Ruth Otte, President and Chief Operating Officer, The Discovery Channel  228

Frank Scott, Director, Voice of America (VOA) Europe  261

Phil Tower, Midday Show Host, WOOD-AM/FM  282

Allison Payne, News Anchor, WGN-TV  286

Valerie Voss, Senior Meteorologist and Weather Department Manager, CNN  290

Lisa Goich, Copywriter, Bruce & Chato, Inc.  292

George Lois, Chairman, Chief Executive Officer, and Creative Director, Lois/GGK Advertising  301

Peter Michael Goetz, Television, Film, and Stage Actor  305

Kevin Campbell, Manager, AV Communications, Dow Corning Corporation  310

Michael Anderson, National Sales Representative, Firstcom/Music House  314

Charles Nairn, Audio Engineer and President, Com Tec, Inc.  320

Pattie Wayne, Videographer, KXAS-TV  326

Philip Sgriccia, Editor/Owner, Trapline Productions  330

James Gartner, Commercial Director, Gibson/Lefebvre/Gartner  334

Valerie Tuttle, General Sales Manager, WWJ/WJOI  344

Cynthia Braunlich, Group Research Manager, Petry Television, Inc.  346

Gary Lico, Vice-President, Eastern Region, Columbia Pictures Television  349

Kris Kelly, Commercial Producer/Director, WKBD-TV  351

Arlene Lehmann, Vice-President Marketing, Magnetic North  353

Brad Fuhr, Program Director, WLTO-FM  358

Paul Boscarino, General Sales Manager, WOOD AM/FM  366

William Shearer, Vice-President and General Manager, KGFJ  369

Rick Sykes, Assignment Editor, WDIV-TV  374

Danielle Claman, Manager, Television Series Development, Aaron Spelling Productions  380

Roger Bodo, Group Creative Director, Intergroup Marketing and Promotions  383

Andrew Schmittdiel, Field Operations Director and Account Executive, DDB Needham Worldwide, Advertising  386

Jay Campbell, Broadcast Supervisor, W.B. Doner & Company Advertising  389

Thomas Elkins, Owner and General Manager, KNUI/KHUI  392

Ruth Whitmore, Owner and President, Whitmore Communications, Inc.  395

Patricia Diaz Dennis, Attorney and Former FCC Commissioner  402

Gerald Udwin, Washington Vice-President, Westinghouse Broadcasting Company, Inc.  409

Stephen Serkaian, Director, Democratic Press Office, Michigan House of Representatives  412

James Gammon, President, Gammon Media Brokers, Inc  417

Mary Kukowski, Media Analyst, Bear, Stearns & Co.  420

Don Peppers, Executive Vice-President, Business Development, Lintas: USA  423

Russell Mouritsen, Media Consultant  427
Susan Hill, Vice-President, Library and Information Center, National Association of Broadcasters  431

Jay Rouman, High School Media Production Teacher  434
Louis Day, Media Professor, Louisiana State University  436 ♦

## LIST OF **ILLUSTRATIONS**

### Chapter 1

1–1    The Communication Loop  2
1–2    American Medical Association "Ashes to Ashes" Photoboard  4
1–3    *Broadcasting* Magazine Cover  9
1–4    Moviegoer Pie Charts  11
1–5    Typical Teletext 'Page'  12
1–6    Basic Broadcast Signal Transmittal  15
1–7    Cable Network (Nonbroadcast) Transmittal  16
1–8    Combined Broadcast/Nonbroadcast Transmittal  17
1–9    Hand-Held EARS Wireless Response Instrument  18
1–10   Focus Group Moderator at Work  19

### Chapter 2

2–1    Unmodulated Carrier Wave  22
2–2    Amplitude Modulation  22
2–3    Frequency Modulation  25
2–4    Sky Wave Ionospheric Bounce  26
2–5    AM Nighttime Ground and Sky Wave Activity  27
2–6    FM/TV Direct Wave Coverage Possibilities  28
2–7    VOA Shortwave Antenna System  31
2–8    Microwave Relay Installation  35
2–9    MMDS (Wireless Cable) System  39
2–10   SMATV Antenna  40
2–11   DBS Windowsill Antenna  42

### Chapter 3

3–1    Electronic Media Dichotomies Pie Chart  47
3–2    Cable System Expenditures in 1984 and 1988  50
3–3    Addressable PPV Device  51
3–4    On-Screen Teletext Index  55

3–5     C-SPAN I Transmission   57
3–6     Satellite-to-Home Signal Descrambler   62
3–7     VCR/Pay Cable Penetration   63
3–8     Video Store Interior   64


## Chapter 4

4–1     GTE "Fingerpainting" Photoboard   72
4–2     Worker's Compensation Script   73
4–3     Edison Tinfoil Cylinder Phonograph   77
4–4     Columbia Grafonola Disc Phonograph   78
4–5     Classic Wurlitzer Jukebox   79
4–6     Audio Recording Control Room   81
4–7     AP Wire Machine   86
4–8     Nielsen Viewers in Profile   91
4–9     Arbitron Radio Market Report   92
4–10    Fiber Optic Strand   93


## Chapter 5

5–1     Nathan Stubblefield   101
5–2     Reginald Fessenden at Brant Rock   102
5–3     Lee De Forest in 1958   103
5–4     KDKA Transmitter Room   106
5–5     Detroit's 8MK Staff in 1920   107
5–6     Tuning a Crystal Receiving Set   108
5–7     De Forest 1925 Radio Receiver   110
5–8     Edwin Armstrong and His Portable Radio   111
5–9     Radio Receiver Sales   112
5–10    Laying the Transatlantic Cable   113
5–11    Mechanical Television System Transmitter   116
5–12    Mechanical Television System Receiver   117
5–13    Early RCA Videotape Recorder   121
5–14    John Walson, Cable Pioneer   123
5–15    GTE Spacenet Satellite   125


## Chapter 6

6–1     The *Titanic*   128
6–2     Guglielmo Marconi Late in Life   129
6–3     ASCAP's Founders   131
6–4     Secretary of Commerce Herbert Hoover   132
6–5     Bruno Richard Hauptmann   137
6–6     An Early BMI Directors' Meeting   138
6–7     FCC Chairmen James Lawrence Fly and Frank McNinch   140
6–8     ABC Founder Edward Noble   142
6–9     Senator Joseph McCarthy   144
6–10    Leonard Goldenson   146
6–11    Dean Roscoe Barrow   147

6–12    Charles Van Doren    148
6–13    Lar Daly on the Air    149


## Chapter 7

7–1     Dancing in Detroit to Experimental Radio    170
7–2     1928 Radio Studio    173
7–3     Atwater Kent 1930 Radio Receiver    175
7–4     FDR, the "Radio President"    176
7–5     *The Lone Ranger* Cast Rehearsing    177
7–6     Edgar Bergen and Charlie McCarthy    180
7–7     Orson Welles in 1938    181
7–8     Father Coughlin Greets Babe Ruth    182
7–9     Air-King Wire Recorder    185
7–10    Bing Crosby with his Audiotape Machine    186
7–11    Number of On-Air U.S. Radio Stations, 1920–1990    190
7–12    WXYZ Deejays    192
7–13    Underground Radio Innovator Dick Kernen    195
7–14    FM Share of Audience    197


## Chapter 8

8–1     David Sarnoff at the 1939 World's Fair    202
8–2     1945 Telecast of "The Perfect Alibi"    204
8–3     Newscaster John Cameron Swayze    206
8–4     The Pat 'n' Johnny Show    208
8–5     TV Comedian Ernie Kovacs    210
8–6     Edward R. Murrow    210
8–7     The Kennedy/Nixon Debates    215
8–8     Growth in Advertising Media Expenditures    217
8–9     1964 "Daisy Petals" Political Spot    218
8–10    Spiro Agnew on the Tube    221
8–11    Richard Nixon Confronting Broadcasters    224
8–12    Where People Got News    224
8–13    C-SPAN Cameraperson    226
8–14    LPTV Antenna    227
8–15    Television Stations Operating in the United States, 1946–1990    231
8–16    United Artists Cablesystems PPV Logo    233


## Chapter 9

9–1     Rural Students Listening to a 1930 Instructional Broadcast    243
9–2     Ohio School of the Air 1930–1931 Schedule    244
9–3     FCC Commissioner Frieda Hennock    246
9–4     Scope of MPATI    248
9–5     1960's Instructional Television Production    250
9–6     NBC's John Royal    256

9–7    VOA News Operations Center   259
9–8    VOA Satellite Dishes   260
9–9    CNN *World Report* Frame   268

## Chapter 10

10–1    Radio Format Popularity Chart   280
10–2    TV Anchor Team   285
10–3    *San Francisco Examiner* "Babble" Commercial   288
10–4    Loveland Ski Resort Radio Spot   294
10–5    TCP "Wasp Attack" TV Script   295
10–6    Advertising Agency Salaries   296
10–7    Sacred Heart Storyboard   298–299
10–8    KNET Logo   300
10–9    WPVI-TV Logo   300
10–10   TVQ Logo   306
10–11   TVQ Program Report for *Cheers*   307
10–12   Corporate Video Crisis   311

## Chapter 11

11–1    Maintenance Engineer with Calibration Instruments   318
11–2    Setting Lights for an In-Studio Production   322
11–3    Dura Soft "Circus" Photoboard   324
11–4    ENG Mobile Systems, Inc., Van   328
11–5    Cost-Per-Thousand (CPM) Trends   341
11–6    WOOD Radio Rate Card   342

## Chapter 12

12–1    Arbitron Format List   360
12–2    Z-Format Hot Clock   362
12–3    Trends in Cable Operations Expenditures   372
12–4    Sigma Delta Chi Photoboard   376
12–5    Average Broadcast News Salaries   377

## Chapter 13

13–1    Best Ten TV Advertising Revenue Markets   416
13–2    Virginia Department of Economic Development Photoboards   426
13–3    *Married . . . with Children* Cast   430

## Chapter 14

14–1    HDTV/NTSC Comparisons   442
14–2    Eureka 95 Image   443
14–3    ACTV-2 Off-Screen Image   444

xvi

14–4    Household Media Penetration   446
14–5    Hughes HS601 High-Power DBS Satellite   449
14–6    REQUEST TELEVISION Logo   458
14–7    Farmer Tuning to 1920s Radio   460

## Chapter 15

15–1    Fred Jacobs   464
15–2    Weekly Reach of Radio by Band, 1990   466

# PREFACE

Welcome to the electronic media world! In formally introducing you to a subject to which you were informally oriented soon after your birth (if not before), this book unequivocally reflects four of the author's fundamental beliefs.

*Belief number one* is that the electronic media are serviced and directed by true professionals. A *profession* is usually thought of as an educated calling to which someone permanently devotes his or her working life. As we see in the following chapters, and in the personal profiles they contain, such devotion is a prerequisite to success in radio/television. Inevitably, our industry is marked by long hours, continuous training, substantial stress, and periodic personal risk. If you want a comparatively stable, predictable career, look elsewhere. If you want rapid change, unanticipated opportunities, and a zigzag career path that might lead from stations to advertising agencies, to government service, to marketing management and back again, a career in the electronic media may fill the bill. Contrary to popular belief, this is not a field for which you can train in six months or can even learn in six years. Instead, to devote yourself to a radio/television career is to devote yourself to a thirty- or forty-year internship—the completion of which is always just beyond the next big assignment or job change.

*Belief number two* is that electronic media careers are personally gratifying. Sometimes you can make a lot of money. But more often, you earn a comparatively modest living in which the limited financial returns are partially compensated for by the diversity of people and problems with which you are able to become involved. Some of the brightest, most industrious, most passionate, and most compassionate people on earth are involved in radio/television enterprises. Unfortunately, the industry also shelters some who are not. Part of the gratification you derive from being in this profession is discovering how to tell the difference—and learning to react accordingly. Because of their scope and intrusive place in our society, electronic media operations can make a fundamental impact on the way audiences see their world and themselves. If you can feel good about how you contributed to this vision, there are few more intense satisfactions.

*Belief number three* is that the electronic media now encompass much more than over-the-air broadcasting. As the title, *The Electronic Media,* implies and the text chapters demonstrate, an ever-expanding number of vehicles and careers are being established beyond the boundaries of the conventional radio or television station. Given the range of technologies now available, the delivery system (the hardware) is becoming less and less crucial. Much more important are the content we are able to disseminate via that system and whether that content possesses the capability to inspire, entertain, comfort, educate, and sell (not necessarily in that order). In the United States, at least, our profession did begin with local stations. But where it is going is much less clear. Technologically, local station are no longer the only avenue by which we can electronically communicate with our audiences. Some authorities would argue that stations are no longer even necessary in the accomplishment of that linking task. What is unequivocally required, however, is the ability to plan, design, target, and execute audiovisual messages so that they reach the right people efficiently, effectively, and in the most timely manner possible. Authentic members of our profession are well attuned to the fact that they are engaged in the practice of mass communication and not the broadcasting or cable 'biz.'

*Belief number four* is that you are reading this book to ascertain whether you wish to launch an electronic media career. Or, at least you are attempting to better understand how these media operate so as to put them to appropriate use in another profession as well as in your personal life. By the time you have completed the fifteen chapters that follow, you will have been exposed to information, issues, and people that should serve either or both of these purposes.

tent and those who technically package and sell it. You also learn how managerial roles are apportioned and are introduced to the men and women who evaluate and analyze our field.

Finally, Section Four, "Sneak Preview," isolates trends and speculations for the future. Given the accelerating events in the electronic media, you may find that some of these speculations have already come true or been disproved. Either way, you will have been exposed to how timelocked any book becomes when it attempts to keep up with change in the electronic media.

## Plan of the Book

Section One of *The Electronic Media,* "The Big Picture," introduces you to the entire mass communication spectrum and to how the radio/television media specifically fit within this spectrum. You also learn about the forces that subdivide the electronic media themselves and become acquainted with the associated enterprises that are important to radio/television functioning.

Section Two, "Chronicles," provides the historical background necessary to comprehend why our profession is now the way it is. To make this information more digestible, it is divided into individual discussions of technological, legal, and radio and television operational evolution. A separate chapter on the development of noncommercial and international systems (Chapter 9) gives you a glimpse of these less publicized endeavors.

Section Three, "Professional Perspectives," then details the specific operations and responsibilities carried out by electronic media personnel. In Chapters 10, 11, 12, and 13, you are exposed to the tasks and issues facing professionals who create radio/television con-

## Special Features of *The Electronic Media*

*Professional Profiles.* No single author can provide you with the insights you need to begin to grasp the complexity of today's radio/television scene. Therefore, interspersed among the chapters are professional profiles composed by key individuals who hold vital positions throughout our industry. These media practitioners come from large and small enterprises. Some are persons relatively new to the field. Other profile authors have devoted more than a quarter-century to their calling. The twin commonalities binding them are a love of this profession and each person's demonstrated ability to succeed in it. Through their written profiles, these dedicated communicators have fashioned brief conversations with you, conversations intended to give you an accurate and unvarnished view of what is required to function effectively in our field today.

*CNN Connection.* Special CNN video signposts are scattered throughout the book. These boxed inserts highlight a segment of CNN video footage relevant to the chapter material under discussion.

## Instructor's Teaching Aids

*Instructor's Manual with Test Questions.* This includes a sample course syllabus, suggested projects, lecture and discussion topics, as well as essay and multiple choice questions.

*Computerized Test Bank.* More than 400 objective questions from the Instructor's Manual are also available in computerized form, compatible with either IBM or Macintosh systems.

*CNN Video Enhancers.* An important teaching and learning tool, this one-hour video is free to adopters of *The Electronic Media* and contains twenty separate segments from CNN that cover key electronic media issues, technologies, and operations. The video segments are arranged in chapter order and are keyed to the appropriate text discussions via brief boxed inserts.

## This Book's Ultimate Goal

The electronic media offer a wide range of "love it or leave it" career paths. This text will have succeeded if it helps each individual reader to decide whether loving or leaving is his or her more appropriate choice.

## Acknowledgments

First, and most obviously, thanks are extended to the dozens of media professionals who contributed profiles to *The Electronic Media.* Each contributor is a top practitioner in his or her own branch of our industry, and each took time from the intense scheduling pressures that are the hallmarks of our business to share personal insights with you, the reader. Any profession remains strong only when its veterans willingly give of their expertise in tutoring their successors. The profile authors in *The Electronic Media* have amply demonstrated such a willingness. Special gratitude is extended to Jay Rouman, who, in addition to composing his own pro-

file, lent his technical expertise to critiquing and improving Chapter 2; and to *Broadcasting* Magazine's John Eggerton for locating several antique photographs.

Thanks are also extended to Dr. B. R. Smith, chairman of Central Michigan University's Broadcast & Cinematic Arts Department, who provided the resource and clerical assistance essential to project completion. Additional appreciation is expressed to department administrative secretary Patti Hohlbein who, while providing secretarial support for a 300-student department, also made time for the flawless word-processing of this entire manuscript.

Gratitude is expressed as well to the following colleagues who reviewed portions of the manuscript, and made many valuable suggestions for its improvement: Don Agostino, Indiana University; Karen Buzzard, Northeastern University; Larry Collette, Michigan State University; Louis A. Day, Louisiana State University; Franklin Donaldson, University of North Carolina at Greensboro; John Doolittle, American University; John E. Fryman, Texas Technological University; Lincoln M. Furber, American University; Lynn Hinds, Pennsylvania State University; Don LeDuc, University of Wisconsin at Milwaukee; John Spalding, Wayne State University; Vernone Sparkes, Syracuse University; Sam Swan, University of Tennessee at Knoxville; James W. Welke, University of Central Florida.

I am likewise indebted to Steve Hull at Allyn and Bacon and to Grace Sheldrick of Wordsworth Associates for their editorial and book-production support and expertise. Writing a text is never an easy endeavor, but it is a manageable one when an author is supported by skilled and enthusiastic editors.

Finally, special acknowledgment and love are extended to my wife, Chris, and our two children, Darcy and Blaine. This text was written atop my normal teaching responsibilities, which meant that family life had to suffer so that "author life" could proceed. Their support and encouragement never faltered, and for this I am deeply grateful.

C H A P T E R    **1**

# Bringing Mass Media into Focus

❏ *Before we can learn about the careers and issues pertaining to our increasingly complex profession, we should establish the boundaries by which that profession is defined. In the case of the electronic mass media, these boundaries are determined as much by a task as by a series of delivery systems. So let us examine the task first.*

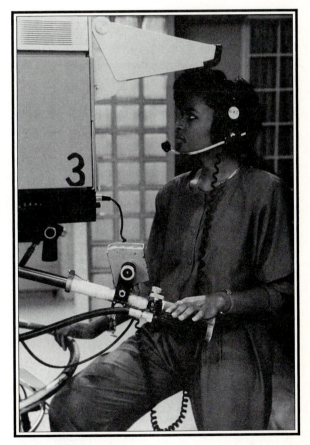

## Clarifying the Communication Task

We have all heard the term *communication*. Likewise, we have all been exposed to the concept of *mass communication*. But exactly what do we mean by these terms? Where does one term leave off and the other begin? Are they mutually inclusive or mutually exclusive? We might say, for example, that the electronic mass media are vehicles for achieving mass communication; but this statement gets us nowhere if we do not understand what such achievement entails.

### A Communication Definition

As a first step in making sense of all of this, let us begin with the following basic presumption:

Communication among human beings is the process of conveying and exchanging information, assertions, and attitudes.

Because this is not a book on horticulture or animal husbandry, we are not interested in how plants or animals converse. Nor are we computer scientists plotting interactions between banks of silicon chips or psychiatrists seeking to explain how people relate to their inner selves. Instead, we are simply (or not so simply) concerned with what happens in the establishment of linkages *between people,* or, as the definition puts it, "among human beings."

Also, we must realize that such communication is an ongoing *process;* it is not the flipping of a switch or a one-way burst of data, but an ongoing stream of interactions to which both the initiator and receptor of the initial cue contribute. Every successful communicator discovers that receivers are more than passive sponges who merely soak up data. Rather, these receivers are communicators in their own right who might respond in a variety of ways to the apprehended message. In fact, the process of human communication is so circular, so ongoing, that it is sometimes difficult to detect which party initially set the

activity into motion. Even though we tend to refer to the initiating stimulus as a *message,* and to the receiver's response as *feedback,* (see Figure 1–1), it is often difficult to distinguish one from the other.

For example, little Billy tells Johnny to "buzz off" or "get out of my face." Is this the initial *message* or is it *feedback* in response to a perceived gesture or verbal comment from Johnny? A third party might not be able to figure this out and, perhaps, neither will the two children. Johnny's earlier gesture or comment may not have even been directed to Billy. Consequently, what Billy intended as *feedback* is misinterpreted by Johnny as an unfriendly introductory *message.* Communication is a *process,* a loop, the beginning and end of which may defy easy identification.

As this example suggests, the *transmitting* function of communication can be both verbal and nonverbal. We communicate with posture, gestures, touches, and facial expressions as well as with aural sounds and words in order to bridge the physical and/or psychological distance between people. Sometimes, as in the case of a friendly wave across a parking lot or the typical telephone conversation, we rely exclusively on either nonverbal or verbal communication. More frequently, our

**Figure 1–1**

The communication loop

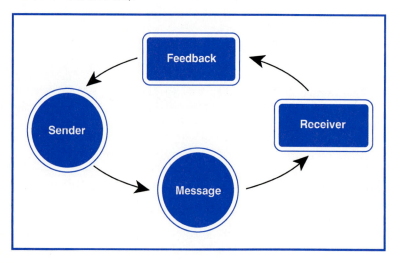

linkage with another person is a blending of these two modes. Usually, such a combination strengthens the communication bond. But when the verbal seems to contradict the nonverbal—when the words say "It's true" while the eyes shift away—the transmission becomes more complicated to decode, though no less meaningful.

## Communication Content

Whether verbal, nonverbal, or both, our messages transmit three categories of content, and they are often conveyed simultaneously. As our definition indicates, this content trio consists of (1) information, (2) assertions, and (3) attitudes.

Taken by itself, *information* is simple conveyance of fact. "The flight will leave at 9:35." "Elvis Presley is dead." "Lima beans make me puke." These are three seemingly straightforward pieces of knowledge that one person might share with another. Yet each item, under certain circumstances, may also be perceived as a debatable *assertion*. Coming from a harried ticket agent, the promise that the flight will leave at 9:35 may be taken more as hope than certainty, particularly by passengers who have already been twice delayed. Elvis probably is departed, but that is arguable conjecture to the faithful who believe they saw him in a Kalamazoo Burger King. And despite your distaste for lima beans, your physician may disagree with your contention that they possess the chemical capacity inevitably to make you nauseous. So, depending on the receiver of the communication, each of these messages may be perceived, not as objective information, but as subjective assertion.

Finally, *attitude* also comes into play in any human communication transaction because it is impossible for people either to send or receive a message without encasing it in an opinion-suggesting wrapping. People are not robots. They make evaluative judgments on every subject they encounter and look for signs of such judgments in the transmissions of other people. If such a sign is difficult to detect, they might conclude that the other person is either devious or insensitive. Thus, the ticket agent's scrupulously emotionless recitation of the flight's alleged departure time may be seen as a deliberate cover-up by some people and as cold indifference by others. The recited fact (or assertion) of Elvis's demise will carry with it an inevitable suggestion about the reciter's feeling toward that celebrity/condition. And the biochemical slang chosen to describe the lima beans' effect will convey as much about the speaker's appraisal of the listener's breeding as it does about the vegetable's impact. (See Figure 1–2.)

The remoteness of *written* words on a page may make an assertion seem like unadorned fact and disguise the attitude behind it. *Spoken* communication, however, carries many more judgmental clues. Tone and pitch of voice, length of pauses and speed of delivery, eye contact, posture, facial expression, and gestures all carry intended or accidental hints as to the feelings and beliefs that accompany and motivate the statement. These hints may be distortive or inaccurate, but they will be taken into account nonetheless. Inevitably, interpersonal communication is *expected* to convey information, assertions, and attitudes. If a given message seems devoid of one of these factors, we as receivers are likely to supply that factor from our own storehouse of presumptions gathered from past human interactions.

## Communication as Social Process Carrier

Another way to define the communication task is to assert that "communication is the carrier of the social process." This is certainly a task statement, but it doesn't tell us much unless we know what that conveyed social process involves. To pioneering communication theorist Harold Lasswell, the phenomenon consists of three major components: "(1) the surveillance of the environment; (2) the correlation of the parts of society in respond-

**Figure 1–2**

What elements of this public service message are information? Assertion?
Attitude?

## American Medical Association

Campaign: Anti-Smoking
Film Title: "Ashes to Ashes"
Film Length: :30

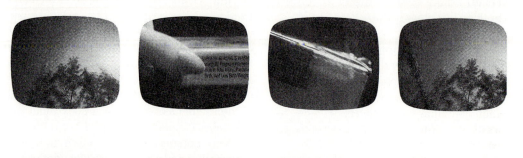

V.O.: Sooner or later everyone
quits smoking,

one way,                    or another.                    For your health from the
                                                            American Medical
                                                            Association

ing to the environment; (3) the transmission of the social heritage from one generation to the next."[1] The first two elements can be accomplished by any living entity. The third separates human beings from lower life forms and therefore constitutes the crucial ingredient of the human communication task.

In a plant, the tap roots survey for moisture. If the eastern-most root detects it, the correlated response directs more root capacity in that direction. A sparrow looks around and sees a cat ready to spring on it. The bird's correlated response is to fly to a safer locale. Yet, future generations of plants and sparrows do not move beyond these simple reactions. Plants do not learn to build irrigation systems to bring themselves distant water, and sparrows do not construct cat traps. Each succeeding generation begins at about the same place as previous ones, with only the lengthy process of biological evolution to offer any chance of enhanced adaptation.

Through their possession of advanced communication skills, however, human beings can use that vital third step of *transmitting social heritage;* they record and convey new methodologies and insights so that each generation can build on the advances made by its immediate predecessor. Unlike the lower life forms, human beings have a history that, when conveyed by human communication, has the capacity to promote generational progress and development. Thus, this component of social process not only separates human communication from that practiced by lower life forms but it also defines and enhances humanity itself.

This transmission of social heritage, in its simplest form, is achieved through the memorization of truths, principles, and skills that are then orally passed along from person to person. Often, these insights are put in the form of songs, poems, and stories (fables) to make memorization and recitation easier. The biblical psalms, for example, were perfect for an overwhelmingly nonliterate soci-

ety. They required neither the ability to read nor the then-considerable expense of writing equipment in order to be conveyed. Instead, their lyrical imagery made the task of memorization a pleasant and attainable accomplishment. Often, as in the case of the *rhapsodes* of ancient Greece, a whole profession was created to facilitate such heritage transmission via poetry. "As this poetry becomes more popular and addresses itself to a wider public," art historian Arnold Hauser points out, "so the style of delivery becomes less and less formal and approaches that of everyday speech."[2] Thus, with the psalmists, rhapsodes, and similar ancients, we may confront the conversational ancestors of today's electronic media professionals.

## Communications as Communication Extender

Passing social heritage solely through face-to-face encounters, however, is an inefficient and time-consuming enterprise. The number of psalmists, rhapsodes, minstrels, and similar history passers available to any society is exceedingly small compared to the population to be served. To cope with this shortage, more advanced societies further progress themselves through the development and use of *communications* (with an *s*).

### Defining Communications

In a nutshell, communication*s* are implements that enable us to extend our ability to interact over time and space. Unlike the rhapsode's voice, these vehicles are not part of the human anatomy. Instead, they are separate tools that allow us to communicate in situations in which face-to-face contact is not possible.

At 8:00 A.M., a teacher writes an assignment on the chalkboard for a 10:00 A.M. class and then leaves town on an emergency errand. Even though that absent professor may be more than a hundred miles away by the time the 10:00 A.M. students arrive, she has still communicated with them. Through use of as simple a 'tool set' as a piece of chalk and a sheet of slate, the instructor has managed to leap both time and space in completing her transmission. In a modern society, such communications tools are all around us and are readily available. The fax machine and telephone answering device represent the more sophisticated of such mechanisms, and the note on the refrigerator or pile of rocks that mark a forest trail constitute more primitive communications vehicles. Yet, because all of these methods extend our ability to disseminate over time and distance, all are powerful out-of-body amplifiers of the communication process. They are technical implements through which the impact of our information, assertions, and attitudes can be magnified.

Communications vehicles therefore possess the associated capacity to build *dispersed communities.* A second-century Roman physician may have resided hundreds of miles from other healers. But through common access to written scrolls (technical implements) detailing certain medical procedures, he could join other such healers to create a community of physicians, even though most would never meet each other face-to-face. Despite today's vastly improved transportation systems, trade and professional communities of all types still owe their existence, not to eyeball-to-eyeball interchange but to the more or less continuous mechanical linkages that communications vehicles provide.[3]

### The Mass Communications Dimension

Obviously, a great variety of such linkage tools are currently available. As we begin this introduction to the electronic media, however, we need to focus our attention on the category of professionally operated commu-

nications tools that offer the greatest potential for communication carriage. Known as *mass communications* (again with an *s*), this "intricate, many-faceted machinery"[4] provides the technological wherewithal to deliver information, assertions, and attitudes proficiently to vast segments of the population. More precisely, mass communications can be defined as

> those hyperefficient and highest capacity communications tools that permit timely transmittal to the largest number of dispersed individuals.

Clearly, we are talking now about more than the chalkboard or the telephone. True mass communications mechanisms give us the potential to reach even millions of people at roughly the same time. And, even though captured audience members may share similarities of age, occupation, or locale, they are just as likely to be highly diverse in these and other characteristics. In short, it is the fundamental *mass*iveness of mass communications tools and their achievable audiences that sets these delivery systems apart from other, less potent communications vehicles.

## Achieving Mass Communication

Up to this point we have distinguished between *communication* (a process) and *communications* (the tools that can extend this process over time and space). We have also isolated *mass* communications as the tools possessing the greatest efficiency and capacity. What remains is to delineate *mass communication* (no *s*), the process made possible only through the use of mass communications devices.

## A Mass Communication Definition

For comparison and consistency, therefore, let us modify our original definition of *communication* and propose that *mass* communication is

the process of rapidly conveying identical information, assertions, and attitudes to a potentially large, dispersed, and diversified audience via mechanisms capable of achieving that task.

There are obviously some key differences between this statement and our earlier communication definition. Four of these differences relate to the addition of the relative terms *identical, large, dispersed,* and *diversified.* Let us look at each requisite separately.

### The 'Identical' Characteristic

When something is *identical,* of course, it is exactly the same as another entity with which it is being compared. Real mass communication offers this "same as" quality. Even though 50,000 different people may read our town's morning newspaper today, it is expected that, through a uniform printing process, they are all reading exactly the same material arranged in exactly the same way. Similarly, even though 30 million different people may watch a particular network situation comedy this evening, and watch it in four or five different time zones, they are all being exposed to precisely the same program content as has been preserved on film or videotape.

On the other hand, if you separately meet three friends on the street and tell each the new joke you've just heard, these three retellings will not be identical. No matter how hard you try to be consistent, you will use different words, phrases, and gestures each time you relate your witticism. There will be even less uniformity, of course, if you tell the story only to the first friend, who passes it on to the second, who, in turn, conveys it to the third. In this case, different communicators as well as different phraseology will impact the joke's transmittal, with the subsequent likelihood of some very unidentical messages, including at least one that may mangle the punchline.

Through its ability to make a virtually unlimited number of impressions of the exact same original, however, mass communication can transmit identical content to every person in a position to receive the message. Whether these people *respond* identically is another matter, of course. As we've mentioned, each person is a unique receiver whose feedback (or lack of same) constitutes a completely individualized, discrete, and often unpredictable response.

### The 'Large' Characteristic

Our second relative term, *large,* is more ambiguous. We can come to grips with it only by taking a "compared to what?" orientation. Two thousand people in a theatre watching a new Broadway musical is a large crowd compared to 200, but not compared to the 2 million who might easily be exposed to the play if it were telecast over the Public Broadcasting Service. A presidential address to a United Auto Workers convention may reach 6,000 delegates, but how much larger will the audience be if the address is reprinted in one or more major newspapers? Clearly, there is a quantum leap in what constitutes large once we recruit one of the mass communications vehicles to transmit our consequently *mass* message.

### The 'Dispersed' Characteristic

Our third relative term, *dispersed,* pertains to the location of the audience members. A vast auditorium may be packed with a comparatively large crowd made up of many diverse types of people who are all receiving an identical message from the speaker or performance on stage. Yet, because these people are all in the same locale, they are not dispersed. All were required to travel to the event in order to experience it. The process of mass communication, in contrast, brings the event to the audience rather than the other way around. This fact provides great flexibility in both group size and group location.

We could, for example, bring together substantial numbers of viewers to watch educational programs on community television sets in their respective neighborhoods, something regularly done thirty years ago in India.[5] At the other extreme, we can follow standard U.S. practice of reaching millions of geographically separated families or even solitary viewers who are watching in affluent isolation from each other on their own personal sets. Either way, our audience is dispersed, and the size of each viewer group is less important than the fact that the televised event was actually delivered simultaneously to all of these groups.

### 'Diversity' and 'Potentiality'

The *diversified* element in our mass communication definition provides our fourth comparative, though imprecise, benchmark. Even though the 30 million people from our earlier example who watched that situation comedy certainly represent a broader spectrum of society than do the 2 million who watched the Broadway show on PBS, both are much more variegated than is the populace attending that UAW speech or the three friends exchanging jokes. To a considerable degree, the larger a group, the more diversified it is likely to be. Nevertheless, the factors of audience size and composition must be considered separately in gauging whether a given situation possesses the potential for mass communication.

The word *potential* (or *potentially*, as it appears in our definition) is extremely important. There are times when a mass communicator deliberately chooses *not* to use the full

mass communication capacity that a vehicle offers. *Broadcasting,* for example, is a trade magazine that seeks to serve professionals working in, or offering services for, the commercial radio and television industries. (See Figure 1–3.) It is disseminated only by subscription and only to members of this target audience; it has an average weekly circulation of 30,000 copies.[6] Compared to other national magazines such as *Time* or *People, Broadcasting's* readership is not particularly large and is certainly not diversified. Instead, the publishers of *Broadcasting* (and of many other specialty magazines) have made the conscious decision not to exploit the national magazine format's *potential* for a sizable and heterogeneous audience. Rather, they closely control circulation so that advertisers seeking exclusively to reach people in the radio/television business will be attracted to *Broadcasting*. These advertisers know that they are paying to reach only individuals who might actually be in a position to use their products or services with no waste circulation among uninterested readers.

Using the same printing press, manufacturing, and basic mail distribution process, *Broadcasting* could decide to *function* as a mass communications vehicle simply through content changes. The articles on leveraged buyouts of cable systems could be replaced with discussions of cohabitation in Connecticut, and the two-page ad for a new field camera could be exchanged for a bikini-clad centerfold with a staple in the navel. What would have changed? Not the *form* of the magazine, but rather its *content*. It is important to recognize, therefore, that while *content* determines whether a given entity is actually functioning as a system for mass communication, it is *form* that decrees whether such potential could exist. In other words, *Broadcasting* (and, in fact, any trade publication) is a mass medium in form that chooses not to exploit that mass communication ability in its featured content.

**Figure 1–3**

*Broadcasting* Magazine. Mass medium in form, nonmass in content.

NAB CONVENTION ISSUE

# Broadcasting Apr 15

Reaching over 117,000 readers every week                    60th Year 1991

**TELEVISION** / 64
*Networks square off
on Saturday morning;
syndication scorecard*

**RADIO** / 72
*AOR fragmenting as it
crosses generation gap;
annual format survey*

**BUSINESS** / 82
*How the pros
forecast next year's
ad revenues*

**WASHINGTON** / 90
*Children's TV rules
adopted imposing ad limits,
renewal requirements*

U N I V E R S A L
P I C T U R E S

·L·I·S·T·
OF A
LIFETIME

35 major motion pictures.
Primetime entertainment at its best.

PRIMETIME ENTERTAINMENT *from*

© 1991 MCA TV. All rights reserved.

Broadcasting
1931 1991
60

Vol. 120 No. 15   $2.50

No-win decision
on fin-syn
NAB PERSPECTIVE
Sizing up the business
on convention eve

## Comparing Delivery Systems

This brings us to the last phrase in our definition of mass communication: "via mechanisms capable of achieving that task." By applying the other aspects of our mass communication yardstick, and combining these criteria with our definition of what constitutes true mass communications tools, we find general agreement as to what these tools are:

Newspapers
Magazines
Movies
Radio
Television

All of these tools *permit timely transmittal to the largest numbers of dispersed individuals.* All have the capacity *rapidly to convey identical* messages to *diversified* audiences. Thus, the full exploitation of any of these vehicles of mass communications ignites true mass communication activity.

### The Concept of Timeliness

Even though the five media listed above all meet the requirements for mass communications vehicles, *how* they meet these requirements varies by degree. Radio and television, for example, are more timely (rapid) than are newspapers, magazines, and movies because the messages generated by the latter three must first be committed to paper or film stock, duplicated, and then physically transported to consumers. A live radio or television transmission, on the other hand, can be distributed in real time, direct from communicator to consumer; it can be received by millions of people at virtually the same moment it is being sent.

There are, of course, some further qualifications to this timeliness. Most modern television programs outside of the news arena are not delivered live, as was the case in the 1950s, but on videotape that was recorded days, months, or even years before. The content of the tape can be transmitted around the country or the world instantaneously, but the original occurrence captured by that tape may be anything but contemporary. Similarly, even though most radio programming is held together by live announcers, disc jockeys, and newscasters, these air talents are usually manipulating recorded (non-real-time) music, commercials, and news reports. In some nationally syndicated music formats, in fact, virtually all the program content—disc jockey included—has been prerecorded before distribution.

Movies involve additional timeliness qualifications. First, when we speak of "*The* Movies" as an independent mass medium, we are referring either to film prints that are physically shipped to theaters for exhibition ("theatricals") or to television cassettes dispatched to video stores for individual sale or rental. (See Figure 1–4 for a glimpse of recent changes in the composition of movie theater audiences). In either case, the process is much more extended over time than that required by the other mass media. When a movie is transmitted over a pay cable network like HBO or an over-the-air system like CBS, however, we are no longer dealing solely with the movie medium but with a combination of movie medium production and television medium distribution. The movie's timeliness factor may thereby be improved, but only after it is married to the real-time transmission capabilities of television.

### Combining Systems

Whether the movie has been captured on film stock or on videotape ultimately makes no real difference. From a mass communication standpoint, we are interested only in

**Figure 1–4**
The maturing moviegoer

11

CHAPTER 1
Bringing
Mass
Media
into Focus

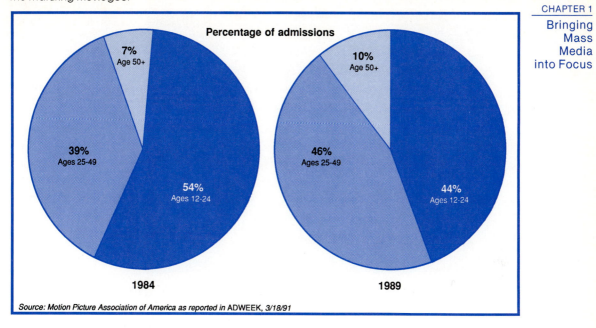

**Percentage of admissions**

7%
Age 50+

10%
Age 50+

39%
Ages 25-49

46%
Ages 25-49

54%
Ages 12-24

44%
Ages 12-24

1984

1989

Source: Motion Picture Association of America as reported in ADWEEK, 3/18/91

whether, in a given instance, the movie medium is self-standing or has become the content for a colleague mass medium (television). The importance of the movie medium is not necessarily diminished when it is conveyed by television. In fact, film theorist Siegfried Kracauer argued more then thirty years ago that "like the conqueror who surrenders to the culture of the conquered, television increasingly feeds on the fare of the moviehouses; indeed, it may be in part the continued impact of the old medium which accounts for the attractiveness of the new one."[7]

A similar hybridization takes place when we deal with *teletext* type operations in which print is conveyed and consumed electronically rather than mechanically committed to paper. The editorial process may be the same as that practiced by a standard newspaper, but the subsequent distribution is via a cable or broadcast television system that results in text read by the public off their television screens. Because there is no printing press

production required and no need physically to bundle and transport sheets of newsprint, teletext is thus the more timely alternative. (See Figure 1–5.)

## Special Print Aspects

Newspapers (even in their traditional form) are generally thought to be more timely than magazines, but this timeliness has more to do with publishing schedule convention than with any fundamental technological difference. Newspapers are normally defined as folded, nonstapled sheets published on a daily or weekly basis. Magazines are usually considered to be bound pamphlets that appear weekly, monthly, or even less frequently. For all practical purposes, of course, a weekly magazine is probably just as timely as a weekly newspaper.

Both of these print media, like their radio, television, and movie mass communications cousins, are capable of reaching large numbers of people. As we have discussed, the only

**Figure 1-5**
A typical teletext 'page'

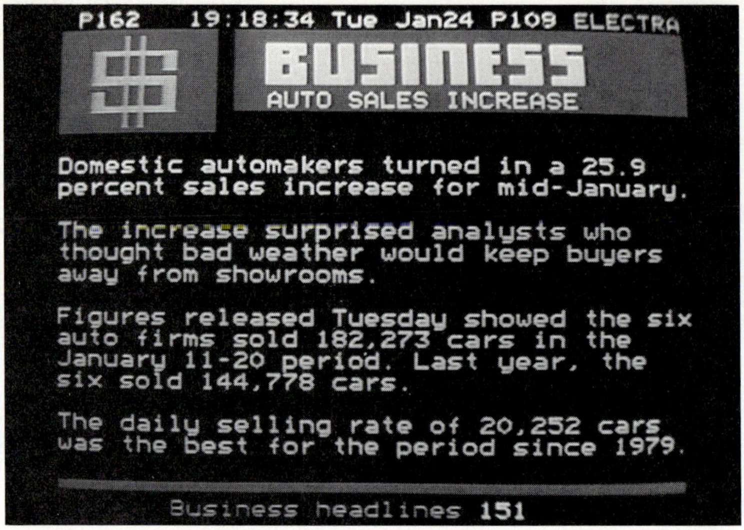

differences are in the time it takes for the various technologies to make these connections. When it comes to communicating with dispersed individuals, however, additional distinctions emerge. A newspaper or magazine's dispersal, for example, is limited by the available transportation system. If it takes too long (or is too expensive) physically to distribute the publication, timeliness and economic feasibility are lost. The same conditions apply to the shipment of film prints to movie houses or of their tape cassette counterparts to video stores. In all of these instances, more concentrated populations can be reached more easily (and more quickly) than can the scattered inhabitants of rural areas.

## Special Electronic Aspects

Dispersion factors apply somewhat differently in the case of radio and television. Using over-the-air broadcast signals, everyone within a station's coverage pattern can receive the message at the same time. People need not have access to a video store or movie house, a newsstand, or a carrier person's delivery route in order to take advantage of initial message availability.

This is why broadcasters are fond of pointing out that it costs as much to reach a million people as it does a hundred. The signal is out there regardless of how few people choose to tune it in. Of course, it is in the commercial broadcaster's best interests to aim for the million instead of the hundred because advertising revenues are directly tied to audience size and composition. The print media also are largely dependent on advertising, of course, but they can adjust number of copies printed (and, therefore, operational expenses) to the actual number of paying reader/subscribers.

Limited access radio/television systems such as cable, meanwhile, fall somewhat between these two extremes. The cable signal is available only to people who hook up to (and pay for) it, just as movie house admission is granted only to people who buy a ticket. However, cable trunklines usually pass significantly more homes than those who agree to have the service installed. This is reflected in cable penetration figures. "Cable penetration is the percentage of television households subscribing to basic cable service."[8]

Like the newspaper, the cable system need only provide its goods to people who actually pay for them. But similar to the broadcaster, that system must still blanket (wire) the geographic area prescribed by its franchise. It cannot, as is the case with movies or print, restrict proximity only to actual customers. In the way lines are strung, cable can, of course, more precisely limit its operating area than can a broadcaster whose signal will not magically stop at the city limits. Still, because not everyone whose home is passed by cable will subscribe, a system will still have paid to disperse its lines past more homes than those contributing to that system's operating revenues.

Direct-to-home satellite transmissions known as DBS (Direct Broadcast Satellite) are another variation on this dispersal theme. Like a broadcast station's signal, the satellite's so-called footprint can blanket an entire geographic area without respect to the dispersal of people within that area. But as with the print or movie media, the DBS operator can restrict actual access only to paying consumers through scrambling of signals and rental of decoders. Further, the footprint from but one satellite transponder is so vast that a profit can be made if even a small percentage of the households under it sign up for the service.

# Key Nonmass Media

All these peculiarities notwithstanding, the five mass media we have identified still permit comparatively quicker connection with large, dispersed, and diverse audiences than does any available nonmass alternative. Chief among these nonmass alternatives are the telephone, recording, and book publishing industries.

## The Telephone and Recording Industries

Taken as a whole, the telephone system in the United States is certainly ubiquitous, meaning its instruments are virtually everywhere. Why, then, isn't the telephone a mass medium? Because, even though telephone messages can reach virtually everyone, these transmissions are all produced and routed to be received only by very small groups of people—often, by only a single person. Telephone messages certainly possess real-time immediacy, but no one message is meant for a large number of diverse and dispersed individuals. Rather, even in the case of conference calls, each transmission is a private, point-to-point interchange.

Recall here that our definition of mass communication requires that identical information, assertions, and attitudes be disseminated. Any time a large number of people are using the telephone, they are engaged in highly individualized and very *un*identical message exchange. Granted, this is not the case when the telephone call is part of a radio talk show, but in that instance, the radio, not the telephone, is the determining medium.

Radio also functions as the determining medium in the recording industry. Many different tapes and discs are produced each year by recording companies, with thousands or even millions of pressings of certain titles manufactured. Yet, for any one title to reach a large and dispersed audience, a record company must expend months, if not years, in that title's distribution and promotion. Timeliness certainly suffers. If the selection is exposed on the radio, however, this dissemination process can be reduced to a matter of weeks, or, in the case of the biggest break-through releases by famous artists, just days. The company will make significantly greater profits from the sale of pressings than from the tune's exposure via radio, but this second operation helps to stimulate the first. Airplay converts a nonmass activity to a much more immediate mass communication endeavor.

As in our earlier examples of theatrical movies carried on television and telephone calls aired via talk shows, the radio industry's exposure of the recording industry's product is another example of the interdependency of mass and nonmass communications structures. In fact, the mass media rely on a great many outside enterprises and persons for most of their content and economic support while, in turn, providing these enterprises with an efficient means of reaching their target audiences. As media theorists Ball-Rokeach and DeFleur have pointed out, "the mass media are not all powerful. The media depend upon resources controlled by the political, economic and other social systems, resources that the media need to function effectively. . . . Relationships between the media, on the one hand, and other large social systems, on the other, are interdependent because neither could attain its respective goals without being able to use the other's resources."[9]

### The Book Publishing Industry

Book publishing also is a nonmass enterprise that can be partnered with a mass delivery system. From the time a manuscript is accepted by a publisher, it normally takes anywhere from seven to fourteen months to produce a hardcover trade volume and distribute it to vendors. This is not a rapid activity. Further, because of their expense and subject matter, most hardcover volumes are outside the economic reach and subject matter interests of all but a select few people for any given title. Thus, even though that title's audience may be dispersed (recall what we said about the building of dispersed communities) it is unlikely that the audience will be large or particularly diverse in proportion to the total population.

Paperback books, on the other hand, are a hybrid. Because they can be produced cheaply and quickly, paperbacks can be categorized as one-issue magazines. Like any magazine, a paperback can inexpensively address subject matter designed for a mass audience (like a supermarket-distributed Harlequin romance) or choose not to exploit the format's mass communication capacity by becoming a specialty publication (such as a pocket guide for coin collectors). In a more extended manner, a book can be released in a hardcover (nonmass) format and then, if it enjoys initial popularity, be re-released in paperback to tap a wider and perhaps mass audience. It might even be serialized by a regularly issued magazine and enter the mass communications mainstream.

In short, books can be considered mass or nonmass vehicles depending on the form selected to accomplish the publishers' audience goals and the impact of this format decision on readership delivery.

# Tuning in
# the Electronic
# Mass Media

Having defined communication and mass communication activities and discussed the tools available to facilitate each, we can orient ourselves more precisely to the central focus of our professional interests—the electronic mass media.

Our earlier discussion touched on the fact that the electronic mass media generate and disseminate a signal (technically, an electromagnetic signal) over the air and/or down a wire to permit timely transmittal to the largest number of dispersed individuals. This description, of course, isolates radio and television.

### The Essence of Broadcasting

In the most basic electronic media application (see Figure 1–6), a radio or television station

**Figure 1–6**
Basic broadcast signal transmittal

**15**

CHAPTER 1
Bringing
Mass
Media
into Focus

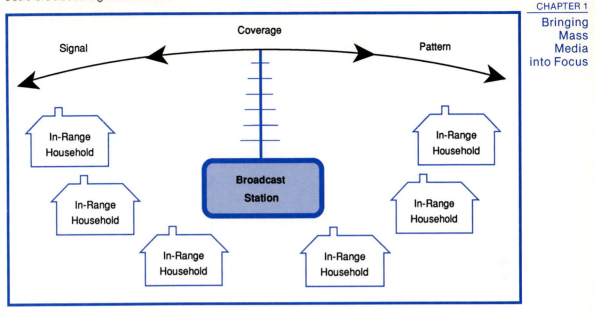

catapults its message into the air over an assigned frequency. This *broadcast* communication is then capable of capture by all receiving sets within range of the signal for the benefit of the listening/viewing public.

The term *broadcast* is an appropriate descriptor of this process even though that word did not originate in the mass media field. *To broadcast* originally meant to strew seeds in all directions, as a farmer would do in planting a freshly tilled field. Today's broadcast professionals are engaged in planting and germinating ideas, assertions, and attitudes rather than corn or wheat. Yet, the concept of scattering the commodity in all directions remains as relevant to electronic endeavors as it does to agriculture. In neither case does all that you sow bear fruit. But if you harvest too few plants (or too few listeners) you cannot realize the profit necessary to continue your work. Of course, your efforts could be subsidized by the government—as in crop price supports or public broadcasting. Such schemes do not alter the fundamental nature

of your business, however; they only modify the sources and measures by which your labors are compensated.

## Nonbroadcast Mechanisms

As our "over the air and/or down a wire" description implies, electronic communicators sometimes use nonbroadcast delivery systems or combine such systems with broadcast applications. A cable network like USA or Arts & Entertainment, for example, is entirely nonbroadcast. Instead of scattering their signals in all directions over the open airwaves, cable networks use super high frequencies to uplink their signals from their main control rooms to communications satellites that then downlink them to the receiving dishes owned by individual cable systems. The signals are then downconverted to normal broadcast frequencies and distributed closed-circuit by a coaxial or fiber optic line only to viewers who have contracted and paid for the service (see Figure 1–7).

Roughly the same thing happens in a DBS

**Figure 1–7**
Cable network (nonbroadcast) transmittal

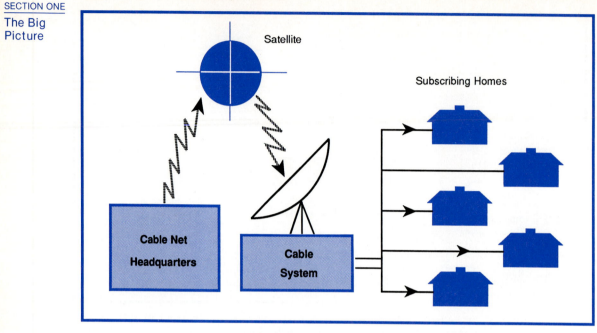

(direct broadcast satellite) situation. In that instance, however, the cable system is eliminated because the satellite signal is received and downconverted at each subscriber's residence rather than channeled and refined by an intermediary cable company.

A combination of both over-the-air (broadcast) and down-the-wire (nonbroadcast) technologies is represented by superstations such as Turner Communications' WTBS in Atlanta. In these operations, the station provides normal broadcast coverage to homes in the city to which it is licensed. At the same time, its signal is also being uplinked to a satellite for distribution to distant cable systems that offer it as another programming service to subscribers (see Figure 1–8). The same signal may also be marketed directly to home satellite dish owners who are outside the cable systems' service areas. These HSD (home satellite dish) homes pay a fee for the signal to an authorized dealer who also provides the descrambler necessary for the receiving set to make sense of the picture. In such a case,

these HSD homes are referred to as TVRO (television receive-only) installations to distinguish them from DBS. A TVRO dish merely intercepts signals being generated by other program delivery systems (such as broadcast and cable networks). A usually smaller DBS dish, in contrast, picks up signals intended *exclusively* for subscribers of that DBS enterprise.

# Facing
# One-Way Realities

Despite the sophistication of mass communications systems such as those just examined, we must recognize their common limitation: mass communication is also one-way communication. Even though, as electronic communicators, we have the capacity to reach large, diverse, and dispersed audiences in an espe-

**Figure 1–8**
Combined broadcast/nonbroadcast transmittal

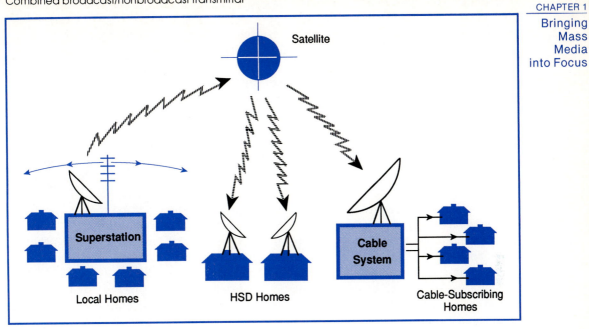

cially timely (even instantaneous) manner, our systems do not presently permit receipt of feedback from these audiences. Instead, radio and television professionals must wait for such delayed and limited responses as ratings reports, in-store customer traffic counts, and product sales computations in attempting to determine the success of their transmissions. Programs and advertising campaigns can be modified or replaced as a result of such subsequent feedback, of course. But unlike face-to-face communication, there is little to help us monitor our success during the moment of actual message delivery. If we have miscommunicated, this fact will not usually be known until well after the occurrence.

## One-Way Exceptions

There are some exceptions to this one-way condition, but their limitations demonstrate the imprecision of immediate mass communication feedback. The radio talk show, for example, seems to offer a rich vehicle for two-

way mass communication—until we examine its real purpose. Certainly the host of the program is conversing directly with the listener/caller. But that host's primary job is to make what the caller says of interest to the audience in general. Host and caller may be having an extended and seemingly productive interchange. Yet, if that conversation's subject or direction bores the rest of the listeners, the program will not hold its audience. The talk show host has no feedback from this audience at the time and thus can rely only on professional experience and intuition as to whether this call is helping the program succeed.

Similarly, many television situation comedies, talk shows, and game programs are taped or filmed "before a live studio audience." Theoretically, the feedback performers receive from this audience should be a guide as to how viewers at home are reacting. In reality, however, that studio audience has been subjected to much additional stimulation not present in the home. Applause signs, exuberant preshow warm-up by program assistants, and even the excitement of being in a real television setting can generate much more enthusiastic feedback from the in-studio audience than is being felt by viewers at home. The performer who relies solely on the captive audience's reaction may be unpleasantly surprised when, weeks later, ratings weakness or decline evidence a much different reaction on the part of the general viewing public.

## Research as Feedback and Prediction

Programmers and advertising agencies engage in a variety of research techniques to try to compensate for the absence of complete and immediate feedback about their shows and commercials. One research method is the *auditorium test,* in which a room full of participants react to programs, commercials, or individual music selections or blends via hand-held response instruments (dials). Among the most advanced of such devices is EARS (Electronic Attitude Research System), a trademarked service of FMR Associates, Inc., of Tucson, Arizona (see Figure 1–9). Resembling large television remote-control pads, the EARS units are transported in honeycomb design boxes, each of which holds twenty-four individual wireless response devices.

Through circuitry built into these carrying-case boxes, the units are programmed with survey instructions for a specific project and then uploaded after each session to a lap-top personal computer with a hard disk. The data are converted to 3½-inch disks for back up and then transmitted via modem to FMR's Tucson processing center each night following the sessions. The EARS System has been used extensively around the world for testing programs, music, and television commercials for broadcast companies such as CapCities/ABC, CBS, and the Australian Broadcast Corporation, and by the Corporation for Public Broadcasting for evaluating nationally distributed programs and concepts.[10]

Conventional focus groups, on the other hand, rely on participant comments for their data. A trained moderator leads no more than a dozen individuals (selected to represent the audience being targeted) through conversations designed to reveal more open-ended perceptions about the product, station, or service. Other research techniques include mall intercept interviews and telephone call-out research. These procedures sample hundreds or even thousands of consumers to try to anticipate their reactions to future messages or to tabulate their exposure and response to previous ones (see Figure 1–10).

Unfortunately, no matter how skillfully

**Figure 1–9**
A hand-held EARS wireless response instrument

**Figure 1–10**

**19**

A focus group moderator at work as observers monitor the session through one-way glass

planned or conducted, these evaluative methods can provide only an approximate gauge of actual listener/viewer feedback. As professors Fletcher and Bowers caution, "the supposed magical qualities sometimes associated with the word *research* and the apparent mystery attached to research may be responsible for the blind allegiance frequently paid to it."[11] This poses the ultimate challenge for our profession because wrong guesses will seem to be wrong only long after the content in question has been irretrievably produced and transmitted.

Mass communications vehicles in general, and the electronic media in particular, provide unparalleled opportunity to reach large and widely scattered groups of people quickly. The constant challenge is to maximize these opportunities in the face of inevitably postponed, after-the-fact feedback. As we stress throughout this book, success in our profession comes not merely from using electronic media technology but also from achieving planned and specified mass communication success *through* that technology.

## Chapter Flashback

Everything we do in our profession is grounded in communication principles. Fundamentally, human communication is the ongoing process of conveying and exchanging information, assertions, and attitudes. These transmissions include both verbal and nonverbal components, which may sometimes contradict each other. Human communication is also the carrier of social process, which involves the constant surveying of our environment, formulating responses to perceived environmental conditions, and then passing on successful responses to other people as heritage.

To extend their ability to communicate over time and space, societies develop communications tools. Some of the most basic of these tools are the chalk and chalkboard, the note on the refrigerator, or the pile of rocks that mark a wilderness trail. Mass communications vehicles are the hyperefficient and highest capacity communications mechanisms that permit timely transmittal to the largest number of dispersed individuals. We use mass communications systems in the process of mass communication, which involves rapidly conveying identical information, assertions, and attitudes to a potentially large, dispersed, and diversified audience. Five media can accomplish this mass communication task: newspapers, magazines, movies, radio, and television. Sometimes these media combine with each other or with nonmass media to accomplish their goals. Prominent among such nonmass media are the telephone, recording, and book publishing industries.

The electronic mass media of radio and television can be divided into broadcast and nonbroadcast mechanisms. Broadcast transmissions are generally accessible as over-the-air signals by all receivers within each station's coverage pattern; nonbroadcast systems deliver their content only to subscribers via wire and/or scrambled transmissions.

Any mass communication enterprise must contend with the virtual absence of immediate feedback because mass communications tools are one-way in their operation. This fact makes audience research an important activity in evaluating past messages and attempting to predict the success of future ones.

❑ Review Probes

1. Compare and contrast *communication* and *communications*.
2. Compare and contrast *communications* and *mass communications*.
3. How does social process separate human beings from lower life forms?
4. What is meant by the concept of media *interdependency?*
5. What are the key characteristics of *dispersed* and *diversified* audiences?
6. Is it possible to achieve mass communication without using mass communications? Explain why or why not.

❑ Suggested Background Explorations

Budd, Richard W., and Brent D. Rubin. *Beyond Media: New Approaches to Mass Communication.* New Brunswick, NJ: Transaction Books, 1988.

DeFleur, Melvin L., and Everette E. Dennis. *Understanding Mass Communication.* 3rd ed. Boston: Houghton Mifflin, 1988.

DeFleur, Melvin L., and Sandra J. Ball-Rokeach. *Theories of Mass Communication.* 5th ed. New York: Longman, 1989.

Fisher, Glen. *American Communication in a Global Society.* Rev. ed. Norwood, NJ: Ablex Publishing Corp., 1987.

Fiske, John. *Television Culture.* New York: Methuen, 1988.

McQuail, Denis. *Mass Communication Theory: An Introduction.* 2nd ed. Newbury Park, CA: Sage, 1987.

Stanley, Robert Henry. *Mediavisions: The Art and Industry of Mass Communication.* New York: Praeger, 1987.

# CHAPTER 2

# Subdividing the Electronic Landscape

❏ *Now that we have surveyed the entire mass communications field, we can focus more specifically on the mass communications vehicles that collectively comprise the electronic media. As you read in the previous chapter (and probably knew beforehand) the electronic media can be broadly segmented into the twin categories of radio and television. There are, however, a number of components to each category, separated one from another by technological variations. Because radio is the older vehicle, it is appropriate to examine the sound medium first.*

## Hanging in There: AM Radio

For most of the U.S. public, radio was exclusively AM until the late 1940s. The term *AM* is the abbreviation for *amplitude modulation*, which denotes how this type of signal is propagated. All broadcasting begins with an electromagnetic carrier wave that operates at a constant (unmodulated) amplitude (power) and frequency (tone) (see Figure 2–1).

**Figure 2–1**
An unmodulated carrier wave

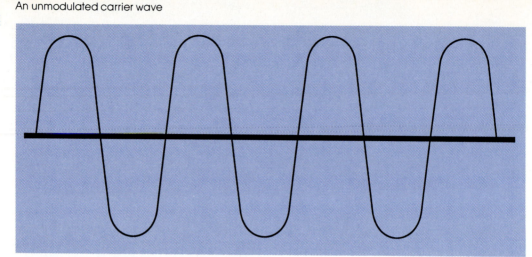

### The Essence of AM

An AM transmission is superimposed onto this carrier wave by rapidly changing (modulating) power through frequent voltage variation. As Ronald Seidle explains, *amplitude* "is just a big word for the height and depth of a wave. Someone discovered that if you vary the amplitude, or the height and depth of the wave, you change the sound of this carrier wave."[1] Thus, in AM, the frequency remains constant while the quantity of energy is manipulated, with the percentage of modulation determined by the audio signal's strength (see Figure 2–2).

Typically, modulation is maintained at between 85 and 100 percent. Anything above 100 percent is known as overmodulation, which distorts the generating wave form and

**Figure 2–2**
Amplitude modulation

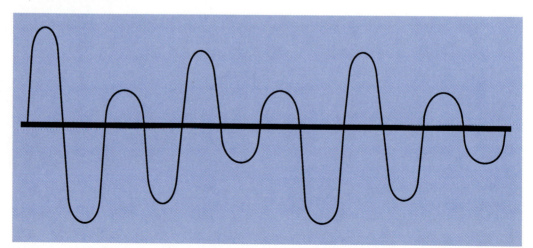

**23**

CHAPTER 2
Sub-
dividing
the
Electronic
Landscape

creates additional undesired frequencies that interfere with the signals of other AM stations. Even when modulation is properly controlled, AM signals are susceptible to electrical interference. This interference occurs because the AM system works on the basis of the quantity of energy received. It therefore attracts extraneous bits of distorting energy to its signal. This energy might be received from natural causes, such as lightning, or man-made causes, like electric motors or automobile spark plugs.

In recent years, the public as well as some broadcasters have tended to overemphasize AM's signal problems when comparing it to frequency modulation (FM) broadcasts that do not share these traits. More and more music formats thus have fled the AM band in favor of FM. Younger listeners have followed this migration. As of 1989, about 75 percent of radio listening in the United States had shifted to FM. AM's remaining 25 percent is now made up primarily of older listeners.[2] News, talk, and similar limited-music formats remain popular on AM, as do certain music stylings that originated in the AM era, such as big band, traditional country, and nostalgia/golden oldies. Older audiences who grew up listening to such music on AM remain comfortable with the marriage, but this condition does not attract younger people to the AM band. Unfortunately, many of today's AM station owners see every funeral as carrying off one more irreplaceable listener, which does not bode well for the future of the service.

## AM Tries New Directions

Some new talk-emphasizing concepts such as business, motivational, and home shopping formats have recently been developed. After tryouts on individual stations, these formats are marketed as a program service to other troubled AM outlets. Usually, the owners of the originating station are also the developers of the format and thus strive to build a network-type distribution service for which their station can be the flagship.[3] One AM facility in the Midwest has even converted itself into a loudspeaker for the amusement park to which it has moved its studios. Whether this sort of specialty AM activity becomes the rule or remains the exception is yet to be determined.

To counter AM's perceived fidelity disadvantage as compared to FM, various systems for AM stereo were developed in the late 1970s. Even though the creators of these systems made significant progress in overcoming the limitations of the relatively narrow AM channel, their efforts to this point have not been widely adopted by the marketplace. This was largely due to the 1982 decision of the Federal Communications Commission (FCC) not to adopt any one of the competing AM stereo methods but rather to let the marketplace determine the winner. In the absence of a single government standard, radio manufacturers and broadcasters alike have been leery of building or buying equipment that might become obsolete if a competing system triumphs. This reluctance has deprived the public of AM stereo stations and has discouraged the purchase of receivers, the cost of which remain artificially higher because of lack of customer demand. In short, the promise of AM stereo seems a long way from realization.

Other proposals for stemming the decline of AM radio have involved such schemes as allowing stations to increase power, banning the reissuance of licenses of stations that go off the air so that remaining outlets are subject to less interference, and permitting a single owner to operate more than one AM outlet in the same market to reduce operating costs. Some proposals have even suggested radio receivers with continuous-dial tuning rather than separately switched AM and FM bands. This would not, of course, change the technical differences between AM and FM but would make them less obvious to listeners in terms of receiver design. That such actions are being seriously proposed indicates both the seriousness of AM's problems and the desperation of people who operate stand-alone AM facilities (those without an FM sister station).

As of July 1, 1990, international agreements extended the top end of the AM band from 1605 kilohertz (kHz) to 1705 kilohertz, making room for a new set of stations. Rather than adding more outlets to the struggling service, the FCC, as of this writing, has decided to give assignment preference on this new portion of spectrum to existing stations that are causing interference to other stations in their present location. By allowing them to simulcast on both their old and new frequencies until enough receiving sets capable of dialing 1605–1705 kHz are on the market, the FCC hopes eventually to improve AM listenability by spreading out the same number of outlets over a wider spectrum space. This plan will not cure all of AM's problems, especially because given the higher frequency, stations eventually moving to the new band will have much less coverage area than they possessed with their old assignments. As then-chief of the FCC's Mass Media Bureau Alex Felker commented, however, "the service will not suffer from the degree of interference that is characteristic of much of the AM service today. So that's sort of a plus. There's a little bit of a gain and a little bit of a loss."[4] In a medium that has already suffered plenty of loss, band expansion thus is a mixed blessing. Still, as one desperate Minnesota AM broadcaster reacted, "I'll take anything I can get."[5]

## Today's Audio Mainstream: FM Radio

Just as FCC inaction on stereo has damaged AM, governmental action helped boost FM. In 1961, the commission permitted FM stations to broadcast stereo signals—and via a single industry-endorsed standard. Then, to encourage more substantial use of the FM band, the FCC gradually increased requirements for separate (nonduplicated) programming on co-owned AM and FM facilities. These expanded requirements forced more music, and different kinds of music, onto the air over an FM transmission system that also offered better fidelity and true stereophonic channel separation. While nonduplicated programming certainly benefited the delivery of classical and "beautiful" melodies, it also contributed even more to the growth of a variety of youth-grabbing rock formats and allowed a new generation of people and stations to grow up together.

### The Essence of FM

FM's fidelity advantage owes much to the fact that the signal is propagated by *frequency modulation*. This means that the *pitch* of the signal is manipulated while its loudness/strength remains constant. In other words, FM energy derives from the up and down movement of the signal within the frequency range provided in each station's assigned channel. Therefore, because FM does not vary the amplitude, its signal does not respond to, or become degraded by, energy emissions from natural or man-made electrical fields (see Figure 2–3).

The width of an FM channel and the characteristics of its signal generation make stereo broadcasting relatively easy. Within its transmission on the channel, the stereo station is actually sending different signals on slightly different frequencies. Stereo radios are then able to separate these signals, and the audio information each carries, to realize a true dual-sound effect or, alternatively, to provide an acceptable combined signal for monophonic receivers. At the same time, the FM station also has room within its channel to carry totally separate program matter. These auxiliary services (or *SCAs*, as they are called in the industry) can provide additional sources of revenue for the station. Among the

**Figure 2–3**
Frequency modulation

25

CHAPTER 2
Sub-
dividing
the
Electronic
Landscape

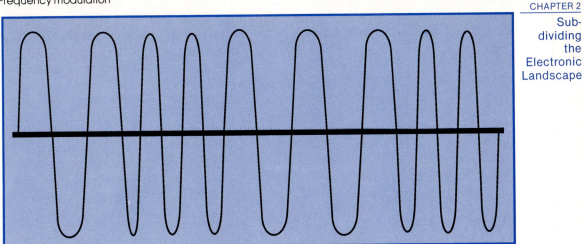

most common uses for an SCA is the Muzak-type system that carries background music to leased SCA receivers in stores and offices. Special interest financial or agricultural commodity prices, paging services, and data exchange activities are other uses to which SCAs can be put. By their nature, these are limited access, nonbroadcast endeavors but ones that can efficiently ride piggyback on the main broadcast signal.

## FM Dominance

As we indicate in our AM discussion, at least three-quarters of U.S. radio listening is currently devoted to the FM band; this is a complete reversal of AM/FM comparative audience numbers of a dozen years previous. The number of FM stations continues to increase while the number of AM stations is declining. It is highly unlikely that this trend can be reversed and even doubtful whether it can be stabilized.

With its multiplicity of stereo-delivered music formats and a strong youth orientation, FM dominance of the audio mass media scene seems unassailable. A clear indication of this situation was a 1990 proposal that would rescue certain AM broadcasters by allowing

them to simulcast their programming over new low-power FM facilities. These facilities would be squeezed, as feasible, onto the existing FM spectrum as long as they did not interfere with the higher-power stations already there. Such a plan, of course, might save some AM *broadcasters,* but it does nothing to assist AM *broadcasting.*

## Shortwaves and All Waves

Though most U.S. radio listeners are oblivious to it, shortwave radio is a prominent part of the audio service in many countries and is the prime vehicle for international radio broadcasting. Shortwave transmissions are AM in nature and can cover vast distances through use of high-power transmitters operating on high frequencies (HF) that take maximum advantage of *ionospheric bounce.* Let us take a moment to examine this phenomenon because, in so doing, we can also become acquainted with the properties of radio waves in general.

## Sky Waves and the Ionosphere

The ionosphere is a layer of the earth's atmosphere that possesses special electrical properties. Among these properties is its ability to bend certain kinds of radio waves back to earth; thus, the waves do not dissipate in space. This bending means that the signal will skip. It will emanate upward from the transmitter, hit the ionosphere, and bounce back to earth, perhaps hundreds of miles away. Depending on a variety of factors, this bounce may recur several times. The practical result is that the station may be received at a succession of distant locations but not in vast stretches of land between these locations (see Figure 2–4).

Radio transmissions that are subject to ionospheric bounce are known as *sky waves.* These waves may be of medium or high frequency. Medium-frequency waves (which are used in regular AM broadcasting) are subject to ionospheric bounce only at night when the ionosphere cools. This is why smaller AM stations are required to reduce power in the evening or, in the case of a *daytimer,* to go off the air entirely in order to avoid causing interference to other local stations in distant markets. This is also why full-power (50,000 watt) AM outlets such as WJR in Detroit or WCCO in Minneapolis can offer reasonably consistent nighttime service to areas very distant from their daytime coverage zones (but not to areas in between).

High-frequency waves, the type of carriage used by short wave broadcasters, skip off the ionosphere *both* day and night and so are the vehicle of choice in intercontinental broadcasting. But because temperature changes modify the degree to which the ionosphere bends high frequency sky waves, shortwave operators must operate on several successive frequencies to adapt to time of day and to seasonal shifts in the sun's heating of ionospheric layers.

## Ground Waves and Direct Waves

*Ground waves,* in contrast, tend to follow the curvature of the earth. They occur in me-

**Figure 2–4**

Sky wave ionospheric bounce

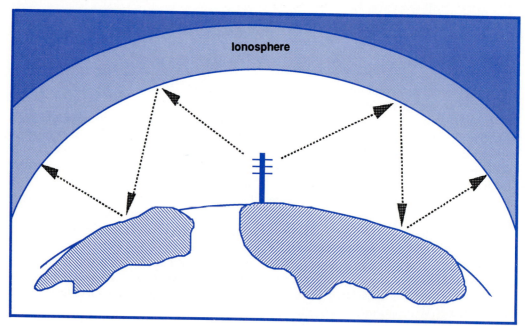

**27**

CHAPTER 2

Sub-
dividing
the
Electronic
Landscape

**Figure 2–5**

AM nighttime ground and sky wave activity

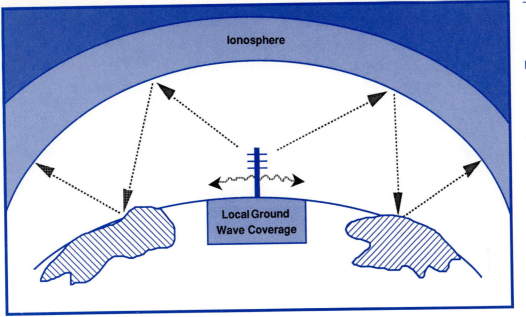

dium-frequency transmissions and so are an additional factor in domestic AM broadcasting. As Figure 2–5 shows, an AM station reaches its local market via ground waves but may also secure additional (though less consistent) nighttime coverage in distant locales via sky wave propagation.

Very-high-frequency (VHF) broadcasts (the type used by FM and some television stations), in contrast, emit *direct waves*. These waves are essentially straight-line phenomena; they travel from the antenna as far as the horizon and then shoot off into space. Thus, beyond a certain range, it does the broadcaster no good to increase power because the increase will only propel the signal farther into space rather than stretch it beyond the horizon to blanket a larger land area. Raising the height of the antenna extends the line of sight somewhat, but there are practical limitations as to how high a steel tower can be built (see Figure 2–6.)

The ultimate extension of this line-of-sight

principal is the communications satellite, which, placed in a geostationary orbit 22,300 miles above the earth, may have a usable horizon (a *footprint*) that embraces up to 30 percent of the planet below it. The term *geostationary* or *geosynchronous* means that the satellite remains over the same point on the earth's surface because both are orbiting at the same speed.

Because of their very high frequency, direct waves are not normally subject to ionospheric bounce. Occasionally, during periods of intense sunspot activity, radiation changes in the ionosphere create some very-high-frequency bounce, but this occurrence merely creates unpredictable interference problems rather than predictable or productive coverage increase.

## International Considerations

We began this exploration of wave characteristics as a means of explaining shortwave broadcasting. From what we have discussed,

**Figure 2–6**
FM/TV direct wave coverage possibilities

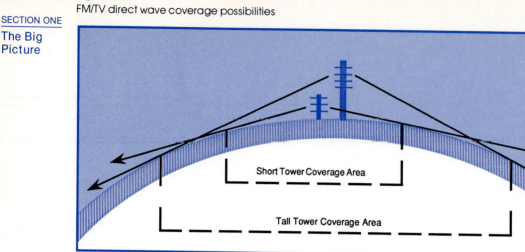

Short Tower Coverage Area

Tall Tower Coverage Area

it should be clear to you why a rich, more or less uniformly populated, and technologically advanced country like the United States relies on higher quality medium-wave and FM signals at home while using shortwave radio mainly to communicate with other nations. The Voice of America (VOA) and Radio Free Europe/Radio Liberty (RFE/RL) are governmental operations of this type. As of 1989, seventeen private stations licensed in the United States were also engaged in shortwave international broadcasting in addition to a global system of stations organized by the Christian Science Publishing Society.[6]

Spectrum use and apportionment for shortwave and most other services are coordinated on a worldwide basis by the International Telecommunication Union (ITU). The ITU began in 1865 as an organization to facilitate telegraphic communication across national borders and gradually extended its span of activity as new electronic media came on the scene. Even though it has no specific mechanism for enforcing its regulations, the ITU can exercise significant moral force because its decisions are really the collective determinations made by the more than 150 countries that comprise its membership.

At its most efficient, spectrum management

is a three-step cooperative process between the ITU and each individual member country with the ITU operating at only the first two decision-making stages. International broadcasting expert Sydney Head describes this arrangement:

First comes *allocation,* in which the ITU sets aside specific bands of frequencies for specific classes of stations. The ITU allocates bands for either exclusive or shared use by one or more services. Broadcasting is only one of thirty-seven services enumerated by the regulations. Long-, medium- and short-wave AM broadcasting all need their own allocations, as do FM radio and VHF and UHF television. In the next step, *allotment,* the ITU designates specific channels in some bands for use by stations within specific countries or regions. Finally, a given country *assigns* its allotted channels to licensed users (stations or broadcasting authorities) within its own territory.[7]

Because of their long reach and the complications arising from seasonal changes in ionospheric bounce factors, international shortwave broadcasting is handled in a more complex manner. What remains constant, however, is the need for international cooperation in the use of a common physical resource (the spectrum) that transcends national borders.

---

## Comparing Frequencies and Wavelengths

In the previous sections, we toss around terms like *short wave*, *medium wave*, *medium frequency* and *high frequency* in an attempt to explain the three basic systems, (AM, FM, shortwave) of radio broadcasting. There is a uniform relationship between wavelengths and wave frequencies that helps to explain why each of these various radio services is where it is on the spectrum.

### Making Sense of Cycles

As John Hasling describes it, "radio transmission is effected by electromagnetic waves which move through the air in a fashion similar to waves that move through water. Just as a pebble creates a disturbance on the surface of a pond, so a radio or television transmitter creates a disturbance in the air."[8]

Let's start by positioning ourselves at a fixed point, past which an electromagnetic transmission is being directed. Each individual electromagnetic wave going by our point represents one *cycle*. The number of such cycles to pass each second determines the *frequency* of the transmission. For example, symphony orchestras typically tune their musical instruments to *middle A*, which is also known as *A 440*. This designation means that the fundamental pitch (frequency) of that tone is made up of 440 cycles passing our point of reference each second. As we move to higher frequencies, we measure by *kilocycles* (thousands of cycles per second) and *megacycles* (millions of cycles per second).

So far so good. To avoid the need to translate the term *cycle* into various languages, it has been replaced by the uniformly expressed designation of *hertz*. This term honors Heinrich Hertz, a nineteenth-century German physicist who, in 1887, created and then detected electromagnetic waves in his laboratory. As medium waves, AM signals are conventionally identified in *kilohertz*, and the very high frequencies used in FM are more conveniently expressed in *megahertz*. These frequency abbreviations are frequently written kHz and MHz with a capital letter *H* to represent Hertz, the proper noun for which it stands.

We now are ready to plug the concept of *wavelength* into the picture. Wavelength is the distance (expressed in meters rather than miles) between two individual waves. Electromagnetic waves travel at the speed of light— 186,000 *miles* per second, or 300,000,000 *meters* per second (actually 299,792,500 meters, but the rounded figure is normally used). The higher the frequency becomes, the shorter is the wavelength. Why? Because there are more waves (cycles/hertz) in a higher frequency, more of these waves pass by our reference point within a second, shortening the distance between each two waves.

Through a simple division problem or two, we can convert wavelength to frequency and back again and thus better understand the interrelationship of these two factors. As an example, let's take an AM station operating at 830 kilohertz. We can divide this into the speed of electromagnetic energy expressed in *kilometers* per second (300,000) to find the wavelength.

$$\frac{300,000}{830}$$

Because we express the frequency in *kilohertz* rather than in individual hertz, we express distance in kilometers rather than in individual meters. This is why we are dividing 300,000 rather than 300 *million*, thereby eliminating a number of extraneous zeros. In a sense, we have already divided both our top and bottom numbers by 1,000 before begin-

**29**

CHAPTER 2
Sub-
dividing
the
Electronic
Landscape

ning the problem so the result will still be in meters (per second).

$$\frac{300,000}{830} = \text{a wavelength of 361.4 meters}$$

As compared to wavelengths in general, 361.4 is of medium length. This result coincides with our earlier statement that domestic AM stations use the medium-wave portion of the spectrum.

In contrast, let us look at a shortwave station to see *why* these sky wave AM transmissions are called shortwave. Assuming our shortwave facility is operating at 15,160 kilohertz, we divide this number into 300,000:

$$\frac{300,000}{15,160} = 19.79 \text{ meters}$$

Clearly, this is a much *shorter* wavelength (distance between each individual wave) than is the 361.4 meters of the regular AM station we examined earlier.

Remember, to avoid squeezing lots of zeros onto our radio dial indicators, shortwave and FM station frequencies are usually expressed in megahertz rather than kilohertz. Thus, the shortwave station we've just discussed would be found at close to 15.2 MHz as the shortwave receiver dial is typically calibrated. Similarly, a given FM station identifies itself as being at 98.5. The label on the FM receiver band tells us that this number is expressed in MHz so, for purposes of working our formula, this spectrum position is 98,500 kilohertz. Let's calculate its wavelength.

$$\frac{300,000}{98,500} = 3.05 \text{ meters}$$

Recall our earlier information that FM signals are transmitted at very high frequencies and that the higher the frequency, the shorter the wavelength. The magnitude of the difference between normal AM and FM broadcasts in terms of wavelength is illustrated by our two examples. Our AM station, at 830 kHz, exhibits a wavelength more than 100 times greater than that of the FM outlet at 98.5 MHz (361.4 meters compared to 3.05 meters).

Our equation can also be used the other way, of course. If we know AM station KTRE is broadcasting at 261 meters, we divide this number into our standard figure for the speed of light to get the frequency:

$$\frac{300,000}{261 \text{ meters}} = 1149.4 \text{ kHz}$$

You would therefore turn to 1150 on your standard AM dial to tune in this station.

## The Antenna Equation

From an equipment standpoint, there is a direct relationship between wavelength and antenna size. This relationship also can be expressed in mathematical terms. For most broadcast applications, the length of the actual signal radiator is either one-quarter or one-half the size of the wavelength on which the station is operating. Because VHF and UHF waves are relatively short, their antenna prongs are short as well, but they are located as high as possible on towers and hilltops to lengthen the horizon the signal can blanket. (Refer again to Figure 2–6.)

The ground wave signals generated by medium-wave AM stations, on the other hand, result in the *entire tower* acting as the radiator/antenna, with extensive underground cabling to maximize conductivity of the earth's surface. A medium-wave AM station usually uses an antenna that is one-quarter of the wavelength in size. Thus, we can determine the typical antenna length of the aforementioned KTRE as follows:

1. We already know that the station broadcasts at a wavelength of 261 meters (or could have roughly calculated that fact from its announced frequency position at 1150 kHz).

2. One meter equals approximately 3.28 feet. Therefore, KTRE's wavelength:

   3.28 (feet) x 261 (meters) = 856.1 feet

3. Because the antenna length for AM stations is usually one-quarter of the wave-

length, we divide by four to get the probable tower (radiator) height:

$$\frac{856.1}{4} = 214 \text{ feet}$$

High-frequency-wave antennas as used by shortwave broadcasters follow similar principles but consist of cables strung between towers in several configurations to match the multiple frequencies they must use in coping with daily and seasonal ionospheric changes. (Figure 2–7 shows a portion of a VOA shortwave array.)

**31**

CHAPTER 2
Sub-
dividing
the
Electronic
Landscape

sand megahertz, one million kilohertz, or one billion hertz.

It must be realized that broadcast-related activities are not the exclusive occupiers of these bands but only use certain portions of them. Still, Table 2–1 does provide a comparative spectrum orientation to the location of mass-media-related services. Recognize also that the higher the frequency, the greater the transmitter's power requirement in serving the same coverage area. This relationship becomes an especially important characteristic as we turn to the subject of television.

### A Band Overview

In summary, international agreements via the ITU divide the spectrum into certain bands to accommodate common activities. The most important of these bands to electronic mass communicators are those listed in Table 2–1. GHz, the top item in Table 2–1, stands for *gigahertz*. A single gigahertz equals one thou-

## Television's Dual Spectrum

Most of us are aware that there are two main types of television stations—VHF and UHF. And, as Table 2–1 reveals, UHF outlets operate on a higher frequency band and therefore with greater power requirements. Even

**Figure 2–7**
A small part of the shortwave antenna system at the Voice of America's relay station near Greenville, North Carolina

**Table 2–1**

**Major Electromagnetic Spectrum Segments**

| Frequency | Range | Service |
|---|---|---|
| Super high frequency | 3–30 GHz | Satellite transmissions and most microwave relays |
| Ultra high frequency | 300–3,000 MHz | UHF TV |
| Very high frequency | 30–300 MHz | FM radio and VHF TV |
| High frequency | 3–30 MHz | Shortwave radio |
| Medium frequency | 300–3,000 kHz | AM local radio |

within the VHF spectrum, however, there are significant differences between channel assignments. These differences have both power and coverage area implications.

### Viewing VHF

In the United States, VHF channels are divided into low and high band operations. Channels 2 through 6 are low-band and collectively operate between 54 and 88 MHz. (Channel 1's frequency still exists in the spectrum, of course, but was deleted from television service by the FCC in May 1948 and reassigned to land mobile/two-way radio use. In exchange, these services gave up their right to share channels 2 through 13 with television.[9])

Other things being equal (including terrain and the absence of man-made signal barriers such as skyscrapers), any low-band VHF station can put a maximum signal over a twenty to twenty-five mile range by generating a visual signal of 100,000 watts. High-band channels 7 through 13, however, do not begin at the upper end of the low-band spectrum (88 MHz). Instead, they extend from 174 MHz to 216 MHz. The space between TV channels 6 and 7 (88–174 MHz) has been set aside for a number of other activities, including the entire FM radio spectrum at 88–108 MHz.

The most obvious result is that a high-band VHF station, because of its significantly higher position on the spectrum, must generate up to 316,000 watts of visual signal power to achieve the same coverage as a low-band facility operating at only 100,000 watts. However, this does not mean the station would be operating a 100,000-watt transmitter. Rather, we are talking about *Effective Radiated Power* (ERP). In VHF and UHF transmissions, ERP is the result of the transmitter power, minus power loss in getting the signal to the antenna, times signal gain generated by that antenna:

$$ERP = (\text{Transmitter power} - \text{loss}) \times \text{Antenna gain}$$

### Viewing UHF

UHF television, meanwhile, does not begin until 470 MHz (channel 14) and goes up to channel 69, which ends at 806 MHz. This puts UHF stations at a tremendous power/coverage area disadvantage. The FCC recognizes this disadvantage, and thus FCC regulations allow 'U's' to generate a visual ERP of up to five million watts in an attempt to achieve picture parity with VHF operations. The resulting equipment and electricity costs ensure that few UHF facilities attain this maximum and further demonstrate the technical obstacles that UHF broadcasters have faced. Little wonder that the first telecasters in a locale snapped up either low-band VHF assignments, or, if these were already taken, put a high-band V on the air. UHF was primarily for latecomers or for broadcasters in the smaller all-UHF markets, which the FCC belatedly created to stem abandonment of the band. Strangely enough, UHF was also the band of choice for some entrepreneurs who mistakenly thought the limited-capacity VHF band would become obsolete. (A summary compar-

**33**

CHAPTER 2

Sub-
dividing
the
Electronic
Landscape

**Table 2–2**
**Summary Table of the U.S. Broadcast Spectrum**

| Frequency Range | | Broadcast Use | Specific Allocations |
|---|---|---|---|
| ⌐3000 MHz | | | |
| | Ultra high frequency | UHF-TV Channels 14-69 | 470–806 MHz |
| └300 MHz | | | |
| | Very high frequency | VHF-TV Channels 7-13 | 174–216 MHz |
| | Very high frequency | FM Radio | 88–108 MHz |
| | Very high frequency | VHF-TV Channels 2-6 | 54–88 MHz (except 72-76) |
| ⌐30 MHz | | | |
| | High frequency | Shortwave radio | Several separate bands |
| ⌐3000 kHz/3MHz | | | |
| | Medium frequency | Domestic AM radio | 535–1705 kHz |
| └300 kHz | | | |

ison of U.S. broadcast bands is presented in Table 2–2.)

Network affiliations also followed VHF popularity, leaving the great majority of UHF stations as *independents* who had to fill their entire program day themselves. UHF difficulties initially were further compounded by early receiving set design that made tuning in UHF stations considerably more difficult and approximate than simply clicking to a VHF channel. Each VHF channel had a precise slot in dial turning. UHF frequency dials, however, were like a radio knob. The viewer was forced to twist the dial back and forth in a sometimes frustrating attempt to locate the center of the UHF signal.

The expansion of cable television in the last two decades brought some significant benefits to UHF broadcasters. Once the cable is run into the home, every channel can carry a signal, unlike regular over-the-air broadcasting, where adjoining channels must be kept vacant to avoid interference. Because cable systems cannot process UHF signals, cable operators must convert these signals to VHF, sometimes placing them between existing VHF broadcasters. Alternatively, through use of a *midband converter* on top of or within the

home set, the viewer can enjoy continuous and discrete tuning of all channels. UHF signals carried by the cable may still be a higher number than VHF, but they are now just as easy to tune as are true VHF stations. At least in terms of ease of use and picture quality, cable has thus brought the UHF broadcaster to parity with VHF operations.

## Cable and Microwave Systems

Many channels on the cable system are not available over the air as local broadcast stations but can be received only by cable subscribers. These added viewing services can be divided into three main categories:

1. Local origination (LO) channels programmed by the cable system itself.
2. Distant broadcast signals delivered to the cable system by satellite or microwave relay. (A popular station carried by a large number of cable systems far outside its

own market is generally referred to as a *superstation*.)

3. Regional or national cable networks that are also satellite-delivered but do not originate as over-the-air station broadcasts.

## The Essence of Cable

Once a program source is assigned a channel position by the cable system, all spectrum-based distinctions evaporate as far as the viewer/consumer is concerned. The program becomes much more important than how it has been delivered, rendering all viewing options a certain equality of access. People don't set out to watch "network television" or "local television." Rather, they decide to view television in general or a specific program that vehicle can deliver.

Cable obscures, even bypasses, the technological distinctions of spectrum location and signal type. It redefines and redistributes the large aggregate mass audience for television by adding new options to old ones and by making them all relatively easy for viewers to locate. Cable can also efficiently deliver all local radio signals over its wire and can supplement these signals with national cable-exclusive audio services.

The cable system itself is an apparatus made up of three main components. Cable experts Baldwin and McVoy describe these components:

> First is the *headend,* which is the point at which all the program sources are received, assembled, and processed for transmission by the distribution network. Second is the *distribution network,* consisting of coaxial cable leaving the headend on power or telephone company poles or, in some cases, buried underground, and going down each street within the community served. Third is the *subscriber drop,* which consists of the coaxial cable going from the street into the individual subscriber's home, and the related equipment required to connect the cable to the

subscriber's television receiver and other devices.[10]

## The Microwave Connection

Signals are transported to cable systems via super-high-frequency microwaves (measured in gigahertz). They are then downconverted to frequencies the cable is capable of distributing and that customer television sets are capable of receiving. Broadcast stations make the same use of microwaves to receive their material. Network programs, commercial feeds, newsstories, and even financial information from corporate headquarters about the station's business affairs can be shipped via terrestrial or (more typically) satellite microwave avenues. The cable/broadcast difference, of course, is that the television station is using these relays to put together a *single* program feed whereas the cable system is assembling multiple microwave transmissions in order to simultaneously fill *dozens* of channels.

Consumers, of course, need not be aware of any of this, and cable systems or broadcast stations themselves are primarily recipients rather than initiators of microwave transmissions. Still, one can get a better understanding of the total electronic media landscape by seeing how microwaves fit into the picture. Figure 2–8 shows a microwave relay tower.

First, because their wavelengths are extremely short, microwaves travel only in a narrow line of sight. For land-based *(terrestrial)* applications, this means that each microwave tower must have a straight shot at the next installation to which it is sending a signal. The distances between these towers, therefore, must be relatively short. In the case of satellite use of microwaves, of course, line of sight is no problem for an electronic 'bird' situated over thousands of miles of real estate. Further, because it is communicating through the physical vacuum of space rather than within earth's dense atmosphere, the microwaves generated from a satellite make

**35**

CHAPTER 2
Sub-
dividing
the
Electronic
Landscape

**Figure 2–8**
A typical terrestrial microwave relay
installation

much more efficient use of their power than
do their land-bound counterparts.

Communications satellites actually use two
distinct sections of the super-high-frequency
band. The more established satellite relay service has been in the so-called C-band (4–6
GHz), whereas newer satellites have tended
to operate in the higher Ku-band (11–15 GHz).
Because terrestrial microwaves are often located within C-band frequencies, satellite

transmissions in the 4–6 GHz range may be
afflicted with interference on completion of
their trip to earth. Ku-band activity, on the
other hand, is concentrated considerably
above conventional microwave operations
on the spectrum and so is spared such interference. On the other hand, the extremely
short wavelength of Ku-band waves means
that even very small objects can block passage of these waves.

## Associated Video Vehicles

Even though television stations and cable systems are the most widely recognized structures on the television landscape, they may not be the only game in town. Some additional options have entered the fringes of the field and now present further opportunities for electronic media professionals. Among these comparative newcomers are LPTV, MMDS, SMATV, and DBS.

### LPTV (Low-Power Television)

*LPTV* stands for low-power television. Intended to provide local television service to isolated hamlets or specialty service to more populated environs, low-power stations operate with 10 watts of power on the VHF band or with up to 1,000 watts on the UHF band. They may serve merely as *translators* to extend the range of regular full-power broadcasters or as self-standing, independently programmed entities. Some of the more than 800 LPTV outlets operating in 1991 received virtually all of their on-air material via satellite in much the same way that cable network programs are distributed. Other LPTV outlets try to program themselves or air a mix of satellite and *bicycled* (mail/freight delivered) content with perhaps some local production thrown in. The FCC considers LPTV stations to be *secondary services*. This means that they may not cause interference to any existing or future regular television outlet but are not protected from receiving such interference themselves.

At this time employment opportunities in the LPTV branch of the industry are very limited. If the LPTV outlet is no more than a translator, it may have no employees of its own but may be serviced by the engineers of the parent station. That station's sales staff will also market it, but usually only as a bonus audience extender for existing advertisers. If the LPTV facility is separately programmed, it will have its own crew; but the limited coverage area and consequently limited revenue possibilities will tend to keep staff size small, with perhaps no more than three or four full-time employees.

### MMDS (Wireless Cable)

Whereas LPTV operations are modeled along station lines, *MMDS* entities are more like cable systems; in fact, the delivery system is often called *wireless cable.* Operating on the ultra-high and super-high-frequency bands, *Multiple Multipoint Distribution Services* (MMDS), like any microwave relay station, can transmit direct, line-of-sight waves out to approximately a twenty-five-mile radius. These signals are then downconverted at their destination so as to be receivable on open channels of regular television sets. (A diagram of an MMDS/Wireless Cable system is presented in Figure 2–9.) MMDS is really a marriage of older MDS and ITFS activity. MDS was originally a business data carrier until the early 1970s, when the FCC permitted its use in television service. Typically, this service consisted of a movie channel that was radiated to hotels in a large city from a tall, central transmission point. The movie was then downconverted for hotel guests, who paid an additional charge for the entertainment. *ITFS (Instructional Television Fixed Service)* used essentially the same technology, but the receiving dishes were on the roofs of school buildings rather than hotels and the programming was instruction instead of cinematic entertainment.

As cable gradually began to wire urban areas, however, single-channel MDS operations were unable to compete with the multiple channels that the new competitor could provide. Many ITFS channels, meanwhile, remained vacant because no educational institution had applied to operate them. In the mid-1980s, therefore, the FCC promulgated new regulations whereby MDS and ITFS as-

37

CHAPTER 2
Sub-
dividing
the
Electronic
Landscape

**JOHN KOMPAS**/PRESIDENT
KOMPAS/BIEL & ASSOCIATES, INC.

Low power television (LPTV) was born in the early 1980s after Congress instructed the Federal Communications Commission to create a service that would give more people access to television station ownership and diversify broadcast television programming. The FCC did not mandate local programming in its rules for the new LPTV medium, but local programming was encouraged and the concept of localism was clearly at the heart of the service.

The idea of small local television stations was the perfect answer to an old dilemma for me. In my early days in broadcasting, I worked as a radio disc jockey and ad salesman. During this period, I became increasingly frustrated by my larger ad clients—the fast-food restaurants and national chain stores, for example. These clients would insist on buying television ad time—on a station sixty miles away! I tried the logical approach—reminding them that the television station's high prices could never be cost-effective for them, that most of the people who would see their commercials lived too far away ever to come to their stores. But my radio station couldn't compete with television—even expensive, inefficient television. And I wasn't closing those sales.

But in 1982 I suddenly found myself right in the middle of the low-power heyday. When more than 14,000 applications for new stations were filed with the FCC, my partner, Jacquelyn Biel, and I realized that a new industry was being born. We also realized that the new industry would need informa-

tion. So we began writing about it for every trade magazine that would print our articles. In 1986 we started our own trade monthly, *The LPTV Report.* Five years later, *The LPTV Report* was a subscriber- and advertiser-supported trade magazine read by more than 3,000 people every month.

As its publisher, I am responsible for selling the ad space—not an easy job in this day of declining ad budgets! I have to make a lot of sales calls every week in order to keep the magazine growing at its present rate. My job also includes drawing up sales contracts, setting ad rates, and helping Jackie Biel, the editor, with the general preparation of each issue.

But that's not all of my job. In 1984, Jackie and I realized that the new LPTV industry needed a trade association to help it establish its own identity in the television marketplace. So, with the invaluable help of many other people, we started the Community Broadcasters Association (CBA), and I became its president in 1987. We now have nearly 200 members and a host of new frontiers to explore.

One of the most difficult parts of my job as CBA president is almost constant fund raising. We need money for so many things, including services for the members, legal counsel, publicity. I must also make monthly trips to Washington, DC, to represent the association on various issues. Twice now, for example, I have testified before a Senate subcommittee investigating cable re-regulation. I am also sort of a working ambassador for LPTV and the CBA. I often answer calls from people across the country looking for information on how to start their own LPTV stations.

As a consultant, I work to help these newcomers plan, build, and sign their own stations on the air. In order to get a construction permit (the go-ahead to begin building a station), one must submit a very thorough application to the FCC. My consulting company, Kompas/Biel & Associates, helps LPTV clients prepare and submit these applications. Absolute accuracy is a must; the FCC will return applications that are not letter perfect. If that happens, a client could lose the frequency he or she wants. We also help our clients analyze the market potential of the areas in which they want to build their stations. We help them decide what programming will best suit that market. We engineer and build their stations. And we assist them with budgeting, staffing, and other aspects of station operation.

Finally, I have my own LPTV station on the air. W43AV has been broadcasting to Waukesha County, Wisconsin, since July 1990. Before it signed on, I had to help find investors for the project, interview and hire responsible employees, work with the station's chief engineer to choose and buy equipment, work with the general manager to decide on programming, and take care of the myriad details that any new project entails.

Even though my days and weeks can be very hectic and stressful (and my desk can be piled rather high at times) I love my work and I look forward to watching the seeds that I have planted grow. I believe in the value of local television. I believe that television is a wondrous medium that we have only begun to understand how to use. Helping LPTV grow is my way of helping the communities it serves to become better places.

---

signments would be grouped into sets of four and licensed to qualified applicants on a lottery basis. ITFS frequencies for which no educational institution had applied also were made available for commercial MMDS assignments. Educational institutions that did hold ITFS assignments, however, were permitted to lease all or part of their spectrum space to commercial operators and thereby receive additional revenues for their regular instructional activities. These FCC actions meant that up to 33 MMDS channels thus were available for use in a given city. Programmers could operate four channels of their own and

**Figure 2–9**
An MMDS (wireless cable) system

39

CHAPTER 2
Sub-
dividing
the
Electronic
Landscape

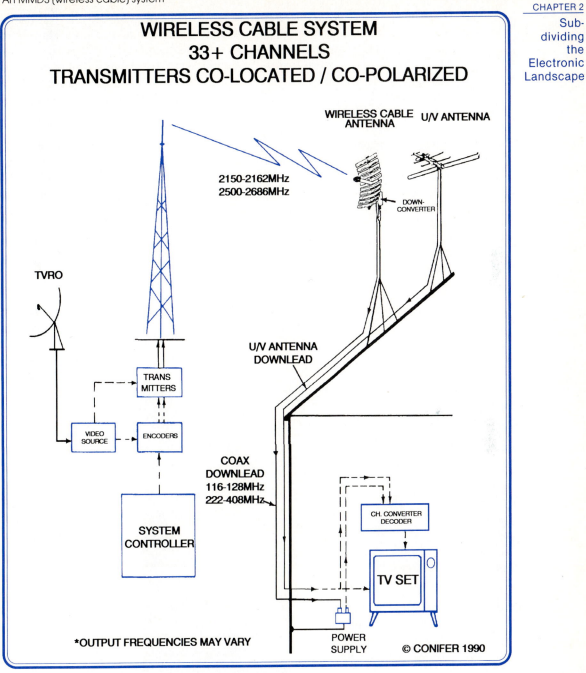

# WIRELESS CABLE SYSTEM
# 33+ CHANNELS
# TRANSMITTERS CO-LOCATED / CO-POLARIZED

WIRELESS CABLE ANTENNA     U/V ANTENNA

2150-2162MHz
2500-2686MHz

DOWN-CONVERTER

TVRO

U/V ANTENNA DOWNLEAD

TRANS MITTERS

VIDEO SOURCE     ENCODERS

COAX DOWNLEAD
116-128MHz
222-408MHz

CH. CONVERTER DECODER

SYSTEM CONTROLLER

TV SET

*OUTPUT FREQUENCIES MAY VARY

POWER SUPPLY

© CONIFER 1990

lease the channels of other companies to deliver a wide range of pay services to urban residents. Many of these services the MMDS company receives via satellite.

Compared to cable, MMDS remains a small, fledgling industry with slightly more than a dozen active systems at the start of the 1990s.[11] Robert Schmidt, president of the Wireless Cable Association, has charged that one constraint on MMDS development has been a conspiracy on the part of the cable industry to keep the new industry from getting programming. "One [cable] operator," Schmidt complained, "had the audacity to put his finger on my chest and say, 'If you even think of coming here, I'll keep you from getting product.'"[12] Men and women seeking a career in MMDS should thus prepare themselves for contentious times.

## SMATV (Satellite Master Antenna Television)

*SMATV* (Satellite Master Antenna Television) installations are another potential challenger to cable's multichannel market. An SMATV operator services a single building or apartment complex with television service by mounting a satellite receiving dish on the roof and then downconverting and distributing the multiple channels thereby received. The SMATV facility, unlike MMDS, really does not transmit any signal itself but merely captures programming by means of its large *TVRO (Television Receive-Only)* satellite antenna (such as the dish pictured in Figure 2–10). Thus, building an SMATV installation requires no license from the FCC (as do broadcasting and MMDS) or specific franchise from a municipality (as does cable) to operate. Pro-

**Figure 2–10**
A high-capacity 2.8 meter SMATV antenna

vided that its dish does not violate local zoning ordinances, the SMATV entrepreneur need only secure the approval of the landlord.

Cable operators accuse SMATV of *cream skimming*, of grabbing the most affluent and concentrated subscribers while leaving cable with poorer and more dispersed customers. Consequently, the cable industry has encouraged its members to pursue legal actions designed to require landlords to provide equal access for cable lines on SMATV-served property. The success of such actions has varied from state to state, but it does illustrate the complex turf battles that can be waged by rival electronic media interests.

## DBS (Direct Broadcast Satellite)

In a sense, *DBS (Direct Broadcast Satellite) is* SMATV without the intermediary operator or landlord. With DBS, the signal shoots directly from the satellite to the homeowner's small receiving dish. The transmission is then downconverted and descrambled right on the property to make regular viewing possible. Descrambling is necessary because most types of programming (superstation, cable network, pay channels, etc.) are manipulated electronically to prevent viewing by people who have not paid for the service. DBS had a brief initial trial during the mid-1980s in the United States, but high costs and few subscribers forced the shutdown of the United Satellite Communications experiment.

A semi-by-product DBS has emerged as an outgrowth of the cable industry. By 1989, some 2.5 million owners of large backyard TVROs (receive-only dishes) were being provided with many of the same program services available to cable customers. For the most part, these homes are in rural or sparsely populated areas that are uneconomical to reach by cable lines. Cable companies and program suppliers license these TVROs to receive their shows and arrange for the descramblers, often through home satellite dish dealers. But because these private dishes must pick up the same signals as do the head-

ends of entire cable systems, they usually have to be equally as large, averaging ten to twelve feet across and costing an average of $3,000. With a true DBS system, such as is currently being put on line in Europe, higher-power satellites are used and therefore require receiving dishes of only 60 centimeters (less than two feet) that can be acquired for approximately $300. (A Hughes Communications high-power DBS consumer antenna is shown in Figure 2–11.)

The 1990 status of DBS in the United States then, was that of ancillary enterprise enabling the cable industry, its programmers, and receiving dish dealers to reach isolated homes that would otherwise be uneconomical to service, with the consumer being directly responsible for the substantial reception equipment costs. For at least the near future, U.S. job opportunities in DBS seem inseparable from employment in cable. Cable executives appear willing to tolerate the activity as a spin-off of their own business but will be highly resistant to a whole new competitor. *True* DBS (as opposed to the current TVRO-based activity) may challenge cable for at least a portion of its subscriber base and thus is likely neither to be welcomed nor given easy access to cable program product. (A discussion of future DBS ventures now in the planning stages appears in Chapter 14.)

# Keeping Technology in Perspective

This chapter introduces you to a number of technical and equipment-intensive subjects. Because the electronic media *are electronic,* we can never dismiss the importance of these hardware concerns in the successful execution of mass communication tasks. There is, however, a tendency in our profession to let equipment overshadow the ultimate goals of

**41**

CHAPTER 2
Sub-
dividing
the
Electronic
Landscape

**Figure 2–11**
A DBS windowsill antenna

establishing linkages with those unseen listeners and viewers. Any technical system or application must be judged not on how high tech it is but on whether it has improved our ability to communicate with our target audiences in a timely manner and in a way that somehow benefits their lives. The electromagnetic spectrum can be counted on to resonate our messages via a variety of energy-manipulating methods. The constant question is whether any given message is *worth* resonating.

This worth is measured by whether the communicator's goals were attained. This attainment, in turn, is dependent on physically reaching our audience with material to which they want to attend. Some electronic media projects have failed because the message could not be delivered with technical clarity in an economical manner. The kilowatt-gobbling, hard-to-tune-in UHF stations of the

1950s are a prime example of that principle. Yet, failure also occurs when a technologically perfect transmission delivers a message that is unpalatable to, irrelevant to, or unnoticed by the mass of individuals for whom it was intended.

Radio and television technology gets you into that home, car, or office. But professional message planning, framing, and content are necessary to achieve an impact once you're there.

## Chapter Flashback

While the electronic media are generally thought of as simply radio and television, these two elements are comprised of a number of subdivisions. Radio is conventionally

**43**

CHAPTER 2
Sub-
dividing
the
Electronic
Landscape

**RON HERMAN**/VICE-PRESIDENT, MARKETING AND DEVELOPMENT
GENERAL TELEVISION NETWORK

Anyone thinking about pursuing a career in teleproduction must be able to thrive on change because the industry and its jobs are constantly being redefined by new technology and an evolving marketplace. As the vice-president for marketing and development at one of the nation's leading teleproduction facilities, my primary responsibilities are to develop and sell services that our clients can use.

A teleproduction facility is a special kind of factory that creates customized video and audio programs at the direction of producers. Most of these producers work for advertising agencies and other communications businesses. They lease our factory and the services of the technicians operating its complex equipment. Our primary concerns are to keep all the manufacturing equipment performing at the highest levels and to keep our clients happy. It takes talented technicians who can work with each other and with clients as a team to get the job done. A gifted technician who is not a people person will not go far in this business.

One of my jobs is to make recommendations about what our facility should purchase or lease. This is not easy because so much new teleproduction equipment is introduced each year. To help me make intelligent decisions, I attend trade shows where these new products are featured. Clients, co-workers, and trade publications also provide valuable information. Because a wrong decision can be very costly, recommendations are not made lightly. Losing sleep over equipment acquisitions is an occupational hazard.

Providing the right equipment is just one way we serve our clients. Analyzing each project as it comes in and designing equipment packages to tackle the right job is another. This aspect of my job demands a thorough understanding of a facility's resources and an ability to visualize and anticipate the needs of a particular project. Jobs are often won or lost in this process.

Another responsibility I have is attracting new business. This involves letting potential clients know who we are and how we can help them. We do this with calls from our sales representatives and by distributing news releases to business and teleproduction trade publications. We also advertise and use promotions to get the word out. I direct these efforts.

The teleproduction industry demands special skills and temperaments. It is a hands-on business in which skills are developed by doing. Entry-level positions are available for people interested in getting their feet in the door. Once inside, opportunities to try different jobs present themselves to people who work hard. As I have discovered, diligent *labor* is the best way to learn the business and to determine if you have a place in it.

On the down side, you can expect long hours with tight deadlines. On the up side, expect interesting workdays that are never quite the same. For people who have what it takes, this is a career with a bright future.

segmented into AM, FM, and shortwave activities. AM stations function on the principle of *amplitude modulation*, which involves voltage variation that changes the height and depth of the radio wave. Fidelity limitations of such a system, particularly in the transmission of music, have contributed to serious audience declines for AM broadcasters and have caused them to explore new formats. The FCC is examining several options to improve AM service and viability. FM, or *frequency modulation*, stations manipulate the pitch of the signal while keeping the amplitude constant. This creates a signal that is not subject to degrading from other forms of electrical energy and that can be segmented into parts for true stereo and auxiliary service (SCA) transmission. Approximately three-fourths of listening in the United States is now done on the FM band.

Shortwave stations are used to communicate over long distances. Their transmissions are AM in nature and generate *sky waves* that take maximum advantage of *ionospheric bounce* to skip the signal to target areas. Regular AM stations emit both *ground* and *sky* waves. Ground waves tend to follow the curvature of the earth. In contrast, FM and television services transmit *direct waves*. Direct waves are essentially straight-line phenomena that travel to the horizon and then shoot off into space. Spectrum management for all of these services is coordinated on a global basis by the International Telecommunication Union (ITU).

All electromagnetic transmissions are based on *cycles*—the number of individual waves per second that pass a given point. Frequencies are measured in *kilocycles* (thousands of cycles per second), *megacycles* (millions of cycles per second), and *gigacycles* (billions of cycles per second). The term *cycle* has largely been replaced by the designation *hertz*, honoring the German physicist who conducted pioneering electromagnetic experiments.

*Wavelength* is the distance between two individual waves expressed in meters. Therefore, the higher the frequency (the more waves passing a point per second), the shorter will be the wavelength (the space between the individual waves). The length of an antenna bears a direct proportional relationship to the wavelength on which the station is operating.

Television stations are either *VHF* or *UHF*. VHF *(very high frequency)* outlets are divided into *low-band* (channels 2 through 6) and *high-band* (channels 7 through 13), with the FM radio service operating in the spectrum space between the two bands. UHF *(ultrahigh frequency)* stations must generate much more power than VHF outlets because they are located at a much higher part of the spectrum. This fact illustrates the general rule that the higher the frequency, the more power is required to propel a signal over a comparable area. Cable television, as a common retransmission system, has helped to narrow the disparity between VHF and UHF broadcasters.

Cable television systems can carry four types of content: *LO* (local origination) mate-

45

CHAPTER 2
Sub-
dividing
the
Electronic
Landscape

rial they program themselves, rebroadcasts of local television stations, rebroadcasts of distant television stations (the most widely popular of which are known as *superstations*), and presentations of cable-exclusive regional and national networks. Cable systems physically consist of three components: the *headend,* the *distribution network,* and the *subscriber drop.* Cable systems as well as television stations and satellites make use of *microwaves* (super- high-frequency transmissions measured in *gigahertz*) for program receipt and/or distribution.

Some additional video delivery services are now present on the television landscape. These services include *LPTV* (low-power television stations), *MMDS* (multiple multipoint distribution services or wireless cable), *SMATV* (satellite master antenna television), and *DBS* (direct broadcast satellite).

## ❏ Review Probes

1. What is the difference between the way AM and FM signals are generated?
2. Define sky waves, ground waves, and direct waves. What types of stations transmit each?
3. What is the relationship between frequency and wavelength? Calculate the wavelength of your favorite FM station.
4. Engineers tell us that increasing the power output of an FM station beyond a certain point will not result in any increase in coverage area. What is the reason for this?
5. Which electronic media services use each of the following?
   Medium frequency
   High frequency
   Very high frequency
   Ultra high frequency
   Super high frequency
6. How has the growth of cable helped many UHF broadcasters? Are there ways in which cable might also hurt UHF operations?

## ❏ Suggested Background Explorations

Bennett, Hank, et al. *The Complete Shortwave Listener's Handbook.* 3rd ed. Blue Ridge Summit, PA: TAB Books, 1986.

Busby, Linda, and Donald Parker. *The Art and Science of Radio.* Boston: Allyn and Bacon, 1984.

Noll, A. Michael. *Introduction to Telecommunication Electronics.* Norwood, MA: Artech House, 1988.

O'Donnell, Lewis B., Philip Benoit, and Carl Hausman. *Modern Radio Production.* 2nd ed. Belmont, CA: Wadsworth, 1990.

Oringel, Robert S. *Audio Control Handbook for Radio and Television Broadcasting.* 6th ed. Boston: Focal Press, 1989.

Pellegrino, Ronald. *The Electronic Arts of Sound and Light.* New York: Van Nostrand Reinhold, 1983.

Smale, P. H. *Introduction to Telecommunications Systems.* Blue Ridge Summit, PA: TAB Books, 1986.

Whitehouse, George E. *Understanding the New Technologies of the Mass Media.* Englewood Cliffs, NJ: Prentice-Hall, 1986.

## CHAPTER 3

# Industry Dichotomies

❏ *A* dichotomy *is defined as the division of a whole into two separate and sometimes opposing parts. The electronic media industry embraces a number of key dichotomies; the basic radio/television pairing is but the most obvious. Certainly, the differences between radio and television are easy to comprehend and are technologically detailed in Chapter 2. But even though they are less visible, other electronic media segmentations are just as important in determining the environment within which industry professionals must function. Figure 3–1 graphically summarizes these other dichotomies with the two parts of each dichotomy presented directly opposite each other on the 'wheel.'*

## Broadcast/Nonbroadcast

As we mention in Chapter 1, true *broadcasting* represents only a portion of the electronic media landscape. We know that broadcast signals are propelled into the air for reception by anyone who lives within that signal's coverage pattern and possesses a receiver. In a sense, broadcasting is thus the most democratic of media because the richest mansion on the hill and the poorest shack near the

**Figure 3–1**
Electronic media dichotomies at a glance

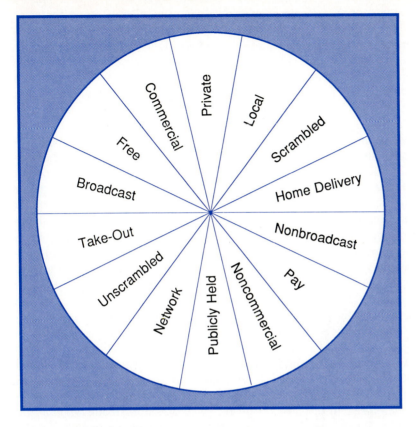

swamp have access to exactly the same product. Granted, the mansion may install a much better receiver, but the content it captures will be no different. Once some sort of radio or TV set is obtained and the electricity bill paid, all broadcast product is free to all area residents without regard to class or creed.

Because of this unique attribute and its use of the common spectrum, broadcasting is considered to be a public activity, with the people engaging in it acting as public trustees. In the United States, the Radio Act of 1927 was the first law clearly to reflect this public trustee consciousness. According to former FCC Chairman Wayne Coy, debate leading up to the act's adoption demonstrated that "Congress intended that radio stations shall not be used for the private interest, whims, or ca-

prices of the particular persons who have been granted licenses."[1] The 1927 law's emphasis on broadcasting in the "public interest, convenience, or necessity" (a phrase borrowed from earlier railroad-regulating legislation) was maintained in the much more comprehensive Communications Act of 1934. As amended, the 1934 statute remains in place today and repeatedly cites "public interest, convenience, or necessity" as the guiding principle for FCC actions.[2]

### The Common-Carrier Distinction

With its enactment, the Communications Act also established important distinctions between *broadcasting* and *common-carrier* activities. Section 3 of the law defined broadcasting as "the dissemination of radio communications intended to be received by the public." On the other hand, a common carrier meant "any person engaged as a common carrier for hire, in interstate or foreign communication by wire or radio . . . but a person engaged in radio broadcasting shall not . . . be deemed a common carrier." This delineation represents another facet of our broadcast/nonbroadcast dichotomy. Common carriers, like telephone companies, are expected to provide their transmission avenues to all comers, on a first-come, first-served basis. They typically have no control over the content their customers choose to have sent, and their rates are frequently subject to governmental regulation. The deliberate exclusion of "radio [and, by later extension, television] broadcasting" from common-carrier status helped free mass–communications-related activities from several regulatory mandates while still requiring an overall "public interest" type of operation. By using the phrase *intended to be received by the public* to define broadcasting, the Communications Act also sifts out such nonmass activities as police and amateur radio transmissions. From a legal standpoint, then, broadcasting is clearly a *mass communication* enterprise in its most fundamental sense.

The delineation between broadcasting and common-carrier endeavors was clear and unequivocal to federal legislators in 1934. However, a number of hybrid systems have subsequently emerged to enlarge the standard of comparison from the basic broadcasting/common-carrier focus to a broadcast/nonbroadcast orientation. Certainly, a telephone company is a common carrier, and a television station is a broadcaster. But what about a cable system, an MMDS facility, or a DBS operation?

### Neither Fish nor Fowl

The Cable Act of 1984 (which amended the basic Communications Act) put cable in a nebulous middle ground between broadcasters and common carriers. Cable uses the air-waves to receive most of its programming, but it then delivers this programming to customers via private lines rather than over the public spectrum. Despite the fact that several of its channels are devoted to retransmission of over-the-air broadcasters, the cable system is not itself that broadcaster and does not radiate a signal outside the wires it has strung. Even though cable is franchised by a community potentially to service the entire populace of that community, it will be made available only to people who pay for the privilege. Further, cable is not really a common carrier for those home subscribers because it does not routinely offer them the opportunity to contract for channels in order to initiate their own messages (as we do when we use a telephone circuit). However, when cable systems lease specified channels to other businesses, they must serve all leasees on a nondiscriminatory basis like any common carrier—without legally assuming actual common-carrier status.

In contrast, the intermediary companies that pick up and satellite-deliver superstation programming to cable systems are common carriers, as are most terrestrial or satellite microwave relay operators. If and when a true DBS service is permanently mounted in the United States, a more specific decision will have to be made about whether DBS operations should be similarly classified as common carriers, defined as broadcasters, or consigned to the neither/nor category, as is cable.

MMDS operators, meanwhile, have been allowed to choose their own regulatory status even though the medium and its predecessors historically have been considered common carriers. Beginning in 1987, the FCC permitted MMDS systems to specify which of their channels were common carriers and which were noncommon carriers (the latter status is comparable to most cable activities).[3]

Even though all of the electronic media that come under the FCC's jurisdiction are expected to operate in the "public interest, convenience, and necessity," a broadcaster's link with that public is much more direct, widespread, and automatic than is that of nonbroadcast operators. Customers might complain to the telephone company about the availability or clarity of its service, but not about the content that service carries, which is, for the most part, customer-initiated. Alleged abuse of the phone lines by telemarketers (telephone salespeople) or dial-a-porn panderers is protested, of course, but no one believes that the phone company is itself responsible for the content. Broadcasters, however, are seen as both the operators of the delivery system and the creators of what goes over it and are thereby held fully accountable by both the citizenry and the FCC.

From this perspective, too, cable operators stand on a somewhat unstable middle ground. They can be attacked for the services they choose to carry (such as an 'adult entertainment' channel) or fail to carry (such as Congress-covering C-SPAN). They also are subject to vilification from broadcasters as to the cable channel to which that broadcaster's signal has been consigned or the complete deletion of that signal. Citizens might also respond negatively to programs aired on the cable system's public access channels, even though the near common-carrier status of these channels limits the operator's discretion in denying access. Still, as in the case of the telephone company, the public usually holds cable accountable for whether an entire service is received rather than for the individual program content decisions such as those a broadcaster must make on a continuous basis.

## Free/Pay

A second and closely associated dichotomy involving the electronic media is whether the service directly charges the public for its product. Conventional broadcasting is heralded by its industry associations as a "free" medium that is there for the taking by anyone who wishes to enjoy it. In July 1989, the National Association of Broadcasters kicked off a "Free TV" campaign designed to contrast broadcast television advantageously with cable and other competitors to which consumers must pay actual fees. In the on-air message that launched the promotions effort, no less a personage than news legend Walter Cronkite reminded station viewers across the country:

What you are watching is called Free Television. It's part of a system—born 50 years ago—that is unlike any other in the world. Through your Free TV window, you've been witness to triumph and tragedy—to love and laughter, learning life. It's offered free to all, even the cable systems that carry it. Imagine the impact if it were gone. Join us in the coming months, as we celebrate and stand watch, over Free TV.[4]

### Qualifying 'Free'

Yet, as with many electronic media dichotomies, the distinction is not quite so simple. At a time when almost 60 percent of U.S. households received all of their television service (broadcast stations included) from a cable company to which a monthly charge is paid, even "free" TV signals no longer seem free. As NBC-TV executive Pier Mapes asserted to the New York State Broadcasters at the time, "The campaign is probably ill-conceived. The average American who's paying $28 or $15 or $50 a month cannot differentiate. It's not free to him."[5]

What we really have, then, are degrees of "free." If you receive the signal over-the-air direct from your local broadcaster, the service *is* essentially free because you need expend only your time and electricity. Once that broadcast station is delivered by a cable system, it becomes less "free" because the customer is paying for rental of the cable line through which it comes. Still, the cost of this signal is probably very low because that same fee is also bringing fifteen, twenty, or more other *basic* services into the home. Basic cable packages are the lowest tiers of service that the cable system provides. They usually include broadcast stations as well as cable networks that secure much of their revenue from advertising. Assuming a monthly basic cost of $23, the customer is probably paying only a few cents to receive each station that could be captured "free" if picked up off the air. Figure 3–2 illustrates recent trends in how cable systems spend their customer/ subscribers' fees.

## Specific-Charge Services

What most people characterize as real "pay" television is when a single service or two closely associated services are specifically and separately charged for. HBO, Showtime/The Movie Channel, The Disney Channel, and a multiplicity of regional sports networks are among the most active pay services. Whether delivered by cable, MMDS, or a licensed satellite dish in your own backyard, these services are transmitted in delib-

**Figure 3–2**

Cable rates: facts and figures. Recent trends in where your cable subscription dollars are spent

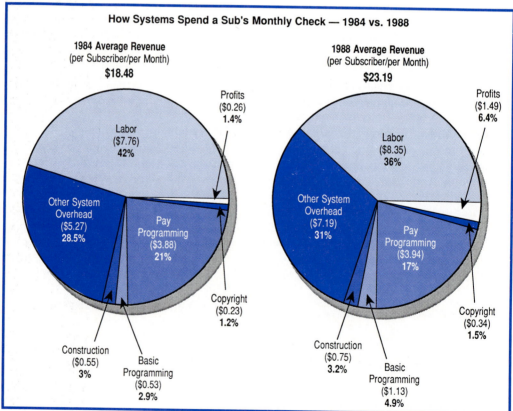

(Source: MSO Magazine, a publication of Transmedia Partners, I, L.P.)

erately scrambled form and are descrambled only after the payment of a monthly fee. In the older, *nonaddressable* technologies, the actual descrambling box must be installed at your home or on a pole nearby. When you cancel the service, this box must be physically removed or disconnected (deactivated). With newer, more sophisticated *addressable* technologies, the service can be switched on or off automatically from the cable or other program provider offices, thereby avoiding costly physical service calls.

In the most advanced addressable pay technologies, a telephone call from the customer to a central computer (via a device like that in Figure 3–3) is all that is necessary to descramble/deliver the channel. Because these computers are capable of handling thousands of calls instantaneously, they are expected to greatly increase *PPV* opportunities. PPV (pay-per-view) means that customers connect for one event (such as a movie, boxing match, or live stage show) rather than for continuous service. This availability, of course, is the ultimate in "pay"; it makes the purchase of TV product analogous to buying a theater admis-

sions ticket or a single copy of a magazine or newspaper.[6]

## Other Pay Vehicles

Though the mechanisms are less obvious, radio also can function as a pay medium. In the early 1960s, for example, the author got his first media job working for a commercial listener-supported radio station. People who enjoyed the jazz/show tune/classical format were implored (frequently) to send in a good-faith subscription to the station. The signal, of course, was not scrambled, and there was no way to detect nonpaying subscribers or do anything about it even if they were identified. This was a primitive way of mounting a service that lacked advertising support by depending on the consumer beneficiaries of that service voluntarily to pick up the cost. Public radio and television pursue this same strategy today with membership drives and subscriber auctions.

The SCA services such as Muzak (mentioned in Chapter 2) are a more technologically sophisticated form of pay radio. Because they are designed to pull the subcarrier out

**Figure 3–3**
The VIDEOpal ® Order Recorder plugs into the phone line to permit instant (addressable) ordering of PPV home-satellite (HSD) events

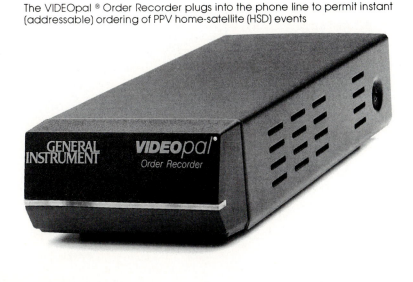

from the body of the main FM signal, SCA receivers function much like television descramblers by converting otherwise indecipherable electromagnetic patterns into content that the customer can use. Cable-exclusive radio networks are another pay audio option, of course. In this case, the cable system pipes the music into the home as another optional-purchase tier.

## Who Provides the Free Ride

In all of the above instances, direct consumer payments replace fees paid by advertisers as the sole or primary means of revenue for the electronic media company supplying the service. Free media, then, are only free to consumers because sponsors have paid for those program events (and the commercials within them) to be delivered. In exchange for enduring commercial breaks and programming that is conceived or edited to accommodate them, U.S. listeners and viewers can receive over-the-air broadcasts without charge. This massive advertising revenue has stimulated every phase of the U.S. television industry from programming to outlet construction to receiver sales.

In many other countries, media consumers have to pay an annual license fee in order to operate their radio and television sets. Revenues from these licenses help only partially to offset the absence of advertising dollars, and the direct cost to consumers is often the equivalent of more than a hundred dollars per year. Particularly in Europe, where movement to private commercial broadcasting is accelerating, both the license fee concept and advertising limitations are being re-examined. This process will likely result in redefinition, expansion, and innovation in free as well as in pay operations. Table 3–1 provides a glimpse of how U.S. TV receiver penetration compares to that in other countries—many of which had little or no advertising to support system development.

**Table 3–1**
**TV Receivers per 1,000 Inhabitants in 40 Selected Countries, 1986**

| Country | # Receivers | Country | # Receivers |
|---|---|---|---|
| United States | 813 | Cuba | 202 |
| Japan | 585 | Bulgaria | 189 |
| Canada | 546 | Brazil | 188 |
| United Kingdom | 534 | Mexico | 117 |
| Finland | 480 | Colombia | 102 |
| Australia | 472 | South Africa | 93 |
| Switzerland | 411 | Egypt | 83 |
| France | 402 | Nicaragua | 59 |
| Hungary | 399 | Iran | 57 |
| Sweden | 393 | Morocco | 54 |
| West Germany* | 379 | Viet Nam | 34 |
| East Germany* | 363 | Paraguay | 23 |
| Spain | 322 | China | 10 |
| U.S.S.R. | 321 | India | 7 |
| Belgium | 301 | Afghanistan | 7 |
| Saudi Arabia | 269 | Nigeria | 6 |
| Israel | 261 | Haiti | 4 |
| Hong Kong | 232 | Congo | 3 |
| Bahamas | 223 | Ethiopia | 2 |
| Argentina | 214 | Burma | 1 |

(Source: UNESCO Statistical Yearbook, 1988
*Before unification)

## Commercial/ Noncommercial

As we have just discussed, no electronic media service is entirely free. Someone or some institution must cover the substantial costs involved in providing radio and television service. In free media, these costs are borne by advertisers. In the various pay options a greater and greater percentage of the tab is shifted to consumers. With noncommercial systems, of course, advertising revenues are precluded, and so other means of revenue must be found. This commercial/noncommercial dichotomy thus represents a different but associated dimension of the free/pay division.

Until relatively recently, most European broadcasting was of the noncommercial variety, with license fees and other governmental grants covering the bills. Consumers paid for the services both directly (through the license fees mentioned earlier) and indirectly (via general governmental taxation of which a portion was diverted to support the state radio/television activities). Now, however, a combination of cable, private broadcaster, and DBS interests is rapidly expanding the options available to European consumers. With the sudden political changes in Eastern Europe, these options are proliferating at least as fast there as in the West. Even though most of these electronic media activities are commercial in nature, not all of them will sell *commercial advertising*. Therefore, it is important to define our terms carefully.

### In Pursuit of Profit

A *commercial* electronic medium, in simplest terms, operates with the intent of making a financial profit or of generating a loss that results in tax benefits for other parts of the company. Even though this usually means that the medium is owned by business and financial firms, in some countries the government itself may hold a part interest and use its share of the profits to help underwrite other public expenditures. From our discussion of free and paid media, you know that there are other methods for acquiring the money that leads to profits. The selling of commercial time to advertisers is certainly, from a U.S. broadcasting standpoint, the device that has been relied on the most and for the longest period of time. Nonetheless, there are newer alternatives that commercial operations not wishing to pursue advertising can use or that can be supplemented with advertising ventures.

Basic cable, DBS, MMDS, SMATV, and SCA accrue most of their income by leasing their services to subscribers. Particularly in the case of basic cable, this revenue stream can be coupled with the sale of local advertising by cable systems or national advertising by cable networks. The resulting commercials are inserted into cable programming in much the same manner as in over-the-air broadcasting. Like their broadcast counterparts, cable networks provide *local avails* in their schedule. Local avails are short openings into which the cable system can place commercials that it has sold to local advertisers. The system can keep all the proceeds from this activity, which helps offset the cents-per-month-per-subscriber levy that most established cable networks charge the systems who carry them.

Pay cable services like HBO, on the other hand, do not usually include advertising; instead, they charge subscribers several dollars a month to receive a largely *commercial-free* (but still *commercially* profit-making) service. In practice, of course, the pay cable service charges the cable system to receive its programming, with fees usually predicated on the number of subscribers. The cable system then levies on consumers a marked-up retail price in order to accrue its own profits. The cable network normally sets a ceiling on how much the local system can charge to make

## WAYNE HINDMARSH/SALES MANAGER
### CONTINENTAL CABLEVISION ADVERTISING

Get involved with a new business and you get a roller-coaster ride of alternating successes and failures. The cable advertising business is the newest electronic advertising game in town and one that might provide a very exciting ride for you.

In reality, our account executives sell television commercials that are inserted (aired) over our local cable systems on cable channels, like CNN and ESPN. As with all new businesses and new technologies, a lot of time is spent in so-called missionary selling both to local businesses and advertising agencies. In other words, we must convince our potential customers of the value of the *new* product we offer.

What kind of employment possibilities are possible in cable advertising? If you like production, there is a need for talented writers/producers/videographers to make low-cost but professional-looking video commercials. This is a great opportunity to work with a script and a mental image of what the commercial will look like and to put your creative talents to work. In cable, you can stay with your concept from the first rough script to the airing of the final, finished spot.

How about cable advertising sales? Initially, you may not make as much money as broadcast salespeople, but as television broadcast shares decline and cable viewing shares increase, the revenues will follow. You need to be ready to work long hours and be willing to spend time building up your account list. People getting into this business will find that with persistence and time, financial rewards are sure to follow.

After a couple of decades in the communications/advertising business on both the broadcast and cable sides, I'll pass along these four tips. (1) Never stop learning about your industry. Stay on top of technological developments. They can generate great opportunities in your future. (2) Make integrity and honesty basic values in your life. In business, your reputation is a key determiner of what opportunities may come your way. (3) In the end, hard work usually pays off in both satisfaction and success. Few people become successful without an investment in time and sweat. (4) Speaking of time, reserve time in your life for family. Too many successful business people are lonely individuals who chased the dollar and forgot everything and everyone else.

Finally, I encourage you to learn well from your mistakes and failures. Accept them. Take lessons from them. Then move on and enjoy this great industry.

certain that the programming is not priced out of reach of target consumers. PPV operations work in much the same way, except that customers are billed on a per-event rather than on a service-per-month basis.

A more specialized fee-for-service profit option is available to television broadcasters who sell space literally between certain lines of their regular picture to clients who wish to transmit or receive printed data. (See Figure 3–4 for an example.) Such use of the *VBI* (vertical blanking interval) is somewhat akin to FM's leasing of SCAs in that special receivers are required to strip the VBI material from the main transmission in which it is hidden. VBI offerings can diversify the broadcaster or cable originator's revenue stream with only minor expansion of existing transmitting equipment .

In the last few years, a new profit approach has arisen in the form of direct television merchandising operations. The largest of these endeavors, the Home Shopping Network (HSN), owns a large group of broadcast stations as well as a cable network arm. HSN's programming is devoted exclusively to offering consumer goods to viewers. A product is demonstrated on the screen and purchasers have a limited amount of time to call a toll-free number and make a credit-card purchase. HSN, and companies like it, accrue their profit from the mark up on these wares—just like any store-front retailer.

## Break-Even Servants

In contrast to all of these activities, *noncommercial* electronic media applications are not

**Figure 3–4**
On-screen index of the ELECTRA teletext system as carried on the VBI of WTBS, Atlanta

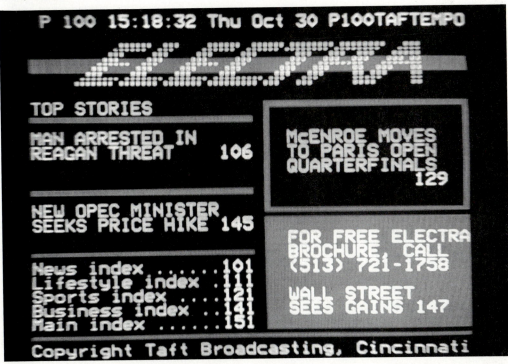

designed to make a profit. Instead, they are intended to serve a particular governmental or societal need, with their revenues supposed to do no more than offset operating expenditures. A noncommercial application of VBI technology, for example, is the nationwide practice of *closed-captioning* for the hearing impaired. Hearing-impaired persons obtain VBI decoders that pull subtitles out of the main television transmission and print them at the bottom of the screen. Hearing viewers without these decoders are unaware of the captions.

Not all television programming is closed-captioned. Program producers and transmitters participate on a voluntary basis, and the actual captioning is done at the studios of a separate nonprofit institute. Commercial broadcasters and other disseminators carry this service at no charge as a good will gesture, with this noncommercial venture electronically submerged in their regular for-profit signals. A potential boost for closed-captioning activities was provided by the 1990 Television Decoder Circuitry Act requiring that *all* television sets with at least 13-inch screens sold in the United States after July 1, 1993, must be capable of closed-caption display.

Noncommercial broadcasters, meanwhile, are primarily nonprofit in all their activities. In the United States, they operate on channels specifically reserved by the FCC for noncommercial use. The first 20 FM band assignments (88–92 MHz) were set aside for educational radio in 1945, and 242 of the initial 2,000 television slots (two-thirds of these UHF) were allocated for noncommercial television in 1952. This number was later increased to about one-third of all potential television assignments. As of mid-1991, 1,442 noncommercial FM stations plus 124 VHF and 229 UHF noncommercial television stations were on the air in the United States.[7]

These broadcasters obtain funding from a variety of sources. Some are owned by state or municipal governments that appropriate their budgets from general operating funds. Others are run by community boards whose members seek to attract revenue from a variety of corporate and private donors within that community. Additional facilities are operated by schools or religious groups that assume primary responsibility for finding the money necessary to keep the outlets on the air. All but the smallest stations also qualify for grants from the federal government, chiefly through the Corporation for Public Broadcasting. Throughout the 1980s, however, federal dollars for noncommercial broadcasting became less and less plentiful, which led to revenue shortfalls that had to be supplemented from other sources.

The commercial/noncommercial broadcasting dichotomy becomes less clear-cut in the area of *underwriting*—one of the options that drew increased attention as federal monies diminished. Through underwriting, a corporate endower of a program or station is mentioned on the air as the donor who is helping to make the transmission possible. Formerly, underwriting credits were limited to a statement of the corporate name and (for television) a picture of the company *logo* (key identifying graphic symbol). In the mid-1980s, however, the FCC liberalized rules to provide for *enhanced underwriting,* which allows for such things as mention of store locations and available products or services.[8] Enhanced underwriting has, in some critic's minds, dangerously narrowed the distinction between commercial and noncommercial broadcasting. From our vantage point, however, it does not alter the fundamental profit/not-for-profit yardstick that separates the two activities.

In Chapter 2, we introduce ITFS (Instructional Television Fixed Service) in conjunction with an examination of MMDS. When not used as a teaching tool, ITFS presents another source of funding for educational entities. They can lease these microwave channels to for-profit MMDS operators. In this case, however, the actual electronic media activity is entirely commercial, with the noncommercial aspects being limited to the passive sharing of the proceeds.

The essence of cable noncommercial activity is represented by *C-SPAN* (Cable-Satellite Public Affairs Network). This two-channel enterprise tirelessly covers the Congress. C-SPAN I (see Figure 3–5) focuses on the House of Representatives, and C-SPAN II (the newer service) concentrates on the Senate. When not following the actual proceedings of these two chambers and their committees, these cable networks feature a variety of seminars, speeches, and other important governmental and political events. Cable systems carry one or both channels as a public service to their communities, paying a few cents per month per subscriber for the privilege. Along with limited underwriting identifications between programs and the subleasing of some of its ex-

cess satellite time, these subscriber revenues allow C-SPAN's staff to keep a constant spotlight on important Washington activities and decision makers.[9]

Noncommercial media are best positioned to perform this kind of continuous ministration to public needs. Even the most civic-minded commercial vehicle, in contrast, must always weigh every activity on the basis of its contribution to, or deduction from, a projected profit margin.

## Private/Publicly Held

The profit-seeking (commercial) sector is itself segmented into a dichotomy based on how a

**Figure 3–5**
C-SPAN I transmission from the House of Representatives

given media company is controlled. *Private* (independent) ownership means that the company is the property of a relatively small group of individuals who exercise total control over its operation and are responsible only to themselves in setting profit goals and the means of attaining them. Of course, if a bank or other financial institution has lent money for facility purchase or upgrading, certain promises must be made as to a payback schedule. Beyond this, however, the media outlet's fate is very much in its own hands.

## Stocks and Partnerships

*Publicly held* companies, conversely, have raised revenue by selling stock on the open market and are thus owned by stockholders who elect the board of directors and are interested in a timely and continuous return on their investment. Often the founders/operators of the company own some of this stock—perhaps even a majority interest. Still, the conversion of an enterprise to publicly traded status tends to put added pressure on "moving revenues to the bottom line" (profit-enhancement) because pursuit of dividends are why outside stockholders have invested.

A variation on this arrangement is the sale of *limited partnerships* rather than stock. The company technically remains private because only the partners share in its ownership. However, limited partners are precluded from taking any active role in the company's management, which is left to a comparatively small number of *active partners.* Practically speaking, this arrangement means that limited partners are in the same position as outside shareholders. Their primary reason for involvement in the business is to receive dividends rather than to inject themselves into the company's actual operation and development.

## Control Shifts

Much of the electronic media landscape was originally staked out by private entrepre-

neurs who founded broadcasting stations, cable systems, networks, or advertising agencies because they saw a future in the business from a personal career as well as a money-making standpoint. Often, these were mom-and-pop (small, family-run) businesses in which the success of the business and the livelihood of the family were intertwined. The small cable system that began as a way for an appliance dealer to sell his television sets or the radio station that started because a local insurance agent wanted to hear more country music are classic examples of the modest roots from which the electronic media have often sprung.

Even the three major broadcast networks, though more broadly financed undertakings, owed much of their early development to a single family's hands-on management. David Sarnoff (NBC), William Paley (CBS), and Edward Noble (ABC) built and controlled their respective organizations for substantial periods of time before the full force of publicly traded status changed their corporate cultures.

In private companies, the organization's owner-operators are the key players. The long- and short-term goals of the company, therefore, tend to mirror the career goals of the people who manage it. Short-term profits are often postponed in deference to long-term facility development and achievement. In publicly traded enterprises, on the other hand, the managers are employees of a board of directors who are responsible to the stockholders for the timely payout of dividends.

Under such conditions, the *stock analyst* becomes an additional and critical player. By advising the investment community on the strengths or weaknesses of the companies they follow, the dozen or so electronic media specialists working for the major brokerage houses exercise tremendous influence over the operations of the media firms they scrutinize. If the media company's return on investment is seen as limited, then its ability to sell its stocks or bonds will be harmed. Even

**GARY STEVENS**/PRESIDENT
GARY STEVENS & COMPANY MEDIA BROKERAGE

Marketing and winning—two distinct pursuits with a common thread. What thread, you might ask? The answer is quite simple—it's hard to succeed in communications without either.

As a young collegian, I decided that playing records on the radio was a noble profession. It was only later that I discovered there weren't too many people over age forty doing that sort of thing. Where had they gone? Sales and management seemed to be the spots, and after a few years, that's where I found myself. Running businesses (with lots of employees who played records for a living).

Having endured what I perceived to be unbearable pressure to win ratings and audience adulation, and the nice rewards that come with them, I finally figured I had found a place to work, create, manage, and lead a normal work existence. Still, I needed to summon every marketing skill available to convey that success into the marketplace.

Then came the 1980s—the fast-paced '80s with their financial engineers. They discovered broadcasting, and soon we moguls of the airwaves learned that we could be bought and sold overnight. Thirty years of history were changed with a handshake between eager buyers and sellers. Now, *these* were the ultimate marketers and winners. Nothing wrong. It was just evolution, and a time in my life when professional growth meant moving along to the banking side.

Today, I run a successful media brokerage firm. This career followed two years on Wall Street in broadcast investment banking. Still marketing and still trying to win. When I hear someone wants to sell a station, I want that listing as badly as I ever used to want a station of mine to win a rating. And I know I'm going to need every marketing skill I possess to sell that property if I'm asked.

The bottom line is that, although my career has moved through several distinct phases, I am still using those same winning and marketing skills I started to develop in the early phases of my broadcasting career.

While it is probably true that winning isn't everything, I've never found anything redemptive in the alternative. In some ways the beauty of the broadcasting business is the incredible exhilaration in the win. Even the depths of losing is something worthwhile, however, for it only makes the next win that much more poignant. And it's all driven by the two distinct pursuits of marketing and winning.

though this situation helps ensure that these large companies are fiscally well managed, it also brings increased pressure to deliver dividends that the analysts' clients are seeking— perhaps at the expense of enhanced service to listeners and viewers.

The complicated fiscal pronouncements of some Wall Street analyst may seem remote and irrelevant to a disc jockey in Des Moines or a TV street reporter in Sacramento. But if that analyst has advised that their stations' companies are spending too much on personnel, it could mean the elimination of both the d.j.'s and the reporter's jobs.

## Local/Network

The larger the electronic media business, of course, the more likely that it will be publicly held in order to have ready access to the vast amounts of working capital needed to remain progressive and competitive. By this yardstick, networks seem more likely to be publicly traded entities than are local outlets. However, given the increasing consolidation of station/system ownership and the downsizing of mature network operations, this is not always the case.

The local/network dichotomy is somewhat akin to the manufacturer/retailer relationship that provides us with everything from automobiles to soda pop. A broadcast or cable network *manufactures* (or contracts others to manufacture) the programming product. This product is then distributed to the local retailers (the stations and systems) who make this product available to individual listener/ viewer consumers. Sometimes, as in the case of certain satellite services, an intermediary distributing company may move the product between its builder and ultimate seller, but this does not change the fundamental relationship between the two.

## U.S. Localism

From the beginning, electronic mass media in the United States have reflected local rather than national orientations. While European countries were building highly centralized state systems to distribute national programming exclusively, the United States was allowing a host of individual stations and operators to serve their local communities in their own ways. Some of these stations later voluntarily joined to share programs (to *network*), but individual responsibility and decision making remained at the local level. When a U.S. broadcaster receives a license from the FCC, that license is tied to a local community that the broadcaster is expected to serve. Even when broadcasting programs from other sources (such as networks), the local station is still held responsible for content decisions. Even though it signs a contract with the network to carry network programming, that local station can never be required to air a network show that it believes contrary to the interests of its local community.

Cable systems exhibit a similar local orientation. The local government (municipality, village, township) grants the cable company a franchise to operate and must decide whether to renew or terminate that franchise. The basic responsibility of the cable system thereby remains anchored to its community rather than to any of the national programmers with whom it does business. Increasingly, individual stations are being gathered together as station *groups*, and cable systems are being bought up by *MSOs* (multiple system operators), but such collective ownership does not change their legal responsibility to serve the local communities in which these outlets operate.

Should it prove practical in the United States, DBS would seem to constitute our only electronic mass media system not grounded in the concept of localism. This is true because, with DBS, the only local presence is the small satellite receive-only dish in the possession of each property owner. Programming would be distributed on a national or wide-region basis and thus could not be customized to provide local content. Therefore, no DBS service could ever supplant the specific community orientation of a local broadcaster or a cable access programmer. For stationless developing countries or for countries that have known only a national/centralized service, however, DBS offers significant cost advantages by eliminating the need to build an expensive string of local television facilities from scratch. (See Chapter 14 for a discussion of proposed satellite-delivered audio services that raise similar issues for radio.)

## What Networks Offer

In essence, *networks* are nothing more than efficient delivery devices. They allow the same programs to be shared more or less simultaneously by a number of localities or retransmission facilities. DBS, of course, is a network that goes directly and exclusively to the most basic localities of all—individual residences. Broadcast and cable networks, on the other hand, distribute to stations and systems (retransmission facilities) that then stack the program units for local use. Much like grocery stores, our industry's local broadcast, cable, MMDS, and SMATV proprietors acquire program packages from their suppliers and then get these out on the shelves for consumers to select. (The number of available channels on a cable system, in fact, is referred to as *shelf space.*)

Network vehicles bridge every dichotomy we have so far discussed. They may be broadcast or nonbroadcast, free or pay, commercial or noncommercial, and private or publicly held. But the one thing they all have in common is their ability to share programming (and hence, program *costs*) efficiently with a number of individual outlets. The most prominent networks are national in scope, but international networks have long been the rule in shortwave radio and may soon be the rule in European DBS. At the other end of the net-

work spectrum, state and regional networks make possible program exchange tailored more precisely to the needs and interests of a smaller geographic area. College and professional sports teams frequently set up networks in their home regions to carry their games, and state news nets are cost-effective ways of sharing regional information programming. A number of urban cable systems, meanwhile, have joined together in regional *interconnects*—not to share programming but to allow advertisers to make a single time buy that includes several adjoining cable operations.

The ability to facilitate national broadcast advertising through a single transaction has always been a fundamental service of, and reason for, commercial broadcast networks. Some media executives, in fact, would argue that the common carriage of the commercials is a more central function than is the delivery of the programs these commercials make possible. *Unwired networks* carry this idea to its ultimate conclusion. They put together large lists of stations on which they sell time. The unwireds do not convey programming, however. Advertiser clients of unwireds thus accept the fact that their commercials will air on all of these stations at somewhat different times and adjacent to many different programs but often at significant cost savings over what the conventional full-service networks would charge. Because of this advantage, observes broadcast sales authority Charles Warner, unwired nets "have continued to proliferate and are now a significant source of revenue for stations."[10]

As we have discussed, *cable* networks meanwhile may obtain their revenues from (a) separate viewer payment for the particular service; (b) a cents-per-subscriber-per-month levy on cable systems that carry the network on their basic tier; (c) conventional national advertising transmitted with their programming; or (d) some combination of these three revenue streams. In any event, networks are designed to provide efficiencies of scale for everyone involved—programmers, advertisers, local media outlets, and for the consumers, who are the ultimate beneficiaries of the information and entertainment services that such efficiencies make possible.

# Scrambled/Unscrambled

Networks can also be classified by another electronic media dichotomy—whether or not they garble their transmissions to prevent unauthorized reception. Pay cable nets are perhaps the most well-known scramblers; they require their subscribers to pay a substantial fee for each signal they want decoded. From the mid-1970s to mid-1980s, *STV* (subscription television) stations were also prominent in some urban areas. An STV was like any other television outlet except that, for all or part of its operating day, its broadcast signal was manipulated so as to be decodable only by viewers leasing a converter. Like the old MDS systems, however, STV's single-channel offering could not compete with pay cable's multiplicity of choices once the city in question had been wired. When cable arrived in town, STV facilities usually went dark or converted

themselves back to conventional broadcasting.

## Scrambling Expands

With the growth of the TVRO (home satellite) market, basic cable networks and superstation carriers also began to scramble their feeds to system affiliates so that home dish owners would not receive for free what cable subscribers had to pay for. Often, this action was initiated at the urging of the systems themselves to protect the local exclusivity of their product and, perhaps, to build up a sideline TVRO business. (Figure 3–6 illustrates a consumer decoder that facilitates such an enterprise.

Even the broadcast networks now became engaged in scrambling activities, though for a slightly different purpose. The networks discovered that some TVRO owners were intercepting their *backhaul feeds*—the original microwave relaying of sports and news events from their point of origin back to network headquarters for recording or retransmission. Because some backhaul material is never meant for public consumption or is intended to be intermixed later with the commercials that help pay for it, unrestricted consumer capture of backhauls created business and legal difficulties for their originating net-

**Figure 3–6**
The VideoCipher ® II Plus IRD (Integrated Receiver Descrambler) processes and decodes satellite-to-home signals

works. Scrambling therefore became a logical and efficient way to neutralize the problem.

From a mass communications standpoint, local broadcast signals thus constitute one of the last remaining unscrambled transmission activities. In comparison to all these other encoded/restricted operations, local broadcasters throw their product out for use by any consumer who wants it; advertisers or government grants and private donations are expected to pick up the tab. Broadcasters argue, in fact, that cable systems are really picking up something for free (the local television or radio signal) and then selling it to consumers as part of the total bundle of basic signals for which these consumers are charged. The systems respond that by amplifying and retransmitting this programming, they are offering the broadcasters' product to more people and with improved signal quality, thus making possible larger broadcast audiences and increased advertising rates.

## Decoding Home Video

Before we leave the matter of scrambling/unscrambling, the subject of *home video* must be mentioned. The term *home video* basically refers to all the program matter that consumers can put on the screen themselves without the aid of any outside transmitter. The *video cassette recorder* (VCR) and home computer are the two main tools in this regard. (VCR penetration is compared to pay cable penetration in Figure 3–7.) Through their use, a consumer can (1) watch prerecorded programs that have been purchased, rented, or recorded off the air or the cable; (2) play video games from prepackaged computer software; and (3) pursue electronically aided typing (word processing), personal finance, record keeping, or other computer-generated activities.

While most of this programming/software is available to the initial purchaser in unscrambled form, scrambling devices are frequently used to prevent user *copying* of these

**Figure 3–7**
Top 10 market VCR and pay cable penetration

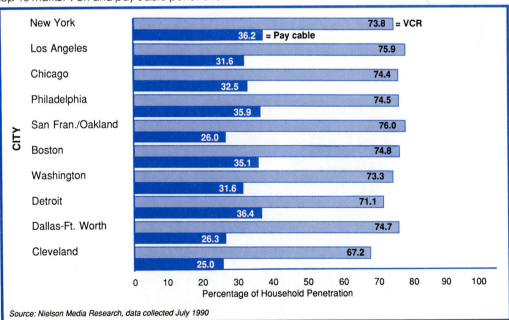

Source: Nielson Media Research, data collected July 1990

materials. A variety of scrambling modes have been developed by software programmers and still others by video cassette recording companies to protect their creative investment. Understandably, they don't want buyers to use one purchased copy to make unauthorized duplicates from which the program's creator will not derive any compensation. This problem has long plagued the audio industry. No feasible technological device is available to protect against widespread copying *(pirating)* of sound discs and tapes by people seeking to enjoy the song or album for free. Because computer software and video recordings must carry hundreds of times more electronic information than do audio recordings, anticopying scrambling systems in home video product are much easier to achieve, even though this does add to manufacturing costs.

## Home Delivery/Take-Out

The development of the home video market has also given birth to the seventh and final dichotomy this chapter discusses. Before home video, electronic mass media were all home delivery vehicles. A person turned on the radio or TV set and programming was instantly available. (One could go to the record store for discs and tapes, of course, but this, as we discuss in Chapter 1, was not a true *mass* media activity.) Broadcast stations, cable systems, and eventually SMATV, MMDS, and DBS operations, all were conceived to bring programming to the consumer's doorstep.

Now, however, a significant portion of television viewing results from *take-out* transactions. The customer goes to a video store like the one pictured in Figure 3–8, rents a particular piece of cassette programming, and physically transports the tape home. On the one hand, this is very inconvenient as compared to the ease of the instantaneous, home-delivered, electromagnetic transmission. On the other hand, this new enterprise liberates consumers from any dependence on the programming decisions and scheduling patterns of station and network executives. Due in no small part to their low cost and ease of copying, audio programs have not been similarly take-out available. To take the sound recording home, you had to buy it for your perma-

**Figure 3–8**
The video store multiplies viewer choices

nent collection—a decision that is much more irrevocable than is the rental of something for one or two plays. For a lower charge than the sale price of even the shortest audio recording, the video rental store provides a lengthy program that can keep you occupied for hours—and with moving images as well as sound.

Even though virtually all successful home video titles, like audio recordings, owe their success to previous mass media exposure, the timely manner in which these pieces of extended video programming are hand-carried into millions of homes makes them rival the immediacy of a magazine issue. It may not constitute a separate mass medium, but the video store certainly extends the reach of selected products that the true mass media vehicles have introduced. Just as important, the video store is using these products to compete with programs that those actual mass media are, at that same hour, showing in their theaters or feeding to their transmitters.

## The Dichotomy Dynamic

As we again see in our brief discussion of home video, contrasting aspects of the electronic media can enlarge markets for the radio/television industry as a whole while, at the same time, intensifying competition within it. This is perhaps the ultimate dichotomy—successful innovation by one media system sets countering industry forces in motion that present significant threats to the original system's dominance.

Putting this dynamic in its simplest terms, listeners and viewers can attend to only one thing at one time. Thus, "*Are they patronizing us or them?*" is a continuous, top-of-the-mind question for the men and women who shape and direct the productivity and plans of radio/television enterprises. This us-or-them tension seems destined to remain a central

characteristic in the electronic media and guaranteed to keep our profession intensely competitive.

At the same time, newer technological advances have increased our profession's diversity and, therefore, the number and type of employment options available within it. Particularly for persons possessing a blended background in media and sales, marketing, economics, or management, expanding competition will also mean enhanced career opportunities.

## Chapter Flashback

A *dichotomy* is a division of something into two separate and sometimes opposing parts. The electronic media are segmented into several such pairings, many of which overlap as different ways of dissecting the same operations.

*Broadcasting* propels signals into the air for reception by anyone within the coverage pattern. *Nonbroadcast* activities restrict or narrow signal reception in some way to facilitate more of a selective or point-to-point linkage. Many nonbroadcast entities are *common carriers* who must provide transmission avenues to all comers. *Cable television* currently occupies a tenuous middle-ground between broadcast and common-carrier status, whereas MMDS companies have flexibility in choosing how they are legally defined.

Even though we often talk of *free* versus *pay* programming, there is probably no such thing as a truly free system. Free media costs ultimately must be borne by taxpayers or by advertisers, who then pass on advertising expenditures as part of the price of their product. Specific-charge *(pay)* media receive their money more directly through actual per-service or per-program fees collected from listeners/viewers. *Commercial* operations have profit making as their main goal. *Noncom-*

*mercial* enterprises seek to serve a particular governmental and societal need while breaking even—staying within the limitations imposed by available financial resources. In some instances, a noncommercial medium can lease out part of its facilities to a commercial one in order to generate operating revenues.

*Private* ownership of a media agency means that it is the property of a relatively small group of individuals who exercise complete control in operation and goal setting. The larger the company, however, the more likely that it will be *publicly held,* with stock sold on the open market and key decisions made by a board of directors responsible to the stockholders. As they and their industry grew, more and more electronic media enterprises evolved from private to publicly held ownership.

*Local* outlets service a single community, whereas *networks* provide the same programming (and advertising efficiency) to a large number of outlets throughout a region or the country as a whole. In a sense, the network is like a product manufacturer/distributor. The local station or cable system is the retailer that makes the product available to consumers. Radio and television in the United States have a long tradition of media localism that has modified the dominance of networks. With systems like DBS, however, it is now possible for a network entirely to do without local outlets.

The availability of new delivery systems and consumer options has established the need for the deliberate scrambling of program content with devices for descrambling made available as part of a direct consumer pay arrangement. Scrambling is a factor in over-the-air, cable, and home-video operations. Even though most electronic media, scrambled or unscrambled, are delivered to the home electronically, the emergence of the VCR has created the video store as a vehicle for take-out video service to expand viewer options of what and when to watch.

## ❑ Review Probes

1. What is the key distinction between a *broadcast* and a *nonbroadcast* media system?
2. Where does cable fit in the broadcast/common-carrier pattern?
3. From an economic standpoint, why is it said that no electronic medium is completely free?
4. List four revenue streams that an electronic medium can use to make a profit. Which of these sources are available to commercial broadcasters?
5. What is the chief difference in operating control between a private and a publicly held corporation? Which is more likely to concentrate more on short-term profit generation than on long-term development? Why?
6. What is meant by a take-out system? What is the prime example of this activity?

## ❑ Suggested Background Explorations

Bagdikian, Ben H. *The Media Monopoly.* 3rd ed. Boston: Beacon Press, 1990.
Dominick, Joseph R. *The Dynamics of Mass Communication.* 3rd ed. New York: McGraw-Hill, 1990.

Donlan, Thomas G. *Supertech: How America Can Win the Technology Race.* Homewood, IL: Business One Irwin, 1991.

Eaman, Ross A. *The Media Society: Basic Issues and Controversies.* Toronto: Butterworths, 1987.

Orlik, Peter B. *Critiquing Television and Radio Content.* Boston: Allyn and Bacon, 1988.

Powell, Jon T., and Wally Gair, eds. *Public Interest and the Business of Broadcasting: The Broadcast Industry Looks at Itself.* Westport, CT: Quorum Books, 1988.

Salvaggio, Jerry L., ed. *The Information Society: Economic, Social, and Structural Issues.* Hillsdale, NJ: Lawrence Erlbaum Associates, 1989.

# Associated Enterprises

❏ *The previous three chapters focus primarily on the actual operators of electronic media systems and facilities. This is natural, of course, because most people think of stations, cable companies, and networks when the topic of radio/television arises. Nevertheless, electronic media professionals also labor in a number of other employment situations that are crucial to the effective functioning of media outlets, even though these jobs are not a part of the outlets themselves. This chapter examines such associated enterprises.*

## Advertising Agencies

As we know from Chapter 3, when advertising funds radio/television transmissions it alleviates the need for consumers to pay for these services out of their own pockets. The key facilitator of this activity, as most people recognize, is the advertising agency. It is the agency's job to serve as the linking agent between the businesses of client marketing and consumer programming. In other words, the agency is the bridge between the advertiser and the electronic media. Its endeavors typically cover print as well as a number of nonmass-media responsibilities; here, however, we focus primarily on the advertising agency's role in the radio/television sector.

## Agency Heritage

The forerunners of modern advertising agencies were anything but the glamorous message sculptors that the term *Madison Avenue* conjures up (Madison Avenue is the New York City street address of many of the country's largest ad shops.) Instead, the agency function grew out of the mundane business of *space brokerage.* As nineteenth-century print media in the United States began to expand from narrow political or financial content to reach a broader populace with general interest news, so, too, did these media shift their revenue base from direct political party or reader funding to fees charged individual businesses for carrying their announcements. The advertiser could contract directly with the print medium for the message space, of course. However, this procedure became increasingly burdensome as the number of such advertisers mushroomed. Space brokerage was a means of streamlining the process for the publisher by adding an intermediary.

In essence, space brokers function much like real estate developers. Each broker buys large tracts of a commodity (be it land or page sections) from its owner and then subdivides this commodity for sale to a number of individual customers. In both cases, the agent may also buy and combine space from a number of different sellers to meet the total needs of the client. Space brokers thus enabled newspapers and magazines to service a large number of advertisers through a relatively small number of intermediaries. Also like real estate developers, space brokers made their money from the difference between what they charged their clients and the lesser amount they originally had to pay to the commodity's owner.

Gradually, the media standardized this difference as a 15 percent commission. If the asking price for a half-page advertisement was $1,000, for example, the space broker would charge the advertiser that full amount. The print medium, however, would rebate 15 percent of that sum to the broker as a commission for selling the space. Thus, that broker would receive $150 as compensation for this go-between service. Even though a number of different compensation variations subsequently have emerged in the modern sale of print space and radio/television time, some form of commissioning is usually still a part of this business arrangement.[1]

As more and more companies began to advertise, many of them discovered that they lacked the expertise as to how best to fill the space they had purchased. Consequently, the more astute space brokers began to expand their client service by designing/writing the layouts that filled the space their clients were buying. The brokers thereby included *creative* as well as *media buying* functions in their operations, and the modern advertising agency concept was born.

## Modern Agency Scope

Today, creative and media departments constitute two of the four basic functions that a full-service advertising agency performs. *Creative,* as we have just seen, involves the design/writing of the advertisement. In the electronic media, most of these advertisements are known as *commercials* or, more simply, as *spots. media* selects the stations/systems/networks on which a given client's advertising will be placed and then executes the purchase of time on these outlets at the most favorable rates possible. (Like most businesses, the more of the commodity you wish to buy, the cheaper will be the individual units because sellers can give you greater volume discounts to get your order.)

*Research,* the third basic agency function, gathers and analyzes data to enhance the effectiveness of both (1) how the message is constructed and (2) which media are chosen to carry it. By helping to fine-tune campaign strategy and by targeting prospects, research

## GERALD DOWNEY/CREATIVE DIRECTOR
VISUAL SERVICES, INC.

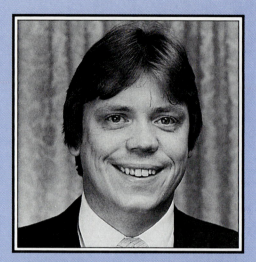

Creative director is about as high as you can go on the creative (or fun) side of the advertising business. The next step would be agency ownership, retirement, or becoming a share cropper!

Typically, a creative director begins life as either a copywriter or an art director. It has been my experience that the art director-turned-creative director often has a bit of an edge over the copywriter-turned creative director, in that skills as an illustrator enable a person to sell a raw concept more easily to the creative team, account executives, or clients. So, my first bit of advice is this: Writers, learn how to draw!

As a good advertising agency creative director, you must know a little about every aspect of creative—and a lot about one, specific area. For example, you must be at least as good a copywriter as anyone in the creative department and yet also be able to communicate intelligently with art directors and the production staff about every aspect of their jobs. As creative director, you must distinguish good from bad artwork, recognize a good layout, and know when a storyboard is on target.

And because, at many ad agencies, the creative director is also the producer of that agency's radio commercials and video productions, you must know your way around radio studios, sound stages, and editing suites. A creative director should be conversant with broadcast production terminology, the titles and roles of various crew members, and also with videotape and film formats and the advantages and disadvantages of each.

You must be prepared to critique without criticizing, because creative temperament is fragile. And you must be quick to congratulate your staff for creative victories, because creative egos must be fed.

Some of the best creative directors are people with fat Rolodexes. The creative department of an ad agency is equipped to take most projects only to the client-approval stage. From that point, the creative director must know where to find the best people and facilities for such specialized work as finished art, illustration, animation, photography, performing talent, radio production, video production, or whatever else is needed to complete the job.

The best creative directors often have experience in client contact. This enables them to sell their concepts first to their own account executives, and later, if necessary, to the client as well. The creative director should be able to provide solid reasons for the approaches taken and copy used in every commercial, video, and print ad.

Being a creative director for an advertising agency isn't exactly a day at the beach. It has more than its share of headaches caused by unreasonable deadlines, insensitive clients, nervous account executives whose allegiances often seem to lie more with the client than with their own creative department, and a creative staff filled with sensitive egos and, shall we say, unique personalities.

On the positive side, the job exposes you to a variety of people, places, and things that few other endeavors can match. Knowing that your work is often seen or heard by thousands of people, affecting the spending decisions and lives of many of them, is a tremendously satisfying experience. And it beats the heck out of working on the assembly line.

Keep your ambition under control early in your career, solicit and accept advice, and recognize your weak points. Inevitably, later in your career, you'll review some of your earlier efforts and recognize that your work matures even as you do.

---

tries to ensure that the client's advertising dollars are spent wisely in an effort to secure the maximum consumer impact. Finally, *account management* functions as the liaison between the agency and the client. Account executives see that client wishes are adhered to by agency creative, media, and research staff. They also convey agency findings and recommendations back to the client to help clarify and, perhaps, modify those wishes in order to improve advertising effectiveness.

The ultimate result of all of these activities is billions of dollars channeled from clients, through agencies, and to the commercial electronic media. The Radio Advertising Bureau and the Television Bureau of Advertising estimate that, in 1988, for example, commercial broadcasting in the United States enjoyed total advertising revenues of almost $33 billion.[2] This money pays for the massive programming costs incurred in developing the entertainment and information smorgasbord that U.S. consumers have come to expect from the radio/television industry.

Small, local businesses may not operate through an advertising agency. They often place spots directly with their local station or system. And the strictly pay cable networks function with other than advertising dollars. For the bulk of U.S. radio/television service, however, the advertising agency serves as the essential financial facilitator of a vast, costly, and profit-driven endeavor. Fewer professionals would be working in our stations, systems, and networks were it not for the cash flow generated by the agency professionals working outside these electronic outlets. The advertising expenditures that agencies make possible provide U.S. consumers with unparalleled program choices and U.S. businesses with a wealth of message delivery options.

## Public Relations Firms

Many people consider advertising agencies and public relations firms to be the same thing—and, in fact, many advertising shops do have a public relations arm. However, the thrusts of advertising and public relations are

**Figure 4–1**

Is this message an example of advertising, public relations, or both?

# GTE Corporate Advertising

## "Fingerpainting" :30

AGENCY: DDB Needham

COMM'L NO.: GNCP 8070

ANNCR: Imagination. Creation.
Application. At GTE

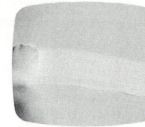

we know the power of people. At GTE, that
power becomes

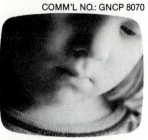

an operator's voice when you need it most.

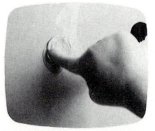

Your company's telecommunications
system,

a nightlight for your child.

One to one, person to person,

GTE to you. It's the power of the human
touch.

And at GTE, the power is on.

THE POWER IS ON
*(Courtesy of GTE)*

somewhat different and tend to be serviced by different people.

## Advertising and PR Compared

In the main, advertising is designed to market a particular product or service via communications that are clearly labeled *as advertising*. We know a commercial when we see or hear it and recognize the common unit size (ten, fifteen, thirty, or sixty second spot) in which these commercials are typically cast.

Public relations may use advertising as part of its overall tactics (see Figure 4–1), but the aim is to influence public opinion rather than to stimulate sales. Or, as Professors Newsom and Carrell put it, "PR is the brokering of goodwill between an institution and its publics."[3]

Unlike advertising, public relations efforts are much less likely to surface in easily identifiable chunks of airtime. Instead, public relations often involves the dissemination of information via a number of mass and nonmass means in such a way that the attitude it expresses becomes intertwined with the information and attitudes being expressed by journalists, decision makers, and opinion leaders. For example, the hairnet industry's public relations efforts had a lot to do with mandated hairnet use by food service employees and swimming pool users—but when was the last time you saw a commercial for a hairnet?

Corporate *image* or *issue* commercials constitute an overlapping of advertising and public relations functions. Like any piece of electronic advertising, they occupy a distinct and recognizable unit of time, with the source/beneficiary of the message clearly identified. At the same time, like any public relations enterprise, image or issue spots seek to influence or stabilize *public opinion about* something rather than to generate the *sale of* a commodity. In the spot in Figure 4–2, for example, the Minnesota Chamber of Commerce is using television advertising as one aspect of its total public relations campaign to have the state's worker's compensation regulations tightened.

## PR Premises

Edward L. Bernays, who is sometimes called the father of public relations, referred to his craft as the "engineering of consent." In the years immediately following World War I, Bernays and similarly oriented professionals set up firms designed to make business communication more responsive to public concerns and attitudes. Increased governmental scrutiny of commerce and industry in the early twentieth century meant that the captains of free enterprise could no longer operate without regard to public feelings. At about the same time, the success of the U.S. government's Committee on Public Informa-

**Figure 4–2**
Minnesota Chamber of Commerce TV Script

| VIDEO | AUDIO |
|---|---|
| MAN IN A WHEELCHAIR STRUGGLES TO GET TO A CASHIER'S WINDOW | ANNOUNCER (VOICE-OVER):   If you think there's no need to reform the Minnesota Worker's Compensation system, consider this. For every person receiving |
| JUST BEFORE HE GETS TO WINDOW 9 PEOPLE CROWD IN FRONT OF HIM | permanent benefits who can't work, there are nine people receiving the same benefits who can. |
| TITLE CARD:    Phone numbers and theme statement. | Tell your legislator to get to work on Worker's Comp. Call now. |

*(Courtesy of Gary LaMaster, Lacey LaMaster Nelson Farmer, Inc.)*

## ROBERT BRADSELL
POLITICAL MEDIA CONSULTANT

U.S. Senator Malcolm Wallop's 1988 campaign for reelection in Wyoming started out predictably. Wallop, a Republican from a state where that's a good thing to be, looked likely to win against a lack-luster Democratic challenger—a state senator named John Vinich. Senate races are rarely predictable, however. I was Wallop's media consultant.

In 1988, certain Washington-based interests—most notably labor interests—surveyed the landscape to see where they could put their money and have the greatest chance of picking up another Senate seat that would be favorable to their legislative agenda. Their gaze was drawn inexorably to beautifully mountained, and lightly populated, Wyoming. The reason? You can buy a lot of air time there for not much money. By late September, thousands of dollars in out-of-state contributions were flowing into the Vinich-for-Senate campaign.

It didn't take long for the attacks to start flying. Wallop was accused of everything from "selling out to the special interests" to being a "Mooney" (he had once spoken to a group in which some people in the audience were members of the controversial religious sect). At seven weeks out from election day, our own polls showed Wallop in some trouble. The escalating attacks were taking their toll. What was worse, to counter the attacks directly wouldn't have worked; there were too many of them. And it would have cast Wallop in a damaging, chronically defensive posture. What we needed was a truly credible advocate; someone whom the voters of Wyoming knew and trusted. Former Senator (and former Governor) Clifford Hansen fit the bill perfectly.

I wrote a commercial that set a tone of accomplishment and caring and capped it with a strongly worded, direct-to-camera endorsement of Wallop by Hansen. The commercial was a standard thirty seconds in length; Hansen's part of it would take up some seven seconds; seven of the most crucial seconds in the Wallop campaign. We had most of what we needed to produce the commercial "in the can" (footage from previous shoots, still photos, freeze frames, and graphics). All we lacked was Cliff Hansen's all-important seven seconds. To meet our production deadlines, it was absolutely imperative that we have the Hansen footage by noon, Wednesday, September 21. One small problem: Hansen was only available to us at his home, near Jackson Hole, Wyoming—and not until Tuesday, September 20.

Dawn on September 20 saw me on a plane—to Dallas, of all places! The only way I could get to Jackson Hole from New York on short notice that day was to fly to Dallas, then to Denver, then to Salt Lake City, then to Jackson Hole. I'd be there about 1:00 P.M. and at the location about 2:00 P.M. I'd arranged to have the local production crew (whom I'd never met) pick me up at the airport. We'd go directly to the Hansen home and set up. With some luck, we'd still have a couple of hours of good daylight in which to shoot. Governor Hansen did a superb job. With the magnificent Tetons behind him, he leaned against his backyard fence, looked directly into the camera, and delivered his heart-felt endorsement like a Hollywood pro. We had exactly what we needed. Now to get it back to New York by noon the next day!

The last commercial flight had long since gone. A charter would get me to Salt Lake City. From there I'd fly to L.A. And on to New York on the "Red Eye." As with everything else in this project, timing would be tight. But it should work. Well, maybe. By 6:00 P.M., when my small plane was to take off, a September snow storm had descended on the Teton range. Jack, the pilot, wasn't at all sure we'd be able to take off. We waited. A little after 7:00, I asked Jack if he could make it. He said he didn't know for sure. But the snow seemed to be letting up a bit, and if I was willing, he'd give it his best shot.

At 7:25 we were strapped in and taxiing. I couldn't see a thing out the windows except a blinding curtain of snow moving horizontally past us, reflecting the landing lights of the small plane. About half way down the runway, we seemed to leap into the air, and began a sickening dance through the black sky that didn't let up until we'd cleared the highest mountains and the welcome lights of Salt Lake City defined a horizon for the first time that night.

The flight to L.A. was uneventful, but it got me there too late for the last nonstop "Red Eye" to New York. I had one option—a flight that stopped in Chicago that would get me to Newark by 10:00 A.M. We left L.A. at midnight, but my body—still on Eastern time—thought it was 3:00 A.M. I'd now been up for twenty-four hours. I was mentally and physically exhausted, and can't remember a thing until we landed in Chicago—amazed that the sun was up.

The final leg, my flight departed Chicago on schedule at 7:00 A.M. I remember watching Lake Michigan drift by beneath a cloud layer when the normal mix of sounds in the cabin changed noticeably. We started a steep descent. The pilot announced that we were returning to Chicago! There had been a fire in one engine. It was out. There was nothing to worry about. He said it all so calmly. I'd learned years before that Murphy's Law was always at work in this business. It proved to be just a routine precaution—but I know I'd burned off a little more adrenalin by the time I got to a phone and alerted the staff back in New York. Yes, I'd get the tape there, but I had no idea what time. Just hang tight and wait for my next call.

I called from an "air phone" aboard a flight that would get me in at 11:00. Make it noon at the studio. On the cab ride into New York, I couldn't help but reflect on how I'd just spent the last thirty-six hours. *Why would anybody willingly do this for a living?* But I made it to the studio. We finished the spot. We got it on the air in time.

On election day, I knew the answer to that question I'd asked myself in the cab seven weeks earlier. Malcolm Wallop had won in one of the closest U.S. Senate races ever. Some two thousand votes statewide had deter-

mined the outcome. Campaigns frequently provide the kind of "rush" not found in the average media work environment. But I can't remember ever having had a greater sense of accomplishment than I did the night of election day, 1988.

tion demonstrated that government, too, stood to benefit from well-planned communication to the constituency. Under George Creel, the committee had been quite successful in stimulating citizen support for the war effort in general and for the purchase of war bonds in particular. This groundbreaking work by Bernays, Creel, and other individuals gradually propelled the practice of public relations into a mainstream activity that few corporate or governmental entities could afford to be without.

Like (and through) advertising, public relations activities can involve communication with mass audiences. At the same time, however, PR firms often engage in client-enhancing activities *within* an industry or single firm. One public relations campaign may be designed to convince travel agents that a particular resort is better tailored to the needs of vacationer clients. Another campaign might be intended to give news directors and reporters a favorable and informative view of the lumber industry's land management practices. Still a third PR effort might be focused on

members of Congress and their staffs in seeking to block proposed regulation of a given electronic medium (or to encourage its adoption in restraining a competitor). Whether using radio and television to carry messages to the public at large, or working behind the scene to engineer the consent of the professionals within those mass communications vehicles, public relations executives must themselves become knowledgeable in the ways of the electronic media. This is why many public relations professionals often begin their careers at an electronic media outlet or working for an advertising agency that handles a significant amount of radio/television business.

Electronic media outlets themselves usually handle their own PR efforts via their promotions or creative services departments. Therefore, a growing number of public relations practitioners remain full-time employees *within* the radio and television enterprise. In an increasingly competitive electronic environment this in-house expertise is vital. Promotion and other marketing activities, says Professor Susan Eastman, "have become cru-

## CNN Publicists

Publicists are public relations professionals who specialize in promoting celebrities. The publicist serves as a liaison between the star and the mass media.

cial to the success of television and radio stations, the commercial broadcast networks, the major pay and basic cable networks, and public broadcasting. Each marketing situation calls for a particular set of strategies to gain and hold viewers or listeners and advertisers or underwriters."[4]

## Audio Recording Companies

As mentioned in Chapter 1, the recording industry depends heavily on the electronic media to publicize and popularize its product. These media in turn (especially radio) use this recorded material as an inexpensive mainstay of their programming. This close interdependent relationship has not always existed. In fact, the emergence of radio broadcasting was almost responsible for the recording business's demise.

### Disc Development

Beginning with Thomas Edison's first successful recording experiments in 1877, the capturing of sound and the devices that made it possible proceeded at a slow and uneven pace for about the next forty years. Gradually, the mechanical tinfoil cylinder pictured in Figure 4–3 gave way to the disc and then, following World War I, to the electronically powered phonograph and master recording equipment. These devices captured sound much more efficiently and effectively by converting mechanical energy from a moving needle into electrical impulses and back again. By about 1925, the dominant record companies and manufacturers of recording equipment were rushing to convert to electrical systems, although mechanical players long remained popular with consumers (see Figure 4–4). The public was buying the new phonographs (often with radios attached) as well as a mushrooming number of records to play on them.

With the onset of the Depression, however,

**Figure 4–3**
The 1878 Edison Tinfoil Cylinder Phonograph. In this picture, half of the foil sheet has been recorded on (scored).

(Lautman Photo 77200)

**Figure 4–4**

Mechanical (crank-wound) Columbia Grafonola Disc Phonograph. Even though phonographs were soon converted to electrical power, hand-cranked models remained in use for decades, especially where electricity was not readily available.

(Lautman Photo 77352)

phonograph records became a luxury that few households could afford. Also, the rapidly expanding radio broadcast industry brought into the home all the music that you could want—and for free (once the radio set was paid for). Often, this music was live rather than recorded, which made the broadcasts more exciting but further lessened the demand for products that the recording companies had heretofore provided.

Indeed, the record business was at the point of virtual extinction when the economy started to improve and disc sales took a minor upswing. More important at the time, the massive introduction of coin-operated juke-boxes at young people's hang outs (see Figure 4–5) presented a new marketing opportunity for the comparatively small number of recording companies that remained in existence. "In the 1930s," observes music histo-

**Figure 4–5**
West Virginia teens groove to swing music from a Wurlitzer jukebox in 1942

rian David Dachs, "there were three major producers of popular recordings—Victor (its label was then called 'Just Victor'), Columbia, and Decca. Perhaps two dozen other independents—or fewer—were active. From the movies, Broadway, Tin Pan Alley, and the swing bands poured forth what many have termed 'The Golden Age of Popular Music.'"[5]

Swing music blared out of the jukeboxes and stimulated increased purchases of recordings by teens and young adults. About this same time the advent of multidisc albums also helped reinvigorate sales of symphonic and operatic works. All of this product was still on low-capacity 78 rpm (revolutions per minute) discs, of course; but prices had fallen and consumer demand had increased.

After World War II, new technologies and new directions in the structure of the radio industry fueled unprecedented growth of the recording business. In 1948, Columbia Records introduced the vinyl microgroove disc that could accommodate up to twenty-three minutes of playing time on each side (four to five times that of standard 78s). This created the 33⅓ LP (long-playing) record. Its vinyl composition was much more durable and suffered from less surface noise than did the old shellac-covered 78s. The 33⅓ vinyl discs also featured the new high fidelity audio sound that had been developed as a spin-off of military sound detection research during the war.

RCA Victor countered with the shorter and cheaper 45 rpm record. This third type of disc meant that phonographs must now be capable of playing tunes recorded at three different speeds. The durability, price, and reproductive quality of the 33s and 45s, however, gradually made 78s obsolete. Simultaneously, inexpensive magnetic audiotape (another product of war-time research) entered the field to provide another option for the consumer—one that permitted home recording as well as playback.

Meanwhile, the postwar boom in television had brought fundamental changes to the way radio operated. As the networks and *group* (multiple station) owners sought every available dollar to stake out their claims in the new medium, the expensive network radio programs were, one by one, abandoned. Local shows had to fill the gaps on existing stations and constitute the entire program day for new *independent* (nonnetwork) stations that had arisen. By the early 1950s, radio was well on its way to being a local music/news/weather endeavor increasingly dependent on the recording industry for its on-air product.

Simultaneously, the development of the new *rock and roll* (primarily a repackaging of black rhythm and blues with elements of white hillbilly music thrown in) brought a heretofore unavailable sound to the radio waves. "Rock and roll of the '50s was a thundering, ear-shattering mixture of C & W and R & B. The rhythm of rock was overpowering, monotonous, and youngsters played it at a deafening volume."[6] Rock and roll did for local radio what the early swing music had done for the jukebox, and the recording industry, of course, benefited from this development as well. New *disc jockeys,* record labels, artists, and formats elbowed their way into the recording and radio industries, cementing a profitable and interdependent relationship between the two.

Certainly, the relationship continues to this day, with the music videos on television further helping to solidify it. As Charles Turner explains, cable television by the end of the 1970s "had access to spare. Caught out by their medium's overexpansion, nervous programmers were looking for fresh and inexpensive content. Enter an army of music merchandisers dispensing free 'product' for 'promotional consideration,' and the success of MTV and its spin-offs is explained. Almost. The cumulative effect of all those quickie news clips and zoomy ads, those thousands of replays and video games, provides the rest of the story."[7]

## The Record Business Today

Whether cable or broadcast, within the electronic media, program and music directors are the key points of contact with recording companies. For its part, the recording industry is served by a number of players who all strive to stimulate mass exposure to, as well as individual purchase of, the audio product that the record companies are marketing.

In a dichotomy akin to some of those discussed in Chapter 3, record companies can be roughly divided into the majors and the independents. Majors like MCA and EMI/Capital are huge companies whose vast financial resources accrue from their function as subsidiaries of vast multifaceted corporations known as *conglomerates.* The majors sign recording artists and produce their records (via sleek equipment like that pictured in Figure 4–6). They also manufacture the discs and tapes, distribute them to wholesalers (and sometimes direct to retailers) and promote them among radio/television programmers. This consolidation of creative, financial, and distribution clout means that fully three-quarters of the best-selling albums each year are the properties of the majors.

Independents, in contrast, are very small companies that try to make their marks with artists and music that are either new or as yet outside the popular mainstream. Most of rock and roll's first generation of talent and tunes were discovered by independents, for example. These little companies fought, with varying degrees of success, to maintain their hold on the new artists once their careers, and the

*(Photo courtesy of Studer Revox America, Inc. and Lighthouse Recorders, N. Hollywood. Equipment Featured: Studer Custom 905 Console [with 2 Studer A820–24 & A820–2 recorders].)*

music they performed, skyrocketed to popularity. Even today, most independents only shepherd their product through the manufacturing stage. At this point, they sell it to intermediary distributors who are responsible for placing the recording in retail outlets and promoting it among the electronic media most likely to give it on-air exposure. By assigning these functions to other people, independent record companies can get along with very small staffs—perhaps fewer than a dozen people altogether. On the other hand, independents are thereby very dependent on the expertise and success of the outside distributors to whom they have entrusted their wares.

Often, retail outlets lack the ability to select which records to stock from the vast quantities of product available. In such cases, they turn to another go-between, the *rack jobber*. These companies specialize in selecting the most likely 'hot' sellers from available recorded product and then stocking their selections on the client retailers' in-store racks. Jobbers subsequently share in the profits that the record sections generate. Usually, this in-store success is inextricably tied to the amount and type of exposure that the recording has received over radio and television and, to a lesser degree, in clubs and similar entertainment spots. Sometimes it is difficult to pinpoint whether a given song or album received its initial boost from airplay or retail sales because stations and stores (or their jobber associates) so closely monitor each other. What is most important, however, is that this dual product stimulation system exists to enrich both business enterprises as well as the consumers they service.

The record business remains a high-risk venture; at least 75 percent of album releases fail to reach the revenue break-even point. But the minority of recordings that do succeed have the potential to realize immense profits for the companies that issue them. These profits can cover the costs of a number of new attempts in the continuing quest for the latest chart buster.

# Television and Film Producers

Video production firms, of course, have much the same relationship to the television industry as audio recording companies have to radio. Yet, as we discuss in Chapter 1, the movie industry also constitutes a self-standing mass medium in terms of its ability to deal directly with large and diversified audiences via theaters and home video releases. The dual mass medium/associated enterprise nature of this business is often encompassed within the same studio that produces for both theatrical and television distribution. Even a single product of that studio might reflect this dichotomy, such as the made-for-TV movie that later shows up in theaters under a different title or the theatrical release that then flows to succeeding pay cable and broadcast network exposures.

As in the case of the recording industry, television and film producers can be divided into the majors and the independents. But in the visual media, this division is a more equal one. Generally speaking, the major studios continue to dominate in movie-length produc-

tion (including televised miniseries) while independents make up the bulk of program series producers. The majors also serve a vital distribution role for independent movie producers by contracting to serve as conduits for their films. In addition, the costs and risks of production increasingly have led to a variety of coproduction activities in which majors and independents frequently join forces. The distinction between the two camps is further blurred by the majors' common practice of serving as distributor/syndicator for independently produced program series as well.

## Dealing with Networks

Due to legal antitrust restrictions and/or to the simple lack of in-house production capabilities, most entertainment programming aired by the broadcast and cable nets has been obtained from these outside suppliers. Thus, the growth in the number of networks available to consumers has meant a concomitant expansion in opportunities (and risks) for the visual production community. Before the 1980s, prime-time shows that were not sold to one of the three major broadcast networks never saw the light of day. *Syndicated* (direct-to-station) series that were not purchased by the major station group owners were likewise stillborn. With the advent of superstations and cable networks, however, a new list of options emerged for producers and viewers. The new avenues into the home that were paved by cable and other new delivery systems have made possible innovative and special-interest programming that had not been economically viable before.

When it is a television network that has commissioned a program, the theoretical separation between the mass media customer and its nonmass supplier often becomes blurred. Because shows are so costly to make, the network does not simply issue a contract and wait for the completed episodes. Rather, network executives exercise continuous and powerful guidance over every aspect, from script approval to talent (performer) selec-

**DAVID SALZMAN**/PRESIDENT
LORIMAR TELEVISION

Life in the broadcast entertainment industry is virtually nonstop. Because the pace is relentless, it is important to carve out occasional time for reflection and to conserve my energies so I will perform effectively over a daily twelve to sixteen hour span.

Up each morning by 6:30, I make a "To-Do" list for the day and compare it to the list I made the prior evening so I have a consolidated gameplan. I've been a list freak since my adolescence. The practice serves me well because as the leader of an operating business unit, I must maintain an expansive overview while making sure that there is follow-through on all cylinders.

My drive to work takes about an hour. Usually, I'm talking on the phone for 30 minutes, making notes on my Dictaphone for 15 minutes, and ruminating for 15 minutes—about new show ideas, fixing troubled projects, and closing deals. Once at the office, much of my day is taken up by meetings. Running a major production studio involves interaction with several departments: program development, current programs, casting, research, advertising and promotion, physical production, finance, and business affairs. I talk to these department heads regularly, as well as to the buyers of our product. Then there are the producers of our shows and the vast array of intermediaries—agents, lawyers and managers.

My scope of responsibilities involves production not only for the networks, but also for first-run syndication and cable. Beyond the exigencies of overseeing day-to-day operations, I regularly devote time to strategic planning, developing new business opportunities, positioning our company in the marketplace, and interfacing with other branches of our vast Time-Warner corporation. Each work day has its own unique mix of activities. Like most fast-paced industries, ours is filled with crises that arise as unexpected explosions.

Today is Monday, and it promises to be eventful. First is an 8:30 breakfast with the president of a network. Last Friday evening, this executive said he wanted to rescind his order for nine additional episodes of our first-year dramatic series whose ratings had declined in the past two weeks. My mission is to change his mind while buying time to retool the series. So I get him excited about a new direction in storytelling for the show. We then discuss another of our one-hour series. It is showing growth against the champion sitcoms on competing networks.

We agree to speed up the first half-hour and provide a better midpoint cliff-hanger to keep viewers hooked for the second half-hour.

Next, we talk about original series for the summer; this is an atypical practice for networks because summer advertising revenues are usually inadequate to cover the costs of new production. But the network president has an intriguing idea for a limited series that could cause a sensation and be done at low cost. Our studio has an exclusive deal with a writer perfect for the project, so we agree to meet again soon to pursue this further. Finally, we discuss international coproduction of television movies. I mention that Lorimar can deliver a package of five two-hour films for about 70 percent of the normal license fee. He is interested, requesting that we come to his network first—and do so quickly.

Back at the office by 10 A.M., I give my secretary a completed dictation tape and a briefcase of work I did over the weekend and meet with a producer of a hit network series that is "unencumbered"; in other words, the rights to sell reruns of this reality program are available. A former producer of reality programming myself, my relationship with this producer goes back more than ten years. But the cost of updating the stories appears too high, prompting alternative approaches. We set up a conference call for the end of the week to see if we can close a deal for Lorimar to syndicate the series.

I call in our network research director. I need research for the troubled network drama that was the subject of my breakfast—specifically, for alternative time-period suggestions to improve the show's performance. I also ask him for past examples of new network series that were restructured and went on to be successful.

Now it's time for a brief lunch with an employee who wants to pitch for a higher job that is rumored to be opening up. However, an urgent call comes in from the executive producers of another network series. One of the two leading stars has quit after a boisterous argument over a scene. They begin to explain what a disruptive force the star has become but are reminded that there is no series without the actor. They develop an approach to solve the problem.

At the delayed lunch, the employee pitches her experience, contacts, and loyalty. I explain that if the position becomes available, she will be a candidate, albeit a longshot.

A new list of phone calls to return is on my desk, and I start with one from our top comedy producer. He is upset that our merchandising-licensing division has failed to follow through on promises to create toys and other consumer products based on his hit sitcom. He wants to hire his own merchandising bird-dog. Though I feel it's a good solution, I ask him to ruminate for a few days before I say "yes."

The research director walks in with material on the dramatic series. The best time period is isolated. Even though I had breakfast with him this morning, my instinct tells me to call the network president. But he presents a dire view of prospects for moving the show that catches me off guard. So the next hour and a half is spent strategizing. Our head of creative affairs puts pressure on his network counterpart. I persuade a former colleague of the network president to exert influence on our behalf. The do-or-die decision on the fate of our series will be made tonight—and more work is necessary.

It is now nearly 7 P.M. and time for a meeting of the Harvard Alcohol Project. An ardent nondrinker myself, I have taken an active role to help this project get its designated driver message into television programs. While the meeting goes on, I dart in and out to make calls concerning the network drama. By 9:45 P.M. we have the time period we wanted, thanks to the arm twisting of the network president's old colleague.

The Alcohol Project session is concluded by 10:30 P.M., and I drive home to make tomorrow's "To Do" list and start all over. On the way home, I squeeze in three more phone calls.

tion. The end product does issue forth from the supplier studio or independent producer, but its development is, in fact, the collaborative result of that supplier's reactions to ongoing network guidance. CBS commentator Eric Sevareid once equated this guidance to "being nibbled to death by ducks."[8] In the recording industry, the song or album has already been completed and it becomes a matter of whether media outlets choose to air it. In most television/film production enterprises, by contrast, the outlets shape the product's very creation.

## Nonnetwork Markets

Because they are sold to individual or groups of stations rather than to a single network customer, *first-run* syndicated programs (programs without previous network exposure) are more completely the creatures of the producer who developed them. With first-run syndicated product, the project has usually been solidified to the *pilot* (sample program) stage before an attempt is made to sell it to individual outlets. Even though the major station groups may condition their purchase on certain modifications to the show, the producers are still much more in control of product development based on the perceived and general preferences of the stations with whom they expect to do business.

For most of their projects, the major and independent production companies must keep in mind the needs of a number of markets. Even when developing a show for initial network airing, the producer must calculate how well the concept and its execution will perform later in off-network syndication and foreign sales. As a global marketplace emerges, this last category is greatly increasing in its importance to a program product's ultimate profitability. Typically, the license fee a network pays for the program does not cover the cost to produce it, particularly in the critical first and second years. Thus, the producer must attempt to satisfy the network's content directions today while still building a show that will do well enough in subsequent markets (the so-called back-end) to make up the difference between profit and loss. We examine this economic dynamic further in Chapter 12.

## News Services

In terms of electronic journalism, the news services are much more analogous to how the recording industry functions with radio than to how the television and film production community interacts with video outlets. Like the record companies, news services primarily provide individual pieces of completed content, which the electronic media then assemble into packages to meet their own needs. As the radio format assembles music selections into a succession of on-air hours, so the newscast puts together a number of news service stories to serve the particular interests of its listener or viewership.

A large outlet (a network or a major market station, for example) gathers most of the news it uses itself, relying on outside services only for supplemental material originating outside the area covered by its own reporters. The smaller the outlet, however, the greater is its dependence on news products from other sources. A music-heavy FM station, for example, may air only brief newscasts that consist of nothing more than printed wire service copy "ripped and read" by the station's talent. (A wire machine is pictured in Figure 4–7.) An alternative may be voiced audio feeds from the same outside supplier that require only the throwing of a switch to transmit.

In the United States, the two major wire services are the Associated Press (AP) and the financially troubled United Press International (UPI). With bureaus and cooperating agencies all over the world as well as in every region of the country, AP and UPI offer stations (and a small but increasing number of local cable news shows) a wealth of up-to-the-minute material at a very economical cost. Both services strive to outdo each other in making their supplied content user-friendly so that stations can plug it into their own

**Figure 4–7**
An Associated Press printer of the type that retrieves AP newscopy at thousands of media outlets

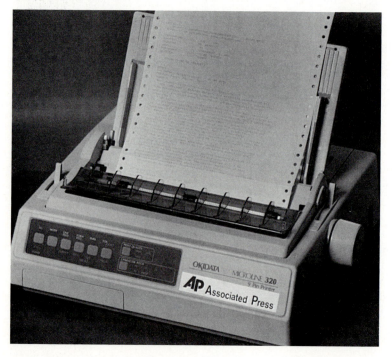

news programs with the least possible invest-ment of time and personnel. AP and UPI wares include everything from the conven-tional wire copy to complete voiced news-casts and supplementary audio actualities to spice up a local outlet's own features.

With the easy availability of satellite com-munications and small dishes to receive them, a number of video news exchanges have also arisen to provide television outlets with a wealth of visual news inserts. Some of these news exchanges, such as Visnews, sell their services for a set fee; others, like Hubbard Broadcasting's Conus Communications, are news exchanges or cooperatives to which users also contribute stories from their own regions. Whatever the arrangement, video news services can make even the small mar-ket station newscast seem as visually dy-namic as the journalistic products of one of the big three networks. If this sense of ex-panded coverage is accomplished at the ex-pense of local coverage, however, the ulti-mate benefit to local viewers (and stations) may be substantially diminished. "Local sta-tions will have to be more local," warns Gan-nett Broadcasting news executive Richard Mallary. "That's how to defend against cable television competition," a task made much more formidable by CNN's 1991 triumph in Persian Gulf War reporting. Nevertheless, ar-gues Post-Newsweek Stations' executive Jim Snyder, "what impresses people is local cov-erage."[9]

Finally, in addition to AP, UPI, and the na-tional visual news exchanges, a number of state and specialty news networks have been organized with varying degrees of success to provide agricultural, financial, sports, weather, and regional-oriented material. On the audio side, complete talk nets have been formed as an ancillary activity by established radio network companies to enhance local conversation formats with national-appeal guests and hosts. Though some people would be reluctant to call such offerings "news,"

they serve the same purpose as conventional news services in making informational prod-uct readily available to local electronic media outlets in an efficient and affordable form.

# Audience Measurement Services

Another service provider even more central to the economic well-being of radio and tele-vision outlets is the ratings service. Through a variety of sampling techniques, these compa-nies seek to determine the size and composi-tion of station/channel/network audiences so that advertisers can obtain estimates of who and how many consumers are being ex-posed to commercials placed on those outlets.

For print media, audience measurement is a fairly concrete and straightforward opera-tion. Since 1914, the Audit Bureau of Circula-tion (ABC) has monitored and documented the circulation of most magazines and daily newspapers in the United States and Canada. Because a copy of a publication is a tangible commodity, the dissemination of these com-modities is relatively easy to track and use in estimating probable readership figures. An electronic signal, on the other hand, does not bundle itself into countable copies. Instead, its audience is determined by how many people choose to tune to its initially invisible trans-missions. Broadcast ratings services, then, arose as attempts to estimate how many peo-ple within range of the signal were actually being exposed to it.

## Research Evolution

Beginning in the 1930s with the Crossley Re-ports and the Hooperatings, broadcasters and advertisers initiated a variety of sampling techniques to ascertain who was listening to what. Hooperatings (from the C. E. Hooper

## JOHN DIMLING/EXECUTIVE VICE-PRESIDENT
### NIELSEN MEDIA RESEARCH

On a typical day, I arrive at the office at 8:00 A.M. After sorting out some work I've done overnight, I meet with the marketing director for Nielsen Television Index (NTI) and several of her people to review the lower viewing levels that are being reported in NTI. (Using data from peoplemeters, NTI is the daily measurement on a national basis of all network programs.) The declines since February have been sharper than one might expect, and the networks are understandably concerned that something has gone wrong with our measurement system. We have a meeting with them scheduled for Friday, and much of this week will be spent preparing for that meeting.

At about 9:15 I consult with the marketing director for Nielsen Syndication Services to review with him what I will say at an Advertiser Syndicated Television Association panel tomorrow morning. His people will review what I put together and will make some changes.

I then meet with my boss to assess where we stand on the viewing decline. At 10:00 I confer with the new vice-president for micro products. He has been on the job for about three months, and we review a first draft he has put together of a strategy for Nielsen Media in the microcomputer area.

Following that conference, my boss and I call each of the network research VPs, as well as the networks' consultant, to discuss the Friday meeting. We need to garner some understanding of their expectations for the session and to communicate to them what we intend to cover.

Shortly after 12:30 P.M., I go to a luncheon with a client, the head of media research for a major Chicago advertising agency. We have a wide-ranging discussion covering various industry topics, including the decline in viewing. She is concerned that there may be a problem in the Nielsen system. Last October, a restructuring in Nielsen operations eliminated a number of positions, and she wonders if this move could have created problems. I agree to call her back with some specific information.

After lunch, I huddle with senior management of other Nielsen divisions and the head of marketing for a major health and beauty aids company. This group has been charged by the chairman of Nielsen to develop an overall strategy for Nielsen that takes full advantage of synergies between Nielsen Media and Nielsen Marketing Research. This meeting is one of approximately twenty we will have over a four-month period in order to deliver the strategy by mid-June.

After the meeting, I spend some time with the marketing director for Nielsen Station Index (NSI), Nielsen's local service. We discuss how to handle an Electronic Media Rating Council edict that will forbid the purchase of extra viewer sample by stations for NSI's local rating reports. Although it appears that the EMRC believes that such extra sample can bias the ratings in favor of the station ordering it, both theory and empirical evidence convince us that no such bias is created.

At 6:45 P.M. I leave the office to have dinner with the other participants on tomorrow's ASTA panel to discuss how the panel will proceed. I leave the restaurant at 9 P.M. and am home by 10:15 P.M. to prepare for the next round of challenges.

---

Company) innovated the *telephone coincidental* technique whereby a statistically selected sample of people were called in a given quarter-hour and asked questions about their radio listening at the moment. From their responses, estimates were derived as to the actual size of the listening audience during that quarter-hour and the percentage of these listeners who were tuned to a given station or network. Ratings methodologies and technologies have subsequently become much more sophisticated, but the basic operations of population sampling to determine audience size and apportionment remains the core of modern audience measurement activity.

Today, three companies provide the bulk of audience measurement data about U.S. broadcasters and cablecasters. Television ratings are compiled by the A. C. Nielsen Company (a subsidiary of Dun & Bradstreet) and the competing Arbitron Company (a subsidiary of Control Data Corporation). Arbitron is also the leading radio measurement firm. However, Arbitron is encountering increasing competition from the Birch Radio Ratings. These ratings are compiled by the Birch/Scarborough company, which first introduced them in 1978.

In the 1940s, Nielsen pioneered use of the audimeter, an electronic attachment to a radio or television set that, via continuously improving methods, kept track of every signal to which that set was tuned. As broadcast research expert Jhan Hiber recounts:

> The Nielsen radio meter must have been a fascinating development. The instrument was installed inside the radio cabinet (remember those large console models?) and it recorded (on tape) which stations were being tuned to. The tapes were then picked up, transcribed, and boiled down into a ratings report. Although because of the cost of the meters local audience measurement was too expensive, national network data were feasible. Respondents were paid 50 cents for every two weeks they participated in the sample.[10]

Like their much-improved descendents, these early audimeters chronicled when a set was turned on and to what station, but they were unable to determine how many members of the household were listening/viewing at the time. In fact, they could not even detect if anyone was in the room at all!

## People Meters, Diaries, and Coincidentals

In 1987, therefore, Nielsen converted its national television sample from audimeters to *people meters*. These devices pinpoint audience composition by having members of the household punch in their personal code numbers when they start and cease viewing. Unfortunately, this greater involvement on the part of consumers may also inject greater error into the system. Children's viewing patterns in particular seem subject to distortion because young people either neglect to punch in or use incorrect codings. Research is now being undertaken toward development of *passive* people meters that use infrared devices to recognize automatically and record the presence of specific persons in front of the set.

Nielsen and Arbitron also use *diaries* to gather audience data although Nielsen's use of this methodology is limited to small market measurements that cannot economically be measured by meter. Most Arbitron radio research is currently diary-based, but it is moving toward a people-meter type of system called ScanAmerica in its television operations. Diaries require that respondents write down their listening or viewing for a given week. Like the placement of phone calls or meters, diaries are also distributed so that the active sample at a given time mirrors the composition of the total population being measured.

*Telephone coincidentals* are the methodology of choice for Birch/Scarborough's radio measurement service. Birch issues monthly and quarterly reports for the markets that it monitors. Stations and specialty research firms also use the telephone to obtain more precise data on local audience perceptions and preferences as to stations and music selections. The only tracker of *network* radio, RADAR (Radio's All-Dimension Audience Research from Statistical Research, Inc.) also uses phone calls to compile its national measurement data.

Audience measurement services make their money from substantial subscriber fees paid by advertising agencies, networks, individual stations, and similar parties. (The covers of the two most widely consulted local reports are reproduced in Figures 4–8 and 4–9.) Because billions of dollars (and thousands of careers) hinge on the results and accuracy of ratings data, these parties are constantly looking for ways to make these data as reliable and current as possible. Whatever the measurement company or system, broadcast authorities Howard and Kievman point out that all "modern audience research essentially relies on the concept of statistical inference, which permits the estimation of charcteristics of a population (such as all TV households in an area) from data obtained by sampling a cross-section of the population being measured. When a sample is carefully selected, following valid statistical procedures, the information gained may be projected confidently to the total population."[11]

As we discuss in Chapter 1, mass communication is essentially a one-way enterprise. But trustworthy audience measurement can provide an after-the-fact feedback that enables electronic media professionals to capitalize on discovered successes and to remedy detected failures.

## CNN   Passive People Meters

Passive (advanced) peoplemeters use a set-top camera to monitor automatically who is watching television. Specific viewers are identified by their facial characteristics.

**Figure 4–8**

The Nielsen Station Index (NSI) reports local market television viewing via *Viewers in Profile*

## Telephone Companies

In addition to the avenue they make available for phone-based audience measurement, telephone companies (telcos) have long provided other kinds of service to electronic media ventures. Radio stations frequently rely on temporary audio loops to allow them to cover on-location sporting events and other happenings of interest to their listeners. Terres- trial (land) lines provided by the telephone companies were also the chief carriers of radio and television network programming until they were replaced by satellite delivery. Such land lines remain an option in various short-distance televised events that do not lend themselves to microwave or satellite pick-up. For cable, the telephone companies' poles presented a convenient way to string its lines, although excessive charges for the priv- ilege over the years have resulted in cable/telco lawsuits and *pole attachment* reg- ulation.

**Figure 4-9**
Arbitron's Radio Market Report is the most widely used estimate of local market radio station listenership

1 1 2  Reno
Fall 1989

# Radio Market Report

Audience Estimates in the Arbitron Defined
Metropolitan Area and TSA for:

**Reno**

*ARBITRON*

**Fall 1989**
September 21 - December 13

Now, however, many executives within the telephone industry are looking at possibilities for playing a much more direct and active role in the electronic media. Currently prohibited (via a variety of FCC regulations and judicial consent decrees) from most electronic mass media ownership or content generation, some regional telcos are pushing for change. For example, the telcos would like to generate their own business data and other electronic information services rather than just carry content owned by others. More significant from our perspective, the telephone industry also sees itself as a future broadband

**Figure 4–10**
A fiber optic strand. Will it convert telcos into mass media players?

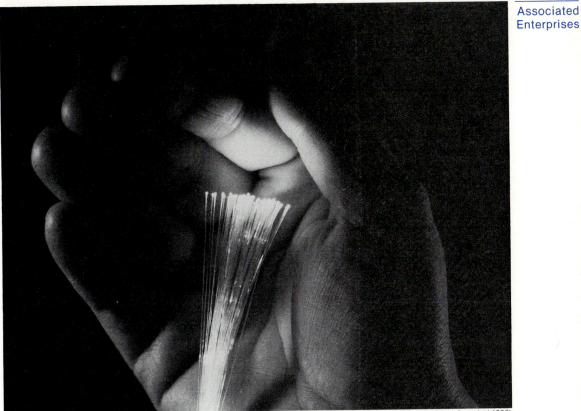

*(© Stock Imagery Inc./Mark Sparshot 1990)*

communications service for the U.S. home. As immense-capacity *fiber optic* technology (see Figure 4–10) becomes economically feasible, the telcos envision a time when one fiber optic line into the home (their line and your home) could accommodate all telephone, personal computer, electronic mail, security alarm, and mass entertainment services.

This scenario is particularly worrisome to

## ⓒⓃⓃ   Fiber Optics and the Telcos

Fiber optic technology has heightened the battle by telephone companies to enter the video and interactive data businesses. Broadcasters and cable companies fear this will result in one giant telecommunications monopoly.

cable interests, who see the size and financial clout of their own industry dwarfed by the vast resources of the telco establishment. How, they ask, could a local cable company compete with such a multifaceted monolith like that envisioned by some telco executives? Ironically, observes communications attorney Frank Lloyd, "It was, in fact, the hope of the FCC in 1970, when it kept the two industries separate, that cable would become a future competitor in providing telephone service. Yet every time the cable industry has attempted to bring consumers this diversity, the telcos have fought them to a standstill before the state public service commissions and the FCC."[12]

Though they never envisioned themselves as a telephone company competitor, broadcasters also worry about telco motivations. Some telco spokespersons have indicated that their broadband operations would agree to carry broadcast signals over their lines for free. But conventional radio and television owners view the prospect of a telephone company gatekeeper between them and most of their audience as a significant threat to their continued survival as independent entities. Broadcasters wonder if they would become no more than passive content providers to the telco rather than audience assemblers in their own right.

The role of the telcos in terms of electronic mass media activities is a vast and complicated issue likely to evolve through, and impact on, most of your professional life. As new technologies have blurred some of the old distinctions between purely broadcast and purely common-carrier activities (recall our earlier Chapter 3 discussion), so might even newer technological capabilities erase the boundaries between broadcast and cable interests, on the one side, and telephone interests on the other. If the telcos break out of constraints that currently limit them to the status of associated enterprises and instead become mass communications purveyors,

then the entire electronic media profession will be transformed. If you are at all interested in a radio/television career, following developments in the telephone industry should be a mandatory activity.

## Electronics Manufacturers

Before leaving the subject of technology and this chapter on associated enterprises, we must mention the part equipment manufacturers play in determining the boundaries and shape of electronic media operations. Though this is not a scientific textbook on physics or electronics, we should realize that, directly or indirectly, much of our jobs as electronic media professionals is shaped by what engineers have built, sold, or failed to sell. We only need look at two examples to illustrate this interdependence: AM stereo and HDTV.

As you recall from our Chapter 2 discussion, many people saw AM stereo as a way to make the older radio service more competitive with its newer FM cousin. By 1980, four major competitors were lobbying the FCC for selection of their equipment and system as the designated standard for AM stereo in the United States. When the commission decided a year later to avoid making a choice in favor of letting the marketplace decide, no system was able to garner enough support to become the de facto standard that broadcasters and other equipment manufacturers could adopt with confidence. AM stereo remained a largely unfulfilled promise, with stations that choose to broadcast it more the exception than the rule.

As of this writing, a much broader technological issue is being debated within the Congress, the FCC, and the television industry as a whole: HDTV. High definition television, in any of its several possible formats, would approximately double the 525 lines in the stan-

**DENISE GALLANT**/ADVANCED SYSTEMS PLANNER
THE CHYRON GROUP*

Being involved with advanced systems planning in a company such as CMX and Chyron is a synthesis of both technical and creative occupations and necessitates a broad base of experience in video as well as other media fields.

Thinking about and designing product ideas that might be the next step in the industry is not just a theoretical process. Answering how-to phone calls; being a liaison between marketing and engineering; knowing what has been attempted, what has succeeded, what has failed, and why— these are all very much hands-on tasks. Advising what feature is important to add to the next version of computer software, operationally what keystrokes should access this new feature, or what user interface would make life a little easier for the editor on the other end of that phone call are all parts of the daily routine.

At the other end of your visionary yardstick is the ideal. You create new tools that will allow new programming to be created—a new environment to spawn new graphics, new art, a new look. New technology to allow the artist new possibilities.

Other challenges also periodically arise. One of the interface engineers needs you to test new versions of software. Or, because a trade show is about to begin, your job description explodes to include being ad writer, spec sheet interpreter, demonstration coordinator, display producer, direc-tor, and editor, as well as party coordinator and speaker.

As a systems planner there are always secrets to be learned and hints to be taken. Customers may have a particular need for a particular communicative function. They may have suggestions that spark new directions or confirm a solution that might have been overlooked.

Then, there are moments when you hang up the phone, close the door, and turn to the computer and lay out a system concept. A new idea, not just for today, but also for tomorrow. Pushing the envelope just a little bit further. This is the most fun.

*The Chyron Group is a leading manufacturer of digital electronic graphics equipment and systems and computer-assisted videotape editing systems.

dard U.S. television picture. The result is a picture that offers the quality of 35-mm film without noticeable lines or other unwanted electronic artifacts. Yet, in order for broadcasters to transmit a *true* HDTV picture, their assigned channels would have to be significantly enlarged. A number of compromise systems are available as alternatives. Although they are not true HDTV, these other EDTV (Enhanced-Definition Television) options would noticeably improve picture quality without requiring additional spectrum.[13] The picture would not be as good as genuine HDTV, but neither would it be incompatible with existing television sets sitting in people's homes. Meanwhile, because they are not subject to the same spectrum constraints, cable, DBS, home video, and even telco adoptions of true HDTV present no fundamental problem. But should these delivery systems be allowed to implement it and thereby make conventional broadcast television a comparatively grainy and outmoded curiosity?

As they develop and refine their own EDTV or true HDTV systems, equipment manufacturers are engaged in a high-stakes game in which one big winner and several big losers are likely to emerge. The stakes are too high for the FCC to walk away as it did in the case of AM stereo. HDTV's military and world trade implications alone make it a topic of intense interest on the part of several governmental agencies. Whatever pure, compromise, or transitional system is authorized, its positive and negative impact on the television industry cannot be overestimated.

Like it or not, as an electronic media professional, the boundaries of your business and your options within those boundaries continue to be molded by the laws of physics and the inventiveness (or disinventiveness) of technologists. Programming may be an art, but it is equipment science that enables the radio/television industry to capture this art in time, deliver it to consumers, and thereby sell the collective attention of those consumers to advertisers as audience.

We see the influence of this relationship over and over as we more closely explore electronic media history in subsequent chapters. So stand by.

## Chapter Flashback

Several related businesses have an interdependent relationship with electronic media proprietors. Advertising agencies are the linking agent between client advertisers and the radio/television outlets that bring their commercials to the public. Agencies began as space brokers and gradually expanded their activities to include a multiplicity of functions that are generally divided into four categories: creative, media, research, and account management. Advertising is typically recognizable, product-driven, and mass media-delivered; public relations efforts, on the other hand, are much more diverse in their dissemination and in their focus on influencing public opinion. Sometimes, as in the case of corporate image commercials, advertising and public relations overlap. But in many other instances, PR is a more subtle, behind-the-scenes endeavor. The promotions departments of radio/television outlets themselves engage in both advertising and public relations tasks on behalf of their parent facilities.

The audio recording industry depends heavily on the electronic media to popularize its output, and the media rely on the record industry for a great deal of their programming. The onset of the Depression brought serious problems for record companies, but swing music on the jukebox, and then rock and roll on the radio, restimulated the industry. Today, the record business is an intensely competitive collection of large (major) and small (independent) companies that struggle to expose their product in the stores and over the airwaves.

Television and film producers are similarly

separated into major and small/independent businesses, with frequent distribution and other cooperative arrangements between these two branches. Supplying programming to the networks can be very lucrative, but it also entails network oversight of content development. Nonnetwork markets include first-run syndication, off-network syndication, and foreign sales, which are rapidly increasing in importance.

News services specialize in gathering and packaging information modules that individual media outlets can then select and adapt to meet their own needs. The Associated Press (AP) and United Press International (UPI) are the two dominant news services in the United States, but the networks, station groups, and a variety of international, regional, and state news exchanges are also prominent players. Local stations strive mainly to cover their own communities in order to distinguish themselves from competing media.

Audience measurement (ratings) companies are essential in helping to document listenership/viewership as a means of justify-

ing advertising rates. Begun with the Crossley Reports in the 1930s, electronic media measurement is now dominated by Nielsen and Arbitron for television and Arbitron and Birch for radio. People meters, diaries, and telephone coincidentals are all widely used in audience size-and-type computations. All rely on the concept of statistical inference based on carefully weighted sampling of the population.

Telephone companies have long provided services to electronic mass media outlets but now threaten to become active media participants in their own right. A great deal of political maneuvering involving the telcos, Congress, the courts, the FCC, and the broadcast and cable industries is likely to continue for decades. However the telco question is resolved, the electronic media will still depend heavily on electronic manufacturers to provide the technological devices and innovations that will drive continued advancements in our profession's ability to serve its audiences.

## ❑ Review Probes

1. What is a space brokerage? How did it function and of what is it the ancestor?
2. What are the key similarities and differences between the practice of public relations and that of advertising?
3. How did radio first hurt, and then help, the recording industry?
4. What two media-associated businesses are subdivided into majors and independents? What are the relationships between the two subgroups in each of those businesses?
5. How do news services assist radio and television stations? What type of news content must a station handle on its own?
6. What are the three main audience measurement methods used today? How does each one operate?

## ❑ Suggested Background Explorations

Ailes, Roger. *You Are the Message: Secrets of the Master Communicators.* Homewood, IL: Dow Jones-Irwin, 1988.

Barnouw, Erik. *The Sponsor: Notes on a Modern Potentate.* New York: Oxford University Press, 1978.

Beville, Hugh M., Jr. *Audience Ratings: Radio, Television, and Cable.* Rev. ed. Hillsdale, NJ: Lawrence Erlbaum Associates, 1988.

Hood, James R., and Brad Kalbfeld, comps. and eds. *The Associated Press Broadcast News Handbook: Incorporating the AP Libel Manual.* New York: Associated Press Broadcast Services, 1982.

Jamieson, Kathleen Hall. *Packaging the Presidency: A History and Criticism of Presidential Campaign Advertising.* New York: Oxford University Press, 1984.

Jewler, A. Jerome. *Creative Strategy in Advertising.* 3rd ed. Belmont, CA: Wadsworth, 1989.

Matrazzo, Donna. *The Corporate Scriptwriting Book: A Step-by-Step Guide to Writing Business Films, Videotapes & Slide Shows.* (revised). Portland, OR: Communicom Publishing Company, 1985.

Ries, Al, and Jack Trout. *Positioning: The Battle for Your Mind.* New York: McGraw-Hill, 1981.

Stone, Alan. *Wrong Number: The Breakup of AT&T.* New York: Basic Books, 1989.

C H A P T E R  **5**

# Technological Maturation

❑ *Radio and television did not suddenly spring upon the world. Scientific experimentation with electrical conduction beginning in the eighteenth century and with electromagnetism in the nineteenth paved the way for the modern electronic media.*

*The first practical communications application of this electrical knowledge came in the form of Samuel F. B. Morse's telegraph. By 1844, Morse had built a telegraph line from Washington, D.C., to Baltimore. Using electrical current sent down this line to convey a series of dots and dashes, Morse was able to transmit coded messages in which each letter of the alphabet had its own dot and/or dash designation (Morse Code). When he clacked out that first message ("What hath God wrought?") along his system, the carrier pigeon's days were numbered and a new era of wired communication began.*

*Thirty years later, in 1876, Alexander Graham Bell was able to vary the wire-bound electrical current's intensity so as to convey the shape of human speech. His telephone thereby carried voices rather than mere dots and dashes over its wire and further increased our ability to bridge space with instantaneously delivered messages. The common limitation of both telegraph and telephone, of course, was that this wire had*

*to be physically strung between two locations before people could communicate with each other. Once this was accomplished, point-to-point conversations were made possible, with one person or station talking to another person or station. Even though these were wonderful inventions, the telegraph and telephone did not possess the capability for mass communication as we define that term in Chapter 1. To achieve mass communication, a way had to be found to escape the bonds of the current-carrying wire. And here is where what we today call radio enters the picture.*

## The Roots of Radio

In 1873, Scottish physicist James Clerk Maxwell provided the theoretical basis for the development of wireless transmissions. Maxwell argued that electromagnetic waves existed and that these invisible types of radiant energy traveled at the speed of light. Fifteen years later, German scientist Heinrich Hertz borrowed Maxwell's theory as the basis for a successful laboratory experiment. Using a primitive spark discharge device, Hertz was able not only to create electromagnetic waves but also to detect them and measure their wavelength by means of a simple receiving antenna. As Maxwell had surmised, these waves did travel at the speed of light. But what he did not envision was that they would also serve as the vehicle for powerful new mass communications systems.

### Enter Marconi

While the scientific community of the time explored the theoretical implications of the Hertz experiments, a young scion of a wealthy Italian family, Guglielmo Marconi, saw real *practical* applications for the phenomenon Hertz had isolated. Financially well off, Marconi was able to devote all his energy

to his subsequent technical pursuit, although his businessman father initially felt the project to be a dreadful waste of time. Once the young man demonstrated the device to him, however, the elder Marconi agreed to provide the developmental funds. In 1894 and 1895, Guglielmo continuously improved on Hertz's early equipment. By 1896, he had successfully transmitted and detected electromagnetic signals beyond hilltops and over a distance of up to nine miles.

To develop the apparatus fully would require much more money than Marconi's father could provide. When the Italian authorities showed no interest in the project, Marconi's Irish-born mother decided they should see if the British government was more receptive. With the assistance of the British Post Office's engineer-in-chief, William Henry Preece, the young inventor conducted a series of demonstrations that convinced the British government to issue him a patent in 1897. At the same time, a small group of powerful English financiers joined with him to form a company that came to be known as Marconi's Wireless Telegraph Company, Ltd.—an enterprise that would soon be worth billions of dollars. The twenty-three-year-old Marconi had certainly made the most of his time and more than justified his father's tolerance of his frivolous tinkering.

By 1899, Marconi's wireless telegraph was sending coded messages across the English Channel, and his invention was attracting attention throughout Europe as well as in the United States. In 1901, the Marconi device successfully transmitted three dots (the Morse Code designation for the letter *S*) across the Atlantic ocean from the English Coast to Newfoundland, where Marconi and his assistants used a high-flying kite antenna to detect the signal. The entire world soon was talking about the wireless telegraph. Wireless sets were installed on ships, and over the next decade, this new communications tool came permanently to bridge oceans and span continents. Meanwhile, during an 1899 visit to the

United States, where he used his wireless to report the America's Cup Race, Marconi had set up a U.S. subsidiary of his company. By 1913, American Marconi enjoyed a virtual monopoly over the country's wireless communication activities. What had been one young man's technical fascination twenty years before had now become a hugely profitable and vitally important enterprise.

## Stubblefield and Fessenden

Up to this point, we have discussed only the sending of *code* messages over the airwaves. Radio as a mass communications vehicle (the sending of actual speech and music) required the contributions of additional innovators. As early as 1892, a Kentucky farmer and amateur inventor named Nathan Stubblefield (see Figure 5–1) was transmitting his voice a distance of some three miles via what was known in the Murray, Kentucky, locality as a "vibrating telephone."[1] Whether Stubblefield's device was based on Hertzian principles or on some other system not involving the generation of radio frequencies is unclear in the historical record. His efforts to promote his discovery through an awkwardly capitalized company were miniscule in comparison to the resources of more famous inventors and were largely unknown outside his home region. Stubblefield died of starvation in 1928; certainly a tragic conclusion to the life

**Figure 5–1**
Nathan Stubblefield—parent of our profession?

of the man who may have been the first voice broadcaster.

Much better documented is the work of University of Pittsburgh professor Reginald Fessenden. He correctly theorized that a continuous radio (Hertzian) wave had much the same character as a sustained musical note and therefore could be modulated to assume the shape of articulate speech. Fessenden conducted groundbreaking work on how the voice (the program content) could be placed onto a carrier wave for transmission as a series of amplitude *modulations* (review our discussion of modulation in Chapter 2). Fessenden also conceived of the radio transmission as a continuous wave rather than as the interrupted wave used by Marconi and other wireless telegraphers. With backing from two Pittsburgh financiers and the assistance of F. W. Alexanderson, a General Electric Company engineer, Fessenden's experiments reached their culmination in a 1906 Christmas Eve transmission from his Brant Rock, Massachusetts, station (see Figure 5–2) to ships far out in the Atlantic.

Imagine the surprise of seamen who, instead of the familiar dots and dashes, suddenly heard music and voices emanating from their wireless sets. Briefly pioneering the role of on-air performer, the inventor played "O Holy Night" on his violin, read verses from the Bible, and wished his stupified audience a Merry Christmas. On New Year's Eve, Fessenden aired another program that was picked up as far away as the West Indies by the United Fruit Company's banana boats.[2] Seeking a more efficient means to direct those boats to waiting cargos, United Fruit subsequently purchased a quantity of Fessenden equipment for use in the Caribbean. But unfortunately for Fessenden, his company, like that of Stubblefield, ran into a tangle of financial and legal difficulties and he was forced from the scene before profiting from the results of his technological contributions.

## De Forest and Herrold

At about the same time, a third brilliant and likewise financially naïve inventor, Lee De

**Figure 5–2**
Reginald Fessenden (seated) and co-workers at his Brant Rock station

(Smithsonian Institution Photo No. 52,214)

Forest, improved on J. Ambrose Fleming's two-element tube by placing a grid between the tube's filament and plate, all of which were encased within a glass housing. When a small electrical voltage was applied to this grid, the flow of electrons between filament and plate could be much more precisely controlled. De Forest's *triode* (three-element) tube, in short, provided the means by which weak electromagnetic signals could be greatly strengthened.

Taking his invention (now called the Audion tube) to France in 1908, De Forest transmitted voice communication (*radio telephony*) from the top of the Eiffel Tower to receivers up to 500 miles away. Two years later back in the United States, he placed a transmitter in the attic of New York's Metropolitan Opera and carried the vocal artistry of Italian tenor Enrico Caruso to listeners around the city and to ships at sea. Such events gained De Forest, and what would become *radio,* a great deal of publicity. Unfortunately, unscrupulous business associates and running battles over his patents subsequently consumed much of De Forest's strength and

activity. Even though his Audion tube became an essential ingredient in the development of a reliable broadcasting apparatus, De Forest, like Stubblefield and Fessenden, was unable to convert his electrical genius into business success. De Forest's accomplishments were duly noted by the NAB a half-century later—see Figure 5–3.

Meanwhile, on the West Coast, inventor Charles D. Herrold was introducing the citizens of San Jose, California, to the phenomenon. Using an umbrella antenna strung in all directions from the top of a downtown bank building, Herrold began transmissions in 1909 to publicize his own School of Engineering. Soon his Wednesday evening programs attracted a considerable local following, and schoolchildren were brought to the station to see this new scientific marvel that could be heard forty miles away in San Francisco. In fact, when Lee De Forest exhibited his reception equipment at the 1915 Panama Pacific Exposition in that city, Herrold's San Jose station was the source of the programming.

Like virtually all similar radio activities, Herrold's station was shut down by wartime

**Figure 5–3**
Eighty-four-year-old Lee De Forest accepts an award for his groundbreaking engineering contributions from the National Association of Broadcasters in 1958

priorities and he lacked resources to resume operations after the 1918 Armistice. Nevertheless, his efforts, like those of Fessenden and De Forest, had served to generate significant if highly localized public excitement for what many people were calling the "radio telephone." While the serious business of military and commercial communication continued to be conveyed via the dots and dashes (radio *telegraphy*) of the big Marconi facilities and others using their patents, the idea of wireless entertainment was quietly germinating.

## Radio Telephony Blossoms into Radio

With the onset of World War I, wireless activity and research were focused on the needs of the military. On the one hand, this activity spurred the further development of radio technology. On the other hand, most of this attention was devoted to the telegraphy aspect of the enterprise. Armies and governments were much more concerned about increasing their ability to send and detect dots and dashes than they were about generating the curiosity that was voice communication. Nevertheless, by 1915 the U.S. Navy was conducting transatlantic voice tests from its Arlington, Virginia, station. Because the United States was not yet at war, such experimentation could still be accommodated and helped keep interest in the radio telephone alive.

### Dreams and Innovations

The following year, a young employee of the American Marconi Company named David Sarnoff wrote a memo to his superiors in which he advocated the expansion of the firm's focus beyond point-to-point wireless telegraphy to encompass wireless *telephonic* transmissions to the public at large. Four

years before, Sarnoff had been one of the Marconi wireless operators processing messages from rescue ships engaged in picking up survivors from the *Titanic*. He knew firsthand the power of the wireless and also understood that its applications should be greatly broadened:

> I have in mind a plan of development which would make radio a "household utility" in the same sense as the piano or phonograph. The idea is to bring music into the house by wireless. . . . The receiver can be designed in the form of a simple "Radio Music Box" . . . supplied with amplifying tubes and a loudspeaking telephone, all of which can be neatly mounted in one box. . . . Aside from the profit to be derived from this proposition the possibilities for advertising for the company are tremendous, for its name would ultimately be brought into the household, and wireless would receive national and universal attention.[3]

While the Marconi company was trying to decipher this fantastic notion, Lee De Forest had improved his Audion tube to the point at which it could function as an *oscillator* (a Hertzian wave generator). This meant that the Audion could now be used in the radio *transmission* process as well as in reception. Setting up a transmitter in his Bronx, New York, home, De Forest tested his improved system by airing phonograph recordings and such live singers as could be convinced to perform into his microphone. De Forest even sent out the 1916 election night returns with the help of a special tie line from one of the New York City newspapers.

With the entry of the United States into the war in 1917, most radio telephony advances had military point-to-point objectives rather than civilian entertainment goals. Bell System engineers pioneered the transmission of conversations between airplanes and ground stations as well as plane-to-plane exchanges.[4] Meanwhile, the U.S. Navy took over all wireless telegraphy stations not already under Army control, enlisting these facilities in various phases of the war effort. Even though any thought of radio as a public entertainment medium was thus pushed into the background, the war years did advance the cause of modern radio in two significant ways. First, the needs of the military stimulated a rapid increase in wireless research and development. This development was relevant to voice as well as code communication. Second, the armed forces trained thousands of young men in the operation and maintenance of wireless systems. At the war's end, these servicemen comprised an already-trained pool of engineering talent on whom an emerging radio industry could draw in the years ahead.

Nevertheless, the 1918 Armistice did not signal a sudden explosion of radio service for the U.S. public. Most wireless companies saw their business as a future of point-to-point communication, with voice transmissions serving as an extension of the telephone. The old De Forest and even older Fessenden activities were seen as little more than sidebar curiosities. Further, the financial troubles experienced by both of these men (as well as by others) seemed indicative of what would befall anyone seeking to make the wireless more than a vehicle for data transmission by government and commerce.

## Conrad Builds a Business

However, the postwar United States was ready for something more, as events in Pittsburgh soon proved. There, Westinghouse Electric Company engineer Frank Conrad was operating a small radio telephony station in his garage as a field extension of his laboratory experiments in the factory. While Conrad transmitted, an assistant checked signal strength and quality from a variety of area locations. As a means of putting something on the air, Conrad began by reading items from the newspaper; but he soon realized that he could not monitor his equipment and read at the same time. Thus, an arrangement was

made with a local music store. The store would provide Conrad with musical recordings he could transmit in exchange for mention of the store's name over the air. Conrad's two sons soon became involved in announcing and in planning informal wireless concerts, which were regular events by the summer of 1920.

Keep in mind that the main purpose of Conrad's 8XK (his experimental station's call sign) was to explore new patent ideas for Westinghouse. It might have remained no more than an industrial curiosity were it not for the merchandising opportunism of Pittsburgh's Joseph Horne department store. In September 1920, the retailer ran the following item as part of a display ad:

> Victrola music, played into the air over a wireless telephone, was "picked up" by listeners on the wireless receiving station which was recently installed here for patrons interested in wireless experiments. The concert was heard Thursday night about 10 o'clock, and continued 20 minutes. Two orchestra numbers, a soprano solo—which rang particularly high and clear through the air—and a juvenile "talking piece" constituted the program.
>
> The music was from a Victrola pulled up close to the transmitter of a wireless telephone in the home of Frank Conrad, Penn and Peebles avenues, Wilkinsburg. Mr. Conrad is a wireless enthusiast and "puts on" the wireless concerts periodically for the entertainment of the many people in this district who have wireless sets.
>
> Amateur Wireless Sets, made by the maker of the set which is in operation in our store, are on sale here $10.00 up.[5]

Seeing this ad, Conrad's boss at Westinghouse, Harry Davis, sensed a whole new marketing possibility. Up to this time, the only wireless receiving sets in use had been built and operated by electrical apparatus companies and university engineering departments or by skilled hobbyists who used them to talk to each other. But the department store ad introduced the concept of preassembled receivers that could be sold to the general public. If Conrad's transmissions could be upgraded and extended, then the people of Pittsburgh would have a new source of entertainment—and Westinghouse would have a demand for a new product line of prebuilt wireless sets.

Davis immediately scheduled a meeting with Conrad and other Westinghouse employees. Plans were laid to increase the station's power to 100 watts and move it from Conrad's garage to the roof of one of Westinghouse's East Pittsburgh warehouses. By November 2 (the date of the 1920 presidential election), the relocated facility was ready (see Figure 5–4) and operating under the Department of Commerce-designated call sign KDKA. The success of this election night transmission and the interest it aroused around Pittsburgh showed Westinghouse's Davis that he had a commercial windfall on his hands. More important, this comparatively powerful new station, deliberately transmitting to the public rather than point-to-point to other stations, marked the transition from wireless telephone to *broadcasting*.

## The First Real Broadcasters

While most of the rest of the world would continue to use the generic *wireless* designation for decades to come, people in the United States soon appropriated the more descriptive term *broadcasting* in referring to over-the-air voice transmissions to the public. The term was not a new one. It could be found in most dictionaries of the time as a word to describe how a farmer sowed seeds by scattering them in all directions. Such agricultural imagery was certainly appropriate to this new concept of wireless use. Instead of directing its signal to a single ship, a shore installation, or a sister station, the *broadcast* station threw material out on the air for the benefit of everyone within range of the transmission. The transformation from communications to mass communications vehicle was suddenly under way.

As the Pittsburgh experiment became replicated in more and more localities, different

**Figure 5–4**
KDKA's original transmitter room

motivations for broadcasting gradually emerged. Some stations, like the University of Wisconsin's 9XM, continued to function as testing laboratories but added weather and musical programs as by-product public services. Other stations, such as the *Detroit News*'s 8MK (see Figure 5–5), were seen as low-cost public relations devices for their parent companies. Still others, like KDKA itself, were in the business of stimulating sales for their company's own electrical products. While the spotlight was now on broadcasting rather than on wireless telephony, no one as yet saw the activity as a self-standing business, let alone a promising new profession.

In 1921, the Department of Commerce issued thirty-two radio licenses, a number that would increase tenfold over the course of the following three years. Wisconsin's 9XM became WHA, and the *Detroit News*'s 8MK became WWJ; it was purchased in 1989 by CBS. By July, the Radio Corporation of America (formerly American Marconi) was also dabbling in broadcasting from its Hoboken, New Jersey, facility by retransmitting a telephoned description of the Dempsey–Carpentier heavyweight boxing match from a stadium in Jersey City. The first newly designated broadcast license was issued as WBZ to a station in Springfield, Massachusetts, and the Crosley Radio Corporation began mass-producing radio receivers with a $35 price tag. In short, the year 1921 proved a transition between the raw experimentation of the first mass wireless telephonic episodes and the emergence of radio as a true broadcast medium in 1922.

The course of events accelerated as major players entered the field. RCA acquired Newark station WJZ from Westinghouse (a station

**Figure 5–5**
The 1920 staff and control room of the *Detroit News*'s 8MK

**Figure 5–6**
Tuning an early crystal receiving set

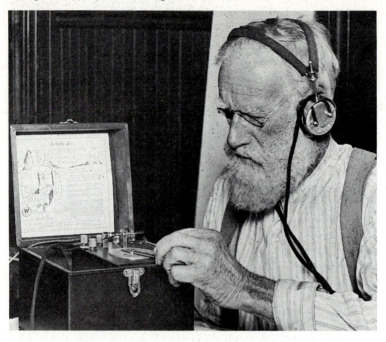

that had been built only months before) and relocated it in Manhattan. It was soon joined in the market by WEAF, owned and operated by the dominant telephone company, AT&T. The attention two such giant stations attracted did much to stimulate the building of other stations by these and many other companies.

Unfortunately, the Department of Commerce, in creating the new class of broadcasting stations in 1921, allocated only one place on the spectrum for such operations: 360 meters (833 kilohertz). Thus, every newly authorized station was given the same place on the dial! The escape from the mounting congestion was just as bizarre. Because 485 meters (619 kHz) had been specified for weather, crop, and similar governmental reports, stations frequently moved to that frequency to broadcast that type of content and then moved back to 833 to transmit all other programming. Listeners were expected to follow

along and somehow continue to locate their favorite station despite the increasing interference of other outlets now working those same frequencies.

In the true hands-off spirit of the Republican administrations of the 1920s, the Department of Commerce simply told stations to work out sharing arrangements among themselves. As a partial solution, a new class of operation, the B stations, was created and allowed to transmit at 400 meters (750 kHz). Occupants of this channel had to operate at significantly less power, however, and were not allowed to broadcast any phonograph records. Finally, as we see in Chapter 6, the airwaves became such a tangle of interference that responsible broadcasters had to convince the government to take corrective action.

By the midtwenties, radio equipment had vastly improved and the number of home receiving sets mushroomed. Everyone was talking about *radio,* and the much less glamorous work of the wireless telegraph receded into the shadows. As early as 1923, low-cost vacuum tube receivers were replacing the old crystal sets with their awkward cat's whisker wire that detected radio waves in silicon, iron pyrite, or galena and then converted them into a weak electrical current you needed headphones to hear. Figure 5–6 illustrates one of these devices. Now, a listener could sit in front of a handsomely wood-encased radio like the one in Figure 5–7 rather than huddle over an ugly pile of wires. The expenditure on radio sets and parts in the United States rose to $150 million in 1923 alone.[6] In addition, newly improved triodes required only 5 percent of the electrical current that De Forest's older tubes had used to heat their filaments. This meant much more efficient transmission and reception and over much wider distances.[7] By the following year, radio was already ranked as the 34th largest business in the country and sales of sets and parts had jumped to more than $350 million.[8]

Using its WEAF as the anchor and its long-distance telephone lines as the vehicle, AT&T set up a temporary twenty-two-station coast-to-coast radio network in 1924 to cover a speech by President Calvin Coolidge. Two years later, this arrangement had evolved into a permanent network of twenty-four stations carried over much improved equalized circuits. By 1928, this network spanned the continent. At about the same time, the new Federal Radio Commission took over broadcast spectrum management from the Department of Commerce and instituted new policies requiring stations not to deviate more than half a kilohertz from their authorized frequency. Summarizing the FRC's first few months of intense activity, Commissioner O. H. Caldwell observed in December 1927:

> We have forced hundreds of stations to divide time. . . . Other stations are being assigned for daylight operation only. . . . Some stations are operating simultaneous during day hours and dividing time on night programs. Stations are operating on two coasts using the same wave depending for clearance on the time difference and isolating effect of the sunset. . . . But the limit of loading our broadcasting channels is now absolutely reached.[9]

## Radio Comes of Age

The year 1928 witnessed a complete reorganization of the broadcast spectrum as an essential prelude to the stabilizing of U.S. broadcasting activities. The Federal Radio Commission's new allocation plan arranged channels into local, regional, and national groupings. The country was divided into five zones. Each zone received eight exclusive channel assignments that were nationally cleared for the use of a single high-power station. These clear channel outlets were designed to restore the feasibility of long-distance listening and to provide more assured radio service to the country's rural inhabitants. (Later, these clears would be standardized with power of 50,000 watts.) By decade's end, more than 10 million U.S. homes were equipped with radios,[10] and these would be joined by 4 million more over the next year. A populace wracked by the economic Depression saw radio as their only source of free entertainment. As broadcast historian Erik Barnouw relates:

> Social workers reported cases of families that had lost their installment-bought car, icebox, vacuum cleaner and sofa and canceled the milk but still met payments on the radio. It was their link with humanity.[11]

### Armstrong's Contribution

By this time, shortwave broadcasting had firmly established itself in most parts of the world. Most people in the United States, however, were content to listen to their regular domestic (AM) stations. To these audiences,

**Figure 5–7**
A De Forest 1925 radio receiver outfitted with 1923 Western Electric loud-speaker

*(Lautman Photo 77355)*

radio *was* AM and had been since they had built or bought their first set. In fact, the AM designation was seldom even used; radio dials simply called it the broadcast band.

But in 1933, the brilliant Edwin Armstrong unveiled his static-free FM (frequency modu-lation) system to RCA engineers. Previously, as an undergraduate at Columbia University,

Armstrong had developed a feedback circuit that made De Forest's Audion tube capable of efficient radio reception. He was awarded a patent in 1914 but subsequently lost a tangled legal battle to De Forest in 1934. Now, even though RCA did not seem impressed by FM, Armstrong pressed on with his new invention in an attempt to recoup his fortunes.

Unfortunately, like Stubblefield, Fessenden, and even De Forest himself, Armstrong's technical genius (another of his innovations is pictured in Figure 5–8) far outstripped his business and legal acumen. RCA's real interest was television, not FM radio, because FM seemed to pose a threat both to the corporation's profitable AM empire and to its spectrum plans for video. Once Armstrong detected the real cause of RCA's foot-drag-

ging, he struck out on his own and opened experimental station W2XMN at Alpine, New Jersey, in 1939. Through his persistence, the Federal Communications Commission (which had succeeded the old FRC) authorized commercial FM broadcasting.

Almost immediately, World War II shut down any possible exploitation of this opportunity. By the time the war was over, RCA had helped convince the FCC to move FM to a higher frequency in order to make spectrum room for television. This move made the half-million existing receivers obsolete and fatally undermined Armstrong's financially fragile endeavors. He sued RCA for patent infringement in its use of FM television sound transmission and eventually settled out of court five years later. Armstrong died in a suspi-

**Figure 5–8**
A young Edwin Armstrong displays another of his inventions—the six-tube portable radio

cious fall from his thirteenth floor New York apartment in 1954, leaving behind a medium with great but unfulfilled potential.

Even though the number of FM stations increased to more than 700 by the end of the 1940s, many of them were operated by long-established AM broadcasters who grabbed FM assignments solely as a means of protecting their existing stations against possible future competition. Most merely *simulcast* (duplicated) their AM programming on FM. The public therefore saw little need to buy FM receivers and so, in absence of significant demand, the cost of these receivers remained artificially high. Between 1950 and 1958, the number of FM stations actually declined by hundreds of outlets, and AM's position as the dominant radio system seemed secure.

### The FM Sun Rises

In 1961, however, FM's fortunes began to change when the FCC permitted FM stations to broadcast in stereo, via a hybrid system that combined elements of Zenith and Gen-

eral Electric proposals. This allowed broadcasters to exploit the new stereophonic capability that the recording industry had introduced in 1953. The commission followed up its stereo action a few years later with the *nonduplication rule* that prohibited major (and, later, middle) market broadcasters from using their FM assignments as passive repeaters of AM fare. Both of these pronouncements resulted in new and acoustically appealing programming that captured public interest and stimulated FM receiver sales (see Figure 5–9). The separate offering of SCA-type services (see Chapter 2) had been authorized years before, but FM stations could now regard such activities as a secondary rather than an essential means to raise revenue. FM became salable to advertisers in its own right, and more and more music formats migrated to the FM dial.

By the end of the 1970s, a generation of young music listeners had grown up with the contemporary music formats on the FM band. To them, AM stood for "antique melodies"

**Figure 5–9**
U.S. radio receiver sales

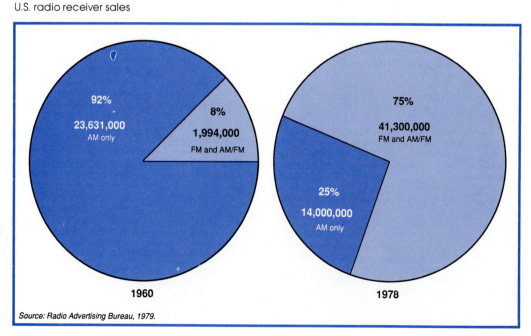

1960

1978

Source: *Radio Advertising Bureau, 1979.*

and was avoided like the plague. By 1989, almost 80 percent of listening in the United States was done on the FM band, and it was AM that needed resuscitation. Ironically, the FCC dropped its nonduplication rule in 1986 so that co-owned AM stations could echo what their sister FMs were broadcasting! This only reemphasizes that the future of AM seems precarious unless radical new ideas for the band can be found and executed.

## The Video Venture Begins

Technological discoveries that ultimately led to television were occurring throughout the years of radio's development. That it took somewhat longer for video to capture attention was due to two factors: (1) most early television work took place in laboratories well outside general public notice; and (2) television progress was hobbled by the existence of two competing and quite different systems, the *mechanical* and the *electronic*. Both systems depended on the use of light-sensitive materials to break up a picture and put it back together again at the point of reception. How this disassembly and assembly were accomplished varied greatly, however.

### Laboratory Groundwork

In 1873, Willoughby Smith, a telegraph engineer at the Irish end of the new transatlantic cable project (see Figure 5–10), made an interesting observation. Resistance components made of the new element *selenium* (chiefly a byproduct of copper refining) exhibited a variation in their electrical conductivity depending on the amount of light to which they were exposed.[12] The brighter the light, the better was selenium's conductivity. The underlying implication of this finding was that electronic impulses could take the form of light. Following up on this revelation, scientists in both England and the United States experimented to see if visual data could be conveyed via an electrical current. After all, Alexander Graham Bell had fashioned a telephone to replicate the function of the human ear, so why couldn't another device be built that was patterned after the human eye?

With a bank of selenium cells as a substitute for the eye's retina, researchers used a lens to capture the light/shadow patterns of the sim-

**Figure 5–10**
The steamship *Faraday* lays transatlantic cable between Ireland and the North American continent. This project indirectly stimulated initial television research.

ple object at which that lens was pointed. In essence, the scientists were attempting to construct an electrical camera in which unexposed film had been replaced by a bank of unexcited selenium cells.

When light comes through the lens selectively to expose a frame of film, a chemical reaction occurs that results in what we call photography. On the other hand, when the light and dark elements of the scene were focused onto the selenium bank, each cell either increased or decreased its ability to carry current depending on whether its portion of the framed subject was light or dark. This constituted an electrical rather than a chemical response—the basic video/film distinction that still pertains today.

In 1884, the father of mechanical television, German scientist Paul Nipkow, took the process a significant step further. Nipkow's invention pointed the light-focusing lens onto a rapidly rotating disc. This spinning wheel contained a spiral pattern of perforations with each hole progressively closer to the center of the disc. Behind this disc was a light-sensitive photoelectric cell (a refinement on the older selenium bank concept). As the disc revolved, the succeeding perforations allowed light (or its absence) from different portions of the scene to reach the cell. When the first hole was between the lens and the photoelectric cell, the top of the scene was scanned. If that segment of the scene was bright, the cell would be excited to conduct the maximum current. If it was dim, little or no current would be passed. Each successive hole then scanned a slightly lower band of the scene.

Meanwhile, at the receiving end, another synchronized disc was used to scan a luminous surface; bands of this surface were caused to glow, partially glow, or remain dark (unexcited) depending on the amount of current being sent down the wire that linked the transmitting apparatus with this receiver. The resulting picture was extremely crude—but it was television. An observer of the Nipkow invention described the effect this way:

The picture, measuring about 4 by 5 inches, was in tones of pinkish-red, a color which represented the spectrum of the gas neon contained in a special electrical lamp capable of extinguishing and relighting itself as many as 100,000 times per second. The picture was divided up into 48 thin strips, each strip being separated by a very thin line of black. Much like the movies of old, the reproduction at times stubbornly drifted from the field of vision only to be coaxed back into position by the operator.[13]

## Mechanical Television Runs Its Course

The Nipkow system was *mechanical*, of course, because it relied on the rapid motorized spinning of two synchronous discs (one in the transmitter and one in the receiver) to convert the picture into a series of electrical current fluctuations. These fluctuations then recreated the light and dark patterns of the original picture/subject on the luminous surface of the receiver. At this stage, it was also telephone vision because it relied on current sent down a closed wire rather than on an electromagnetic transmission propelled into the air. Still, these laboratory achievements captured the imagination of other inventors eager to pick up where Nipkow had left off.

By 1923, John Baird in Great Britain and Charles Jenkins in the United States were demonstrating primitive black-and-white silhouettes in motion. Two years later, Jenkins transmitted television pictures of President Harding from Washington to Philadelphia and had added a series of prismatic rings to the transmitter as a means of double-scanning the picture for greater clarity. In fact, by the end of the decade, the Jenkins Television Company was making plans for the production of a radio-visor through which the public could receive television pictures over the air by adding the contraption to an existing multiple-tube radio set.[14] AT&T's Bell Laboratories conducted similar mechanical television experiments in the mid-1920s. Two of the devices that Bell Labs contrived are seen in Figures 5–11 and 5–12.

The 1930s proved to be the high-water mark for mechanical television. Even though public demonstrations of the system by Jenkins, Baird, Bell Laboratories, and RCA multiplied, the latter company was already focusing on an all-electronic system in its behind-the-scenes research. More and more, the inherent limitations of the mechanical apparatus were becoming clear. As R. H. Mansen, president of the Institute of Radio Engineers, remarked in 1931:

> It is reasonable to expect that any great stride in the advancement of television will be through some new invention for simplifying the transmission problem. Otherwise progress will be comparatively slow and the public will have to wait several years for commercial results.[15]

Another television authority added:

> We are just as far from that goal [television service to the general public] today as we were from modern sound broadcasting in, say, 1902, when wireless telegraph communication was conducted clumsily and precariously by the aid of spark coils and coherers.[16]

Still, the proponents of mechanical video found it difficult to abandon a project on which they had labored so hard. In 1932, an English cinema audience was treated to the telecasting of a horse-race scene in which the normally tiny television picture had been tripled in size through the use of a series of *three* synchronized drums.[17]

But four years later the mechanical and electronic systems went head-to-head in London, and the result of this competition signaled the death knell for the scanning disc. The scene was the British Broadcasting Corporation's experimental television studio at Alexandra Palace. For three months, from November 1936 through January 1937, alternate transmission tests of Baird's mechanical system and the new all-electronic method de-

veloped by the Marconi–E.M.I. Television Company were conducted. In February, the BBC selected the clearly superior 405-line electronic apparatus[18], and the British Empire's sun set on scanning disc TV. Meanwhile, in the United States, RCA and, to a lesser extent, several other companies were making rapid strides in electronic system development that outstripped anything the mechanical method could hope to achieve. In 1946–47, CBS attempted to revive mechanical television as the basis for its color television system, but the process was not compatible with existing black-and-white receivers and would have required its own separate band on the spectrum. The FCC thus refused to approve it, and the prospect of video discs spinning merrily in homes across the country was permanently foreclosed.

## The Ripening of Electronic TV

During these years of mechanical television's well-intentioned but ill-destined progression, discoveries that would lead to today's electronic system were taking a different course. In 1878, British physicist Sir William Crookes invented the cathode ray tube. Simply put, this tube was a glass container to house high-speed electrons. These electrons possessed the capability of being deflected and focused by electrical and magnetic fields. By 1897, Germany's Carl Ferdinand Braun had built a similar tube and was actually able to direct the path of cathode rays through the primitive manipulation of magnets. Braun also added a fluorescent surface to the tube to increase its light-sensitivity properties significantly. The cathode ray tube would prove to be the cornerstone of electronic television in the same way that the scanning disc was central to the mechanical method.

Ten years later, Russian scientist Boris Rosing used Braun's tube as the basis for a prototype *wireless* television receiver. For a time, a young student named Vladimir Zworykin worked as Rosing's laboratory assistant at the

**Figure 5–11**
Performer seated in front of a mechanical television system transmitter

St. Petersburg Institute of Technology. By 1917, Zworykin had decided to leave crumbling Czarist Russia and immigrate to the United States in order to pursue this television research. In two years, he was working for Westinghouse and had persuaded his reluctant superiors to allow him to phase out of his job as a production-line assembler of vacuum tubes and into research exploration of electronic television. Before 1923 was over, the Russian-born inventor had developed an all-electronic television pickup tube he called the *iconoscope.* This device used a scanning gun or eye rather than a spinning disc to convert a light image into electrical energy for transmission.

Meanwhile, Philo Farnsworth, a young Salt Lake City scientist, was completing his own work on a similar device labeled the electronic *image dissector* camera. Before long, Zworykin, Farnsworth, and several lesser inventors became embroiled in patent litigation over their competing devices. Farnsworth would eventually be paid a million dollar settlement by RCA so that it could continue to develop Zworykin's concepts with a free hand.

Zworykin had continued to work for Westinghouse until 1930, when General Electric, Westinghouse, and RCA merged their research efforts into a powerful development effort located at the RCA Laboratories in Camden, New Jersey. By 1933, both Farnsworth and Zworykin had developed their still-competing systems to the point at which they could electronically transmit pictures of 240 lines of resolution. At the receiving end, however, these lines were still being assembled via mechanical means.[19]

Still, the electronic transmitter was a tremendous improvement over its mechanical counterpart. With the cathode ray scanning

**Figure 5–12**
A viewer uses a mechanical television system receiver. The picture appears
in the small square aperture.

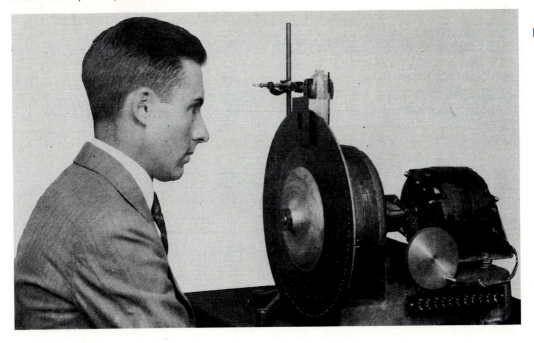

device, the entire picture surface was illuminated all the time, and the heat and friction
caused by rotating discs were eliminated. By
1935, RCA engineers had produced a television picture of 343 lines. This was a great improvement over the 50- or 60-line images of
just a few years earlier, because the greater
the number of lines, the greater the picture
resolution (clarity). Nevertheless even RCA's
comparatively advanced system produced a
very small picture that could not be transmitted more than twenty-five miles and was subject to significant static caused by automobile
ignitions and other electrical fields. RCA president David Sarnoff announced plans to build
an experimental television station and produce a small number of receivers, but he predicted that full-scale consumer service was
still a long way off. Whether he truly believed
this or was trying to lull competitors into a
false sense of security, events progressed

faster than Sarnoff's pronouncement suggested.

The following year, the Philco Radio and
Television Corporation held a demonstration
of their 345-line system. It featured an im-
proved-contrast black-and-white picture
rather than the murky green-and-white that
had heretofore been a hallmark of electronic
television. After the demonstration, Philco's
head research engineer, a former RCA employee named A. F. Murray, was much more
optimistic than his former boss had been.
"With the information we now have and with
the breaks that seem to be coming our way,"
said Murray, "we hope to put TV on a commercial basis within 5 years. The sets should
cost the customer about $500, but they'll re-
ceive good pictures, at least from a technical
standpoint."[20]

By 1937, there were no less than seventeen
experimental television stations operating in

some fashion, and Sarnoff's earlier prediction seemed much too conservative. New players, including CBS, Philco, and Zenith, were bringing their own technical expertise to bear, and such competition intensified the pace of development. At the New York World's Fair in 1939, RCA cameras captured the welcoming speech by President Franklin Delano Roosevelt on a 441-line system, and the public was able to view the latest prototype receiver at the RCA pavilion. RCA/NBC's New York station, W2XBS (later to become WNBC–TV) began regularly scheduled public broadcasts of two full hours each week to the few hundred receivers in existence. It looked like real broadcast television was about to arrive.

Seeking to avoid a repetition of radio's chaotic early years, the Federal Communications Commission held hearings in 1940 to determine how to convert television most efficiently from an experimental to a regular broadcast medium. A new National Television System Committee, made up of a number of technical experts, was constituted to set standards for video operations. The committee subsequently selected a picture made up of 525 lines with the picture surface being completely scanned by the cathode ray eye at a rate of 30 times (30 frames) per second. The picture portion of the television transmission would be amplitude modulated (AM). The sound would be generated by frequency modulation (FM) means. These standards were officially adopted on April 30, 1941, and they remain the cornerstone of the U.S. (NTSC) television system to this day.

Within six months, it was estimated that between 10,000 and 20,000 television receivers were in use. Half of these were in New York, and the rest were divided among Philadelphia, Chicago, and Los Angeles. Both NBC (the network owned by RCA) and CBS mounted expanded schedules of fifteen hours per week on their New York stations, and eight other commercial outlets were also fully established by the end of 1941. In the wake of the attack on Pearl Harbor, however, four of these ten commercial operations shut down and the other six converted to noncommercial, limited-service status for the war's duration. Wartime research and development continued, nonetheless, and served to improve the technology whereby commercial television would be relaunched in 1946.

## Television Becomes a Mass Medium

The video industry rapidly took shape in the postwar years. In 1945, RCA unveiled the *image orthicon* (IO) camera tube as the successor to Zworykin's old iconoscope. The greatly increased sensitivity of the IO meant that much less studio illumination was needed. TV performers no longer broiled under intense light and could throw away the thick makeup and purple lipstick that had been required. AT&T, for its part, had used the war years to improve the coaxial cables that would carry network television signals from station to station and was already beginning installation of intercity links. The question of color television was still to be resolved, however, and FCC spectrum allocations to the new medium were based on purely theoretical projections as to both number of stations and the interference to which they would subject each other.

### Technical Decisions
At the beginning of 1946, the total television medium in the United States consisted of 6 noncommercial stations serving no more than 8,000 sets with screen sizes of either 7 or 10 inches. Two years later, the number of stations had increased to 48 outlets serving 23 cities. With more applications being filed every day, the FCC realized that its earlier spectrum plan of providing only 13 VHF channels to serve the entire country was

going to be less than adequate. Therefore, on September 29, 1948, the commission announced it would not process any more applications until spectrum considerations had been revisited. "The Freeze," as it came to be known in the industry, lasted until 1952. Nevertheless, stations whose construction applications had already been approved were allowed to take the air, which meant that 108 fortunate facilities had the television audience all to themselves for a period of up to four years as the number of sets rose to well over 17 million.

Meanwhile, as mentioned earlier, the FCC decided that the CBS mechanical color system would not be a viable option. But it also refused to endorse the RCA electronic system because this system also was incompatible with existing black-and-white receivers. In a more positive development, NBC, Western Union, and several other companies were beginning to put microwave relays into service as an alternative means of networking because the AT&T coaxial cable capacity was becoming overcrowded. AT&T, through a variety of actions, tried to stifle this new source of competition and was subsequently sued by Philco, Western Union, and the fledgling Du-Mont network. But if it seemed as though television was awash in unresolved problems, the U.S. public's enthusiastic purchasing of sets did not wane. In some neighborhoods, in fact, people who could not yet afford a receiver put an antenna on their roof just to impress the neighbors!

As the United States entered the 1950s, CBS took another run at the color prize when it showed the FCC a 405-line field sequential color system that would work on black-and-white sets with the purchase of a special adapter. This was not quite the mechanical system that the commission had earlier turned down, but neither was it a completely electronic device. Still, CBS was allowed to begin field testing because the color it attained was superior to that offered by any other company. Unfortunately for CBS, a variety of circumstances, including RCA's legal actions and the onset of the Korean War, precluded further development of its system. By the time of the Korean Armistice in 1953, RCA/NBC had developed a completely compatible and all-electronic color system that won NTSC approval.

Spectrum questions had been resolved the previous year when the FCC lifted the Freeze via its Sixth Report and Order. In it, the commission retained its 1948 shift of old Channel 1 to land-mobile communication and then reconstituted other television spectrum space as follows:

VHF channels 2–13 54–216 mHz
UHF channels 14–83 470–890 mHz
(channels 70–83 were subsequently diverted to land-mobile use, and channel 37 was granted to radio astronomy operations)

As mentioned in Chapter 2, differing maximum powers were specified for low-band VHF, high-band VHF, and UHF telecasting respectively, and minimum mileage separations between users of the same channel were also established. This plan provided for a potential of more than 2,000 individual stations assigned to almost 1,300 communities and reserved 242 of these stations for noncommercial use (these numbers were later enlarged). Even though this new spectrum plan was much more realistic than its 1945 predecessor, its location of almost two-thirds of the assignments on the less efficient UHF band caused continuing difficulties for years. Still, the FCC had finally released a medium that had been artificially restrained for more than a decade. By 1953, television was finally free to expand at its own pace.

Almost immediately, UHF broadcasters ran into trouble. Their equipment and operating (power) costs were much higher than those for VHF. Transmitters that would have allowed a UHF station to reach maximum power did not even become available until the 1970s. Furthermore, most receivers sold were VHF-only. Consumers either had to buy a separate converter or pay an exorbitant cost for an all-channel set. Either way, the UHF channel dial lacked the click slots of its VHF counterpart, making tuning difficult. Major broadcasters grabbed up the VHF allocations and the network affiliations that followed, resulting in UHF's technical difficulties being compounded by a lack of appealing programming. Almost 40 percent of the 125 UHF stations on the air in 1954 had gone dark six years later. This dire situation continued until several FCC actions and market events eventually provided partial relief. Some smaller markets, primarily those not yet served by any local VHF station, were made all-UHF by the FCC. But this remedy did little to improve the television service to those markets and did nothing for UHF broadcasters elsewhere.

## Improving Picture Capture, Distribution, and Color

In 1956, a different technical development made life a little easier for telecasters in general when the Ampex Corporation successfully demonstrated *videotape* recording at the 31st annual convention of the National Association of Broadcasters. Up to this time, the only means of recording a live television event was via a *kinescope*—the grainy capturing of an image off a television monitor by a specially adapted film camera. With videotape, however, even recorded programming could continue to look live. CBS became the first network to exploit videotape on November 30, 1956, when it recorded its 15-minute evening newscast, *Douglas Edwards with the News,* for delayed broadcast over the three western time zones.[21] Unlike the patent squabbling and governmental delays that had inhibited other advances in broadcast technologies, all the major equipment manufacturers adopted a common standard so that videotape quickly became the normal recording procedure within most television stations. (One of the first mass-produced professional videotape machines is shown in Figure 5–13.)

Television entered the space age in 1962 with the launch of AT&T's Telstar I communications satellite. An active repeater bird, Telstar possessed the capability to receive microwave signals from earth, amplify them ten billion times, and then retransmit them back to the ground. On July 10, as the satellite came in line-of-sight of the Andover, Maine, tracking station, the three U.S. television networks presented a twelve-minute news program that interrelayed TV pictures between the U.S., France, and England.[22] Even though broadcast television was not Telstar's primary purpose, this breakthrough event paved the way for today's commonplace use of satellite relaying of both international and domestic programming.

Also in 1962, and of much more "down-to-earth" importance for UHF operators, Congress and the FCC agreed on an "all-channel requirement." As of April 30, 1964, all new television sets shipped over state lines would have to be capable of receiving both VHF *and* UHF stations. This regulation, by itself, would not eliminate UHF's plight, but it did ensure that virtually all television households would eventually be capable of UHF reception.

After more than a decade of slow and stumbling growth, color television also came of age by the mid-1960s. Until 1964, only NBC regularly broadcast a significant number of color programs. This, of course, was to be expected because the FCC-approved color system had been developed by that network's RCA parent. Still, the cost of a color set was high, and the scarcity of color programming hardly provided an incentive for its purchase.

By the midsixties, however, when color receiver technology had been improved and the price of sets had dropped, more than one-quarter of all receivers sold were color-capable. The perfection of color videotape recorders by both Ampex and RCA to replace the

**Figure 5–13**

Engineers minister to the control panel of an RCA TR–1, one of the first production model videotape recorders. The complete unit consisted of several more racks of tubes and wires not shown in this photo.

first generation black-and-white models meant that nonfilm color programming and commercials now could be dependably captured for later play and distribution. Further, the launch of Early Bird, the first satellite intended primarily for television transmission, restimulated public interest in enjoying state-of-the-art video at home. By 1966, all three networks had all-color prime time schedules and, for the first time, the number of black-and-white sets sold decreased while the sales of color sets jumped by almost 70 percent.

In an age of astronauts and intercontinental satellite communication, black-and-white was dull. Advertisers discovered that consumers paid more attention (at least initially) to commercials in color. This fact accelerated the conversion because color advertisements made stations' adjacent black-and-white programming look antique by comparison.

Even though much later developments such as increased transistorization, the home VCR it made possible, and the prospect of HDTV (high-definition television) would further enhance television technology, the medium had come of age by the midsixties. As had been the case with radio by the mid-1930s, the U.S. public now thought of television (even *color* television) as a household necessity rather than a luxury. In fact, TV viewing seemed to be replacing more traditional forms of entertainment. When cable television service to the town of Somerset, Kentucky, was suspended because of a 1968 franchise dispute, the isolated community was completely deprived of television service for thirty-one days. Nine months after the blackout, the birthrate at Somerset City Hospital had risen by 300 percent.[23]

## The Cable Option

Over the years, cable television has made some technical strides of its own—not in how a signal is produced but in how it is distributed.

In one sense, cable shares a certain commonality with early mechanical television in that both involve the sending of a single picture/program *by wire*. In another sense, most of the other developments we have discussed were concerned with the actual *broadcast* of video into the open airwaves. People stuck an antenna on the roof and pulled in whatever signals were in range. But what about individuals living in outlying areas or in valleys not being reached with viewable pictures? For them, an additional technology was needed and began to emerge almost as soon as the television medium was released from its wartime bonds.

### CATV Pioneers

In 1948, John Walson, an employee of Pennsylvania Power & Light, was also running the family appliance store in Mahanoy City. Because the city is in a valley, local residents could not receive television signals from the new Philadelphia stations eighty miles away. Walson was forced to drive prospective TV set buyers to an antenna he had constructed on top of a nearby mountain in order to demonstrate his wares. When the disadvantage of this method became apparent, he used his connections with the power company to string a cable from the mountain top to his store, wiring several homes (including that of

a PP&L official who had allowed him to use company poles) along the way. By the summer, Walson had hooked up 725 residences and began to charge $2 per month for providing three Philadelphia stations (see Figure 5–14).[24]

At about the same time, Ed Parsons of Astoria, Oregon, mounted a master antenna atop the local hotel, pulled in the signal of the new Seattle television station, and used a combination of retransmitters and coaxial cables to pipe the signal to residences in the community. In the Parsons system, there was no monthly fee. Instead, subscribers paid $100 for installation and became a part of the community cooperative. In classifying such arrangements, an FCC staff attorney coined the term *CATV* (community antenna television), and a new branch of the electronic media was on its way.[25]

Notice that even from its inception, CATV was not *broadcasting*. It did not send signals into the VHF/UHF airwaves for everyone who wanted to grab them. Instead, the programming was fed down a private line to subscribers or co-op members who contracted to receive its services. Initially, CATV was merely a retransmission device that extended broadcasters' signals into areas not reachable by over-the-air means. Thus, it was embraced by station owners as a way to increase potential viewership (and, therefore, advertising rates) at no cost to them.

Other entrepreneurs, such as Robert Tarleton of Lansford, Pennsylvania, soon entered the field. Using his background in electronics, Tarleton created the first commercially viable cable system by modifying existing signal amplifiers specifically for coaxial cable use. This greatly improved the quality and strength of the cable retransmission. His Panther Valley TV Company also followed systematic utility-company practices of running lines on poles up and down the streets.[26] Through the activities of Walson, Parsons, and Tarleton, the prototype for the modern cablecaster had been established.

**Figure 5–14**
John Walson, cable television founder, over-
looks the town he first wired

## Cable as Competitor

Throughout the 1950s, a number of mostly small, family-owned CATVs helped bring the benefits of television to rural and mountainous areas of the United States. A hint of things to come was unveiled in 1957, when the FCC gave permission for an experimental pay cable system in Bartlesville, Oklahoma. Although too far ahead of its time, the Bartlesville innovation of *originating* programming (in this case, first-run motion pictures) rather than merely relaying existing broadcast signals, helped point the way to a new series of options for cable service and development. As of yet, however, the U.S. public was not willing to pay for cable-only programming if it could continue to receive broadcast programming for free.

During the next two decades, cable expanded throughout the country, and systems began to be consolidated as large MSOs (*multiple system operators*) were formed. Now, many systems were relaying distant station signals into local broadcasters' own back-

## CNN  Consumer Electronics

The home electronics industry believes HDTV eventually will prove to be as hot a retail item as were the VCR, camcorder, and CD player in the 1980s. Until HDTV reaches the market, it is hoped that DAT and versatile pocket computers will continue to boost electronics sales.

yards. Some cable operations also were originating their own programming. CATV thereby had become a threat to local broadcasters rather than a friendly extender of their signals, and a long and involved series of legal skirmishes continued throughout this period (see Chapter 6).

The real establishment of cable as a self-standing and competitive industry, however, came in 1975, when Time Inc.'s Home Box Office (HBO) married satellite technology and cable's selective distribution capacity to create a national premium service that delivered uncut movies and exclusive sporting events directly into subscribers' homes. Before HBO, each cable system wishing to originate material had either physically to obtain and show the movies themselves, or enter into expensive land-line or microwave interconnections with other systems in the region. With HBO and a satellite dish, however, pay programming literally dropped out of the sky at the cable system's headend for easy and immediate sale to local households.

HBO paved the way for scores of other pay or advertiser-supported cable networks. These networks brought exclusive programming to the industry's subscribers and introduced a range of new competitors to the television broadcaster's audience. Meanwhile, broadcasters and broadcast networks also came to use the satellite as a cost-effective way to relay network programs and grab local news stories. But the most dramatic contribution of so-called birds such as the one pictured in Figure 5–15 was their conversion of cable from a predominately repeater service to a self-standing originator in its own right. By the end of the 1980s, little more than a century after Alexander Graham Bell put those first tentative impulses into a wire, a vast amalgamation of telecommunications enterprises was well established.

As we discuss in Chapter 14, these enterprises stand at the brink of even more massive technological change. High Definition Television (HDTV), Digital Audio Broadcast-ing (DAB), fiber optics, audio/video compression devices, and a whole range of applications that such tools make possible are promising both to enlarge and transform how we reach our audiences in the years immediately ahead. As National Association of Broadcasters President Eddie Fritz told his organization's 1991 convention, "We face challenges to the structure and technology of television and radio that will require all the strength and persuasiveness we can muster. These are challenges of a new order."[27]

## Chapter Flashback

Radio and television owe their beginnings to eighteenth- and nineteenth-century laboratory experiments in such fields as electrical conduction and electromagnetism. First the telegraph and then the telephone demonstrated that electricity running down a wire could be manipulated to carry human communication, through either simple stop/start code (the telegraph) or the more complex shaping of the current's intensity to mirror speech (the telephone).

The work of Hertz and Marconi subsequently used the energy in electromagnetic waves to generate coded communication through space rather than within the confines of a strung wire. The wireless telegraph paved the way for the wireless telephone, which could send speech and music over the air. Stubblefield, Fessenden, De Forest, and Herrold each made his own innovative if uncoordinated contribution to this new delivery system. The years immediately before and after World War I bridged the gap between point-to-point and true mass communication in wireless utilization, with the radio telephone blossoming into *radio broadcasting*.

The early 1920s saw the birth and mushrooming growth of radio. Frank Conrad's experimental Westinghouse station in Pitts-

**Figure 5–15**

**125**

CHAPTER 5
Technolo-
gical
Maturation

GTE Spacenet satellite used to distribute cable network programming

burgh became a source of entertainment and popular interest. Other companies and educational institutions built their own outlets to promote their experiments or products. Before long, stations became businesses in their own right. Major corporations like AT&T and RCA entered the fledgling broadcasting field, and fundamental principles for commercial and network operations were established. The Depression further solidified radio's appeal to the U.S. public because the medium provided free entertainment once you finished the payments on your radio set.

Edwin Armstrong's work led to FM (frequency modulation) as both a new class of stations and a means of transmission, but he lacked the corporate power and financial resources to profit from his innovations. FM broadcasting did not come into its own until the 1970s. During the following ten years it far surpassed its AM predecessor in listener appeal, particularly among young people.

Starting from a series of laboratory experiments with light-sensitive selenium, what would become television progressed in two directions: mechanical and electronic. Ultimately, the electronic system proved the more practical, but only after a contest that, in the case of color television, lasted until the 1950s. World War II and the necessity of establishing viable operating standards meant that the television medium was not fully unleashed in the United States until 1952 with the lifting of the FCC's "Freeze." Rapid expansion followed and was further stimulated by breakthroughs in compatible color, videotape, and satellite delivery. The UHF part of the television service lagged behind, however, due to several technical disadvantages.

The growth of the cable industry helped bring UHF broadcasts to more viewers, but it also created new competition for the broadcast industry as a whole, including the concept of pay programming.

## ❏ Review Probes

1. What were Marconi's main contributions to modern broadcasting?
2. What roles did David Sarnoff and Frank Conrad play in transforming the concept of radio from a point-to-point to a mass-communication orientation?
3. What spectrum problems did pioneering broadcasters face in the early 1920s?
4. Rank the importance of the contributions made to the development of radio broadcasting by the following people: Fessenden, Armstrong, Herrold, Stubblefield, De Forest.
5. What are the key distinctions between mechanical and electronic television systems?
6. What factors prompted the birth and growth of cable television?

## ❏ Suggested Background Explorations

Abramson, Albert. *The History of Television: 1880 to 1941.* Jefferson, NC: McFarland, 1987.

Binkowski, Edward S. *Satellite Information Systems.* Boston: G. K. Hall, 1988.

Brand, Steward. *The Media Lab: Inventing the Future at MIT.* New York: Viking Press, 1987.

Douglas, Susan J. *Inventing American Broadcasting, 1899–1922.* Baltimore: Johns Hopkins, 1987.

Inglis, Andrew F. *Behind the Tube: A History of Broadcasting Technology and Business.* Boston: Focal Press, 1990.

Marconi, Degna. *My Father Marconi.* New York: McGraw-Hill, 1962.

Stephens, Mitchell. *A History of News: From the Drum to the Satellite.* New York: Viking Penguin, 1988.

Sterling, Christopher H. *Electronic Media: A Guide to Trends in Broadcasting and Newer Technologies, 1920–1983.* New York: Praeger, 1984.

# C H A P T E R  **6**

# Legal Legacies

❏  *Any industry is subject to certain legal constraints and shaped by a variety of governmental regulations. Broadcasting, however, because of its use of the public airwaves and virtual automatic access to U.S. homes, invites unusually extensive scrutiny. Electronic media such as cable, MMDS, and DBS that do not use the normally accessible spectrum have somewhat more latitude than do conventional broadcasters, but the exact limits of this latitude are still being probed. In exercising our responsibilities as media professionals, therefore, we must understand the nature of our statutory and regulatory limitations and how these limitations came to pass.*

## Early Precedents

The first U.S. law to regulate what would become our industry dealt neither with broadcasting nor with voice communication. Instead, the Wireless Ship Act of 1910 simply mandated that no ocean-going passenger steamer carrying fifty or more persons could leave a U.S. port unless it was equipped with "an efficient apparatus for radio-communication, in good working order, in charge of a person skilled in the use of such apparatus." More germane to the future of broadcasting, the 1910 Act assigned regulatory responsibility for wireless to the secretary of commerce and labor, but without delineating the precise power the secretary might exercise. This delegation of responsibility without real authority would become a major problem once point-to-point wireless evolved into radio broadcasting.

## Beyond the Wireless Act

Even within its narrow safety scope, the Wireless Ship Act proved inadequate. As the *Titanic* disaster demonstrated, the requirement of having a wireless on board was of little utility if the set was not manned. (See Figure 6–1.) Because many of the ships in the *Titanic's* vicinity did not have a wireless operator on duty that fateful night, and thus could not respond to her distress call, Congress subsequently passed Public Law 238. This law required staffing of the wireless room whenever the ship was in transit.

Only a month after Public Law 238's enactment in 1912, Congress approved a much more comprehensive piece of legislation that brought U.S. policing of the spectrum in line with new international radio agreements to which this country was party. Most important, the Radio Act of 1912 made it illegal to operate a radio station "except under and in accordance with a license" to be obtained from the secretary of commerce and labor. Once again, however, the law failed to specify criteria by which the secretary could grant or refuse to grant such licenses. It did provide for the closing or takeover of any station by the government "in time of war or public peril or disaster" (a provision that would be invoked during World War I). But outside of such emergency situations, the 1912 Radio Act shed no light on qualifications that could allow the secretary to choose one license applicant over another. Technical interference was specified as something to be avoided, but the law failed to make clear how overuse of the spectrum through the awarding of too many licenses was to be avoided.

Once the war was over, governmental attention was concerned more with radio threats to national security than with any thought of nurturing a new mass medium. Having helped, in President Wilson's words,

**Figure 6–1**

The sinking of the liner *Titanic* brought increased legislative attention to radio

"to make the world safe for democracy," U.S. public opinion became increasingly focused on ways by which future foreign entanglements could be prevented. In the midst of such sentiment, the American Marconi Company stood as a potential threat. Here was a British subsidiary founded by an Italian (see Figure 6–2) on our own shores that controlled patents and facilities essential to the continuation and development of radio in the United States. Through a complicated series of maneuvers in 1919 with the U.S. Navy and the White House, General Electric's chief lawyer, Owen D. Young, spearheaded the "governmentally suggested" sale of American Marconi's stock to General Electric for $3.5 million. In its new, domestically owned configuration, the GE subsidiary was christened the Radio Corporation of American (RCA).

AT&T and Westinghouse also invested in RCA, allowing it to emerge as by far the most powerful company in U.S. radio. AT&T sold its stock in 1923 and, under antitrust pressure, General Electric and Westinghouse divested themselves of RCA stock in 1932. By this time, however, the now independent company's extensive electronics and radio broadcast activities were more than enough to ensure continuation of its dominant presence on the electronic media landscape.

In the early 1920s, as radio *broadcasting* activities came to overshadow the industry's earlier *wireless telegraphy* enterprises, corporate maneuverings intensified. During the summer of 1922, AT&T put a powerful and well-equipped station (WEAF) on the air in New York City. With it came the new concept of toll broadcasting that AT&T borrowed

**Figure 6–2**
The elderly Guglielmo Marconi makes an NBC broadcast in the 1930s, two decades after the conversion of his operations in the United States to American ownership

(Smithsonian Institution Photo No. 81–12110)

from its telephone operations. Anyone wishing to use the station would pay a toll for the amount of time they wished to buy. The purchaser could then put whatever he wanted on the air during that time period. In essence, this practice was like using the telephone to make a long-distance call, except that the message could now reach thousands of people over the air rather than a single individual at the other end of the line. When the Queensboro Corporation bought five 10-minute timeslots to promote its real estate development in Jackson Heights,[1] commercial radio had arrived.

### Groundrules for a New Business

For the first time, broadcasting had the capacity to be a money-making industry in its own right rather than merely a sideline promotion for equipment manufacturers, stores, or newspapers. The immediate success of Queensboro's campaign and of other companies that followed it onto WEAF's airwaves soon stimulated other stations to pursue similar revenue-producing activities.

AT&T was not about to share this lucrative new business with other companies, however, and began to use both its patent rights to radio transmitters and its control of the phone lines to thwart competition. The company attempted to enforce a ban on the use of AT&T-licensed transmitters for the carriage of rival toll programs and denied or inhibited access to long-distance lines by potentially competing stations. Four years later, and after numerous skirmishes between AT&T and its sometime partners RCA, General Electric, and Westinghouse, AT&T agreed to leave the broadcast field. It sold WEAF and gave up its rights to the partners' pooled patents on transmitters. In exchange, however, AT&T obtained virtually exclusive control over wire and wireless relay systems that were essential to networking and remote broadcasts. RCA took over AT&T's rights to broadcast commercially, but without the patent and phone-line clout that could prevent

competitors from engaging in the same activity. These new alignments resolved the key squabbles between the major electronics companies and allowed their attentions to be fully directed to development of the blossoming business of broadcasting.

The success of toll broadcasting exposed stations engaging in it to another liability, however—the responsibility of paying copyright fees on the music being used in their programming. As soon as broadcasting became a revenue-generating service, the American Society of Composers, Authors and Publishers (ASCAP) began to demand fee payments from stations as compensation to the composers whose works were being broadcast in both live and recorded form. (See Figure 6–3.) In 1923, ASCAP got the most obvious profit-maker, AT&T's WEAF, to pay a one-year license fee of $500. ASCAP followed this success by winning a lawsuit against station WOR for playing the ASCAP-protected tune "Mother Machree" without a license.[2] Because ASCAP-affiliated composers were the creators of virtually all popular music, stations now faced the prospect of either paying up or ceasing to play the tunes the public expected to hear.

Perceiving themselves to be at ASCAP's mercy, the major station owners formed the National Association of Broadcasters (NAB) to do battle with ASCAP. Their radio concerts were becoming dull without the melodies ASCAP controlled, but the license fees were seen as being too high for some stations to pay.[3] The NAB subsequently expanded into U.S. commercial broadcasting's major trade association and lobbying agency while its sparring with ASCAP became a continuing and escalating crusade.

### Federal Reluctance to Regulate

As these various legal contests unfolded within the industry, the federal government was very much on the outside looking in. On orders from President Harding, Secretary of Commerce Herbert Hoover convened a

**Figure 6–3**
ASCAP's charter members gather in 1921, seven years after their society was founded, to ensure that composers and publishers would be paid for performance of their music. Left to right: Gustave Kerker, Victor Herbert (at piano), Raymond Hubbell, Harry Tieney, Louis A. Hirsch, Rudolph Friml, Robert Hood Bowers, Silvio Hein, A. Baldwin Sloane, Irving Berlin.

Washington Radio Conference in February 1922 with representatives of the major broadcasting, amateur radio, and governmental interests in attendance. As Hoover told them in his opening remarks:

It is the purpose of this conference to inquire into the critical situation that has now arisen through the astonishing development of the wireless telephone; to advise the Department of Commerce as to the application of its present powers of regulation, and further to formulate such recommendations to Congress as to the legislation necessary.[4]

The broadcasters agreed that the airwaves were becoming clogged with interfering signals and that some government action was badly needed, but they did not engage in specifics. For its part, Congress was divided on whether the secretary of commerce should be given more authority over the medium or, as an alternative, an independent regulatory body should be established. Some lawmakers feared that the first option would make Hoover much too powerful in controlling what was coming to be a key means of communication. Others believed that another commission was an unwanted step toward big government. Lacking a consensus, the Congress did nothing, and the spectrum continued to degenerate into chaos. (See Figure 6–4.)

A year later, Hoover found himself calling a second Washington Radio Conference to enlist more support from the industry itself. The secretary pointed out that "Since the last conference of a year ago, the number of broadcasting stations has increased from 60 to 581, and it is estimated that somewhere between 1,500,000 and 2,500,000 receiving sets are now in use."[5] Letting this unrestricted marketplace continue to bloat was clearly not an option. The Conference responded by telling Hoover he had the power under the 1912 Radio Act to regulate hours and wavelengths in order to prevent harmful interference, and it passed a resolution to that effect. Armed with this endorsement, the secretary soon released a spectrum reallocation plan that divided stations into three groups: high power (500 to 1,000 watts), medium power regional facilities (up to 500 watts), and some low-power local stations that also included most educational and religious broadcasters.

Not surprisingly, the high-power group was dominated by the big players such as RCA, AT&T, GE, and Westinghouse, which had already established stations capable of serving large areas of the country. Rather than having to share the same channel, they were now scattered over a variety of channels from 550 to 1,000 kilohertz. The medium-power group was spread out in the spectrum between 1,000 and 1,350 kilohertz, but all of the lowest tiered stations were still consigned to a single channel—833 kilohertz (360 meters)—amidst the squeals and hisses that such multiple occupation caused. Although the new allocations may not have been equitable, they were the first attempt at modern spectrum delineation based on power and area of service considerations and thus formed the basis for actions by future regulatory bodies.

As the number of stations continued to in-

crease, the new frequency plan provided only a temporary respite for Hoover and for broadcasting. There were still no clear standards about who might obtain a license, and a sort of spectrum land-rush continued to escalate. Subsequent radio conferences were called in 1924 and 1925, with the latter evolving proposals that would pave the way for long overdue legislation.

Meanwhile, two court cases had precluded the possibility that the Radio Act of 1912 could be interpreted to give the secretary of commerce more organizational power over the spectrum. In 1923, a federal appeals court found in *Hoover* v. *Intercity Radio Company, Inc.* that the secretary could not refuse to grant a broadcast license to anyone who qualified under the vague terms of the 1912 law. Even worse, a 1926 decision (*United States* v. *Zenith Radio Corporation et al.*) decreed that the secretary could not limit a licensee to broadcast only on certain channels or restrict the times at which such broadcasts could take place. In short, there was scant justification to deny anyone a license even if there was no

**Figure 6–4**
Secretary of Commerce Herbert Hoover experienced the impracticality of a completely unregulated marketplace

*(Smithsonian Institution Photo 79–88)*

place left to put a new station and no way to inhibit what they did with that license once they obtained it!

Little wonder, then, that even a "business of the country is business" president like Calvin Coolidge felt compelled to call for a legislative solution. In a December 7, 1926, message to Congress (H.R. Doc. 483), he observed:

> Due to decisions of the courts, the authority of the department [of commerce] under the law of 1912 has broken down; many more stations have been operating than can be accommodated within the limited number of wave lengths available: further stations are in course of construction; many stations have departed from the scheme of allocations set down by the department, and the whole service of this most important public function has drifted into such chaos as seems likely, if not remedied, to destroy its great value. I most urgently recommend that this legislation should be speedily enacted.

## The Rules of the Game Solidify

Two months after President Coolidge's plea, the years-long struggle for more comprehensive radio legislation resulted in the Dill-White Radio Act of 1927. A five-member Federal Radio Commission (FRC) was created to oversee radio until such time as Congress decided otherwise. The part-time conception for the body was evidenced by the fact that the law provided for commissioners to receive "a compensation of $10,000 for the first year of their service" but "thereafter a compensation of $30 for each day" that they were actually needed for duty. Nevertheless, the 1927 Radio Act was our first modern piece of broadcast legislation. It established "public interest, convenience, or necessity" as a standard by which licensees and their performance could be gauged, erected barriers to the creation of radio monopolies, and, in Section 18, provided for "equal opportunities" for political candidates.

### The FRC Takes Charge

After years of virtually unregulated frequency-grabbing and operation had left the spectrum in chaos, there was now a statutory-based belief that the interests of the public rather than those of individual broadcasters were more in need of protection. As an editorial in the May 1927 issue of *Radio Broadcast* sought to remind the new regulators:

> Gentlemen of the Radio Commission, let but one voice rule you! The voice of the broadcast listener! Give him fair, efficient and equitable service! Remember, not one of those who seek to broadcast has anything but a selfish purpose, however disguised, in seeking a place in the ether.

Cognizant of this trust, the FRC took several actions in 1928 to police and reorganize the spectrum. It determined that 550 to 1500 kilohertz should be reserved for radio broadcasting and took pains to provide for equitable service throughout the country by encouraging high-power stations in the major cities and lower power facilities for smaller population centers. In a statement on the public interest released on August 23 (2 FRC Ann. Rep. 166 for 1928), the commission justified its support for a limited percentage of stations "so equipped and financed as to permit the giving of a high order of service over as large a territory as possible. This is the only manner in which the distant listener in the rural and sparsely settled portions of the country will be reached." The FRC's statement concluded:

> Since the number of channels is limited and the number of persons desiring to broadcast is far greater than can be accommo-

dated, the commission must determine from among the applicants before it which of them will, if licensed, best serve the public. In a measure, perhaps, all of them give more or less service. Those who give the least, however, must be sacrificed for those who give the most. The emphasis must be first and foremost on the interest, the convenience, and the necessity of the listening public, and not on the interest, convenience, or necessity of the individual broadcaster or the advertiser.

The three concepts of (1) different classes of license to serve different needs, (2) spectrum scarcity that requires careful governmental allocation, and (3) the discretionary granting or withholding of licenses based on "public interest" standards all flow from this statement, and they remain embedded in U.S. broadcast regulation to this day.

Subsequent actions in the spirit of this declaration resulted in the FRC's termination of sixty-two stations and mandating of power reductions for dozens of others. By the end of the 1920s, the Federal Radio Commission was firmly established as an effective spectrum traffic cop. Regulation of the actual *content* of broadcasts over licensed stations, however, was another subject. This would raise constitutional issues that the country and the industry were not yet ready to explore.

In an attempt to stave off possible governmental intrusion into programming questions, the National Association of Broadcasters issued a tentative Radio Code in 1929. The first in a series of Code documents to which most major broadcasters subscribed, this self-regulatory approach sought particularly to encourage prudent advertising practices that would preserve the profitability of the industry on the one hand but make governmental intervention unnecessary on the other.

In 1932, however, court-sanctioned justification for at least overall governmental scrutiny of program content came about as a result of the actions of a renegade radio preacher. Rev. Robert Schuler, pastor of the Trinity Methodist Church in Los Angeles, was

also the owner of station KGEF. For years he had used his electronic pulpit to attack local judges, city officials, Jews, and the Roman Catholic Church. Such activities drew a number of complaints, but his ultimate excess may have been the use of his broadcast license as an instrument for blackmail. As the Federal Appeals Court decision in *Trinity Methodist Church, South* v. *Federal Radio Commission* unsmilingly attested, "On one occasion he announced over the radio that he had certain damaging information against a prominent unnamed man which, unless a contribution (presumably to the church) of a hundred dollars was forthcoming, he would disclose. As a result, he received contributions from several persons."

The appeals court upheld the FRC's denial of Schuler's license renewal. This ruling thereby established that even though the First Amendment prohibited prior restraint of broadcasts, subsequent punishment could be administered. In other words, the government could use after-the-fact appraisals of a station's program performance to determine whether it met the public-interest standard for continued operation.

Meanwhile, a long-simmering antitrust issue was also put to rest in 1932 when General Electric and Westinghouse agreed to divest themselves of RCA stock, thus making RCA a completely independent company for the first time. For the radio industry as a whole, the important result of this agreement was the loosening of a number of patent rights that the three companies had controlled in a shared pool. Now, other companies could have easier access to these patented radio components in building their own equipment. This arrangement created a more competitive market that benefited both station and consumer equipment purchasers.

## The FCC is Born

Even though radio was a healthy industry, the Depression-wracked economy of the country as a whole continued to suffer. By 1934, the twin factors of (1) a rapidly expanding communications industry and (2) President Roosevelt's New Deal reorganization of government to fight the Depression intersected in a new and broadly encompassing piece of legislation, the Communications Act of 1934. The Act set up a seven-member Federal Communications Commission and consolidated all wire and wireless communication under its regulatory umbrella. Responsibilities formerly exercised by the Federal Radio Commission, the Interstate Commerce Commission, the postmaster general, and even the president were now all vested in a single independent agency.

As the law that still governs the electronic media today, the Communications Act clearly delineated "broadcasting" from "common carrier" activities (see Chapter 3) as well as from private radio (such as citizen's band transmissions) intended for point-to-point linkages. The legislation continued the 1927 Radio Act's conception of broadcasting as a privately owned but nonmonopolistic enterprise rather than as a government-operated entity. In its Section 315, the 1934 statute also carried forward the earlier legislation's provision for political candidate equal opportunity over the airwaves. FCC commissioners were to be presidential appointees with the advice and consent of the Senate and their regulatory actions subject to court challenge.

This Communications Act also included an important no-censorship provision. Specifically, Section 326 decrees that

nothing in this Act shall be understood or construed to give the Commission the power of censorship over the radio communications or signals transmitted by any radio station, and no regulation or condition shall be promulgated or fixed by the Commission which shall interfere with the right of free speech by means of radio communication.

Despite its honorable aims, this provision has had the effect of placing the FCC on a precarious legal tightrope: trying to enforce the public-interest mandate on stations without becoming embroiled in questions of program content. In other words, if a station's programming determines whether the public interest is being served, then how can the commission judge that programming without assuming the role of censor? Conversely, how can the commission enforce the public interest standard without evaluating program content?

Some broadcasters saw the Communications Act as the forerunner of sweeping new regulation. But their fears were somewhat lessened at the first meeting of the new FCC on July 11, 1934, when it unanimously voted to maintain the status quo regulations that it had inherited and to proceed cautiously in proposing any new ones. Nevertheless, the much more comprehensive nature of the Communications Act and the much larger agency it created (more than triple the staff size of the FRC) clearly suggested that the FCC would be more than a spectrum traffic cop (and perhaps *needed* to be) given the increasing complexities of government, society, and technology.

As early as the following year, the FCC sent citations to twenty stations for their having advertised certain personal medical-care products. Choosing to accommodate rather than challenge these initial government thrusts into specific content regulation, two networks and a number of stations obligingly refused to renew contracts for laxative commercials. Then, a few months later, the Federal Trade Commission decided to preempt FCC control over radio advertising. Stations were given the option of signing stipulations in which they agreed to abide by any FTC rulings pertaining to questionable commercials. If and when an FTC cease-and-desist order was issued against any advertiser, stations would be notified of such action and would stop airing the advertising in question. This action would absolve the station from involvement in any governmental litigation that might follow.[6] Clearly, the transactions between expanding broadcasting and expanding government were to become more complex the more each grew.

Growth was certainly the hallmark of 1936 as the FCC adopted new rules promoting the use of experimental broadcast services. Among these services were superpower (500,000 watt) AM, plus FM and television ventures. While creating a certain amount of excitement in the electronic media establishment of the time, such prospects also raised the anxiety level of many established broadcasters who saw little need to allow new competitors into what was becoming a very profitable business. In the case of television, the FCC did seem to be barring the door to quick authorization of regular service by indicating that picture clarity would have to be increased to at least 450 lines before any such approval could be considered.[7] Still, a 1937 RCA demonstration showed that company, at least, was close to achieving this technical standard. The enormous financial consequence of FCC actions began to be readily apparent to current and prospective video interests.

### New Restrictions

Even though electronic technology seemed to be making great strides, radio journalism suffered a significant setback in 1937, when the American Bar Association supplemented Canon 35 of its Code of Judicial Conduct with the recommendation that microphones as well as cameras be barred from courtrooms. This action came as a result of the chaotic coverage of the 1935 trial of Bruno Hauptmann, the alleged kidnapper and killer of aviator Charles Lindbergh's baby son (see Figure 6–5). An ex-soldier in the German army who had illegally entered the United States in 1923 as a stowaway, Hauptmann was the ideal villain. From the time of his arrest through his indictment, trial, conviction, and execution, Hauptmann's case was decided by the press, newsreels, and radio long before the judicial process had a chance to work.

Microphones were allowed in the actual courtroom only for the verdict, but temporary radio facilities had been set up throughout the area, and jurors were able to hear broadcast speculations from a studio below their hotel rooms.[8] The resulting circus atmosphere led lawyers and judges to fear that justice itself was being compromised, and their Canon 35 language reflected this concern:

> The broadcasting of court proceedings are calculated to detract from the essential dignity of the proceedings, distract the witness in giving his testimony, degrade the court, and create misconceptions with respect thereto in the mind of the public and should not be permitted.

As part of an ethical code for the legal profession, Canon 35 (later renumbered as Canon 3A[7]) did not have the force of law, but it substantially influenced the subsequent actions of judges and state legislators. Their bench rulings and state statutes in support of the philosophy Canon 35 expressed would restrict broadcast courtroom access for decades to come.

The federal government also seemed to be exhibiting a predisposition to restrict the programming latitude that broadcasters had come to enjoy. In 1938, Congress passed the Wheeler-Lea Act that gave the Federal Trade Commission jurisdiction and expanded its power over food, drug, and cosmetic advertising. The intent was to enable the FTC to exercise closer scrutiny over false and misleading advertising in such areas. However, it caused radio networks special concern because one-third of their commercial revenue was derived from these categories.

The highly profitable networks were already on edge due to increased FCC interest in their business. Even though the question of whether the Communications Act of 1934 gave the FCC power over networks (as opposed to individual stations) remained open, the commission nonetheless issued Order No. 37, which launched a formal inquiry into net-

**Figure 6–5**
Bruno Richard Hauptmann in the Flemington, New Jersey, courtroom that became the site for a trial by mass media

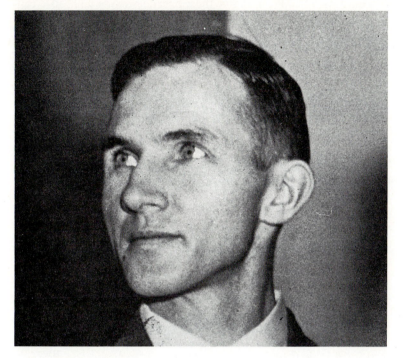

work operations and the contractual relationships of these networks with their affiliates. This chain-monopoly study, as it came to be called, soon blossomed into a full-scale inquiry of broadcasting in general. A mass of data was accumulated and, if nothing else, the industry was served notice that the FCC was prepared to look at the internal operations of broadcasting much more closely. In self-defense, the National Association of Broadcasters adopted a much more extensive code of conduct and an NAB Code Compliance Committee to administer it on an ongoing basis. Though it lacked enforcement machinery, the Code was embraced as a prudent business decision by the majority of large broadcasters. Among other things, the code stipulated that "fair and impartial presentation of both

sides of controversial issues is a duty of the broadcasters and should be done without pay."[9]

## Wars of Many Kinds

Of more immediate pocketbook concern to NAB members was the continuing war with ASCAP over music licensing fees. Since the battle had first been joined in 1923, broadcasters had sought to resist ASCAP's monopoly power over the music they played, while ASCAP, in the interests of its member composers and publishers, had consistently raised its performance rights licensing fees. Legal skirmishes, Congressional hearings, and a justice department antitrust probe of ASCAP over the years had served only to intensify the financial stakes and NAB/ASCAP antagonisms. When, in 1939, ASCAP demanded another increase in their license rates, radio fought back.

### Arming an Ally—BMI

The NAB moved to create a competing music licensing organization that could counter ASCAP's dominance in the field. As a result, in 1940, about 600 broadcasters and broadcast-related companies pledged the equivalent of 50 percent of their 1937 ASCAP payments for the purpose of creating a new licensing organization to be known as Broadcast Music Incorporated (BMI). The stock in BMI that these broadcasters purchased to capitalize the new company did not pay dividends, and BMI itself was organized as a non-profit venture.[10] (See Figure 6–6.)

Many broadcasters stopped playing ASCAP music (and did not renew their ASCAP licenses). These actions, however, meant that they no longer had access to most of the music then on the commercial market. Thus began what came to be known as "The-Jeanie-with-the-Light-Brown-Hair" Era, named after the nineteenth-century song by Stephen Foster. For several months, the anti-ASCAP stations played nothing but music by old composers like Foster, whose tunes had entered *public*

**Figure 6–6**
A 1940s BMI board of directors meeting sets goals for the new licensing organization

*domain* (meaning that their copyrights had expired). Meanwhile, the fledgling BMI moved to build a music catalogue of its own. Eight songs were commissioned from non-ASCAP composers, and a massive effort was undertaken in Latin America to sign composers there to BMI affiliations.[11] The sudden popularity of rumba, tango, and samba music on U.S. radio was the result of this enterprise. Over the next fifteen years, BMI came to parity with ASCAP principally by signing creators ASCAP had ignored: (1) young mainstream composers disaffected by ASCAP's royalty payout system, which favored more established writers; (2) country and western composers from the hinterlands; and later (3) the rock and roll songsters who combined black blues and white country stylings into a new, rhythmically pulsating phenomenon.

## An Editorial Skirmish

Much less noticeable than the battle over radio music was the question of broadcasting's right to editorialize. True, the NAB Code advocated the impartial and noncommercial presentation of controversial issues, but all stations did not subscribe to this theory. A test case, decided in 1941, involved Boston's WAAB, which had regularly aired the editorials of its management. Mayflower Broadcasting Corporation challenged WAAB for the license to its frequency and cited WAAB's editorializing as proof that the station was being used to serve private rather than public interests. Even though the station had ceased editorializing by this time, the FCC was persuaded to reexamine the grant of its license renewal. Ultimately, WAAB's incumbent owners were allowed to keep the license, but the language the FCC used in its January 16, 1941, decision seemed to decree a ban on radio editorializing:

Under the American system of broadcasting it is clear that responsibility for the conduct of a broadcast station must rest initially with the broadcaster. It is equally clear that with the limitations in frequencies inherent in the nature of radio, the public interest can never be served by a dedication of any broadcast facility to the support of its own partisan ends. Radio can serve as an instrument of democracy only when devoted to the communication of information and the exchange of ideas fairly and objectively presented. A truly free radio cannot be used to advocate the causes of the licensee. It cannot be used to support the candidacies of his friends. It cannot be devoted to the support of principles he happens to regard most favorably. In brief, the broadcaster cannot be an advocate.

Because it had been allowed to keep its license, WAAB did not challenge this FCC pronouncement. For its part, the broadcast industry as a whole was too preoccupied with other matters to take up the cause of editorializing. Consequently, this Mayflower Case assertion that the broadcaster did not have the same rights as a newspaper publisher remained uncontested until years had passed.

## Duels with the Nets and the Axis

Later in 1941, the FCC released its Report on Chain Broadcasting that attacked several broadcasting practices. One target was RCA's National Broadcasting Company, which was operating two networks, NBC-Red and NBC-Blue. Believing this practice to constitute a monopolistic consolidation of power, the commission ordered that "no license shall be issued to a standard broadcast station affiliated with a network organization which maintains more than one network." This skillful statement avoided the question of whether the FCC had the power to regulate networks directly by seeking to regulate them indirectly through the station licenses they held. Even though political pressures forced the commission to put implementation of this

**Figure 6–7**
Attorney James Lawrence Fly (left) takes over what would become a turbulent FCC chairmanship from his predecessor, Frank McNinch, on September 1, 1939

position on temporary hold, RCA saw the handwriting on the wall and initiated actions designed to give its less powerful Blue network separate corporate status.

The Columbia Broadcasting System (CBS), for its part, was stung by the Report on Chain Broadcasting's proposed banning of *option time* through which CBS enjoyed the contractual right to take over any time period in its affiliates' schedules. The Mutual Broadcasting System, on the other hand, supported the FCC document because the advocated restrictions would make it easier for that weaker network to compete with the big three. By the end of the year, the commission had turned over much of its option time material to the justice department for pursuit of possible antitrust action. In a more conciliatory spirit, however, the FCC increased station licenses from one to two years in length and did the same for permissable network/affiliate contracts. (The Communications Act allowed for stations to be licensed for up to three years at the FCC's discretion. Previous network/station contracts, unregulated under the Act, had typically been for five years.)

Amidst all this contention and the ensuing involvement of various powerful Congressmen on both sides of the issue, FCC/broadcaster relations seriously deteriorated. FCC Chairman James Lawrence Fly (see Figure 6–7) was invited to attend the 1941 Annual Convention of the National Association of Broadcasters to give his views on the *Report on Chain Broadcasting*. Much to Fly's discomfort, he found himself sitting on a panel on which he and his policy making were attacked without his being given the opportunity for a rebuttal. In an angry news conference, Fly lambasted what he saw as an arrogant domination of the NAB by the networks and charged that this alliance reminded him of "a dead mackerel in the moon-light—it both shines and stinks."[12]

Within a few months, U.S. involvement in World War II pushed the FCC/NAB conflict into the background but not entirely off the stage. A freeze was put on the construction of new radio and television stations, and the War Production Board brought all manufacture of civilian receivers to a halt by April 1942. An Office of Censorship set up under Byron Price banned man-on-the-street interviews, ad-lib programs, and similar unscripted broadcasts through which enemy agents might pass on coded instructions to other Axis subversives. Most stations were closed to the public, and weather reports were forbidden because they might prove of assistance to enemy planes. President Roosevelt authorized an Office of War Information (OWI), headed by CBS news commentator Elmer Davis, as a clearinghouse for all government agencies that released material for broadcast. The OWI also took over every private shortwave station in the country and either shut them down for the war's duration or exercised control over what they broadcast overseas. (These shortwave broadcasts later gave birth to the Voice of America.) Given the gravity of the international situation, broadcasters cooperated fully with such restrictions and activities.

The industry's enthusiastic support of the war effort did not extend to support of further FCC incursions into the purely business aspects of broadcasting, however. In May 1943, the Supreme Court upheld the right of the FCC to regulate contractual dealings between networks and their affiliates (*National Broadcasting Co., Inc., et al.* v. *United States et al.*). This case remains a landmark today because it also established that FCC denial of a broadcast license for failure to operate in the public interest did not constitute a violation of the freedom of speech guaranteed under the First Amendment.

Together with a November FCC ruling that banned multiple ownership of standard (AM) stations in the same market, the NBC case spelled the end of the company's dual network ownership. The Blue network and its three owned-and-operated stations were sold to Edward Noble, chairman of the board of Lifesavers Corporation (see Figure 6–8). The Blue was subsequently rechristened the American Broadcasting Company. On another front, the FCC did provide broadcasters with one piece of good news in 1943 by finally extending license terms to the full three years permitted by the Communications Act.

## Postwar Scrutiny

In 1945, as World War II came to its long-awaited conclusion, broadcasters looked to postwar opportunities with great anticipation. The FCC was preparing to resume processing of AM, FM, and TV license applications and had expressed its intent to open up new spectrum space for both VHF and UHF activities. Yet, the commission was also unhappy with some of the program practices indulged in by existing broadcasters. Commissioner Clifford J. Durr was especially concerned and instructed his staff to compare the program promises that stations had made on their license applications with their actual performance as reflected in their operating logs. What Durr's staff found was massive commercialization at the expense of local and public affairs programs. So heavy was the commercial load (the amount of advertisements) on some outlets that Durr and his fellow commissioners put dozens of stations on temporary licenses rather than renewing them for full three-year terms. Chairman Paul Porter called for a thorough review of the entire promise-versus-performance issue, and a special task force was set up to supervise the project.

**Figure 6–8**
Lifesavers Chairman Edward Noble bought the Blue Network from NBC for
$8 million and renamed it the American Broadcasting Company

*(Photo copyright 1990 Capital Cities/ABC, Inc.)*

### The Blue Book

What resulted was the 1946 document officially called *Public Service Responsibility of Broadcast Licensees.* Unofficially this document was known as the "Blue Book" because of the color of its cover and the attempt by its opponents to equate it with the blue-penciling indulged in by wartime censors. The Blue Book raised a storm of protest from the broadcasting industry. Even though few industry executives attempted to defend the overcommercialized practices of the individ-

ual stations the document had cited, the National Association of Broadcasters saw the Blue Book's publication as the FCC's attempt to move deeper into actual program regulation and thus into actual censorship.

The commission's cause was hurt when it was unveiled that one of the Blue Book's authors had been Charles Siepmann. Though now a U.S. citizen, Siepmann was a native Englishman who had once served as director of program planning for the British Broadcasting Corporation. The NAB wasted no time in using Siepmann's background to indict the purpose and relevance of the report he had helped to author. How, it was charged, could the former executive of a foreign *state-run* broadcasting system be expected to understand the dynamics of free-enterprise radio in the United States?

This challenge to the Blue Book's credibility along with attacks from pro-industry Congressmen about the dangers of peacetime censorship meant that the ultimate impact of the report was muffled almost to silence. The Blue Book episode did raise the promise-versus-performance issue to the point at which broadcasters realized they should do what they had said they would do—if for no other reason than to protect themselves from competing applications at license renewal time. From this point on, FCC scrutiny of a station's record would extend beyond a strictly engineering assessment of its technical operations. The public-interest character of a licensee's overall programming service would now also be examined, although the actual impact of this examination remained unclear.

### Of Candidates, Fairness, and Films

The FCC did achieve more clarity, however, in its pronouncements on political broadcasts. In a 1948 decision involving the license renewal of WHLS (Port Huron, Michigan), the commission ruled that a station could not be held accountable for libelous statements made by a political candidate over its airwaves. Even though it seems that this decision should have pleased broadcasters, it instead enraged them by re-affirming their constitutional inferiority as compared to print media. Section 315 of the Communications Act (as had Section 18 of the preceding 1927 Radio Act) required stations to provide competing candidates with equal access to the airwaves while forbidding the outlets from censoring what those candidates said. To

broadcasters, the *Port Huron* decision simply fleshed out this abridgement of their rights of free expression. It made them second-class citizens to newspapers, which were free of any such restrictions.

Similarly, broadcasters were becoming increasingly unhappy with the apparent ban on editorializing that the 1941 *Mayflower* (WAAB) case had imposed. Hearings were scheduled in 1948 and led to FCC reversal of *Mayflower* when the Commission created the Fairness Doctrine the following year. The Fairness Doctrine now permitted on-air editorializing, but the FCC also seemed to impose new burdens when it stated that stations had

an affirmative duty generally to encourage and implement the broadcast of all sides of controversial public issues over their facilities, over and beyond their obligation to make available on demand opportunities for the expression of opposing views.[13]

In short, with the Fairness Doctrine, broadcasters got more than they bargained for. Beyond acquiring an *option* to express their own opinion, they seemed to have been saddled with "an affirmative *duty*" to present not only controversial issues, but also the varieties of opinion that had given rise to such controversies. For the next four decades, the implications of the Fairness Doctrine would be debated by the Congress, the courts, the FCC, and the broadcast industry itself.

As 1949 drew to a close, the fledgling television industry won a more unequivocal victory when a U.S. District Court ruled in *Du-Mont* v. *Carroll* that the Pennsylvania state board of censors did not have the right to pre-censor television films as it did movies shown in theaters. Television, ruled the judge, was a product of interstate commerce and could thus be regulated only by the federal government. Furthermore, because stations were already licensed by the FCC, this general oversight was more preferable because it "avoids the danger of whittling away the constitutional guarantees of freedom of speech and the press." As they entered the 1950s, broadcasters were still pondering what directions this FCC oversight would be taking.

## The Red Scare

As we discuss in the previous chapter, the early 1950s saw much of the FCC's and the industry's attention directed toward the unfreezing of the TV spectrum and the repercussions of this for the new FM services. Internally, meanwhile, broadcasting became embroiled in the red scare and the search for Communists that was preoccupying much of the government. Spurred on by political opportunists such as Wisconsin Senator Joseph McCarthy (see Figure 6–9), fears that the country was being subverted from the inside led to a number of misguided actions meant to demonstrate that the U.S. broadcasting industry was 100 percent patriotic. A number of stations required their employees to sign loyalty oaths as the Korean War further inflamed passions. Simultaneously, in June 1950, a

**Figure 6–9**
Senator Joseph McCarthy intimidated people both inside and outside the media with his allegations of Communist affiliation. Such accusations were exempt from civil defamation suits because members of Congress enjoy immunity from libel actions when their remarks are related to their official activities.

group of ardent anti-Communists who had published a weekly newsletter called *Counterattack* released the 250-page *Red Channels: The Report of Communist Influence in Radio and Television.* The document included the names of 151 "unfaithful" creators and performers whom the industry was alerted to avoid. Included on this list were such notables as composers Leonard Bernstein and Aaron Copland, actors José Ferrer and Edward G. Robinson, writers Arthur Miller and Lillian Hellman, and radio celebrities Ben Grauer and Orson Welles.

Both CBS and NBC now demanded that staff members disclose whether they were members of the Communist Party. Even though the people named in *Red Channels* were guilty of nothing more than being politically liberal, this publication soon found its way onto the desks of many broadcast executives as a guide to talent to avoid lest their own loyalties be questioned. Variety TV show host Ed Sullivan, after drawing much heat for booking a dancer with alleged Communist sympathies, then consulted with *Red Channels* publisher Theodore Kirkpatrick in selecting future acts for Sullivan's *Toast of the Town* program.[14] Eventually, the industry and the country recovered from the self-inflicted excesses—unlike the careers of many of the people who had been blacklisted in the process.

---

## Midcentury Corrections

Fortunately, some regulatory activity of the time was conducted by governmental due process rather than by behind-the-scenes coercion.

### McFarland, Paramount, and Barrow

In addition to the FCC's Sixth Report and Order, which lifted the TV Freeze (see Chap-

ter 5), 1952 saw Congress pass the *McFarland Bill,* which was the first significant overhaul of the 1934 Communications Act. The legislation was the result of a series of compromises between government and industry interests and, in the main, served to streamline and clarify FCC processes. Under *McFarland,* the commission lost the power automatically to revoke the licenses of stations found guilty of antitrust violations and assumed the burden of proof in demonstrating that any licensee was not qualified for renewal. Time deadlines by which the FCC had to act on cases, protests, and petitions for rehearings were also specified, as was the requirement that a former FCC commissioner must wait at least one year after resignation before practicing law before that body. On the other hand, the FCC was granted the power to issue immediate cease-and-desist orders to stations rather than having to wait until that outlet's license came up for renewal. Broadcasters, for their part, were prohibited by the legislation from charging political candidates more for air time then they charged regular advertisers. This latter provision again demonstrated that public-spectrum-using broadcasters had less freedom then the print media, who could overcharge, undercharge, or ignore candidates as they saw fit.

One network was the beneficiary of FCC action the next year when the commission approved the 1953 merger of struggling ABC and United Paramount Theatres. UPT had been split from Paramount Studios three years before in the culmination of a Justice Department antitrust action against the movie industry. ABC, the old second-string Blue network while part of NBC, had never become a truly competitive radio network, and so its prospects were just as bleak as those of the divorced theater chain. Overseen by Paramount's Leonard Goldenson (see Figure 6–10), the merger of these two entities strengthened each of them and provided a climate in which a multinetwork battle for tele-

**Figure 6–10**
Leonard Goldenson, head of United Paramount Theatres, became the dominant figure at ABC for almost forty years following the merger of the two firms

*(Photo copyright 1990 Capital Cities/ABC, Inc.)*

vision viewership could be fought on more equal ground. All television stations also benefited from another FCC action in 1953 when the commission set in motion procedures to extend TV license terms from one to three years to bring them in line with radio.

A variety of Congressional inquiries into broadcasting in general and network practices in particular continued throughout the fifties as television became a dominant player in providing the nation with information and entertainment. In 1957, the FCC's Network Study Staff released the Barrow Report (named after the University of Cincinnati Law School dean, pictured in Figure 6–11, who directed the project). The Barrow Report suggested several actions designed to restrict network power over affiliates, advocated tightening the limitations on the number of stations that a single company could own (the multiple ownership rules), and lobbied for the right of the FCC to levy fines against stations in violation of its rules. The assertion that the commission should have the power to regulate network activities directly (beyond their role as individual station owners) was immediately challenged by network executives and by many other people throughout the broadcast industry. The Barrow Report was not immediately acted on by the FCC, but many of the issues it raised formed the basis for commission action in subsequent years.

**Figure 6–11**

**147**

CHAPTER 6
Legal
Legacies

Roscoe Barrow, chief author of the 1957 study of network practices

## Payola and Quiz Show Apologies

If the broadcast industry was serious about preventing more intrusive government regulation, the revelations of 1959 did its cause no good. First, radio was rocked by the payola scandals. On-air personalities and their bosses were shown to have taken undisclosed cash and gifts from record promoters in order to get certain tunes heavily played over the air. Both the Federal Trade Commission and the FCC initiated sweeping probes to determine the pervasiveness of the practice. Before long, RCA Records had entered into a consent decree with the FTC in which, although not admitting past guilt, the company agreed to refrain from paying broadcasters to air its tunes in the future. "'Payola is a rotten mess and it has been getting worse in the last five years,'" admitted King Records President Sydney Nathan, who then supplied a Congressional investigating committee with cancelled checks his company had slipped to certain announcers.[15] The next year, Congress amended the Communications Act to make payola a federal crime punishable by extensive fine and/or imprisonment.

Television, for its part, was under a similarly dark cloud when it was discovered that certain popular quiz programs had been rigged. Contestants had been told when to win and/or when to lose and had frequently been supplied in advance with the questions they would be asked on the air. The scope of the scandal first came to light when Charles Van Doren, a young assistant professor of English from Columbia University, admitted

**Figure 6–12**
Charles Van Doren (center) confesses to the press that he participated in quiz-show rigging

that he had received both questions and answers from the producer of NBC's popular quiz show *Twenty-One.* Van Doren, who won $129,000 plus a $50,000-a-year consultancy contract to NBC's *Today* show, also revealed that he had been taught how to act in the program's isolation booth in order to increase the suspense. (See Figure 6–12.) In a masterpiece of contradictory reasoning, the professor lamented that he had been persuaded to participate in the rigging so that his triumph would bring honor to "the intellectual life, to teachers and to education in general by increasing public respect."[16] Upon announcement of his resignation from Columbia, a student there yelled out a dorm window: "Hey, Charlie's going to be in the quad tomorrow to give out the answers to the Comparative Lit exam."[17]

Other shows, producers, and their sponsors were subsequently found to have engaged in similar practices. Top network officials has-tened to tell the investigating Congressmen that they had been as deceived as everybody else. Several shows were cancelled and contracts with their producers severed. For its part, Congress passed Section 509 of the Communications Act that made quiz show rigging, like payola, illegal. The networks took back control of the game shows from the sponsors that had heretofore been allowed to produce them, and the NAB amended its self-policing TV Code specifically to ban quiz-show manipulation.

## Narrowing Equal Time

If there was one regulatory bright spot amidst all this turmoil, it seemed to benefit broadcast journalism as Section 315 (the equal time rule) was amended. Broadcasters had long argued that the rigid application of this section was inhibiting their news coverage. But it remained for Lar Daly (see Figure 6–13) to prove their case.

**Figure 6–13**
Lar Daly using his Section 315-mandated access to solicit support

**149**

CHAPTER 6
Legal
Legacies

Daly, a perennial candidate for public office who often liked to dress up as Uncle Sam, was engaged in a one-man campaign to be mayor of Chicago. When the incumbent mayor, who was running for re-election, was shown in a local newscast greeting the president of Argentina at the airport, Mr. Daly demanded that the FCC force the Chicago station to grant him equal time. The commission agreed with Daly. An enraged Congress (seeing broadcast coverage of themselves thereby put in jeopardy) passed the so-called "Lar Daly" amendment that exempted bona fide newscasts, news interviews, news documentaries, and on-the-spot news coverage from the equal-time requirement. Debates between candidates were not considered to be bona fide news events, however.

Therefore, another significant (if temporary) modification to Section 315 was made the following year when Congress passed a law that suspended it "for the period of the 1960 presidential and vice-presidential campaigns." The action permitted the so-called Great Debates between candidates John F. Kennedy and Richard M. Nixon to take place without the equal time necessity to involve minor party candidates. The measure was only passed because both parties projected these debates to be of advantage to their particular candidate. Such a convergence of partisan interests was not present in the next three presidential elections, however. The experiment would not be repeated for fifteen years, at which time the FCC further liberalized the rules to include debates sponsored by a third party (like the League of Women Voters) under the exemption. (This exemption was further extended to broadcaster-sponsored debates in 1983.)

## More Issues, More Media

Following John Kennedy's close 1960 election victory (which some people say was decided by his visually superior but not substantively persuasive debate performance), a young Chicago lawyer named Newton Minow was appointed FCC chairman. Minow had been in office only two months when he used a speaking appearance before the 1961 NAB Convention to label television programming "a vast wasteland" and to warn "Renewal will not be pro forma in the future. There is nothing permanent or sacred about a broadcast license."[18] Even though Minow served only a little more than two years before returning to better-paying private practice, his speech signaled a renewed regulatory activism on the part of the FCC, an activism that broadcasters kept firmly in mind as they built their programming schedules.

### FM Encouragement, Courtroom Discouragement

Even though television seemed to be drawing most of the public attention and the regulatory fire, the FCC also took some actions of long-term significance in regard to radio. In 1964, the FCC thawed the freeze on new AM

applications and major facilities changes that it had adopted two years earlier. Accompanying the lifting of the freeze, however, were new regulations designed to slow the growth of large-city AM radio while encouraging it in smaller towns. More important, AM broadcasters in urban areas were no longer able to use their co-located FM facilities merely to repeat the AM signal. Instead, the commission set a *nonduplication* requirement which stipulated that at least 50 percent of the programming of an FM station that was owned in combination with an AM station must be separate if the two were licensed to a city with a population of 100,000 or more. The practical effect of this requirement was that major broadcasters had to develop their FM stations as discrete entities. This development, in turn, generated new music (and new, young listeners) on the FM band and laid the groundwork for the modest service's substantive growth and later dominance.

While the FCC was stimulating FM activity, the Supreme Court was putting the clamps on television, at least as far as courtroom coverage was concerned. In an echo of the Hauptmann Case that had given birth to the American Bar Association's Canon 35 almost thirty years before, the Supreme Court reversed the swindling conviction of Billie Sol Estes in a Texas state court because the trial had been televised. By ruling that "the circumstances and extraneous influences intruding upon the solemn decorum of court procedure in the televised trial are far more serious than in cases involving only newspaper coverage" (*Estes* v. *Texas*, June 7, 1965), the Supreme Court erected another barrier to broadcasting's enjoyment of the same First Amendment rights that print media possess. Furthermore, the *Estes* case established that a defendent's right of judicial due process under the Fourteenth Amendment took precedence over the broadcaster's right of free expression under the First Amendment. The *Estes* decision also inspired more states to pass laws barring cameras from their courtrooms. (Not until 1982 in

*Chandler* v. *Florida* did the Supreme Court's reluctance to allow any courtroom cameras moderate. By that time, most state—but not federal—courts were already permitting at least some courtroom coverage.)

## Putting CATV in Its Place

Meanwhile, another aspect of the television industry was seeing its flexibility restricted as the FCC took steps to regulate CATV (cable television) directly. Relying on 1958 and 1962 court cases affirming its power to regulate microwave relay facilities serving CATV systems, the commission issued rules in 1965 requiring such systems to carry all local television signals (*must carry*) and prohibiting them from importing programs from distant stations within fifteen days of their airing by a local outlet.

At the same time, the FCC asserted that it had the right to regulate *all* CATVs, regardless of whether they used microwave relays for distant signal importation. The following year, this assertion was formalized in a commission rule that reduced duplication protection from imported signals to twenty-four hours on smaller systems but banned *any* distant signal importation by CATV into the top 100 markets. Congress failed to pass legislation specifically justifying these actions. But the FCC proceeded with them under the assumption that this power was already granted under the Communications Act.

Also in 1966, cable suffered a further setback in *Fortnightly* v. *United Artists Television Inc.* In this case, a federal judge ruled that two West Virginia cable systems were liable for copyright payments for the programming they relayed. The implication of this decision was that cable was an active user of copyrighted programs rather than a passive antenna. This decision further challenged the basic assumptions about CATV that had allowed it to secure programs without payment for almost two decades. (The industry earned a temporary reprieve two years later when the Supreme Court overturned *Fortnightly.*

But the 1976 Copyright Act then subjected cable systems to fee payments for distant station signals that they imported into their markets.)

## More Players at Renewal Time

By the midsixties, broadcasters as well as cablecasters were facing new regulatory challenges. In the 1966 *United Church of Christ* case, for example, a federal appellate court reversed FCC renewal of WLBT-TV's license and returned it for rehearing. At issue was whether citizens could challenge a station's renewal if they themselves were not seeking to obtain the license. The commission had taken the position that such citizens lacked legal standing to intervene directly in the license renewal process. Members of the United Church of Christ living within range of WLBT's Jackson, Mississippi, signal thought otherwise, however. They felt they had the right to challenge WLBT's renewal directly on the basis of the station's racially discriminatory hiring and programming practices. When the courts agreed with the citizens group, in proceedings stretching over the next three years, the way was paved for an unprecedented number of renewal challenges. Many of these challenges would be legitimate; others would prove to be mere harassment. In either case, broadcasters could no longer take automatic license renewal, or community complacency, for granted.

## Fairness Revisited and Cable Clarified

The Fairness Doctrine was also becoming a sharper regulatory instrument. In 1967, the FCC ruled that the health question involving the smoking of cigarettes did constitute a controversial issue of public importance. Therefore, under the Fairness Doctrine, this issue required balanced treatment by stations. Outlets airing cigarette commercials thus were expected to balance these messages with appropriate coverage of the anti-smoking viewpoint. The federal courts later upheld this commission ruling, and, for several years, it appeared that all commercial speech might be vulnerable to similar challenge. (The FCC finally retreated from this premise in a 1974 policy statement.)

At the same time, the commission put broadcasters on notice that they incurred special responsibilities when an individual was attacked over their facilities. In such cases, the FCC's strengthened personal attack rule required stations to inform the person so attacked, provide that person with a transcript of the attack, and offer them the free opportunity to respond over the air—all within one week. When it was pointed out that this rule could have chilling consequences for broadcast journalism, the commission backed off to the extent that bona fide news programs, specials, and on-the-spot coverage were exempted.

Just two years later, the Fairness Doctrine and personal attack rule were given firm judicial grounding in the 1969 *Red Lion* Decision. WGCB-AM/FM, licensed to Red Lion, Pennsylvania, had been involved in a five-year battle with author Fred Cook. In a syndicated program carried by the station Cook was accused of having Communist affiliations. When the station refused on First Amendment grounds to give Cook reply time, he took his demand to the FCC, which ruled that such time must be provided. Ultimately, the case wound up at the Supreme Court, which concluded

as far as the First Amendment is concerned those who are licensed stand no better than those to whom licenses are refused. A license permits broadcasting, but the licensee has no constitutional right to be the one who holds the license or to monopolize a radio frequency to the exclusion of his fellow citizens. There is nothing in the First Amendment which prevents the Government from requiring a licensee to share his frequency with others and to conduct himself as a proxy or fiduciary with obligations to present those views and voices which

are representative of his community and which would otherwise, by necessity, be barred from the airwaves. . . . The First Amendment confers no right on licensees to prevent others from broadcasting on "their" frequencies and no right to an unconditional monopoly of a scarce resource which the Government has denied others the right to use. (*Red Lion Broadcasting Co., Inc., et al.* v. *Federal Communications Commission et al.*)

Not only did *Red Lion* thus affirm the Fairness Doctrine and personal attack rule, but it also articulated once again the spectrum scarcity argument as a fundamental reason that stations must be regulated even though print media are not.

At about the same time, the Supreme Court also dealt cable a blow by unanimously ruling (*United States et al.* v. *Southwestern Cable Co. et al.,* 1968) that the 1934 Communications Act did indeed empower the commission to regulate cable television as part of its broad authority over interstate communication. Only a few months later, the FCC used this authority to require cable systems with more than 3,500 subscribers to originate their own programming. Trying to make this directive less bitter, the commission also granted systems the right to air their own commercials. Clearly, CATV was starting to move (or was being pushed) out from under the shadow of its broadcast television predecessor.

## New Content Incursions

The electronic media's First Amendment privileges suffered further battering in 1970 when Congress, in a behind-the-scenes compromise worked out with the tobacco industry, passed a law banning cigarette advertising from the airwaves while allowing it to continue in the other media. Tobacco manufacturers simply shifted more money into print advertising, and Congress was spared the Constitutional question of whether it could exercise prior restraint over the press.

For broadcasters, of course, the cigarette ban *was* prior restraint—a rare example in the United States of overt governmental censorship. Worse, in turning down the subsequent challenge to the legislation in *Capital Broadcasting Co.* v. *Mitchell*, 1971, the federal courts reached their decision "in part on the ground that commercial speech was entitled to less than full first amendment protection."[19]

While the courts and the Congress made their impact on the solidification of broadcast regulation, the FCC staked out its own new ground with the 1970 Prime Time Access Rule. Designed to limit the programming power of the television networks while encouraging greater program diversity, PTAR, as it came to be called, prohibited affiliates in the fifty largest markets from carrying more than three hours of network or off-network programming between 7 and 11 P.M. (prime time, when the most viewers are watching). This convoluted regulation thus controlled the networks (which the FCC does not license) by focusing on their affiliated stations (which are licensed) and thereby avoided the question of whether the commission could dictate to the network companies directly. The rule pertained only to entertainment programming so that news, public affairs, and (later) children's programs were exempt. The courts refused to block the regulation, and different (if not diversified) shows were quickly provided by syndicators to fill the network-vacated hour.

Meanwhile, the Justice Department had also moved against the perceived network monopoly. As a means of settling the suit, ABC, CBS, and NBC entered into consent decrees in which they agreed to get out of the domestic program syndication business and all but eliminate their financial interests in entertainment programs produced for them by outside suppliers. Dubbed the *financial interest and syndication rules* (or fin/syn for short), these agreements did allow the three networks to produce up to 17 percent of their own prime time entertainment shows, though they have seldom seen it to their advantage to pursue this limited option.

By the early 1970s, it thus was clear that electronic media regulatory complexity was growing at least as fast as the media themselves. In 1971, Congress passed the Federal Election Campaign Act that required broadcasters to provide "reasonable access" to candidates for federal office. This amendment to the Communications Act specified that willful or repeated failure to provide such access could result in the loss of the offending station's license. Up to this time, it was possible for broadcasters to avoid equal-time considerations simply by refusing to carry candidate-related content outside of bona fide news programs. This was no longer an option, at least as far as federal election races were concerned.

In addition, the legislation added to Section 315 the further stipulation that

> the charges made for the use of any broadcasting station by any person who is a legally qualified candidate for public office in connection with his campaign for nomination for election, or election, to such office shall not exceed—
>
> (1) during the forty-five days preceding the date of a primary or primary runoff election and during the sixty days preceding the date of a general or special election in which such person is a candidate, the lowest unit charge of the station for the same class and amount of time for the same period. . . .

In other words, not only must broadcasters provide reasonable candidate access, but they also were required to provide it before elections at the discount rates normally available only to their most preferred (high-volume) advertisers.

For its part, cable, too, was now firmly under the regulatory gaze of the FCC. Definitive cable rules that, among other things, required systems to offer channels to educational institutions and a minimum of at least twenty channels overall, had been adopted in 1972. At the same time, the Supreme Court affirmed the FCC's right to mandate that CATV systems (as they were still called) originate their own local programs. Four years later, with the passage of the Copyright Act of 1976, cable systems were, for the first time, subjected to specific copyright liability for programming they imported into their communities via their carriage of distant broadcast signals. Systems were required to obtain a *compulsory license* that allowed them to relay distant signals in exchange for the semi-annual payment of a royalty fee to the new Copyright Royalty Tribunal, which then disbursed these fees among the various copyright-holder interests.

As cable's copyright liabilities were being clarified, broadcasting's content regulations were becoming more complex with the Supreme Court's ruling in the 1978 *Pacifica* case that the FCC had the power to regulate indecency over the airwaves. At issue was the 1973 broadcast by Pacifica Foundation's WBAI (New York) of a recorded monologue by comedian George Carlin called "Filthy Words." On an afternoon drive with his fifteen-year-old son, a parent heard the broadcast over the car radio and complained to the FCC, which cited WBAI for airing indecent material at a time when children were likely to hear it. In supporting the commission's right to take such punitive action, the Supreme Court held that

patently offensive, indecent material presented over the airwaves confronts the citizen, not only in public, but also in the privacy of the home, where the individual's right to be left alone plainly outweighs the First Amendment rights of an intruder. Because the broadcast audience is constantly tuning in and out, prior warnings cannot completely protect the listener or viewer from unexpected program content. To say that one may avoid further offense by turning off the radio when he hears indecent language is like saying that the remedy for an assault is to run away after the first blow. One may hang up on an indecent phone call, but that option does not give the caller a constitutional immunity or avoid a harm that has already taken place.

Second, broadcasting is uniquely accessible to children, even those too young to read. . . . Pacifica's broadcast could have enlarged a child's vocabulary in an instant. Other forms of offensive expression may be withheld from the young without restricting the expression at its source. Bookstores and motion picture theaters, for example, may be prohibited from making indecent material available to children. . . . The ease with which children may obtain access to broadcast material . . . amply justifies special treatment of indecent broadcasting. (*Federal Communications Commission* v. *Pacifica Foundation*, July 3, 1978)

Not only did this decision reiterate the distinctions between broadcasting and other mass media that make it more susceptible to

**CNN  Indecency**

The FCC's attempt to ban indecency on a 24-hour basis arises from a concern that children may be in the broadcast audience at any time of the day or night. Programmers charge that the regulatory action inhibits their creativity.

## ALAN CAMPBELL/ATTORNEY AND PARTNER
### DOW, LOHNES & ALBERTSON

The communications attorney's role has changed substantially over the past twenty years. The philosophy and attitude of the FCC have shifted from the detailed regulation of station operation to the concept of marketplace oversight. Now, there are signs that re-regulation is in vogue. The function of the communications attorney has likewise varied.

For example, two decades ago, all broadcast stations filed renewal applications every three years. This was a major project for station personnel and legal counsel. Each station provided detailed programming information; the FCC rules defined the types of programs a station broadcast, such as news, public affairs, religious and the evil "entertainment." Each station was expected to broadcast an acceptable percentage of nonentertainment, that is, "good" programs. The renewal application also reported the source of each program, whether it was carried live, and the amount of commercial matter (advertising) that was aired. The station's promise of what it would broadcast during the upcoming license term was also a part of the renewal.

This process epitomized much of the work and value of the communications attorney at that time. The attorney explained how a public affairs show broadcast at 6:00 A.M. on a Sunday served the public interest. The attorney could pigeonhole questionable programs in the "good" categories and excuse a station's excessive commercial load during certain hours. The attorney knew the safe amount of "good" programming to

promise for the upcoming renewal term and fashioned creative explanations for past shortfalls.

The administrative process also influenced the attorney's role. The easiest and least expensive ways to regulate an industry are to quantify standards and reduce the review process to yes–no and check-the-box answers. Individual narratives require more time to evaluate and make comparisons difficult. This factor was best illustrated by the requirement that broadcasters ascertain the needs and interests of their communities. Because broadcasters are in the business of communicating, this would appear to be a painless burden. However, the FCC, as is often the case in the regulatory process, elevated form over substance. The FCC mandated what types of groups should be interviewed and established the minimum number of community leaders that must be interviewed each year. Eventually, forms were developed to report the survey results to the FCC.

This type of regulatory overkill has been replaced by the theory of marketplace regulation, with much of the FCC's recent emphasis placed on creating more competition. As a result, the function of the communications attorney likewise changed and became more complicated. When the FCC had regulations for every aspect of station operation, the attorney's primary role was to know, interpret, and apply those regulations. There was at least a degree of certainty. But when FCC regulations are replaced by more general concepts such as the public interest, answers are more difficult to find. For example, it was easier to advise a station as to the minimally acceptable amount of nonentertainment programming than to capsulize a station's obligation to serve community needs.

The FCC decision with the single greatest impact on communications attorneys was the elimination of the three-year (antitrafficking) rule. That rule required the buyer of a station to operate the outlet for three years before it could be sold for a profit. Then, in 1982, the FCC concluded that marketplace regulation required entrepreneurs to be able to profit by improved station performance without an arbitrary holding period. Consequently, the pace, size, and sophistication of broadcast deals changed dramatically, and the broadcast attorney's expertise expanded to include contract, tax, financing, and the myriad other legal issues associated with the transfer of any business.

Now, as in other industries that have experienced a shift to marketplace regulation, such as airlines and banking, abuses have developed. There thus is an overpowering urge by the FCC, Congress, and the public to re-regulate problem areas. As the emphasis shifts, not unlike a pendulum, the role of the communications attorney as the expert in FCC regulations is likely to re-emerge.

---

content regulation, but it also upheld the FCC's assertion that indecency could be restricted. Pacifica had argued that, unlike obscenity, which can be banned because it appeals to "prurient interest," indecency could not be restricted because it lacks this prurient-interest element. The court did not agree and thereby supported both the FCC's decision and its interpretation that actionable indecency is "language or material that, in context, depicts or describes, in terms patently offensive as measured by contemporary community standards for the broadcast medium, sexual or excretory activities or organs." Battles over this definition, and over the

government's right to restrict or completely ban indecency from the airwaves, continue to this day. (See Chapter 14.)

## The Dynamics of Deregulation

As the 1970s came to a close, it became clear to policy makers of all political persuasions that some regulatory heritage had, in a new technological environment, simply become underbrush. Even though the Republican Reagan administration is credited (or blamed) for this deregulatory movement, it was actually begun two years before Ronald Reagan took office. In 1979, the FCC, under the chairmanship of Democrat Charles Ferris, initiated a rulemaking proceeding "looking toward the substantial deregulation of commercial broadcast radio." The commission argued that because of the greater competition in the aural medium due to increased numbers of stations and its conversion "from being the major mass medium to being more of a secondary and often specialized medium," stations should be allowed more latitude in their programming and commercialization practices.[20]

At about the same time, and in response to a number of unfavorable court decisions, the FCC withdrew its restrictions on the number of distant signals that a cable system could import. The commission also deleted its syndicated exclusivity (*syndex*) rule that prohibited cable from carrying distant-signal programming that duplicated programming being aired by a local station. (Syndex would be reimposed on January 1, 1990, as the FCC sought to encourage more program diversity in the now mature cable industry.)

## Discarding Both Radio Rules and the NAB Code

By 1981, a new and much more deregulatory minded FCC formally adopted radio reforms by eliminating nonentertainment program requirements, limits on the number of commercials that could be aired, and the mandate that detailed program logs be kept in stations' public files. Congress, meanwhile, extended license terms from three to seven years for radio and from three to five years for television.

Even the Supreme Court seemed to get into the deregulatory act when it declined to overturn a five-year-old FCC policy statement that, in the court's characterization, "prefers reliance on market forces to its own attempt to oversee format changes at the behest of disaffected listeners." (*Federal Communications Commission* v. *WNCN Listeners Guild,* March 24, 1981). For years, the commission had been trying to extricate itself from the questions of whether radio format changes raised substantial public interest issues, and the Supreme Court now agreed that such programming decisions were best left to marketplace forces rather than to governmental edicts.

Preoccupation with marketplace forces also led to the demise of the NAB Codes in 1982. Focusing on the time standards in the television code, the Justice Department three years earlier had initiated antitrust action against this self-regulatory structure. Government attorneys felt that the code's limits on the amount of commercial time had the effect of artificially reducing television time inventory and therefore drove up the price advertisers had to pay for the slots that were available. Bowing to this assault, the NAB entered into a consent decree with the Justice Department and withdrew both the radio and television codes from operation. Each station was now left to formulate commercial time and

**CNN** **Syndex**

Cable systems often must now black out distant station programming that replicates shows aired by local outlets. Cable operators claim that the reimposed syndicated exclusivity rules are anticonsumer.

content acceptance policies on its own. Then, two years later, the FCC removed the last specific limitations on television commercial time in the same manner that it had deregulated radio in 1981.

## Ownership and Cable Liberalization

Ownership regulations were also liberalized in 1984. After some sparring with the Congress, the FCC increased the number of stations that could be owned by a single group from seven AM, seven FM, and seven TV to *twelve* of each type of facility. The television increase was delayed for some months until further agreements were reached. These agreements stipulated that in no case could the over-the-air signals of a television group reach more than 25 percent of the nation's homes. To promote further the development of stations in that band, UHF signals would have only 50 percent of their reach charged against them, however, and minority-controlled stations were given a similar advantage.

Cable deregulation was not neglected, either. The 1984 Cable Communications Policy Act largely freed the industry by placing significant restrictions on the right of municipalities and the federal government to regulate it. Cable companies were prohibited from owning television stations in their areas of service. But in their cable business itself, they were protected from any local franchise fee greater than 5 percent of their gross revenues. Further, federal and state governments were entirely forbidden from regulating basic cable rates, and no government agency (local, state, or federal) was given the right to regulate *pay* cable rates. For their part, franchising cities retained the power to require a specific number of public, governmental, and educational access channels, the overall upgrading of channel facilities at franchise renewal time, and cable availability to the entire franchise area. All in all, cable acquired a great deal of flexibility in its operation and business practices. Old regulations designed

to protect free broadcasting from cable competition were now gone.

Within the next few years, the courts also decided that the FCC's requiring of cable carriage of all local television signals (the *must-carry rules*) was unconstitutional. Even though the impact of this decision is still being negotiated between cable and broadcast interests, it is clear that cable's ability to compete with broadcasting is no longer inhibited by governmental restrictions. With no must-carry requirement, some authorities would argue that cable is now in the driver's seat when it comes to determining programming access to the nation's homes.

## Pending Business

Also still to be decided is the fate of the Fairness Doctrine, which the FCC repealed in 1987. However, some powerful members of Congress want to enact the document into law, thereby requiring the commission once more to use the doctrine to monitor stations' coverage and their balancing of controversial issues.

Among other hot and continuing regulatory issues are many that have simmered for years. Cable is threatened by proposals either to (1) abolish its right to a compulsory license to carry local as well as distant broadcast signals or (2) substantially increase fees for some new equivalent of that license. Even more important, Congress is considering whether to revisit the entire 1984 Cable Act in response to constituent complaints that the cable industry has misused its freedom in raising subscriber fees while lessening customer service. For its part, the cable establishment is complaining to the FCC that utility companies are levying exhorbitant so-called pole attachment charges for cable company lines designed to carry such new nonvideo services as personal communications networks (PCNs). PCNs are seen as the next generation of cellular telephones. Not surprisingly, cable companies are seeking to enter this emerging business and also plan to use nonvideo wires to deliver security systems, data links between schools, and institutional networks for a variety of corporate users. The cable interests claim that the 1978 Pole Attachment Act (which regulated the rates that utilities could charge cable systems for supporting their video service lines) should also be applied to strands cable installs for these new enterprises. Otherwise, argues the cable industry, the utilities will continue to charge excessive rates for nonvideo lines on their poles in order to keep cable operators out of new businesses that pole-owning telcos and power companies also are interested in pursuing.

Other recent regulatory actions have both broadened and narrowed electronic media flexibility. Broadening policies include the 1990 striking of Canon 3A(7) by the Judicial Conference of the United States. The immediate result is that electronic coverage of civil cases in federal courts will be permitted on a trial basis for a three-year period that began in July, 1991. The allowing of continued coverage after that time, and the possible expansion of the policy to encompass federal *criminal* cases, presumably will be based on the results of this experiment.

The broadcast networks also were given more lattitude in 1991 when the FCC liberalized the financial interest and syndication (fin/syn) rules. ABC, CBS, and NBC obtained the right to acquire ownership in shows produced for them by others and to syndicate these shows in foreign markets. The nets also were granted limited domestic syndication rights for prime-time shows they produced themselves, and such in-house productions could now fill up to 40 percent of a network's prime-time schedule. As of this writing, however, the networks are challenging the FCC ruling for not going far enough, while a variety of studio interests are charging that the rules go too far in injecting networks back into program ownership.

Some *re*regulation actions also occurred as the nineties began. In November 1990, Congress passed legislation granting broadcast and cable programmers a three-year exemption from antitrust laws—but an exemption to be used in development of industry guidelines to limit televised violence. Even though the programmers are not *required* to construct such self-policing standards, Congressional "preference" for some industry action unmistakably has been communicated.

At about the same time, Congress also passed the Children's Television Act of 1990. This piece of legislation limits commercials to 10½ minutes per hour on weekends and to 12 minutes per hour on weekdays during programming targeted to viewers under twelve years of age. Stations (and cable systems originating their own programming) are also required to air material specifically designed to serve the educational and informational needs of children aged sixteen and under. What is more, broadcasters' license renewals are to be conditioned on their having served children's "educational and informational needs."

Whether deregulation thus is giving ground to reregulation remains to be seen. What is clear, however, is that technological developments in the electronic media continue to outpace the ability of government to deal with

## CNN Megastations

FCC willingness to allow some radio broadcasters to simulcast two same-band stations in the same market was motivated by the desire to assist struggling AM operations. However, FM outlets have taken greater advantage of this chance to create so-called megastations.

them. This has been the case since the Wireless Act tried to mandate maritime communication. The *Titanic* sank amidst its desperate transmission of unmonitored distress calls. Therefore, new regulatory approaches had to be fashioned. In today's world of mushrooming media options and blurring distinctions among media, however, the harried distress calls are coming from the regulators themselves.

# Chapter Flashback

Regulation of the electronic media in the United States began with a simple law requiring a wireless set on board passenger ships. This 1910 Wireless Act was succeeded by two pieces of legislation in 1912 that mandated the ship's wireless set be manned and, more important, required that radio stations must obtain operating licenses from the Secretary of Commerce and Labor.

Immediately following World War I, public fear of future European entanglements forced the conversion of British-owned American Marconi into U.S.–owned RCA. AT&T's substantial involvement in RCA and toll broadcasting was subsequently curtailed due to antitrust considerations, but the phone giant maintained its dominance in the new intercity lines that were making networking possible. Once advertising demonstrated that broadcasting could be a money-making enterprise on its own, the business mushroomed. ASCAP demanded payment for the airing of its composers' music, and the National Associa-

tion of Broadcasters was formed to deal with ASCAP demands. So many new stations were being built that the airwaves were soon a jumble of interfering signals. Lacking the power to rectify the situation, the Secretary of Commerce called several conferences in a vain attempt to get voluntary cooperation.

Congress therefore passed the 1927 Radio Act that established the Federal Radio Commission and proved to be the first true piece of broadcast regulation. This law was replaced by the Communications Act of 1934 as part of Franklin D. Roosevelt's sweeping New Deal. The FRC gave way to today's FCC, which was given authority over virtually all wired and wireless telecommunications. The FCC was required to ensure that stations operated in the public interest, but the no-censorship provision of the 1934 Act (Section 326) has raised continuing legal questions as to how far the commission can go in judging program content.

Among the most significant and long-term issues dealt with by the FCC are the power of networks, a station's promise versus its performance, the scrutiny (in conjunction with the FTC) of advertising quantity and content, broadcaster rights to editorialize, political candidate access to the airwaves, and the treatment of indecency on the air. More technical decisions have had to be reached in such key areas as station and program ownership, duplication of aired programming, and the interrelationships of traditional and emerging electronic media systems. Finally, the subject of industry self-regulation has proved a knotty one, with questions of content standards frequently clashing with antitrust concerns.

## ❑ Review Probes

1. How did the 1912 Radio Act pose problems for workable broadcast regulation in the 1920s?
2. What is ASCAP and why was BMI formed to combat it?
3. What is meant by the "scarcity argument" that is frequently used to justify broadcast regulation?

4. How has broadcast coverage of court proceedings evolved from the time of the Hauptmann trial to the present?
5. Compare and contrast the Fairness Doctrine with Section 315.
6. Define the source, intent, and impact of (1) The 'Blue Book' and (2) *Red Channels*.

## ❑ Suggested Background Explorations

Bensman, Marvin R. *Broadcast Regulation: Selected Cases and Decisions.* 3rd ed. Lanham, MD: University Press of America, 1990.

Carter, T. Barton, et al. *The First Amendment and the Fifth Estate: Regulation of Electronic Mass Media.* 2nd ed. Westbury, NY: Foundation Press, 1989.

Gillmor, Donald M., and Jerome A. Barron. *Mass Communication Law: Cases and Comment.* 5th ed. St. Paul, MN: West Publishing Co., 1990.

Horwitz, Robert Britt. *The Irony of Regulatory Reform: The Deregulation of American Telecommunications.* New York: Oxford University Press, 1989.

Le Duc, Don R. *Beyond Broadcasting: Patterns in Policy and Law.* New York: Longman, 1987.

Paglin, Max D. (ed.) *A Legislative History of the Communications Act of 1934.* New York: Oxford University Press, 1989.

Pember, Don R. *Mass Media Law.* 5th ed. Dubuque, IA: Wm. C. Brown Co., 1990.

Ray, William B. *FCC: The Ups and Downs of Radio-TV Regulation.* Ames: Iowa State University Press, 1989.

# Benchmarks

| Year | Technological | Legal |
|------|---------------|-------|
| 1844 | Morse completes Washington–Baltimore telegraph line | |
| 1873 | Maxwell provides theoretical foundation of electromagnetism | |
| | Conductivity properties of selenium discovered | |
| 1876 | Bell creates working telephone | |
| 1878 | Crookes builds cathode ray tube | |
| 1884 | Nipkow invents scanning disc—basis of mechanical TV | |
| 1888 | Hertz creates and detects electromagnetic waves | |
| 1892 | Stubblefield propagates wireless voice transmissions | |
| 1896 | Marconi transmits electromagnetic signals a distance of 9 miles | |
| 1897 | Braun directs path of cathode rays | |
| 1899 | Marconi's wireless telegraph regularly sends messages across English Channel | |
| 1901 | Marconi transmits code message across the Atlantic | |
| 1906 | Fessenden sends musical program to ships at sea | |
| 1907 | Rosing builds prototype electronic television receiver | |
| 1908 | De Forest uses Audion tube in Eiffel Tower transmissions | |

| Year | Technological | Legal |
|------|--------------|-------|
| 1910 | | Wireless Ship Act passed |
| 1912 | | Radio Act passed |
| 1916 | Sarnoff's memo proposes radio as a "household utility" <br> De Forest broadcasts election returns | |
| 1919 | | American Marconi converts to U.S. ownership as RCA |
| 1920 | Conrad's 8XK conducts regular Pittsburgh transmissions | |
| 1921 | Commerce Department issues 32 radio licenses | |
| 1922 | | Pres. Hoover convenes first Radio Conference |
| 1923 | Baird and Jenkins demonstrate mechanical silhouettes in motion <br><br> Zworykin develops electronic TV pickup tube (*iconoscope*) | ASCAP negotiates first broadcast license agreement <br><br> NAB formed as industry's legal action arm <br><br> Second Radio Conference endorses greater operating regulation <br><br> *Intercity Radio* case limits government discretion in granting of licenses |
| 1924 | AT&T demonstrates temporary coast-to-coast radio network | |
| 1926 | AT&T creates permanent 24-station network using equalized circuits | Zenith case narrows government power to regulate station operations <br><br> Under antitrust pressure, AT&T agrees to divest itself of broadcast interests |

| Year | Technological | Legal |
|------|---------------|-------|
| 1927 | | Dill-White Radio Act passed, creating FRC |
| 1928 | | FRC reorganizes spectrum to accommodate modern radio |
| 1929 | | NAB issues tentative Radio Code |
| 1932 | | GE and Westinghouse forced to divest themselves of RCA stock |
| | | *Trinity Methodist Church* case supports public-interest standard in license renewal decisions |
| 1933 | Farnsworth and Zworykin independently create 240-line electronic pictures | |
| | Armstrong unveils frequency modulation system | |
| 1934 | | Communications Act passed; FCC created |
| 1935 | RCA produces 343-line picture | |
| 1937 | BBC tests show electronic TV superior to mechanical | ABA's Canon 35 revised to prohibit microphones and cameras in courtrooms |
| | 17 experimental TV stations in operation in U.S. | |
| 1938 | | Wheeler-Lea Act expands FTC power to regulate advertising |
| 1939 | Armstrong opens experimental FM station W2XMN | NAB Code and its administration strengthened |
| | RCA demonstrates 441-line TV system; begins public transmission and sale of receivers | |

| Year | Technological | Legal |
|------|---------------|-------|
| 1940 | | BMI formed to break ASCAP's music monopoly |
| 1941 | NTSC 525-line system adopted as U.S. standard | *Mayflower* case bans station editorializing |
| | | Report on Chain Broadcasting challenges network practices |
| 1942 | | OWI set up to clear broadcast information, take over private shortwave stations |
| 1943 | | NBC forced to sell Blue network |
| 1945 | RCA unveils Image Orthicon, first modern camera tube | |
| 1946 | | "Blue Book" issued and debated |
| 1947 | CBS promotes mechanical color TV system | |
| 1948 | TV Freeze as FCC restudies spectrum needs | *Port Huron* case frees stations of liability for candidate statements over their air |
| | Walson constructs cable TV system to demonstrate TV sets | |
| 1949 | | FCC creates Fairness Doctrine |
| 1950 | CBS promotes 405-line "field sequential" color system | *Red Channels* publishes names of industry "subversives" |
| 1952 | Lifting of TV Freeze with higher spectrum slot for UHF | McFarland Act overhauls FCC procedures |
| 1953 | RCA compatible color system approved | ABC/United Paramount Theater merger approved |
| 1954 | Regency introduces first consumer transistor radio | |

| Year | Technological | Legal |
|------|---------------|-------|
| 1956 | Ampex demonstrates practical video-tape recording | |
| 1957 | | Barrow Report advocates restrictions on network power |
| 1959 | | Congress exempts news programs from equal time |
| 1960 | | Payola and quiz-show rigging made federal crimes |
| 1961 | FM stations permitted to broadcast in stereo | |
| 1962 | Telestar communications satellite launched | |
| 1964 | "All Channel" requirement for new TV sets takes effect | FCC nonduplication requirements force separate programming for AM/FM combinations |
| 1965 | Early Bird, first dedicated TV satellite, put into orbit | *Estes* case cites televised trials as threats to judicial due process |
| | | FCC *must-carry rules* require cable systems to relay local stations |
| 1966 | Three networks develop all-color prime-time schedules | FCC bans CATV distant signal importation into top 100 markets |
| | | *Fortnightly* case makes CATV liable for copyright payments |
| | | *United Church of Christ* case supports right of citizens to challenge license renewals |
| 1968 | | *Southwestern* case establishes FCC power to regulate cable |
| 1969 | | *Red Lion* case upholds Fairness Doctrine |

| Year | Technological | Legal |
|------|---------------|-------|
| 1970 | | Congress bans cigarette advertising from airwaves |
| | | Prime Time Access Rule limits network evening programming |
| | | Fin/Syn rules limit network financial interests in programs |
| 1971 | | Congress requires that stations provide "reasonable access" and "lowest unit rate" to federal candidates |
| 1975 | HBO uses satellite to relay pay-TV to cable systems | |
| | Sony introduces Betamax home VCR | |
| 1976 | | Copyright Act provides for compulsory cable license |
| 1978 | | *Pacifica* case affirms FCC power to regulate indecency |
| 1981 | | Radio deregulated by FCC |
| | | *WNCN* case supports FCC decision to leave radio format decisions to marketplace |
| 1982 | HDTV first demonstrated in U.S. by CBS | NAB Codes withdrawn due to antitrust concerns |
| 1983 | FCC reallocation of microwave spectrum creates MMDS | Congress downsizes FCC from 7 to 5 members |
| 1984 | | Television deregulated by FCC and station ownership limitations raised to 12 AM, 12 FM, and 12 TV outlets |
| | | Cable Communications Policy Act substantially deregulates cable |

| Year | Technological | Legal |
|------|---------------|-------|
| 1987 | | FCC repeals Fairness Doctrine |
| 1990 | Television Decoder Circuitry Act mandates that most new TV sets must reproduce closed captioning by 1993 | Syndex rules reinstated |
| | | Children's Television Act impacts programs aimed at young people |
| 1991 | | FCC modifies Fin/Syn rules |

# Radio
# Operational History

❏ *As we discuss in the previous two chapters, technological evolution provided the hardware for our profession while regulatory developments attempted (sometimes unsuccessfully) to ensure that this hardware was used in an orderly and equitable fashion. With that discussion as background, we can now more meaningfully explore the actual operations of electronic media businesses. We can more easily understand why they matured as they did in response to the scientific and legal progressions we've just studied. Let's begin with the older medium of radio. As the announcer on* The Lone Ranger *used to intone, "Return with us now to those thrilling days of yesteryear."*

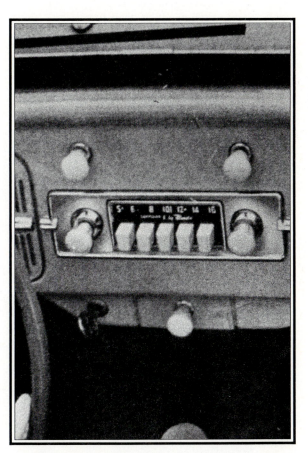

## Stumbling
## on a Moneymaker

When we recall radio's early inventor period, we are reminded of Fessenden's impromptu Christmas Eve concert in 1906 or De Forest's pioneering election coverage ten years later. Such wireless telephone experimentation was mainly concerned with the field testing and improvement of equipment so that valuable patent rights could be staked out. Like

Conrad's 1920 transmissions, the work of De Forest, Fessenden, Herrold, and (presumably) Stubblefield constituted the innovations of applied scientists rather than mass communicators. Program content considerations were incidental to the fact that this content was being successfully delivered by its originator's invention. Only after the public started to eavesdrop (see Figure 7–1), increasingly via pre-assembled, store-bought receivers, did radio become a mass *entertainment* as well as an electrical equipment enterprise.

## The Great Awakening

Even though this transformation came quickly, it did not come immediately. Historian Frederick Lewis Allen surveyed the scene in recalling the year 1921:

Dr. Van Etten of Pittsburgh permitted the services at Calvary Church to be broadcast, the University of Wisconsin gave radio concerts, and politicians spouted into the strange instruments and wondered if anybody was really listening. Yet when Dempsey fought Carpentier in July, 1921, and three men at ringside told the story of the slaughter into telephone transmitters to be relayed by air to eighty points throughout the country, their enterprise was reported in an obscure corner of the *New York Times* as an achievement in "wireless telephony"; and when the Unknown Soldier was buried at Arlington Cemetery the

**Figure 7–1**
Society couples dance to the music of *The Detroit News* experimental station 8MK (later WWJ) in September 1920

**171**

CHAPTER 7
Radio
Opera-
tional
History

following November, crowds packed into Madison Square Garden in New York and the Auditorium in San Francisco to hear the speeches issued from huge amplifiers, and few in those crowds had any idea that soon they could hear all the orations they wanted without stirring from the easy-chair in the living-room. The great awakening had not yet come.[1]

As we discover in Chapters 5 and 6, the great awakening *did* come by the following year as scores of new stations came on the air to promote the newspaper, store, or equipment manufacturer that owned them. Even more important, when WEAF's sale of airtime to the Queensboro Corporation demonstrated that a station could make money in its own right, the programmers and salespeople pushed the inventors and engineers out of the industry's driver's seat. Within a few months, three new trade magazines (*Radio World, Radio Dealer,* and *Radio Broadcast*) had been launched to serve the emerging industry, and several universities (Wisconsin, Iowa, Nebraska, and Rensselaer Polytechnic) put stations on the air or were making plans to offer courses by radio.[2] Six outlets—WOO (Philadelphia), KSD (St. Louis), WJZ (New York City), WHAZ (Troy, New York), WGN (Chicago), and KDYL (Salt Lake City)—were now powerful enough to be heard from coast to coast[3], and when heavy November snows in the Rocky Mountains crippled telegraph lines, 1922 election returns got through on the radio. The print media trade magazine *Editor and Publisher* lauded this election service in an editorial entitled "Radio's Increasing Value to Public"[4]—but the print establishment would soon come to perceive radio as more competitive threat than public servant.

Regular networking, or *chain broadcasting* as it was often called, began just a few months later when AT&T linked its WEAF (New York) with a Boston area facility, WMAF. Although earlier station-to-station relays had been tried, the WEAF/WMAF linkage was the first to use the new high-quality radio ca-

bles that AT&T engineers had developed specifically for chain broadcasting applications. Another AT&T-licensed station, WJAR (Providence), soon joined the chain, and a total of six outlets were permanently connected by the end of 1923. Informally known as the Red network because of the red ink that AT&T engineers used to map out their interconnections, this operation expanded to a coast-to-coast link up in little more than a year and would eventually become the cornerstone of the NBC empire.

These mushrooming radio activities were not always viewed in a positive light, of course. Many people thought commercials were an unconscionable stealing of the public airwaves for private gain, and newspaper publishers began to wonder whether such activities might eventually lure advertisers away from their pages. Even the clergy were becoming concerned. By 1923 several church services were being broadcast regularly. But some clerics protested the practice because it seemed to be diminishing actual church attendance. One bishop even declared that sinners couldn't be converted by wireless because the apparatus could not fully convey the necessary magnetism of a clergyman's personality.[5] Despite such concerns, the public as a whole remained wildly enthusiastic about broadcasting. As the *Scientific American* commented at the beginning of 1924:

> The past year has been marked by an increase in the number of highpower stations, proving again that radio is firmly established in the commercial world as a means of rapid and dependable communication. . . . Looked upon as a fad in the beginning, radio broadcasting has now intrenched itself pretty firmly in the routine of American life. This is due to the commendable effort of the broadcasters who, during the past twelve months, have been steadily improving their programs.[6]

With the 1924 presidential campaign, radio demonstrated both its penetration and its broad appeal. Millions of listeners tuned in as the Democratic Convention struggled ballot after ballot in an attempt to pick the party's presidential candidate. People never before involved in the political process now found it to be a highly charged enterprise and eagerly followed developments from the comfort of their own living rooms. This intense interest in radio's coverage of news events did not go unnoticed by the newspaper industry, however. Dominated by its large-publisher members, and fearing a new electronic competitor, the Associated Press's board of directors voted to withhold all AP news copy from stations.

Meanwhile, RCA Vice-President David Sarnoff was encouraging the new industry to stand on its own through the self-sufficiency that the sale of airtime could bring. "Broadcasters must be able to pay their own way in order to stabilize the industry," Sarnoff said.[7] Many stations did just that by starting to peddle time blocks to advertisers, even when this practice violated the terms under which they were using AT&T patented transmitters. (As mentioned in Chapter 6, AT&T was trying to leverage its patent control to reserve toll broadcasting activities for itself.) The names of sponsors now began appearing in the titles of musical shows, insurance companies started to associate themselves with health and exercise programs, and home recipe broadcasts specified the brand name of the flour that should be sifted. By 1925, stations were charging as much as $500 an hour for program sponsorship,[8] and the true business of broadcasting had emerged. In fact, the National Association of Broadcasters now formally decided to use the term *broadcasting* in reference to their enterprise because the older term, *radiocasting,* had been grabbed by the Associated Manufacturers of Electrical Supplies.[9]

### Enter NBC and CBS

The growth and solidification of network activities further helped to anchor the new broadcasting business. When AT&T withdrew from broadcasting in 1926 in order to protect its domination of land lines and long-distance activities, it transferred its station properties and the associated Red network to the so-called Radio Group, which was made up of Westinghouse, General Electric, and RCA. RCA then formed the National Broadcasting Company as a subsidiary to manage both the Red network and its own much smaller Blue network. Soon after, a loose combination of talent agents and independent stations who feared they would be closed out by the new NBC network monopoly, formed United Independent Broadcasters as a competing chain. The Columbia Phonograph Company subsequently became interested, and the organization was renamed the Columbia Phonograph Broadcasting System. Before the network was scarcely launched, however, Columbia became dismayed with the mounting costs and lack of sponsor support. It pulled out of the project, leaving only its name behind.

Fortunately for the struggling company, a young cigar manufacturing executive had done a little radio advertising and liked the results. William S. Paley's family owned the Congress Cigar Company, which had been one of the Columbia Phonograph Broadcasting System's first clients. When the twenty-six-year-old executive found that radio commercials for his La Palina cigars had doubled the brand's sales,[10] the power of this new vehicle became clear. For about $500,000, Paley's family purchased a majority of CBS stock and sold a minority interest to Paramount Pictures in order to increase the network's prestige and credit standing. Renamed the Columbia Broadcasting System, the 16-station CBS was now ready to compete with NBC's Red and Blue chains for the national advertising dollar. (Paley remained active in directing CBS affairs until his death in 1990.)

### Patterns for the Future

By this time, the new Federal Radio Commission was hard at work bringing order to the broadcast spectrum, which was an essential

**173**

CHAPTER 7
Radio
Opera-
tional
History

prerequisite to radio's health and growth. The FRC also brought order to call signs. Under international agreements, the United States had been given the letters *K* and *W* to identify its stations. The Commerce Department subsequently decided that stations east of the Mississippi River would use *W* and those west of it would be assigned a call sign beginning with *K*. (Nonconforming stations that predated this regulation, like KDKA in Pittsburgh, were allowed to keep their original calls.) But with the continued and projected growth of broadcasting, the FRC realized that three-letter calls such as WJR (Detroit) and KOA (Denver) would not provide sufficient options. These and other pioneer stations identified with three letters were grandfathered, and all new assignments contained four characters.

Thus, by 1929, U.S. radio could boast of a more orderly system of spectrum and call sign management, three healthy radio networks, fancier facilities (see Figure 7–2), and a substantial influx of advertising revenue from both national and local sponsors. In that year

alone, advertisers spent $40 million[11] to propel their pitches into the ether. Dance programs from hotel ballrooms, chamber music and orchestra concerts, dramatic series, children's educational offerings, and even increasing amounts of news via radio now filled the airwaves.

The biggest programming breakthrough was a ten-minute daily comedy called *Amos 'n' Andy*. Begun three years before on WGN (Chicago) under the title *Sam 'n' Henry*, the show starred Freeman Gosden and Charles Correll, two white entertainers who specialized in black dialect. In 1928, the program moved to Chicago's WMAQ, where it was performed live while disc recordings were made for shipment to more than two dozen cooperating stations. This was one of the first examples of program syndication. Ultimately in 1929, the popularity of *Amos 'n' Andy*'s serial comedy led NBC to obtain the show on behalf of Pepsodent toothpaste.

One of the first national telephone surveys of the radio audience found that more than half of the people called were listening to

**Figure 7–2**
A comfortably appointed 1928 radio studio

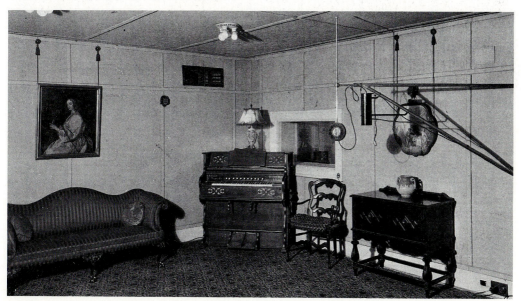

*Amos 'n' Andy.*[12] This astonishing and unparalleled broadcasting hit made nightly radio listening a national pasttime. At the time, very few people thought the concept of two white men performing black caricatures to be racist or even of questionable taste. In a society that was still segregated in its day-to-day activities, *Amos 'n' Andy* was enjoyed as easily packaged comedy. It relied on the naïveté of the roles portrayed to convey plot and laughter quickly to an audience equally oblivious to the show's distortive assumptions. Like the vaudeville stage from which it had sprung, *Amos 'n' Andy* sacrificed truth for selective simplicity in order to appeal to the largest audience possible. The show proved how popular radio could be. In hindsight, it also demonstrated that broadcast popularity and social consciousness do not automatically go hand in hand.

## Prospering in the Depression

As the United States entered both the 1930s and the economic Depression that became that decade's hallmark, it was feared that this financial calamity would stifle the further growth of radio. As it turned out, the medium hardly broke stride. Listeners gravitated toward their ornately encased radios (see Figure 7–3) as a form of free entertainment. Advertisers saw it as the most efficient way to stay in touch with consumers. And performers found it vital to the sustenance of their careers and their bank accounts. The average cost of an hour of radio time on a station had dropped to $310[13], but this was still a healthy figure when compared to the free-falling prices in other industries. To stimulate their own sales, newspapers began to accept advertising from broadcasters, and the radio page became an important source of program announcements, reviews, and paid layouts promoting individual shows.[14]

This cross-media cooperation did not last long. By 1931, the American Newspaper Publisher's Association (ANPA) had decided that the infant radio industry was now a fast-maturing rival. Noting that more and more stations were airing news, features, and advertising, ANPA urged that the legality of advertising over the public airwaves be examined because government licensees were competing with private enterprise. Fueling the publishers' concern was the fact that radio profits for both the networks and the individual stations were up substantially while newspaper advertising revenue had declined between $40 and $50 million.

However, the newspaper establishment was not of a single mind when it came to radio. In 1932, the United Press signed an agreement with KNX (Los Angeles) that allowed the station to use UP wire service stories to produce four newscasts daily, and WCAU (Philadelphia) reached a similar agreement with the *Philadelphia Daily News.* The debate over whether radio was a good customer or an evil competitor continued to divide the publishing community.

Certainly, the new occupant of the White House understood that radio was something more than an entertainment medium. Beginning even before his first "Fireside Chat" on March 12, 1933, President Franklin Delano Roosevelt demonstrated his ability as a radio communicator. Rather than stiffly approach the broadcast microphone as though it were a public address system, Roosevelt talked to it conversationally, as if each listener were being individually addressed. (See Figure 7–4.) The power of FDR's voice soothingly masked the fact that his legs were crippled. Radio therefore constituted one of the most potent tools of his presidency. Meanwhile, the chief executive's affinity for radio provided the medium with increased stature. Roosevelt and radio, in many ways, were an ideal, mutually supportive match.

Radio listenership continued to increase even as the full impact of the Depression caused radio revenues to decrease. Comedy and variety programs like the *Eddie Cantor* and (Rudy) *Vallee Varieties* shows on NBC-Red, *Amos 'n' Andy* on NBC-Blue, and *Burns*

**Figure 7–3**
A 1930 state-of-the-art Atwater Kent floor-model radio

**175**

CHAPTER 7
Radio
Opera-
tional
History

*(Lautman Photo 77377.)*

*and Allen* on CBS provided listeners with a momentary escape from the troubles of the times. Serials like *Little Orphan Annie* (NBC-Blue) and *Just Plain Bill* (CBS) continued to reinforce daily listening habits. Coverage of college and professional sporting events increased while team owners debated whether such broadcasts helped or harmed stadium attendance.

For their part, major newspaper interests had largely reached a decision about radio by the end of 1933, and their decision was a negative one. The Associated Press membership, dominated by old-line publishers, voted to ban network use of AP news and to limit local use of their wire copy to brief bulletins that credited the local AP–member newspaper. The American Newspaper Publishers Association decided that radio program schedules were no longer news but would be printed only if paid for as advertising. An awkward pact between the two media culminated in early 1934 with the set up of the Press-Radio Bureau. Through this agency, the wire services agreed to provide station and networks with two five-minute summaries per day (one

**Figure 7–4**

Franklin Delano Roosevelt, the "radio President," engages in one of his later chats with his fellow Americans

that must be broadcast after 9:30 A.M. and the other after 9 P.M. so as not to beat the release of morning and afternoon editions). These newscasts had to be *sustaining* programming (unsponsored). Furthermore, CBS and NBC were required to dismantle their fledgling news-gathering offices.

The networks were willing to abide by these restrictions, but a number of stations were not. News exchanges like the Transradio Press Service, the Continental Radio News Service, and the Radio News Association were constructed to serve the journalistic aspirations of client stations. Before long, they surpassed the Press-Radio Bureau in the scope and quality of their activities, and the

networks found themselves at a competitive disadvantage as the public's appetite for instantaneous news grew.

Earlier in 1934, a new network came on the scene with the organization of the Mutual Broadcasting System. Distinct in its operating philosophy from the other networks, MBS owned no stations and was primarily concerned with securing advertising for its member outlets, who were each completely free to make their own programming decisions. Pioneered by its four charter members (WGN Chicago, WOR New York, WLW Cincinnati, and WXYZ Detroit) Mutual gradually added more and more independents to its fold. Beginning with the immensely popular *The*

**177**

CHAPTER 7

Radio
Opera-
tional
History

**Figure 7–5**

A mid-1940s rehearsal of WXYZ's *The Lone Ranger,* the series that had inaugurated the Mutual Broadcasting System a decade earlier. The Lone Ranger, by this time played by Brace Beemer, is gesturing, with a balding Tonto (John Todd) at his side.

*Lone Ranger* from WXYZ (see Figure 7–5), MBS was able to serve its members' commonality of programming interests and advertising needs without compromising the right of each station to operate as it saw fit.

possessed receivers, and revenues from the sale of advertising time increased 20 percent over the previous year. Almost 600 regular stations were on the air (all AM, of course), and a few insiders thought viable FM broadcasting might not be far away. Even important segments of the newspaper industry became convinced of the financial potential of radio. By the middle of the year, 114 of these stations were owned by publishers.[15]

## Radio's Glory Years

Despite the continuing Depression, by 1935 the radio industry was riding a rapidly rising wave of profits and popularity. A CBS survey indicated that seven out of ten homes

### Broadcast News and Measurement

This move toward increased station ownership was only one of a number of cracks in the newspaper industry's antiradio ramparts. The success of Transradio Press, which had now also acquired the rights to use copy from Reuters, the major British wire service, demonstrated that broadcasting's journalistic tendencies were not to be denied. Adopting a pragmatic "if you can't beat 'em, join 'em" approach, the two profit-seeking U.S. wire services, United Press and International News Service, agreed to sell their material to radio.

The Associated Press, however, continued to hold out. A news cooperative of old-line publishers rather than a profit-seeking independent business, AP had little fiscal or philosophical reason to embrace the upstart audio medium. AP did agree to increase the amount of daily news that the Press-Radio Bureau could provide to stations, but, along with the American Newspaper Publishers Association, it still insisted that these newscasts be aired on a sustaining (nonsponsored) basis.[16] NBC and CBS decided they would honor their agreements with the Press-Radio Bureau for one more year, but the days of artificial restrictions on broadcast journalism seemed about over.

By 1936, in fact, such prominent newspaper companies as Hearst, *The Washington Post,* and Scripps-Howard had all acquired broadcast properties as important profit centers. This escalating trend toward newspaper ownership of radio did not go unnoticed in government. The chairman of the Senate Interstate Commerce Committee, Senator Burton Wheeler, warned that a monopoly was in the making. Few people listened, however, because healthy Depression-era businesses were too rare to be tampered with.

For its part, radio turned its attention to being able to measure audiences accurately. Newspapers and magazines could rely on the Audit Bureau of Circulation (ABC) to validate the sale of their issues, but radio signal receptions could not be physically counted like stacks of publications. Advertisers wanted evidence of how many people were exposed to their broadcast commercials. Random surveys by broadcasters themselves were no longer credible, either to sponsors or to the

publishers who themselves now owned stations.

A.C. Nielsen, a small market research company, therefore proposed that a device be attached to receiving sets to measure automatically radio use and station selection. Called the Audimeter, this meter had been developed by professors at the Massachusetts Institute of Technology, from whom Nielsen acquired it. Unlike the then-existing Crossley and Hooper ratings services, which asked listeners questions over the telephone, the Audimeter required no overt response from people and measured radio use continuously. After six years of further development, the Nielsen system would emerge as a dominant player in the justification of station audience claims.

Taken as a whole, the radio industry did not need Nielsens to demonstrate its public appeal. In 1937, 80 percent of the homes in the United States contained a receiver, and there were almost 5 million additional sets installed in automobiles. Traffic safety experts considered the bulky devices to be a major hazard while driving because they were difficult to tune. Yet, calls for banning in-car radios went unheeded. People wanted to listen wherever they could because there was just too much appealing programming to miss.

## Program Elements and Issues

Serials, comedies, musical varieties, and quiz shows were massively popular; but so too were serious drama, education, and music offerings. CBS's *Columbia Workshop* aired outstanding aural theater by writers like Archibald MacLeish. NBC produced four Eugene O'Neill plays, and both network companies competed with each other as to who could mount the finest radio adaptations of Shakespeare. CBS broadcast New York Philharmonic concerts, and NBC countered by securing the services of renowned conductor Arturo Toscanini to lead its own in-house orchestra. To compete with the CBS *American School of the Air,* NBC launched *University of* the Air and thus made even educational programming a competitive battleground. Clearly, these were glorious times for cultured dial-twisters.

Still, the golden age did have its tarnishing elements. For one thing, local stations increasingly injected their own commercials into sponsored programs they received from the networks. These spot commercials (or just spots for short) brought in additional revenue but were not welcomed by the national clients who had paid handsomely for exclusive program sponsorships. Ford Motor Company declared that the spots were "unfair to the sponsor and to the public,"[17] but the networks were leery of totally outlawing the practice at the risk of losing important affiliate stations.

Programming itself came in for increasing negative criticism, too, as the tastes of urban listeners and broadcasting executives sometimes clashed with the sensitivities of rural consumers. With four powerful networks (NBC-Red, NBC-Blue, CBS, and MBS) now serving virtually the entire country, it was perhaps inevitable that regional taste divergencies would cause friction. A 1937 case in point was an NBC Sunday evening presentation of an "Adam and Eve" skit on the *Chase and Sanborn Hour* in which the voluptuous Mae West played Eve. Even though Ms. West's prodigious dimensions were not discernible over the radio, her racy reputation was well known. The casting of this actress in a skit based on biblical characters raised a storm of protest that ended up in *The Congressional Record* via a Congressman's complaint addressed to the Secretary of the Federal Communications Commission.[18]

My Dear Mr. Slowie,

It is my desire to most vigorously protest against the actions of the National Broadcasting Company in allowing the Chase and Sanborn Company to broadcast over their network the filthy and indecent program that was given last Sunday night between the hours of 8 and 9 P.M.

The featured performer was a certain Mae West, who served a jail sentence in New York City for presenting an indecent theatrical performance. She was assisted in a later part of the skit by Edgar Bergen.

The radio, entering as it does into the homes of millions of our citizens, must at all costs give clean, decent, and high-class entertainment.

To date every father and mother felt it was perfectly safe to turn the radio on in the presence of their adolescent children. After last Sunday night, no such feeling of freedom can exist.

I wonder if the persons responsible for this program are accustomed to staging such entertainment in their own homes before their own children. Frankly, I believe them capable of stomaching most anything.

It is my intention to force congressional action on this matter.

Very Sincerely Yours,

U.S. Rep. Donald L. O'Toole

Although no formal action was taken on Congressman O'Toole's subsequent resolution, his complaint mirrored concerns that would resurface anytime broadcasting's ready access to the home and children was intertwined with media First Amendment issues (recall our discussion of the *Pacifica* case as well as the 1990 Children's Television Act in Chapter 6). The host of the *Chase and Sanborn Hour* was ventriloquist Edgar Bergen, who held forth with his dummy, Charlie McCarthy (see Figure 7–6). As a puppet presented at 8 o'clock, Charlie presumably commanded a *family* listenership, in front of whom even Ms. West's aural appearance was perceived as inappropriate.

The unsettling effect of radio content on *adults* also was a source of dismay the following year. In 1938 radio brought the prospect of real war and the clever devices of science-fiction war into U.S. homes. When Hitler

179

CHAPTER 7
Radio
Opera-
tional
History

**Figure 7-6**

Ventriloquist Edgar Bergen and sidekick Charlie McCarthy became the recipients of Congressional scolding when they featured the racy Mae West on their radio program

marched into Austria and dismembered Czechoslovakia, CBS, NBC, and MBS all brought the events and the German dictator's speeches directly to the living room via recorded and, later, live transatlantic shortwave relays. A new breed of authentic radio journalists such as Edward R. Murrow, H. V. Kaltenborn, William L. Shirer, and Fulton Lewis, Jr., introduced U.S. listeners to a fascinating and forboding world they would no longer be allowed to ignore.

This ominous reality programming may, in fact, have made fictionalized news seem real, too. Orson Welles's "War of the Worlds" broadcast on Halloween Eve was only the dramatization of an H. G. Wells book. But people had been conditioned to receive bad news instantaneously. Welles's *Mercury Theater on the Air* depiction of a Martian invasion caused thousands of listeners to panic and led CBS to drop the use of simulated news bulletins within entertainment programming. (See Figure 7-7.)

From the trivial plaything of inventors and musicians, radio had evolved into a device perhaps too credible for its own good. Nonetheless, few people in the business were complaining, because radio's average salary, according to *Broadcasting and Broadcast Advertising*, was now the highest of any in-

**181**

CHAPTER 7

Radio
Opera-
tional
History

**Figure 7-7**

Orson Welles inadvertantly demonstrated radio's believability in his 1938 "War of the Worlds" adaptation

dustry. The average weekly take-home pay for its 17,000 workers was $45.12.[19]

As war broke out in Europe, the broadcast industry took special pains to solidify its prosperity and appeal while adopting precautionary measures designed to avoid content pitfalls. A new and formal version of the NAB Code was adopted in 1939 and machinery for administering it established. Among the Code's key provisions were regulations governing the conduct of children's, educational, and religious broadcasts in order to present positive role models, assist the educational process, and promote "spiritual harmony and understanding of mankind." Limits were established as to how many minutes of commercials should be allowed in various length programs, and both news and public affairs shows were urged to cover controversial issues with fairness, accuracy, and balance.[20] Sponsorship of controversial issue programs was banned by the Code. This provision most

directly influenced the activities of Father Charles Coughlin, the so-called Radio Priest (see Figure 7-8).

Broadcasting throughout the 1930s on an increasingly far-flung network of stations from his parish in Royal Oak, Michigan, Coughlin's commentary evolved into extended attacks on President Roosevelt that took on anti-Semitic overtones. By the mid-thirties, the priest's right-wing National Union for Social Justice was seen as a potentially dangerous political movement that had little to do with religion. That his broadcasts were politically controversial is seen in this excerpt from an April 1937 transmission:

Oh, you poor laborers and farmers. We have tried again and again to tell you that there can be no resurrection for America, until Congress begins to coin and regulate the value of money. We have endeavored to teach you time and again that there can

**Figure 7–8**
Father Charles Coughlin's skillful exploitation of radio brought him wide-spread recognition and influence. Here, he chats with baseball legend Babe Ruth

be no coming out of this Depression, until what you earn goes to sustain your wife and your children. But somehow or other you're satisfied to sustain the wives and children of those who do the coining and regulating of money; who live in their palaces and travel in their yachts. You want that. You voted for that. You have that. And it's time that you take that.[21]

At its height, as an announcer indicated at the start of one of his 1937 broadcasts, Coughlin's programs were "paid for at full commercial rates. And in no sense are they donated by the broadcasting corporations. They represent a weekly expenditure of more than $10,000."[22]

These sponsor revenues, of course, were crucial to Coughlin's continued radio activities. But when his stridency began to cast a negative reflection on radio itself, the NAB Code's suggested prohibition on controversy program advertising was a way to deal with the problem, and others like it, without making it seem that the industry was censoring itself. Deprived of advertising revenue, Coughlin's station carriage began a rapid decline by the end of 1939, and industry self-regulation was, for good or ill, shown to have teeth.

## The Wartime Airwaves

In 1940, with important war news breaking every minute, even the Associated Press gave up the fight to keep radio out of the news business when it agreed to accept stations as members. With Edward R. Murrow's chilling actualities of bombs raining on London and the William Kierker (NBC) and William L. Shirer (CBS) broadcasts of France's surrender to Hitler, radio journalism acquired increased stature and dramatic appeal. Buoyed by a *Fortune* magazine survey of a few months earlier that "70 percent of Americans relied on the radio for news and 58 percent thought it was more accurate than that supplied by the press,"[23] broadcast correspondents and commentators became full partners in the dissemination of vital information to the people of the United States. Not surprisingly, the Press-Radio Bureau went quietly out of business; it had been an artificial news bottleneck that neither the public nor broadcasters would miss.

The Japanese attack on Pearl Harbor a few months later impacted all aspects of the broadcast industry—not just news gathering. Military priorities meant the diversion of electronic parts and equipment and personnel to more essential uses than commercial broadcasting; and radio had to make do for the duration. Entertainment programming turned more and more to war-related themes. Popular songs like "Praise the Lord and Pass the Ammunition" shared the airwaves with war bond drives, *Little Orphan Annie's* serialized run-ins with Nazi spies, and soap operas in which characters anxiously discussed the fate of their men and boys in the service. In a special radio address on December 9, 1941, President Roosevelt set the tone and the groundrules for broadcasting in the years to come with these words:

To all newspapers and radio stations—all those who reach the eyes and ears of the American people—I say this. You have a most grave responsibility to the nation now and for the duration of this war. If you feel our government is not disclosing enough of the truth, you have every right to say so. But, in the absence of all the facts as revealed by official sources, you have no right in the ethics of patriotism to deal out unconfirmed reports in such a way as to make people believe they are gospel truth.[24]

With former CBS news commentator Elmer Davis at its head, the Office of War Information (OWI) worked to ensure that Americans at home and abroad received as much news as possible consistent with national security needs. Broadcasters cooperated fully with the content restrictions imposed immediately after Pearl Harbor (see Chapter 6). In addition, a number of government/industry cooperative programs were launched, including *Command Performance* and *The Army Hour*. The eleven private shortwave stations that OWI took over helped make such programs available to servicemen abroad as a means of countering the propaganda of Tokyo Rose and Berlin's Axis Sally. Out of such activities grew the Armed Forces Radio Service.

Meanwhile, at home, war priorities served to give broadcasting a competitive edge over the print media because paper rationing forced both newspapers and magazines to downsize. Advertisers who could no longer purchase adequate page space therefore bought more time on the air, and radio advertising revenues reached new highs. Even dramatic and symphony orchestra presentations were given a consequent boost, as sponsors clamored to support any available programming, no matter how highbrow, if it would keep their names in the public's memory.

As the war dragged on, the country and the radio industry were forced to come to grips with another threat—the increasing polarization and hatred spawned by more noticeable racial discrimination. A product of its times, the U.S. military was uncompromisingly segregated, a fact that Axis Sally's Berlin broadcasts constantly exploited with fabricated reports of the cowardice of black units. To counter these lies, War Department officials joined with some of the finest writers in U.S. radio to produce programs that accurately reflected the contributions of black people to the war effort. An episode of William Robson's *Man behind the Gun* dramatized the exploits of the Coast Guard Cutter *U.S.S. Campbell's* all-black crew, which sank a half-dozen enemy submarines. Soap operas introduced heroic African Americans into their plot lines, and Mutual's *Fighting Men* and *Men O'War* on CBS provided vehicles for black servicemen to relate their training and combat experiences.

Such efforts came none too soon. In 1943, a race riot in Detroit killed almost three dozen people. The CBS response was the preparation and airing of *Open Letter on Race Hatred*, a half-hour dramatization that *Time* magazine called "the most eloquent and outspoken program in radio history."[25] Produced by William Robson as a replacement for that week's episode of his *Man behind the Gun,* the show was first sent down the network's closed circuit lines for affiliate preview. Several southern stations refused to carry the show. Closer to home, the CBS affiliate's owner in Detroit, who had taken out full-page newspaper ads promoting the program, was furious when he learned that the show was not anti-black, as he had assumed.[26] (This owner, George A. Richards, had previously provided his station as the flagship that built Father Coughlin's network.) Nonetheless, the broadcast of *Open Letter on Race Hatred* went forward with an announcer introduction that framed the show's courageous stand and warning:

> Dear fellow Americans. We ask you to spend thirty minutes with us facing quietly, and without passion or prejudice, a danger which threatens all of us. A danger so great, that if it is not met and conquered now, even though we win this war, we shall be defeated in victory. And the peace which follows will for us be a horror of chaos, lawlessness and bloodshed. This danger is—race hatred.[27]

Ultimately, almost 100 CBS affiliates carried the broadcast, and radio demonstrated its potential, if not its complete dedication, to serve the public interest, regardless of the consequences.

Radio braved a different kind of fire the following year when correspondents armed with portable transmitters were among the first to storm ashore on D-Day. Commercials and regular programs were preempted so that listeners in the United States could follow the progress of the battle for the Normandy beaches. News had never been so dramatic for such an extended period of time, and broadcasting proved it could capture and focus the entire nation's attention as immediacy unfolded.

Later in 1944, the Republicans chose Thomas E. Dewey, possessor of a pleasing radio voice, to challenge FDR for the White House. Previous Republican standard bearers had been woefully inadequate over the airwaves, and it was felt Dewey was up to the challenge. Roosevelt, the radio President, won again, but the unprecedented use of the medium by both parties and the convention coverage involving more than 300 radio professionals signaled broadcasting's new indispensability to the political process in the United States.

A few months later, Roosevelt was dead, and a grieving nation communally followed his funeral procession on their radios. The Japanese surrender ceremony on September 1, 1945, was covered from the deck of the battleship *Missouri* in Tokyo Bay. The event was recorded via both the old wire (see Figure 7–9) and new acetate (audiotape) technologies for delayed transmission ninety minutes after it occurred. This was arranged so that newspapers would not be beaten to this historic story by radio's instantaneous technology.

The FCC now made plans to free up pending station construction permits for both AM and FM stations. FM service had been reassigned to a higher and more spacious section of the spectrum but this action made pre-war FM receivers obsolete. Fortunately, there were scarcely more than 400,000 of them because FM activities had largely been put on hold during the hostilities. The last vestiges of wartime censorship and restrictions on ad lib programs were removed, and broadcasters eagerly looked toward the predicted postwar consumer boom. New quiz shows like Mutual's *Break the Bank* came on the air, and

**185**

CHAPTER 7

Radio
Opera-
tional
History

**Figure 7–9**
An Air-King Wire Recorder, the low-fidelity predecessor of the audio tape
machine

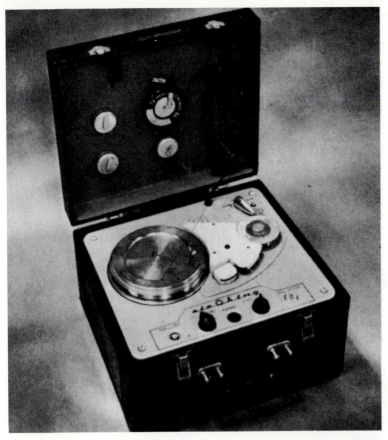

*(Lautman photo 77360)*

existing ones improved their prizes. Radio's prospects and riches, it seemed, could only get better.

## Postwar Perplexities

The future, however, held bleaker surprises. In addition to a more activist FCC (recall our previous discussion in Chapter 6), radio soon faced a threat from within the broadcasting industry itself as the new television medium emerged from its wartime cocoon.

### Rising Disenchantment

For a while in 1946, indications remained rosy. With equipment and parts once again available for civilian use, some fourteen million radio receivers were sold to replenish and expand the industry's prewar consumer inventory. The number of AM stations jumped from approximately 1,000 to more than 1,500, and almost 400 FM outlets were authorized. Improved recording techniques led the networks to loosen their bans on transcribed programs. In 1947, singer Bing

Crosby (see Figure 7–10) was able to convince ABC to record his show on the new audio tape and thereby eliminate the need for him to replicate his performance for western time zones.

In contrast, recorded music was about all FM stations could afford. FM was referred to as the free music medium because scarce advertiser support inhibited more expensive and varied live programming. Still, the new service was expected to be on solid ground once manufacturers had time to produce enough new receivers. Everything was just taking a little longer than expected.

Soon, however, an advertising slump materialized. Plenty of sponsor money had been available during the war, not only because of print media space limitations, but also because high taxes on excessive wartime profits had coerced companies to plow these profits into advertising rather than pay them as taxes to Uncle Sam. With these taxes now lifted and paper readily available for unrestricted newspaper and magazine use, the competition for fewer sponsor dollars intensified.

To make matters worse, radio advertising was increasingly coming under attack for its pervasiveness and questionable taste. This at-

**Figure 7–10**
Crooner Bing Crosby's use of new audiotape technology overcame network opposition to transcribed (recorded) programs

**187**

CHAPTER 7
Radio
Opera-
tional
History

tack came not only from the FCC's "Blue Book" mentality but also from one of the medium's own pioneers. Speaking to a National Association of Broadcasters Chicago meeting via a letter to the editor in the *Chicago Tribune* (October 28, 1946), Lee De Forest minced no words in his assessment of what broadcasters had done to what he called "his child":

> You have sent him out in the streets in rags of ragtime, tatters of jive and boogie woogie, to collect money from all and sundry for hubba hubba and audio jitterbug. You have made of him a laughingstock to intelligence, surely a stench in the nostrils of the gods of the ionosphere; you have cut time into tiny segments called spots (more rightly stains) wherewith the occasional fine program is periodically smeared with impudent insistence to buy and try.

Such bad press notwithstanding, radio's monetary fortunes seemed to rebound in 1947. Even though *Fortune* magazine scoffed that many network programs of the time "would affect any person of modest discrimination somewhere between complete indifference and acute illness"[28] total network time sales increased some 12 percent over 1946 levels. On the local level, meanwhile, a new low-cost format was enjoying increasing popularity. With the improved high-fidelity records, a station could now employ a radio *disc jockey*—a glib announcer whose main task was to string these recordings together in a way that filled up hours of airtime at almost no production cost. Beyond the deejay's salary and the price of such discs as couldn't be obtained free from record promoters, a station's ASCAP and BMI performance licenses took care of the copyright fees involved. Soon, almost 90 percent of stations had instituted at least one disc jockey program in order to lessen reliance on network programming and increase airtime sales to local advertisers. National sponsors preferred the glossier environment of a network program, but local clients found the deejay show to be a very affordable and high-profile way to hawk their wares to their own hometowns.

## TV Steals the Spotlight

As the 1940s drew to a close, the promise of FM was being overshadowed not only by the older AM service, but also by the public's fascination with television. Many consumers seemed to be foregoing the purchase of a comparatively low cost FM receiver in favor of saving up for the much more expensive TV set. After all, you could already listen to radio on your trusty old AM. About 700 FM stations were now on the air, but, in 1949, scarcely 900,000 new receivers were produced—only about 1,300 new receivers for each operating station! Many of these FMs were co-located with established AM outlets and carried the same programming so there was little incentive for the consumer to invest in a new set. Most AM operators grabbed an FM allocation simply to keep it out of the hands of possible competitors but had little interest in developing it separately.

Particularly at the network level, AM was facing a much more dangerous threat from television as industry executives started to reposition themselves for the new medium. On the surface, network radio seemed as vibrant and competitive as ever. CBS, through skilled application of the tax laws, lured major radio stars from the other networks by helping these stars become independent corporations. CBS then offered these corporations hefty monetary incentives to leave their current networks. As corporations rather than individuals, the stars' salary increases were considered capital gains rather than regular income and so were subject to a much lower tax rate. Taking advantage of the offer, some of radio's most popular personalities and their programs made the jump to CBS. *Jack Benny, Ozzie and Harriet, Amos 'n' Andy, The Edgar Bergen and Charlie McCarthy Show,* and *The Red Skelton Show* all moved from NBC, and

Bing Crosby's vocal chords were enticed away from ABC.

Actually, CBS Chairman William Paley was less interested in the continuing radio careers of these stars than he was in their TV potential. Paley understood the value of prepackaged success, and so he went after not only big stars but also stars who could make the transition to video when the proper time came. Even before the end of 1949, some established radio properties were now being seen rather than just heard. CBS's *The Goldbergs,* ABC's *Stop the Music* and *The Lone Ranger,* as well as DuMont Television's *The Life of Riley* were among the first programs to migrate to television; and before long, this migration assumed the dimensions of a wholesale evacuation of network radio.

## Network Eclipse and FM Stagnation

The 1950s dawned unpleasantly for the sound medium. Network radio revenues declined significantly. At least some of this decline was attributable to sponsors' following their stars to television. The onset of the Korean War brought renewed interest in radio news, but General Douglas MacArthur, supreme commander of the U.S. armed forces, imposed extensive censorship on reports from the war zone. Big network radio shows continued (in fact, NBC premiered a new all-star variety program called *The Big Show* starring Tallulah Bankhead), but radio personalities like Henry Morgan and Martin Gabel were finding their names on blacklists as the Communist-seeking witch hunts intensified. By 1951, NBC, CBS, and Mutual all succumbed to advertiser pressure and lowered the cost of their airtime between 10 and 15 percent. Even the one bright spot for FM, transit radio (by which commercial FM broadcasts were piped into city buses), disappeared when a U.S. Appeals Court ruled that the captive passengers were thereby deprived of their "liberty without due process of law." After thirty years of steady advances, the radio industry now seemed to be retreating on every front.

The Supreme Court reversed the finding against transit radio in 1952, but few FM stations could make a profit by relying on the distracted listenership found in trolleys and buses. At the same time, all four radio networks announced further rate cuts, and research showed that individual consumer listening on a daily basis had dropped more than an hour from what it had been only two years earlier. Much of this drop was occurring in the evening, of course, as former listeners were now becoming viewers of television's nighttime fare. The radio networks began to turn more airtime back to their affiliates to program and sell, and the affiliates most often responded with disc jockey shows.

## The New Localism

Meanwhile, station owners Todd Storz in Omaha and Gordon McLendon in Dallas were experiencing significant success with a format called "Top 40," in which the most popular songs of the day were endlessly replayed by youth-appealing deejays who communicated in short bursts between records. Simultaneously, a Cleveland disk jockey named Alan Freed dominated the local airwaves by spinning a pulsating blend of rhythm-and-blues, country, and gospel music he dubbed "rock and roll." With its almost hypnotic appeal to teenagers, rock and roll soon became a national phenomenon that gave radio a new franchise with young people even as their parents were deserting it for comfortable seats in front of the tube. The music licensing organization BMI (see Chapter 6) also greatly benefited from the trend because most rock and roll composers were outside of ASCAP's traditional constituency. BMI scooped up these new songwriters as members and gradually came to parity with ASCAP in terms of who licensed the music that U.S. broadcasters were playing.

**189**

CHAPTER 7
Radio
Opera-
tional
History

Thus, by the midfifties, radio was becoming much more of a local than a national medium. Network dramas, documentaries, situation comedies, and action/adventure programs were moving to television in droves. Increasingly, the radio networks emphasized news and musical segments that would augment rather than dominate the recorded tunes being programmed by local affiliates. In short, radio became something used as an accompaniment to other activities rather than a vehicle to captivate your full attention.

This shift in audience listening patterns was enhanced when Regency (a division of Industrial Development Engineering Associates) brought out the first practical transistor radio.[29] Much smaller and much more durable than tubes, the solid-state transistors had been introduced to the U.S. electronics industry by engineers John Bardeen and William Shockley in 1948. Transistors required no warm-up time and made possible a radio you could carry around in your pocket. Expending only a fraction of the power of a tube-type receiver, the transistor set could be run by a tiny battery. Radio could now accompany you anywhere, as rock-and-roll-fixated teens were eager to prove.

In 1954, television advertising sales surpassed those for radio for the first time, and the network companies accelerated their move to where the money was. For the moment, radio daytime soap operas remained strong because housewives could do their chores while listening. Appreciating this fact, NBC president Sylvester "Pat" Weaver moved to bring a similar dynamic to weekend radio with *Monitor,* a potpourri of interesting modules strung together from 8 A.M. Saturday until midnight on Sunday. *Monitor* was the archetype of the new network radio. It served both listener life-styles and affiliate scheduling needs by providing a wealth of easily digestible segments designed to enhance a variety of listener and local station use patterns. Mutual soon followed with *Companionate*

*Radio.* Announcing the service, MBS program head Robert Monroe rightly observed that "radio should no longer produce shows, but friends instead . . . companions providing information, enjoyment, and entertainment."[30]

Lacking both receivers and listeners willing to use them, FM was hard pressed to serve as anyone's companion. There were approximately 160 fewer FM stations on the air in 1955 than in 1949 (see Figure 7–11), and profits were almost unheard of. The FCC moved to shore up the industry by allowing both *simplex* and *multiplex* operations. Basically stated, *simplex* involved using the main FM broadcast in nonconventional ways, such as transit radio. *Multiplex* services, on the other hand, relied on special equipment to transmit additional program content along with the main over-the-air signal. Chief among these services was commercial-free background music that could be leased to stores and offices (recall our discussion of SCAs in Chapter 2). Such additional revenue streams, it was hoped, would keep more FM stations from folding while regular broadcast FM attempted to establish a niche.

Almost imperceptibly, the radio industry seemed to stabilize in 1956–1957. For the first time in almost a decade, radio network sales figures actually increased. A half-dozen intrepid companies filed applications for new FM stations. Radio may have surrendered its place in the living room to TV, but the new portability in both equipment and programming vastly increased the sound medium's presence in cottages and workshops, and on beaches and patios. Buoyed by rock-and-roll's pied-piper impact on the youth, local radio was posting impressive revenue gains as advertisers flocked to reach this fresh, young consumer market in its members' formative years. The number of FM stations on the air actually increased and more than one million FM receivers were sold. Network radio nonetheless continued to contract to the point that the A.C. Nielsen Company discontinued its

**Figure 7-11**

Number of on-air U.S. radio stations, 1920–1990

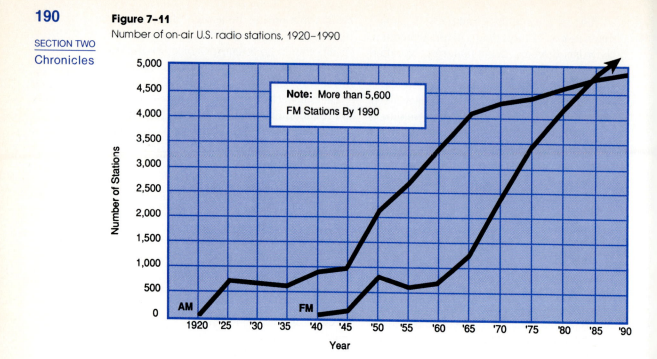

compilation of the top ten radio programs. But local radio was strong on AM and was showing signs of enjoying salable life on the FM side as well.

## Deejay Dangers and Dominance

The prominence of local radio, and its importance to the recording industry, naturally if not inevitably propelled segments of the industry into the practice and scandal of payola (see Chapter 6). With an average of 200 recordings a week being released, some promoters felt that giving undisclosed payoffs to key disc jockeys was the only way to ensure that their tunes had the on-air prominence needed for success. Through such bribes, some deejays in the key Los Angeles market were found to be making from $300 to $500 extra per week by riding certain tunes during their air shifts. Disc jockey morale was already low because the top-40 format was evolving to more tunes per hour and less chance for air personalities to establish themselves as stars. Pushed into a subordinate state in which their on-air persona was less valuable, some disc jockeys grudgingly fol-

## CNN Payola

Play-for-pay is still a factor in the music business. Some industry observers and radio programmers claim that payola is as prevalent as ever—and cite recent prosecutions as evidence.

**191**

CHAPTER 7
Radio
Opera-
tional
History

lowed the format's demands. They talked less and spun more records but augmented their diminished status with under-the-turntable payments for the records they chose.

ASCAP added fuel to the fire when its spokesmen maintained that rock and roll, largely the creative product of BMI-affiliated composers, would never have gotten off the ground without payola. This charge was meant to indict BMI at least as much as rock and roll itself. As if to validate the charge, WABC fired rock-and-roll guru Alan Freed when he refused to sign a statement certifying that he had never received payment for playing certain records. Yet, it was not only the deejays who were at fault. As Dick Osgood, a prominent broadcaster of the time, observed:

The stations themselves were not entirely innocent. One Los Angeles station had charged $225 to play one record 8 times a day, but limited such deals to 3 records a week. This was not called payola; it was called the "test record plan." A station in New York was reported to be offering 6 "plays" a day for $600. One music publisher was paying a weekly fee to have his music played on a TV show. When the cabbage was kicked, [when the practice came to public notice] the agreement was quickly and quietly cancelled.[31]

With the passage of Federal antipayola amendments to the Communications Act, the issue faded from view in the early 1960s, but whether it had also faded from the radio industry remains the subject of periodic debate.

Undebatable in the new decade was the final conversion of network radio into a purely supplemental service for local stations. On November 25, 1960, the last four long-running soap operas (all CBS properties) left the air for good. *Young Dr. Malone, Right to Happiness, The Second Mrs. Burton,* and *Ma Perkins* wound up their plot lines and faded away as their sponsors abandoned them for the greener pastures of video soaps. Virginia Payne, the actress who had played Ma Perkins since the show's first broadcast on December 4, 1933, shuttered her mythical lumberyard in Rushville Center as she and full-service network radio retired together.

But if Ma's national notoriety was gone, a lot of disc jockeys had collectively taken her prominent place in their respective local communities. As a study by the Radio Advertising Bureau revealed, more people knew the names of their area disc jockeys (such as those in Figure 7–12) than could identify the U.S. Senators and cabinet members then making headlines.[32] Radio, it seemed, was not any less popular, only a lot less national.

## (Mostly) Profitable Fragmentation

By 1961, prospects for FM were definitely looking up. FCC authorization of the Zenith/General Electric system for transmitting stereophonic sound created a product that grabbed the attention of the public and receiver manufacturers alike. Simultaneously, advertisers began to show more interest in FM when an industry survey revealed an already available FM audience of seventy million people—about 44 percent of the U.S. population.[33] The appeal of the new stereo receivers seemed likely to expand this penetration rapidly.

### "America's Roommate"
Despite the recent payola scandals, even regulators seemed to be looking at the radio industry (AM as well as FM) in a more favorable light. While new FCC Chairman Newton Minow was labeling television a "vast wasteland," (recall our discussion in Chapter 6), he was refering to radio as "America's roommate." In a speech to the CBS Radio Affiliates

**Figure 7-12**
In the heyday of the deejay, power-house pop music stations trumpeted the identity and quantity of their on-air personalities, like these local stars from the early 1960s

Association, Minow went on to observe the medium's changed role:

Radio is also America's traveling companion. It travels with us like a welcome shadow. . . . We all recognize that entertainment—that music—is the core around which the day's programming is built. But we also know that more people depend on radio for news as it happens, and for news of community affairs, than they do any other means of communication.[34]

**193**

CHAPTER 7

Radio
Opera-
tional
History

There was, however, a downside to radio's localism and reinvigorated popularity. With more stations coming on the air, listening audiences were fragmenting to the point at which national advertisers in particular were finding it difficult to use the medium. With about 3,600 AM facilities and more than 1,000 FM outlets in operation by 1962, competition for sponsor dollars resulted in a jungle of confusing and contradictory rates that made radio time difficult to buy, especially on a regional or national basis. Certainly, the medium's comparatively low cost made it accessible to many small local clients, but the slivering of the listening audience among competing stations made it more and more difficult for a large company to determine which, and how many, stations should carry its advertising.

Relentlessly, both AM and FM operations intensified their search for new and unique formats that would allow them to stand out from the crowd. A singular image was seen as crucial in attracting specific types of listeners and thus, the advertisers striving to reach them. As one means of heightening listener involvement, phone opinion programs were on the upswing. Listeners were encouraged to call in and chat with the show host while the rest of the audience eavesdropped on the conversation. Soon, these offerings evolved into entire talk-radio blocks that attempted to harness local radio's intimate "roommate" quality to which Chairman Minow had referred.

Billing himself as a sort of radio psychiatrist, San Francisco air personality Michael Jackson soon developed a large late-night following as he conducted a sort of on-going group therapy between callers and the listening audience as a whole. Occasionally, this format involved Jackson and similar hosts in unnerving conversations with people allegedly contemplating suicide. Such occurrences raised questions about whether such shows amounted to practicing medicine without a license. Nonetheless, these and more mundane programs like recipe exchanges and on-air swap shops helped make the telephone an important programmatic device for radio stations seeking to air something other than music.

Increasing transistorizing and consequent miniaturization of radio sets meant that the medium, and its talk or music, could now follow the consumer anywhere. This extreme portability helped bolster radio listenership even as the radio ratings companies attempted to find ways of properly documenting such out-of-home use. While both AM and FM benefited from this development, FM alone was given an additional boost when the FCC limited to 50 percent the amount of time FM stations in major cities could duplicate the programming of a commonly owned AM outlet. The resulting creation of new music-heavy (and inexpensive) formats took full advantage of FM's stereophonic appeal while keeping programming costs low. Young listeners in particular gravitated toward the contemporary music that increasingly found exposure on the FM band.

## Format Innovations

Beginning in 1966 on New York's WOR-FM, the format known as Progressive or Free Form rejected shouting top-40 deejays and the formal voices found on adult stations. In their place, progressive enlisted laid-back, conversational communicators who featured albums cuts excluded from conventional playlists.[35] Forerunners of today's AOR (Album-Oriented Rock) outlets, these stations abandoned the rigid structures of conventional programming to give the youth of the sixties an anti-establishment radio service they could call their own. Thus attracted to FM, many of these young listeners came to forget that AM ("antique modulation") even existed.

Other than a few old 50,000-watt powerhouses like WCCO in Minneapolis and WJR in Detroit, or tiny facilities in one-station towns, the something-for-everybody radio station was ceasing to exist. For the most part, a radio station now targeted its programming to a specific segment of the available audience that could then be sold to interested advertisers in pursuit of those particular demographics. Increasingly intercompetitive, both AM and FM stations sought a population sliver they could call their own, and the mechanics of format design became even more important.

A few commercial stations tried to be different by avoiding advertising entirely. They sought, instead, to secure direct listener support for their specialty programs through on-air appeals. Usually offering such off-beat material as jazz, folk songs, operas, and show tunes, such stations pleaded with their audience to send in money as a fair return for not having to listen to commercials. Unfortunately, these on-air appeals were often much more intrusive, and much less entertaining, then real advertisements would have been. (The pledge drives on today's noncommercial stations sometimes resemble these unrelenting listener-subscription efforts.)

Perhaps the most obvious sign of radio fragmentation was ABC's 1967 decision to split itself into four separate networks to better serve the supplementary needs of diversely programmed affiliates. (See Table 7–1.) In putting together this new design, ABC Radio's president, Ralph Beaudin, adroitly avoided violating the FCC's chain broadcasting rules (see Chapter 6) by making certain that the four networks were transmitted at different times of the day rather than simultaneously. ABC could thus claim that it was still operating only one network but choosing to subdivide its functions. (The FCC subsequently eliminated the prohibition on multiple radio network ownership by a single company in 1977.)

In future years, NBC, CBS, and newer players followed the ABC strategy as network radio came full circle. Instead of mounting a full program schedule to which stations had to adapt, an audio network was now an enhancement tool that must conform to operational patterns established by those stations. In short, the local outlets, rather than the national chains, now called the shots.

Many music stations continued to rely on a network as a convenient source for news but, as the 1960s came to a close, another category of outlets was airing more news than any of the networks. Beginning earlier in the decade with Gordon McLendon's XTRA (a Tijuana, Mexico, station serving Southern California) the all-news format caught on in several major markets—most successfully on stations owned by Westinghouse and by CBS. All-news was the ultimate extension of radio's portability and capitalized on a mobile society's need to get quick bursts of information on demand at any time of the day or night. As its performance during the 1965 Eastern Seaboard power blackout had proven, radio could provide instantaneous information under even the most trying circumstances. If a station possessed a back-up power generator, and a listener owned a bat-

**Table 7–1**
**ABC's Four-Way Split, 1967**

| Network | Focus |
|---|---|
| American Information Network | MOR (middle-of-the-road) and talk format stations |
| American Entertainment Network | MOR stations having a greater blend of news, music, and feature programs |
| American Contemporary Network | Rock-and-roll and top-40 stations |
| American FM Network | News and public affairs material designed especially to complement FM's music-heavy emphasis |

tery-powered transistor receiver, radio communication could continue when most other services and media were shut down. All-news built on this always-there premise. Although it was expensive to program due to its high personnel costs, All-news could turn significant profits through its appeal to upscale listeners and the advertisers seeking to reach them. All-news was also a format that was not at a noticeable fidelity disadvantage when programmed on the AM band. This fact was not lost on veteran AM broadcasters who were finding it more difficult to compete with the superiority of FM's music-delivery.

Still, most stations on both bands continued to offer music-oriented formats, which became more precisely delineated as greater competition resulted from additional facilities coming on the air. A format success in one market was quickly cloned in another as format doctors (program consultants) like Bill Drake developed and shipped programmatic concepts around the country. Sometimes, a format that worked wonderfully in one city would bomb miserably in another; but this occurrence did not stop the race to hire the best consultants as broadcasters sought to import someone else's ratings breakthrough into their own market.

## Seventies Sounds

One branch of radio, however, was immune to the influence of program doctors because it was too unstructured to duplicate, even in succeeding days on the same station! This format, or antiformat, was known as underground radio. An extension of the sixties' progressive FM phenomenon, the underground radio of the early 1970s mirrored the social turbulence of its times and provided anti-establishment youth with a broadcast voice for their disaffection. As Dick Kernen (see Figure 7–13), one of its chief practitioners, recalled:

> The FM stations that were showing growth were the, quote 'Underground Free Form,' unquote, radio stations that were playing not only what has now come to be called progressive rock. But they were playing Wagner; they were playing Czechoslovakian folk music; they were playing just an incredible gamut of music. And they were talking a lot. They were playing 20 and 30-minute segments from philosophers like Marcuse. In some instances, it was extremely creative, but no one can be extremely creative 24 hours a day 7 days a week. The bursts of creativity were few and far between but they were brilliant when they occurred.[36]

**Figure 7–13**
Underground radio innovator Dick Kernen

## CNN Rock Trends

Consultants narrowed progressive rock to a set playlist that has resulted in the so-called classic format. College radio stations are the primary remaining outlet for true progressive music product.

Through the influence of master programmer Lee Abrams, underground would eventually mellow out in the post–Vietnam era into more formula-based album-oriented rock (AOR) patterns with narrowed playlists and predictability. As broadcast consultant Joel Lind points out, "Underground of the 60s and Progressive of the 70s didn't really make an impact until Lee Abrams developed AOR by tightening the playlist and bringing structure."[37]

At about the same time, in 1971, automobile manufacturers began offering FM receivers as original equipment on about 20 percent of their new models. This figure rapidly became larger as the decade continued. Because morning and afternoon drive times were now the most important dayparts for urban area stations (the time when radio was the only usable medium for commuters stuck in their cars), FM's inclusion in the dashboard helped significantly to bring the medium to parity with its AM counterpart.

Radio formats continued to multiply in an effort to reach out to listeners in more customized ways. The number of stations playing country music was eight times greater in 1972 than it had been a decade before as advertisers discovered that the country music audience was large, loyal, and not necessarily residing in the country. Black radio stations enlarged their orientation and their numbers by adding jazz, gospel, and African music to their original soul focus.

In 1974, the Associated Press recognized the healthy character of the radio industry and its special formatic needs by launching Associated Press Radio, a twenty-four-hour service of hourly five-and-one-half-minute newscasts designed for easy drop-in into music-heavy schedules. The United Press had begun UPI Audio some fifteen years before, and the entry of the venerable AP into the condensed voice newscast business marked the final armistice in the press-radio war. That same year, even radio drama made a brief comeback under veteran producer Himan Brown with the *CBS Radio Mystery Theater*. Modern U.S. listening patterns proved to be intolerant of the attention demands made by such long-form literary programming, but the brief return to radio's golden age demonstrated that nothing was automatically out of the question in the search for ways to capture listener attention.

In the midseventies, some forty years after Edwin Armstrong's first on-air experiments, FM was finally able (and required) to stand on its own. The FCC strengthened its nonduplication requirements to limit replicated programming on co-located AM/FM facilities to 25 percent in cities with more than 100,000 people  and to 50 percent in communities with a population of 25,000 to 100,000. By this time, AM's share of the radio audience had dropped to about 60 percent, which meant that FM was coming close to achieving equal status with the older service. More important, the bulk of FM's audience was youth-oriented, whereas AM listenership was skewing older. (See Figure 7–14.) FM, in other words, was strengthening its franchise with the new generation, who would stay with that service as they aged.

**197**

CHAPTER 7
Radio
Opera-
tional
History

**Figure 7–14**
1973–1978: FM share of all radio listening Monday–Sunday

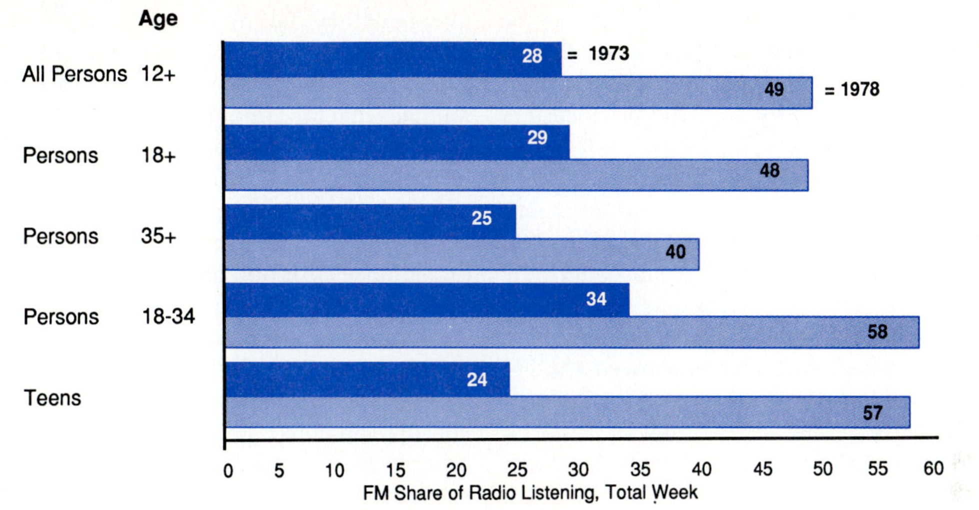

Source: Statistical Research Inc. Spring 1973 and Spring / Fall 1978 RADAR Studies.

## Expanding Services and Flexibilities

By the early 1980s, new networks like NBC's The Source, CBS's RadioRadio and the first of the RKO Radio Networks arose to service the FM boom with music features attractive to younger listeners. New program syndicators also came on the scene with both short-form (individual features) and long-form (complete format) offerings. Once satellite delivery of these services became readily available in the 1980s, this activity multiplied as stations and suppliers were now freed from the limitations and costs of land-line distribution. Gradually, the distinctions between syndicators and networks melted away, to be replaced by the concept of program service. Both AM and FM stations could now get virtually whatever type of material they wanted, and in virtually any length, from any of a wide range of companies that might or might not use the term *network* in their self-descriptions. The name of the game was flexibility, and satellite delivery made that game a convenient one for stations to play. They could mix and match fea-

tures and formatic elements from a number of suppliers as local needs required.

In 1981, even the FCC gave flexibility a boost by eliminating nonentertainment programming and commercial guidelines for radio stations. Each outlet would be free to air as little news and public affairs, and as much advertising, as it saw fit—provided that somewhere in its overall programming it addressed the key issues and problem areas of its community. In many instances, music stations began to play more music, and news stations expanded their news coverage, with even greater distinction between the two being the end result.

At the same time, the Supreme Court's ruling that the FCC had been correct in leaving entertainment format decisions up to individual licensees meant that stations could now pick and change formats as market conditions required. A disgruntled group of listeners could no longer challenge a license renewal because their favorite format had been dropped by the operators of that station. But the FCC's flexibility approach showed a downside as well when it came to AM stereo. When the commission refused to choose a standard from among four competing systems in favor of letting the marketplace decide (see Chapter 2), it seriously impeded adoption of any stereo system by both AM broadcasters and manufacturers.

Overall, however, the 1980s were good to radio in general if not to AM in particular. FCC liberalization of the multiple ownership rules meant that a single group could now own up to twenty-four stations (twelve AM and twelve FM), and the 1986 abandonment of nonduplication regulation allowed AM/FM operators to program their two facilities together or separately as they saw fit. Unfortunately, much of the impetus for this change was the increasingly grim outlook for AM. The ultimate irony was that the nonduplication rules, which had been first adopted to force broadcasters to develop their FM properties, now had to be abandoned because this development had worked *too well.* By 1988, approximately 75 percent of radio listening was devoted to the FM band. Some older AM stations were actually going dark even though the absolute number of AM facilities rose slightly as new stations elsewhere went on the air.

Carried along on the high-capacity and high-fidelity wings of the satellites, national program services expanded their operations even though their numbers declined. Westwood One, which began as a program syndicator, best epitomized the trend as it purchased first the Mutual Broadcasting System and then NBC Radio. That two historic networks could be swallowed up by one syndicator showed that old allegiances were much less important than was the ability to compete in a changed audio environment. Later, as the 90s began, both Westwood and ABC realigned their multiple networks to provide more rational packaging for national advertisers in search of precise target audiences.

The old affiliate/network relationship now became as fragmented as the radio industry itself. Sometimes stations pay for the programming they receive from an outside supplier (whether that supplier calls itself a syndicator or a network). In other instances, the supplier pays the station for carrying the commercials that programming contains. In other situations, a combination of both revenue patterns is used. However it is obtained, a station chooses outside-produced program content because that content possesses the capacity to minimize costs and maximize profit by appealing to the particular listener segment that the station tries to claim as its own.

This does not mean that today's local radio stations are merely passive conduits for satellite-supplied news or entertainment. Local programming is still vital to meeting the listenership's local needs and to distinguishing that station from other outlets with which it might be confused. A few years ago, Arbitron, the largest national radio ratings service, listed 18 format types and subdivided them into 155 variations by which stations attempted to stand out from the crowd. (See Chapter 12.) Whatever the format, however, and whatever national, regional, or local segments used to assemble it, every modern radio station shares a common operational philosophy. As star program consultant Kent Burkhart says,

A programmer is a programmer regardless of format. I have been hired numerous times to program a variety of formats, including News, Talk, Contemporary Hit, Album Rock, Country, Classical, Urban, Black, and Hispanic. I have found that there is not a vast difference in the skills needed to program a News or Contemporary Hits format. The bottom line is that they both require heavy repetition, announcer communication, community awareness, and all the other elements that add up to producing a great radio station.[38]

The search for the great—for the perfect—radio station has been a vibrant part of the in-

**199**

CHAPTER 7

Radio
Opera-
tional
History

dustry since the 1920s. Only the rules and the tools have changed.

## Chapter Flashback

Radio was transformed from wireless experimentation into a self-standing mass communications vehicle in the 1920s. The public's imagination was captured by entertainment and information they could pick off the air with preassembled receivers now available in stores. WEAF's sale of airtime demonstrated that radio could be a money maker in its own right. Large numbers of new stations therefore began operations, and AT&T initiated the first networking activities to link major facilities together. When AT&T withdrew from station ownership to concentrate on intercity distribution lines, NBC (owned by RCA) and CBS soon came to the fore as centers of broadcasting power.

By 1929, radio was already a $40 million business with three healthy networks and the first national hit show in *Amos 'n' Andy*. Even the onset of the Depression did not stop the medium's growth because many people clung to it as the only form of entertainment they could afford. Much of the newspaper industry now perceived radio as an advertising competitor and responded by restricting the amount of wire service material made available for broadcast. Radio countered with news cooperatives of its own and was further bolstered by President Roosevelt's frequent use of the airwaves for direct communication with the citizenry. Some publishers themselves bought radio properties, and the broadcasting business was further solidified with the introduction of the first systemic audience measurement procedures.

Before the end of the 1930s, programming ran the gamut from outstanding cultural presentations to low brow and disparaged fluff. Still, radio's immediacy made it indispensable in monitoring the gathering war clouds. Before long, broadcasting's average salaries were the highest of any industry. Once the United States entered World War II, radio marshalled its resources to help the war effort through news coverage and morale-building entertainment that reflected war-related themes and concerns.

After the war, radio encountered a host of problems. FM suffered from a lack of interest on the part of advertisers, listeners, and even broadcasters themselves. As the network companies and other major operators shifted their resources to the new television, radio as a whole became less national and more local, with deejay programs replacing more and more of the network shows. The development of the transistor receiver helped accelerate the conversion of radio into a highly portable keep-you-company medium to which people could listen in random spurts. The payola scandals demonstrated the potential abuses of the new and music-heavy local programming. Yet they also illustrated the power of the medium in shaping the recording industry.

From the midsixties, radio formats became more fragmented. Newer listeners and music gravitated to the FM band, which, by FCC rule, could no longer merely echo what co-owned AM outlets were playing. Gradually, FM grew to be the equal of AM, and then it surpassed the older medium, with many young listeners avoiding AM altogether. FCC deregulation in the 1980s left stations free to choose and refine whatever format they wished in trying to carve out a salable sliver of the total audience pie. Syndicators and networks now use satellites to supply both individual programs and complete formats to client stations via low-cost satellite delivery.

❏ Review Probes

1. What dual role did AT&T play in the early days of radio broadcasting?
2. Compare and contrast how NBC and CBS were formed.
3. What were some of the factors that made FDR the first real radio president?
4. Why did the Associated Press hold out longer than the other wire services before agreeing to make its material fully available to radio stations?
5. Who was Father Coughlin and why did his activities lead to the NAB Code prohibitions on the sponsorship of controversial issue programs?
6. Why did William Paley of CBS lure away radio personalities from rival networks in the late 1940s? What financial mechanism did he use to accomplish this?

❏ Suggested Background Explorations

Allen, Robert C. *Speaking of Soap Operas.* Chapel Hill: University of North Carolina Press, 1985.

Bannerman, R. LeRoy. *Norman Corwin and Radio: The Golden Years.* University: University of Alabama Press, 1986.

Hilmes, Michelle, *Hollywood and Broadcasting: From Radio to Cable.* Urbana: University of Illinois Press, 1990.

MacDonald, J. Fred. *Don't Touch That Dial! Radio Programming in American Life, 1920–1960.* Chicago: Nelson-Hall, 1979.

Paper, Lewis J. *Empire: William S. Paley and the Making of CBS.* New York: St. Martin's Press, 1987.

Rosen, Philip T. *The Modern Stentors: Radio Broadcasters and the Federal Government, 1920–1934.* Westport, CT: Greenwood Press, 1980.

Routt, Ed, James McGrath, and Fredric Weiss. *The Radio Format Conundrum.* New York: Hastings House, 1978.

Smith, Wes. *The Pied Pipers of Rock 'N' Roll: Radio Deejays of the 50s and 60s.* Marietta, GA: Longstreet Press, Inc., 1989.

# Television Operational History

❏ *While radio service was first capturing broad public attention, television technology remained hidden in laboratories and was discussed only on the pages of technical and electronics hobbyist publications. During these early years, devising a way to transmit video was more important than the content being televised. Real television programming did not begin until members of that public possessed sets on which to receive it. As we discuss in Chapter 5, regularly scheduled U.S. telecasts were initiated by RCA in 1939 immediately after the company's receivers were introduced for sale at the New York World's Fair. Thus, we'll "fade in from black" at that moment.*

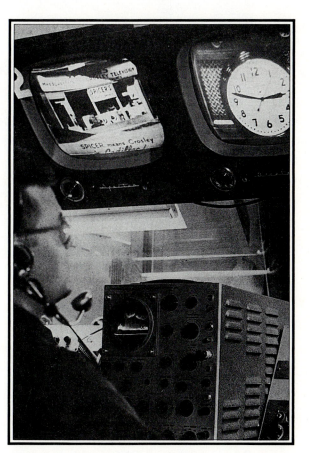

## Big Excitement from Small Pictures

If you were to encounter a 1939 model television set, you might meet an apparatus in which the picture appeared, not on the front of the console, but reflected in a mirrored lid, hinged to its top. This arrangement enabled the small (five- or nine-inch) cathode ray tube surface to be magnified to a comparatively

**Figure 8–1**

RCA boss David Sarnoff dedicates the RCA World's Fair pavilion on April 20, 1939

large ten or twelve inches. The tube was thus mounted in the console vertically rather than horizontally, a compromise made necessary by its unwieldy length. This early receiver presented a tiny, murky view of the world, but a nonetheless magical one.

## Prewar Video

Watching that 441-line NBC picture in New York in April 1939, you would have seen President Roosevelt delivering the dedicatory address for the World's Fair and RCA's David Sarnoff performing a similar rite to initiate television (see Figure 8–1). In the days that followed, studio snippets of plays, puppet shows, comedy and singing acts, and remote sporting events captured by NBC's cumbersome two-bus mobile unit showed what television could accomplish and even more graphically, its limitations.

Despite these restrictions, NBC pressed on and increased its New York transmission schedule to an ambitious 11½ hours a week by the end of August, including the pledge of a no-repeats policy. Some of the few thousand viewers apparently had already complained that certain film programs were being aired more than once.[1] TV's propensity for reruns,

**203**

CHAPTER 8
Television
Opera-
tional
History

it seemed, began very early. Speaking of repetitive programming, the NBC technicians chose to broadcast the Six-Day Bicycle Race from Madison Square Garden. Even though bikes going round and round may have lacked visual variety, the remote was the perfect opportunity to test equipment durability and the specially amplified telephone circuits that Bell Telephone had installed between the Garden and the broadcast transmitter in the Empire State Building.

The following year, NBC used improved video landlines (now called coaxial cables) to relay the Republican Convention from Philadelphia to New York and from there to the RCA experimental station in Schenectady, New York. TV networking was born. Using its own equipment, Philco covered the same event for airing over its own experimental outlet in Philadelphia. By mid-1940, almost two dozen television operations run by RCA/NBC, CBS, DuMont, Philco, and other pioneers were on the air, but only in a tentative, "experimental status." The FCC had rescinded earlier "limited commerical" authorization due to confusion over the specific line system to be used. Not until 1941 was the 525-line picture chosen to supplant 441-line technology and commercial operating authority restored effective July 1 (see Chapter 5).

## Waiting For the Shooting to Stop

Commercial telecasts lasted only five months. Once the United States entered World War II, television was put into moth balls. Its components and inventors were needed for wartime research that eventually resulted in radar. Soon only six stations were left on the air and performed in very subordinate roles. NBC's New York station devoted most of its efforts to video instruction for air raid wardens who gathered around TV sets that had been loaned to city police precincts for this purpose. Some very limited and low-cost programs were aired by the surviving stations for the benefit of the few thousand sets that had been sold. But no new receivers were being produced, and the older models were soon rendered obsolete by parts unavailability and rapidly changing television technology.

For almost four years, real television broadcasting was kept in a straitjacket as military needs superceded civilian applications. This did not mean that no one was thinking about the restoration and development of video broadcasting, however. By mid-1944, with the end of the war now seeming to be in sight, *Newsweek's* radio editor, Robert Conly, put television's status and prospects into focus when he wrote:

> It is evident that the sale of receiving sets and transmitters alone will not make television broadcasting a paying business. Someone must be found to foot the bills. It looks now as if television is going ahead on the same formula as radio, as an advertising medium. . . . The full significance of television, after commercial exploitation has brought it into wide use and near to technical perfection, is not yet clearly apparent. Once it has become a means of mass entertainment, it will automatically become also a system for mass education, culture and travel—and for mass propaganda and deception as well. It may well turn out to be a more useful tool and a more powerful weapon than radio, press, and cinema combined. Like all great technical advances, its value will depend on the wisdom with which it is used.[2]

As early as 1945, telecasters were preparing to retake the stage. NBC's New York studio increased its ability to create television drama through production of such plays as "The Perfect Alibi (see Figure 8–2)." CBS was again promoting its color television system, and the FCC had contrived spectrum allocations that it felt would be sufficient for the new medium. Everything seemed to be in place—or was it?

## Another False Start

Even though 1946 marked the emergence of television from its wartime cocoon, this re-

**Figure 8–2**

Scene from the NBC television broadcast of "The Perfect Alibi" in 1945. Actors (from left to right) are E. J. Ballentine, A. P. Kaye, and Hall Shelton.

birth was anything but spectacular. At the start of the year, only a half dozen stations were on the air, broadcasting to no more than 8,000 surviving sets. All of these stations were functioning without advertising. Instead, their operating costs were being absorbed by the research and development arms of their parent companies. The FCC had resumed processing station applications in October 1945. Almost half of these applications were subsequently withdrawn, however, because many would-be telecasters believed that it would take at least four years for any station to become profitable. Receiving sets were expensive and scarce, and no one seemed to know

whether color would make these sets as obsolete as were the prewar models. Nonetheless, some new stations were under construction in the hopes that the video industry would soon get on track.

In 1947, television first started to hit its stride, much in the same way that radio had begun to blossom in 1921. Before the year was out, twelve stations were commercially broadcasting. Advertisers were lining up to buy airtime, the public was waiting cash-in-hand for the sets that were now rolling off the production lines, and enterprising tavern owners in cities served by television were finding that a receiver over the bar was a potent method for attracting new clientele. Bab-O (a powdered cleanser) became one of television's pioneer sponsors when female viewers were offered a green plastic replica of a good-luck scarab once worn by the ancient Egyptian queen Hatshepsut. Soon ABC was flooded with envelopes containing the required quarter and Bab-O label, and the TV hook or premium commercial began. In the absence of video audience measurement, and because entire neighborhoods often watched television on a single set, such hook spots helped both sponsors and broadcasters estimate how many people might have seen their televised messages.

Some experts still believed that the building of a television system was too costly to be met by advertising revenues alone. Zenith, a pioneer broadcaster and set manufacturer, therefore proposed a pay-as-you-view system it called Phonevision. Viewers would receive programming over telephone lines with the charges for the shows they watched added to their phone bill. Many newspapers welcomed the idea because it would have removed television as a competitor for advertisers' dollars. But few broadcasting industry executives thought such a system could generate the kinds of profit margins they felt advertising would eventually be capable of providing. Phonevision also had substantial technical problems that needed to be overcome.

The experienced broadcasters who were then engaged in television recognized that, as had been the case in radio, networking was the best way to increase program quality while decreasing operating costs. AT&T's coaxial cables and microwave relays were the means to this end. By June 1947, AT&T announced it would develop a regular commercial rate schedule for telecaster use of its linkages. By the end of the year, NBC had established a live network that interconnected its stations in New York, Philadelphia, Washington, and Schenectady, and competitors at CBS, ABC, and DuMont were poised to do the same as soon as AT&T could establish service. It took a bit more time to accomplish, but with the first riveting telecasts of a World Series and the video coverage of the Joe Lewis versus Jersey Joe Walcott heavyweight championship, consumers were ready and waiting. As *Fortune* magazine commented, "Public interest in TV as a gadget is so great that there is no question but that receiving sets in quantity can be sold . . . . Buyers will be willing to take their chances on the quality of the programs."[3]

# Mixed Metaphor: The Freeze Heats Up an Industry

By 1948, people everywhere in the United States wanted TV, and potential telecasters everywhere wanted to bring it to them. That neither group immediately got their wish was attributable to a variety of supply problems. As we discovered in Chapter 5, the first problem dealt with spectrum supply as the FCC came to realize that its earlier blueprint for TV allocations was entirely inadequate. Therefore, before the television band had a chance to become overoccupied, the commission's TV freeze put a moratorium on the granting of new station construction permits. The body of new stations coming on the air was thus limited to those that had already been authorized. This scarcity seemed only to increase public interest in the new medium as the facilities that did begin operation enjoyed immense prominence.

Television sets were still scarce as well, but the full conversion to a peacetime economy was generating new production lines at a number of manufacturing plants. The price of a standard set was now about $300. This amount of money was a working person's monthly wages but an amount that many excited consumers were willing to pay.

**Figure 8–3**
John Cameron Swayze hosts NBC-TV's first continuing evening newscast, the *Camel News Caravan*

## Early Breakthroughs and Drawbacks

The 1948 political conventions were carried by new coaxial and microwave relays to eighteen stations serving ten million viewers. This further stimulated network activities and the expansion of landlines that would make live networking possible. Following the 1948 conventions, regular television network news made its formal debut via two competing newscasts. Having moved from NBC radio to cover the televised conventions, John Cameron Swayze stayed on the tube to initiate the *Camel News Caravan* (see Figure 8–3). Wholly sponsored by a cigarette company, this quarter-hour of straight story-reading and brief film clips remained on the air until *The Huntley-Brinkley Report* replaced it in 1956. Swayze's show was a counter to CBS's *Douglas Edwards with the News* (initially called the *CBS TV News*) that had begun a few weeks earlier and was reaching 30,000 viewers in New York, Philadelphia, Boston, and Washington. Edwards was also a news reader, but his fifteen-minute program proved more durable. It remained on the air until 1962, when

Walter Cronkite took over. Soon after, both networks permanently expanded their newscasts to a half-hour.

ABC, which for several years lacked the resources to be competitive either in news or television programming in general, did manage to put its New York flagship station on the air in 1948 and began lining up affiliates. Meanwhile, the DuMont network (the only company that had carried on with extensive program activities through the war years) linked up its stations in New York, Pittsburgh, and Washington. Founded and controlled by electronics expert Allen B. DuMont, this independent company manufactured cameras, transmitters, and associated station equipment as well as a line of television receivers. Even though it would ultimately lack the clout to compete with the big three, DuMont pioneered television networking in a number of ways and also introduced significant innovations in consumer sets, including a giant thirty-inch oval picture tube. Some people had to tear out doorways to get this set in the house. "Who wants to look at the world

**207**

CHAPTER 8
Television
Opera-
tional
History

through a knot hole?" asked DuMont,[4] and his pursuit of big pictures stimulated larger manufacturers to similar tube-stretching efforts.

For the fifty stations in operation by the end of 1948, costs still exceeded advertising revenues, but sponsor and consumer interest was escalating rapidly. Profitability now seemed just around the corner, with many advertisers following the old radio practice of wholly sponsoring programs. One of the first breakthrough successes in such endeavors was NBC's *Texaco Star Theater,* an outlandish video return to vaudeville in which star comedian Milton Berle costumed himself as everything from a heavily made up matron to a gigantic pumpkin pie. With running sight gags and slapstick to tie a number of acts and performers together, the Berle show was television's first runaway hit, garnering a 1948 Hooperating New York audience share of more than 80 percent.

To relay this and other programs to affiliates not yet reachable by cable or microwave facilities, networks made film recordings (*kinescopes*) off the face of control room monitors as the show was airing live. These foggy, low-definition movies were then bicycled (physically shipped) to distant affiliates for airing on subsequent evenings. It was all incredibly primitive but welcomed by viewers who were intrigued even by stations' pre-sign-on test patterns.

When network offerings or old films weren't available, stations put on any local production they could think of to keep viewer interest and get advertiser attention. Often, these were little more than radio concepts at which a television camera was pointed! A typical example was the *Pat 'n' Johnny Show* on WXYZ-TV in Detroit. Every weekday afternoon, beginning in 1949, a rotund deejay from the co-owned radio station (Johnny Slagle) and a statuesque young blonde (Pat Tobin) carried on for an hour or more with drop-in guests, chitchat, record spinning, and shots of studio pets. If nothing else was working, the audio engineer would cue up the tune "*Rag Mop,*" and the camera would focus on the show's guinea pig in the hope that the furry little creature would be doing something of interest. (See Figure 8–4.) More often than not, he was snoozing under the hot studio lights. But viewers were still enthralled, and *Pat 'n' Johnny Show* "became one of the first real hit shows on Detroit television."[5]

In this same year, the Academy of Television Arts and Sciences was formed to give out program awards labeled Emmys (after the "immy" or image orthicon tube which had made television cameras much more light-efficient). The first Emmy for "Outstanding Personality of the Year" was won by ventriloquist Shirley Dinsdale for *The Judy Splinters Show,* which bore the name of her dummy. Both Dinsdale and her wooden partner showed an affinity for straw cowboy hats and plaid shirts, and Judy spent a lot of time telling child viewers how to brush their teeth—no real coincidence given the prominence of toothpaste advertisers on the television airwaves. Even though these first Emmys covered only Los Angeles, *Judy Splinters* and the award system that honored her soon spread across the country.

Audience measurement was assuming a national posture as well; 1949 was the first year in which Hooper, then the largest television ratings operation, extended its activities to all areas of the country being served by network television. By this time, at least 40 percent of the U.S. population was reachable by at least one television station even though there were fewer than two million sets in use. Viewership was much higher than the set figure suggests, however, as millions more people watched with a neighbor who had purchased a receiver. Kids would crowd into that living room in the afternoon to watch *Judy Splinters, Howdy Doody,* and *Kukla, Fran, and Ollie,* to be replaced in the evening by men watching the fights or couples enjoying *Your Show of Shows* with Sid Caesar and Imo-

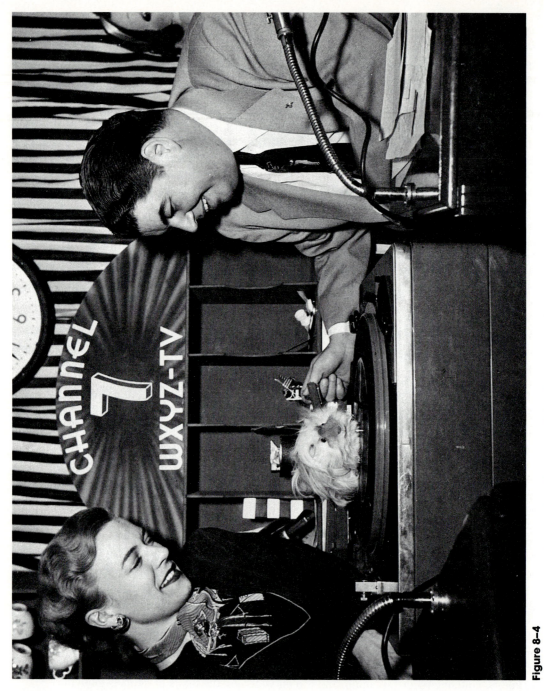

**Figure 8–4**
Pat, Johnny, and animal side-kick Rag Mop of WXYZ-TV's *Pat 'n' Johnny Show*. Recycling radio to create early TV.

gene Coca and Mike Stokey's *Pantomime Quiz*. Those first TV's gathered people together in front of their flickering images like cave dwellers must have been drawn to the first campfires. The phenomenon was new, it was exciting, and (once you finished the installment payments on the set) it was free.

## Free TV Hits Its Stride

As early as 1950, however, television's free attribute was being challenged by alternative concepts. Zenith was given FCC approval for a Chicago field test of its Phonevision—the pay-TV-via-telephone line system. In New York, the Skiatron Corporation was using WOR-TV for a different kind of pay TV in which an over-the-air broadcast signal was decoded by a special device attached to the customer's set. Both of these systems immediately encountered opposition from the film industry, however, which was contemplating the idea of theater television—big screen broadcasts of prestige programs that would keep the public coming to the movie house. Consequently, both Zenith and Skiatron discovered that film product was somehow not available for their experimentation.

For its part, the viewing public seemed content with the advertiser-supported free TV that was building the medium. By the end of 1950, more than 100 stations (all authorized before the freeze) were on the air. About 60 percent of the public was now served by at least 1 station, and 7½ million sets were in use.[6] Microwave relays had been improved to the point at which they were fully competitive with coaxial cables as a means of networking signals,[7] and network activities expanded even more rapidly as a result. NBC's *Kate Smith Hour* became the first daytime program to be shown coast-to-coast and was soon joined by *The Gary Moore Show* on CBS. At night, a new crop of quiz shows such as *What's My Line?* and *Beat the Clock* on CBS shared the evening audience with immigrant programs from radio such as Groucho Marx's *You Bet Your Life* and *Your Hit Parade* on

NBC and *The Jack Benny Show* on CBS. Lacking a radio operation from which to draw, DuMont had to develop original properties of its own. The most notable DuMont offering was *The Jackie Gleason Show*, a comedy/variety extravaganza.

The following year, the most successful television situation comedy of all time, *I Love Lucy*, made its CBS debut. On NBC, a much less heralded but much more innovative comedy program was launched from Philadelphia. *The Ernie Kovacs Show* (see Figure 8–5) stretched the boundaries of the medium with ingenious use of visual devices, direct close-up conversations with the camera, and Dutch Masters cigar commercials that were as zany as the show they sponsored. Comedian Kovacs demonstrated that true television was not just radio in front of a camera, or a movie projected on a cathode ray tube, but a unique technology. When he moved his show to CBS in early 1953, Kovacs pioneered the exploitation of special effects and became the first producer willing to spend thousands of dollars to achieve a 4- or 5-second shot.

The fifteen million sets in service in 1951 carried other breakthroughs as well. President Truman's address at the San Francisco peace conference officially ended the war with Japan at the same time it inaugurated AT&T's permanent transcontinental video network. Only 13 of the country's 107 stations were not yet interconnected, and these outlets received coverage of the event via film (kinescope) recording. A few months earlier, CBS had aired its first color program, a variety special featuring several big stars and sixteen commercials in order to demonstrate color's impact to and for advertisers. Other colorcasts were sporadically programmed throughout the remainder of the year, but color sets were few and the CBS color system would soon be supplanted by one developed by RCA (see Chapter 5). As if to mark television's coming of age as a responsible medium, the NAB (temporarily renamed the National Association of Radio and Television

**Figure 8–5**
The comedy of Ernie Kovacs probed the potentialities of television technology

Broadcasters) implemented a self-regulatory TV Code to parallel the document developed for radio decades before.

The self-protective Code came none too soon. In 1952, crime-fighting Senator Estes Kefauver launched a probe of the relationship between rising juvenile delinquency and violent television and radio programming. Ironically, TV had given Kefauver national stature the year before with its complete coverage of his Crime Investigating Committee's hearings into organized crime. As the senator was being accused by some broadcasters of biting the hand that had so lavishly enlarged his prominence, the lifting of the freeze by the FCC diverted attention to a much more far-reaching—and positive—development. The pent-up demand for television service was released as the FCC began accepting new applications for the restructured VHF and UHF bands. Within a year, the number of on-air stations tripled, and television injected itself into almost every nook and cranny of the land.

## Regroupings

Freed from Freeze constraints, the television industry seemed to expand in all directions.

The nation's video networking capabilities were extending into more remote areas as AT&T and lesser players improved their co-axial cable and microwave relay installations. Network programming had pushed into the early morning hours with NBC's *Today*. Hosted by low-key Dave Garroway, who was frequently assisted by a rambunctious chimpanzee called J. Fred Muggs, *Today* demonstrated that a day-opening blend of news, weather, interviews, and cast conversation could assemble a potent audience of housewives as well as people preparing to go off to work. Even though the news component on *Today* was limited, it compared favorably with the network quarter-hour newscasts in prime time.

In a last-ditch effort to become competitive, ABC strengthened itself by merging with the United Paramount Theater chain that the Justice Department, in an antitrust action, had caused to be spun off from its parent studio. Leonard Goldenson, the Paramount Theater executive who became the new ABC president, made it clear that FCC approval of the merger would give the network the resources it needed to offer programming that was the equal of what NBC and CBS were providing.

But if ABC's prospects seemed improved, those of UHF broadcasters were already grim as high operating costs and limited numbers of receivers threatened to kill the baby in its cradle. Several UHF owners urged the FCC to allow them to convert to "subscription television" (pay TV) in order to raise the revenue to survive. However, after three years of experimentation by Zenith, Skiatron, and others, the FCC was not convinced of the viability or propriety of such a use of the public airwaves. Thus, pay TV and UHF continued to languish as graphic exceptions to television's prosperity.

As we learn in Chapter 5, the commission did act favorably on RCA's new compatible color system. Beginning with *The Colgate Comedy Hour* telecast on November 22, 1953, NBC began its regular, if limited, schedule of colorcasts that culminated in an all-color schedule some thirteen years later. The following year, CBS tentatively reentered the color arena (via the RCA system, of course) when it presented its popular *Toast of the Town* with Ed Sullivan in color. NBC countered with a number of 90-minute color spectaculars that featured big stars, lavish production numbers, and often mismatched colors when the picture switched from one camera to another! Lacking the resources for such endeavors, both DuMont and ABC remained entirely black and white for the time being.

ABC did turn its competitive disadvantage to advantage, nonetheless, in its gavel-to-gavel coverage of the Army-McCarthy Hearings (see Chapter 6) before the U.S. Senate's Permanent Investigations Subcommittee. When the committee insisted that the coverage be unsponsored, NBC and CBS opted for brief film segment use in order to preserve their extensive advertising revenues in regular programming. On the other hand, with comparatively few daytime programs and sponsors anyway, ABC executives wisely decided that end-to-end live coverage would not be much of a financial sacrifice and might attract new audience to its affiliates. The ploy worked, and ABC's competitive position was given a substantial boost. DuMont carried complete coverage as well but, with fewer affiliates and a shrinking program schedule, the smallest network was already terminally ill.

## Army-McCarthy Effects

In addition to building viewership for ABC, the Army-McCarthy hearings proved to be the downfall of Senator Joseph McCarthy, who had manipulated public fears of Communist infiltration into a power-grabbing witch hunt. Key preludes to the hearings had been two *See It Now* broadcasts in which newsman Edward R. Murrow exposed the smear and bullying tactics that McCarthy had used so successfully in his showcase committee search for "Reds." CBS carried the Murrow pieces, but they refused to promote them.

Consequently, Murrow and his producer, Fred Friendly, paid for newspaper ads out of their own pockets. In fact, to provide balance, CBS gave the Senator the opportunity to prepare a response of his own in which he characteristically labeled Murrow "the leader and the cleverest of the jackal pack that is always found at the throat of anyone who dares expose Communists and traitors."[8] (see Figure 8–6.)

McCarthy's attack backfired. President Eisenhower, who, up to this time, had remained largely silent on McCarthy's activities, publicly stated that he counted Murrow as a friend. The stage was thus set for the Army-McCarthy hearings, which probed the Senator's charges that the Army was full of subversives. Already primed by the Murrow broadcasts as to McCarthy's unsavory methods, viewers clearly saw a man who would use any device to accomplish his ends. When the soft-spoken attorney for the Army, Joseph Welch, dramatically rebutted a McCarthy charge that one of Welch's young associates was a Communist, the hearings, and the Senator's political power, were fundamentally finished. Television, however reluctantly, had demonstrated its capacity to expose abuses of power. Less positively, this string of episodes also showed that the medium was much more adept at depicting struggles between riveting individuals than it was at illuminating philosophical ideas and Constitutional issues.

## Surmounting the Fifties

By the mid-1950s, television's engaging if not always insightful programming had firmly established the medium as a central facet of U.S. life. More than 450 stations were on the air, and two-thirds of U.S. households now contained a television receiver. The success of NBC's late evening *Tonight Show* with Steve Allen indicated that viewer and sponsor interest in network fare was not restricted by time of day—as long as the shows were appealing. On the other hand, audiences were highly intolerant of companies lacking the financial resources to compete fully. By the middle of 1955, DuMont had shrunk to a single network show (Monday night boxing) and two owned stations as a prelude to the firm's total disengagement from broadcasting later that same year.

Taken as a whole, the entire UHF business was in almost as bad shape as DuMont, with

**Figure 8–6**
Legendary broadcast journalist Edward R. Murrow proved that television could successfully take on a powerful political figure

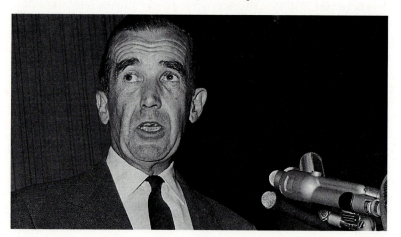

several broadcasters turning in their licenses. Meanwhile, subscription television remained a highly controversial and solely experimental concept. The movie interests, the hugely successful VHF telecasters, and their networks were more than happy to leave this idea pigeonholed at the FCC. A small cable television (CATV) industry had emerged to extend existing broadcasters' signals into rural or mountainous areas, but this merely assisted the already profitable outlets by providing their advertisers with bonus viewers. In short, the medium was consolidating its successes and unceremoniously burying its failures.

One breakthrough success in 1956 was television's obtaining of feature films for broadcast. Almost since the medium's commercial beginning, television had been denied access to movies by a film industry that viewed video as a competitive threat. In much the same manner that the newspaper establishment had sought to keep news off the radio, Hollywood interests had done whatever they could to prevent their products from migrating to the tube. At the same time, however, they were aggressively entering the video marketplace with TV series produced by their subsidiary corporations!

Several inconclusive antitrust skirmishes over movie access had accomplished nothing, but now, some profit-seeking studios could no longer resist the substantial telecaster market. RKO, 20th Century Fox, and Columbia Pictures' Screen Gems division were among those companies agreeing to make certain of their theatrical films available for broadcast. However, in an attempt to protect box office exclusivity for first- and second-time releases, the producers did not provide any movie made after 1948 to the broadcasters. Meanwhile, some television executives and critics were warning that extensive airing of movies, new or old, would dilute video's potential to be a truly unique medium. RCA's David Sarnoff, for example, felt that a "film invasion" would cause television to turn from its

innovative "live" character and "ride a toboggan of decline."[9] *Time* magazine critic John Crosby agreed. "The best of TV," wrote Crosby, "are the 'unrehearsed' things like conventions, ball games, the McCarthy hearings."[10] (Today's political conventions, conversely, are *scrupulously rehearsed* in an effort to achieve maximum impact from this free coverage as politicians have become much more sophisticated in their manipulation of television.)

Among the TV original events in 1957 were lavish productions of *Annie Get Your Gun*, Richard Rodgers's musical version of *Cinderella*, and Mark Twain's *Prince and the Pauper*. Yet, as Crosby had predicted, it was the unrehearsed actualities that generated the most attention. When Soviet Premier Nikita Khrushchev was featured in a taped Moscow interview on CBS's *Face the Nation*, and Yugoslavian strongman Marshal Tito appeared on Edward R. Murrow's *See It Now*, television's ability to create a global forum was clearly demonstrated. In fact, some members of Congress felt that such appearances by Communist leaders should not be permitted unless they had first been cleared by the State Department. Fortunately, the McCarthy era had largely passed, and such suggestions were not seriously entertained by most government officials.

Television's power was felt in the commercial entertainment arena, too, as the appeal of the tube seriously undercut the attraction of the silver screen. In 1957 alone, some 12,000 movie houses closed their doors. Of the 17,800 U.S. theaters left in existence, one-third were drive-ins,[11] which offered young couples an environment for more participatory pastimes than just watching the movie. If there was a bright spot for theater operators, it was that pay television was not evolving as an additional competitive threat. The FCC and the Congress had both been successfully lobbied to prevent any quick authorization of over-the-air subscription TV, and the pay cable experiment in Bartlesville, Oklahoma, failed after just nine months due to lack of consumer interest (see Chapter 5).

Regular CATV was faring better, with about 600 small systems serving perhaps a half-million homes. Even though most of these homes would otherwise have been outside the service areas of existing stations, the FCC was beginning to worry that the presence of a cable system in a smaller market might preclude the establishment of a financially viable local station.

A more broad-based concern of the time was being expressed by educators who perceived the non-dominant television medium as a serious threat to childrens' physical and mental development. "TV is reducing our children to a race of spectators," warned an article in *School and Society*. "Last year in homes with television sets, three-fourths of all the families in the country, more total time was spent watching television than in any other single activity except sleep."[12] In response both to this kind of criticism and to the negative fallout from the quiz show scandals (see Chapter 6), commercial telecasters set up the Television Information Office (TIO) in 1959 to research television's societal impact and to provide educational data about the medium to schools, professional groups, and other opinion leaders.

The industry the TIO began defending was clearly a much more financially and technologically secure entity than it had been at the beginning of the decade. For one thing, ABC was now closing the competitive gap with the other two networks by pioneering the strategy of *counterprogramming*—putting on a show as divergent as possible from what the other two nets were airing at the time. Rather than engage heavily in the specials and spectaculars of CBS and NBC, ABC largely stuck to regularly scheduled series in an attempt to establish audience viewing routines. Even though it remained a black-and-white programmer, this did not put the smallest network at much of a disadvantage because CBS offered only a few random hours of color, and

even NBC's schedule was limited. Color-set costs remained high, but the perfection of color videotape was about to provide a highly flexible recording format that would gradually make colorcasting the norm as both advertisers and consumers came to expect and demand it.

## TV's Young Adulthood

Nevertheless, as the 1960s began, only about 1 percent of the fifty million TV sets in the United States were color receivers. The new decade's start thus was marked not so much by increased colorization as by tightened network control of a still black-and-white viewing environment.

Partly in response to the quiz show scandals in which sponsor packaging of the properties had contributed to fraud, and partly because they could no longer afford to maintain a sponsored show viewers weren't watching, the networks themselves now licensed more than 80 percent of the programs. Instead of a sponsor's producing a property and bringing it to the net, the network now contracted for development of the show and then sold advertisements around it to a number of clients. Thus, a series that was doing poorly in the ratings could be cancelled at any time rather than continue to wither on the air because its sponsor/packager had already contracted for a full thirteen or more weeks.

Meanwhile, an increasing number of prime-time series were being produced for the three networks by the major film studios. Hollywood may still have recoiled from allowing its major movies to be shown on the tube, but it was very willing to produce original series under lucrative television contracts. For more and more studios, in fact, network program production was essential to fiscal survival.

215

CHAPTER 8
Television
Opera-
tional
History

## News and Numbers

In 1960, a proper accommodation with television seemed important for politicians as well. More candidates were spending vast sums of money on TV advertising, and exposure on news programs was essential to establish voter recognition. The most notable exposure, of course, was that enjoyed by Senator John F. Kennedy in the four so-called Great Debates with Vice-President Richard M. Nixon (see Figure 8–7). Initially, Kennedy wasn't as familiar a figure as Nixon, but their joint debate appearances brought him to national recognition parity with his opponent. In the first debate, on September 26, 1960, some 75 million people (the largest audience yet assembled) saw a relaxed and well-made-up Kennedy in a dark suit and a haggard, ill-shaven Nixon clothed in washed-out gray. On radio, Nixon's responses seemed more knowledgeable and to-the-point. But on U.S. TV screens, his drawn, almost devious appearance spoke much louder than his words.

Some theorists attribute the vice-president's extremely close election loss to this first debate and thus, to this visual shortcoming. Whether Kennedy's victory margin was due to Great Debate #1 was less important than the fact that a number of politicians believed so. Kennedy became our first television president in the same way that Roosevelt had become our first radio chief executive. In

**Figure 8–7**
Kennedy and Nixon square off in one of the later television debates. Nixon had now learned the importance of makeup and is wearing a dark suit.

skillfully adapting to the new medium of their respective times, each man enhanced his own image as well as that of the communications vehicle that had grown up in time to carry that image. As Roosevelt began the live fireside chats, so Kennedy soon inaugurated the *live* TV press conference to establish a powerful and direct link between himself and the citizenry. (Kennedy's predecessor, Dwight Eisenhower, had allowed *filming* of news conferences, but he reserved the right to edit them before broadcast.)

Scarcely fifteen years since its postwar hatching, television was now a fully grown industry with almost 600 stations. In the early sixties, virtually every household had access to a set by which to view a wide array of film and increasingly *taped* entertainment programming. With the common availability of videotape, the risks inherent in live shows and commercials had largely been abandoned in favor of safer prerecording. Newscasts remained live, of course, and were thus in place to cover the flights of astronauts and the murder of the television president in Dallas on November 22, 1963. Audience measurement studies showed that more than 90 percent of U.S. homes watched at least a portion of President Kennedy's telecast funeral and demonstrated that the visual medium was now firmly positioned as a U.S. household necessity. Many elitists scoffed at much of the programming, but few felt they could afford to isolate themselves from the medium itself.

That the great majority of the people in the United States watched television was certain. But what and when they watched was becoming a subject of major contention. The House Special Subcommittee on Investigations, in a wide-ranging exploration of radio and television ratings practices, found numerous shortcomings in how these audience figures were being calculated and presented. For one thing, three of broadcasting's top ratings services, including A.C. Nielsen (the leading television measurement firm), were claiming that their figures were 100 percent accurate.

When this assertion could not be proven to the Congress or the Federal Trade Commission, the companies agreed to abandon the claim and to call their figures what they were—audience estimates. Stations were also put on notice by both the FTC and the FCC that any contentions they made about audience size would have to be substantiated. Merely quoting a ratings service would no longer be sufficient.

Despite these problems, ratings continued to be a powerful and irreplaceable determiner of programming and advertiser decisions; and those advertisers were predisposed to spend more and more dollars in television (see Figure 8–8). So, to strengthen both ratings credibility and accuracy, the NAB set up the Broadcast Rating Council as a vehicle for setting standards for and monitoring performance of the various ratings services. This effort at self-policing helped dissuade the FTC and FCC from adopting additional regulations in this area, but both government agencies continued to monitor the situation closely. From this time on, the Broadcast Rating Council (renamed the Electronic Media Rating Council in 1982) made certain that measurement companies provided significant disclosure of the methodologies, sample sizes/compositions, and data adjustment policies being used.

One branch of television that did not require a ratings service to document its problems was pay TV. In 1962, the FCC authorized RKO's WHCT in Hartford, Connecticut, to broadcast a scrambled picture that viewer decoder boxes would unscramble for a fee. A year later, only 2,200 households had agreed to subscribe to the service, even though RKO had spent millions of dollars in lining up special sports, movie, and entertainment events.[13] Despite this lack of success, another pay-TV effort emerged on the opposite coast in 1964. Initiated by former NBC executive Sylvester "Pat" Weaver, Subscription Television Inc. in Los Angeles used wires rather than a scrambled over-the-air signal to distrib-

**217**

CHAPTER 8
Television
Opera-
tional
History

**Figure 8–8**
Growth in advertising media expenditures, 1955–1974

*Source: McCann Erickson*

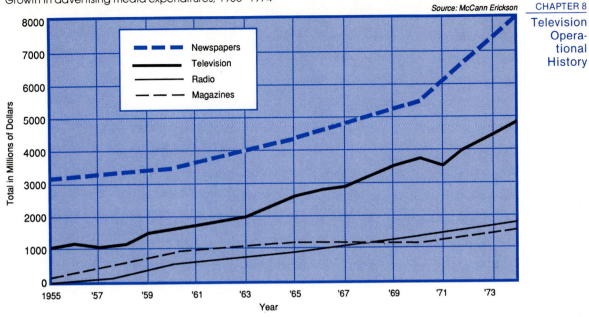

ute exclusive Los Angeles Dodgers and San Francisco Giants baseball telecasts plus theatrical productions and select United Artists movies to some 2,500 subscribers. In reaction, antipay forces put a state proposal on the California ballot that sought to outlaw pay television as contrary to public policy. This successful referendum was subsequently declared unconstitutional, but the public sentiment it mirrored had, by that time, caused the company to fold.

Nationwide, 1964 saw unprecedented election coverage by the television networks and the emergence of hard-hitting negative political commercials. In one such commercial, the Democrats showed a little girl counting daisy petals while a voiceover announcer counted down to a nuclear explosion. This spot attempted to capitalize on Republican candidate Barry Goldwater's alleged willingness to use tactical atomic weapons (see Figure 8–9). Republicans countered with a 30-minute film called "Choice" that purported to show the moral decay of the United States under the

Democrats. It was capped by a shot of a Lincoln Continental automobile bouncing recklessly across a field while the unseen driver periodically pitched out empty beer cans—a reference to a reported Easter ride taken across his ranch by President Lyndon Johnson. In response to protests from the other side, "Daisy Petal" only ran once and Goldwater himself stopped the airing of "Choice" before it was ever shown nationally. Nonetheless, attack commercials had now come to television with a vengeance.

## Technology to Praise and Blame

Also coming in with a vengeance by the mid-sixties was color television. After years of slow set sales and limited programming, improvements in home receivers, broadcasters' color videotape recorders, and color technology in general finally provided the stimuli the industry needed. By the end of 1966, both CBS and NBC were airing almost all-color primetime schedules and ABC was striving to catch up. This programming, in turn, forced

# IN 1964, LYNDON JOHNSON

CHILD: One. Two. Three.

Four. Five. Seven.

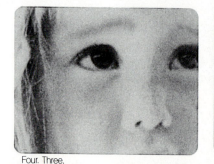

Four. Three.

Two One.

To make a world in which all of God's

children can live.

**Figure 8–9**
The ''Daisy Petals'' negative political spot

# WON THE ELECTION IN 60 SECONDS.

Six. Sev... Eight. Nine.    Nine...

MAN: Ten. Nine. Eight. Seven.

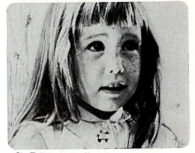

Six. Five.

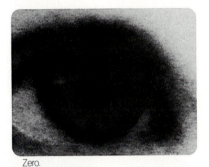

Zero.

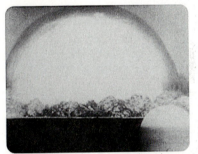

LYNDON JOHNSON: These are the stakes.

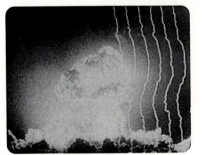

Or to go into the dark.

We must either love each other or we must die.

VOTE FOR PRESIDENT JOHNSON
ON NOVEMBER 3.

VOICE OVER: Vote for President Johnson
on November third. The stakes are too high
for you to stay home.

Many believe this powerful message ruined Senator Goldwater's chances of reassuring skeptical voters of
his commitment to peaceful solutions. Nothing informs, educates and motivates people to action like advertising.

## ADVERTISING. ONE OF THE MOST EFFECTIVE TOOLS EVER INVENTED.

*This ad is brought to you in the interest of advertising by Levine, Huntley, Schmidt & Beaver and Adweek.*

stations to colorize so that their local news-casts did not look obsolete by comparison. The NBC Peacock was introduced as the symbol of that network's polychrome commitment, and sales of color sets skyrocketed while black-and-white sales actually declined. After twenty years of doubt, it was now clear that the entire television industry would be converted to color in the near future.

At the same time, the Early Bird and Lani Bird relay satellites, together with spectacular coverage of the astronauts' Gemini flights and Surveyor's unmanned pictures from the moon, raised the curtain on an era of space telecommunications that would have significant ramifications for domestic and international program distribution.

Almost immediately, the twin technologies of color and satellite distribution were enlisted to cover the war in Vietnam. For the first time, viewers saw battlefield carnage up close, in living, bloody color, and with only a few hours' delay between the time the pictures were filmed and when they were aired following satellite transmission to network headquarters. Some voices in the military complained that this enhanced communication system was undermining the national will to win. Other people welcomed it as a chance for the public at home to comprehend the real challenges faced by U.S. armed forces in carrying out the administration's Southeast Asian policies. Both sides now recognized, as did television journalists, that video-encapsulated warfare had moved the psychological frontlines into the living room and with public reactions that could not always be predicted or controlled.

By 1968, television's technical capacity for the graphic coverage of real-life violence was demonstrated in the cities of the United States as well as in the hamlets of Vietnam. The assassination of Martin Luther King and the riots that followed, the murder of Senator Robert Kennedy in a California hotel, and the chaotic confrontations between Chicago po-

lice and protestors outside the Democratic National Convention all made for television coverage that was as compelling as it was anxiety-producing. Often, there was a tendency to blame the messenger for the event. As some military officials were criticizing video for undermining the war effort, so Mayor Richard Daley lambasted television's revelations that showed Chicago police pummeling news personnel as well as protesters. "They're in the crowd and many of them are hippies themselves in television and radio and everything else," the mayor charged. "They are a part of the movement and some of them are revolutionaries and they want these things to happen."[14] Only five months previously, President Johnson's National Advisory Commission on Civil Disorders had concluded that, even though radio and television made an effort to give factual reports of riots, the overall effect of their activities was "an exaggeration of both mood and event."[15] Clearly, television was being taken seriously as a national force, but this recognition proved to be a mixed blessing, at least as far as governmental relations were concerned.

The following year, the new Republican vice-president, Spiro Agnew, heightened television/politician tensions even more (see Figure 8–10). In a Des Moines speech to Midwest Republicans, given nationwide network coverage, Agnew blasted television commentators for their analyses of a Vietnam policy speech by President Nixon the previous week. The networks had been told that Agnew's speech would be newsworthy, but they were not aware until it was being delivered that their own practices would be the subject. The following key portions of the Agnew attack reveal the dimensions to which the industry had grown as well as the vice-president's concern about these dimensions:

The audience of 70 million Americans—gathered to hear the President of the United States—was inherited by a small

**Figure 8–10**
Spiro Agnew using television to berate television

**221**

CHAPTER 8
Television
Opera-
tional
History

band of network commentators and self-appointed analysts, the majority of whom expressed, in one way or another, their hostility to what he had to say . . . .

The purpose of my remarks tonight is to focus your attention on this little group of men who not only enjoy a right of instant rebuttal to every Presidential address, but more importantly, wield a free hand in selecting, presenting, and interpreting the great issues of our nation.

First, let us define that power. At least 40 million Americans each night, it is estimated, watch the network news. Seven million of them view ABC, the remainder being divided between NBC and CBS.

According to Harris polls and other studies, for millions of Americans the networks are the sole source of national and world news.

In Will Rogers' observation, what you knew was what you read in the newspaper.

Today, for growing millions of Americans, it is what they see and hear on their television sets . . . .

As with other American institutions, perhaps it is time that the networks were made more responsive to the views of the nation and more responsible to the people they serve.

I am not asking for government censorship or any other kind of censorship.

I am asking whether a form of censorship already exists when the news that 40 million Americans receive each night is determined by a handful of men responsible only to their corporate employers and filtered through a handful of commentators who admit to their own set of biases. . . .

We would never trust such power over public opinion in the hands of an elected government—it is time we questioned it in the hands of a small and unelected elite.

The great networks have dominated America's airwaves for decades; the people are entitled to a full accounting of their stewardship.[16]

In response, former CBS news chief Fred W. Friendly brought to bear his knowledge of the inner workings of all three networks' news departments in fashioning this observation:

> There is an independent, sometimes awkward complex of network executives, producers, station managers and reporters whose joint production is the news we see. They represent a geographic, ethnic, political profile nearly as far ranging as American society itself. The news program emerges from a complicated system of argument, conflict, and compromise.[17]

Supporting Friendly's assessment, sociologist Herbert Gans added:

> Network newsmen do not function the way Agnew said they do. I have been studying the networks as well as news magazines for the past several years, and insofar as there is bias in their product it stems, I find, far less from their own prejudices than from the nature of modern journalism.[18]

# More Expansion and Tougher Choices

Even though television's societal effects and alleged biases continued to be hotly debated in the early 1970s, this controversy did not retard the medium's continued growth. By the end of 1972, more than 900 television stations were on the air and approximately 2,500 cable systems were serving more than 5 million homes, mainly in rural areas. For the first time, the number of color sets sold actually exceeded sales of black-and-white receivers, attesting to the almost full-color schedules now offered on virtually every station. Using terrestrial relays, cable programmer Home Box Office (HBO) produced the first original pay TV event when it distributed the Pennsylvania Polka Festival from Allentown on March 1, 1973. Over-the-air subscription television may have been stymied, but pay-cable

was about to break loose to offer viewers a new set of options.

## Social Impact

Television, by now, was such a central part of the U.S. life-style that few people could recall how we ever did without it. In fact, the idea of TV abstinence was probed in a German study by the Society for Rational Psychology in Munich. Researchers paid 184 habitual viewers for every day they stayed away from the tube. Despite the monetary incentive, one man went back to television after only three days and no one held out for more than five months. While under video deprivation, subjects reported increases in moodiness, child spanking, and wife beating with decreased interest and performance in marital sex. In exquisite seriousness, psychologist Henner Ertel postulated, "With people who watch regularly, many behavior patterns become so closely related to TV that they are negatively influenced if one takes the set away. The problem is that of addiction."[19]

The allegedly addictive nature of television was also being discussed in the United States from a different perspective. The newly founded Action for Children's Television (ACT) petitioned both the FCC and the FTC to ban commercials in child-oriented programming. ACT argued that young folks could become hooked by unrealistic product expectations that had been overblown by distortive advertising. At the same time, a two-year report by the U.S. Surgeon General indicated that violent TV programs could trigger violence in children already predisposed to overt hostility. On the other hand, the study also found no direct causal link between violent television fare and aggressive behavior by normal children, but the fact that the Senate had initiated such a probe put the industry under a cloud nonetheless.

Between 1974 and 1975, FCC and television industry attempts to dissipate this cloud led to more difficulty in an abortive series of actions subsequently known as the family

**223**

CHAPTER 8
Television
Opera-
tional
History

viewing debacle. To satisfy Congressional demands to clean up early evening primetime programs (when children were most likely to be in the audience), FCC Chairman Richard Wiley met with key executives of the networks on November 22, 1974. The outcome was a recommendation to the National Association of Broadcasters' television code review board that the first two hours of prime time exclude programs whose sexual or violent content made them inappropriate for a family audience. Even though broadcaster reaction to such self-censorship was mixed, the code was obediently amended to include the family viewing concept. Subsequently, the networks enforced this self-regulation by moving certain shows out of family time (or off the air entirely) and by dictating more stringent content guidelines for programs that remained in this time period.

In October, 1975, a number of writers and producers (including *All in the Family's* Norman Lear) joined the Writers Guild of America, the Screen Actor's Guild, and the Director's Guild in bringing suit against Wiley and the TV Code. Family viewing, the plaintiffs charged, had violated the creative community's First Amendment rights and had caused financial harm to the creators whose programs had been moved as a result. A year later, Judge Warren Ferguson agreed. The case was appealed and bounced around the courts for the next eight years, but family viewing, as a simplistic answer to a complex issue, was as dead as some of the programs it caused to be relocated.

If children's and family programming was a hot issue, so, too, was television's journalistic performance in covering Watergate. As the Nixon administration's potential involvement in the burglary of the Democratic Campaign Headquarters became enmeshed with other 1972 election dirty tricks, relations between the White House and most of the press establishment worsened. Because network television had been seen as an administration enemy since the events leading up to Vice-President Agnew's Des Moines broadside, TV became a particular lightning rod. The Senate's Watergate hearings in 1973 were extensively covered by the three networks and evoked in some observers' minds the specter of the Army-McCarthy hearings almost twenty years previous. Now, of course, television was much more pervasive, and the revelations caught by its lens had a more immediate impact.

Unfortunately, both Nixon and the network newspeople began to lose some of their decorum. At an October 1973 news conference, CBS reporter Robert Pierpoint asked the president why he seemed so upset about television's Watergate coverage and was met with a curt retort: "Don't get the impression that you arouse my anger . . . . You see, one can only be angry with those he respects."[20] The running battle continued and a few months later was again captured on television at the NAB's 1974 Convention in Houston, where President Nixon had agreed to hold a news conference. (See Figure 8–11.) When Dan Rather of CBS was applauded as he stood to ask a question, the President taunted, "Are you running for something?" Rather reactively responded, "No sir. Are you?"[21] No one's image benefited from such exchanges, but they did demonstrate the potency of the televised sequence in dramatizing events and the actions of its own professionals.

Scarcely three months later, the networks mounted rotating coverage of the Nixon impeachment hearing in the House of Representatives, including the debate between the Select Committee's members before the actual vote to impeach. Soon after that affirmative vote was taken, the president resigned and left the White House following a tearful goodbye to his staff, which the cameras also captured live. Looking back on this string of events, some people wondered and worried if television had been as much participant as documentor in this almost Shakespearean drama. At the least, the medium conspicuously thrust the stage into virtually every

**Figure 8–11**

A combative Richard Nixon makes an appearance at the 1974 NAB Convention. NAB President Vincent Wasilewski shares the stage.

home, where the residents became eye witnesses. (Television's increasing prominence as a conveyor of news of all types is illustrated in Figure 8–12.)

## Diversifying Delivery

Beyond such encompassing events as a live walk on the moon or the Congressional probe of a president, television constituted not one

**Figure 8–12**

Where did people get most of their news? 1959–1976

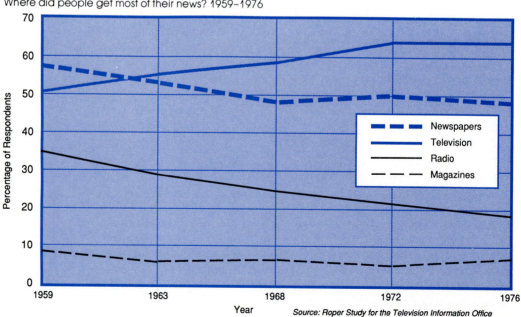

Source: Roper Study for the Television Information Office
(Multiple answers accepted when respondent named more than one medium.)

**225**

CHAPTER 8
Television
Opera-
tional
History

but several stages, and by the midseventies, their number began to multiply. The broadcast networks still constituted the three dominant arenas, but other operators were positioning themselves to offer their own options. Independent stations without network affiliations (known as indies) were discovering that well-promoted sports and movie programming could lure audiences of a profitable size as a counterprogram to network half-hour and one-hour series. Such divergent programming also made it more likely that cable systems would choose to carry an indy's signal beyond the limits of its over-the-air coverage pattern, thereby increasing the station's potential audience and making it more competitive with network affiliates.

In the cable sector itself, Home Box Office, in 1975, first used a satellite to deliver its exclusive pay-cable programming. Now, a cable network could offer its service to any cable system in the country possessing a receiving dish without the high cost and geographic limitations of terrestrial distribution by microwave (recall our previous discussions in Chapters 2 and 5). Before long, independent broadcaster Ted Turner established a relay company, Southern Satellite Systems, to carry the programming of his Atlanta station to distant cable operators around the country. This first *superstation* (now called WTBS) was a brilliant integration of the broadcast, satellite, and cable businesses and provided a new way to package audiences for advertisers. Unlike broadcasting or land-line distribution, the satellite allowed Turner to reach pockets of viewers spread throughout the continent without having to pay to cross the unprofitable geography in between.

Televangelist Pat Robertson followed in Turner's footsteps only a few months later as his television station evolved into the Christian Broadcasting Cable Network (since renamed The Family Network). Viacom put its Showtime movie service on the bird in order to compete with HBO, and satellite carrier United Video uplinked WGN in Chicago (although without its consent) to cash in on the

superstation business Ted Turner had stimulated. These new options for cable subscribers were the vanguard of a host of program services that came to challenge conventional broadcasters for viewer attention and (in the nonpay services) for advertiser patronage.

Between 1976 and 1980, newly liberalized rules helped cable take full advantage of the opportunities technology was providing. The compulsory license (see Chapter 5) now allowed the pick up of distant over-the-air signals at very low fees. The federal courts overturned the FCC's pay cable rules and thus permitted the new industry to compete with broadcasters for exclusive rights to sports and movie telecasts. Later, the FCC abolished the requirement that distant signals be blacked out when they replicated local broadcaster programming (a rule recently reinstated) and repealed limits on the number of distant signals that could be imported. Buoyed by such events and by the rapidly expanding cable subscriber base, a number of additional cable networks were launched. Among the most important were Figure 8–13's Cable Satellite Public Affairs Network (C-SPAN), which provided live coverage of the House of Representatives; the ESPN and USA entertainment/sports networks; and Ted Turner's Cable News Network (CNN).

Ironically, while cable was being freed, the broadcast networks still squirmed under FCC restrictions imposed by the financial interest and syndication rules (fin/syn) and the prime time access rule (PTAR) (both are discussed in Chapter 5). The new competitive environment demanded flexible responses, but the flexibility advantage was now enjoyed by cable interests. Nonetheless, only about one-sixth of U.S. homes were as yet wired for cable by 1980, and so over-the-air broadcasting and its networks still garnered the lion's share of television viewers and advertising revenues.

Programming innovations like the miniseries reaped large audiences; ABC's 1977 blockbuster, *Roots*, became the then-most-watched program in television history. Together, the three networks spent almost $2 billion on their programming the following year, according to Fred Silverman, then president of NBC. Silverman took an aggressive stance on the new program deliverers. Speaking on July 24, 1979, to the California Association of Broadcasters, the master programmer stoutly maintained:

> Whatever our competitors may do, we have no intention of diverting our resources into the production of theatrical motion pictures. Whatever our competitors may do, we are not going to dissipate our creative energies by producing software for other media or other technologies. We are broadcasters and we are going to remain broadcasters.[22]

Thus, as television entered the 1980s, many conventional broadcasters seemed to be circling the wagons as no-longer-so-primi-

tive alternative delivery systems came to surround them.

Over-the-air subscription television, which had languished for many years, finally took advantage of the FCC's relaxation of restrictions. Nine STV stations were on the air at the beginning of 1980; the largest, KBSC Channel 52, outside Los Angeles, served 282,000 subscribers. All of these outlets offered their customers a mix of movie and sporting events. The facility in Milwaukee, WCBG, created a special variation. For an additional five dollars per week, WCBG's viewers had access to *Night Owl Theatre*, a 10:30-to-midnight event featuring films strong on violence, nudity, and adult situations. Whether such fare would make STV a viable alternative to more staid conventional broadcasting remained to be seen. But it was significant that 90 percent of the Milwaukee station's customers paid the additional fee to receive *Night Owl Theatre*.[23]

**Figure 8–13**
Gathering public affairs footage for C-SPAN's cable networks

**227**

CHAPTER 8
Television
Opera-
tional
History

Also in 1980, the FCC began to accept applications for low-power TV stations (LPTV). VHF LPTV outlets were limited to a power of either 10 or 100 watts depending on whether they were operating within the FCC's existing table of channel assignments. UHF facilities were restricted to 1,000 watts. With a range of no more than twelve to fifteen miles, LPTV stations were seen as a way to bring specialty programming to more populated areas and local service to small towns that could not support their own regular television station. (A typical LPTV antenna is depicted in Figure 8–14.) Almost immediately, the commission was buried with more than 5,000 LPTV applications and, red-faced, had to put a freeze on applications until it sorted the matter out. For the most part, the only grants made initially would be in locales served by fewer than two conventional stations.

Another potential but likewise undemonstrated threat to established telecasters was direct broadcast satellite service (DBS). Before the end of 1980, Comsat, the privately owned satellite carrier set up by Congress in 1962, announced that its subsid-

**Figure 8–14**
Zig-Zag, UHF transmitting antenna for an LPTV station. The antenna emits a directional signal and can be used in multi-antenna arrays to create various coverage patterns.

**RUTH OTTE**/PRESIDENT AND CHIEF OPERATING OFFICER
THE DISCOVERY CHANNEL

Being president of a cable television network requires constant commitment to business and human concerns in several different arenas. To succeed, our company must be effective in delivering on our promises and providing benefits to several key constituencies:

a. More than 500 current advertisers who advertise their products on our air.

b. 7,000 cable companies that carry our service and expect good programming and solid marketing support from us.

c. One million nightly viewers who rely on us to deliver on our programming promise of educational, informative, and entertaining programs eighteen hours a day.

d. Our owners, who have expectations for our financial and marketplace performance.

e. Some 4,000 producers of television product from around the globe who sell programming to us and expect us to edit, package, and promote the product as we promised.

f. Our suppliers of key technology, such as our production house, uplink and satellite vendors, etc.

g. Other organizations with which we have formed strategic alliances for programming and marketing.

Because the company must deal effectively with each of these constituencies in order to succeed and grow, I have to be effective in setting direction, resolving breakdowns, and empowering my team in all of the many facets of our business.

On just about any day, I wrestle with concerns in all of these areas. For example, last Friday started with a call on my car phone from our sales manager regarding an advertiser who wants to spend $1.8 million on our network but is insisting on a rate below our standards. Do we walk away from such a good-sized order? Do we give him what he wants and perhaps set a dangerous precedent? Together, the sales manager and I structure a deal that would be more tolerable for us and hopefully acceptable to the advertiser.

Then we discuss the need to add two or three people to our traffic department (which schedules advertisers' commercials and gets them on the air) because the people in that group are working until 8 or 9 every night and are burning out. Adding new traffic positions would put us over the total headcount my board authorized for the year, so I make a mental note to revisit the other departments' needs to see which can put off hiring a new person. We agree to add some temporary help immediately.

I ride up in the elevator with our head of programming, who gives me a verbal report on this month's ratings. The news is good. We are up 25 percent over last year. I ask how we are doing on finalizing the schedule for the next four quarters. Our new season advertising sales begin in just six weeks. It is going to be very difficult to finalize all the programming decisions and contracts in that period of time, as well as meet the advance deadlines that our marketing department needs to create sales tapes, sales brochures, and other material. Because so much money is at stake, we discuss which personnel can be taken off other projects and put on this one.

Now begins the first of today's twelve regularly scheduled meetings. Each has a concrete agenda. First, our senior vice-president of marketing reviews our consumer campaign plans for next quarter and the press conference agenda for an upcoming industry convention. We agree to meet later in the afternoon so I can look at the initial trade ads promoting one of our new originally produced series.

I then take a call from our European division informing me that we have had requests from Spain and Poland to bring Discovery to those countries.

We discuss potential partners, how soon we can assemble and translate sufficient programming, how we can re-organize the London-based staff to potentially accomplish the feat, plus certain new developments in Spain that might open up additional possibilities for us.

Throughout the rest of my day, I meet with various department heads to discuss (1) issues they are facing for which we have no precedents; (2) breakdowns or problems we are working on; (3) milestones that have been achieved (or haven't been achieved); and (4) areas in which we need to set or change standards for what we will accomplish, by when, and at a cost of how much money, time, and human resources.

If I contrast what I learned in business school with my actual management of Discovery, I find that the human element is virtually absent from business school curricula. Yet, this element is the most frequently discussed and most vital aspect of virtually every real-world enterprise. I have come to see that work is accomplished through the coordination of action between individuals. This coordination includes nurturing people's dignity, respecting their desire to make a valuable contribution, and the willingness of both parties in any interaction to take each other's concerns seriously. This attitude holds true for all the people with whom one interacts, whether employees, colleagues, customers, suppliers, or investors.

iary would be providing three channels of pay programming to subscribers' home dishes by the middle of the decade. For its part, the FCC announced two separate inquiries into policy matters designed to pave the way for possible full-scale commercial DBS activity.

The three broadcast network companies were not oblivious to the new technologies. In fact, all three now mounted attempts to diversify by moving into cable. CBS formed CBS Cable; NBC's parent, RCA, announced a similar cultural programming channel to be called Rockefeller Center Television (RCTV); and ABC checked in with its ARTS service, bought a piece of sports-minded ESPN, and (with Westinghouse) set up the Satellite News-Channel to compete directly with Ted Turner's CNN. Unfortunately for the networks, their dominance in over-the-air operations did not automatically translate into cable expertise. CBS Cable and RCTV never got off the ground, and Turner's aggressive pricing plus the addition of a Headline News channel to his CNN soon led the Satellite NewsChannel to sell out to him. Other ABC ventures fared better; ARTS merged into a broader A & E (Arts and Entertainment) service, and ESPN increased in popularity and system carriage.

Meanwhile, new cable players like the music-video rocking MTV and its later subsidiaries (Nickelodeon and VH-1), the Nashville Network's country capers, the Discovery Channel's documentaries, and the Disney Channel's family fare established their niches as providers of cable-exclusive specialty programming. Clearly, television was no longer one business but at least two (broadcast and cable), with other technologies waiting in the wings. Some established broadcast corporations became financially involved in both businesses in an effort to protect their stake in the industry at large, and other interests new to the electronic media saw cable as a way to establish a foothold in the mushrooming but risky world of 1980s television.

## Competition Unlimited

In 1982 the FCC opened the competitive floodgates even wider. First, it finally adopted LPTV rules that, in addition to providing for new stations, allowed existing TV translators (passive relayers of regular stations) to convert to independent LPTV status if their operators so wished. Meanwhile, eight construction permits (CPs) were awarded for DBS systems, with one each going to CBS and RCA. Even over-the-air STV was finally fully freed when the commission allowed its entry into markets of any size and scrubbed the requirement that an STV station must air at least twenty-eight hours of free unscrambled programming per week. The following year, the FCC permitted another new player onto the field when it began accepting applications for MMDS—multichannel multipoint distribution services. (We discuss these wireless cable operations in Chapter 2).

### Viewer Power

By this time, a home video cassette recorder (VCR) was in 11 percent of U.S. homes (it penetrated two-thirds of all homes by decade's end), and more and more viewers were purchasing these devices as prices continued to drop. A piece of equipment that only two decades before filled several racks in a station control room could now, with slightly lower picture resolution, fit on a home bookcase or end table. For broadcasters and cablecasters, the VCR was a two-edged sword. On the one hand, it allowed consumers to watch shows they would otherwise miss by having the machine's timer automatically record them for later viewing (*time-shifting*). On the other hand, the VCR also paved the way for the video store and the use of the television set to play programs other than those provided by

**231**

CHAPTER 8
Television
Opera-
tional
History

broadcast stations and cable networks. Take-out video (as mentioned in Chapter 3) now constituted an expanding alternative demand on viewer patronage. It further threatened the audience levels, and thereby the advertising income, of both broadcasters and advertising-supported cable channels.

Even viewer time-shifting of their shows was not unequivocally advantageous for advertiser-based services because (1) such later watching was not detected by most audience measurement (ratings) services; (2) later viewing of time-shifted programs meant that those receivers were not available to watch the programs being broadcast/cablecast at that moment; and (3) many viewers zip through commercials during tape replay. Any legal impediment to home taping of television programs for personal use was removed on January 23,1984, when the Supreme Court ruled (*Universal City Studios, Inc.* v. *Sony Corporation of America*) that such home copying was

fair use and did not constitute any infringement of copyright.

Both in number of stations (see Figure 8–15) and in total delivery systems, viewers now had an unprecedented variety of ways to receive television and a variety of options as to what to do with a program once they got it. Watching television, by the mideighties, was no longer having to choose between what the three networks, a struggling independent, or the noncommercial Public Broadcasting Service happened to be airing at the moment.

## Giants Remolded

This new freedom of choice significantly cut into the networks' share of audience. The resulting competitive pressures sent tremors through the three old-line networks and caused fundamental changes in the ownership of each. In 1985, ABC was bought by Capital Cities Communications, a well-managed group of stations that included several of

**Figure 8–15**

Television stations operating in the United States, 1946–1990 (not including LPTV)

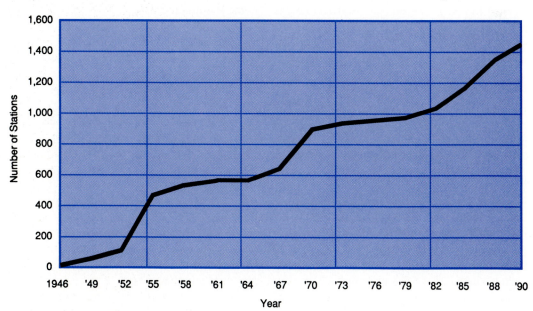

that network's key affiliates. RCA and its NBC subsidiaries were purchased by General Electric, which had been a partner with RCA in the assumption of AT&T's broadcast properties in 1926 (see Chapter 7). CBS, faced with a takeover attempt from Ted Turner, put itself $1 billion in debt by buying back about 21 percent of its stock. This crippling debt led, a few months later, to Loews Corporation stepping in to buy almost 25 percent of CBS; Loews chairman, Laurence Tisch, became CBS's chief executive officer. Cost-cutting and sale of nonbroadcast divisions became the rules at all three networks as their new owners sought to (1) pare away fat that had accumulated over decades of dominance and (2) move resources around to meet the technological challenges of the nineties.

Meanwhile, other new players were making their influence felt. Australian media baron Rupert Murdoch became a U.S. citizen (a federal requirement for station ownership) and bought six major-market television facilities from the Metromedia group. He then increased his half ownership of major program producer 20th Century Fox Film Corporation to full ownership. With a key station group and a key studio/syndicator now under his control, Murdoch announced plans for the Fox Network, which would begin by programming weekend prime time for its affiliates and gradually expand into other nights and dayparts.

Local stations were largely passive observers to these network machinations, but they were shaken when, on July 22, 1985, the U.S. Court of Appeals struck down the FCC's *must-carry* rules (see Chapter 6). A cable system was now free to delete a local station from its carried channels at its discretion. For example, if 45 percent of the television households in a given city were cable subscribers, a local broadcaster's failure to secure cable carriage would cause its potential audience to be cut almost in half. True, a consumer could disconnect the cable to receive the signal over the air (or could install a so-called *A/B switch* to make disconnect/reconnect simpler) but stations knew that few viewers would go to such trouble. Television broadcasters were now threatened with actually being walled off from their audience. As of this writing, must-carry discussions among broadcasters, cable interests, and government continue, but clearly, guaranteed over-the-air access into every television household can no longer be taken for granted.

## The Ways to Pay

As the 1980s came to a close, the shake out and realignment of television services continued. STV, so long kept captive by the FCC, was unable to establish a foothold against cable. Some twenty-seven Subscription Television stations did go on the air, but their signals were often pirated by unauthorized descramblers. Furthermore, an STV's single channel of pay programming was no match for cable's multiple pay and basic options. Once cable came to town, STV shut down; the last such outlet ceased operation in 1986. Some of these stations went dark, others became regular independent facilities, and still others were converted to the new rage—TV home shopping.

The Home Shopping Network (HSN), the first and largest of such enterprises, began as a cable service in 1985 and soon expanded to carriage on over-the-air stations as well. Before long, HSN itself owned several stations via subsidiary Silver King Broadcasting. By late 1989, in fact, Silver King became the fourth largest group broadcaster, trailing only the three major networks. Armed with a TV set, a telephone, and a credit card, a viewer could now brouse and purchase from HSN or any of several other competing twenty-four-hour televised catalogue services. These shows feature compelling product demonstrations by glib on-camera talent and once-in-a-lifetime opportunities that usually expire in a matter of minutes.

By this time, some consumers could also purchase individual video events program-

**233**

CHAPTER 8
Television
Opera-
tional
History

**Figure 8–16**
Logo used by United Artists Cablesystems to identify its multiple PPV services.

ming via Viewer's Choice or Request Television. Such pay-per-view (PPV) enterprises (see Figure 8–16) used cable system channels to deliver special movie, theatrical, and sporting events. Subscribers paid on an individual event basis by using their telephone or via a code sent back over the cable wire to place their order. As equipment providing easier *addressability* between consumer and cable system is put on line, PPV promises to become a significant new option for viewers and also for programmers seeking new revenue bases for and through television.

On the other hand, DBS and MMDS had yet to establish their viability by the end of the decade. DBS was making some progress in Europe, but it encountered many more established competitors in the United States. Only one U.S. DBS operation actually got underway in the 1980s, and this effort, by United Satellite Communications, Inc., did not get beyond an East Coast trial run. As mentioned in Chapter 2, some home satellite dish owners (TVROS) were now receiving programming direct from the bird but merely as an alternative to cable delivery rather than as a separate and distinct DBS-only service. Just recently, however, new genuine DBS ventures have been announced by powerful media partnerships. (See Chapter 14 for more about this development.) MMDS, meanwhile, is making some headway in certain cities, particularly where a strong cable service has not yet been established.

## Focusing on Fragmentation

All of these new choices, of course, mean that the television audience—like the radio audience in the early 1950s—is becoming more and more fragmented. Thus, in the fall of

CNN **PPV**

Rock concerts and major sporting matches are making pay-per-view (PPV) a viable entertainment form. The 1990s are projected to be the PPV decade once addressable technology becomes more widespread and permits impulse buys.

1987, Nielsen shifted to measuring national television audiences via the *peoplemeter* rather than by the old passive Audimeter or diary. Individual viewers must now punch into the hand-held peoplemeter device when they enter the room and punch out when they leave. Some small children can't, some older adults won't, and the credibility of the system has been brought into question. Nielsen, however, maintains that its research proves that the peoplemeter is superior to previous methods of estimating audience size and composition. Arbitron, Nielsen's key competitor, is seeking to implement a peoplemeter system of its own known as ScanAmerica. Whatever the measurement system, more viewing options lead to smaller audience levels for each individual option. Thus, ratings companies must find more precise ways of tallying and describing thinner and thinner segments of total viewership.

From a few thousand viewers watching experimental live television on a half-dozen stations, fifty years of television had, by 1989, now brought 24, 36, or even 108 separate channels into the home, in addition to video cassette material that, with a camcorder, the consumers might have created themselves. The VCR's presence in more than two out of every three U.S. homes means that people can now watch whatever they want whenever they want. Three decades previous, TV consumers adjusted their lives to meet the scheduling dictates of programmers at three networks and no more than four or five local stations. By the end of the eighties, these and dozens of other industry professionals were frantically scrambling to mesh with the viewing whims exhibited by those now empowered audience members.

In 1991, CNN's breakthrough coverage of Persian Gulf hostilities demonstrated that broadcast network news dominance could no longer be taken for granted. In a larger sense, the ratings CNN garnered also signaled that alternative delivery systems were coming close to parity with conventional broadcasting. Broadcast network share of audience dropped to 62 percent as the television audience exercised their increasing ability and willingness to explore newer viewing options.

Charting and catering to these continually diversifying consumer preferences will make the business of television more challenging as a new century approaches. Some of the cutting-edge video opportunities are explored in Chapter 14.

---

# CHAPTER FLASHBACK

Television's availability to the U.S. public began in 1939 with small screens reflected in the top of expensive receivers. Commercial telecasts via the modern 525-line standard had been on the air for only five months when U.S. entry into World War II forced the suspension of most television operations. After the war, the medium was beginning to emerge from its cocoon when the FCC imposed its four-year Freeze while it re-examined television's spectrum requirements. Most of the stations that did manage to receive pre-Freeze construction permits profited from rapidly escalating consumer and advertiser interest.

Early television programs, particularly those originated by local stations, were often primitive, but the novelty of the new medium outweighed their content limitations. The first neighborhood household to obtain a TV set often became a gathering place for the entire block as people viewed with rapt attention whatever was broadcast. Until AT&T interconnections were constructed, early networking was often done by the bicycling of *kinescopes* that had been filmed at the time of the show's original broadcast.

Not all phases of the new television industry were successful. Even after FCC selection of the RCA system, color transmissions were limited by their expense, technical imperfections, lack of advertiser interest, and high cost

**235**

CHAPTER 8
Television
Opera-
tional
History

of receivers. UHF stations encountered serious problems due to a similar lack of receivers and the high cost of signal transmission. Various pay TV systems met with opposition from Hollywood, FCC roadblocks, and viewer contentment with free TV service. Network newscasts were only one-quarter of an hour in length, but television's power as a journalistic medium was demonstrated in the exposure of the tactics of Senator Joseph McCarthy, which helped pave the way for his downfall.

By the late 1950s, television was firmly established in 75 percent of U.S. households and seriously impacted movie theater revenues. Hollywood turned increasingly to producing material for the new medium. In the following decade, TV became a mature industry; most national shows now were produced under contract to the networks rather than packaged by individual sponsors. Politicians learned how to deal with the new medium as John F. Kennedy effectively used it in both his pre- and postelection appearances. The widespread availability of videotape meant that programs could now be easily prerecorded as a more controlled and economical production method. Ratings services were scrutinized and their findings subject to more precise qualification.

Relay satellites and improved colorcasting were both in place by the late 1960s to cover the carnage in Vietnam as television made war more immediate and less palatable. Assassinations and civil disturbances were also brought into U.S. homes, with some authorities charging that TV was as much an instigator as a messenger. The impact of the medium on society in general and on children in particular was widely debated and led to the abortive family viewing scheme, which attempted to create industrywide uniformity in early evening programming.

The rise of independent stations and of cable (both free and pay) as separate programming forces brought escalating industry fragmentation beginning in the late 1970s. FCC liberalization of cable rules accelerated this trend, and other regulations like fin/syn and PTAR limited the flexibility of the networks in program acquisition and distribution. LPTV, DBS, and STV all came on the scene, but the first two were slow to catch on and the last died out as soon as its operating areas were wired for cable. Home VCRs gave viewers unprecedented power over what and when they wanted to watch and brought further audience fragmentation. This, in turn, has led to new procedures for audience measurements (peoplemeters) and more attempts at niche programming, especially by cable networks. Home shopping, pay-per-view, and the consumers' ability to produce their own programming via camcorders are now widening television options and increasing industry competition even more.

## ❑ Review Probes

1. What were the factors that greatly inhibited the growth of U.S. commercial television in the twelve years following its introduction?
2. What various systems for subscription (pay) television were introduced over the last forty years?
3. Trace the origin and history of the DuMont Network.
4. How did Hollywood respond to the growth of television? What movie industry and political events served to make ABC more competitive?
5. How and why did the cable industry change after HBO's 1975 innovation?
6. What were notable aspects of television's political coverage of the presidential elections of 1960, 1964, and 1968?

SECTION TWO

Chronicles

Berry, Joseph P., Jr. *John F. Kennedy and the Media: The First Television President.* Lanham, MD: University Press of America, 1987.

Boyer, Peter J. *Who Killed CBS? The Undoing of America's Number One News Network.* New York: Random House, 1988.

Comstock, George. *The Evolution of American Television.* Newbury Park, CA: Sage, 1989.

Erickson, Hal. *Syndicated Television: The First Forty Years, 1947–1987.* Jefferson, NC: McFarland, 1989.

Hawes, William. *American Television Drama: The Experimental Years.* University: University of Alabama Press, 1986.

Shapiro, Mitchell E. *Television Network Prime-Time Programming, 1948–1988.* Jefferson, NC: McFarland, 1989.

Udelson, Joseph H. *The Great Television Race: A History of the American Television Industry 1925–1941.* University: University of Alabama Press, 1982.

Watson, Mary Ann. *The Expanding Vista: American Television in the Kennedy Years.* New York: Oxford University Press, 1990.

# Benchmarks

| Year | Radio Operations | TV Operations |
|------|------------------|---------------|
| 1922 | Queensboro Corporation contracts for first commercials | |
| 1926 | NBC created by RCA to manage Red and Blue networks | |
| 1927 | United Independent Broadcasters (soon to become CBS) is formed | |
| 1929 | *Amos 'n' Andy* first national program hit | |
| 1933 | FDR's first fireside chat | |
| 1934 | Press Radio Bureau set up as limiter of radio use of wire service material | |
| | Mutual Broadcasting System begins | |
| 1938 | *War of the Worlds* broadcast demonstrates radio's potency | |
| 1939 | | NBC begins regularly scheduled telecasts to the public |
| 1940 | AP accepts stations as members; Press Radio Bureau abandoned | NBC uses coaxial cable to network Republican Convention |
| 1941 | | Commercial TV mothballed for duration of war |
| 1943 | CBS airs controversial *Open Letter on Race Hatred* | |
| 1946 | Number of AM stations increases by 50% | Rebirth of commercial TV over existing 6 stations |
| 1947 | | NBC establishes permanent network linking 4 eastern stations |
| 1948 | | NBC's *Texaco Star Theater* first breakthrough hit |

| Year | Radio Operations | TV Operations |
|------|------------------|---------------|
| 1949 | FM in serious trouble; many stations but few receivers | First Emmy awards given |
|  |  | Hooper begins national television measurement |
| 1950 |  | Zenith field-tests Phonevision wired pay TV |
|  |  | Skiatron tests over-the-air pay TV |
| 1951 | Network radio rates lowered in face of TV growth | TV's most successful situation comedy, *I Love Lucy*, debuts |
|  |  | AT&T inaugurates permanent transcontinental video transmission lines |
|  |  | NAB introduces Television Code |
| 1953 | Deejay Alan Freed brings rock and roll to national prominence | NBC begins limited colorcast schedule |
| 1954 | NBC introduces *Monitor* as new approach to network packaging | TV advertising sales surpass those of radio |
| 1955 | FCC approves multiplex as way to increase FM revenues | DuMont network abandoned |
| 1956 |  | Hollywood begins to make films available to TV |
| 1960 | Last radio soaps are cancelled | Television Information Office established |
|  |  | Kennedy–Nixon great debates televised |
| 1962 | Talk radio programs take hold | FCC authorizes over-the-air pay TV in Hartford, CT |
| 1966 | Progressive format pioneered on WOR-FM (New York) | Color set market booms; black-&-white set sales decline |

| Year | Radio Operations | TV Operations |
|------|------------------|---------------|
| 1967 | ABC network split into 4 separate services | |
| 1969 | | Agnew attacks network news power |
| 1972 | | 2,500 cable systems in operation; increased wiring of cities |
| 1973 | | Surgeon General's report cites dangers to children of violent programming |
| 1974 | Associated Press Radio launched | |
| 1975 | | Family viewing suit brought against FCC chairman and TV Code |
| 1977 | | Turner completes conversion of Atlanta UHF to superstation |
| | | *Roots* demonstrates drawing power of miniseries |
| 1980 | | FCC permits regular subscription television service |
| | | First LPTV applications accepted |
| 1982 | FCC decides to let marketplace select AM stereo standard | FCC awards first DBS construction permits |
| | | First MMDS applications filed |
| 1984 | | Supreme Court boosts VCR fortunes by ruling home taping as legal |
| 1985 | Mutual purchased by Westwood | Home Shopping Network initiated |
| | | Fox Network formulation plans announced by Murdock |
| | | ABC and NBC change hands; control of CBS shifts |

| Year | Radio Operations | TV Operations |
|------|------------------|---------------|
| 1986 | FCC abandons nonduplication rules to shore up AM | Last STV outlet closes down |
| 1987 | Westwood purchases NBC Radio Networks | Nielsen converts national measurement to peoplemeters |
| 1988 | 75% of U.S. radio listening now done on FM band | Cable penetration reaches 50% of U.S. homes |
| 1989 | | Television Information Office closed in industry economy move |
| 1990 | Westwood and ABC networks reconfigured to correspond better to advertiser marketing plans | |
| 1991 | | CNN breakthrough coverage of the war in the Persian Gulf outclasses broadcast network news |

# Noncommercial and International Adventures

❑  *To this point, our attention primarily has focused on the development of the domestic and commercial applications of our electronic media system. Unquestionably, these comprise the great majority of U.S. radio and television activities. There also are significant professional opportunities in the noncommercial and international sectors. The evolution of these diverse enterprises occupies our attention in this chapter.*

## Orienting Definitions

Before beginning an exploration of noncommercial radio and television activities, it is important to define some terms. As we discuss in Chapter 3, *noncommercial* electronic media enterprises are not designed to make a profit. Instead, they are intended to serve a particular governmental or societal need, with their revenues supposed to do no more than offset operating expenditures. Noncommercial stations are maintained by religious organizations, educational institutions, and other nonprofit foundations such as Pacifica. Even though most of their programming (and, indeed, a good deal of commercial station con-

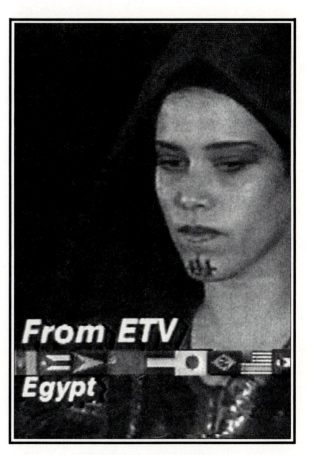

From ETV Egypt

tent) may be considered broadly educational in nature, actual *educational* broadcasting/cablecasting is defined more precisely as endeavors in support of a specific educational goal. In other words, teaching the audience about the program's subject is the prime and perhaps sole priority.

If the educational material is designed to be part of a formal curricular effort (such as in-school modules for a high school physics class or a college-credit history course broadcast over PBS), it is even more narrowly referred to as *instructional* radio or television. Finally, as we see later in this chapter, the term *public broadcasting* was coined in the late 1960s to emphasize multifaceted enrichment programming rather than single-purpose and limited-appeal instructional endeavors. In other words, it became the dream of public broadcasters to offer a wide variety of special-interest shows, each of which served the precise needs of a different audience group underserved by commercial media.

## The Postponed Promise

As we discover in Chapter 7, several of the earliest radio broadcasting facilities were operated by universities, usually as laboratories for their engineering and music students. With the mammoth success of commercial radio in the mid-1920s, however, many educational stations either lost their frequencies or were given the least desirable spectrum assignments. Because the 1927 Radio Act made no special provision for such noncommercial operations, their numbers declined from 170 to less than 2 dozen. Thus, while educational and cultural programming mushroomed in countries served by a noncommercial state-owned broadcasting corporation, such offerings in the U.S. free-enterprise system became increasingly rare.

## Forces in Early Educational Broadcasting

In an attempt to revitalize educational broadcasting, a group of U.S. educators formed the National Committee on Education by Radio on December 30, 1930. As stated in its by-laws, the organization was committed

> to secure to the people of the United States the use of radio for educational purposes by protecting the rights of educational broadcasting, by promoting and coordinating experiments in the use of radio in school and adult education, by maintaining a Service Bureau to assist educational stations in securing licenses and in other technical procedures, by exchange of information through a weekly bulletin, by encouragement of research in education by radio, and by serving as a clearinghouse for research.[1]

The committee also led the fight to convince the Federal Radio Commission to set aside 15 percent of the nation's AM frequencies for use by educational broadcasters. This policy was vigorously opposed by commercial interests.

Meanwhile, a somewhat competing agency, the National Advisory Council on Education by Radio, had also been organized with grants from the Carnegie Fund and the Rockefeller Foundation. According to its executive secretary, this council was

> attempting to do two things: First, to assemble and disseminate facts about radio in education; second, to induce qualified educators and authorities in various fields to devise radio programs that will be notable contributions to educational broadcasting.[2]

With representatives of both NBC and CBS on its board, however, the National Advisory Council seemed more intent on promoting occasional educational broadcasts on commercial stations than on supporting the cause of separate frequency allocations for educational outlets.

However, there were some examples of successful cooperation between commercial and educational interests. Notable among

**243**

CHAPTER 9

Noncom-
mercial
and
Interna-
tional
Adven-
tures

these in the early 1930s was the Ohio School of the Air, carried into schools (see Figure 9–1) as *sustaining* (nonsponsored) programming by the Crosley Radio Corporation's high-powered Cincinnati station, WLW. Each weekday, WLW and Ohio State's WEAO (Columbus) relayed well-produced *instructional programming* (in the specific sense of that term) into the schools, where principals often used a master radio switchboard to route the show to the appropriate classrooms. A typical School of the Air curriculum is detailed in Figure 9–2.

Unfortunately, in most of the country, such joint efforts became increasingly rare as the Depression constricted funding. In addition, some educators' condescending attitude toward commercial broadcast professionals encouraged these professionals to leave the educators to their own devices. Thus, what instructional or educational programming remained in donated time slots was often dull and primitive in comparison to the slick commercial material that surrounded it.

Soon after its establishment, the Federal Communications Commission revisited the subject of reserved frequencies for educational broadcasters. After ten days of hearings, in October 1934, it reaffirmed the decision of its FRC predecessor that such action was unwarranted. The educational community was itself split on the issue; some members feared that station operation would divert scarce funds from other more traditional instructional endeavors. Thus, the future of educational radio (and, indeed, of any noncommercial broadcasting service) did not appear bright. Occasional sustaining programs, such as Dr. Walter Damrosch's incisive music appreciation series over NBC, achieved a national following. But the dream of a separate system of educational stations and networks seemed more farfetched than ever. By the end of 1935, the National Committee on Education by Radio had itself ceased operation due to lack of funds and, apparently, lack of interest on the part of some of the constituency for whom it claimed to speak.

**Figure 9–1**
Students at the Virginia Ridge one-room school at Philo, Ohio, listen to a lesson from the Ohio School of the Air

**Figure 9–2**
A comprehensive radio curriculum

## THE SCHEDULE FOR THE OHIO SCHOOL OF THE AIR
### 1930-1931
### Showing Suitable Grade Placement

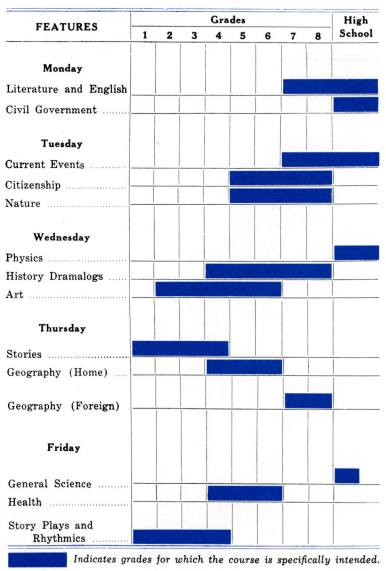

| FEATURES | Grades | | | | | | | | High School |
|---|---|---|---|---|---|---|---|---|---|
| | 1 | 2 | 3 | 4 | 5 | 6 | 7 | 8 | |
| **Monday** | | | | | | | | | |
| Literature and English | | | | | | | ██ | ██ | |
| Civil Government ........ | | | | | | | | | ██ |
| **Tuesday** | | | | | | | | | |
| Current Events ........... | | | | | | | ██ | ██ | ██ |
| Citizenship .............. | | | | ██ | ██ | ██ | | | |
| Nature .............. | | | | ██ | ██ | ██ | | | |
| **Wednesday** | | | | | | | | | |
| Physics .............. | | | | | | | | | ██ |
| History Dramalogs ...... | | | ██ | ██ | ██ | ██ | | | |
| Art ..................... | | ██ | ██ | ██ | ██ | | | | |
| **Thursday** | | | | | | | | | |
| Stories ..................... | ██ | ██ | ██ | | | | | | |
| Geography (Home) .... | | | ██ | ██ | ██ | | | | |
| Geography (Foreign) | | | | | | | ██ | | |
| **Friday** | | | | | | | | | |
| General Science ......... | | | | | | | | | ██ |
| Health ............... | | | ██ | ██ | ██ | | | | |
| Story Plays and Rhythmics ............ | ██ | ██ | | | | | | | |

██ *Indicates grades for which the course is specifically intended.*

*(Courtesy of State of Ohio Department of Education.)*

**245**

CHAPTER 9
Noncommercial
and
International
Adventures

However, there was one positive development as the FCC set up the Federal Radio Education Committee to attend to the needs of the noncommercial sector. More than three dozen educational radio stations were broadcasting in 1936 and, even though these outlets were not operating on reserved frequencies, they did provide a service to at least some areas of the country. Recognizing that a large expansion of this number was neither technologically nor financially possible, some educators asked the FCC to dictate specific times for educational programming on commercial stations. This proposal was never given much chance of success, but it did at least serve to keep alive the discussion of educational radio's needs. As a result, when the commission authorized full-scale FM broadcasting in 1940, five of the forty original channels were earmarked for the use of educational institutions. Seven school systems and universities actually were granted FM noncommercial licenses[3] before wartime shortages brought most FM activity to a temporary halt.

Instructional *television* now made its impromptu debut as NBC's New York station turned its attention to training air raid wardens (see Chapter 8) and the CBS outlet offered courses in first aid. Although limited in both subject matter and coverage area, the events did demonstrate the visual medium's potential for quick and efficient mass teaching. Beyond this special-purpose 1942 curiosity, educational broadcasting during World War II was little more than a byproduct of such news, public affairs, and cultural programs as the commercial networks chose to carry.

## Staking FM and TV Claims

In 1945, however, the FCC paved the way for substantial and self-standing educational radio when it moved the FM band to a higher frequency and thus accommodated 100 channels—60 more than the prewar authorization.

The first 20 of these channels (88.1 through 91.9 mHz) were specifically reserved for noncommercial broadcasters. For the first time, a large and discrete section of the band (four times bigger than the prewar allocation) had been provided to noncommercial users, and they moved to take advantage of it. During the remainder of the decade, some 60 educational FM facilities were built. Many of these were low-powered (10-watt) outlets. Though their signals seldom went farther than seven or eight miles (and, then, only with a high-gain antenna), such stations were inexpensive to build and operate. A typical example was WNAS in New Albany, Indiana, which went on the air in 1949:

> Superintendent Henry Davidson wanted a "voice" for his schools. He couldn't see a way to finance the only kind of station then possible—a high-power station costing from $50,000 to $100,000. He waited until the low-power FM station became a possibility for schools. Then he went into action.
> He found that a 10-watt FM station would cost about $3,000 to build and equip. (Actual final cost $3,500)[4]

But just as they were beginning to develop their allocated channels in FM radio, noncommercial broadcasters were forced to divert some of their attention to television. Decision making at the FCC preparatory to ending the *TV freeze* (see Chapters 5 and 8) was about to determine the use of the television band for the foreseeable future. Educational broadcasting interests recognized that failure to secure video spectrum space now would seriously undermine the prospects for any noncommercial television stations later. A consortium of seven educational groups, backed by money from the Ford Foundation, created the Joint Committee for Educational Television (JCET) to press their case.

JCET filed a petition with the FCC asking that 25 percent of television assignments be reserved for noncommercial licensees. They had calculated their actual needs at 10 percent but thought that petitioning for the higher percentage would give them a stronger base from which to compromise. The National Association of Broadcasters opposed the request, arguing as they had in the 1930s that because *all* stations had to operate "in the public interest," reserved channels for noncommercial interests were redundant. The NAB further pointed out that the few old AM educational facilities, as well as the more numerous new FM outlets, had been able to attract only very small audiences. Why waste valuable television spectrum space in pursuit of such a limited market?

Fortunately for the JCET, it found a strong and adept advocate in FCC Commissioner Frieda Hennock (see Figure 9–3). The first woman to serve on the commission, Hennock

agreed with the educators that the postwar baby boom, shortage of teachers, and explosion of knowledge created challenges that educational television could help address. Largely through her efforts, almost 12 percent of the post-freeze assignments (242 of 2,053 slots) were exclusively reserved for bona fide educational institutions or organizations. Eighty of the 242 were VHF. In subsequent FCC rulemakings, both the number of overall assignments and the number of noncommercial slots were increased.

Commenting on this action, a *New York Times* editorial of April 15, 1952, cautioned:

The world of education must give thought to the possibility of pooling its resources to use whatever channels it can in order to bring both the humanities and the vocations into the home. Such a golden opportu-

**Figure 9–3**
FCC commissioner Frieda Hennock, champion of educational television

**247**

CHAPTER 9
Noncom-
mercial
and
Interna-
tional
Adven-
tures

nity for education to extend its horizons must receive the most earnest and sincere study; it must not be lost by default.

The FCC has risen to the challenge of television, now others must be willing to accept it.

Part of the concern of the *Times* was that the educational assignments were good for one year only, after which frequencies not applied for would be available for commercial application. Under Congressional pressure, however, the FCC modified this decision in 1953, when Chairman Rosel Hyde announced that the noncommercial reservations would not expire but were, in fact, permanent.

### ETV Comes Alive.

Even though the immediate pressure was off, prospective educational telecasters moved as fast to take to the air as their limited resources would allow. The University of Houston's KUHT was the first station to begin operations on May 23, 1953. Meanwhile, several philanthropic organizations provided their help. The Ford Foundation offered a matching grant program that could bring a station up to $150,000. The National Appliance and Radio-TV Dealers Association donated money for the promotion of educational television as well as for station operating expenses, and the Emerson Radio Corporation pledged $10,000 to each of the first ten ETV (educational television) stations able to get on the air.

Still, progress was slow. Outlets that were built usually lacked the programming and recording resources necessary to produce shows that compared favorably with their commercial counterparts. Consequently, ETV came to be perceived as the medium with dull pictures and shoddy production values. By the middle of 1954, only seven educational telecasters were operational. One of the most successful, Pittsburgh's WQED, pioneered a new noncommercial ownership pattern by

being the first TV station to be operated by a community group rather than by a single educational institution.[5] Bringing together a coalition of interests, the community licensee arrangement offered the potential for a broader support base than could be provided by a single university or school system.

Gradually, ETV began to stabilize. The Ford Foundation increased its funding for the Educational Television and Radio Center (known after 1963 as NET, National Educational Television). Originally located in Ann Arbor, Michigan, the Center assisted individual stations in producing programs that were then made into kinescope recordings and bicycled to other ETV outlets around the country. Pictorial quality and timeliness were not hallmarks of this system, but the enterprise did provide many more programs than any one station could have secured on its own. By 1956, two dozen ETV stations were on the air. Three of these outlets belonged to the Alabama ETV system. Alabama was the first state network to reach more than 90 percent of its state's population with its signal.[6] Closed-circuit applications of instructional video were also being explored. About 100 CCTV systems were in use, including a public school operation at New York's Port Chester High School.[7]

## New Support, New Missions

As the 1960s began, educational broadcasting seemed a permanent, if minor, part of the electronic media landscape. NET had moved to New York and was bicycling *videotapes* rather than kinescopes to member stations. This breakthrough was made possible by the Ford Foundation's purchase of videotape recorders for NET headquarters and for each

ETV station. Almost 4 dozen such stations were now on the air and, together with the 162 operational educational FM facilities, they provided a viable if modest core on which noncommercial broadcasting could build.

## Airborne and Terrestrial ETV

In 1961, a different delivery system designed specifically for instructional television was launched. MPATI (the Midwest Program for Airborne Television Instruction) took to the air. First tried commercially in 1948 by Westinghouse as Stratovision, MPATI used a plane circling at 23,000 feet over Montpelier, Indiana, to transmit history, science, and foreign language videotaped programs to rural school districts in six midwestern states.[8] (See Figure 9–4.) In essence, the lumbering DC-6 constituted a moving UHF antenna atop a

23,000-foot tower in order to extend the transmission's line-of-sight (see Chapter 2) over a 300-mile diameter. Using Purdue University's airport as its base of operations, MPATI broadcasts continued for seven years.

Although its technical premise proved valid, MPATI's key weakness was in on-the-ground coordination. Funds from the Ford Foundation, the U.S. Office of Education, and other interested groups did not provide for adequate staff to communicate properly with the hundreds of school districts nestled under the airplane's signal. Thus, programming often went unwatched because it did not meet the particular curricular or scheduling needs of individual schools. The promise of satellite communications also made MPATI seem antique by comparision, and financial support waned. Still, the pioneering effort did demonstrate that television technology, if

**Figure 9–4**
MPATI's design for multistate instructional television

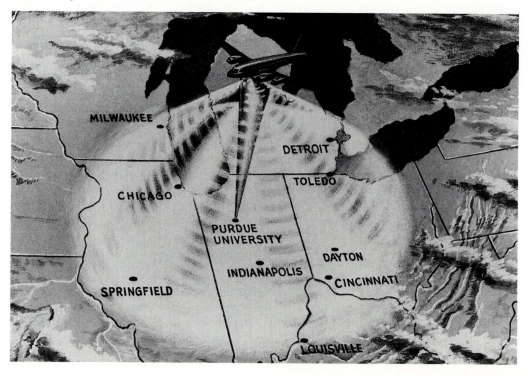

properly coordinated, could narrow the instructional resources gap between have and have-not school districts.

Terrestrial stations were not being ignored during the MPATI period. In 1962, Congress passed the Educational TV Facilities Act, which authorized $32 million over a five-year period to provide up to 75 percent of the cost of new station construction or upgrading of existing station facilities. Largely due to this support, the number of ETV stations nearly doubled (from forty-seven to ninety-two) during the following three-year period. At about the same time, the Ford Foundation gave a further boost to educational television in two significant ways. First, it helped purchase Channel 13 in New York (WNDT) as the flagship station for a national ETV hook-up. Then, in a related manner, it helped National Educational Television (NET) organize a programming staff that made possible both original program production and a unified network schedule.

Meanwhile, some schools (particularly Catholic parochial districts) were putting ITFS (Instructional Television Fixed Service) installations on line. These microwave relays operating on reserved noncommercial frequencies enabled districts to share televised lessons with all their school buildings simultaneously. (As mentioned in Chapter 2, unallocated ITFS channels were subsequently reclaimed by the FCC for MMDS use. Other licenses held by educational institutions have been leased back to MMDS operators as a much-needed source of revenue to support other instructional activities.)

## Ups and Downs of Educational Radio

By this time, NET, in both name and action, was out of the educational radio enterprise. And NERN (the National Educational Radio Network) was largely limited to tape exchange activity. To a large extent, noncommercial radio thus became a collection of unassociated entities with no clear national direction. Some of these stations were organized into state networks or, like the nonprofit Pacifica outlets, were held together by common philanthropic ownership. Others were linked by their religious purpose. But there was little national visibility for the medium, and large areas of the country were without noncommercial radio service. Like the commercial broadcasting establishment, educators were viewing television as the preferred medium, and its high costs were draining off money that might otherwise have been available for radio. (Recall our Chapter 7 discussion of 1950s commercial network radio.) "Money, time, energy, and skilled personnel have been absorbed by educational television," wrote educational radio manager James Mead in 1965.[9] John Stiehl, the chief engineer for the Wisconsin Radio Council Network, added:

> In talking about radio, I feel, I suppose, somewhat like the doctor must feel when he does a post mortem. Although radio is by no means dead, it is not nearly as glamorous, I guess, as television.[10]

One aspect of educational radio that seemed to do well even in the face of television was the public school radio station. Glorying in their relatively low-power localism, the forty-six outlets (forty-four FM and two AM) operated by independent school districts programmed a mix of in-school lessons (instructional programming), general enrichment offerings (such as classical music and dramas), and community-oriented services from basketball games to school board meetings.[11] Mainly operated by entities that could not afford to build a television station, these outlets adapted to the same realities as did their commercial radio counterparts by stressing their localism and customized responsiveness to select groups and needs.

## Becoming Public

Nevertheless, while the public school and other noncommercial radio stations kept learning how to do more with less, government and foundation attention focused to a greater extent on how to provide educational television with more. Low budgets were resulting in a primitive on-air look (see Figure 9–5) that drove away all but the most sympathetic or teacher-assigned viewers. Accordingly, in 1965, the Carnegie Corporation formed a blue-ribbon panel to study educational television and make recommendations about how it could better serve the public as a whole. Chaired by James Killian, president emeritus of the Massachusetts Institute of Technology, the thirteen-member Carnegie Commission on Educational Television issued its report in January 1967. The document advocated creation of a Corporation for Public Television (CPT) which would be the conduit for federal and other grants for the system. While the government would contribute substantial sums to CPT (via an excise tax on new television sets) the earmarked nature of these revenues and CPT's independent status would

ensure that politicians would not be able to influence noncommercial programming. In addition to funding station facilities and program development, the corporation would develop live interconnection capabilities among outlets to create the infrastructure for a national TV network. Just as important, the Carnegie Commission advocated changing the name of the venture from *educational* to *public* television in order to broaden its role and constituency beyond instructional implications.

With the prodding of President Lyndon Johnson, legislation reflecting the core of the Carnegie Commission's recommendations was adopted the following November with passage of the Public Broadcasting Act of 1967. A permanent funding mechanism was not provided, however. Instead, the new organization would have to depend on periodic Congressional appropriations. The other significant change from the Carnegie Report was

**Figure 9–5**
Early 1960s instructional television, like educational television as a whole, was long on enthusiasm but often short on production values

that CPT became CP*B*—the Corporation for Public *Broadcasting*—in order that it be charged with supporting and developing noncommercial *radio* service as well. Despite its lack of guaranteed funding, the Public Broadcasting Act and the CPB that it created signaled a much more stable, visible, and comprehensive approach to development of noncommercial radio and television services for the U.S. public.

Meanwhile, the Ford Foundation, which had already contributed so much to the growth of noncommercial television, donated $10 million for production of a two-year program enterprise to be known as the Public Broadcasting Laboratory (PBL). Administered by NET, but independent of it in terms of program content, PBL's two-hour Sunday evening news and public affairs program ran for two years. Even though its quality was uneven, the series did serve the important function of pioneering season-long interconnecting of public television stations, an essential prelude to the development of more extensive cooperative activities.

Soon after, in early 1968, a public television organization destined to have a much longer and more successful life was initiated under the title of the Children's Television Workshop (CTW). With major underwriting by the Ford Foundation, the Carnegie Corporation, and the U.S. Office of Education, CTW set about making teaching programs for children more involving by imitating many of the techniques of commercial television. The workshop's director, Joan Ganz Cooney, used slick, spot-length segments to communicate linguistic and mathematical concepts and surrounded these segments with interesting characters, storylines, and instructive musical tunes and jingles. Beginning with *Sesame Street* in 1969, CTW proved that educational and self-esteem-building children's television could be as engaging and fast-paced as any commercial entertainment fare. (*Sesame Street* was also the first example of true instructional television designed entirely for in-*home* rather than in-school consumption.)

In order to distribute *Sesame Street* and other new program projects that were being planned, CPB moved to set up the interconnection mandated by the Public Broadcasting Act. Because the Act prohibited CPB from operating the system (or any production facility) itself, CPB marshalled the forces of public television stations in setting up the Public Broadcasting Service (PBS) as the autonomous interconnection agency. Governed by a board representing the interests of station managers and the general public, PBS began formal operations in the 1971 fall season. With PBS on line, NET lost much of its networking reason for being. Consequently, its assets were folded into the New York flagship station, which reflected this merger by changing its call sign from WNDT to WNET.

On the radio side, National Public Radio (NPR) was created as a distributive agent for audio broadcasters. Although similar in structure to PBS, with stations having member clout, NPR differed from PBS in that it *produced* programs as well as distributed those created by NPR member stations. PBS, on the other hand, remained an exclusively distributive rather than creative organization. Together, the two now gave public broadcasters unprecedented opportunities for obtaining the programs of other stations and a wider potential for exposure of shows that outlets themselves produced.

## Political Turbulence

Even as it began its first year of full-fledged activity, however, PBS's seeming role as a network was challenged by Clay Whitehead, director of the Nixon administration's Office of Telecommunications Policy. Already suspect by the White House because of the liberal slant to some programs it carried (but did not produce), PBS was put on notice that "a centralized, national network" was not looked on favorably. In his October 1971 speech to the National Association of Educational Broadcasters Convention in Miami Beach, Whitehead quoted the Carnegie Commission as maintaining that the structure of public broadcasting "was to be built on a bedrock of localism." Alluding to public affairs shows from NET in New York and Washington's National Public Affairs Center for Television (NPACT) that had drawn the administration's ire, the OTP director warned:

> When you centralize actual responsibility at a single point, it makes you visible politically and those who are prone to see ghosts can raise the spectre of government pressure. . . . When the struggle is simply between the Washington center and the New York center, it doesn't matter much who wins. It probably isn't even worth the effort.[12]

Using a battle cry of localism, the Nixon White House made it clear that a strong, powerful, noncommercial network, independent of both commercial pressures and government content oversight, was not in the best interests of stations expecting additional monetary support from the federal government.

Some public broadcasters subscribed to Whitehead's appeal for decentralization, even though they did not support his underlying motivation. They believed that PBS operating as a true network would dominate public television. These broadcasters, along with Whitehead, felt that the historic independence of individual noncommercial stations could be assured only if PBS were limited to *interconnect* activities, to passive distribution of programs produced at the local level. This, of course, was what the old NET had done for years. The contribution of PBS, it was argued, was that it could now bring live interconnection to the distribution process rather than rely on the mailed bicycling of NET days. PBS should not, however, involve itself in the scheduling or promoting of national issue programming.

President Nixon, stung by some of the NPACT coverage of his administration car-

ried over PBS, vetoed the CPB authorization bill in July 1972. His press secretary reiterated the contention that this was done because CPB and its PBS creation were exercising too much control over local station schedules. People supporting a true PBS network were further disheartened later in the year when the CPB board, now dominated by Nixon appointees, itself moved to take a greater programming role. CPB announced that funding would no longer be available for most NPACT offerings or for other PBS series noted for a liberal bias. After further months of wrangling, a tentative truce was reached. PBS remained in control of the interconnection system but would be ineligible to receive any CPB money for program production. Instead, program production funds were channeled by CPB directly to individual stations, which could use these allocations to pay for the programs they wished to receive down the interconnect. Localism was thus reaffirmed while the attempt by a politicized CPB board to affect the system's program choices and availability had also been blunted.

## Revised Mechanisms

In early 1974, the process of station/PBS cooperative decision-making was refined with creation of the Station Program Cooperative (SPC). Through this mechanism, PBS submitted lists of programs to member stations that indicated which programs they were willing to support with their CPB-derived or other revenues. A succession of shorter and shorter lists of shows thus resulted in a money-driven consensus among stations from which a substantial portion of the PBS schedule was subsequently fashioned. Notice how this from-the-bottom-up decision-making process in the public sector was the exact opposite of the commercial network television top-down arrangement. In commercial broadcasting, of course, the network organization determines the schedule and then pays local affiliates for carrying the commercials that the schedule contains. PBS maintained its from-the-bottom

**253**

CHAPTER 9
Noncom-
mercial
and
Interna-
tional
Adven-
tures

**Table 9–1**
**CPB's Escalating Schedule for Public Radio Funding Eligibility**

| Minimum Criteria | 1973 | 1974 | 1975 | 1976 |
|---|---|---|---|---|
| STAFF: | | | | |
| Full-Time | 3 | 3 | 4 | 5 |
| ON-THE-AIR SCHEDULE: | | | | |
| Weeks per Year | 52 | 52 | 52 | 52 |
| Days per Week | 7 | 7 | 7 | 7 |
| Hours per Day | 12 | 14 | 16 | 18 |

approach until 1990, when decreasing federal dollars precipitated a more commercial-like pattern.

While the much more visible world of public television was embroiled in midseventies political and philosophical conflicts, National Public Radio discretely assumed the role of radio network without opposition. Furthermore, through a series of gradually increasing facility, schedule, and personnel requirements, (see Table 9–1) NPR membership came to embrace and assist both established and new stations to become major and more or less full-time voices in their localities. In a variety of ways, CPB and other federal funding sources dovetailed their requirements with those for NPR membership so that a system of strong and professionally managed stations emerged. Unfortunately, many of the public school and student-operated college stations could not meet CPB/NPR standards and were bypassed in this upgrading process. Thus, by the midseventies, noncommercial radio became a two-tier entity. The top tier comprised the qualifying public stations, and the bottom tier consisted of low-power, limited-staff outlets whose only funds were derived from meager local resources.

## Raised to Chase Dollars

With the upgraded public radio system well on the road to realization, and the public television sector having put its worst political battles behind it, noncommercial broadcasters moved to take advantage of their now-solidified status. A second Carnegie Commission was convened in 1977 and reported its conclusions in January 1979. To solve public broadcasting's continuous battles for federal appropriations while also better insulating it from the political pressures inherent in those battles, Carnegie II called for the creation of an autonomous Public Telecommunications Trust. Funds for this trust were to come, most significantly, from a spectrum-use tax levied on commercial broadcasters. Not too surprisingly, this tax, and the trust as a whole, lacked the political support needed for implementation.

### New Tools: Satellites, NAPTS and APR

On a more positive note, both public radio and public television converted their distribution systems to satellite relays before the end of the seventies. CPB provided all but $7 million of the $39.5 million needed to put PBS (in 1978) and NPR (in 1979) on the bird and therefore increased both the quality and the flexibility of public broadcast networking. PBS could now develop regional transmissions and also feed four separate programs at any one time for live airing or taping for later use. Similarly, NPR now had four audio channels available for programming, and excess capacity it could lease to commercial entities as a revenue-raising device.

In 1980, public television moved further to improve its operational coordination by creating the National Association of Public Television Stations (NAPTS). A nonprofit membership organization formed by the PTV licensees, NAPTS took over the lobbying, research, and planning functions for public telecasters in order that both they and PBS could devote more attention to programming matters. The radio side of public broadcasting also added a new organization about this same time with the founding of the American Public Radio Network (APR) in 1982. APR was established by five public radio stations that wanted an alternative to NPR program distribution. As a nonprofit corporation rather than a station membership organization like NPR, APR sells individual programs to interested stations and delivers them by satellite. The success of APR's a la carte approach to program distribution led, in fact, to NPR's decision at the end of the eighties to unbundle its programming. This means that a station can now obtain certain groups of NPR offerings rather than being forced to take or leave basic NPR service as a whole.

## Shifting Revenue Sources

Despite its unprecedented success in building a national infrastructure, public broadcasting throughout the 1980s was preoccupied with fund-raising problems. Even though almost every U.S. home was now within range of a PBS and NPR signal, money to pay for these signals was in scarce supply. Reagan administration cuts in CPB and related activities meant that by fiscal year 1986, total federal contributions made up no more than 15.5 percent of public television's income.[13] To compensate for this drop, the system and its stations were forced to depend more and more on corporate underwriters, individual listeners/viewers, and a host of unconventional fund-raising schemes.

In 1982, for example, ten PTV stations participated in a Congressionally authorized test that allowed them to solicit and air actual commercials. The results were inconclusive and seemed only to suggest that a public station airing spots would not be able to attract

enough advertising to offset the reactive loss of foundation and viewer donation support. Some FCC loosening of the underwriting credit rules was undertaken to allow more specific product mention on noncommercial radio as well as on television outlets. But commercials per se were ruled out.

Three years later, the FCC initiated a proceeding on the feasibility of allowing PTV stations operating on VHF channels to swap their assignments with a commercial UHF broadcaster. The PTV station would receive the difference in value in cash. Almost no one came forward in support of that plan, but even more unusual ventures were being attempted. In the minus column was a Sacramento PTV outlet that lost $35,000 trying to run its own restaurant. In the plus column was North Dakota's Prairie Public Broadcasting, which in 1985–86 raised almost 20 percent of the income for its six TV and three radio stations through the operation of a chain of blackjack and bingo parlors.[14] For most licensees, however, the more conventional if less exotic on-air auctions, telephone solicitations, and member festivals served as the main local revenue devices.

In fact, CPB's calculations for 1986 (compiled in 1988) showed that local viewers and listeners had become the sources of more than one-fifth of the dollars received by public broadcasters. Specifically, income sources were as cited in Table 9–2.

## Seeking Fiscal and Role Stability

Despite decades of development and generous support from the Ford Foundation, the Carnegie Corporation, and the fluctuating appropriations through CPB, public broadcasting entered the 1990s still in search of an assured funding mechanism. True, the 1967 Public Broadcasting Act had built the system and created CPB as a separate, if not completely politics-free, dollar disseminator. Getting dollars to CPB in the first place, however, remains a highly uncertain enterprise and one subject to standard Washington power struggles. After sixty years of trying, a stable

**255**

CHAPTER 9

Noncom-
mercial
and
Interna-
tional
Adven-
tures

**Table 9–2**
**Revenue Sources of Public Broadcasters**

| Income Source | Percentage of Income |
|---|---|
| Member subscribers | 21.6% |
| State governments | 18.8 |
| Businesses | 15.0 |
| Federal-CPB | 14.0 |
| State-supported colleges and universities | 10.2 |
| Local governments | 4.3 |
| Foundations | 3.4 |
| Federal government grants and contracts | 2.3 |
| Private colleges | 2.3 |
| Auction participants | 2.0 |
| Other sources | 5.9 |
| Unspecified sources | 0.2 |

*Source: Adapted from "CPB Renews Pitch for More Funding,"* Broadcasting *(April 25, 1988), p. 61.*

support scheme for U.S. noncommercial broadcasting has yet to be implemented. The Children's Television Act of 1990 (see Chapter 6) did provide approximately $6 million for the production of "educational programming" but this amount is hardly significant.

Of greater operational, if not fiscal, enhancement was PBS's 1990 decision to replace the cumbersome State Program Cooperative with a more streamlined National Programming Service. Under the new arrangement, the PBS chief programming executive oversees a centralized National Programming Service that selects and provides about 1,600 original broadcast hours to PBS member stations each year. The NPS is funded by a commitment of dollars from the stations (dollars they used to spend in making their SPC selections) as well as from the transfer of funds from CPB, which has greatly reduced its role in program development. In short, public television stations now subscribe to a program service rather than select individual programs as they did through the old Station Program Cooperative. By consolidating decision making and working toward a uniform prime-time schedule, it is hoped that the new structure will bring greater visibility to PBS and expend existing dollars more effectively, and thereby increase governmental and private support for public television.

By itself, however, the National Programming Service cannot resolve public television's recurring identity crisis. PBS's claim of being the main source for top-notch cultural and artistic programming is being challenged by commercial cable services like Discovery and Arts & Entertainment. Its franchise on more in-depth news and public affairs analysis has been significantly preempted by C-SPAN and CNN. Even the strictly instructional sector has now been invaded by Whittle Communications' Channel One and a special educational service from CNN, both designed for in-school viewing and use. In the midst of this diversifying media environment, public television is finding it increasingly difficult to define itself as a unique service worthy of continued financial contributions from government or individual viewers.

## External Ventures— Private Shortwave

We now turn our attention from domestic noncommercial broadcasting to the even less understood world of international transmissions. Because this is an introduction to electronic media in the United States, we do not examine the radio and television systems operated by other countries to serve their own citizens. Instead, we focus on the various efforts by U.S. broadcasters to reach the ears and eyes of people beyond our own borders.

## Prewar Opportunities

As early as the 1920s, U.S. electronics manufacturers and later both CBS and NBC set up sideline shortwave operations to target European and South American listeners. In March 1932, the Federal Radio Commission authorized U.S. broadcasters to relay sponsored as well as unsponsored programs to foreign audiences, activities which both RCA and AT&T soon incorporated into their transoceanic operations. Seven years later, on June 1, 1939, the FCC enlarged this policy to permit the actual sale of commercial time over the private shortwave facilities.[15] At this juncture, Crosley, Westinghouse, and General Electric,

as well as NBC and CBS, were engaged in such officially experimental shortwave enterprises. With an eye toward tapping into a profitable Latin American market, CBS set up a shortwave "Network of the Americas"[16]. NBC countered by dispatching its vice-president for programs, former vaudeville impresario John Royal (pictured in Figure 9–6) to that same region to explore possibilities for local rebroadcasts of NBC shortwave shows.[17]

Because Congress had no wish to create government-run stations, it was felt that such network activities, and the fourteen private shortwave licensees then in operation, were the best way to establish a U.S. presence on the increasingly propaganda-filled international airwaves. "A straight, unbiased synopsis of what is happening in the world," wrote one commentator, "is the best proof of American freedom and integrity, the most effective and unanswerable propaganda." Consequently, President Roosevelt's fireside chats

**Figure 9–6**
John Royal, NBC's prospector for Latin American business

were always accorded airtime on the stations and translated into Spanish, French, Portuguese, German, and Italian.[18] By mid-1940, the commercial shortwave stations were reportedly receiving 10,000 letters a month from Latin America alone and seemed on the brink of real profitability. Prospects appeared so good that William Paley himself, the founder and head of CBS, traveled to South America in search of new business relationships for his company.[19]

With the U.S. entry into World War II, however, such ambitious commercial ventures became impossible as the federal government first appropriated blocks of time on the private shortwave stations and then took over the eleven surviving stations themselves (see Chapter 7). Under the auspices of the Office of War Information (OWI), these stations originally were devoted to serving the listening needs of U.S. servicemen overseas. In fact, the *Command Performance* series was literally that—a show made up of the big stars and features requested by such units as the Flying Tiger pilots serving in China and the doomed troopers surrounded by Japanese on Bataan. Eventually, the Armed Forces Radio Service, made up primarily of portable stations programming transcribed material received from stateside, assumed this role, and the shortwave stations returned to their original purpose of broadcasting to the citizens of other nations. Under the rubric of the Voice of America, this service officially began on February 24, 1942, with most VOA programming produced by NBC and CBS under contract to the OWI. New transmitters were put on line to complement those leased from the private shortwave stations, and, in 1943, some twenty-three facilities were in operation, broadcasting in almost two dozen languages.

## Decline and Rebirth

After the war, the leased shortwave stations were returned to their owners, but the market for a profitable commercial shortwave service was now much softer. Furthermore,

CBS and NBC were devoting every resource they could spare to the development of their domestic television operations and retained little interest in the seemingly outmoded field of shortwave. Thus, for more than three decades, the only private international radio engaged in by U.S. interests was done by religious broadcasters, who sold time exclusively to religious groups. Only four such stations remained by the end of the 1970s.

In 1980, however, commercial international radio revived in the U.S. when 100-kw WRNO New Orleans was licensed by the FCC. The station simulcast the programming of its sister FM station to Canada and Europe. The station's slogan, "The Rock of New Orleans," was adapted to become "The Rock of the World." Two years later, KYOI went on the air from the U.S. trust territory of the Mariana Islands with a top-40 format voiced in Japanese and aimed at listeners and advertisers in Japan.[20] By the end of the decade, KYOI changed hands to become one of three transmitting facilities making up the shortwave service of *The Christian Science Monitor*. With installations in Maine and South Carolina as well as two in the Marianas, the Monitor network's 1,700 kw combined output made it the largest private international broadcaster in the world. Providing news and informational programming in two-hour blocks interspersed with religious and inspirational offerings, the Monitor's signal now blankets the world. Sale of commercial time is planned, with the Monitor network eventually projected to be self-standing and profitable.[21]

At the beginning of 1990, a total of eighteen U.S.-licensed private shortwave broadcasters were on the air—a number almost equaling those at the end of World War II. Most of these facilities have a religious purpose in whole or in part. At least three of them, however, (KUSW Salt Lake City; NDXE Opelika, Alabama; and previously mentioned WRNO New Orleans) emphasize commercial music formats.

To U.S. inhabitants unaccustomed to relying on shortwave for their radio service, such stations may seem to be an outmoded curiosity. Yet, in regions where shortwave signals have historically been the only economical means of covering vast distances with limited monetary resources, the delivery system makes sense. In preparing to sign his station on the air on July 4, 1986, NDXE President H. Dickson Norman commented, "We intend to propagate the best of American radio to audiences around the world because there is a hunger for that programming."[22] As with any commercial venture in the electronic media, it remains to be seen whether such outlets can create reasonably documented audiences of a type global advertisers will pay to reach.

## Voice of America Development

As we've just discussed, the Voice of America was born over leased transmitters in 1942 to give the United States its first official presence on the international broadcasting scene. Before long, VOA activities had been expanded to seven days a week, twenty-four hours per day, in twenty-four languages.

### The First Thirty Years
Whether broadcasting news, information, or entertainment, the service's programming tried to become a vehicle to which people everywhere would want to listen. Therefore, it was the result of "a continuous search for interesting and vigorous methods of presentation."[23] Royal "Arch" Gunnison, the Mutual Broadcasting System's Manila correspondent, gained first-hand knowledge of VOA's effectiveness in the Far East. Repatriated in 1943 after seventeen months in a Japanese concentration camp, Gunnison testified that

although the Japs have a single punishment (death) for the possession of a shortwave

set, there are plenty around and they'll never find them. . . . San Francisco's powerful shortwave station KWID (100,000 watts), KGEI and KWIX (50,000 watts each) send a clear signal into all parts of the Orient. When U.S. propaganda broadcasts stick to the facts in the Far East . . . [VOA] is well received and widely distributed by the grapevine.[24]

Indeed, in its first transmission in February 1942, the VOA's German-language announcer articulated the service's guiding goal of accuracy:

Daily, at this time, we shall speak to you about America and the war. The news may be good or bad—we shall tell you the truth.[25]

Such high purpose notwithstanding, Congress was ready, at the end of the war, to dismantle VOA as part of the general demobilization. The ABSIE (Armed Forces American Broadcasting System in Europe) branch of VOA was closed down only two months after Germany's surrender, and the Office of War Information (VOA's parent) was abolished almost immediately following the Japanese capitulation later in 1945. President Truman transferred the now orphaned VOA to the Department of State. But Congress, suspicious of an international radio system operated by the Executive Branch, required that 75 percent of the network's programs be prepared by CBS and NBC. The networks did not want this sensitive job, and, after a few of the programs they produced had antagonized some Congressmen, they were able to extricate themselves from any further VOA participation by 1948.[26]

With Cold War tensions between the United States and the Soviet Union on the increase, however, it seemed unwise to abandon VOA as a weapon in the information war. Therefore, Congress passed the United States Information and Educational Exchange Act of 1948 that committed the country to engage in international broadcasting while prohibiting the retransmission of such programming to U.S. listeners. Here, again, Congress feared a domestic propaganda voice that could be controlled by any presidential administration and so made certain that VOA material was earmarked exclusively for external consumption. Nevertheless, the State Department remained uncomfortable managing such a public enterprise, and VOA continued to be a neglected stepchild. In 1953, Congress created the United States Information Agency (USIA) to handle all overseas informational tasks and placed VOA under USIA's span of control.

Gradually, VOA improved its technical facilities and began to tailor its broadcasts more toward news and informational programming and less to the primarily entertainment offerings that had characterized it previously. To bolster its credibility, and that of USIA in general, President Kennedy appointed CBS newsman Edward R. Murrow as USIA director in 1961. Consistent with both VOA's tradition and his own philosophy, Murrow composed a statement that was reprinted in VOA publications long after his departure:

The Voice of America stands upon this above all: The truth shall be the guide. Truth may help us. It may hurt us. But, helping or hurting us we shall have the satisfaction of knowing that man can know us for what we are and can at least believe what we say.[27]

In its subsequent reports about the shooting down of a U.S. U-2 spy plane over the Soviet Union and in its coverage of the racial unrest and brutalities that engulfed the United States throughout the sixties, VOA added substantially to its stature abroad (and to some Congressional irritation at home) by fully disclosing negative as well as the positive outcomes of U.S. life and policies. Credibility meant listenership. In reply to announcements aired during a single week in 1964, for example, VOA received 35,000 letters from listeners in Latin America and 85,000 responses to its English-language broadcasts from almost every country in the world.[28]

## Philosophy and Facility Refinements

Fortunately, Congress came to recognize that long-term credibility of the VOA was more

**Figure 9–7**
"The Bubble," VOA's long-time news operations center in Washington, D.C., where telephone reports from correspondents are received, recorded, and duplicated for broadcast

important to the national interest than were short-term propaganda ploys. On July 12, 1976, therefore, new legislation was passed to bolster continuance of the Voice's hard-won tradition for veracity and independence. Specifically, the Congress directed that

1. VOA will serve as a consistently reliable and authoritative source of news. VOA news will be accurate, objective, and comprehensive.
2. VOA will represent America, not any single segment of American society, and will therefore present a balanced and comprehensive projection of significant American thoughts and institutions.
3. VOA will present the policies of the United States clearly and effectively, and will also present responsible discussion and opinion on these policies.[29]

Nevertheless, five years later, the newly installed Reagan administration sought to make the Voice a much more affirmative propaganda arm. On the plus side, this meant sub-

stantial new funds for facility upgrading, including enhanced satellite capability (see Figure 9–8) and the addition of powerful AM transmitters to serve Central America. On the downside, it also brought a number of changes in VOA senior management, with more emphasis placed on the idea that the Voice should be a cheerleader for the United States. For the most part, the system withstood the more extreme attempts to convert it into a public relations arm for the administration and emerged from the 1980s with its credibility intact.

Along the way, VOA added two significant new services. VOA-Europe began experimentally in October 1985 through a leased-time arrangement with an English-language FM station in Paris. The first VOA service intended specifically for Western Europe since the 1945 shutdown of ABSIE, VOA-Europe's programming soon came to be modeled after full-service, contemporary hit radio in the United States. Designed to reach the young, postwar citizens of Western Europe, much of VOA-Europe material is assembled in Wash-

**Figure 9–8**
Satellite dishes at the VOA relay station near Greenville, North Carolina

**261**

CHAPTER 9
Noncom-
mercial
and
Interna-
tional
Adven-
tures

## FRANK SCOTT/DIRECTOR
### VOICE OF AMERICA (VOA) EUROPE

Like most things there is good news and bad news about my job. The good news is that I am pioneering on an international scale in a communications world that almost defies imagination. The bad news is that I seldom see most of my family members, even when they are at home, and, in many ways, I don't really know where home is. I live in Munich, but I am seldom there. I am in the same city as my wife less than 150 days a year and my twin sons less than fifty. My other four children and their families I see even less. I have not seen one son, his wife, and three children for nearly two years.

But I love what I do! In the last five years I have devised a plan and led a team of broadcasters in the creation of the first satellite-driven, commercial, pannational radio network. It broadcasts twenty-four hours a day, mostly CHR (contemporary hit radio) music in a full-service format, all in stereo. It now reaches some 223 major cities, towns, and regions of East and West Europe in twenty-four countries. Every day it gets bigger. We started in Western Europe with a service designed for Europeans that would also provide information about what people in the United States are really like. Now we continue to add affiliates in the West and are also expanding in the East. We made history again on March 15, 1990, when Radio Bridge signed on the air in Budapest as the first-ever privately owned commercial radio station in Hungary, the first in Eastern Europe, and the first Eastern European affiliate of VOA Europe. We are the broadcasting of the future, operating now. Soon truly global radio and TV networks will be on line.

A representative few weeks sees me leave home early on a Thursday. I fly to London for meetings with the chairman of our affiliates board and with TSMS, the international advertising sales representative organization that sells commercials on the VOA Europe Network. On Friday, I board a Pan Am Jet at London Heathrow airport for Atlanta and the annual National Association of Broadcasters convention. There, I talk and negotiate with any number of people and organizations from program syndicators and equipment suppliers to prospective affiliates. All in all, I might squeeze at least twenty-five meetings into three working days at the NAB. Then I fly to my Washington office to check in with our program production center. Even though my headquarters are in Munich, my network program center is in Washington. There, programming either originates or is inserted into the network string. Even though I keep in close contact with the Washington office by telephone and other links, I try to *be* there at least four times each year.

After three or four days of intensive meetings in Washington and a weekend in which I try to see some members of my family, I'm back on a plane to London, where I arrive very early in the morning for meetings all that day and the next before heading home to Munich. Arriving on a Wednesday or Thursday, I spend two or three days in my office catching up on paperwork, try to spend the weekend with my wife, and maybe get in a little skiing or golfing, depending on the time of year. (Last year I was able to find time to play golf only twice and go skiing just once!)

On Monday, I am off to Warsaw for meetings that afternoon and Tuesday morning. Tuesday afternoon I fly to Sofia for meetings there through Wednesday before flying to Prague. In Prague I have late afternoon meetings and conferences Thursday morning and then fly to Bucharest for meetings there through Friday. Sometime Friday evening I get home.

I live on airplanes, run up huge telephone bills, and sometimes feel too much like a workaholic in perpetual motion. But it's fascinating and rewarding, as well as being on the cutting edge of the media future.

ington and then satellite-relayed in stereo across the Atlantic for pick up by radio stations and cable FM channels. With a twenty-four-hour blend of news, public affairs, pop music deejay shows, and short Americana features, VOA-Europe strives to offer an entertaining U.S. broadcast presence to a new generation. Still, some U.S. foreign service (State Department) officers question the need for this outreach effort, and VOA-Europe's funding battles have been more or less continuous.

For its part, Congress has firmly supported the service, which has therefore continued to expand. In December 1989, VOA-Europe assumed commercial status, with all proceeds from network spots going to its terrestrial affiliates. The affiliated stations themselves were already carrying their own commercials in local windows built into the network programming and had been engaged in this business activity since VOA-Europe's inception.

More contentious is the subject of support for Worldnet, the USIA's expensive television

## CNN  Worldnet and Radio Marti

USIA's Worldnet was created as a television tool for communicating unfiltered U.S. policy to the international community. In contrast, the U.S. government's much more controversial Radio Marti aimed at Cuba is considered by some observers to be an instrument for electronic invasion.

service. An interactive system that began in November 1983 to explain the U.S. invasion of Grenada, Worldnet deployed satellite interconnections to enable foreign journalists gathered in U.S. embassies and USIA libraries to listen to and interview U.S. policy makers back in Washington. Subsequent to that first presentation on Grenada, Worldnet mounted a regular daily schedule featuring news, sports, documentaries, and a USIA version of the *Today* show geared to bring morning talk and information to most of Europe and North Africa. These activities, of course, are in addition to frequent multipoint live press conferences that can bring together experts and officials from a number of countries. Worldnet service is no longer just intended for reception at U.S. embassies and libraries. It is also designed for pick up by foreign cable systems, hotel master antenna (SMATV) arrays, and home satellite dishes.

Congressman Dan Mica, whose subcommittee oversees USIA operations, has called Worldnet "the superstation that America will never see." Like many of his colleagues, Mica supports the system as long as its content does not restrict itself to the views of the administration in power. "We want to be sure," he warns, "that there is a true balance and not just tokenism—that they don't throw in just enough opposition spokesmen to say they had a balanced presentation when in fact they did not."[30] Unfortunately, in the late 1980s, USIA director Charles Wick undercut such Congressional support when he grossly overstated the foreign viewership garnered by the system. Though reactive threats to close down Worldnet later subsided, some of Worldnet's more ambitious outreach plans were aborted as a result of this miscalculation. Even in governmental electronic media, it seems, audience delivery estimates are expected to be reliable and also to demonstrate cost effectiveness!

In a stated attempt to improve such cost effectiveness, USIA Director Bruce Gelb merged VOA, Worldnet, and the Cuban-serving TV and Radio Marti into a new Bureau of Broadcasting in 1991. This Bureau was itself folded into general USIA operations in terms of budget, personnel, and public affairs activities. Some people in VOA have charged that the USIA's so-called policy advocacy mission on behalf of U.S. interests and VOA's "journalistic credibility and independence" cannot be co-managed. Meanwhile, Worldnet was suffering a further setback during the Persian Gulf War when commercial CNN used its own unduplicated access to Baghdad and the cable network's worldwide signal delivery capability to function as an effective electronic intermediary and forum for combatants, neutrals, and their citizens. CNN proved itself to be a much more potent linkage than was the comparatively obscure Worldnet, placing the future role of USIA's video branch into question.

## Surrogate Services

A government-operated international outlet like the Voice of America strives to be a reflection of its country of origin. *Surrogate* services, on the other hand, are set up by a foreign power as a substitute for another country's own domestic stations. Usually this is done because the foreign power believes that the target country's own media are concealing the truth from the citizenry and that such an absence of truth is harming that same foreign power's interests.

### The Martis

The most recent surrogate services to be set up by the United States are Radio Marti and TV Marti, stations designed to give residents of Cuba an alternative to the Castro-run media. Although operated from an existing VOA station in the Florida Keys and nominally under VOA control, Radio Marti has its own presidential advisory board and, for the

## CNN TV Marti

Cuba's Fidel Castro calls TV Marti "tele-aggression." He has jammed its signal and threatened retaliation in the form of increased electromagnetic interference for U.S. AM broadcasters.

most part, functions independently, even after the USIA reorganization. Beginning full AM operations in 1985 with a staff of 175, Radio Marti was the product of a coalition between Reagan administration activists and Florida Democratic Congressmen, who count large numbers of anti-Castro refugees among their constituents. With a blend of news, music, and Spanish-language soap operas, Radio Marti's impact is uncertain, although it initially goaded Fidel Castro to increase the power of some of his own stations and thereby interfere with a number of U.S. commercial AM broadcasters.

A counterpart TV Marti went on the air in 1990 with signals transmitted from a tethered balloon swinging high above the Florida Keys. The long-term technical and practical potential for such a project remains the subject of heated Congressional debate. (A few months after its launch, the balloon broke free of its moorings and crashed in a Florida swamp.) TV Marti's signal (when operational) is extensively jammed by the Cuban authorities. They also have threatened additional spectrum retaliation against U.S. domestic broadcasters.

### Radio Free Europe and Radio Liberty

The much older and much more extensive U.S. surrogate operation is Radio Free Europe/Radio Liberty (formerly called Radio Liberation). Originally thought to be a purely private endeavor of prominent U.S. patriots, Radio Free Europe (RFE) began broadcasting

to the Soviet-dominated countries of Eastern Europe on July 4, 1950. In an era of the Berlin blockade by the Soviets and the Red Chinese-backed invasion of South Korea, RFE was seen as a way to present the truth to Eastern Europe without the restrictions VOA faced as the official service of the U.S. government. Radio Liberty (RL) began operations only a few months later, targeting the Soviet Union itself as well as Soviet Army units stationed in other East Bloc countries.

Together, RFE and RL soon operated massive transmitter banks in West Germany, Portugal, Spain, and Taiwan. Funding for the facilities seemed to flow from the associated National Committee for a Free Europe and American Committee for Liberation. Public service announcements on U.S. commercial radio and television stations also solicited contributions to a coordinating office in Valley Forge, Pennsylvania.

RFE and RL on-air staffs were made up of anti-Communist exiles from the target countries, and so the political philosophy of the stations was well known. Nevertheless, both RFE and RL worked for credibility in their news presentations. A 1964 policy statement from the RFE management for example, proudly maintained:

RFE newscasts must be accurate, objective, truthful and complete as possible. In general, unconfirmed, opinionated, or interpretive material will not be used in newscasts. Newscasts must carefully avoid slanting or taking material out of context. Primary responsibility for newscasts lies with the individual broadcasting departments, whose selection and presentation of newscast material is guided by the needs and interests of their audiences and the general objectives of RFE.[31]

Although prominently featured, RFE editorials have always been separated from news reports. Furthermore, as Cold War tensions eased, music and other entertainment content came to occupy a greater proportion of the on-air schedule. RFE/RL news and information programming continues as the mainstay of the two systems, however, and is supported by a huge research library in Munich. This library includes books and periodicals from East Bloc countries as well as transcripts of their domestic broadcasts and material gathered from interviews with travelers and recent emigrants.

Such policies and resources helped bolster the credibility of RFE/RL broadcasts behind the Iron Curtain, but this credibility was shaken (perhaps more among Americans than Eastern Europeans) when as early as 1966 news reports began circulating that linked the stations to the Central Intelligence Agency. Before long, the U.S. Senate found out that this not-so-well-kept secret was true. Almost from the beginning of their operations, the difference between private donations and what it cost to operate RFE/RL had been made up from CIA discretionary funds. A book by a former CIA operative later claimed that the agency's own internal policy studies had frequently recommended phasing out this support. At every juncture, however, "a few old-timers in the CIA, whose connection with the stations went back to their beginnings, would come up with new and dubious reasons why the radios should be continued."[32]

Some members of Congress felt that the time had come to end all federal underwriting of the stations because their origins had been exposed and tensions between the U.S. and the Communist world were easing. Eventually, however, the decision was made to legitimize the operations by funding them directly through a new nonprofit Board of International Broadcasting. Beginning in 1973, the BIB, whose nine members are appointed by the president with Senate approval, assumed overall and public responsibility for RFE/RL activities. In the new arrangement, the two stations were molded into a single operating unit, although the different geographic emphases of each remained unchanged.

By the 1980s, the old RFE/RL stridency had softened to reflect changing world conditions and the fact that a large percentage of their target listeners had by now lived their entire lives under Communism. Eugene Pell, a former foreign correspondent for NBC and Westinghouse who had also once served as director of VOA, took over as RFE/RL president in 1986. Pell further tightened journalistic standards and insisted on following basic U.S. journalistic practice that two credible sources must be found to validate any story before it will be aired. Meanwhile, Pell's director for RFE, former *Time* magazine staffer Gregory Wierzynski, took great care to understand the potential bias of his emigré staff and to institute procedures designed to com-

**CNN   RFE and VOA**

Questions are raised about the relevance of these two radio services in a post–cold-war world. Each organization is struggling to formulate a clear rationale for its continued existence and also for Congressional support.

pensate for this before material is aired. "They're politically engaged," observed Wierzynski. "That's why they're here. They have to justify their decision to leave their country. They could get in front of a microphone and yell."[33]

Holding such staffers to U.S.-style journalistic standards may become easier as political reform sweeps the former Iron Curtain countries in the 1990s. But these liberalizing events and consequent decreasing of old antagonisms may also mean that there is no longer a need for a surrogate broadcaster in Eastern Europe. At some time, local independent media may usurp the role that RFE/RL has served. For the present, however, RFE/RL continues with a $77 million facilities improvement program approved by Congress in 1985 and envisions a continuance of its surrogate activities for the foreseeable future.

## AFRTS Expeditions

As we discuss earlier in this chapter, special broadcast services for U.S. military personnel were initiated soon after Pearl Harbor under the title of the Armed Forces Radio Service. Today, with "Television" added to its name, AFRTS maintains approximately 100 stations on military posts located in fifteen countries. Even though the signals of these facilities are intended primarily for consumption by U.S. servicemen and women, their almost inevitable spillover to the host country's civilian populace makes them inadvertent international broadcasters as well.

AFRTS facilities are especially extensive in Frankfurt, West Germany, and in Tokyo, Japan. In Frankfurt, the U.S. European Armed Forces Network maintains a 150-kw AM transmitter that feeds a network of twenty-eight other AM outlets of various sizes throughout the region. The Armed Forces/Europe operation also includes a dozen FM

stations and eight television facilities that are further extended through use of a number of low-power translators. In Tokyo, AFRTS maintains a 50-kw AM and a 10-kw shortwave station to provide radio service to posts throughout the Far East.[34] As has been the case since its founding, AFRTS air schedules contain substantial amounts of news, sports, and entertainment programming from U.S. commercial networks and syndicators. The advertisements, however, have been removed. This material is extensively supplemented with locally produced base news and features to provide the equivalent of full-service broadcasting for the military personnel assigned to that posting.

As is to be expected, most AFRTS staffers are members of the military. Thus, professional opportunities in this far-flung enterprise mesh with the career paths available in the armed services. Despite their specialized mission, many AFRTS stations have helped diversify the broadcast services of their host countries by whetting the local populace's appetite for a wider range of program content and delivery. This accidental byproduct function can, of course, be considered as either a boon or a bane depending on the sort of changes the AFRTS activities end up stimulating.

## Satellites and the Global Village

We cannot end our exploration of international adventures without at least mentioning the tools and organizations that have opened up vast new opportunities for live intercontinental program exchange. As we have just discovered in our look at the USIA's Worldnet (and its functional competition, CNN), communications satellites now allow participants appearing on the same program to be physically scattered around the globe. Interactive,

**267**

CHAPTER 9
Noncom-
mercial
and
Interna-
tional
Adven-
tures

satellite-delivered technologies can bring geographically separated experts, generals, diplomats, and entertainers together for the scrutiny of local and multinational audiences alike. Such a cross-pollination of attitudes and interests may not always have a pleasing or enlightening result, but the capacity for increased political or cultural understanding cannot be ignored.

## INTELSAT

International electronic communication took a giant step forward in 1964, when nineteen nations signed an agreement establishing INTELSAT, the International Telecommunications Satellite Consortium. The United States joined INTELSAT through the Communications Satellite Corporation (COMSAT) that was established by Congress in 1962 to own and operate this country's satellite communications system. Because of its head start in the field, COMSAT was designated as managing agent for the INTELSAT system and supervised the launch of the Early Bird satellite (INTELSAT I) on April 6, 1965.

Parked over the Atlantic in a *geosynchronous* orbit 22,300 miles above the equator, Early Bird, and its later cousins, seem to remain in the same position because the speed of their orbit keeps pace with the speed of the earth's rotation. Early Bird initiated the first regularly scheduled relays of live, intercontinental television transmissions between North America and Western Europe. This capability was first widely appreciated in its international telecast of Pope Paul's visit to the United Nations.

By 1966, a total of fifty-five Western and Third World nations had joined INTELSAT (the Soviet Union and its allies opted for their own, much smaller *Intersputnik* system that was not operational until 1981.) Several more INTELSAT birds were contracted for so that a fully functioning global system could be implemented. By 1969, with additional INTELSAT vehicles now hovering over the Pacific and Indian Oceans, fully one-seventh of the world's population were given the chance to watch the first landing of a man on the moon—a case of one technological breakthrough trumpeting another.

In 1970, the INTELSAT system carried only about a thousand hours of television programming, but this figure increased almost ten times by the end of the decade.[35] Only twenty-five countries had the earth station capability to tie into the system as the 1970s began,[36] but this figure also soared during the next ten years. When INTELSAT V was launched in 1980, it offered a signal capacity fifty times greater than Early Bird had provided. This greatly increased capability on the new birds meant that by 1982, INTELSAT was able to offer customers the option of leasing a full-time rather than only a per-program service. AFRTS was among the first to take advantage of this proposal in relaying programming to its far-flung facilities.

Even though the United States was still a dominant force, INTELSAT by this time was able to assume independent operational control of its system and faced competition from EUTELSAT, a regional system founded by the national telecommunications ministries of several Western European countries. As its influence in the organization declined, the United States also began to look at alternatives to INTELSAT. Ownership quotas in the consortium are proportionate to a country's use of the system and, with more and more nations becoming involved, the U.S. ownership share had fallen to about 25 percent by 1987.[37] Thus, as early as 1984, the Reagan administration was moving toward a national policy to permit the establishment of private companies to compete for international satellite business. Several such companies are now active.

## The Electronic Nervous System

All of these events have brought about the technological realization of what media guru Marshall McLuhan foresaw a quarter-century earlier as the *global village*—a sort of electronic nervous system binding the entire planet together in instantaneous intercommunication, hopefully to the benefit of all concerned. On July 13, 1985, for example, a potential audience of two billion people had access to a telecast fund-raising concert on behalf of starving people in Africa. Featuring music stars like Madonna, Mick Jagger, and Paul McCartney, this *Live Aid* special lasted for 16 hours and was delivered to 150 countries via 13 satellites. Two years later, ABC News sponsored a series of three satellite television discussions between U.S. Congressmen in Washington and members of the Supreme Soviet in Moscow. And talk show host Phil Donahue conducted several syndicated spacebridges that brought together ordinary citizens from selected United States and Soviet cities to share impressions, beliefs, and attitudes.

Among the people in the forefront of these global village linkages is media entrepreneur Ted Turner. As mentioned, his Cable News Network (CNN) is now beamed by satellite to virtually every country in the world, providing an instantaneous planetary forum for the exploration and discussion of events and policies. As an offshoot of this enterprise, Turner has also pioneered *CNN World Report* (see Figure 9–9). Through this show, news agencies around the world can submit television news stories from their own countries for sharing in a two-hour unedited program cooperative that is globally distributed. Finally, with sports broadcasts a popular element in virtually every land, Turner's quadrennial Goodwill Games constitute a satellite-driven athletic event that, at the same time, is designed further to ease East/West tensions.

The mere availability of interactive satellite communication does not automatically insure global good will, of course. Professor Don Flournoy reported in 1989 that although news organizations in more than 100 coun-

**Figure 9–9**
An off-screen frame from CNN's global news compendium

tries have contributed items to CNN's *World Report,* "only 16 countries report they are regular users. It appears the impulse to be heard is stronger than the disposition to listen."[38] (Less than two years later, however, CNN found that between 40 and 50 percent of contributing nations were now airing the compiled program.[39])

The overthrow of a Phillipine dictator, the marshalling of world opinion against brutal repression in China's Tiananmen Square, and the unimaginably rapid transformation of East Bloc regimes from totalitarian to democratic systems have all come about, at least in part, because a satellite signal captured by easily obtainable two-foot dishes makes political isolation virtually impossible. The compactness and availability of VCRs is another major factor in this equation, of course. Once a single video cassette is smuggled into a country, copies can be quickly dubbed and distributed by political activists and resistance groups. The cassette proved to be a significant instrument in the hands of the Polish and Hungarian reform movements.

Of course, the global village raises important implications for electronic media businesses, too. Programmers and advertisers are just now beginning to explore their options in building new markets and in resegmenting others. The practical results of their explorations will undoubtedly shape your own professional life and impact your career choices. But beyond such economic and personal considerations, our evolving electronic nervous system presents an unprecedented opportunity for cross-cultural exchange and understanding, which are the ultimate international adventures.

Anticipating the opportunities that are now within our grasp, science writer and social observer Isaac Asimov labeled satellite communications humanity's *fourth revolution* when, in 1970, he foresaw that

electronic communications must become so widespread that there must be a kind of "electronic literacy" established, with every man owning his own electronic outlet, as every man can now own his own library. . . . The Earth for the first time will be knit together on a personal and not a governmental level. . . . To know all your neighbors on the global level does not mean that you will automatically love them all; it does not, in and of itself, introduce a reign of peace and brotherhood. But to be potentially in touch with everybody at least makes fighting more uncomfortable. It becomes easier to argue instead.[40]

## Chapter Flashback

The *noncommercial* electronic media are a diverse grouping of nonprofit facilities operated by religious, educational, or foundation-based entities. Their purposes vary from the promotion of philosophies and ministries to broadly educational, formal instructional, or public enrichment activities. The earliest U.S. noncommercial outlets were university radio stations operated for the benefit of their electrical engineering and music students. In the 1930s, disagreements over the role of educational broadcasting kept it from establishing a national presence or securing dedicated spectrum space.

Instructional television began in an impromptu manner during World War II with NBC and CBS New York stations offering televised air raid warden and first-aid training. In the postwar era, noncommercial broadcasters received the first twenty channels on the reconfigured FM band. Yet, even as these were being applied for, many educational entities found their energies redirected to television, where 12 percent of the post-Freeze assignments were reserved for noncommercial use. ETV relied on grants from a number of sources to establish a foothold in the late 1950s and early 1960s. Some projects, like MPATI, failed to live up to expectations, but renewed Congressional interest via the 1962 Educational TV Facilities Act and the Public Broadcasting Act of 1967 brought in much needed developmental funds and a mandate to expand service beyond narrowly defined educational boundaries.

A variety of new organizations came to the fore in the new public environment. CTW (Children's Television Workshop) proved that instructional programming could be successfully designed for in-*home* consumption. The Corporation for Public Broadcasting (CPB) became the conduit through which federal funds passed to producers and stations. The Public Broadcasting Service (PBS) gathered television stations together into their own interconnection agency, and National Public Radio (NPR) became a distributive agent for radio broadcasters.

Such centralization trends were viewed unfavorably by the Nixon administration, however, which had philosophical concerns undergirded by a partisan distrust of the perceived liberal bias of some public television programming. In the struggle, CPB's political independence was compromised and PBS developed the Station Program Cooperative (SPC) to ensure that decision making was driven by local station preferences. This has now been replaced by a more centralized National Programming Service. Recently, the public broadcasting sector has had to contend with reduced federal funding and with new (often commercial) competitors airing programming formerly available only on public outlets.

U.S. international broadcasting endeavors first began in the 1920s with private shortwave radio. These were largely taken over for governmental services during World War II and were not a significant force for decades after their reconversion to private use. In the 1980s, however, private shortwave radio enjoyed a modest rebirth.

The Voice of America (VOA), which was launched during the war via many of the converted private shortwave facilities, is the official radio service of the U.S. government. Despite this role, VOA has striven for objectivity and credibility in its programming. In recent years, it has expanded activities to include an FM network (VOA-Europe) and has acquired a sister television service in parent USIA's Worldnet.

U.S. *surrogate* services (operations designed to be a substitute for politically hostile domestic broadcasting operations in other countries) include Radio/TV Marti and Radio Free Europe/Radio Liberty (RFE/RL). The Martis are beamed to Cuba from south Florida, and the much older Radio Free Europe and Radio Liberty are aimed at the countries of Eastern Europe and the Soviet Union, respectively. Cuban reaction to the Marti broadcasts has taken the form of significant signal interference for U.S. domestic broadcasters. The future of RFE/RL is now unclear in light of the massive democratic wave that has swept the East bloc countries and the Soviet Union itself. Through its military, the United States also maintains the Armed Forces Radio and Television Service (AFRTS) on its foreign bases as a means of providing broadcast programming that meets the local information needs of the base communities and offers entertainment programming schedules similar to those enjoyed back home.

Satellites have played a major role in fostering intercontinental program exchange. Since 1964, INTELSAT has been the chief coordinator for international satellite service, but it is now beginning to experience competition from private systems. Satellites have interlocked the nations of the world into what Marshall McLuhan foresaw as "the global village." Together with the compact, low-cost VCR, satellites have made it virtually impossible for any government to isolate its citizens from the voices and ideas of the outside world.

❏ Review Probes

**271**

CHAPTER 9

Noncom-
mercial
and
Interna-
tional
Adven-
tures

1. Compare and contrast the terms *educational, instructional,* and *public* broadcasting.
2. What were the differences in philosophy and membership between the National Committee on Education by Radio and the National Advisory Council on Education by Radio? What impact did these differences have on the shape of educational broadcasting in the 1930s?
3. What forces (a) propelled and (b) retarded the growth of educational FM between 1945 and 1976?
4. Who was Frieda Hennock and what was her major achievement?
5. Of what governmental departments has VOA been a part and how did each impact its operations?
6. What was the real source of much of RFE/RL revenues for the first two decades of the stations' operations? How was this source revealed and what was the ultimate impact of this revelation?

❏ Suggested Background Explorations

Boemer, Marilyn Lawrence. *The Children's Hour: Radio Programs for Children, 1929–1956.* Metuchen, NJ: Scarecrow Press, 1989.

*Broadcasting in the '90s: Competition, Choice and Quality: The Government's Plans for Broadcasting Legislation.* (Paris: UNESCO), Lanham, MD: Unipub, 1988.

Browne, Donald R. *Comparing Broadcast Systems: The Experiences of Six Industrialized Nations.* Ames: Iowa State University Press, 1989.

Helms, Harry L. *Shortwave Listening Handbook.* Englewood Cliffs, NJ: Prentice-Hall, 1987.

Hudson, Heather E. *Communications Satellites: Their Development and Impact.* New York: Free Press, 1990.

Koven, Ronald, *Needs of News Media in Central and Eastern Europe.* Washington, DC: World Pree Freedom Committee, 1990.

Ostendorf, Virginia A. *Teaching through Interactive Television.* Littleton, CO: Virginia A. Ostendorf, 1989.

*World Radio TV Handbook 1990.* New York: Watson-Guptill Publications (Billboard Books), 1990.

# Benchmarks

| Year | Noncommercial | International |
|------|---------------|--------------|
| 1928 | Ohio School of the Air begins instructional broadcasts | |
| 1930 | National Committee on Education by Radio formed | |
| 1932 | | FCC authorizes relay of sponsored broadcasts to foreign audiences |
| 1934 | FCC decides against reserving frequencies for educational broadcasters | |
| 1935 | National Committee on Education by Radio dies | |
| 1939 | | FCC permits shortwave stations to sell commercial time |
| 1940 | FCC reserves 1/8 of new FM channels for educational institutions | CBS and NBC explore commercial shortwave opportunities in Latin America |
| 1942 | NBC and CBS television stations in New York begin war-related instructional programming | OWI takes over shortwave stations, transforms them into VOA |
| | | Armed Forces Radio Service set up |
| 1943 | | 23 VOA facilities in operation |
| 1945 | FCC reserves first 20 channels on relocated FM band for noncommercial use | OWI returns leased shortwave stations to private operation |
| | | Truman places VOA under State Department |
| 1948 | | CBS and NBC cease program preparation for VOA |
| 1950 | Joint Committee for Educational Television founded | Radio Free Europe and Radio Liberty created |

| Year | Noncommercial | International |
|------|---------------|--------------|
| 1952 | FCC reserves 242 TV assignments for noncommercial use<br><br>National Educational Television and Radio Center (NET forerunner) created | |
| 1953 | University of Houston's KUHT becomes first noncommercial TV station | Congress places VOA under new USIA |
| 1954 | WQED (Pittsburgh) becomes first community-licensed telecaster | |
| 1956 | First state ETV network initiated (Alabama) | |
| 1961 | MPATI airborne instructional telecasts begin | Murrow appointed USIA director |
| 1962 | Congress funds ETV expansion through Educational TV Facilities Act | |
| 1964 | | INTELSAT established by 19 nations |
| 1965 | Carnegie Commission begins comprehensive study of ETV | |
| 1967 | Public Broadcasting Act passed, creating CPB | |
| 1968 | Children's Television Workshop formed | |
| 1970 | | 25 countries tied into INTELSAT system |
| 1971 | PBS and NPR begin operations | |
| 1972 | Nixon vetoes CPB authorization, CPB Board cuts off funds to NPACT | |

| Year | Noncommercial | International |
|------|---------------|--------------|
| 1973 | | Board of International Broadcasting created to oversee RFE/RL |
| 1974 | Station Program Cooperative created as public television program selection mechanism | |
| 1979 | Second Carnegie Commission calls for a Public Telecommunications Trust Fund | |
| 1980 | National Association of Public Television Stations formed | Shortwave WRNO (New Orleans) goes on air as commercial "Rock of the World" |
| 1982 | American Public Radio Network organized as alternative to NPR | |
| | Ten PBS stations experiment with commercials | |
| 1983 | | Worldnet initiated as USIA's TV service |
| 1985 | | VOA-Europe created |
| | | Radio Marti begins broadcasts to Cuba |
| | | *Live Aid* concert telecast to potential audience of 2 billion |
| 1986 | CPB contribution to public broadcasting revenues declines to 14% | |
| 1987 | | ABC News sponsors U.S./Russian satellite TV discussions |
| 1989 | | Christian Science Monitor's world shortwave service operational |
| 1990 | PBS program selection centralized under a new chief programming executive | TV Marti launched |

| Year | Noncommercial | International |
|------|---------------|--------------|
| 1991 | | USIA's electronic media activities reorganized |
| | | CNN becomes key international linkage/forum in its coverage of the war in Persian Gulf |

CHAPTER  **10**

# Creative and Performance Functions

❏ *To many people, the electronic media are glamour industries in which the most important players are those whose voices come through our radio speakers and physiques glow on our television tubes. But as you have probably guessed by this point in your reading, on-air jobs are, in many ways, just the tip of the electronic industry iceberg. Glamour, even for media personalities, is a minor part of an enterprise that usually entails long hours and high stress. Nonetheless, because radio/television performers do comprise the first and most prominent impression of what our business is about, it is appropriate to begin our occupational analyses with a look at some of them.*

## Disc and Video Jockeys

As we discover in Chapter 7, the rise of the disc jockey paralleled the conversion of U.S. radio from network-produced, feature-length programs to locally generated music formats. Disc jockeys establish a specific identity for their stations and help string together isolated music selections and announcement segments into a seamless whole. Depending on the format sculpted by the *program director*

278

SECTION
THREE
Profes-
sional
Perspec-
tives

(see Chapter 12), today's disc jockey can be anything from a high-profile personality allowed extensive talk-time to a virtually anonymous presence mouthing little more than song titles, time, and weather.

Either way, the deejays at most local stations are expected to *run their own board*—in other words, to manipulate the controls on an audio console so that the recorded and live, on-mic elements of the program are linked one after the other. It is especially important that the *segues* (transitions) between the elements be so tight that *dead air* (silence) is avoided. Contemporary radio listeners expect continuous and instant gratification and have developed lightning trigger fingers that punch up another station at the mere suggestion of a pause in the action.

From the previous paragraph, it is apparent that air personalities (and our industry as a whole) have a great affinity for jargon. Such in-group terminology is usually an appropriate means of streamlining communication with our colleagues. When it spills into our messages to the public, however, jargon can obscure our meanings and force the public to witness the manufacturing process instead of simply enjoying the communicative product the process creates. Air personalities especially must never forget that the audience is there for its own gratification and is not particularly interested in the procedures (and labels) you use to package that gratification for them.

To be effective on-air professionals, disc jockeys and other program hosts must accomplish two objectives: (1) establish a sense of personal communication, even personal intimacy, with the listener; and (2) blend in with, and use to the fullest, all the elements provided by the format in which they work. Some personalities, on the one hand, know a great deal about the music they are playing but are unable to parlay this knowledge into a sense of sharing conversation with listeners. At the opposite extreme, other air talent possess a superb ability to stimulate a dia-

logue with the audience but are so ignorant of the music or other formatic features that the interchange soon proves to be boring or purposeless.

Like it or not, in the carefully integrated package that is today's program design, the communicator and the format content must be not just compatible but also perfectly synchronized. Nationally respected radio consultant Tim Moore sees this synchronization as vital to the successful positioning of a station in the public's perception. From the standpoint of the air talent themselves, this means, according to Moore, using the precise amount of talk required to "lubricate" this particular format and the sense of *control* that the on-air host seems to bring to and through the microphone.[1]

It is not simply a matter of how much or how little talk is engaged in but how appropriate the talk seems within the dynamics of the chosen format. As radio creative and programming consultant Tyree Ford reports,

In those same focus groups [small numbers of consumers assembled to probe their perceptions] where overly talky announcers received negative ratings, the same respondents gave high ratings to the station with a high-profile personality air staff. What first appeared as a contradiction was later realized to be a qualitative statement. If the content and style were not appreciated by the audience, the perception was negative—overly talky. If those elements were appreciated, the perception was positive—entertainment. . . . Put simply, it's not just what you say, it's what you say *and* the way you say it. Those stations that are successful have a sense of identity that is stronger than the strongest positioning statement. No collection of words can communicate more strongly than the intent of the individual who speaks them.[2]

This intent cannot be effectively projected by merely copying the style of another personality or caricatured personality type. As Ford also observes,

> Don't expect the application of stylistic delivery crutches such as: The Puker, The Big Smile, and The Big O to improve your air person's delivery. (If you're not familiar with these terms, The Puker is the hyper-extension of CHR [contemporary hit radio] delivery. The Big Smile, prevalent on soft-rock and AC [adult contemporary] formats, sounds as if a pre-formed plastic smile insert has been placed in the announcer's mouth. The Big O is the female talent who sounds as though they are on the brink of orgasm each time they open the mike.)

Applying these surface fixes is easy and may give a superficial consistency to the air sound. It is also the mark of a mediocre radio station.[3]

There are, of course, a significant number of mediocre radio stations; but ambitious media professionals try to move beyond them as soon in their careers as possible. The ultimate goal of most radio personalities who want to remain on the performance side of the station business is to appear on a distinctive outlet that dominates its market *and* to appear during *morning drive*. This time period, normally defined as from 6 to 10 A.M., "is always going to be the focal point of the radio station," according to Jay Cook, president of Gannett Broadcasting's radio division. "The more successful it is, the more that show will create the perception of what the station is all about."[4] This, of course, is because early morning listenership (and therefore advertising revenues) far outpaces any other daypart. In the fall of 1988, for example, the national RADAR (Radio All Dimension Audience Research) studies indicated that 61 percent of persons over 12 years of age, 52 percent of men eighteen and older, 66 percent of women eighteen and older, and 79 percent of teenagers ages twelve to seventeen were morning drive listeners.[5]

To succeed in the morning, to tap into people's consciousness at a time when they are once again getting ready to cope with their immediate environment, most radio programmers agree that air personalities must be locally oriented. "I always figure," maintains program consultant Ed Shane, "that if I go into a market and I listen to the station's morning show and I don't understand what they're talking about, they're probably doing it right. Morning shows can't be pulled from one place to another."[6] The same principle usually applies to other local dayparts as well, of course, and these are where air talent most often train to make the move to the morning at their current or a subsequent station.

Midday slots require a less intrusive style that can effortlessly accompany listener tasks at home or in the workplace. With more and more adults engaged in out-of-home employment (and audience measurement firms adjusting procedures to measure these listeners) the importance of midday listening as a way to make the job more bearable is being amplified. In larger markets, where afternoon commutes can be lengthy, afternoon drive is second only to morning as a revenue producer

## CNN Long-Distance Radio

The value of a hot deejay is evidenced by so-called fly-jock Tom Joyner, who commutes three times a week to handle air shifts for stations in both Dallas and Chicago.

**280**

SECTION
THREE
Profes-
sional
Perspec-
tives

for the station. Like the morning deejay, afternoon personalities are generally more in the foreground than are those at midday. In the afternoon, however, the stress is placed on looking ahead to plans and relaxation for the evening. For those air talent drawing evening shifts, the style reflects a more laid-back enhancement of listeners' free-time activities rather than being a center-stage performer who distracts us from the boredom of getting to and from the job.

Eventually, some radio personalities ascend from local to national venues, where their voices may be heard on dozens or even hundreds of stations. Even though they may no longer be required to sound local, they are still expected to structure their delivery to blend in seamlessly with the overall *local sounds* of the outlets carrying their program. Of course, the number of national on-air jobs is minuscule when compared with local station opportunities. More surprising, local salaries may in fact outpace many national ones, particularly for those important morning drive hosts. As early as 1989, Atlanta-based

consultant Kent Burkhart noted that stations were often paying $100,000 for such people, even in medium-sized markets.[7] Certainly, such paychecks are not the norm for radio disc jockeys as a whole, but they do demonstrate the premium placed on people who can truly communicate with their listeners while advancing the identity and format characteristics of the station for which they work. (The key format types, and their comparative share of the U.S. radio audience, are displayed in Figure 10–1.)

Recently, radio disc jockeys have been joined by TV video jockeys. Veejays are most often found on cable music channels or on youth-oriented weekend broadcast events. Unlike their radio counterparts, video disc jockeys are seldom concerned with tying into a given locality. Instead, they must project an aura of national or even international music hipness that assures viewers that the music videos they feature are "where it's happening." Like the deejay, the video host must still be that communicative lubricant that helps tie together and advance all the isolated musical

**Figure 10–1**

Radio format popularity (by percentage of listening audience), Spring 1990

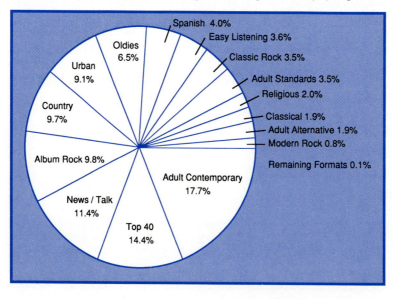

(*Source: The Arbitron Company and Billboard Magazine data.*)

281

CHAPTER 10
Creative
and Per-
formance
Functions

selections. But the veejay carries the added burden of having to resemble physically what he or she sounds like. For a lot of electronic personalities, the beauty of radio is that you don't have to "look like your voice" to succeed.

## Talk Show Hosts

On-air personalities who work in talk rather than music formats must cope with a much more unpredictable environment. Here, the assurance of the prerecorded tune is replaced by the usually live contributions made by people in the studio or at the other end of a telephone line. Whether on radio or on television, talk show hosts must lucidly and revealingly communicate with these contributors while keeping in mind that it is the audience, rather than the caller or guest, who must ultimately benefit from the exchange.

Most television talk shows are recorded on videotape for later airing. Thus, inappropriate comments by guests or audience members and inane exchanges that go nowhere can usually be edited out in post production to remove verbal garbage and quicken the pace. Sometimes, of course, offensiveness can be useful in revealing the topic and enhancing audience interest. But when it is not, videotape editing constitutes a welcome safety net and the assurance that rough spots can be smoothed over before the show is ultimately distributed.

For the most part, this safety net is not available to the radio talk show talent because on radio live spontaneity is the key to listener attention and caller participation. "In fact," observes talk format innovator Bruce Marr, "talk radio is radio waiting for something to go wrong."[8] To lessen the chances of things "going wrong" while taking telephone calls, talk show hosts usually make use of a *squelch button.* The call is either recorded or

sent through an electronic delay loop before reaching the transmitter. If an obscenity or other unwanted phrase is uttered, the host has from four to seven seconds to hit the squelch button and delete the offense before it reaches the airwaves. This delay mechanism is the reason callers must turn down their radios to avoid their own words echoing back to them.

Clearly, the air personality on a radio or television talk program must possess several skills. In addition to articulate speech, the talk host must exhibit an interest in and knowledge of a wide range of subjects that may become the topic of conversation. In other words, it is essential that these personalities be well-read and continuously in search of items that might prove compelling to their audiences. Beyond this, it is necessary to cultivate a quick wit and the ability to use that wit in keeping the program interesting and well-paced. Long-winded participants must be gracefully cut off and timid participants drawn out, without the hosts seeming to dominate the dialogue. Air personalities thus require a good deal of seasoning before they are ready to attempt a talk assignment, and such seasoned professionals can usually demand significantly higher salaries than those accorded most deejays.

Although it takes time to build, radio or television talk hosts are capable of consolidating extremely loyal followings. This following provides their stations and networks with stable audiences that can be promised with assurance to advertisers. There are concerns within and outside our industry, however, that the power this loyalty confers on the host/personality may be abused. One such controversy erupted in late 1988, when Congress was considering granting itself a 51 percent pay raise. Activated by consumer advocate Ralph Nader, about sixty radio talk show hosts discussed the issue on the air and encouraged listeners to send teabags to their Congressional representatives in protest. The teabags were symbolic of the pre-Revolutionary War Boston Tea Party, when colonists

282

SECTION
THREE

Profes-
sional
Perspec-
tives

**PHIL TOWER**/MIDDAY SHOW HOST
WOOD-AM/FM

As a radio personality/talk show host, I often find myself wondering how and why I ended up in this profession. I think that the most obvious answer is that I have the type of job that allows me to be myself, while informing and hopefully entertaining other people. The hardest thing to realize about being an on-air personality is that it's all right to let my audience see me as I really am—a person very much like them, someone who goofs up every now and then, and most important, never takes himself too seriously.

Too many times in this business of broadcasting the on-air types get lost in a personna they have willingly or unwillingly created. Is the Rick Dees we hear on the radio the same Rick Dees at home with his wife and family? Most likely he is not. Many of the biggest names in radio are famous and successful because of the image they portray on-air, but most of us in the business will not reach that level of fame or notoriety.

I feel successful as an on-air personality because I can be myself on the air. If I want my listeners to know my attitude about a book or film or any other topic, I am free to do so. Too many radio personalities today are bound by strict guidelines set by either the station management or the nature of the community in which the station is located. An abrasive talk show host in conservative Grand Rapids, Michigan, would certainly not be as successful as he or she would be in a larger, more liberal market such as Chicago or Los Angeles.

Without a doubt the most vital skill for my job as a radio personality and talk show host is the ability to communicate effectively with the listener. Notice how I stipulated the word *listener* and not listeners. For me, I feel the best way to reach the audience is to picture myself talking to *one* person. It does not matter how young or old that person might be or even what he or she looks like. What's most important is that I visualize the conversation I am having with that person, and then convey that one-on-one approach to my audience as a whole. It is much more difficult to talk "to" your listeners than to simply talk "at" them. Ours is a business of ratings, and if more people choose your station because they feel a kinship with you, then ultimately your position in that market is strengthened because of the bond you have forged between your station and its listeners.

If you are considering a career in broadcasting, take time to know what is going on around you. This means

283

CHAPTER 10
Creative
and Per-
formance
Functions

staying informed not only about issues that interest you, but also on the things that are of no concern to you personally. If there's a morsel of information on some event, place, or person, it will be of value to you or especially to one of your listeners someday, somewhere, somehow. Never take for granted the amount of trust listeners place in *you* as a representative of your radio station. They will call on you for the strangest bits of information when you least expect it, and nothing hurts a station's credibility more than not knowing about an event that is important to the listeners. Being successful as an on-air personality requires being informed. This is certainly one profession where it is a must to know "a little something about everything." Read as much as you can, be involved in community projects, and especially take an interest in the people who make up your audience. The more you know them, the more they will come to know you and your station.

For me, the best thing about being a radio personality is the fun I have walking into that studio everyday and knowing anything could happen. No two days are ever alike, and the biggest challenge I face is being ready to meet the unknown that the listeners will throw at me. Being prepared for that challenge every day, and especially *enjoying* it, is to me the best reason for staying in this profession.

---

dumped tea into the harbor to protest British taxation. Buried in teabags, Congress sidetracked the pay raise for almost a year, but many representatives also expressed their outrage at what they saw to be broadcaster manipulation of the airwaves. Talk show hosts, of course, felt otherwise. As Mills Crenshaw of Salt Lake City's KTKK asserted,

> Any time the citizens of the U.S. are given a chance to talk back to the government, it seems to frighten the politicians to death. I thought they were supposed to represent us, not dictate to us—apparently, they feel otherwise.[9]

This controversy, of course, focuses on the same issue raised by Vice-President Spiro Agnew in his 1969 speech (see Chapter 8). What, if any, are the limits to unelected electronic communicators' use of their audience reach to oppose the actions of elected officeholders? Putting it another way, should the electronic media constitute an unrestricted pipeline of information from government to citizenry? Should it be a critical watchdog? Aren't manipulative air personalities as dangerous as unresponsible politicians? Even though he lived long before talk show hosts, Thomas Jefferson clearly believed that the mass media of his time had a vital role to play in providing the people with "full information of their affairs." In a 1787 letter to Edward Carrington, Jefferson articulated a position that would become codified four years later in the First Amendment to the Constitution.

> The people are the only censors of their governors: and even their errors will tend to keep these to the true principles of their institution. To punish these errors too severely would be to suppress the only safeguard of the public liberty. The way to prevent these irregular interpositions of the people is to give them full information of

284

SECTION
THREE
Profes-
sional
Perspec-
tives

their affairs thro' the channels of the public papers, and to contrive that those papers should penetrate the whole mass of the people. The basis of our governments being the opinion of the people, the very first object should be to keep that right; and were it left to me to decide whether we should have a government without newspapers or newspapers without a government, I should not hesitate a moment to prefer the latter.[10]

## Newspersons

Unfortunately, Jefferson's ideals cannot be as easily applied to the electronic media. Confounding the issue for talk show hosts, of course, is whether they are actually the informers Jefferson sought to ensure or merely entertainers who *draw on* rather than *contribute to* public opinion. The recent move of some network infotainment shows from News to Entertainment Divisions has been one attempt to clarify and respect the distinction between journalism and show business. It is not necessarily that news is superior to entertainment, only that the purpose and function of the two programmatic commodities are quite different.

Most electronic journalists, like their print counterparts, see their job as one of digging out and presenting to the public information the public does not have the time or the capability to uncover for itself. Even though this information may not always be world-shaking, a premium is placed on its ability to increase audience understanding of events or processes and suggest their key implications for the viewers' or listeners' own lives. Talk show hosts are primarily fielding reflections of existing public knowledge and attitudes, whereas journalists seek to expand that knowledge based on new or recently unearthed factors. Distinguished political commentator Walter Lippmann put it this way:

The news is not a mirror of social conditions, but the report of an aspect that has obtruded itself. The news does not tell you how the seed is germinating in the ground, but it may tell you when the first sprout breaks through the surface. . . . It may even tell you what somebody says is happening to the seed underground. It may tell you that the sprout did not come up at the time it was expected. The more points, then, at which any happening can be fixed, objectified, measured, named, the more points there are at which news can occur.[11]

In capturing and packaging these "obtruded aspects" of which Lippmann speaks, electronic journalism is comprised of both the functions isolated in this chapter's title: (1) the performance and (2) the creative. The performance function, of course, refers to the actual voicing of the story through the camera and/or microphone by professionals like those pictured in Figure 10–2. The creative aspect, meanwhile, pertains to the gathering of information and organization of it through how that story is written.

A reporter or correspondent engages in both activities. Whether covering the cop house (police department), state capitol, or State Department, the reporter does the legwork, cultivates sources, writes the story, and is then responsible for delivering this story over the air. Some authorities view this method as the most credible journalism because the same professional has followed the story from inception to delivery. In short, the person who's been there is the one actually chronicling the event or finding for us.

Many times, however, the on-air (performance) and creative functions of electronic journalism are parceled out to separate people. A radio announcer, reading copy pulled from a wireservice machine, or a TV *anchor* (coordinating newscast presenter), conveying stories that have been covered by other staffers, are two examples of the performance function in isolation. This separation of story deliverer from story preparer is not, in itself,

**Figure 10-2**
Anchor teams are assembled to maximize viewer attraction

**285**

CHAPTER 10
Creative
and Per-
formance
Functions

good or bad. It just means that an intermediary (the on-air personality) has been injected between story coverage and audience comprehension.

For persons employed exclusively as air talent, a priority is clearly placed on delivery skills. This means a pleasing, authoritative voice and crisp, clear diction that follows the conventions of Midwestern pronunciation that the networks adopted decades ago as the most easily assimilated national standard. In television, these aural attributes must be combined with a comely (telegenic) appearance that wears well on viewers. Taken as a group, the station's on-air news team should also reflect a balance between male and female deliverers plus include representatives of ethnic groups that constitute a prominent part of the market. In short, persons who seek to break into electronic journalism solely as presenters, and without firm credentials in the harsh street-world of newsgathering, must recognize that their careers are dependent almost entirely on their looks and their sound.

Some anchors, of course, are highly regarded reporters who came to their jobs as the culmination of years of hard work in actual newsgathering. Even though physical attractiveness is also a mandate for them, their credibility gained on the conceptual side helps compensate for scars, wrinkles, and gray hair. Many of these anchors, especially at the networks, try to keep their hand in reporting by working on special assignments or flying to the scene of major breaking stories such as the crumbling of the Berlin Wall, the San Francisco earthquake, or a Scud missile attack in Saudi Arabia. The danger in such expeditions, of course, is that their presence is seen as mere window dressing that detracts from the actual work on the story being compiled by lesser-ranking journalists.

There is nothing inherently deceptive or deficient in employing skilled presenters exclusively to deliver the news. In some environments, this practice is mandated by policy or labor considerations. Irish broadcast journalists, for example, are strictly divided into

SECTION
THREE

Profes-
sional
Perspec-
tives

## ALLISON PAYNE/NEWS ANCHOR
### WGN-TV

News is the kind of job on which you work twenty-four hours a day. Unfortunately, a lot of people think the anchor just comes into the station a half-hour before air time, checks over the copy, and sits down to perform into a camera. Admittedly, there are anchors in the business who get away with that kind of work ethic. But the majority of us take our roles much more seriously. We recognize the great responsibility associated with our jobs, and we work constantly to maintain our knowledge of what's going on in our communities and in the rest of the world around us.

My typical workday begins even before I drive to the station. I start the day by scanning the city's two top newspapers and watching the early morning news programs. Sometime around early afternoon, I call the assignment desk to find out what's cooking. That allows me to do a quick study on any story I may be expected to cover before I actually leave home.

On an average day, I'll get to work about 2 o'clock in the afternoon. If I'm lucky, the key story will be set up when I walk in the door. All I have to do is grab a notebook and I'm ready to go. Once the story is shot, the videographer and I head back to the station, where I immediately sit down with the producer. He or she may make suggestions about how my story should be put together, as well as recommend production values that would enhance the piece. After I write the story, I turn it over to a writer/producer who will work with an editor to put the finished piece together. By this time, it's usually around seven o'clock and the show starts at nine. I probably won't see the final version of my story until it hits the air.

In the meantime, I need to look over the rest of the newscast scripts. A staff of writers have been busy all day putting the show together, but the anchors have final say over style and grammar. My co-anchor and I spend the last few minutes before airtime making any necessary changes. Then it's five minutes in front of a mirror to do that cosmetic stuff, and before you know it, you're in front of the cameras. Thirty minutes later, the show is over.

But an anchor's job is never really done. There's all kinds of mail to answer. Plus, there are requests to appear at charity functions, speak at schools, and perform stunts for the local radio stations. It's all part of the job, and these kinds of involvement help you get to know the community while helping the community get to know you. Even established anchors make public appearances because the public likes to see them out and about.

**287**

CHAPTER 10
Creative
and Per-
formance
Functions

Finally, though some would deny it, being a news anchor *is* glamorous. Television is a glamorous, glitzy business. But it's also a tough business. News anchors get bumped around all the time, and the competition is tough. However, if you get television news in your blood, if you catch the TV news bug, I suspect I'll be working with you sometime in the near future. Because anyone who's ready to make the sacrifices, put in the time, work for free, and start small can expect to reap huge rewards from the wonderful, unpredictable world of television news.

two union groups; the on-air news readers belong to Equity (the national actor's union) and the reporters and writers belong to the National Union of Journalists (along with print news gatherers and writers).[12]

In Ireland, in the United States, or in any other country, the separation of performance and creative personnel can still make for accurate and efficient journalism. This is provided, of course, that the content standards for news remain uncompromised and that the presenters do not try to masquerade as authorities who have gathered the stories themselves. When the surface look or sound of a news program is allowed to override researched substance, you create a near worthless veneer such as that satirized in the Figure 10–3 commercial.

Substantive journalism, and smooth palatable presentation of it, need not be mutually exclusive commodities in the electronic media. And the print media's hypersensationalized tabloid offshoots long predate the "Larry and Judy" approach that has occasionally afflicted some television news operations. It is not the delivery system that makes journalism authoritative or trivial, but rather the way that system is operated. *The San Francisco Examiner*'s management knows this, of course, because their parent, The Hearst Corporation, runs six television stations of its own in other cities. But the commercial in Figure 10–3 is indicative of the intense rivalry between print and electronic journalism (plus the fact that the competing *San Francisco Chronicle* owns the NBC station in town!).

An inherent characteristic of electronic news is that it is delivered to the audience via dynamic human speech rather than by static symbols on a printed page. For radio and television journalism, this situation can make for either greater clarity and audience involvement or worthless babble and audience confusion. However the on-air and creative aspects of electronic news are divided or consolidated among or within the professionals involved, each of them must realize, as veteran television reporter Byron Harris puts it, that "they have been entrusted with the communication of information. And society is only going to be able to continue to have the pillars that it has if that information has real content."[13]

Content, of course, is germinated at the conceptual stage of the journalistic process by news gatherers and writers. Usually, the same person both gathers the facts and impressions and then writes the story. More often than not, that same reporter serves as the on-air presence who delivers the resulting piece to the audience. We have already spent some time examining on-air aspects of electronic news; we can now explore the purely conceptual tasks in a bit more detail.

Every step of the way, electronic reporters and writers must compensate for the fact that they have a much narrower framework in which to cast their piece than do their print

288

SECTION
THREE

Profes-
sional
Perspec-
tives

**Figure 10–3.**

A newspaper knocks babbling TV journalism

(MUSIC:     TV NEWS THEME UNDER)

LARRY:     Hi, I'm Larry Simpleton - - -

JUDY:     And I'm Judy Bimbo with some quick facts about TV news. Larry, why is our reporting so superficial?

LARRY:     Well, Judy, we figure the audience is pretty stupid, and we're none too bright ourselves.

JUDY:     That's exactly right, Larry, and since we don't have much hard news, we have to spend a lot of time agreeing - - -

LARRY:     You bet we do!

JUDY:     - - - and congratulating each other on terrific reporting.

LARRY:     Terrific reporting, Judy. Maybe you could also explain why we have to look like models.

JUDY:     I'd be happy to, Larry. TV news isn't about ideas - - - it's about mascara and high cheekbones. That's why we get these huge salaries - - -

ANNCR:     Tired of the inane babble of TV news? The San Francisco Examiner is a better way to spend your time. To get two months for the price of one, call 800–345–EXAM. That's 800–345–EXAM.

("The Clio Awards," ADWEEK/Winners [July 1987]:21.)

media counterparts. A half-hour news show often includes fewer words than even a single newspaper page. Brevity, clarity, and conciseness thus become crucial. The great majority of potential subjects cannot be accommodated at all, and the subjects that are must be expressed in the fewest words or clearest pictures possible. Fortunately, through the judicious use of sound bites and video clips, the electronic media allows the subjects and aura of a story to flow directly to the audience without the need first to transcribe everything into print description. The writing that

is done can then be devoted to putting this actuality into a context to further listener or viewer comprehension.

For the radio or television journalist, the trick in all of this is to be able to grasp the essence of the story quickly so that only the most meaningful sounds, sights, and words are selected to put the piece together. The result will almost always have to be brief, but it need not be fragmentary. Instead, the astute electronic newsperson will have set reasonable parameters for what can be covered and then will stay within those boundaries to de-

**289**

CHAPTER 10
Creative
and Per-
formance
Functions

liver a narrow-focus insight that makes relevant sense to the newscast consumer. As CBS News correspondent Susan Spencer explains,

> You have to adjust to the fact that television pieces are not documentaries. You may know an awful lot, and everything that you know probably helps what you end up being able to put on the air, makes it more clear. But you can't say everything you know or you'll consume the whole broadcast. . . . Half the time when I get ready to write a piece, I think "This is the one I can't do. This is hopeless. No way can I cram all this stuff into two minutes." But it's always gratifying when I do it.[14]

Spencer's point has even greater ramifications for radio, of course, where there are no pictures to help cover the topic in the time allotted.

The broader the electronic journalist's education, the wider will be the range of subjects on which he or she can quickly hone in. A firm grounding in history, political science, and economics is almost always helpful, with a background in business, science or the arts a required plus in developing special beat expertise. (See the Valerie Voss profile on the following page.) Radio and television news professionals pride themselves on being more than just conduits for raw facts. Despite the limitations of their format, most also strive to develop a context and perspective for those facts. These qualities can only come from an authentic knowledge base that such professionals bring to each story assignment.

## Copywriters

In advertising, the creators who write commercials, public service announcements, station and program promotional messages (*pro-*

*mos*), and similar types of continuity are known as copywriters. Unlike newspersons, copywriters seldom if ever voice their own work. Instead, they script it out for performance by on-air station talent or the professional singers, actors, and actresses who make at least part of their living by bringing these messages to life.

Copywriters are employed by stations, cable systems, or advertising agencies. They also work in-house for corporate, institutional, or governmental units who prefer that their radio/television communications be prepared by their own staffs rather than contracted out to an advertising or public relations firm. Some copywriters even work for themselves as freelancers. Whatever the setting, it is the copywriter's task to fashion those short, persuasive messages that are the lifeblood of a free-enterprise electronic media system. Unlike entertainment program scripts, which are the province of a comparatively few East or West Coast specialists, pieces of copy must be fashioned by writers at almost every station and cable system in the country as well as by their colleagues in the advertising and public relations firms who use the electronic media on behalf of their clients.

The typical piece of copy is ten, fifteen, thirty, or sixty seconds long. Nevertheless, like the full-length script, it must tell a tale or reveal a truth within the time allotted. That is why many writers discover that copy creation experience is invaluable preparation for a career in long-form entertainment writing. Despite their brevity, commercial and other continuity pieces exemplify all the requirements of media form and content demanded in radio/television news as well as in series-length script formulation. In fact, electronic media copywriting has evolved beyond the audio/visual hawking of goods. Audiences now accept the best commercials as entertainment in their own right, with entire television specials built around collections of the copywriter's art. Because the production costs of nationally distributed TV commer-

290

SECTION
THREE

Profes-
sional
Perspec-
tives

**VALERIE VOSS**/SENIOR METEOROLOGIST
AND WEATHER DEPARTMENT MANAGER
CNN

There's more to television weather-casting than what meets a viewer's eye.

Researchers can verify that most TV news viewers tune in with the weather report as their number-one viewing priority. If this is the electronic media aspect you choose, I hope that you major in meteorology with a minor in speech or broadcast journalism. While there will always be a place for smart and talented weather *reporters,* many weather-conscious, competitive TV stations around the country are hiring only credentialed *meteorologists.* And our numbers are growing.

Naturally, station television meteorologists make their own forecasts for their town or market area on a daily basis. But at CNN, we must forecast for approximately 100 cities around the United States and Canada and for an additional twenty to twenty-five European cities daily. This gives us a much smaller margin for error than predicting in a local market—a local forecaster just has to get *one* right! In either case, you'll get some wrong. So learn early on not to be too thin-skinned about making an occasional error.

Every aspiring TV weathercaster should expect to work alone. Although some major markets provide a weather producer, most don't. Therefore, it's important to be friendly with computers. They are used not only to access and analyze weather data but also to create your on-air weather graphics. Computer programming and a few art classes can be extremely helpful. Every day the weathercaster decides what's most important in the weather picture and how to explain it, both verbally and graphically. Weather maps help accomplish this explanation, and the better they look, the more the weathercaster will be understood, watched, and liked!

If you want to work as a television weathercaster, you'd better *thrive* on pressure! You can't report "old" weather, so everything inevitably must be prepared at the last minute, especially on bad weather days. Even more crucial, weathercasters are always allotted a finite amount of time for their presentations by the newscast producer. You have to go through your act (ad libbing) in an organized, straightforward, authoritative yet personable manner, and end *right on time.* At CNN, we often watch a clock on the front of the camera to be out exactly to the second, while pointing at a blank chroma-key wall and cheating to see the maps and your mirror

291

CHAPTER 10
Creative
and Per-
formance
Functions

image on tiny monitors off to the sides of the set. It all looks so casual. The choreography will become second nature, but I guarantee you'll look a little silly as you learn it.

The most important advice I'd give anyone contemplating TV weather as a career would be cautionary: This isn't an entry-level position anymore. One doesn't become a weathergirl (or boy) to work your way up into another news job. The field now demands a dedicated professional with the interest and expertise to grab viewers' attention with a sincere display of knowledge and enthusiasm for the subject. If you've got that, you'll *love* the work. And succeed!

cials may regularly be ten to fifteen times that of comparable-length portions of the shows they help to sponsor, it is not difficult to see why top copywriters are highly prized professionals.

This is not to diminish the importance of *radio* copy and the people who write it. For years, radio was often thought of as a second-class medium, a kind of "television with the picture tube burned out," as writer/performer Stan Freberg once protested. Electronic media copywriters saw the building of their TV reel as the way to fame and glory and looked on radio assignments as hardship duty. As Jerry Siano, chairman of N.W. Ayer Advertising, recalls,

When television came along people started watching that. Radio didn't change. But our perception of it did. We forgot a quarter of a century of people watching their radio sets. And this might be what led to the development of the 'secret' to bad radio advertising. . . . Just stuffing the commercial full of twaddle, wall-to-wall words, endlines and some cheap music is the sure-fire formula for ineffective radio advertising.[15]

Today, radio is being looked at differently, in part, it is true, as a result of the rising cost of broadcast television time that has priced many smaller advertisers out of that medium. But the rehabilitation of radio is also due, ar- gues former Radio Advertising Bureau president Bill Stakelin, to the renewed realization that

radio *is* visual. It is one of the most visual if not the most visual medium in existence today. Where else can you see 5,000 albino rhinos stampeding down Pennsylvania Avenue? Only on the radio. Radio is visual, and as you plan for it, as you create for it, as you write for it, think of it visually.[16]

This visual imagery through solo sound is not, however, easy for a copywriter to capture. Everything the conceptualizer wants to say must be wholly transportable via words, sound effects, and music. There is no camera lens to convey automatically what the product looks like and how it works; the radio copywriter must explain these things through audio-only sensations. Because of this challenge, the creation of radio messages "offers something unique in this day and age," points out advertising executive Ed McCabe; "the opportunity to stand up and be counted, which is why radio can be a scary medium for creative people who aren't so sure of themselves. . . . Radio separates the doers from the talkers."[17]

These doers, the true professional radio copywriters, realize that the audio medium requires the same respect for language as does print, but a respect that must be rationed into

SECTION
THREE

Profes-
sional
Perspec-
tives

## LISA GOICH/COPYWRITER
### BRUCE & CHATO, INC.

It's 8:23 A.M. My alarm clock just went off for the fifth time. As I gaze at the digital display—8:24 now—my brain finally shakes itself out of its deep sleep, and I come to the realization that—OH MY GOSH! I'M LATE! I HAVE TO BE AT WORK BY NINE!!!

This panic and procrastination are typical traits found in most copywriters. We thrive on it. Deadlines have produced some of the best campaigns in the history of advertising. (At least some of the best in my own history). Now my theory will be put to the test.

When I arrive at the office, both my bosses are already there (I *hate* that!). I notice a note on my desk: "Lisa: We need two radio scripts written for Fretter Appliance. Major emergency. Need to see rough drafts in a half hour. Sorry."

SORRY?!? Two scripts in a half hour? I can't do that! As I sit there staring into space, wasting precious minutes silently complaining, in walks Mike, the account executive. "Lisa, Bob from Kentucky Fried Chicken just called. That TV spot you sent out to the stations yesterday? We had the wrong price on the 15-piece meal. Can you get into the studio this morning and fix it? The spots start running tomorrow."

Who do these people think I am? Houdini?

First things first. Call and book some editing time. I make the call and they say they can get me in within a half hour. I rush in to my boss Chato's office, and, pleading insanity, ask for an extension on my radio scripts. He says, "OK but you better have *two*

scripts—not *one*—on my desk when you get back from the studio."

Well, at least a little of the pressure is off for the moment. With my tiny tape recorder in hand, I begin writing my spots in the car on the way to the studio. My mind is blank, though, and the ideas just aren't coming to me. # @ $ * % !

I arrive at the studio, and within 20 minutes the price point is fixed. One down. One to go. A rough idea just hit me for the radio scripts. I ask a secretary at the studio if I can borrow her typewriter for a few minutes. She says yes. And I bang out two conventional scripts I think will suffice for Fretter.

I get back to the office and my bosses are both out to lunch. I find another note on my desk, "Lisa. Forget the scripts. Doug decided to run the old spots from last year."

At this point, totally frustrated, I put my head down on my desk. And while taking one deep breath after another, I try to remind myself of the perks that

**293**

CHAPTER 10
Creative
and Per-
formance
Functions

got me into this business in the first place. Great parties. Interesting people. Free tickets to major concerts and events. Awards and recognition. My stomach growls. Reminding me that I haven't eaten lunch yet, either. I call up my friend, another copywriter,

to ask her if she wants to go get a bite to eat. And while putting on my coat, I think about the long afternoon ahead of me. Full of more of the same stuff I faced this morning.

I love advertising.

segments of a minute or less. Also unlike print, the radio message cannot be re-read by the audience. Nor can listeners slow down the speed at which they consume it. A radio spot exists in real time at one predetermined velocity and then disappears until the next occasion it is scheduled for airing. If the listener doesn't comprehend it the first time, there may not be another chance.

Yet, despite all these drawbacks, a copywriter can make the radio message more integral to a consumer's life than expressions via any other mass medium. This is because appropriate sound cues from the creator can trigger target listeners to recall specifics from their own past experiences or future dreams in order to complete the picture. The well-fashioned radio spot thus becomes a part of the listener, and the listener becomes a part of the spot. Note how the commercial in Figure 10–4 brings skiers' excitement and fears to life.

When a copywriter is given a television assignment, of course, a somewhat different set of opportunities and challenges present themselves. On the plus side, in proportion to the number of words used, television copywriters probably earn more money per word than do writers for any other medium, even when the vital but unspoken words expended on the script's video explanations are figured into the computation. More important, from a psychological standpoint, copywriters in TV advertising experience the fun of dealing with a

communications vehicle that is more flexible than any other channel human beings have contrived, a vehicle that is becoming *more* flexible all the time. The danger, however, is that the writer is so enthralled by television's technical possibilities that the resulting ads are too diffuse. The creator tries to show/present too much in a single spot.

Keeping the message clear and objective-oriented is always a prime communicator concern (recall our Chapter 1 discussion). This concern is further amplified in television given the multitude of available tools but the limited amount of air time that any video spot has in which to use them. Successful television copywriters always remind themselves that, no matter how state-of-the-art the technique, it is irrelevant if it does not promote the one, central point of the message. As veteran TV conceptualizer Jim Dale cautions,

It all keeps coming back to the idea. Being forced to have one. And having everything riding on the idea being great. When you have it, there's always a way to bring it off. When you don't have it, all the techniques and tricks and hot songs and New Wave and blah blah blah aren't enough. And the funny thing is, when you do have a strong idea, finding a way to pull it off isn't even as hard as you thought anyway. Because people *want* to work on a great idea. They can smell it on a storyboard or a script and they start pulling rabbits out of hats from the beginning.[18]

294

SECTION
THREE

Profes-
sional
Perspec-
tives

**Figure 10–4**
Radio's visual potential

(MUSIC:  'BLUE DANUBE WALTZ' UNDER)

ANNCR:  Imagine. It's a clear, cool January morning and the fresh snow spreads out in front of you sparkling in the bright sun. You tighten your boots and pull your goggles down over your eyes. You turn your skis downhill. And you go.

You're skiing, and you look great.

Then one ski crosses over the other. And gracefully you plant your head in the deep powder and all you can see is white. Then you see blue sky. Then white snow again. Then sky, snow. Sky, snow. You're tumbling.

Your skis are gone now. So are your poles. Your goggles are down around your neck and your neck is down around your ankles. And it's getting worse. You're picking up speed.  Under the lift now, you hear the laughter and you wish that you had come up to Loveland early this season and tuned up your technique.

You kick yourself because you could have skied Loveland for only $15 before December 24th. But you didn't come up to Loveland early, and just look at you now.

*(Courtesy of Don Poole, Karsh & Hagan Advertising, Inc.)*

Simple or sophisticated, a television announcement generally must *be* visual in order to attract and hold viewer attention. Therefore, copywriters usually find themselves writing the pictorial descriptions first. They let the sense of sight carry as much of the revelation task as possible and then supplement as needed with music, sound effects, and spoken words. In conceiving television impressions, the best and most extensive writing is not heard by the audience but instead will be *seen* through the produced result of the verbal video design. In the ultimate extension of this principle, notice in Figure 10–5 how many vibrant words have been used by British copywriter John Green to set down the concept for a 20-second commercial promoting TCP antiseptic. Yet, none of these words are actually spoken.

This necessity of conceptualizing pictures before words is a task shared by television copywriters and news writers alike. This is because both journalists and commercial creators are inherently storytellers. And "in doing a television story," declares CBS news correspondent Charles Kuralt, "you must always know what picture it is you're writing to. That is, you never write a sentence without knowing exactly what the picture is going to be. I will say that again. My philosophy is that you must always know what picture accompanies the words you write. You cannot write for television without knowing what the picture is."[19]

The next time you sit down to watch television, try turning off the sound of the commercials and news items to which you are exposed. How many of these messages

**Figure 10–5**

Verbal descriptions of a TV spot's visuals

**295**

CHAPTER 10
Creative
and Per-
formance
Functions

The whole mood of the commercial is tense and unusual. To this end the camera is handheld, without steadycam, and generally thrown around unconventionally. There is no dialogue and no voice over.

SFX: VICIOUS WASP

Open on the camera being the point-of-view of the wasp. The wasp hunts through the grass and finds a young girl. She starts as she senses the wasp.

There follows a succession of quick cuts as the wasp chases the girl through long grass and a field of yellow canola. The camera is alternately the point-of-view of the wasp and the girl.

The sound of the wasp drives the girl on. She spins to avoid the wasp in a blur of legs and skirt.

She nearly stumbles into a cow and slowly backs away; her heart beating and her breathing heavy.

SFX: HEAVY BREATHING FAST HEARTBEAT.

Close up of her legs as she slowly backs into a bed of nettles.

SFX: SHE GASPS AS SHE IS STUNG.

We pull out of focus and a blue flashing light enters the frame.

The blue flashing light becomes the cap of the TCP bottle as it moves up into the frame.

SUPER:     IN ANY LITTLE EMERGENCY
           SOOTHES PAIN, FIGHTS INFECTION

*(Courtesy of John S. A. Green, Saatchi & Saatchi Advertising Ltd.)*

compellingly convey the main point with the visual alone? And of these, how many tempt you to turn up the audio to acquire supporting information? The results of this little experiment should help you see just how important pictorial factors have become to today's messages and the writers who help sculpt them.

## Art Directors and Designers

Electronic media writers compose verbal descriptions of needed visuals, but the actual re-

**296**

SECTION
THREE

Profes-
sional
Perspec-
tives

alization of these visuals depends on the expertise of other professionals. In the case of commercials and the other short messages we call continuity, this pictorial expertise is provided by people known as art directors. (The salaries of art directors, copywriters and other agency workers are compared in Figure 10–6.) The art director possesses the graphic and layout skill necessary to translate the copywriter's words and concepts into finished products suitable for showing to a client or to the production people responsible for capturing the message on videotape or film.

In many instances, the copywriter comes to the project first and carves out the general idea, which is then refined in collaboration with the art director partner. At other times, however, the pair start the assignment together, contributing more or less equally to the commercial's formulation. In either case, the art director almost always then follows the project into production to make certain that the specified look and design of the spot are adhered to in creation of the finished message.

Most often, copywriter/art director television teamwork is directed toward the creation of a *storyboard*, a sequence of selected sketched stills that helps keep the message visually oriented. An example board appears in Figure 10–7. With a visual block on top and an audio box on the bottom, each storyboard frame or panel strives to illustrate the sequence of pictorial action, the camera settings, angles, and optical effects desired, and the dialogue, music, and sound effects being considered for use.

As it is being prepared, the storyboard provides the art director with the opportunity for effective interaction with both the visual concept and the writer who is helping to define it. This interaction can be most beneficial when the art director is not afraid to make suggestions about the spot's soundtrack and recipro-

**Figure 10–6**
Average advertising agency salaries, 1990

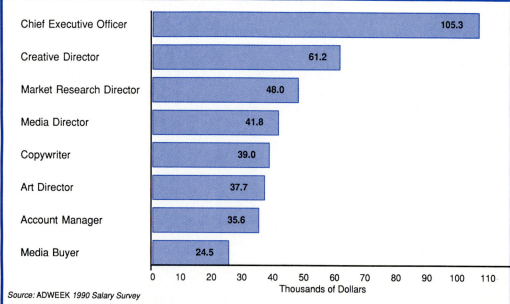

Source: ADWEEK 1990 Salary Survey

| | Thousands of Dollars |
|---|---|
| Chief Executive Officer | 105.3 |
| Creative Director | 61.2 |
| Market Research Director | 48.0 |
| Media Director | 41.8 |
| Copywriter | 39.0 |
| Art Director | 37.7 |
| Account Manager | 35.6 |
| Media Buyer | 24.5 |

**297**

CHAPTER 10
Creative
and Per-
formance
Functions

cally encourages visual recommendations from the copywriter. Art directors have been known occasionally to come up with a better word or phrase than the writer had originally captured. And copywriters, in their own scattered moments of pictorial insight, do stumble on more compelling visual ideas than the artist at first had in mind. Because the professional well-being of both depends on their *collective* ability to derive a successful audio/video communication, the art director and the copywriter each has something to gain from pooling rather than departmentalizing their brilliance.

Today, most successful art directors understand that for a concept to stay on track, continuous dialogue with their wordsmith partner must be maintained. "Traditionally," laments artist Alexander Molinello, "art directors or illustrators take copy and run away with it and then come back with something that the writer never saw that way."[20] When the artist physically works with the copywriter on the 'board, however, the result is much more likely to be a unified idea rather than two mutually exclusive ones.

The television art director's first quick sketches, suitable only for showing to his or her creative teammate, constitute what is referred to as a *rough* or *loose* storyboard. Later versions that are polished enough to exhibit to the client are called *refined, tight,* or *comprehensive* 'boards. In short-deadline situations or low-budget projects, however, it is not uncommon to proceed directly from a *rough* into actual production, provided that the rough is definitive enough to secure executive approval.

With modern computer technology, the distinction between rough and refined 'boards continues to narrow. Personal computers and inexpensive software programs now allow art directors to expand, contract, shift, and otherwise modify their frames on a video monitor before printing out their best effort. Typeface and size can be chosen and

experimented with at will. When the client wants changes, the stored image can be retrieved, adjusted, and reshaped accordingly. Such capabilities can cut the computer-literate art director's time expenditure by at least one-third, with an even greater proportional saving in art materials and photoprocessing costs. Perhaps even more important, the advent of computer-assisted storyboards permits the artist to sit down at the screen with the copywriter and manipulate images *together*—before anything gets locked into uncompromising ink.

To this point, we have focused on art directors who work in advertising agencies. Very similar jobs are available within television stations, production houses, and cable and broadcast networks. But the job title changes slightly to *graphic artist, design artist,* or *scenic designer.* Simply put, the graphics or art department in a media outlet is responsible for coordinating the overall look and visual image of that outlet. Graphics used on-air must be tied in unmistakably with those printed on sales brochures and corporate stationery and emblazoned on station buildings, vehicles, and cameras. Most all of this emanates from the station or network's *logo,* the memorable insignia that should instantaneously characterize the media facility in a distinctive and high-profile manner. Once the logo has been derived, graphic artists carefully oversee its use and reproduction so that the emblem remains consistent and uncluttered no matter what the application. Examples of radio and television station logos are included as Figures 10–8 and 10–9.

For their part, *scenic designers* translate the logo and all other elements of line, shape, and color into the coherent arrangement of the studio sets on which the cameras focus. In production companies, this job also extends to the dressing of outdoor sets and the selection of shooting locations. The creation of series programming and movies further demands the talents of wardrobe and makeup

**Figure 10-7**

But then, I'm not alone
in this, after all.

If you think you can do
the job, call 868-2700.

Sacred Heart Seminary
868-2700

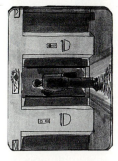

MAN (V.O.): I just hope I can
make a difference
here.

But the rewards are infinite.

NURSE: I think you want 317

MAN: Thanks.

ANNCR (V.O.): The work is hard.

**Figure 10-7** (cont.)

300

SECTION
THREE
Profes-
sional
Perspec-
tives

**Figure 10–8**
KNET logo

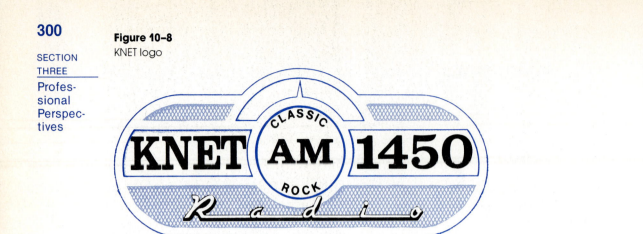

**Figure 10–9**
WPVI–TV logo

artists. Even though such jobs are mainly limited to program production companies, makeup and similar talent appearance specialists are also employed by major stations and the networks to enhance the visual appeal of news and other on-air personalities.

Like their art director counterparts in the advertising agencies, all of these graphics and design experts play a major role in determining the visual values and consequent impact that programs, commercials, and other forms of continuity (such as station promos and IDs) bring to the viewing audience. Even a seemingly static news or interview set depends on such artists for the appropriate conveyance of mood and character. And though radio may be a sightless medium, it, too, relies on artists to extend and magnify its image via such devices as logo development, print piece design, and remote unit decoration. True, art directors and other artists may never be in the electronic media's public eye, but these conceptualizers greatly influence what that public eye perceives.

## Feature Writers and Personalities

Having just discussed the role of artists in entertainment program production, we now turn our attention to the professionals who script and appear in such programs.

In the United States, most television enter-

301

CHAPTER 10
Creative
and Per-
formance
Functions

**GEORGE LOIS**/CHAIRMAN, CHIEF EXECUTIVE OFFICER, AND CREATIVE DIRECTOR
LOIS/GGK ADVERTISING

Any attempt to understand the art of advertising as a serious expression of human creative originality is usually overwhelmed by controversy over morality and ethics. We tend to equate art with virtue and commerce with sin. According to many critics who try to understand its massive impact on modern living, advertising is a twentieth-century love-potion; it arouses wants beyond means, it invites extreme consumption, it conjures a material paradise as life's goals.

It is not easy to explain the complexity of the ethos that inspires my life of creating ideas for selling. Since I was a youngster in public school, I lived to draw, design, and rearrange things. I knew I was going to be an artist. What kind, I didn't know. But I was going to be an artist. When I went to a specialized high school (the High School of Music and Art) I could draw better, design better, sculpt better, paint better, do better in history of art courses than anyone in school. But my special fascination was with art that was expected to persuade, to sell. Like no other art I was studying, it required a cause-effect connection or it simply couldn't work.

Talking to people on a page or in a TV commercial requires what I call "street talk." It has nothing to do with art, other than using art. It has nothing to do with literature other than using today's language. Art and words are merely tools for communicating. But all the tools in the world are meaningless without an essential idea. (An artist, or advertising person, or doctor, or lawyer, or electrician, or factory worker, without an idea, is unarmed.) When that original idea springs out of a communicator's head and intuitions, the mystical and artful blending (or even juxtaposition) of concept, image, words, and art can lead to magic, where 1 and 1 can indeed equal 3.

I have had a lot of breaks in my life (including being raised in a hardworking Greek family and marrying the right woman), but three people recognized my talent and led me to what I do today. My public school art teacher (Miss Engel), my design teacher at Pratt (Herschel Levit), and my first boss (Reba Sochis). After working for Reba Sochis and then Bill Golden at CBS, I plunged into the mediocrity of the commercial world and got myself a reputation as the *enfant terrible* of the advertising world. I'm sure I deserved it, and I'm just as sure that without fighting for my work every second of my life, my work would be just as dull and uninspired as most of the so-called communications in the

302

SECTION
THREE

Profes-
sional
Perspec-
tives

world (the bland leading the bland). To produce work I could be proud of, I've had to shove, push, cajole, persuade, wheedle, exaggerate, flatter, manipulate, be obnoxious, occasionally lie, and always sell.

And with all those lucky breaks of mother and father and teachers and wife and sons and first jobs, I believe a man still decides his own fate, ordains what kind of family life he has and what kind of work he wants to produce. You can decide that no client can make you run a bad ad! A client can kill and kill and kill what you think is right for him (the Abominable No-man), but he can't make you run bad work. (Your choice is to fight back with better work, or find better clients.)

My advice to anyone who goes into the communicating business is this: Be true to your talent, develop it, push it to its limits. Believe in yourself and the work you do. If you're talented, you can make it. Every job is an icon, the most important job in the world. Put in the hours; you have to be competitive to do great work, and energy begets energy. You have to burn out every day. Go your own way; don't take any baloney. Produce the best you can, and remember that this drive has to continue every second of your life. Make manly or womanly decisions, not cowardly ones.

A work of art derives its identity from its visibility and from the response it evokes in other people. I spend my spare moments drinking in that art created by generations of artists who have been the antennae of human sensibility. Artists who understood the art of the past, but who broke with it according to the needs of their time. I see my own role as precisely that of an artist. But my kind of art has nothing to do with putting images on canvas. My concern is with creating images that catch people's eyes, penetrate their minds, warm their hearts, and cause them to act.

If you read this epistle and have some of the feelings I have for what I do, get into the communicating business. Because creative talent, driven by an ethos of the spirit of convincing people to buy a product, vote for a president, or change the world, is rare.

---

tainment programming is created in New York or Los Angeles. The preponderance of daytime soap operas are produced on the East Coast and most game shows, situation comedies, dramas, and action/adventure series emanate from the West. Because the production of television entertainment for national network or first-run syndication distribution is an immensely expensive enterprise, a relatively small number of companies compete in this phase of our industry. This also means there are a relatively small number of jobs for writers and on-air talent, at least compared to the thousands of writers and personalities who make a living at or through advertising agencies and local stations.

Scriptwriters (also called screen writers, staff writers, or just plain writers) are, of course, responsible for coming up with the words and actions that the on-screen talent convey. (We used the term *on-screen* because feature-length *radio* dramatic programming in the United States is virtually extinct; see

Chapter 7.) Many of these scriptwriters are freelancers, preparing one-shot scripts for various studios and producers. These assignments might range from creating an additional episode for a just-extended series, to a movie screenplay, to an industrial promotion or training film. When these writers receive up-front approval and a guaranteed pay for the project regardless of whether it is eventually produced, they are technically known as *contract* or *commissioned* writers.

*Staff* writers, on the other hand, are on-going employees of the studio, production company, or network. Often, their employment is contingent on the continuation of the series on which they are working, but the more well established among them may have negotiated a longer-term arrangement through which they are shifted to other projects within the company if their current show is terminated. For further job security and creative control, the most successful scriptwriters eventually become hyphenates—writer-producers or writer-directors who thus acquire a greater role and financial interest in the creative properties they are developing.

To help them secure equitable salaries, contractual protections, information on new project opportunities, and insurance and pension coverage, electronic media scriptwriters join the Writers Guild of America (WGA), which maintains major offices in New York and Los Angeles. The WGA also helps its members locate reputable *agents,* those important intermediaries who help match their writer/clients with producers in search of scripts or scriptwriter services. Such agents, of course, are particularly important in the earlier stages of the writer's career. Once that writer has put together a string of creative successes, the agent's main function may turn to analyzing and sweetening project offers the writer receives from competing program developers.

There is no sure-fire path to a thriving scriptwriting career. Stephen Cannell, who created such shows as *The A Team, Wiseguy,* and *Hunter,* was an undiagnosed dyslexic who successively flunked out of three private schools. After college, however, Cannell's imaginative talent and urge to write would not let him be satisfied working in his father's interior design business. A *Broadcasting* magazine interview reveals that:

> Determined to become a writer, Cannell sat himself in front of a typewriter every evening after work, including Saturdays, and pounded out stories. Sometimes he would collaborate with a college fraternity brother while their wives played cards. . . . After four years of writing on the side Cannell sold his first script—for $5,000—for an episode of *It Takes a Thief.* That gave him the nerve to tell his father he wanted out of interior design. . . .
>
> In the next six months Cannell got assignments for two scripts, one for *Mission Impossible* and the other for *Ironside,* but he was nearly broke. Rescue came from a source that could qualify as a Cannell plot twist. His house was robbed of the Cannell wedding silver. The insurance brought him $8,000, enough to carry him until payment for his scripts came in.
>
> Cannell's first big break came when he sold a script for *Adam 12* and was hired as story editor on the series. That led to a writing contract at Universal. He began furiously churning out scripts—20 in his first year under contract—and it wasn't long before Universal had him developing and creating his own series. *Rockford Files* was created in 1973, followed by *Baretta* in 1975.[21]

In contrast, Hugh Wilson, who gave birth to *WKRP in Cincinnati, Frank's Place,* and *The Famous Teddy Z,* first tried to break into advertising in New York City after earning a journalism degree. When job hunting got him nowhere, he was forced to become a shipping clerk at the Armstrong Cork Company. There he met two other young clerks, Jay Tarses and Tom Patchett, who were trying to build careers as stand-up comedians. Years later, after working his way up from copywriter to

**304**

SECTION
THREE

Profes-
sional
Perspec-
tives

president of a small Atlanta advertising agency, Wilson founded his own commercial production company. On a 1975 trip to Los Angeles to shoot a commercial, he visited his old friends Tarses and Patchett, who were now writers for MTM Enterprises. They helped Wilson secure employment as an apprentice director, but he spent whatever time he could composing unsolicited scripts. A year later, he was a regular writer of episodes for the original *Bob Newhart Show,* and a year after that he created *WKRP in Cincinnati,* which ran for four years on CBS. Unfortunately, CBS moved the series around in the schedule eighteen times.

"Strangely enough," recalls Wilson, "the week they announced the cancellation, we were ninth. I used to joke if your mother doesn't know when you're on, nobody does. The happy ending is that it went into syndication and far exceeded many times over anybody's expectations. It wasn't long before it made more than $100 million in syndication."[22] (*WKRP* is currently returning to the syndication market with newly produced episodes.)

The path to stardom on the lens side of entertainment television's cameras is no more predictable than it is for behind-the-scenes scriptwriters. In both instances, personal talent, luck, and unquenchable determination all seem to play a part. But in addition to these attributes, every television actor must also understand the uniqueness of the video performance medium if he or she is to prosper. Television series acting is not like stage acting or even like appearing in the movies. The late actor-director John Houseman, who worked in both the film and electronic industries, isolated the differences between them this way:

> Television puts more emphasis on the spoken word; it lessens the importance and effectiveness of the reaction shot, which is the most basic element of most film performances; it encourages a more naturalistic mode of acting; its emotional curves tend

to be shorter, intended for a more direct and immediate effect on the viewer.[23]

In other words, involving viewers in the events on the small screen, and involving them in spite of family-room distractions and the brevity of most television programs, presents a tremendous focusing challenge for actors. As media scholar Horace Newcomb observed, "Even when landscape and chase become part of the plot, our attention is drawn to the intensely individual problems encountered, and the central issue becomes relationships among individuals."[24]

Under such conditions, an actor's believability becomes a function of concentration and controlled movement as well as physical appearance. Certainly, concentration is an essential part of any actor's art, but it must be especially intense in television. Director George Schaefer, for example, recounts that actors in a theater try to develop a bond that reaches beyond the footlights in order to gauge and promote a unanimity of audience reaction. In creating television's tightly framed world, however, Schaefer finds that he must convince his actors to ignore what's out there in the darkness if they are to focus their performances properly.[25]

Even in the case of live-studio-audience situation comedies, performers cannot play *to* that house. Instead, they can use audience reactions only as a partial guide in styling their delivery to the intimate camera and the viewer perspective it represents. Add to this the breakneck production schedule of television as opposed to film or stage work and it becomes clear how rigorously distilled the process of video acting must become. "You don't have time to do your scenes," objects veteran series actor Ken Howard (*Dynasty, The Colbys*). "You have to be ready in two takes. That can be an incredible burden. I think many good feature-film actors would be crushed on TV."[26]

One measure of a television performer's success or failure to connect with viewers

305

CHAPTER 10
Creative
and Per-
formance
Functions

## PETER MICHAEL GOETZ
### TELEVISION, FILM, AND STAGE ACTOR

Even though I have a demo tape with excerpts from more than forty television and film projects,* which helps to remind casting personnel of my potential for any given project, many times I must visit an office peopled by anywhere from three to twenty casting directors, producers, network executives, directors, and others. They conduct a job screening complete with prepared or unprepared readings and/or interviews. Many of my days consist of traveling from one studio to another for various chats about the latest projects.

Once winning the option of participating as an actor in a film or TV piece, my responsibility is to do an enormous amount of preproduction preparation. Unlike theater, very little time is allotted in television for acting rehearsals. Nor is there time for examination of historical significance, experimental rehearsals, character development, or evaluation. Television actors are thrust immediately into the scene. The director and technicians determine the camera angles and blocking marks based on our first rehearsal on the set. Actors can only hope that in the final cut, the editors retain at least a semblance of what the actor put into the scene.

It's very difficult for the video/film actor to totally control the outcome of

his performance. For example, I once played a sinister character who possessed some eccentric redeeming qualities. These qualities were created to keep the character three dimensional, more human, and just plain more interesting. I chose to play him rather inscrutably and mysteriously until one moment when he smiled and reacted to a very tender moment. That "moment" lasted only a few seconds, (hopefully in a poignant close up). However, the editor at that juncture selected a quick cut reaction shot of my fellow actor instead. My character revelation was lost. This gave my finally aired portrayal a very bitter and unredeeming quality. The editor, in short, had removed the key to my character, which I had worked so hard to insert into the production.

For the most part, acting in film and television can be a consistently rewarding experience. If nothing else, there is a certain satisfaction in hit-

---

*Among Mr. Goetz's electronic media credits are continuing roles in two TV series (*After M\*A\*S\*H* and *The Cavanaughs*) as well as guest star appearances on *St. Elsewhere, L.A. Law, Midnight Caller, Golden Girls, Matlock,* and many others.

**306**

SECTION
THREE

Profes-
sional
Perspec-
tives

ting the exact marks, remembering the precise moment we put the cigarette to our lips for continuity, maintaining the eight-foot distance between the car we are driving and the camera truck, being aware of holding our posture so we don't shadow our fellow actors, not being distracted by the maneuvering crew, and somehow even managing to remember our lines.

through the small screen are the Performer Familiarity and Appeal Ratings, or Q Ratings for short. (See Figure 10–10 for their well-known logo.) First used in 1963 by New York-based Marketing Evaluations Incorporated, the Q Ratings annually survey some 30,000 households about their attitudes toward approximately 1,400 actors in order to derive *Performer Q* scores. The same firm uses similar methodologies to determine the appeal of famous athletes (*Sports Q*), animated characters (*Cartoon Q*), and television programs themselves (*TV Q*).

Subjects' appeal and familiarity are broken down by how each fares with consumers in thirty-eight demographic categories. According to The American Society of Advertising and Promotion, these categories are divided

by age, sex, income, Nielsen county size, geographic region, occupation, and race and ethnicity. For a familiarity score, re-

spondents are first asked whether the subject is known to them or not. Then, they are asked to rate the subjects they do know on a five point scale, five points for a "favorite" celebrity, one point for a celebrity who rates "poor" in their judgement. The Q Rating is a percentage arrived at by dividing the total number of 'favorite' responses by the total, who reported they were familiar with the subject. It's a percentage based on 100%—the Hollywood equivalent of a batting average. One result of the formula is that a relatively little known performer can have a relatively high Q Rating, pointing to potentially effective spokespersons outside the ranks of the superstars.[27] (As Figure 10–11 evidences, Marketing Evaluations also "Qs" entire programs as TV Qs.)

The Q Ratings and similar studies by lesser known firms thus help advertising agencies zero in on spokespersons who appear to test well with the demographic group(s) that cli-

**Figure 10–10**
The qualitative ratings of Marketing Evaluations, Inc., measure the appeal and familiarity of television performers, programs, cartoon characters, and famous athletes

# THE QUALITATIVE RATINGS SERVICE

PROGRAMS AIRED: 8/8/88 - 10/09/88  
NBC   THURSDAY    9:00 PM - 9:30 PM

CHEERS  
SITUATION COMEDY

| Category | FAMILIARITY NORMS: PGM TYPE | FAMILIARITY NORMS: ALL PGMS | FAM | TVQ | POSITIVE TVQ NORMS: PGM TYPE | POSITIVE TVQ NORMS: ALL PGMS | FAVORITE | VERY GOOD | GOOD | FAIR | POOR | NOT SEEN | NEG Q | NEGATIVE Q NORMS: PGM TYPE | NEGATIVE Q NORMS: ALL PGMS |
|---|---|---|---|---|---|---|---|---|---|---|---|---|---|---|---|
| TOTAL SAMPLE | 55 | 55 | 76 | 31 | 28 | 25 | 24 | 16 | 19 | 10 | 7 | 24 | 23 | 26 | 22 |
| **TOTAL INDIVIDUALS** | | | | | | | | | | | | | | | |
| 6 - 11 | 55 | 44 | 59 | 28 | 47 | 39 | 17 | 14 | 12 | 12 | 4 | 41 | 28 | 13 | 19 |
| 12 - 17 | 71 | 61 | 86 | 35 | 38 | 31 | 30 | 20 | 19 | 8 | 9 | 14 | 20 | 22 | 24 |
| 18 - 34 | 63 | 62 | 89 | 30 | 24 | 21 | 27 | 20 | 21 | 11 | 10 | 11 | 23 | 28 | 24 |
| 35 - 49 | 55 | 59 | 84 | 33 | 27 | 26 | 25 | 16 | 24 | 10 | 9 | 16 | 22 | 29 | 23 |
| 50 AND OVER | 41 | 49 | 62 | 30 | 24 | 21 | 21 | 12 | 16 | 10 | 3 | 38 | 23 | 26 | 19 |
| 18 - 49 | 60 | 59 | 86 | 31 | 25 | 22 | 26 | 18 | 22 | 11 | 9 | 14 | 23 | 28 | 24 |
| 18 AND OVER | 52 | 56 | 77 | 31 | 25 | 20 | 24 | 16 | 20 | 10 | 7 | 23 | 23 | 28 | 22 |
| **TOTAL MALES** | | | | | | | | | | | | | | | |
| 6 AND OVER | 52 | 53 | 75 | 33 | 25 | 22 | 25 | 16 | 17 | 10 | 7 | 25 | 23 | 28 | 25 |
| 18 - 34 | 59 | 61 | 90 | 31 | 27 | 24 | 28 | 16 | 23 | 11 | 9 | 10 | 23 | 31 | 27 |
| 35 - 49 | 51 | 56 | 81 | 35 | 26 | 21 | 28 | 16 | 17 | 12 | 8 | 19 | 25 | 31 | 26 |
| 50 AND OVER | 33 | 43 | 57 | 34 | 21 | 21 | 19 | 11 | 14 | 10 | 3 | 43 | 23 | 30 | 21 |
| 18 - 49 | 56 | 59 | 86 | 32 | 21 | 19 | 28 | 18 | 20 | 11 | 9 | 14 | 23 | 31 | 26 |
| 18 AND OVER | 49 | 53 | 77 | 33 | 21 | 20 | 25 | 16 | 18 | 11 | 7 | 23 | 23 | 31 | 25 |
| **TOTAL FEMALES** | | | | | | | | | | | | | | | |
| 6 AND OVER | 59 | 58 | 78 | 29 | 31 | 27 | 23 | 17 | 21 | 10 | 7 | 22 | 22 | 23 | 20 |
| 18 - 34 | 66 | 62 | 87 | 30 | 27 | 22 | 26 | 21 | 20 | 9 | 10 | 13 | 23 | 25 | 21 |
| 35 - 49 | 59 | 62 | 87 | 25 | 26 | 23 | 22 | 16 | 31 | 9 | 9 | 13 | 21 | 27 | 21 |
| 50 AND OVER | 48 | 53 | 67 | 33 | 30 | 29 | 24 | 13 | 17 | 11 | 4 | 33 | 21 | 24 | 17 |
| 18 - 49 | 63 | 62 | 87 | 28 | 26 | 22 | 24 | 19 | 24 | 10 | 4 | 13 | 22 | 26 | 22 |
| 18 AND OVER | 57 | 58 | 79 | 30 | 27 | 25 | 23 | 16 | 22 | 10 | 7 | 21 | 22 | 25 | 20 |
| **INCOME** | | | | | | | | | | | | | | | |
| UNDER $15,000 | 57 | 59 | 76 | 34 | 32 | 29 | 26 | 14 | 18 | 9 | 9 | 24 | 23 | 24 | 20 |
| $15,000 - $24,999 | 54 | 53 | 78 | 28 | 27 | 24 | 20 | 15 | 22 | 13 | 6 | 22 | 25 | 27 | 23 |
| $25,000 - $39,999 | 56 | 56 | 77 | 30 | 25 | 21 | 23 | 17 | 18 | 11 | 8 | 23 | 25 | 29 | 25 |
| $40,000 AND OVER | 53 | 53 | 80 | 33 | 28 | 23 | 26 | 19 | 20 | 10 | 5 | 20 | 19 | 24 | 21 |
| **EDUCATION (ADULT)** | | | | | | | | | | | | | | | |
| HIGH SCHOOL OR LESS | 52 | 55 | 75 | 30 | 25 | 23 | 22 | 15 | 19 | 11 | 8 | 25 | 25 | 28 | 22 |
| SOME COLLEGE/DEGREE | 53 | 57 | 83 | 33 | 24 | 21 | 27 | 18 | 22 | 10 | 6 | 17 | 19 | 28 | 23 |
| **OCCUPATION (ADULT)** | | | | | | | | | | | | | | | |
| WHITE COLLAR | 53 | 56 | 80 | 35 | 27 | 23 | 28 | 20 | 20 | 8 | 4 | 20 | 14 | 27 | 22 |
| BLUE COLLAR | 55 | 58 | 82 | 29 | 22 | 21 | 24 | 12 | 23 | 12 | 11 | 18 | 28 | 30 | 24 |
| **RACE** | | | | | | | | | | | | | | | |
| NON BLACK | 54 | 54 | 77 | 31 | 26 | 23 | 24 | 16 | 20 | 10 | 7 | 23 | 23 | 27 | 22 |
| BLACK | 65 | 65 | 78 | 34 | 42 | 37 | 26 | 16 | 17 | 11 | 6 | 22 | 23 | 16 | 14 |
| **COUNTY SIZE** | | | | | | | | | | | | | | | |
| A | 54 | 53 | 77 | 32 | 30 | 26 | 25 | 17 | 21 | 8 | 6 | 23 | 18 | 24 | 20 |
| B | 58 | 57 | 82 | 30 | 26 | 22 | 24 | 18 | 18 | 14 | 7 | 18 | 25 | 28 | 25 |
| C AND D | 55 | 56 | 73 | 31 | 29 | 25 | 23 | 13 | 18 | 10 | 9 | 27 | 26 | 25 | 22 |
| **REGION** | | | | | | | | | | | | | | | |
| EAST | 54 | 53 | 77 | 34 | 27 | 25 | 26 | 17 | 23 | 8 | 3 | 23 | 14 | 24 | 21 |
| NORTH CENTRAL | 54 | 52 | 74 | 32 | 29 | 25 | 24 | 16 | 19 | 10 | 5 | 26 | 20 | 24 | 21 |
| SOUTH | 57 | 59 | 79 | 30 | 29 | 25 | 23 | 16 | 19 | 13 | 8 | 21 | 27 | 25 | 22 |
| FAR WEST | 55 | 56 | 80 | 30 | 27 | 23 | 24 | 17 | 17 | 10 | 12 | 20 | 28 | 29 | 25 |
| **VIEW PRIME TIME (ADULT)** | | | | | | | | | | | | | | | |
| HEAVY | 59 | 63 | 84 | 38 | 29 | 26 | 32 | 16 | 16 | 10 | 10 | 16 | 24 | 26 | 20 |
| MODERATE | 56 | 60 | 81 | 25 | 22 | 20 | 20 | 18 | 24 | 14 | 5 | 19 | 23 | 28 | 22 |
| LIGHT | 47 | 48 | 75 | 27 | 19 | 16 | 21 | 16 | 22 | 10 | 6 | 25 | 22 | 30 | 27 |

**Figure 10-11**  
TV Q program report for *Cheers*. Individual performer Q's may also be compiled for key cast members.

**308**

SECTION
THREE
Profes-
sional
Perspec-
tives

ents are attempting to reach. In addition, casting directors and network and studio executives also use such numbers in selecting actors most likely to deliver (or enlarge) a program's target audience. If this all seems callous and calculating, it must be remembered that nationally marketed products and programs represent investments of millions of dollars on the part of the companies who produced them. Personalities famous enough to be "Q-ed" probably owe much of their notoriety to such investments and stand to benefit additionally if their profiles suggest appropriateness for future commercials, series, or movies.

Who exactly "Q's" the best overall? In 1988, for example, the names at the top of the list were Bill Cosby, Clint Eastwood, Michael J. Fox, Eddie Murphy, Paul Newman, Robin Williams, and Tom Selleck.[28]

Another group of television's on-air professionals who are regularly Q-Rated (and increasingly important parts of syndicated programming's profit picture) are game show hosts. The challenge for these performers, however, is that they must not only register well with viewers at home, but also with on-stage contestants and a studio audience. Game show hosts must also mesh so tightly with the program's fabric and pacing that they control tension build without seeming to dominate it. Above all, game show personalities must bring the same sense of immediacy to their televised tournaments as anchors and reporters seek to inject into their newscasts—and for the same viewer-snaring reasons. In a review of the immensely popular *Wheel of Fortune, TV Guide*'s Merrill Panitt once isolated the key attributes for a game show ringmaster when he testified:

> The host is Pat Sajak, a former television weatherman and public-affairs show moderator. A smooth operator, he is pleasant enough, asks the contestants where they're from and what they do without getting in

the way of the game. . . . As game-show hosts go, he's as good as they come and well worth the half million a year he is paid.[29]

Sajak later unsuccessfully tried his hand as a CBS talk-show host—a seemingly similar performance situation but one, as he found, in which the central performer must be always prepared to take center stage. When a talk show lags, there are no spinning wheels or lit-up game boards to pick up the slack.

## Industrial Performers and Scripters

Although we have mentioned them in passing, we should specifically focus for a few moments on the creatives who work in corporate video. This burgeoning field of training and sales films and tapes is, in many ways, the fastest-growing segment within the electronic media. In some cases, the writers and on-camera professionals involved in corporate video spend all of their time serving this enterprise. In most instances, however, industrial media actors and authors are also engaged in separate *mass* media projects.

Corporate video pays reasonably well, and so many an actor uses its roles to keep bread on the table between public performance opportunities. As of 1989, Screen Actors Guild scale specified that an actor must earn at least $319 a day and an on-camera spokesperson/narrator a minimum of $580. Because these rates apply to the corporate as well as mass media, and because most big companies cannot afford to ignore union regulations, this means that the industrial sector pays at least as well as any other standard radio or television performance opportunity.

"Who cares whether it's corporate?" asks New York stage actress Chris Casady, "I want

**309**

CHAPTER 10
Creative
and Per-
formance
Functions

to work!"[30] Even in Los Angeles, where actors seem more concerned about the type of vehicles in which they perform, corporate opportunities are not looked down on because of their low visibility to the general public. "A serious L.A. actor is more likely to do [corporate video] than commercials," reports casting executive Carol Nadell. "A commercial is *seen*; people will think 'You must need the bread.' But the audience is limited for an industrial; actors do them the way major stars do commercials for Japan. The low profile is a *positive* thing."[31]

None of this should suggest that performing is an industrial production is easier or requires less talent, than do commercials or broadcast series work. By their nature, many corporate presentations are highly technical in nature. Thus, actors in them must not only be convincing as characters, but must also assimilate a great deal of unfamiliar if not downright complex information. To convey this information in a believable and interesting manner takes intellectual curiosity as well as dramatic ability. This is especially true if the role is that of actual spokesperson for the company. In such instance, the image of the firm is on the line, and the actor is expected to project that image to carefully manicured perfection.

This concern for dramatic quality is a relatively new trend in the industrial media. As corporate video expert Fred Cohn recalls,

It wasn't long ago that the cast list of a typical business program may have been headed by the human resources exec with the gimcrack Kirk Douglas imitation or the gregarious woman in accounts payable who played the lead in her high school production of *Oklahoma*. Such amateurs have sunk more than a few productions—inspiring derisive laughter rather than retention with their inept or grandstanding performances. But now, corporate video's actors are likely to be professionals; people who

make their living on stage, screen and broadcast TV.[32]

The perceived need for professionalism in the industrial presentation extends to writing as well. The largest companies employ scriptwriters on their regular staffs on the assumption that full-time employees are in the best position to grasp the complexities of the business. Yet, even in these instances, an outside video writer may be retained to ensure that the content does not clog the program's communicability. "Creativity cannot be parceled out or pushed through amplifiers," warns freelance writer John Morley. "No matter how business-like or systematic we make the process, going from facts and objectives to an exciting, emotional experience requires an intuitive leap of imagination.'[33] And the TV scriptwriting, rather than subject-matter, expert is usually the best one to capture this emotional experience for the camera.

Unfortunately, because companies communicate much more often in print than through radio or television, many in-house training or public relations executives believe they can automatically compose an effective video script. After all, they've written brochures, training manuals, and press releases for years; what can be so different about TV? Thus, people who would never attempt to create a situation comedy script or a broadcast commercial try to write an industrial video that demands the skills inherent in both. This, as the audio/visual scriptwriting team of Carl DeSantis and Phyllis Camesano point out, is a prime example of "the print media trap." They therefore urge people planning a corporate video not to

fall for the myth that 'a writer is a writer.' What you want is someone who writes exclusively for the screen. Someone who does a lot of brochure writing, PR releases or even magazine articles probably is not a scriptwriting pro. When you are deciding

310

SECTION
THREE

Profes-
sional
Perspec-
tives

**KEVIN CAMPBELL**/MANAGER, AV COMMUNICATIONS
DOW CORNING CORPORATION

People tend to think of television only as a mass entertainment medium. However, industrial video/electronic media applications encompass much more. Today, we deal with many forms of constantly changing electronic media to help people and organizations communicate. Computers, electronic visual production, large-screen electronic presentations, electronic still photography, and tele-conferencing are just a sampling of these varied forms. There are constant challenges in applying this technology to effective corporate communications. There are times when we push the technology to its limits and beyond to solve a communications problem. But that's what makes this work fun.

If you're interested in industrial AV, you'll need a strong technical background, but you'll also need good communication skills, a creative streak, and a good business and organizational capacity. Why all these skills and knowledge? Because in this job you will be looked on as an expert in your field. To you this may mean the specific hardware in which you were trained, but to other people in your organization it will be seen as anything having to do with communications technology and ideas.

How do you prepare for this? Start while you are still in school. Take some extra classes in other areas— the sciences, business, and journalism are a few that come to mind. It's much easier to do this now than when you have a full-time job. Never stop learning—it's a requirement of the field. It's not easy when you're pulled in so many directions. But if you stop you will be left behind by those who will not wait for you to catch up.

Patience has been called a virtue. It's also something that will be an asset to you. You will work to complete projects with many highly skilled people from diverse backgrounds. Because of your training, you will create the framework on which they can accomplish their tasks. You will be their mentor and guide. This is where all of your other skills work together. Always remember that you will be working with people who often don't have any idea what you do or how you do it, only that they need a specific result and you have a short deadline in which to help them achieve it.

You must always keep in mind that you and your department are part of the business. You must make intelligent decisions based on the goals of the corporate organization. Sometimes these decisions are difficult to

**311**

CHAPTER 10

Creative
and Per-
formance
Functions

make when you have to say that something can't be done because it's not cost effective or does not meet the objectives that have been established.

The hours are long at times and the competing demands can be frustrating. But just when you think it is never going to get better, someone steps into your office, sends you a note, or, best of all, sends *your boss* a note complimenting you on the job you did for their unit. This makes it all worthwhile, you feel renewed and you're ready to use your hardware and developmental skills to do it again.

on a scriptwriter for an important project, never use a portfolio of print media articles as a factor in your decision. It is like hiring a great plumber to do some carpentry work.[34]

In industrial no less than in mass electronic presentations, then, a professional result requires professional performers and creators.

(Otherwise, a scene like that captured in Figure 10–12 might result!) The comparatively obscure but lucrative world of corporate A/V will likely continue to prosper. But much of this prosperity depends on how well its presentations conform to the media expectations of its audiences. Industrial video need not be as slick or anywhere near as expensive as a typical network program. But it cannot ig-

**Figure 10–12**
Disasters await people who try to build professional corporate video productions from amateurish scripts

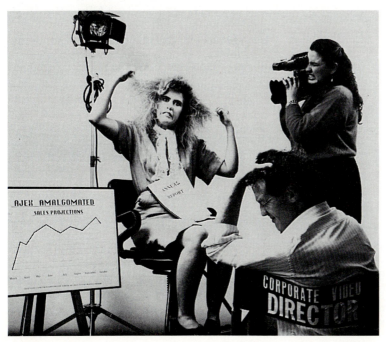

312

SECTION
THREE

Profes-
sional
Perspec-
tives

nore the fundamental production and content concepts that make such programs intriguing to watch and understand.

## Music Suppliers

One of the prime tools for focusing understanding and attention is music. From the most specialized industrial video to the broadly popular network adventure series, music is frequently used to bring a sense of depth, mood, and pacing to the visual presentation.

Like art directors, music specialists come into the electronic media after having been fully trained in their own craft. They then adapt their extensive knowledge of music to the particular requirements of the spot or program soundtrack. As veteran film and television conductor/composer Robert Emmett Dolan explains,

> The musician who works in recording, films, or television is inevitably involved in collaboration with professionals from a broad variety of fields, including sound engineers, tape or film editors, cameramen, etc. Unless he has some knowledge of their possible influence on his music, he will be working with a disadvantage. The aim here, therefore, is not only to expand the musician's technique so that he can work in these areas with confidence, but also to examine the techniques of his collaborators to the extent that they relate to his music.[35]

By the same token, all of these other electronic media professionals, as well as the writers and performers whom Dolan did not list, must be aware of the tremendous contributions that music can make to the success or failure of a project.

Usually, the commercial or program creators have some idea of the type of music bed they want to accompany the words and actions. This idea is then taken to the music specialists who flesh it out. The largest agencies and studios have such experts on staff, but the usual practice is to contract with an outside musical production firm or individual composer. Some of these firms and individuals specialize in the creation of instrumental and lyric treatments for commercials and station promos. A smaller number concentrate on full-length scores for industrial, broadcast television, and feature film projects. In any event, the music supplier's task is to provide tones and rhythms that advance the purpose of the message in question. Successful producers of music for media clients understand that their creations are there to support, not upstage, the product or plot. Production music that calls attention to itself is production music that has failed. Its job is to acquire meaning not for itself, but for the associative role it plays in conjunction with the other presentational elements.

It is easy to discriminate between effective and defective musical applications in program soundtracks. Ideally, the music should be a legitimate heightener of audience involvement; but it is sometimes used as a cover-up for dull dialogue or a ponderous storyline. As an example of the latter, *TV Guide* critic Robert McKenzie once wrote this backhanded compliment about a primetime series:

> This weekly NBC hour . . . is providing a lot of work for violinists. . . . If it makes viewers feel better about life instead of worse, and puts all those string musicians back to work, I suppose it must be OK.[36]

Obviously, it is not "OK" when the music bed is so massive that it overshadows the characters and situations on which the viewer is supposed to be focusing.

Skilled music suppliers and their astute electronic media colleagues know that music can tap, simulate, and stimulate a wide variety of feelings in even a very short passage. They are also aware that if the music says one thing and the dialogue or narration another, it will probably be music's point of view that predominates. Thus, aside from music videos where the tune *is* the message, true professionals do not start off with a music bed and then try to wrap the message around it. To do so can only result in a nice promotion for the melody at crippling expense to the program's main theme or the commercial's selling point.

This same principle applies to the use of *music libraries*—preproduced collections of instrumental beds that a station or corporate A/V department can use to enhance commercials, promos, and industrial videos. But because the library's music beds have all been produced beforehand as generic rather than as custom treatments, special care must be taken that a library cut actually matches the radio or television message now being constructed. Music libraries can greatly reduce the cost of beds for their users. However, if the selected cut sounds tacked on rather than built into the presentation, it is better to use no music at all.

Many potentially useful libraries are available from several reputable music suppliers. One reason for their popularity is that every selection in the library comes with full copyright clearance. As you recall from our Chapter 7 discussion, ASCAP and BMI licenses allow stations and other music exhibitors (taverns, restaurants, concert halls, etc.) to play music composed by ASCAP and BMI-member composers. (A much smaller firm of European origin, SESAC, offers a similar service, and most stations and networks sign licenses with all three organizations.) These licenses, however, cover only *performance* rights—permission to play the tune to the public. They do not entail permission to make dubs of the music (the *mechanical* or *recording right*), to link it with an unrelated piece of audio or video (the *synchronization right*), or to use the performance of the particular musicians on

the recording for any purpose other than the featured playing of that recording.

Thus, holding performance rights licenses from ASCAP, BMI, and SESAC does not by itself allow you to use their licensed compositions in commercials, programs, or corporate videos. As the radio/television producer, you thus have four choices: (1) not to use any music in your production; (2) try to clear all the rights yourself (a frustrating and time-consuming process); (3) commission a custom or preproduced soundtrack from a music supplier; or (4) lease or buy a music library that comes precleared. Assuming you can't abandon music altogether, the supplier-created library or preproduced track is usually the most cost-effective option. Keep in mind, however, that the length and stylings of the selections you obtain must integrate well with the type of media messages you expect to construct. No professional musical supplier can be held responsible if their product is applied like a Band-Aid.

In many ways, electronic media music suppliers are the ultimate performers and creators. Their work imbues almost everything the rest of us produce and heightens the listening/viewing experience for our corporate or mass audiences. "Music," as composer Richard Wagner once observed, "begins where speech leaves off." Professional electronic communicators know how to tap this additional dimension to best serve client objectives and listener/viewer preferences.

## Chapter Flashback

Even though many people believe that on-air media performers are the most important part of our profession, such professionals are just the most noticeable players in a multifaceted enterprise. Disc jockeys exhibit a variety of styles in a variety of formats but share the universal responsibility of providing an ap-

SECTION
THREE

Profes-
sional
Perspec-
tives

## MICHAEL ANDERSON/ NATIONAL SALES REPRESENTATIVE
FIRSTCOM/MUSIC HOUSE

The sales and marketing of music, sound effects, and related audio products has been my career choice since 1978. Then, only a handful of companies serviced the industry. Today, production music marketing is a highly competitive field. One must offer a unique package to excel. An equal balance of people, product, and responsive service is an unbeatable combination and a must for long-term survival.

Production music is prerecorded music created specifically to meet the creative requirements of the electronic media. Films, documentaries, television and radio programs, commercials, as well as informational and motivational programs all use music to help deliver their message. The majority of music used in these programs is prepackaged production music. It's readily available, easily licensed, and cost effective. Yet, it can be of exceptional quality.

Music may be used to open a scene; bridge two scenes; set the stage, the mood, or the tempo; underscore; or herald the finale. Client budgets and production schedules don't generally permit the cost and time required to produce a full-length custom score. With a little preplanning and creativity, using production music can be just as effective in delivering the message.

Music is a very subjective topic. Each project's producers always want what they feel is the best their budget can afford. Balancing quality and selection with prudent budget considerations is not easy. My job is to know my product and how it can meet a producer's specific production requirements. This business encompasses every aspect of sales and marketing. My days are spent locating the users, discovering their particular musical needs, and supplying them with appropriate options.

Telemarketing is a very big part of every day. I call on production companies, recording studios, and television and radio stations. Corporate communications and training and marketing departments in every industry are also potential clients. Local, state, and federal agencies, as well as educational institutions, use music. Advertising agencies and independent producers serve both the broadcast and nonbroadcast sectors. One minute I'll be cold-calling (prospecting) the video manager of a multinational corporation, and the next minute I'll get a call from the production manager of a radio station needing music for local commercials. From educators and teachers to department

**315**

CHAPTER 10
Creative
and Per-
formance
Functions

heads of major communications networks to independent producers—you must be able to communicate effectively in all areas. Each market is as important as the next. Proficient telephone techniques are a must to promote a music product aggressively and successfully in this business.

Outside sales is also an integral part of a well-balanced marketing approach. Personal, one-to-one presentations and trade shows help cement relationships in a way that only face-to-face meetings can. It's a lot of fun visiting the different facilities, meeting the people behind the voices, and experiencing first-hand how the various creative styles integrate music in their work.

In summary—sales . . . sales . . . sales, and more . . . sales! The highly motivated and dedicated sales professional can do very well in the production music business. Being creative and persistent is a must. It's hard work, but it's an exciting field, especially when your efforts help a client attain real communication impact in a cost-effective manner.

pealing linkage between the station and the listener. Usually, this linkage must resonate with local community needs and character. Talk show hosts, in addition, must be consummate conversationalists with broad interests and a constant desire to learn more about any subject that might prove of importance to their listeners.

Newspersons discover and present information the public does not have the time or expertise to gather for itself. Sometimes news presentation and news gathering are handled by different individuals. There is nothing wrong with such a practice as long as the content standards for news remain uncompromised and the people who function solely as presenters do not try to masquerade as authorities. Unlike print, electronic journalists usually must reduce stories to their briefest essence, but without distorting the subject in the process. Despite this inevitable condensation, top news professionals still strive to develop a context within which their reports can be better understood.

Copywriters work in media outlets, advertising and public relations firms, corporate/institutional settings, and independently as *freelancers*. Their brief messages (commercials, promotions, public service announcements) are all designed to *sell* something in the most interesting and memorable way possible. On radio, well-fashioned copy can trigger listeners' recall from their own past experiences in order to complete the picture in their own mind's eyes. On television, the visual usually carries the bulk of the communicative task. Some of the best writing is often the visual directions to the production personnel who will convert those words into filmed or taped images.

Art directors work with copywriters to sculpt a message's visual values. Most often, this collaboration takes place over a *storyboard*, which is the static plan for a fluid television concept. Other artists (graphic, design, scenic) work within media outlets and production houses to coordinate the overall visual image of that outlet and the programming it produces. Feature writers are responsible for the scripts that become full-length entertainment programs. These creators may range from freelancers to writer-producers who oversee the conceptualization of multiple series. Actors/actresses then

**316**

SECTION
THREE

Profes-
sional
Perspec-
tives

strive to translate these scripts into flesh-and-blood characterizations that are compelling and believable despite the distractions and time constraints of the television production process. Q-Ratings are often used to measure the appeal of individual performers and programs to target audiences.

The industrial/corporate sector is growing rapidly and depends on creators and performers who can take often dry and highly technical information and sculpt it into clear and interesting program modules. In this branch of the electronic media as well as in projects intended for a mass audience, music suppliers play a significant role in providing cost-effective soundtracks that can enhance and pace an audio or video production.

## ❏ Review Probes

1. What are some of the differences between the job of disc jockey and that of talk show host? Some of the similarities?
2. List advantages and disadvantages of dividing news gathering and news presentation functions so that these are handled by different individuals.
3. What are some reasons that electronic newsstories are almost always much shorter than their print counterparts?
4. Compare and contrast the tasks of the copywriter and those of the feature (program) writer. Are job opportunities similar in both fields?
5. List five major functions that art directors and designers perform in the electronic media.
6. What are the major rights associated with any copyrighted piece of music? To which of these does an ASCAP or BMI license pertain?

## ❏ Suggested Background Explorations

Blum, Richard A. *Television Writing: From Concept to Contract.* Rev. ed. Boston: Focal Press, 1984.

Blum, Richard A. *Working Actors: The Craft of Television, Film, and Stage Performance.* Boston: Focal Press, 1989.

Dijk, Teun Adrianus van. *News as Discourse.* Hillsdale, NJ: Lawrence Erlbaum Associates, 1988.

DiZazzo, Ray. *Corporate Television: A Producer's Handbook.* Boston: Focal Press, 1989.

Hough, George A. *News Writing.* 4th ed. Boston: Houghton Mifflin, 1988.

Hyde, Stuart W. *Television and Radio Announcing.* 5th ed. Boston, MA: Houghton Mifflin, 1987.

Millerson, Gerald. *TV Scenic Design Handbook.* Boston: Focal Press, 1989.

Orlik, Peter B. *Broadcast/Cable Copywriting.* 4th ed. Boston: Allyn and Bacon, 1990.

Zettl, Herbert. *Sight-Sound-Motion: Applied Media Aesthetics.* 2nd ed. Belmont, CA: Wadsworth, 1990.

# Facilitative Functions

❏ *We use the term* facilitative functions *to isolate the contributions that two separate groups of professionals make to our media industry: (1) the technicians, engineers, and electronic equipment specialists who construct, maintain, and manipulate the delivery system on which all of us depend; and (2) the sales and promotion executives who generate the dollars and public awareness that make it fiscally possible for media businesses to continue to operate. Even though the backgrounds and talents of these two groups generally are quite distinct from each other, they combine forces to provide the stage on which the performers and creators discussed in the previous chapter can showcase their talents.*

## Audio and Video Engineers

This broad employment category encompasses a wide variety of tasks. Sometimes, the term *technician* is used to separate lower-level systems operators from the true *engineers,* who fulfill supervisory, design, and development responsibilities. In most cases, however, the engineering department in a station or production facility is home to both

318

SECTION
THREE
Profes-
sional
Perspec-
tives

groups, with its entire staff conversationally referred to as *engineers*.

Among the more basic technician-level tasks are the monitoring and adjustment of transmission levels; the operation of studio cameras, audio and video control boards, and tape decks; and the setting up of equipment for regular in-studio and remote productions. With advances in solid-state technology, however, a significant number of these tasks have been automated, and others require fewer technical personnel than previously. In 1988, for example, NBC began converting its single-set news shows to robotic cameras and tape machines.

CNN's Studio A in Atlanta carries the concept one step further by remotely controlling the robotic cameras in its compact New York and Washington, D.C., studios. Because the in-studio performers in such situations are relatively stationary, programming cameras for normal shot changes is not all difficult. "Any program with a fixed number of camera shots in predictable locations can use them," said NBC production executive Tom Wolzien in referring to the robotic cameras. Certainly,

not all production personnel, even in a one-set show, can be replaced by automation. But as Wolzien pointed out, "The key is the difference between those adding creative value and those who translate commands from the creative staffers to the equipment."[1]

Robotic cameras are being considered at large and medium-market local stations as well. "We're looking at them real hard," admits Al Dunbar, chief engineer at WRAL–TV in Raleigh-Durham. "They can cut out a lot of the human interface, which slows things down and also causes errors."[2] Mere "translator technicians," in other words, are on their way out.

On the other hand, personnel (like the man pictured in Figure 11–1) skilled in maintaining this more sophisticated equipment and in applying it ("adding creative value") to a host of new production challenges are in great demand. Operating and servicing a state-of-the-art video switcher/special effects bank, or a multitrack audio control console with dozens of inputs, demand both mechanical dexterity and artistic sensitivity. Thus, while job requirements on the technical side have risen

**Figure 11–1**
A maintenance engineer checks his calibration instruments

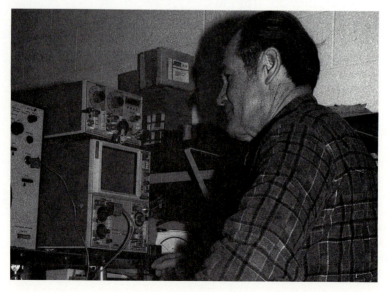

dramatically, so have opportunities and rewarded responsibility. Joseph Flaherty, vice-president of engineering and development for CBS Inc., put this new environment into lucid perspective when he observed that

> engineers, neither artists or writers, are the toolmakers to the arts, craftsmen of fine instruments—instruments that expand artistic horizons, but instruments we cannot play. Yet, this is the engineers' *raison d'etre* [reason for existence]. We live, as it were, on the wrong side of the tapestry, amid networks of strings, knots and loose ends. While this infrastructure is the vital support to the artwork itself, ours is nevertheless the skeletal view.
>   But our fulfillment is this: Without our tools, culture would be diminished, and the arts of modern television and telecommunication would not exist.[3]

Within a station or production facility, the *chief engineer* is the supervisory head of technical-side matters. Depending on the size of the operation, the chief may be a department of one (as at many small radio stations) or may supervise scores of employees in a number of different job classifications (as in a major market television station or production house). In the very smallest facilities (a 500-watt daytime-only AM station or an LPTV outlet, for example) the chief engineer may even be an outside contractor who only calls at the station periodically to check operation of equipment or repair a major component that has broken down. Whatever the case, this professional has usually accumulated considerable experience in the maintenance, installation, and repair of electronic equipment. The bigger the staff, the greater the likelihood that the chief will delegate hands-on operations to other employees while spending more time in administrative, equipment ordering, and facility-design activities. Nonetheless, most chief engineers are still called on to troubleshoot when a technical problem arises that is beyond staff capability or authority.

The marriage of computer science and radio/television technology also means that today's chief engineer (and many engineers below this level) must also understand computer theory and design as they relate to such systems as audio processors, digital editors, and special-effects banks. Computers are also central components of the automation equipment that runs the transmitter, selects and cues program elements, and even keeps track of commercials aired and the billings for them. Thus, today's electronic media engineers are information processing specialists as well as caretakers of hardware. As in the field of automobile repair, the specter of the self-taught tinkerer armed only with a screwdriver and soldering gun is largely a thing of the past.

*Sound* or *recording* engineers should, in addition, possess some musical sense and understanding of how sounds can be alternated and combined for maximum clarity and comprehension. In many instances, however, jobs may not involve the exciting world of mixing a famous rock group or symphony orchestra but rather may include capturing prosaic words from some corporate spokesperson or public newsmaker so that volume levels remain stable and audio reproduction is clear. *Music* recording may be much more exhilarating, but it is also less lucrative. As recording technology professor William Moylan points out,

> The "glamour" positions, and many of the more creative positions, do not pay well (save for a few "name" people). Like musicians, music engineers are underpaid for tasks that appear to be *enjoyable*. These positions are very popular, but are demanding. These are the creative positions that many very talented people pursue because they feel they must.[4]

Technically oriented individuals, then, should set their personal priorities carefully before pursuing an engineering career in the

SECTION
THREE

Profes-
sional
Perspec-
tives

**CHARLES NAIRN**/AUDIO ENGINEER AND PRESIDENT
COM TEC, INC.

Since 1972, when I left the academic world to start my own recording studio, the big question asked by every student sent over by my former colleagues is: "How do I get started in this business?" The honest answer is: It isn't easy. There are always more qualified applicants than entry-level jobs. Like other members of the mass media production community, the audio engineer works in a business that is (1) competitive, (2) dynamic, and (3) fascinating.

Being *competitive,* the field is hard to enter, does not pay particularly well (except at the grand-master level), and provides decent long-term employment only for the resilient and talented individual with superior interpersonal skills. Because the field is *dynamic,* success requires keeping up with changing client needs, marketplace fads, and rapid technical development. And because the field is *fascinating,* the audio engineer enjoys considerable psychic income, which augments the meager paycheck and salves the bruises that come from any competitive business.

For those who truly enjoy audio and can accept these conditions, two additional decisions must be made. The first decision is whether to pursue the more analytical and technical areas of design or maintenance or the more personality and talent-oriented areas of mixing or location recording. To *design* equipment, an engineering or physics degree is typical, although some highly respected designers are largely self-taught. To *maintain* equipment, a technical degree or electronic trade school training is the norm. For mixing or location recording, however, a technical degree is usually unnecessary. Talent, experience, and people skills are much more important.

The second decision is choosing which specific area within audio is most appealing. For the design engineer, the choice is among the various types of technology. For the maintenance engineer, mixer, or location recordist, the basic options are broadcast, film, video postproduction, music, or commercial recording.

Except for a handful of radio stations still doing broadcast production, most radio station work is maintenance. Maintenance engineers also work in every television station. But audio mixers and location recordists are found only in the few cities large enough to support full-time in-house production.

Motion picture sound production is concentrated in a few cities and dominated by craft unions that prescribe most career paths. Because film budgets are large, the highest level of audio quality and craftsmanship is expected. Video postproduction is like films, but tighter deadlines and smaller budgets result in lower quality sound standards. Because it is a newer and less geographically concentrated medium, there are job opportunities in more cities and career paths are not as tightly defined as in film.

Music recording is the most diverse audio area. Many large, well-equipped studios and thousands of smaller facilities are located throughout the country. Entry level jobs at minimum wage are relatively easy to find. But because the music business caters to fads and whims, success or even survival in the smaller studios is rare.

Most commercial studio work involves making radio spots and sound tracks for television commercials, industrial films, and training videos. These studios exist in every metropolitan area. They typically lack the glamour of the more specialized operations, but their broad client base provides exposure to many types of recording.

My personal decision to start a small commercial studio has required me to do it all: design, maintenance, mixing, location recording, and, of course, management. Over the years, I have recorded pop music stars in the studio, internationally famous classical musicians on location, and large musical groups in many performance venues, including Europe. I have made about 15,000 sound tracks for films, videos, and broadcast television and conducted research into several aspects of sound recording.

Hard work? Of course. During the busy season, a week can run seventy or more grueling hours. Challenging? You bet. You deal with difficult clients, lumpy cash flow, more than 100 tax forms every year, equipment that breaks without asking permission, and many other problems. Fun? I wouldn't and couldn't do this if I didn't love it. Is it for you? My advice is choose an audio engineering career only if you're quite sure you'll love it, too.

---

electronic media. Job options exist not only in stations and networks, but also in video production houses, recording studios, corporate and institutional audio/visual departments, and in conventional and wireless cable delivery systems. Some engineers, such as those supervising transmitters, satellite relays, and a cable system's physical plant, spend most of their time in matters of signal sending and reception. Others, like those involved in outlet control rooms and studios, focus on the ongoing process of program production and arrangement. And others (sound and corporate video staffers, for instance) are occupied in the creating and recording of individual projects that associated units or companies will distribute.

The common bond that links all of these situations, of course, is that they are all equipment-intensive with hardware changes dictating job shifts. William Moylan's admonition to would-be recording engineers is thus appropriate for technical aspirants throughout our industry:

A very real danger exists to those employed in an area that is dependent on technology, and that often finds itself reacting

322

SECTION
THREE

Profes-
sional
Perspec-
tives

to a new technology. One can quickly find oneself unprepared to handle a job function. Going into the next century, audio [and video] professionals must be prepared to re-educate themselves to be on top of the *next* new technology. In this business, job security is primarily based on the quality and results of the last "performance," not on history.[5]

## Lighting Directors

Smaller video facilities use regular staff engineers or technicians to handle lighting tasks, whereas larger outlets and production houses employ specialists for this function. Television cameras depend on the proper amount, direction, and quality of light in order to reproduce pictures in which the colors are true and the mood is appropriate to the program's content. Modern cameras require much less illumination than the insensitive monsters of the 1940s and '50s. But the light that is used must still be expertly arranged. Avoiding unwanted glare on the one hand, or dimness on the other, are only the most obvious of a multitude of concerns that impact a lighting design.

At its most basic, illumination can be considered as a purely quantitative commodity that is provided and measured to ensure the proper operation of the cameras. Herbert Zettl refers to this kind of lighting as *Notan*, or "lighting for simple visibility. Flat lighting has no particular aesthetic function; its basic function is that of illumination. Flat lighting is emotionally flat, too."[6] Were this all that video production required, any production assistant could handle the job with a minimum of training.

Lighting directors like the person shown in Figure 11–2, however, seek to facilitate pictures that transcend the two-dimensionality of the television screen by also using illumination to accomplish scene sculpting and visual emphasis. Thus, they move beyond mere Notan approaches into *Chiaroscuro* devices—methods by which illumination can be contrasted with shadow for greater pictorial in-

**Figure 11–2**
Setting lights for an in-studio production

terest. With Chiaroscuro, says Zettl, "the basic aim is to articulate space . . . to clarify and intensify the three-dimensional property of things and the space that surrounds them, to give the scene an expressive quality."[7] In the hands of a competent lighting director, Chiaroscuro makes illumination a key element for pictorial composition and enhancement of whatever mood is most appropriate to the commercial's or program's objectives.

We can illustrate the importance of lighting and shadow by examining the television commercial rendered in photoboard format in Figure 11–3. The shadowy, half-hidden world of dull past and present existence in frames 1–5 contrasts with the cameo clarity of the model's face in frame 6. Yet, in the actual color commercial, her eyes here are shown to be as dull as "big brown shoes". So we rewind to the shadows in frame 7 before advancing in frames 8 and 9 to the divergent and compelling brightness of eyes that the DuraSoft Contact Lenses have turned to blue. Even though the colors are missing in the Figure 11–3 reproduction, the contribution of illuminative shading and emphasis nonetheless comes through clearly in the monochrome version. Note especially the lighting director's accomplishment in frame 2. Here, the precise half-shadowing of the model's face encapsulates the *somber past/radiant future* comparison on which this selling idea is based.

The DuraSoft spot was shot on film, so certain of the lighting director's specific techniques were different here than if he or she were setting up for videotape (electronic) recording. The basic artistic principles of lighting, however, remain the same in both instances, and it is this sense of polished communication that lighting specialists can bring to a production.

For any lighting director, a great deal of work occurs before actual production of the commercial or program. Once the concept and set/location decisions have been made, the lighting director sits down with a set diagram to design a *lighting plot*. The plot specifies the number and type of illumination instruments to be used and where each instrument is to be located in relation to the on-camera action. Rearranging instruments on paper in the planning stage is much easier than moving the actual lights at the time of production, and also much more cost-efficient. With a well-conceived plot, the lighting director can devote actual studio time to final focusing, balancing, and special effects enhancements. In this as in virtually every phase of our industry, professionals always preplan; only amateurs think they can wing it. Lighting expert Joseph Tawail put it his way:

> Time *not* spent for pre-production planning will only be spent later while many more people stand around and watch a few guys sweat. The result will cost more, and rarely looks as good as it could. The light plot is basic to a good production for both economic and aesthetic reasons, and one of its byproducts is peace of mind.[8]

## Camera Operators, Videographers, and Cinematographers

The people who manipulate the cameras that pick up the light and the shadows are known by several designations. Generally speaking, *camera operators* function in television studios or at preplanned events with their electronic instruments mounted on tripods or pedestals. *Videographers* use highly portable (often hand-held) gear to tape location or remote pieces. *Cinematographers* work both in-studio and on location but shoot with film rather than videotape. In all of these situations, the fundamental rules of shot composition remain constant even though the recording medium and style may vary.

As we mention in our discussion of engi-

**324**

SECTION
THREE

Profes-
sional
Perspec-
tives

**Figure 11–3**
DuraSoft 'Circus' photoboard

# "Circus"
# Blue TV:30

*DuraSoft Colors.*

**MUSIC:** ESTABLISH
**WRITER:** THE PAST. WE CARRY IT WITH US IN
WORN LEATHER

BAGS WE CALL MEMORY.
NOT HER.

HER FUTURE WAS ON THE HORIZON,

AND SHE WAS WATCHING FOR IT.

WATCHING WITH EYES BIG AND BROWN AS…

BIG BROWN SHOES… **(FILM PAUSES)**

**VIDEO:** FILM REWINDS AND STARTS OVER.
**WRITER:** NOPE…NOW THAT'S POETIC.

UHHH, BIG AND BLUE AS THE TWILIGHT WITH
ALL OF ITS SECRETS.

**VO:** DURASOFT COLORS CONTACT LENSES.
GET BROWN EYES A SECOND LOOK.

**SUPER:** DISSOLVE TO DURASOFT COLORS
LOGO.

Young & Rubicam Chicago

neers, prospects for persons seeking to function exclusively as *camera operators* are not particularly bright. More and more newscasts and interview shows are likely to be serviced by robotic vehicles—at the station as well as the network level. And because newscasts and interviews are often the *only* in-studio productions found at many stations and cable-origination facilities, the demand for full-time camera operators may gradually evaporate. Instead, camera manipulation will be handled via remote control by an engineer who could also operate the camera directly on those rare projects where such hands-on work might be necessary. Certainly, production houses specializing in commercial and entertainment program recording will continue to require the services of skilled camera operators, as will the producers of sports events coverage. The number of such jobs, however, is relatively small and is confined to big cities and major media companies.

Because of the flexibility and portability of their gear, *videographers,* on the other hand, are a much more plentiful breed. In today's eyewitness-news environment, videographers capture most of the footage we see in local and national newscasts and often edit it for airing. They are thus essential ingredients of every television outlet's news departments. Because much of the success of TV news depends on visual dynamism, adept shooters can distinguish their unit's performance from that of the competition. Everyone may report the same story, and so the best-executed video is a significant factor in determining what viewers perceive as the best overall coverage. Even a star reporter with keen verbal skills cannot long compensate for dull or mishandled videography.

Visual newsgathering is, however, a rough-and-tumble existence in which excitement can gradually give way to aches, pains, and even burnout. Many news videographers, therefore, like the street reporters with whom they labor, eventually seek to move on to other careers. For the videographer, this ca-

reer move might entail involvement with commercials, corporate videos, documentaries, or even entertainment features that require substantial location recording expertise. Some videographers may also advance to director positions, where they combine their camera abilities with greater overall responsibility for the assemblage of the projects on which they work.

The videographer aspect of our profession has blossomed due to the tremendous technological advances in portable camera/recording equipment. Thirty years ago, remote taping required a tractor trailer crammed with equipment and cables snaking to the site of whatever camera operators were trying to shoot. Today, a single unit on a videographer's shoulder can move in tight on virtually any locale or subject. In ENG (*electronic newsgathering*) situations, the videographer often has the capability of either feeding a live microwave signal back to the station or satellite uplink, or taping the event for later transportation or transmission. In EFP (*electronic field production*) applications, the camera/recording technology is similar, but the aim is to capture more polished and preplanned footage from which later to assemble a commercial or program piece. Whatever the case, the videographer's physical dexterity and sense of pictorial composition are the key framers of what we are able to bring to the viewer.

For their part, *cinematographers* may work in-studio like camera operators or out on remote like videographers. But because they use film rather than tape, their recording vehicle must be chemically processed before it can be viewed or edited. Unlike their video colleagues, cinematographers cannot simply rewind their recording stock to check if they have the pictures they needed. Due to these factors, cinematographers have almost completely been replaced by videographers in television newsgathering. Fortunately for the people involved, the transformation was usually accomplished as a technological rather

326

SECTION
THREE

Profes-
sional
Perspec-
tives

## PATTIE WAYNE/VIDEOGRAPHER
### KXAS–TV

I decided, against all odds, that I was going to be a television news videographer. Breaking into what had traditionally been a male-dominated industry was a feat unto itself. I wanted it badly enough to brave Mid-western winters, carrying 85 pounds of gear through wind chills measuring 40 degrees below zero. I've now traded that for blazing hot Texas summers—again, you have to really want it. Enough to withstand the elements, to maintain composure under fire, and to operate under extreme circumstances.

There are risks involved as well. You may find yourself in hazardous situations like shooting an overturned tanker car that is rapidly spewing toxic materials. And I have tempted fate more than once while shooting aerials from a chopper. It helps to be a little crazy in the news business, but the most important requirement, according to twenty-nine-year KXAS-TV veteran photographer Jimmy Darnell is, "first and foremost you must be a journalist and then you must learn the tools of the trade." Technical knowledge and skill are musts, and because developments in the industry are continuous, it is necessary to stay informed as to what is state of the art. Bear in mind, however, that even though anyone can learn the basic operation of equipment, it takes creative ability to be labeled an artist.

An accomplished videographer is aggressive without being pushy, dedicated to the trade, motivated, instinctive, and innovative. About 99 percent of our work involves people, so you must also be adept at public rela-tions. Discipline is imperative when covering a hard news story that involves tragedy. It is necessary to detach yourself from the situation in order to function, but still remain empathetic.

Physical strength, of course, is an asset, but it is more important to be and stay in good shape to protect yourself against injury. A news photographer's worst enemy is the cumulative effect of carrying heavy equipment over a number of years. Full days of shooting off the shoulder can be survival of the fittest, and the videographer who has stamina will prevail. In short, news is a tough business, but it is not without rewards and personal satisfaction.

Now that I work for the station's promotion department, I am not called to shoot all day every day as in news. Instead, my time between shoots is spent editing or producing. A luxury afforded me in my promotion position is that I have complete control of my product from shooting to postproduction.

A television promotion department is not unlike a local ad agency; it is responsible for creating the right image for the product. The keys to good promotion are knowing your consumer (in this case, our viewers) and then developing a campaign that will attract the marketplace to sample your commodity. The process begins with a series of creative sessions that include the executive producer, the producer/director/writer, the art director, and the videographer, who will visually interpret the script. After establishing the marketing plan and determining the look and feel desired, shooting begins.

My frustrations are fewer in promotion as compared to news work. My camera equipment doesn't receive the everyday wear and tear and, therefore, equipment failure is minimal. The greatest stress in promotion occurs when you've hired actors, dancers, and makeup artists; brought in props and animals and extras; and are trying to coordinate "a cast of thousands." The llamas are spitting and eating the ficus trees you've rented; the wind fans are tearing the flags; and someone forgot the helium for the balloons. Top all this off with the realization that your lead actor can't act, at this point you say, "to laugh is not to cry."

Fortunately, a wave of energy and excitement flows when you take promotional spots out of the status quo and into a new realm. Combined with the technology now available, the results are as limitless as the imagination. You now have the option of keeping video in its simplest, purest form, or magically transforming it, adding shape, size, color, and texture. As a result, I am constantly challenged to produce an on-air look that is on the cutting edge.

The news videographer documents events and happenings that occur on a daily basis and receives a first-hand look at life's realities. There is no typical day. It is that anticipation of the unexpected that draws many people to the excitement of television news. Having been a news shooter for five years, I often miss the surge of adrenaline that comes with covering breaking stories. Yet, for me, there is now a much greater challenge in *selling* the news product than in covering it. As a news videographer I captured reality; in promotion, I take the same reality and enhance it.

than a personnel shift. Cinematographers put down their 16-mm film gear, picked up an ENG camera, and went on with their profession.

Before the conversion, television coverage in most cities functionally stopped at about 3:30 P.M. Film crews required time to get back to the station, process and then edit their footage in time for airing on the 6 o'clock local news. (This same timelag occurred for the late news, too, of course; 8:30 was the approximate deadline for what could be shown at 11.) Politicians and public relations people were aware of these scheduling constraints and so planned their announcements and news conferences accordingly. Now, however, videographers can capture events right up to the start of the newscast, and, if their ENG unit (like the van in Figure 11–4) is microwave-capable, can even send live reports di-

**328**

SECTION
THREE
Profes-
sional
Perspec-
tives

**Figure 11–4**

Components of a compact ENG vehicle

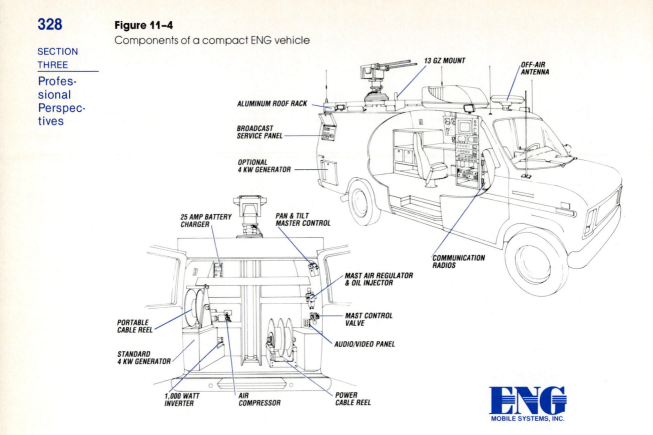

rectly onto the air. These applications are especially exciting, but they also raise serious questions of journalistic responsibility because news directors and editors have no opportunity to screen gruesome or potentially defamatory material before it is sent into viewers' homes.

In commercial, documentary, corporate, and entertainment production, film is still a frequently used vehicle, although much more in mass entertainment than in industrial projects. A number of talented cinematographers thus work in their chemical medium to capture content that is usually then transferred to tape for electronic media consumption. In many spots and long-form projects the look of film is still preferred because, as Time/ Warner's chief technologist Jac Holzman ob-

serves, "Video has a kind of plastic immediacy; film has subtleness and romance. Video brings you up close; film has a softer objectivity."[9] Eastman Kodak staffers further state that "film origination has intrinsic advantages as a reproduction tool because there is nothing between the camera lens and the recording medium. Even with advancement in solid-state technology making smaller video cameras possible, the fact remains that the image processor, in effect, is carried in the video camera. The result is that film production probably always will provide quality and creative advantages."[10]

Kodak's experts made this comment in 1979, however, before the first comprehensive demonstrations of *HDTV* (high definition television). Because it more than doubles the number of lines in a U.S. (NTSC) television transmission from 525 to 1,125 or more (depending on which HDTV system is used), HDTV creates a video image that rivals the clarity of 35-mm film. HDTV thus possesses the capacity to transmit live TV and video-taped images as well as 35-mm film pictures with a uniformly high quality. The film still looks softer, and the video-originated material still looks more like live immediacy, but the depth and coherence of each idiom are now closely comparable.

Film, however, is neither dead nor the adversary of HDTV. Newly developed film stocks provide resolution superior to that of an HDTV video-derived image and can capture acceptable pictures in almost total darkness. Television cameras, HDTV units included, still require significantly higher illumination levels to produce suitably defined images and so cannot attain some of the shadowy nuances that film makes possible. Consequently, many cinematographers and other film advocates see, not the replacement of film with video (as has happened in most newsgathering), but rather, the production community's combining of film and HDTV technology to optimize signal quality as well as production efficiency. Jac Holzman argues:

A production is not just about capturing images, whether it be on video or film; it is equally about post-production, the editing and manipulation and sometimes digital creation of images to form a synthesized whole. It is here that film, computers and video can serve each other seamlessly and well. Routinely, most dramatic television originated in the United States is shot on film, with the use of video assist for instant replay, and then edited either on film or transferred to video and edited within a video environment.[11]

Cinematographers and other experts also realize that transporting HDTV's picture into the U.S. home is a problem still to be solved. HDTV's wider screen (9 units by 16 units compared to the current 3 by 4) and high line count may outmode all current sets—or may result in a compromised system that is not true HDTV at all. For broadcasters, as opposed to satellite or cable deliverers, this also means that current channel assignments probably will be insufficient to carry the amount of electronic information required to produce a true HDTV picture. A combined task force of industry and FCC experts is currently working on these issues. (HDTV trends are discussed in more detail in Chapter 14.)

Meanwhile, as of 1990, about 80 percent of prime-time programming on U.S. networks was produced on film,[12] as were most nationally distributed commercials. Cinematographers not only serve this and related enterprises today, but also are likely to serve them in an HDTV world, where film's mood, and video's editing convenience, can continue in an enhanced collaboration that will result in even higher-quality product.

## Film and Tape Editors

It follows from this discussion that the boundaries between film and tape editing will continue to blur as editors move back and forth between formats. Editors, of course, are the professionals who mix and arrange separate visual segments to further a project's continuity, pacing, and meaning. Editors working entirely in film accomplish this task mechanically by manually splicing together chosen bits (or *rushes*) of film in order to achieve the optimal shot sequence. Tape editors, or film editors who work on tape, perform the job *electronically* by transferring digitally coded segments onto a master tape. The centerpiece device in this process, the *electronic editor,* has the capacity to control both the edit/re-

**330**

SECTION
THREE

Profes-
sional
Perspec-
tives

**PHILIP SGRICCIA** /EDITOR/OWNER
TRAPLINE PRODUCTIONS

A classified ad for a film editor should read: Wanted, one bright and energetic person who needs little sleep and can work under a deadline. A person who can act as artist, computer specialist, baby-sitter, electronic whiz, politician, magician, and ultimately a storyteller.

You need to be all of these things to be a working editor in Hollywood. My job as a film editor is to tell a story in a seamless and entertaining way while keeping my contribution invisible. I think it's a nice compliment when someone tells me they enjoyed the show and didn't notice my editing. If their attention was called to the editing, they are not watching the story and I haven't done my job properly.

Editors function in a highly creative and critical position in the chain of how television is made. I work mostly with executive producers, producers, and directors. Problems are constant in creating a television series, and it's part of my job to solve these problems. Uneven acting performances, out-of-focus shots, film flaws (scratches, etc.), sound break up, and continuity miscues are daily occurrences for me. Each problem is addressed and smoothed out, hopefully to the point of invisibility.

My work week is fifty to eighty hours long. The postproduction schedule dictates my hours. It typically takes anywhere from ten days to a month of editing to finish a show. A one-hour, single camera, filmed TV drama usually requires seven to eight days to shoot. Each day I receive the previous day's footage, called dailies. I screen the dailies, usually with my

assistant editor. We take notes on camera angles, actors' performance and pacing, focus, and lighting and sound quality. We also isolate bad and scratched negative plus continuity problems. I then begin to edit the available complete scenes. I work with smaller sequences at first. Then, as more film arrives, I start to fill in the pieces of the story puzzle. I experiment as much as possible with the pacing and structure of each scene because editing is not a precise science. I sometimes envision the story as a roller-coaster ride complete with it's emotional peaks and valleys, it's lightning-fast action sequences and gentle curving tender moments. I try and mold these scenes into a seamless and clear story.

When I complete the episode, I screen it with the director. We take notes on what the director would like to change and I make the changes. I now screen the show with the producers. We take more notes on which scenes work and which don't. We also keep track of the episode's running time. This process of screening and making changes goes on as long as the schedule permits. As our deadline nears, we *lock* the picture portion of the episode. *Locking* means that the show's visual will not change from this moment on. A locked picture allows the sound and music editors to add their audio contributions. Once the picture is locked, I move on to the next episode and start cutting, fixing the problems, soothing the nerves of producers, telling the story, screening, and making changes. Editing is a process that never ends—it just moves on to other people.

And now, a few words about Hollywood. Car phones, "let's do lunch," and "call my agent" run rampant in Tinseltown. Still, most of the people I've had the pleasure to work with are hard-working and dedicated to their craft. The film and television community here is a small, tightly knit group. Word travels fast in this town. You can be hot as the sun one day and off the planet in a black hole the next. Hollywood can be very unforgiving; but if you keep pounding on the door, it will open. Persistence pays off. Once you get a taste of movie making, it's easy to become addicted to the excitement. I love my work. I must, to put up with the long hours, political maneuvering, and deadlines that are a daily part of the business. The adage "it's whom you know" to get a job seems apropos in Hollywood, but "it's what you know" that keeps you employed. So, study hard and learn your craft.

Philip Sgriccia won an Emmy for his editing of an episode of *The Wonder Years* and subsequently edited and directed episodes of *Midnight Caller*.

cord and playback videotape decks in order to determine precisely where and in what order each edit will occur.

Today, virtually all video editing professionals work on equipment that uses a standard time code developed in 1970 by the Society for Motion Picture and Television Engineers (SMPTE). One second of a television picture contains thirty separate frames. The SMPTE code gives each frame its own separate numerical designator. The numbers are visible both on special editor picture monitors and on the editing machinery's frame counters. With these numbers as reference points, editing personnel can precisely locate the start and end of the segments that they are consolidating into their master product. In this task, they are frequently assisted by computers that have been adapted to make footage control and inventory tasks easier.

Using the SMPTE code as a benchmark, the computer regulates all the equipment involved in the editing process and also stores all the decisions made by the editor about what to edit. This *decision sequence* or *edit decision list* sets down all the determinations made by the editor for assembling the piece. These include the list of segments to be used and their order of placement, each segment's exact entry and exit points onto the master tape, and the type and duration of transitions to be used at each point. A *cut* for example, is the immediate change from one shot/segment to another; a *dissolve* is the gradual replacement of the subject of the first shot with the subject of the second. A *fade in* or *fade out*

332

SECTION
THREE

Profes-
sional
Perspec-
tives

is the progression into or from *black* (a blank screen), and an assortment of *key* and *wipe* transitions provide more distinctive ways of putting one picture within another or pushing one aside in favor of another. With the computer as the control module, editing personnel can call up all of these decisions in their predetermined order and execute each with to-the-frame precision.

Now that the price of computer packages has declined, even middle- and small-size production facilities can offer their editors some sort of computer-assisted operation. Often, this assistance includes the capability to generate graphic and animation effects. Thus, like engineers, editing professionals are being required to become much more computer-wise in order to fully exploit the capabilities with which technology has provided them. Even relatively basic projects now regularly use intricate shot sequencing that was formerly all but impossible for even the most skilled and disciplined editing pro. Today's electronic and computer-assisted equipment makes these tasks comparatively easy and trouble-free—but only for editors who are in control of the sophisticated systems that await their commands.

Even though we have been focusing on video editing, a similar battery of electronic and computer devices are available to improve the audio editor's performance and product as well. With the multiplicity of sound sources and tracks used in today's music releases and video/film soundtracks, the sound editor or editor/engineer requires more than a good ear and nimble fingers.

As in the case of video, electronic control devices allow the audio editor to keep track of and manipulate a number of discrete elements in accomplishing the final product or *mix-down.* Some devices, like the *Lexicon,* further use computer technology to permit the editor actually to compress or expand the soundtrack into other time lengths without altering musical/vocal pitch or comprehension. In other words, a 35-second musical commer-

cial can be squeezed into 30 seconds without listener detection.

---

# Directors: Technical, Assistant, and Main

Film and tape editors work in a *postproduction* environment. They enter the project after the individual rushes, segments, or tracks have been recorded in order to compile them into a final format and arrangement. *Technical directors,* in contrast, have as one of their principal duties the assemblage of multiple video sources in *real time*—that is, during their actual occurrence. Technical directors thus operate the *video switcher* through which all visual sources (cameras, slides, graphics, film or tape machines) are routed. For this reason, they are often referred to as switchers.

By pushing buttons or moving levers and knobs, the technical director (T.D.) can call up and manipulate any of the available pictures for feeding over-the-air (live show) or to the master tape machine (recorded show). In live programs such as newscasts and sporting events, the source the switcher selects is the visual that the audience sees at virtually the same moment. Sometimes, more than one picture is used in order to produce a split-screen, insert, or *superimposition* (a dissolve, which pauses at midpoint so that one picture remains atop the other). Whatever the case, the T.D. executes the command from the main director, who is choosing from among the various pictorial options displayed on individual monitors.

At many outlets, a duty engineer serves as technical director. When the programming being aired is prerecorded or coming from the network, no main director is necessary. The T.D. simply follows along in a program log, bringing up either the network feed or the local prerecorded programs, commercials, and other continuity to be played back by video machines in the control room. Only when a local show is being produced is a main director required, and perhaps not even then if the production is very simple, such as a one-camera news-brief feature. At a small-market station, the main director may be only a glorified T.D. who handles program shot set-up and selection responsibilities as a one-person operation. Conversely, at large outlets or production studios, a T.D. works under a supervising director but exercises a more complicated set of responsibilities. In addition to being the master switcher, the T.D. may oversee the entire technical crew with camera operators, lighting and sound personnel, set construction staff, and control room engineers all under his or her control.

In even larger and more complex settings, an *assistant director* (A.D.) position is also provided. The A.D.'s job is two-fold. First, he or she helps the director in preproduction planning, making certain that the needed props, personnel, and recorded video footage have been identified and are available at the time the program is to be aired or recorded. Then, during the actual production, the assistant director aids in keeping track of shots, anticipating camera and performer cues, and monitoring the running time of program segments and the show as a whole. If postproduction work is necessary, these same functions also carry over to those editing sessions.

Meanwhile, out in the studio, a *floor manager* facilitates the job of all the control room directing personnel by communicating with camera operators and on-camera talent and by otherwise making certain that things in the studio are running smoothly. Sometimes called a *stage manager* (a throwback to earlier theatrical practice), this person is the ultimate studio traffic cop—receiving headset commands from the director in the control room for relay to others on the set. Camera operators typically wear headsets as well but cannot motion to talent, each other, and ma-

nipulate their cameras at the same time. Although important, floor manager slots are seldom lucrative, and most people in this position use it as an entry to higher productional callings.

Near the top of such callings, of course, is the position of main *director* itself. The director is the key person in the entire production process; this individual shapes the look and feel of the final product that the media audience will experience.

In shooting commercials, the director either serves as the camera person or hires another professional to perform that function. Either way, the aim is to translate a script or storyboard accurately into the clearest and most compelling fifteen, thirty, or sixty seconds possible. Commercial directors normally work on a freelance basis or are part of a company that specializes in shooting spots, public relations pieces, and similar assignments. An advertising agency or other creative firm captures the concept on paper and then hires a director to realize that idea on film or tape. Well-established commercial directors command substantial fees because they bring a certain look to their pieces that clients want and to which viewers react positively. In essence, these directors are making micro movies, in which the product must be the star and the plot revolves around how that product dramatically meets a need or solves a problem.

Even though they perform a similar sculpting role for the pieces on which they work, directors of *programs* function somewhat differently. Within a station, directors are regular staff members who supervise the visual design and shooting of the news, interview, and talk programming that make up the bulk of most locally produced offerings on a station or cable system. If the outlet also shoots commercials for its local advertisers, these same staff directors probably handle those tasks as well. Networks, too, use staff directors for their in-studio news and talk shows. Certainly, the crews and audiences are larger

334

SECTION
THREE

Profes-
sional
Perspec-
tives

## JAMES GARTNER/COMMERCIAL DIRECTOR
GIBSON/LEFEBVRE/GARTNER

Hopefully, a director gets involved with a commercial while it first is being conceived. But in reality, it's usually after the spot has been written or storyboarded by the agency. This is unfortunate, because early involvement is part of the plus-ing process, which is the collaborative sum of everyone's skilled contribution. I believe in plus-ing. I think all creative should be plus-ed by all parties. Music. Editing. Camera. Everyone should be adding. And for the director, this should begin at the time of the initial creative. But it rarely happens.

Preproduction. This is where the director and the agency first meet. This is where I attempt to make certain we're all making the same commercial. So Preproduction should be a defining process. Together with the agency, I'll cast the spot. Scout locations. Then I spend a lot of time with my cinematographer, art director, stylist: Defining the look. Light. Filtration. What lenses we should use. All of these define the look. Colors are very important depending on the mood, characters, concept. It's a most important stage. If my art director is making a commercial only 5 percent different from me—and I am making a commercial 5 percent different from the cinematographer, who is maybe 5 percent different from the wardrobe stylist or editor—then add it up. Before long, you have something that is maybe 30 percent out of sync. So you must define the abstract. Because at the preproduction stage, there is nothing. But that's also the magic. The creative process. Defining the abstract.

Most of what you bring to this task is inherent in you. Author H. L. Mencken said, "Nothing can come out of the artist that isn't in the man." But creativity is also a process that evolves. It is surrounding yourself with good art. Good film. Good literature. I believe creativity, largely, is having good taste.

After preproduction comes the execution. The shoot. If in preproduction you have succeeded in defining, the shoot should go well. Alfred Hitchcock said he was bored with the actual shooting, because in his own mind, he had finished the film long before the shooting began.

Then comes the edit, perhaps the most important part of all. I've felt that casting is 70 percent of telling a good commercial. And the storyboard is 70 percent. And postproduction is 70 percent. Sometimes I feel that way. Each element is critical, and that is certainly true with how a spot is finished in postproduction. What performances are chosen. How a scene cuts against another. The pacing. The music. It's the plus-ing process again. It should happen here, too.

It's hard to imagine a Cezanne or a Leonardo working with an art director, a writer, a creative director, an account group, a client. Yet, that's what a director is supposed to balance when creating a commercial. (I don't want to be accused of comparing advertising with Cezanne, by the way. But neither will I concede that film cannot reach these levels). I think if there is a single reason for so much mediocrity in advertising, this is it. Mediocrity is most likely done by a committee of individuals. Good advertising usually is a result of one person—or, if you're fortunate, of a few people with the same vision.

If I were a student, studying advertising, I would first truthfully ask myself if this is what I want to pursue. If the answer is yes, then I would begin in a serious fashion first to surround myself with good art, literature, film. Then to dissect it. What is it about that particular piece that makes it stand out? Notice the cutting. The music. The framing. The dialogue. Where does the light come from? Sit in front of a VCR and play back a scene fifty times. The elements never change. There is a picture. There is sometimes music and dialogue. It's the synergy of how those elements are used. Paying attention to details. The smallest detail is often the difference between good and great. It was Chaucer, I think, who said "a lot of smalls make a great."

James Gartner was named 1988 commercial director of the year by the Directors Guild of America.

---

at the network level, but the director's fundamental coordination role is the same as at local facilities.

In-studio news and talk offerings seldom use visual treatments that are daringly experimental or *avant-garde*. Thus, directors who work in this idiom are not expected to be television artists but instead must create clean, consistent visual progressions that are easy to follow and that make the on-air talent look as good as possible. The best directors here are those whose work goes totally unnoticed by viewers, whose shot transitions are so smooth and sensible that they never call attention to themselves but serve only to propel show content into clearer focus.

Directors of entertainment programs who work for major production studios have more latitude, of course, but they are still expected to turn out shows that a mass public will have no difficulty comprehending. If they are recording before a live audience, the aim is to capture as successful a take as possible the first time around. Unlike true live TV, there is the possibility for retakes or fixing small deficiencies through postproduction editing. Series production works on very tight deadlines, however, so time is limited. A situation comedy director must normally deliver an episode a week, their soap opera counterpart one or even two shows a day, and the game show director perhaps three to five episodes in a single extended shooting session! Under such conditions, the more footage that can be captured in final form the first time, the better.

Game show and daytime soap opera directors record on videotape, but they try to achieve as much of the final shot progression as possible in the initial run, operating much

336

SECTION
THREE

Profes-
sional
Perspec-
tives

as a newscast director would work. A taped situation comedy director may work in a similar manner but with greater opportunity for selected retakes or for shooting corrective inserts that can be added in postproduction editing. For filmed, as opposed to taped, sit coms, there tends to be a greater amount of postproduction work and the director spends much more time on the studio floor with the cast than in the control booth. Film shows especially are shot a little long so that an editor always has more than the absolute minimum footage from which to trim the final product.

A typical five-day schedule for the completion of a single situation comedy episode is described below by John Finger, director of photography for *Cheers. Cheers* is a filmed show, but the progression is much the same for sit coms shot on tape.

> During the first day, there is a production meeting involving all department heads, including props, lighting effects, wardrobe and special effects. We also determine our need for extras for this episode. Later that same day, the cast reads the script to see how it sounds. . . . After the reading, they have the first rehearsal on the stage. Meanwhile, the writers might be busy late into the night making revisions.
>
> Day two, changes are reviewed, and rehearsals begin. Later in the day, there is a complete runthrough. . . . There are generally more rewrites. Day three is more or less a repetition of day two.
>
> On day four, the cameras are brought on stage, and they are used during rehearsals. Afterwards, stand-ins are used while [director] Jim Burrows and I discuss positioning [blocking] of the cameras. There is one last run-through without the cameras, since staging might have changed, Meanwhile, the writers are still fine-tuning.
>
> During the fifth day, most of the cast and crew come in around noon. They rehearse a couple of times. . . . Late in the afternoon, there is a dress rehearsal with everybody present. . . . Many times there are still changes being made in the script. After din-

ner, the show is filmed in front of a live audience.[13]

Throughout the entire process, the director's coordinating input is crucial for quick decision-making and for the communication and execution of those decisions to everyone involved.

Directors of hour-long series, which are virtually always shot on film, work much more like their movie than their situation comedy counterparts. Hour projects combine both sound-stage and location shooting. They are shot out of order and then completely assembled in postproduction just as is a full-length movie. Normally, it takes a production company eleven weeks to complete an hour-long episode. This time includes two weeks of preproduction rehearsal and technical preparation, seven weeks of shooting, and two weeks of postproduction. Because the director must be involved throughout the process, more than one director works on a given series, with the production of episodes assigned to each director frequently overlapping. The complexity and cost of hour shows (and of made-for-TV movies) invest their directors with greater overall creative responsibility. Unlike the situation comedy production environment cited above, industry watcher Neal Koch reports that "Once long-form productions start, the scripts are set and writers are often not even allowed into the filming sessions, which puts the director in control."[14]

We cannot leave the subject of electronic media directors without pointing out that such professionals are found on the radio side, too. Certainly, there are fewer opportunities for U.S. radio directors than in the years when radio drama ruled the networks (see Chapter 7). Nevertheless, some skilled audio professionals still work as directors in two separate areas: syndicated program production and commercials.

Today's national syndicated radio shows are often music-related, like *American Top 40,* and may combine the playing of tunes with host commentary and interview segments. Frequently, the programs require extensive background research into the featured musicians, songs, and environment out of which they came. A director thus coordinates the consolidation of all of this material into a well-paced program that will play effectively in every area of the country, and perhaps overseas as well. These syndicated projects must be consistent in their style and pacing from week to week and must develop a flowing format that is always maintained. Either live or, more frequently, in postproduction, the radio director's job is to ensure this continuity and the comfortable predictability that the show's listeners and affiliated stations expect.

Major-client radio commercials also employ directors to deliver spots that are as well engineered and enacted as anything heard on the air today. A talented radio copywriter can create a wonderfully involving and image-rich script, but it won't play well if the vocal casting or pacing are off the mark. Good radio spot directors hear the optimal product in their heads and are able to motivate and navigate their talent to achieve that sound vision. Award-winning radio writer/director Joy Golden sees her job this way:

The key to making a good radio commercial is to know how to direct the people. . . . What I often do, especially with some of the new people, is set up a visual scenario for them. I'll say, "You're a husband and wife in bed, right? And it's early in the morning, and he's feeling lousy, and she's feeling—". I'll give them a whole physical and personality scenario, so they can perform, in their minds, in a setting that isn't so audio. Because I want a bigger thing to come out. . . . In the studio, most of the time it requires ten, twelve, fifteen takes for the talent to get it right, especially if it's a monologue. We do and we re-do and we re-do.[15]

Golden's description of the radio commercial director's job is probably an apt illumination of the key responsibility of *any* electronic media director. Even though the equipment varies (and there's lots of it), a successful director is still communicating with people (the audience) through the skillful guidance of other people. This guidance, or the lack of it, is most noticeable in how a director handles performers. "All actors," observed veteran television director Peter Dews, "are to some degree nervous, and the director can help them to overcome this by creating the right kind of environment to work in, so that they know where they are with the medium, come to working terms with it."[16] Fellow director Franklin Schaffner adds, "Simply defined, I suppose the director's function really is just staying one jump ahead of the cast."[17]

The special constraints of corporate video present a director with additional challenges, observes industry authority Stephen Barr. "Working with tighter budgets, shorter time frames, smaller crews and less-extensive arsenals of equipment, they don't have the same creative clout; they find themselves walking a tightrope between aesthetic expression and economic reality. The employer may pull the plug before the ideal lighting setup is achieved; time constraints may keep flubbed lines from being reshot; there may not be enough money to rent a dolly—forcing the use of a zoom where a tracking shot would have worked better."[18]

Understandably, it is easy for a television or radio director to lose sight of the human function and to become preoccupied with all the technical tools and procedures of our industry. But like any other craft in the electronic media, accomplished directors realize that hardware is only their avenue, not their destination. Equipment and its manipulation exist to package performances in such a way that these performances strike responsive chords with the target audience. This holds true whether we are producing a radio commercial, a broadcast television series, or a corporate video.

Successful communication with our se-

**338**

SECTION
THREE

Profes-
sional
Perspec-
tives

lected audience is the ultimate justification for the costs any production incurs. Raising money to cover these costs (and turn an appropriate profit) is frequently the job of the sales professionals whose facilitative functions we now examine.

## Station/System Salespersons

Local commercial stations, cable systems, and most of the networks that service them all employ sales staff whose job it is to sell air time to advertisers. For stations and broadcast networks, revenue from the sale of their commercial slots or *avails* constitutes virtually the sole source of income. For a cable system, on the other hand, this revenue stream is still comparatively minor compared to income from subscriber fees for basic and pay channel service. Local advertising activity on cable systems continues to increase, however, and appears to promise substantial rewards in the future.

Whatever the medium, the time salesperson (called an *account executive* at some outlets) makes a living by offering advertisers an intangible commodity (time) that they can use to attract prospects and build brand recognition.

In many ways, electronic media salespeople work in a more difficult arena than do their print counterparts. First, the availability of on-air time is fixed. There are only twenty-four hours in a day (assuming the outlet programs all twenty-four). The air schedule cannot be contracted when advertiser demand is low or expanded when it is high. *Unsold* time is lost revenue; the lack of *enough* time is lost business. Print media, conversely, can add or subtract pages at will to mirror advertiser needs. (Many local papers are much thicker on Wednesday, for example, when grocers are seeking the end-of-week food buyer, than

they are on Tuesday.) So the air salesperson must not only secure advertising dollars, but must also secure them in such a way that the resulting commercials will be more or less equally spread throughout the course of a week.

Also unlike print, the cost of operating a station bears no assured relationship to the number of people reached. A newspaper expecting to sell 10,000 copies will print 10,000 copies (with a few extra to meet unanticipated requests). As the paper's circulation expands, it can increase the press run incrementally to match actual demand. A station, on the other hand, must transmit a full program day whether 100 or 100,000 people tune in. Its program costs are mainly determined by its market and signal dimensions and cannot easily be scaled down because it is failing to attract enough listeners. Advertisers pay rates based on the number and type of people the outlet is delivering. These rates fall as audience levels fall, but operating and programming costs stay relatively the same. If the on-air product is unattractive, the time salesperson is put in a double bind, being forced to sell more inventory at lower rates on a less desirable outlet.

Finally, whereas a print layout is a concrete entity that sits there as long as one wants to look at it, a radio or television spot is a real-time emission that exists only at the moment it is being distributed. The amount of information that even a sixty-second commercial can carry is also significantly less than can be accommodated in a quarter-page or larger print ad. Thus, many local advertisers either avoid the electronic media or have unreasonable expectations as to how much content can be memorably conveyed in a single spot.

Skilled time sellers have learned to surmount these problems while carving out lucrative careers. The specific techniques they use are beyond the scope of this introduction, but a few key principles shaping their task can be illuminated here.

Fundamentally, sellers and buyers of air

time negotiate on the basis of audience *ratings, shares, cost-per-thousand* (CPM), *gross rating points,* and *frequency* (message repetition). A rating measures the number of people or households reached by a given station/channel as compared to the total number of people or households in the market. Radio is normally measured in *persons* and television in *households* (but the introduction of peoplemeters is gradually converting TV measurements to a person-base as well). A rating then, is mathematically expressed this way:

$$\text{Rating} = \frac{\substack{\text{people/households} \\ \text{using your station/channel}}}{\text{total surveyed people or homes}}$$

Thus, if we survey 280 persons and find that 42 of them are listening to our radio station, our station has attained a 15 rating:

$$\frac{42}{280} = .15$$

From this (and assuming the measurement service's sample was representative of the composition of our market as a whole), we estimate that approximately 15 percent of the listeners in the market are tuned to our station (and its commercials!) at the time on which we are focusing. (Basic audience measurement techniques are discussed in Chapter 4.)

A *share,* conversely, is the percentage of listeners/ viewing households attained by our station/channel in relation to the number actually listening or watching at the time:

$$\text{Share} = \frac{\substack{\text{people/households} \\ \text{using your station/channel}}}{\substack{\text{total surveyed people or homes} \\ \text{using the medium}}}$$

Following up on our ratings example, let's assume that the number of people in the sample who report they are listening to the radio at the time is 126. Therefore, our equation is:

$$\frac{42}{126} = .33$$

This means that we enjoy an audience share of 33 (in other words, one-third of the persons using radio at the time in the market are listening to us). These two numbers, the rating and the share, are often expressed together (15/33) in describing the performance of the station or program.

Shares are almost always larger than ratings, of course, because they factor out persons/households not using the medium before station performance is computed. Even though shares are more important to the salesperson in selling against competing stations, ratings are also of interest to the advertiser because they indicate what percentage of the total market is attuned to the station and, therefore, to that advertiser's commercial. The farther we get from prime listening (morning/afternoon drive time) or prime viewing (evening prime time) periods, the wider is the discrepancy between ratings and share numbers because the greater is the number of people or households *not* using the medium. In many markets, for example, *The Tonight Show Starring Johnny Carson* historically pulled a 1 or 2 rating in the 11:45 to midnight quarter hour. Even though this would have been an immense failure by prime-time standards, Carson's *share* might be 45 or higher. For advertisers who wanted to reach the *available* TV viewing audience at that time, the station carrying Carson was certainly the preferred vehicle.

Even with such a dominant share, of course, an advertiser would not pay anywhere near as much for a commercial slot near midnight as for a spot in prime time. This is because commercial rates are figured on the basis of *cost-per-thousand* (abbreviated *CPM* with M being the Roman numeral designator for 1,000). In other words, what does it

340

SECTION
THREE

Profes-
sional
Perspec-
tives

cost to reach each group of 1,000 on the outlet under consideration for a time buy?

Let's go back to our original example and assume that the sample of 280 people is an accurate reflection of the entire market population of 98,000. We divide the total number listening (or viewing) by the total sample size to get our PUR (persons using radio) or HUT (households using television) level:

$$\frac{126}{280} = .45 \text{ (PUR level)}$$

In other words, our numbers indicate that 45 percent of the people in the market are listening to radio at the time in question. We then multiply the radio PUR or the television HUT level by the total number of *actual* people or households to get the number using the medium. Continuing with our original example:

$$98,000 \times .45 = 44,100 \text{ persons using radio}$$

As a salesperson for the radio station in our example, however, we know that the advertiser's cost-per-thousand expectations are based on the number of people *our station reaches*. We therefore multiply our rating (15) by the total market size to convert that rating to people reached:

$$98,000 \times .15 = 14,700$$
persons listening to our station

Now, let's say that advertisers are willing to pay a CPM for radio of about $5. We first divide our number of persons into units of 1,000:

$$\frac{14,700}{1,000} = 14.7 \text{ groups of } 1,000$$

and then multiply the number of these thousand-people groups by what the advertiser is willing to pay to reach each group:

$$\$5 \times 14.7 = \$73.50$$

Thus, as a salesperson, we could be reasonably comfortable in trying to sell our spot positions in this particular time period at a price of somewhere between $70 and $75. (CPM trends for several media are displayed in Figure 11–5.)

In actuality, things are much more complicated than this. The 14,700 people the salesperson is selling may not, in whole or part, be the demographic types of people this particular advertiser is most interested in reaching. Perhaps that advertiser does not think the content of the program is a suitable image vehicle for his or her company. Or perhaps this buy is made contingent on the availability of a number of other time slots in parts of the day in which the station is already sold out. Consequently, the advertiser may not be able to purchase the *gross rating points* (total of all rating points for a specific schedule of spots) or *frequency* (number of times a given listener/viewer will be exposed to the spot) required. These and a multiplicity of other factors enter into the negotiation, and the salesperson must anticipate them before making a pitch.

*Qualitative* factors also come into consideration. Certain clients may be willing to pay a considerably higher CPM in order to reach a more specific/higher quality audience. All-news radio salespersons, for example, can usually out-price their station's rating/share level because all-news tends to reach older, more affluent male professionals who are prime targets for luxury cars, stock/commodities offerings, travel services, and similar clients. On the other hand, certain formats/stations are perceived as delivering down-scale listeners, and thus the salesperson faces a constant battle against pressures to under price the rating/share numbers because they are less valuable prospects for many advertisers.

Most salespeople, whether they work for radio, television, or cable, operate from a *rate card* that sets forth the costs of airtime on different parts of the schedule, in different packages (*volume buys*), and in a variety of spot

**Figure 11–5**
Cost-per-thousand (CPM) changes for major media

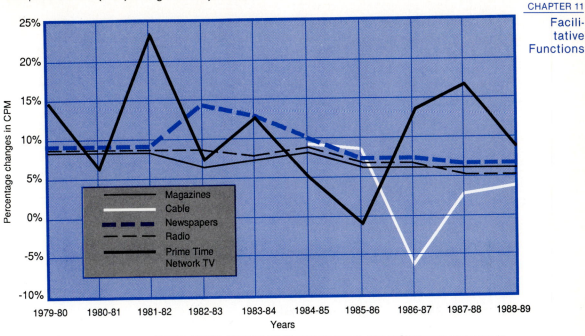

(Sources: For 1979–80 through '87–88: network television—Nielsen CPM Reports; all other media—
Saatchi & Saatchi DFS Compton. For 1988–89; all media; S&SDFSC as reported in ADWEEK.)

lengths. Today, many of these rate cards (like the one in Figure 11–6) are *grids* that list several different pricing options. As demand for the outlet's air time rises, the time seller may move to a higher-priced box on the grid. Fourth-quarter (October to December) demand, for example, is normally significantly higher than first-quarter (January to March) because of the effects of the holiday season and the need for many businesses to reduce end-of-year inventory for tax purposes.

The tasks of broadcast and cable sales professionals are much the same, but local cable selling is effected by two key distinctions. First, the extensive marketing of advertising time on cable systems is still a relatively new enterprise. Advertising agencies and local businesses alike are still attempting to ascertain the real value of local cable buys because audience measurement is not yet able to track the effectiveness (exposure) of commer-

cials placed on this multichannel medium. Thus, cable sales executives must sell the value/prestige of an advertiser's placement on a given channel(s) rather than documented rating and share points.

Second, a given local cable spot is normally inserted on a number (package) of basic cable channels. Virtually all the national basic cable networks (CNN, USA, Nickelodeon, etc.) make available local insert time within their programming into which each cable system can inject spots for advertisers in its market. Consequently, even though many of these individual cable networks don't have enough rating/share numbers to appear in a ratings book, cable salespersons do have great flexibility in packaging a buy. They can sell the advertiser placement on not just one but on a group of several programming channels. Local clients seeking upscale viewers might buy a package on CNN, Arts & Entertain-

**342**

SECTION
THREE

Profes-
sional
Perspec-
tives

**Figure 11–6**
A typical grid rate card

## AM/FM COMBO RATE CARD 4C
### EFFECTIVE NOVEMBER 13, 1989

| **TAP I** | Open Grid Rates | | I | II | III |
|---|---|---|---|---|---|
| 1/3  5:30 a.m. - 10:00 a.m. | :60 | | $125 | $120 | $115 |
| 1/3  10:00 a.m. - 3:00 p.m. | :30 | | $112 | $108 | $104 |
| 1/3  3:00 p.m. - 8:00 p.m. | Yearly Contract Rates | 125x | 250x | 500x | 750x |
| | :60 | $110 | $105 | $100 | $ 95 |
| | :30 | $ 99 | $ 94 | $ 90 | $ 86 |

| **TAP II** | Open Grid Rates | | I | II | III |
|---|---|---|---|---|---|
| 1/4  5:30 a.m. - 10:00 a.m. | :60 | | $110 | $105 | $100 |
| 1/4  10:00 a.m. - 3:00 p.m. | :30 | | $ 99 | $ 94 | $ 90 |
| 1/4  3:00 p.m. - 8:00 p.m. | Yearly Contract Rates | 125x | 250x | 500x | 750x |
| 1/4  8:00 p.m. - 12 mid. and/or | :60 | $ 95 | $ 90 | $ 85 | $ 80 |
| Sun. 8:00 a.m. - 12 mid. | :30 | $ 86 | $ 81 | $ 76 | $ 72 |

| **TAP III** | Open Grid Rates | | I | II | III |
|---|---|---|---|---|---|
| 1/5  5:30 a.m. - 10:00 a.m. | :60 | | $ 95 | $ 90 | $ 85 |
| 1/5  10:00 a.m. - 3:00 p.m. | :30 | | $ 86 | $ 81 | $ 76 |
| 1/5  3:00 p.m. - 8:00 p.m. | Yearly Contract Rates | 125x | 250x | 500x | 750x |
| 1/5  8:00 p.m. - 12 mid. and/or | :60 | $ 80 | $ 75 | $ 70 | $ 65 |
| Sun. 8:00 a.m. - 12 mid. | :30 | $ 72 | $ 67 | $ 63 | $ 59 |
| 1/5  12 mid. - 5:30 a.m. | | | | | |

| **6-DAY DISCOUNT** | Deduct $10 for TAP Plan schedules rotating on 6 of 7 consecutive days. 1/6 of the schedule must air on Saturday and/or Sunday. |
|---|---|

| **WEEKEND/EVENING PACKAGE** | Saturday 5:30 - 10:00 a.m., 10:00 a.m. - 3:00 p.m., 3:00 - 8:00 p.m., 8:00 p.m. - 12 mid. Sunday 11:00 a.m. - 3:00 p.m., 3:00 - 8:00 p.m., 8:00 p.m. - 12 mid. Monday-Friday 8:00 p.m. - 12 mid. No more than one-half of the weekly commercials may air Saturday 10:00 a.m. - 3:00 p.m. Flat $58 rate for :60's or :30's. |
|---|---|

| **DAYPART RATES** | Monday-Friday 5:30 - 10:00 a.m. . . . . . . . . . . . . . . . . . . Add $20 to applicable TAP I rate<br>Monday-Friday 10:00 a.m. - 3:00 p.m. . . . . . . . . . Subtract $20 from applicable TAP I rate<br>Monday-Friday 3:00 - 8:00 p.m. . . . . . . . . . . . . . . . . . . . . . . Use applicable TAP I rate<br>"10:00 a.m. - 3:00 p.m. Package" . . Flat $68 rate with purchase of 10x or more per week. |
|---|---|

| **OVERNIGHT SPECIAL** | Advertisers may purchase Overnight Commercials for 10% of their applicable TAP or daypart rate. These commercials will be aired on a full 12 midnight - 5:30 a.m. rotation. |
|---|---|

| **ON-LOCATION BROADCASTS** | Rates available upon request. |
|---|---|

UNITED ARTISTS ENTERTAINMENT COMPANY • 180 NORTH DIVISION, GRAND RAPIDS, MICHIGAN 49503 • PHONE (616) 459-1919 ment, and Discovery, for example, whereas clients interested in being associated with sports might select a package consisting of simultaneous placements on USA, ESPN, and a regional sports service.

*Network* selling, meanwhile, in both broadcasting and cable involves much bigger decisions and dollar values on the part of all parties involved. The selling task remains fundamentally the same, but the network sales executive is now dealing almost exclusively with *media buyers* (see Chapter 12) at advertising agencies rather than with clients themselves.

In general terms, network sales are divided into the *upfront* and *scatter* markets. During the time the upfront (advance) selling period is held for an upcoming quarter, advertisers are given the opportunity to commit to certain buys at a lower rate and with ratings guarantees. If the network fails to deliver the promised rating levels, additional advertising time is provided free as *make-goods*. Meanwhile, clients who wait until after the upfront market closes must buy in the *scatter* market at presumably higher rates, with minimal or no ratings guarantees, and with fewer choices as to the shows around which their spots may be placed. However, if the network salespersons have been unable to generate extensive enough sales in upfront, or if certain advertisers have pulled their commercials from a show that has become controversial, significant airtime bargains may surface during scatter sales.

More and more, networks are turning to demographic rather than to ratings-level sales. National advertisers are less willing to spend money for undifferentiated tonnage numbers. Instead, these marketers seek assurances that their advertising messages are being delivered to at least the broadly delineated audience segments that make up their prime consumer market. For instance, in looking at ABC's younger and more urban-skewing programs, major advertising agency

time-buyer Paul Isacsson recently observed, "Demographically, ABC is more competitive with NBC than CBS. The household race, which still gets most of the press attention, is largely irrelevant from the advertiser's perspective. TV time just isn't bought that way anymore."[19]

An effective salesperson, whether network or local, broadcast or cable, knows exactly how time is being bought in his or her branch of the industry and proceeds accordingly. This is merely the most obvious facet of the salesperson's most important function: learning and serving the prospective time buyer's needs. "Before I walk into a door," reveals one successful time salesman, "I try to bring to the table what's going to help this person's business. It's the creative ideas that distinguish us from our competitors."[20] From the potential client's prospective, agency time-buying executive Sondra Michaelson adds, "Most salespeople are too interested in making sure that their pitch is heard, at the sacrifice of listening to buyer's needs. Frankly this is a brand of a bad salesperson. Knowledge of client and agency needs creates opportunities."[21]

## Station Representatives

To this point, we have focused on the sale of two kinds of airtime: *local* and *network* (national). There also is an important intermediate category known as *national spot*, or just *spot* for short. Simply put, *spot* is the sale of time on local media outlets to national advertisers. But agency buyers do not have time to see salespersons from hundreds of stations and cable systems. And these stations and systems can't afford to send their sales force to meet with agency time buyers in all those major cities where top agency executives are headquartered. Consequently, a vitally im-

**344**

SECTION
THREE

Profes-
sional
Perspec-
tives

## VALERIE TUTTLE/GENERAL SALES MANAGER
### WWJ/WJOI

Selling radio is not very different from selling or marketing any other product or service. The same four Ps that apply elsewhere also apply to radio: product, pricing, place, and promotion. Radio is the overall product, but how you price, place, and promote that product is different with each station.

For example, an all-news radio station reaches a vastly different audience than does a contemporary hit radio (CHR) station. Therefore, the advertisers to which each station (or product) appeals are also going to be different. This also means that the promotion to reach the audience, and the pricing to reach the advertiser, will be different.

Radio is perhaps different from selling/marketing certain other products in that we are extremely people-oriented. This orientation applies in both the programming side to reach an audience and in the selling side to reach advertisers.

When I first started selling years ago, a person who had been a very successful salesperson and sales manager told me two things that still apply today:

1. If you are out there trying and working at it, you will be so much better than 90 percent of your competition. Hard to believe, but true.
2. Some company is going to pay you a lot of money to go out and make friends.

Making friends is a tremendous side benefit of selling. However, it also takes a great deal of hard work. Substance, in terms of doing the basics over and over and over, is required to achieve and maintain success.

The five basics that must be done over and over are these: *Prospecting* for potential clients, *qualifying* (making sure these clients are the right people for your product), *researching* the benefits that client seeks, *closing* the sale, and *servicing* the client's continuing needs in order to promote future sales. Over and over and over.

These basics also apply when you make the move to sales manager. As manager, you now apply these basics to finding salespeople instead of finding accounts.

The two most important aspects of being an effective general sales manager at a broadcast property are training and motivating salespeople, and inventory control. It also helps if you are part teacher, parent, and psychologist. And, for good measure, throw in a little knowledge of broadcast law and a basic understanding of things financial. The success of a general sales manager depends almost totally on the performance of other people. This can be a difficult transition for a salesperson, who is accustomed to being responsible solely for his or her own performance.

Don't let this deter you, however. The job can be, and is, immensely rewarding. As exciting as it can be to get an order when you're a salesperson, it can be even more exciting when the people who report to you are selling successfully.

---

portant business has grown up to provide this liaison efficiently and make *spot* buying work. This is the business of the *station representative* or *rep firm*.

Every major radio or television station is affiliated with a *rep firm*. This firm may have dozens or even hundreds of stations among its clients. Normally, a given rep will only handle one station in a market, although this rule may be broken in the case of outlets having widely divergent formats (and thus widely divergent and mutually exclusive listenerships). The rep salesperson compiles the avails from his or her client stations and packages them in a virtually endless variety of patterns to meet the specific demographic and CPM requirements of advertising agency clients. Using a rep firm, an agency time buyer can thus purchase time on a number of stations throughout the country in one single business transaction. *Spot* is also a much more flexible vehicle than *network* because the buyer can emphasize a given type of station, or region of the country, without having to purchase the network as a whole. A snowmobile manufacturer, for example, can use a rep firm or firms to purchase an advertising schedule on stations located exclusively in the dozen or so northern states where snowmobiling is most popular.

Through such activities, the rep firm often creates what is known as an *unwired net-*

*work*—an assemblage of stations whose key commonalities are that they have the same representative and are airing the same commercial at about the same time. The program adjacent to that commercial may vary widely from station to station. And these outlets may be network affiliates, independents, or a blend of both. But the essential thing is that the rep salesperson has cleared simultaneous time on all of them on behalf of the same advertiser.

Rep firms earn their money via the commission they make for the time they sell. Let's say that a rep firm collects $5,000 from an advertising agency for spots it has sold the agency on a given station. The rep keeps its commission (usually around 10 percent) and forwards the remainder to the outlet. Thus, in this case, the rep firm makes $500 and the station receives $4,500. There are, of course, some variations on this pattern depending on the size of the buy and the degree of importance that the parties assign to each other. A rep firm that really needs a powerhouse station to fill out its client list may thus be willing to take less commission than when it is selling time on behalf of an underperforming or small market facility. Like any national distributor, a rep firm seeks strong local outlets that offer the dollar volume making for lucrative commission levels.

As a means of strengthening their client

346

SECTION
THREE

Profes-
sional
Perspec-
tives

## CYNTHIA BRAUNLICH/GROUP RESEARCH MANAGER
PETRY TELEVISION, INC.

As research manager, it is my responsibility to act as a source of sales support, information, and communication for Petry's client television stations and sales force. I report to a research director who heads up a department of five research teams. I work alongside Petry and client station sales staffs to produce a master planner report, sales promotion sheets, and individual market studies as well as serve as a consultant on primary research projects. Sales people then used this information to sell spot and local advertising on our client stations.

On a typical day, I usually arrive early for a half-hour of calmness to plan my day. Then I get a request from a client station to check on how upscale its early news is skewing compared to the competition. Our programming department asks me for some background information on the performance of soap operas versus talk shows. A station calls with changes on their master planner. They want the audience estimates for the NFC playoffs and NFC championship to be figured higher than we originally projected. I work on sales promotion sheets for local basketball in one market and next year's sports in another. Lesson plans for new sales trainees are made up for a class I will be teaching next week. In between this, I assign work to my assistants (analysts). This week, I have them working on first-quarter estimates for regular programming and estimates for the upcoming CBS sports schedule. A Petry salesperson in New York calls and asks me what we estimated for the Superbowl audience on one of our CBS stations.

This sounds like a lot of work for one day, but two skills of being a good research manager are learning to organize your time and to juggle the many different requests received. Sometimes the deadline for a project is immediate, and sometimes more than one project is needed right away. Part of my job skills are knowing how to organize my day and, if necessary, to delegate work when a lot has to be done.

Another important part of my job is to be a public relations person for the company. I have a lot of communication (phone and face-to-face) with our client stations, and so part of their image of Petry is based on their contact with me. Simple telephone courtesy and respect for clients are key qualities for this position.

In looking at the research field, a lot of people are intimidated by the word *research* because they imagine a windowless room, a lot of numbers, calculators, and boredom. Not that some of that doesn't exist (when you first start in this field you may spend your first few months strictly pulling numbers from ratings books), but there are other sides, too. There is a creative side that comes to the fore when preparing sales promotion sheets for stations. You need writing skills as well as a sense of design in developing the layout of the sheet. There is always the opportunity to work on new projects or on a different approach to an old idea. I won't lie and say the job is never boring. There are routine tasks I have to do all the time, but these are a necessary function of any research department.

As a research manager I think the most satisfying part of my job is, after putting in a lot of hard work and long hours on a new client pitch, receiving word that the station decided to sign a contract with Petry. On the other hand, the downside is having a station change its mind or go with some other firm.

If you are looking for a job in the television research field, having a background in business and broadcasting is a plus. Basic office skills and etiquette are a must here as they are in any professional job. You don't have to be a calculus whiz, but fundamental math skills are essential. Being able to work with a group of people is an asset, as is being able to work well on your own and under stress. Most of all, keep your expectations realistic. You will not start as a research manager and probably will not be ready to pitch that position for 1½ to 2 years (there are exceptions to the rule, however). You are expected to put in your time as an analyst and to learn the ropes. Television research is not the most glamorous job in the world. But it is extremely important to stations' financial success and it also can be very rewarding for the skillful researcher.

stations (and thus their own revenues), rep firms also frequently offer researched advice on programming to those stations. Reps have access to more sophisticated audience data on shows and formats than do local facilities and also employ the research staff to analyze this data in formulating recommendations. Particularly in the case of television, the rep firm is also given the chance by syndicators to preview their new series. Client stations of the rep thereby enjoy advance information that can help them decide whether to pur-

chase new program properties and how much to bid for them.

## Program Salespersons (Syndicators)

On the opposite side of the negotiation from the rep firm's client station is the seller of the

348

SECTION
THREE

Profes-
sional
Perspec-
tives

## CNN Foreign Syndication

The privatization of European television has heated up the market for U.S. syndicated programming. Overseas sales have become so important that they are now a factor in determining which projects U.S. producers will choose initially to develop for U.S. consumption.

programs that the station, cable channel, or other outlet is interested in running. In both radio and television, syndication firms employ salespersons whose job it is to place on local outlets the shows and formats packaged by their producer clients. In radio, because of the lower cost figures involved and the multiplicity of outlets, salespersons usually work directly for the company (radio network or syndicator) that has created the property.

In television, on the other hand, the sales force is likely constituted as a separate company or division of a studio-owning corporation. Some of this separation has been mandated by a portion of the FCC's *fin/syn* (financial interest and syndication) rules. As of this writing, these rules have been liberalized, but they still prohibit broadcast television networks from subsequently selling (syndicating) to U.S. stations the primetime shows they obtained from outside producers.

The television market, then, is serviced by salespeople who work either for the actual producers of a show or for an independent company that specializes in the placement of program product prepared by others. Broadly speaking, all of this air material can be classified as either *off-network* or *first-run syndication*. Off-network material, as the name implies, has been originally exposed on one of the major national networks with episodes now made available for exposure on local stations or cable channels. A significant factor in a program salesperson's handling of *off-net* properties is the FCC's *Prime Time Access Rule* (PTAR), which basically limits network

programming in the top fifty markets to three hours per evening (see Chapter 6). The practical effect of PTAR is that a network affiliate station in major U.S. cities may not air *off-net* material in the hour before prime time starts (access time). This, in turn, means that program salespeople selling in major markets must either convince an affiliate to buy an *off-net* show for other than access time or must sell the show to an independent station or cable network.

Increasingly over the last several years, hit network series are first marketed as *futures*—contracted for local exposure at least two years in advance and before some of the later on-network episodes have even been produced. A station or cable network takes a risk that the show will still be popular two years or more down the road and may even have to commit to sharing production costs if the network cancels the project before a sufficient number of episodes have been produced. On the other hand, a *futures* buy could be a bargain if the series' network popularity stays stable or increases in the interim.

*First-run syndicated* projects, conversely, have never appeared on a network and will be exposed for the first time at the local station or cable network level. Many times, the syndicator/salesperson will market a first-run series on a *barter* basis. This means that the station may secure the show for free or at a reduced rate by carrying at no charge the commercials that come within the program. What has actually happened is that the production company has presold advertising

**GARY LICO**/VICE-PRESIDENT, EASTERN REGION
COLUMBIA PICTURES TELEVISION

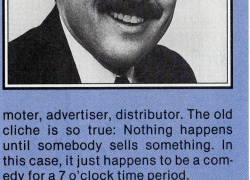

"Did you get the list of movies I sent you?"

"What program will you put at 7 o'clock?"

"Did you hear what your competition just bought?"

Snippets of telephone conversations that comprise most of my day. Servicing the client ("Did you get our promotional material?"), moving a negotiation along ("If I give you more runs, will you raise your price?"), setting appointments or just plain keeping in touch. *Communication* is central to the life of a syndication salesperson.

Meetings are for presentations of programs (and why a station should buy them), to get or take new information in order to get closer to a sale, or to close the deal. Time is too precious to take a meeting without a specific goal. I'm good for three to four meetings per day when I'm on the road, which is at least half the time. Listening skills are mandatory; anyone can talk, but you'll learn nothing from the buyer if that's all you do. I try to go to every meeting with questions that I need answered. That way I'll have a better idea of the client's needs and can devise a deal to meet those needs.

Travel is a big part of the job, which sounds glamorous at first. It is—at first. Then you hate it, dragging yourself into every airplane or hotel room. Finally, you'll tolerate it—or you'll quit and do something else.

A sales job, in this or any business, puts you at the epicenter of your industry: buyer, manufacturer, pro-

moter, advertiser, distributor. The old cliche is so true: Nothing happens until somebody sells something. In this case, it just happens to be a comedy for a 7 o'clock time period.

The pressure to deliver is enormous; the degree of difficulty is very high. The company needs *your* sales for its revenue—to pay talent, producers, writers, and studio overhead, for example. Your own income is directly tied to your performance, in most cases. As a result, one must possess the self-discipline to prioritize one's sales efforts: concentrating on those opportunities likely to yield the greatest revenue. The ability to bounce back from a "no" is crucial. You'll hear that word more than any other.

On the upside, when a sale *is* made, there must be elation, the joy of achieving a goal. The trick is to be able to savor the good feeling long enough to carry you through the chorus of "no's" you're sure to hear.

**350**

SECTION
THREE

Profes-
sional
Perspec-
tives

positions contained in the vehicle to certain clients or their advertising agencies. This money then helps the producer with the up-front financing for project production. (Some high-powered off-network properties are also sold on a partial barter basis to raise more revenue than would be available from stations on a straight-cash deal.) Rather than sell *all* of the advertising time within and around the show, local stations then give up some slots (avails) to the bartered spots on behalf of those national advertisers. In short, the station exchanges some of its commercial time for syndicated programming.

For a barter project to work, the program salespeople must be able to place the series with stations covering at least 70 to 80 percent of the country. Anything less will not give the participating national advertisers the commercial penetration they need to justify their barter costs. Stations, for their part, must be careful not to contract for too much barter programming. For one thing, they thereby incur the obligation to air the bartered spots—even if they pull the program from the air before the contract expires. Furthermore, every minute of bartered time means one less minute that the station's own sales force can sell, one less chance to obtain revenue from local or spot sources. Barter syndication is thus a commodity that both program and time sellers must analyze carefully before offering or making binding commitments.

Other syndicated shows are made available on a straight cash basis. Among these are usually the *evergreens*—series that have been so popular for so long that it is hard to remember whether they began life as network or first-run entities. *I Love Lucy, The Brady Bunch, The Andy Griffith Show,* and *Bonanza* are a few such recurrent properties that continue to draw salable audiences even after years of re-running. Sometimes, as in the case of *Lassie, The New Leave It to Beaver,* or *WKRP in Cincinnati,* an evergreen concept will be brought back into production for release as a first-run syndication project.

Off-network or first-run, evergreen or new, barter or cash, a program salesperson's job is to get the widest possible placement for his or her properties, on the best possible outlets, and at the most favorable price. Recently, for example, the market for off-network hour-long shows has been soft because local stations have found it difficult to accommodate them in schedules already committed to other things. Thus, program sales people have sold several such properties to cable networks on an exclusivity basis. The cable network sale will probably bring in less money than will peddling to individual stations, but this loss is balanced by the fact that the syndicator's administrative costs are much lower when dealing with one cable net than with a multiplicity of individual television stations.

## Promotions People

Once a program is placed on a station, network, or even local cable channel, it becomes the job of promotions people to make certain that the public is made positively aware of the show. Using a combination of *on-* and *off-air* promotions, these professionals do whatever they can to ensure that their outlet is *sampled;* in other words, that listeners or viewers give it a try. If the product is good, this sampling should then be converted into measurable and loyal audience whose predicted attention can be sold to advertisers

*On-air promotion* activities consist of the messages carried by the outlet itself or placed on other noncompeting electronic media vehicles. These messages range from simple identification (ID) slogans, jingles, and graphics to full-scale commercials on behalf of the facility and its programming. These longer promos are often subdivided into three categories: image pieces, generics, and topicals. *Image pieces* try to position the station or network as a whole in the consumer's mind. We

## KRIS KELLY / COMMERCIAL PRODUCER/DIRECTOR
### WKBD-TV

Why would anyone want to go into broadcasting? You have to be enthusiastic, hard-working, and dedicated beyond the call of duty to get ahead in this field. You have to be able to write, to think creatively, to work independently.

A forty-hour week is rare in this business. Work schedules often require nights, weekends, and/or holidays. Cancelled vacations are not unusual. The pay is never enough to compensate for the tremendous amount of stress. The pressure is constant. The deadlines are never-ending. Last-minute changes are commonplace. The work load is heavy, devouring creative ideas at an amazing rate. Projects are often frustrating because there is never enough time, money, personnel, or equipment to do the job the way you think it should be done. The demands never quit.

So why would anyone put up with this? Personally, I love the excitement, the constant change, the creativity, the challenges. I love the adrenaline rush that comes with every emergency.

Promotion is an area that seems to have lots of emergencies. Programming is always changing, ratings need to be improved, contests are starting—and its up to the promotion department to let the audience know about it. That's where on-air promotion comes in.

On-air promotion is really another kind of commercial. Instead of pitching the wonders of a new laundry detergent, it sells the station, its programming, or personalities. In my opinion, on-air promotion can be the most creative writing you will ever do for a station. Promotion producers, if

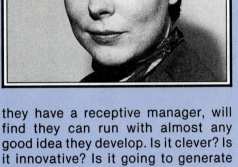

they have a receptive manager, will find they can run with almost any good idea they develop. Is it clever? Is it innovative? Is it going to generate an audience? Let's give it a try!

On-air promotion has its downside, though. Not all promotion managers are receptive. Budgets can be small to nonexistent. Time, as always, is limited. The pressure is high. And, unfortunately, promotion producers are like Rodney Dangerfield—they "don't get no respect" either.

But it's still an area that lets your creativity shine. If you have the right attitude (and the right boss) you'll find on-air promotion frequently involves minimal input or interference from other people. It's one of the few assignments in which the final project can be totally *yours* from start to finish—your concept, your words, your music, your video, and occasionally your heart and soul. It's *your* spot. And that can be pretty exciting. Sometimes, it can even make up for all the long hours, missed lunches, and headaches.

352

SECTION
THREE

Profes-
sional
Perspec-
tives

are the fun station; the station where news comes first; the station where you always hear your favorites; the place to turn for family entertainment; or the people who know your community best. The top image pieces articulate a clear and attainable benefit/promise. The promotions person stakes out a personality for the outlet that is both memorable and appealingly in line with what the target audience is looking for in a radio or television service.

*Generics* are messages designed to publicize a particular show or series. On radio as a whole, or in television news, these generics often focus on an air personality or newscaster because these on-air talents are the most consistent element. The individual musical or journalistic elements change from day to day, but the talent stays the same. In the case of an entertainment series, the focus may still be on the personalities, but the environment and central premise of the program must also be established to aid viewer recall and to pique curiosity.

*Topicals* (sometimes called *episodics*) then stress what is to happen on a particular segment (episode) of the show. Often, a group of topicals will be grouped together to form a *block promo* that teases the happenings the listener or viewer can enjoy on several successive programs.

Promotions or *creative services* staff (as they are also known) balance these on-air efforts with a wealth of off-air activities as well. *Client promotions* endeavors might include printed sales kits and rate cards and also extend to more exotic activities such as recorded sampler tapes touting the outlet's programming or hosting full-scale client theme parties tied to a new station campaign or show concept. *Audience promotions* might involve anything from newspaper ads to bumper stickers to cosponsorship of live concerts or community health fairs where pocket blood pressure charts come emblazoned with the station's logo. A whole range of contests might combine both on- and off-air activities

to enhance consumer recognition and choosing of an outlet. *Value-added* events carry the practice even further by creating station/client joint promotions to give advertisers bonus exposure.

In short, promotions/creative services professionals are in the intense business of marketing their outlet so that their time sales colleagues can more easily sell avails on it. Even in the case of public broadcasting, promotions remains an essential component in attracting the audience attention that justifies and expedites grants, donations, and pledges. With more and more competing electronic vehicles, the job of the promotions or creative services staffer is critical to a given outlet's visibility and survival. At a recent industry seminar, promotions expert Vince Manzi pointed out that in the year 2000, the mandate to "get noticed" will be as applicable as ever, so the need for skilled promotions people can only increase. "You'll have to pay them more and you have to give them some opportunity to do good creative," Manzi advised station managers.[22] "Getting noticed" in our business does not come cheap or easy. But not getting noticed because of deficient promotion means almost certain bankruptcy. Promotions is highly demanding work—but it is also work in high demand.

## Production House Marketers

The last facilitative function discussed in this chapter combines aspects of promotions, direct selling, and equipment operations. The job of *production house marketer* is thus a fitting subject through which to summarize the chapter as a whole. In essence, these marketers explain and publicize their firms' technical capabilities in order to sell those capabilities to other electronic media players.

With state-of-the-art equipment becoming more sophisticated and multifaceted every-

**ARLENE LEHMANN**/VICE-PRESIDENT MARKETING
MAGNETIC NORTH

My typical day at our postproduction house starts before I arrive at the office. The one-hour commute gives me two hours each day free from interruptions and phone calls. During this time I review invoices, write memos, read trade magazines, and organize my thoughts and priorities. Upon arrival, I read today's schedule and yesterday's coordinator reports over coffee. I check which clients are in our editing suites today and if any follow-up is required from yesterday. At a quick meeting with our public relations assistant, we review items with approaching deadlines and talk about the slant of a press release she is writing. She gives me a report on quotes for printing a new rate card.

The head of scheduling drops in and gives me a quick report on current facility workload, revealing conversations she or the others have had with clients and any internal concerns. At this point I try to walk through the facility, making certain that everything looks great and greeting the clients in the rooms. On this particular morning we have a meeting of our executive committee comprised of the company president and VPs of engineering, operations, finance and marketing. These weekly meetings are intense because we not only discuss general issues but also decide on definite courses of action before we leave the room. After the meeting I return my phone messages—two for quotes, one for advertising, one for a tour, and one for the sales person at our sister company. Then off to lunch with a client.

Back from lunch, I return the newest accumulation of phone calls and then read over the press release draft and make changes. Next is a meeting with a potential client at his office. We discuss different postproduction alternatives, budget, available freelance staff in town and arrange for a camera test and Ediflex demo. Back at the facility I take another tour around, check with the coordinators on how things are going, discuss with a computer artist a storyboard that has been faxed in, and have a quick meeting with the outside supplier who designs our advertising.

Our sales rep drops in to go over a couple of quotes on storyboards that have to go out tonight. We also discuss strategy on promoting a new piece of equipment the engineering department is installing on the weekend. I clean off my desk and then prepare to attend another industry dinner/award show, association meeting, cocktail party, film screening, wrap party, or trade show.

**354**

SECTION
THREE

Profes-
sional
Perspec-
tives

The days go quickly, and no two are the same. On this sample day we did not experience the triumph of signing a contract for a new television series nor did we suffer a critical downtime situation with a broken film scanner, no replacement components in all of North America, and the scanner booked wall-to-wall for the next four days. The biggest challenge used to be the continual heavy investment necessary to stay current with capital equipment. That has not changed, but we have the additional problem of escalating expenditures to hire the prominent editors, colourists, and computer artists necessary to attract business.

In this type of environment it is necessary to use every skill you have ever learned and to apply every past experience. Never be afraid to ask a question, and don't overlook the obvious. This is a communication business, but communications are usually where problems arise. If you don't understand it, you can't possibly explain it to somebody else—especially to a client.

Of course, be prepared to start at the bottom and work your way up. The ultimate career choice in the postproduction industry these days is a colourist or editor position. That's where the big bucks are!

Be happy in your work; if you're not, then get out. You cannot possibly do a good job if you're miserable.

Finally, no matter how many hours you work or how rotten your boss is, remember that you are learning. At the very least, that's what's in it for you.

---

day, few media companies are in a position to produce their messages entirely in-house. Advertising agencies, public relations firms, industrial media units, and even stations and networks must often turn to outside companies to obtain cutting-edge audio and video production services. Because their only business is to produce projects brought to them by others, production houses can concentrate exclusively on technical rather than conceptual processes. By booking projects from a variety of clients, they can keep their expensive physical plants and expert staff in continuous use. The marketing managers for these shops therefore have as their top priority the booking of production business so that costly facilities are never standing idle, on the one hand, or are overbooked on the other.

Some production houses specialize in multitrack audio recordings. Others concentrate on in-studio or remote video shoots or on the postproduction editing and sophisti-cated assemblage of footage shot by other professionals. A few houses focus exclusively on computer effects and graphics or even on narrow specialties such as claymation (animation derived from manipulating clay figures such as the famous California Raisins). Whatever the case, the reputations of these firms are only as good as their last project. Thus, their marketing executives must keep abreast of the triumphs that have just come through their shops and must use this information to attract new and repeat business. Having one foot on the technical side and the other on the sales side, these marketers facilitate on two levels: they ensure that the communication projects from other companies are successfully completed while making certain that their own company's client volume goals are sustained.

Because it is exclusively devoted to the optimal consummation of projects brought to it, the production house is the best positioned of any branch of our industry to probe and experiment with new techniques and ways of packaging an audio/visual message. These firms thus constitute the frontier for technology and the application of it to new conceptual challenges. The marketers of such services realize, however, that their clients are not interested in these techniques for themselves but only in how such abilities can create more effective commercials, programs, or training videos. Like any electronic media facilitator, the production house marketer must reconcile his or her services to the communication objective of whoever is paying the bill.

## Chapter Flashback

Technical and sales/promotion facilitators build and sustain the vehicles through which media performers and creators can display their talents. Technology has automated several operations that formerly required the constant ministration of technicians and engineers. This automation has reduced the number of lower-level jobs but has opened up entire new sets of opportunities for people who can manipulate state-of-the-art tools that are often computer-assisted. Some television engineers are responsible for lighting as well as for video equipment, and larger facilities employ specialists who can manipulate illumination to accomplish sophisticated scene sculpting that transcends the two-dimensionality of the television screen. Much of the work of the lighting director/designer occurs at the preproduction stage in the construction of a *lighting plot*.

The individuals who run the cameras can generally be divided into three categories: *camera operators, videographers,* and *cinematographers.* Some operators have been replaced by robotic equipment, and videographers have almost completely supplanted cinematographers in television newsgathering. Both film and videotape are widely used

in commercial, documentary, and entertainment productions, however, with the medium of choice depending mainly on the look desired for the final product. HDTV is blurring the distinctions between the two media, but it is unlikely to eliminate these distinctions in the foreseeable future. Both film and tape *editors* (people who piece together isolated sequences into cohesive wholes) usually perform their tasks electronically for greater efficiency and element control.

Directors also can be divided into three main classifications: *technical, assistant,* and *main,* although in smaller facilities, all three functions can be exercised by a single individual. Technical directors assemble multiple video sources in real time and may oversee the entire technical crew. In more complex settings, an assistant director helps with preproduction planning and keeping track of shot sequences and running times during shooting and postproduction. The main director, meanwhile, exercises the ultimate responsibility for bringing together all the technical and performance elements into a cogent whole; this responsibility holds true for both television and radio projects.

Salespersons generate the revenue that keeps electronic media companies operating. At stations and cable systems, they sell air-time to advertisers. This commodity is fixed. Unsold air-time cannot be retrieved at some later date, and additional air-time cannot usually be created—at least not without cutting into program content. Time sales are negotiated based on a number of considerations, including *ratings, shares, cost-per-thousand, gross rating points,* and *frequency.* Qualitative factors such as the type of programming being aired and the type of audience it attracts may sometimes outweigh purely quantitative considerations. Local salespersons often deal directly with advertisers, but network selling is usually done through media buyers at advertising agencies. *Station reps* also pitch to these buyers by offering spot packages on a number of their client outlets as a single transaction. Reps also often pro-

356

SECTION
THREE

Profes-
sional
Perspec-
tives

vide their stations with research-based programming advice. This advice helps these facilities select what products they should consider purchasing from program salespersons who represent the syndication firms offering *off-net, first-run,* and *evergreen* properties on a cash and/or barter basis.

Whatever programming is selected, it is the job of promotions or creative service staff to see that this programming gets sampled by listeners or viewers. Audience promotion activities take place both on-air and off-air; the latter encompassing everything from bumper stickers to concerts. Simultaneously, client promotions are developed to court current and potential advertisers. Finally, production house marketers must combine the entire range of facilitative functions. They explain and publicize their firms' technical capabilities in order to sell these services to other electronic media enterprises.

## ❏ Review Probes

1. Define the difference between a translator technician and a creative value technician.
2. Compare and contrast Notan and Chiaroscuro lighting.
3. How has the replacement of cinematography with videography changed the practice of television newsgathering?
4. What types of technical activities take place in *pre*production compared to *post*production?
5. How are ratings and shares computed? Why will a share almost always be larger than a rating?
6. Differentiate *local, network,* and *spot* airtime sales.

## ❏ Suggested Background Explorations

Anderson, Gary H. *Video Editing and Post-Production: A Professional Guide.* 2nd ed. White Plains, NY: Knowledge Industry Publications, 1988.

Bartlett, Bruce. *Introduction to Professional Recording Techniques.* Indianapolis: Howard W. Sams & Co., 1987.

Carlson, Verne, and Sylvia E. Carlson. *Professional Lighting Handbook.* Boston: Focal Press, 1985.

Compesi, Ronald J., and Ronald E. Sherriffs. *Small Format Television Production: The Technique of Single-Camera Television Field Production.* 2nd ed. Boston: Allyn and Bacon, 1990.

Kuney, Jack. *Take One: Television Directors on Directing.* Westport, CT: Greenwood/Praeger, 1990.

McLeish, Robert. *The Technique of Radio Production: A Manual for Broadcasters.* 2nd ed. Boston: Focal Press, 1988.

Millerson, Gerald. *The Technique of Television Production.* 12th ed. Boston: Focal Press, 1990.

Nisbett, Alec. *The Use of Microphones.* 3rd ed. Boston: Focal Press, 1989.

Rowlands, Avril. *The Production Assistant in TV and Video.* Boston: Focal Press, 1987.

Schneider, Arthur. *Electronic Post-Production and Videotape Editing.* Boston: Focal Press, 1989.

White, Barton C., and N. Doyle Satterthwaite. *But First, These Messages . . . The Selling of Broadcast Advertising.* Boston: Allyn and Bacon, 1989.

# Directive Functions

❏ *Up to this point, we've looked at the performers who are the most noticeable aspect of our industry and the creators who formulate much of the material these performers deliver. We've also examined the facilitators who maintain and operate our delivery systems as well as other facilitators who bring in the revenues necessary to sustain these systems. Now, it is time to focus attention on the executives who provide the managerial guidance and decision making that determine how all of these other people and resources are used in pursuing the needs of clients and intended audiences. We start with directive functions found within electronic media outlets and then turn to the outside counterparts with whom they conduct business.*

## Program Directors

At both radio and television stations, the program director is responsible for sculpting and scheduling the content progression designed to attract an audience. In radio, this means (1) choosing a particular format that is calculated to appeal to an attainable demographic, and then (2) fine-tuning that format to improve

358

SECTION
THREE

Profes-
sional
Perspec-
tives

**BRAD FUHR**/PROGRAM DIRECTOR
WLTO-FM

You would probably like to program a radio station for a very selfish reason—so you can play the kind of music you like (or the kind you *think* your audience will like).

But as a program director (PD), you'd soon discover that programming to other people's tastes can be a bitter pill to swallow. You can't just play your own favorites. That's not to say that gut feeling isn't a big part of programming, but research and market knowledge are also two of the most important tools you will use.

Although there is never a typical week, here's what the job of program director is all about. Literally everything that goes on the air is my responsibility. This includes news, commercials, public affairs programs, and, of course, the music and personalities. The job requires that I be very detail-oriented, yet very creative. And that mix of personality traits is hard to find. Personality profiles of individuals usually show that creative people are not very organized, and vice-versa.

In any case, my week is divided among these duties:

1. Motivating the listener to stay turned to my station. This means looking for new ways to get listeners talking about my station and listening for something new. This is called planned unpredictability. At the same time, the station needs to be like a good friend—someone you are comfortable with. And you maintain formatics (integrated on-air elements) that make the station consistent.

2. Motivating my air staff to do their homework. This is called "show prep," and it includes being on top of current events as well as finding new ways to introduce the same song in a new and creative way. I'm the coach of my on-air team, and we're *always* performing. And like a coach, you'll have to deal with the fact that your air talent may make more money than you do!

3. Working with the sales department to help make the station profitable. In my years as program director, some of the most unnecessary yet time-consuming problems have arisen because of skirmishes between programming and sales. To be a successful PD, you must get along with the sales department.

The rewards in programming are immense. There's a great sense of pride when you hear your station being aired in businesses, cars, and homes. There's also a sense of accomplishment when the ratings show, in real terms, your share of the market. And there are the perks—free CDs, concert tickets, backstage passes, and recognition. But that elation can quickly turn to exasperation by hearing a few seconds of dead air, a fumbled talk set, or an outdated commercial that slipped past your many systems of checks and balances.

If you can deal with the highs and lows, the struggle between creativity and detail, and the egos of air talent, you are probably suited to program a radio station. It's a worthy career goal.

and solidify this appeal. The owner and/or general manager play crucial roles in the first task, but the second task is the fundamental responsibility of the program director. Today, even a relatively small market may have a dozen or more listenable radio signals from which to pick. The radio dial thus becomes much like a grocery store shelf. A number of competing alternatives are set adjacent to each other, and from these, consumers make a "purchase." In the case of radio, of course, this purchase does not involve the expenditure of money but instead of a sometimes more valuable resource—personal time. How long or how often each consumer uses a given station depends on a number of factors. But the on-air programming constitutes the real product essence.

In selecting, refining, and delivering an on-air 'sound,' successful program directors realize that they are not in the business of manufacturing programming itself. Rather, they are in the business of manufacturing an *audience* that is salable to advertisers. Individual elements are selected for airing because they seem to have appeal for the type of listener the station is seeking. Once these individual listeners are assembled into an audience by the program director's product, this audience is then rented out to advertisers—usually for thirty or sixty seconds at a time. The more similar these listeners are to each other in demographic or life-style characteristics, the more appealing the station's audience is to clients seeking to reach this consumer type. If, on the other hand, the listenership consists of

many dissimilar groups of people, it may be more difficult to 'rent' it to advertisers who do not wish to pay to reach people who aren't prime prospects for their business. Such unwanted listeners, as mentioned in Chapter 1, constitute *waste circulation* as far as an advertiser is concerned. They inflate the cost-per-thousand (CPM) (see Chapter 11) through inclusion of irrelevant ears.

The radio program director thereby seeks to attract not only raw numbers, but also numbers that cluster into population groupings that are desirable to available advertisers. By manipulating music selection, amount of news, prominence or de-emphasis of deejay patter, commercial placement, and other formatic factors, programmers hope to find the key mixture that will attract an easily identifiable audience segment and also clearly distinguish their air sound from that of other stations. Putting it another way, consultant John Parikhal commented in the September 14, 1990, issue of *Radio and Records* that "programming begins with the format, lays in the precise creative components and tries to maintain anticipation and momentum at all times."

As the number of radio facilities has increased (review Chapter 7) formats have been slivered into smaller and smaller segments. During the mid-1980s, Arbitron tried to inventory format types and came up with literally scores of subcategories (see Figure 12–1). Because of such complexity, that rating service has subsequently abandoned its attempts to delineate every format nuance precisely,

360

SECTION
THREE

Profes-
sional
Perspec-
tives

**Figure 12–1**

Arbitron format list

# FORMATS

**ADULT CONTEMPORARY**
Adult Pop
Adult Rock
Contemporary Pop
Pop Adult Rock
Pop Contemporary

**ALBUM ORIENTED
ROCK (AOR)**
Acid Rock
Album Rock
Classic AOR
Classic Rock
Contemporary AOR
Eccletic
Heavy Metal
Mainstream Rock
Progressive Adult
 Contemporary
Rock 'N' Gold
Rock 'N' Roll
Rock 'N' Stereo
Solid Rock
Stereo Rock

**ALL NEWS**
News
News/Information

**BLACK/
RHYTHM & BLUES**
Adult Soul
Basic Black
Black Contemporary
Black Oldies
Black Rock Blues
Caribbean Rhythm & Blues
Contemporary
 Rhythm & Blues
Contemporary Soul
Heavy Soul
Modern Soul
Progressive Soul
Sophisticated Black
Soul

**CLASSICAL**
Concert
Light Classical
Semi-Classical

**CONTEMPORARY
HIT RADIO (CHR)**
All Hits
Contemporary Rock
Contemporary
Contemporary All-Hit
Hit Parade
Hot Hits
Top 40

**COUNTRY**
All-American Country
Beautiful Country
Contemporary Country
Country and Western
Country Gold
Country MOR
Countrypolitan
Cross-Country
Easy Country
Folk
Live Country
Metropolitan Country
Modern and
 Traditional Country
Pop Country
Progressive Country
Town and Country
Uptown Country

**EASY LISTENING**
Album
Beautiful Contemporary
Beautiful Music
Contemporary
 Easy Listening
Fine Background Music
Good Music
Instrumental
Mellow Music
Quality Music
Show and Movie

**EDUCATIONAL**
Childrens Educational
Listener Supported
Public Broadcasting
School Extension Service

**ETHNIC**
French
German
Polish
Polka
Portuguese
etc.

**JAZZ**
Black Jazz
Fusion
Lite Jazz
New Age

**LITE/SOFT ROCK**
Adult Soft Rock
Casual Contemporary
Contemporary Soft Rock
Light Contemporary
Light Adult Contemporary

**MIDDLE OF THE ROAD
(MOR)**
Adult MOR
Big Band
Bright MOR
Comedy
Contemporary MOR
Contemporary Standard
Current/Recent MOR
Diversified
Easy MOR
Full Service
General Popular
Gentle MOR
Modern MOR
MOR
Music of Your Life
Nostalgia
Personality MOR
Pop
Pop MOR
Pop Standard
Standard
Standard Pop
Uptempo MOR

**NEWS/TALK**
Commentary
Farm
Talk Only
Talk-Interview-Discussion
Talk-Service
Talk-Sports
Talk-Telephone
 Participation
Sports

**OLDIES**
Adult Contemporary Gold
Contemporary Gold
Contemporary Oldies
Easy Listening Gold
Gold
Great Gold
Mellow Gold
Pop Contemporary Gold
Pop Oldies
Solid Gold
Super Gold Oldies

**RELIGIOUS**
Black Christian
Christian
Christian MOR
Christian Rock
Contemporary Christian
Gospel
Inspirational
Light Contemporary
 Christian
MOR Gospel
Religious MOR
Christian Country

**SPANISH LANGUAGE**
Contemporary Spanish
Hispanic
Hispanic Hits
Latin
Mex-Tex
Salsa
Rancheras

**URBAN CONTEMPORARY**
Black Adult
Contemporary
Black Dance Music
Black-Oriented
 Contemporary

**ARBITRON RATINGS/RADIO**

leaving this job to the stations and syndicators who claim to program such refinements.

Clearly, radio program directors walk a tightrope. On one hand, if they appeal to a listenership that is too broad in its composition, their station image may be blurred, with many advertisers avoiding the outlet because it delivers too much waste circulation. On the other hand, if the format is too narrowly drawn, it will not attract a large enough listenership to be salable to advertisers at rates high enough to keep the station financially solvent. Maintaining a balance between these two extremes makes a PD job in the larger markets especially challenging.

Even in smaller towns, where there are fewer competing signals, program directors must still wrestle with these image and audience targeting issues. They must set their sights on attracting a larger slice of a smaller audience pie while still making certain that their station is projecting a distinct personality. Sometimes, formatic techniques developed in one market can be applied elsewhere, but a sensitive programmer knows that local conditions must still be accommodated. Programming consultant Bill Hennes therefore advises that

> programmers need to understand what makes a radio format work, then translate that to their market. Go ahead and monitor successful stations, but do it with a grain of salt. A certain percentage of the things you monitor will remain the same, but it's the expansion of those basics that will make the radio station successful. Expand on these basics by applying them to the unique aspects of your own market.
>
> Before you monitor any station, analyze the market. Don't just look at the demographics either. The mind-set of the market is important. What makes the market tick? Getting a handle on the real pulse of the listener base is the first step to understanding why the station you're monitoring is successful. . . .

Once you have found out what makes that radio station tick, then you can come back to your market and take the bits and pieces that apply to your station. I caution you in taking a cookie cutter approach though. Dissecting your market and refining those bits and pieces to fit the uniqueness of your audience is what will work.[1]

Anyone can play the hits. But it's what you do with them or with any other on-air element that distinguishes innovative program directors from drone formula followers.

Even the best radio format design will fail if it is not properly executed. Program directors thus must clearly communicate their managerial plan to the staff in their departments and must continuously monitor performance to ensure that these plans are carried out. In larger markets, PDs are often assisted in these endeavors by *production managers, music directors,* and *traffic directors.* At smaller stations, these functions may be combined.

The production manager is most directly responsible for the sheen of the on-air sound. This includes overseeing of in-studio, remote, and recorded programming to make certain that technical quality and style remain consistent. The production manager must also see that all appropriate personnel are competent in equipment operation. (At the largest outlets, this duty may be delegated to an *operations manager.*) Just as important, the production manager serves as the quality control executive for all commercials, promos, and other recorded messages prepared at the station. Because the commercials pay all the bills, their production standards become a top priority.

The music director helps translate the PD's overall sound goals into specific selections. Often, the music director screens all incoming records (frequently referred to as *product*) to ascertain which songs should be added to the station playlist and with what frequency. Record *rotation* is a key component of any music-

362

SECTION
THREE
Profes-
sional
Perspec-
tives

driven format, and so the music director's categorization of a tune is a key factor in how much airplay it will receive. A "hot clock" like that in Figure 12–2 determines the placement of these categories and other on-air elements within a given hour. Increasingly, computer programs operationalize these decisions.

Focus group (see Chapter 1) and call-out telephone research also can be used to gauge listener perceptions and preferences. To help keep track of new product, the music director also reads trade publications such as *Radio and Records* and *Billboard* and serves as the contact person with record company representatives. This last task is a particularly sen-

sitive one given the *payola* possibilities that can occasionally arise (recall discussions in Chapters 6 and 7). Many stations, therefore, have created a group screening process so that no one person has complete control in specifying the individual tunes that will receive heavy play.

As their name implies, *traffic directors* are the station schedulers. Operating within the patterns and flow developed by the program director (as graphically conveyed via daypart hot clocks), traffic people arrange the specific commercials, promos, and programs and prepare the master log that sets forth everything that is to air on a given day. In final form, this

**Figure 12–2**

Hot clock developed by Broadcast Programming, Inc., for its Z format

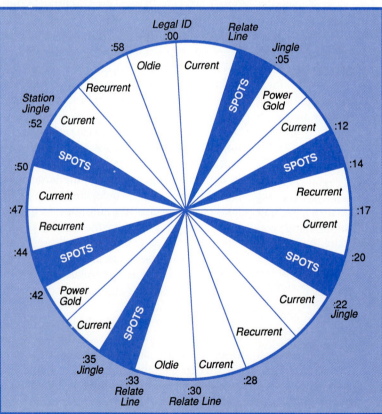

*(Courtesy of Dennis Soapes, Broadcast Programming)*

log becomes a validation that contracted-for spots were aired. At many stations, the traffic director prepares the log via a computer, which automatically generates advertiser invoices as the various advertisements are run.

Up to this point, we have been discussing the span of control exercised by *radio* program directors. Television station PDs play a similar role but with different emphases. Instead of concentrating on the design and maintenance of a format, television program directors must concentrate on the individual and often highly divergent *programs* that make up a given broadcast day. The task here is to encourage audience flow from one show to the next while keeping an eye on the programs being scheduled by competing outlets. If other major local stations are airing material with heavy male appeal, such as a sporting event and an action/adventure cop show, the wise TV programmer may choose a property like a nighttime soap that will skew more to female viewers. If a station is a network affiliate, of course, some of these options are precluded by what the net has decided to slot during that time.

Regardless of a network affiliation, it is important to recognize that no network can dictate what an affiliate station must air. Over the years and via several regulations and policy statements, the FCC has made it clear that a station is licensed to serve a local community. Program decisions, therefore, are to be made at the local level. With the backing of the general manager, any program director can refuse to clear a given network show in their market, though this occurrence is quite rare due to a variety of network disincentives. The reason for preemption could be anything from a time conflict with a local baseball broadcast to a concern that the net show's content will offend local community values. Of course, if the net show is not run, the station will not receive compensation (*net comp*) for the network commercials within the preempted show that were also not run. The

larger the market, however, the less a station depends on net comp, so this factor is not the major deterrent—at least in the top fifty population centers.

On the other hand, networks are not totally at the mercy of their affiliates. A station that consistently fails to clear a significant number of net programs may find the network seeking to move its affiliation to another outlet. This, of course, assumes that there is a local outlet with equal technical facilities in search of such an affiliation. No network would drop a VHF affiliate if it meant its only alternative was a UHF facility. Recently, some of the networks have sought to maintain or improve station clearances by offering cash bonuses, more local avails within net programs, or similar incentives. However it plays out in a given situation, the program director at a network affiliate must constantly reappraise which party (the station or the network) needs the other more. Often, a series of compromises must be fashioned between the optimum local schedule and the offerings being fed from the net.

Independent station program directors have no such limitations to their scheduling flexibility. But the pressure to fill an entire program day generates significant administrative and financial problems in its own right. Purchasing a spate of low-cost properties will make the station *look* cheap and unattractive to audiences and advertisers alike. But spending vast sums on consistently high-appeal programs may put untenable pressures on the sales staff to sell at rates high enough to pay for the on-air product. To lessen this dilemma, many former independents have affiliated with the Fox network. Fox's comparatively limited schedule of offerings allows the former independent to maintain much of its flexibility while still freeing up station resources to purchase better programming for remaining locally determined dayparts.

Television station PDs, like their radio

**364**

SECTION
THREE
Profes-
sional
Perspec-
tives

counterparts, have production/operations managers and traffic directors to assist in the administration of their departments. Given the requirements of a visual medium, they are also responsible for art/graphics departments and for the larger number of technical personnel required to produce local pictorial content. With cable bringing more and more viewing options to town, television station program directors must use these resources more deftly than ever in delineating their outlets from the expanding list of alternatives. As has been the case in radio for years, television PDs must now labor to find and fill what broadcast consultant Clark Smidt labels the "profitable market niche." As Smidt sees it,

> Proper positioning results from understanding a constantly changing competitive field within a defined area. . . . The total packaging of a station is the amalgam of all elements reaching the public, and doing so in synch. It includes a properly tuned presentation, appropriate style and meaningful services. The total package is your station's identity and personality. . . .
>
> Station development is a deliberate and gradual process, requiring step-by-step building and minimal error. A well put-together product invites many vehicles for reinforcing ongoing presence in your competitive arena.
>
> Management must respect its own staff capabilities while carefully monitoring the competition. Ratings are the product of not only what's been on your air but also what everyone else in the market has or hasn't been doing.[2]

Beyond the individual formatic and show scheduling elements, today's station program director thus must be a *marketer* with a marketer's sensitivity to audience targeting and audience expectations.

Over the years, television programmers at the network and station level have devised several basic strategies that have proven successful depending, as always, on what the competing outlets are airing. Because this is not a textbook on programming, we mention only a few of these strategies. *Strip* programming means airing the same show at the same time five or more times a week. The alternative is *checkerboarding,* where several different shows appear in succeeding days. In prime-time access (the hour before network evening programming begins) most affiliate and independent stations alike have gone to stripping for consistency and easier promotability. Checkerboarding is, of course, the common network prime-time strategy—which some independent outlets try to counter via a strip with high appeal to a certain demographic.

*Vertical* programming is the airing of several same-category shows in succession, such as a block of situation comedies, one-hour action/adventure series, or game shows. The assumption is that viewers who enjoy this type of offering are more likely to stay with the channel as long as their preference is available. Another pair of strategies relate to the strength or initial weakness of properties the programmer has available to schedule. *Hammocking* is the placement of a new or untried series between two established successes. NBC used this to great advantage in 1987 when it premiered the lightweight *A Different World* between returning powerhouses *The Cosby Show* and *Cheers. Tentpoling,* conversely, is using a proven series to prop up newer and/or weaker properties scheduled before and after it. To a degree, tentpoling is a desperation strategy that, if it fails, can torpedo the established show as well. That same Fall 1987 NBC schedule also reflected this negative result when the smash *Miami Vice* was hobbled by scheduling it between the soon-to-fail *Rags to Riches* and *Private Eye.*

Before concluding our assessment of program directors, we need briefly to explore how this position functions on the cable side of our business. In the wired environment, PDs are not concerned with individual programs but rather with the total arrangement of entire program channels on their system.

What broadcast signals will be carried and on what cable channel? Will distant broadcast signals, including superstations, be offered? What basic cable networks should be run? How many and which pay cable services are to be offered? And, should these services be grouped into certain packages or *tiers* for which subscribers pay additional fees? Should certain basic cable networks be tiered as well? What about local origination, public access channels for governmental units, or leased access channels to be rented to realtors, home shopping services, or other enterprises? Together with the system manager, a cable program director deals with all of these questions.

In the case of MSOs (*multiple system operators* who own several individual systems) many such decisions may be made by a program director at MSO headquarters, leaving the local staffer with little more than traffic-director duties. Certain other determinations (such as the number and use of access channels) may have been specified in the franchise agreement that the system has signed with the local government in whose territory it is operating. Unlike the situation found at stations, therefore, a cable program director may have limited decision-making powers and may serve more a facilitative than a directive function. Even though they are in their early stages of development, it appears that groupings of LPTV stations as well as wireless cable (MMDS) operations will limit program director roles in similar ways, with key choices about program carriage made at the multiple-outlet group level.

## Sales Managers

The sales-side counterpart of the program director is the sales manager. The time sellers discussed in Chapter 11 report to this executive. The sales manager directs and monitors the efforts of the individual sellers to meet the projected revenue goals of the station, system, or network. This executive must also set the rates specified in the grid card (review Figure 11–6). If the unit for which the sales manager is responsible does not perform to expected capacity, the future of the entire operation and everyone who works for it is in jeopardy.

In setting goals for subordinates, sales executives stress one of two things: *share-of-market* or *budget.* In share-of-market, a computation is made of the total advertising dollars being spent in the particular medium for that geographic area. Then, in light of the outlet's programming performance, the sales manager targets a certain percentage of the total ad dollars that his/her sales staff should be able to obtain. Thus, if increased money is being spent in radio advertising in the market, for example, the radio sales manager using a share-of-market approach expects that the sales force will bring a proportionate increase in revenue into the station. Conversely, *budget* targeting looks at the revenues needed to operate at the expected profit margin and then sets the individual salesperson's dollar goals accordingly. If market expenditures increase, it will be easier for the staff to deliver their goals. If, on the other hand, advertisers are spending fewer dollars in the medium, time sellers must actually increase their share of market in order to meet the budget mandates.

Clearly, sales managers must be adept forecasters as well as skilled motivators. They must project what performance standard and level to set and then activate their staff to reach this objective. By themselves, goals and targets are worthless if the people who must attain them are not given supportive direction and organized assistance by their sales boss. Broadcast sales consultant Martin Antonelli puts it this way:

Managing at a station or rep firm must be approached with a definite plan of action;

366

SECTION
THREE

Profes-
sional
Perspec-
tives

## PAUL BOSCARINO/GENERAL SALES MANAGER
### WOOD AM/FM

Looking back at how I achieved the position of general sales manager of a high-profile AM/FM radio combo operation, I realize that it is virtually impossible for anyone to be *fully* prepared for a job like this when it becomes yours. Like many other people, I figured that the sure-fire way to become my stations' sales manager was ultimately to become the top billing salesperson for the stations. I also felt that once somebody ascended into the sales manager's chair, he or she finally had one heckofa nice, cushy job.

It turned out I was wrong on both counts.

True, the skills you acquire in becoming the top biller on your staff do come in handy as a sales manager because you can credibly offer good guidance and selling ideas to the salespeople you supervise. However, the one thing a new sales manager quickly discovers is that *a sales manager doesn't manage sales; rather, a sales manager manages human relationships with the salespeople who go out and generate the sales.*

Being a professional salesperson is not an easy job, and that's regardless of whether you're selling radio advertising or ice cubes to Eskimos. Let's face it. On any given day, you hear a lot more "no's" or "call me later's" than you do "yes." Mix in a normal dose of personal life pressures and it's clear why every salesperson has a lot of challenges to face, *individually.*

But the unique challenge of being a successful sales manager is that you must have the talent and/or empathy to motivate *a whole group* of people

faced with their own daily challenges (you being one of them!) Sales managers don't garner that kind of essential human relations training just by being the former top dog on the sales staff. A sales manager develops these skills through trial and error on the job—and not sooner.

Being promoted to the sales manager's chair presents another challenge you might not be prepared for, either. It's called "Welcome to 'middle management,'" where on one side you answer to the station's general manager (and also his or her bosses) while on the other side you're dealing with a large group of bright, aggressive salespeople who always manage to keep you on your toes!

Still, being a sales manager can be a very fulfilling position. For me, the best part is watching one of my salespeople nurture a selling idea I gave for a prospect or current client and turning it into a campaign or commercial that generates a lot of customer traffic and sales. This is the kind of win-win situation I love because the client is happy, the salesperson gets all pumped up, and I feel good knowing I had a hand in contributing to the client's success on our station(s).

Other radio sales managers will probably agree that the best things you learn in a job like this are the human relations, time management, and budgeting skills that, taken together, prepare you well for the next rung on the ladder—a general manager's position.

---

One year after writing this profile, Paul Boscarino became general manager of a major AM/FM property in another market.

---

one that involves discipline and organization. Without a plan we see nothing more than activity without action; motion without movement. Salespeople have a right to be managed with competence and dedication. Anything less will lead to breakdown and chaos. . . .

Perhaps the single most important responsibility of the sales manager involves spending time with salespeople. Daily sessions should be scheduled at which the following subjects are covered: pending business; establishing target shares for specific buys; what salespeople are saying to clients; how clients are responding; whether the appropriate areas are being pitched on specific buys; whether specials are being emphasized; what the client requirements are (cost per point, target demo, number of spots, reach, frequency, traffic building, etc.); what type of order it looks like the station will get; determining the problems that exist and possible solutions. Time spent on these areas can be invaluable in determining strengths and weaknesses of the sales staff as well as providing direction and leadership for the team.[3]

In other words, leaders who don't lead are as damaging to a sales effort as they are to programming, engineering, and any other aspect of our industry.

While directing their own staffs, sales managers at electronic media outlets must also work closely with other department heads—particularly the program director. Nowhere must this cooperation be closer than in determining the amount of *barter* programming (see Chapter 11) that will be aired. If the program director accepts too many barter contracts, the sales department's revenue-generating prospects will be seriously squeezed. This, in turn, means not only less money for the company, but also fewer commissions for its salespersons. As in most commercial businesses, time sellers supplement their basic salary with substantial commissions (often in the area of 10 to 18 percent) based on the dollars they generate. An avail filled by a barter spot means no revenue for the station—and no commission for the salesperson.

The sales manager must also come to agreements with programming and promotion heads as to the acceptability and volume of *trade-outs*. In a trade-out, an outlet exchanges its airtime for goods or services provided by the advertiser. A widespread example of this is *TV Guide's* providing advertising space to station promotion departments in exchange for free airtime to pitch *TV Guide* purchases by consumers. The sales department itself may create a barter deal such as giving a restaurant no-cost spots in exchange for restaurant catering of a station client party. Trade-outs may have some resource-providing advantages but, as in the case of barter, they also consume valuable avails. A sales manager who allows too many trade-out and

**368**

SECTION
THREE
Profes-
sional
Perspec-
tives

barter deals to flourish may discover that there is no longer enough revenue potential in remaining airtime to generate a profit!

To complicate the sales manager's life even more, an increasing number of advertisers are seeking *value-added services* from the media with which they do business. As an incentive for buying an extensive spot schedule from the station, an automobile dealer, for example, may want the outlet's popular morning drive personality to make a personal appearance at the dealer's tent sale. Or, he may demand that the morning show be broadcast live from under that tent! In such circumstances, the sales manager and the program director must make a joint assessment as to whether either one or both of these activities will do the station image or air sound more harm than the sales contract with the car dealer is worth. If he or she has the clout, a sales manager may sometimes decide to provide such a client service over the program director's objections—but such heavy-handed tactics will only make an enemy of the person who produces the only product that the sales department gets to sell.

## General Managers

If program director/sales manager disagreement persists, the general manager will probably have to settle the issue because the GM is the boss to whom both of these unit heads report. Settling turf wars is, however, a very unproductive use of a general manager's time and can result in no more than a temporary truce. As the top executive at the outlet, the effective general manager knows that it is much more important to engage in team-building than in arbitration activities. In trying to construct a winning, profit-making operation, the person in the head office must marshall everyone's efforts toward the competitive arena that exists outside. When conflicts inside are so acute that they distract everyone's attention from success-building, the facility is headed for financial disaster.

Management expert Peter Drucker has often stated that management is the task of making ordinary people perform in an extraordinary manner. The astute general manager knows that you can never achieve this extraordinary performance with people who are preoccupied with mundane grudge matches. Unfortunately, however, today's general managers often have less time than did their predecessors to achieve extraordinary results. After a decade of mergers, buyouts, corporate takeovers, and defense against such takeovers, a number of facilities face significant *debt-servicing*. In acquiring the property—or fending off the attempts of other companies to acquire it—owners have assumed high interest payments to lender banks or other financiers. Thus, the general manager must generate increased revenue to cover this expense.

No matter what else he or she delegates to other executives, the GM can never pass on responsibility for P & L (profit and loss). A substantial debt load only adds to this responsibility, making the job of general manager more challenging today than at any time in the memorable past. Under such pressures, rating/share performance and the advertising rates tied to it become concerns of almost overwhelming importance. The current saying that a program director has two (ratings) books in which to succeed—and a general manager two program directors—is no exaggeration in many situations.

The person who can cope with such pressures while still energizing and encouraging the rest of the staff is much in demand in our industry. If you aspire to such a position, it is essential that you identify and gradually acquire experience relative to the four main task areas in which a GM functions. As inven-

# WILLIAM SHEARER/VICE-PRESIDENT and GENERAL MANAGER
## KGFJ

Radio is a very exciting, creative, and deeply rewarding career field. It's different from many other industries because each day is unique and allows you to feel and touch many people in a positive way. Radio helps to entertain, allows listeners to feel good about themselves, and enlightens them about the problems their communities face.

The overall role of the general manager is to give direction to the station and its employees while ensuring that preset goals and objectives are met in a timely manner. The most important resource of any radio station is its staff. These individuals must be consistently reminded that everything we do is directed toward one goal: producing and airing the best on-air product possible. My station has thirty employees. Each employee is an individual who may have any number of dynamics occurring in his or her personal life. Some have domestic problems, financial concerns, a sick relative, or a variety of other mind-distracting problems. I must detect any signal that an employee is bothered and not prepared to function to greatest potential.

Because most radio stations operate very lean, with a minimum number of employees, each person is key and must be counted on to deliver his or her best effort. I must motivate or assist a troubled employee but attempt to do this without becoming emotionally or personally involved. Many employees do not want their boss meddling in their personal lives. Many others do not open up to have an honest discussion. This is where manage-

rial experience and skill come into play.

A second challenge is the selection of key department managers. I have found that most résumés look alike, and many individuals interview well and offer the right answers. So after interviewing an applicant, I find I normally reach inside my gut and react to that feeling. Experience has also shown me that managers forget the importance of ongoing evaluation. Quite often, individuals are placed in a job and as long as nothing drastic goes wrong, we feel all is well. However, the employee may just be getting by. When we accrue enough employees doing just enough to get by, we find we have an average staff producing a mediocre product. In a competitive market, this situation does not produce a winning organization or quality air sound.

The area of sales is also crucial. My radio station happens to be Black-owned, and we program to the Los An-

370

SECTION
THREE

Profes-
sional
Perspec-
tives

geles Black community. Our great difficulty is trying to convince major advertisers of the importance of this market group. The Black consumer has traditionally either been written off or expected to respond to generalized marketing and advertising efforts. Black-owned radio stations have conducted all kinds of research. An advertising agency requests the research, and then challenges it after it is submitted. It's a difficult situation, and many small-to-medium radio stations must therefore exist solely on revenues from local retail advertisers.

Most advertising agencies use rating services as the basis or justification for the decision to buy air time. But many Black-owned radio stations are the smaller signal facilities or those with less desirable frequencies. The reason for this is pure economics; these stations cost less to purchase. The good news, however, is that many Black owners are able to sell these stations, upgrade to stronger-signal outlets, and therefore be more competitive.

The job of senior management is to take all of these ongoing problems and find a way to succeed in spite of them. I have found that one effective tool in achieving our goals is setting the right work climate. Part of that climate involves demonstrating that open, honest, and frank communication is not only allowed, but also encouraged. Other tools include ensuring that each employee feels important, needed, and part of the radio family. Hands-on management allows me to learn first-hand what the real deal is. Thus, effective leadership on my part goes a long way in impacting what does and does not happen within the organization.

You have the potential for effective leadership if you properly prepare yourself, learn to listen, ask questions, and make a strong commitment to do your best to reach your potential. Any career field is crowded, but there's always room at the top for people who know where they want to go. I started in radio as an account executive and steadily moved up through the ranks.

It's been twenty-two exciting years. I have advanced beyond my wildest expectations in the radio industry. But it only happened because I made the commitment to myself and accepted the challenge.

toried by Professors William McCavitt and Peter Pringle, these tasks include:

(1) planning, or the determination of the station's objectives and the plans or strategies to accomplish them; (2) organizing personnel into a formal structure, usually departments, and assigning specialized duties to persons and units; (3) influencing or directing—that is, stimulating employees to carry out their responsibilities enthusiastically and effectively; (4) controlling, or developing criteria to measure the performance of individuals, departments, and the station, and taking corrective action when necessary.[4]

To keep track of the financial information necessary to deal with many of these aspects, the general manager is aided by a *comptroller* or *financial officer*. This staffer monitors and keeps the ledger on the outlet's cash flow and all the related business transactions. In larger operations the comptroller, in turn, is assisted by a *credit manager*. The credit manager works closely with the sales department in ensuring that invoices for airtime are mailed out and that payment is received. With comptrollers and credit managers policing the daily debits and credits, the general manager can concentrate on overall business and organizational goals. Still, the GM must always be prepared to intercede when one of these executives isolates a potential or recurring financial problem that threatens revenue stability.

The comptroller, for example, may point out that the promotions department is committing to too many trade-out deals for contest prizes or the credit manager may sound a warning that too many slow-pay clients are still being allowed to obtain large numbers of prime avails. In such cases, the general manager must step in to enforce the financial discipline necessary for the maintenance of a healthy bottom line.

Even though actual *profit* is not in the picture, the general manager at a noncommercial facility deals with the same fundamental responsibilities as exercised by commercial colleagues. Revenues must be balanced with expenses. However, noncommercial income is most likely to derive from grants, corporate donations, and audience pledge drives. There is no sales department as such, but there probably is a grant or donor development office that coordinates the station's fund-raising and program underwriting activities. Money must still be raised to fire up the transmitter, secure the programs, and pay the staff. The noncommercial GM can no more delegate this responsibility than the commercial manager can shuffle away profit-and-loss concerns.

Cable system general managers (usually called *system* managers) are not that different in their overall perspective. The key difference is that, in cable, the chief executive is dealing with multiple revenue streams: subscriber fees for basic and pay programming,

local cable advertising income, and payments received from shopping services or other leased-channel users. Meanwhile, the system manager must monitor expenses related to such things as the franchise fee tendered to the local governmental body, semi-annual payments to the Copyright Royalty Tribunal (CRT) for importation of distant broadcast signals, and charges from cable networks and satellite suppliers for retransmission of their programming. (Trends in general expense categories are shown in Figure 12–3.) In addition, as a marketer, the cable GM must watch the system's *churn rate* (subscribers disconnecting compared to those adding cable service) and attempt to control the technical and administrative costs associated with such customer turnover. In short, the items on their ledger sheets may be different, but the overall fiscal preoccupation remains the same for general managers throughout our profession.

## News Directors

Station general managers must oversee a media enterprise that Edward R. Murrow once called "an incompatible combination of show business, advertising and news." The GM nonetheless must forge these three disparate activities into a coordinated whole by working through the subordinate executives responsible for each. We have already looked at two of these three elements in our discussion of program directors (the show business aspect) and sales managers (the advertising dimension). To complete the picture, we now examine the executive responsible for the news function—an executive appropriately labelled the *news director*.

Depending on the station's organizational chart, the news director may either be of equal rank with the show business and advertising counterparts or be a subordinate who

372

SECTION
THREE
Profes-
sional
Perspec-
tives

**Figure 12-3**

Cable system operations expenses as a percentage of total expenditures

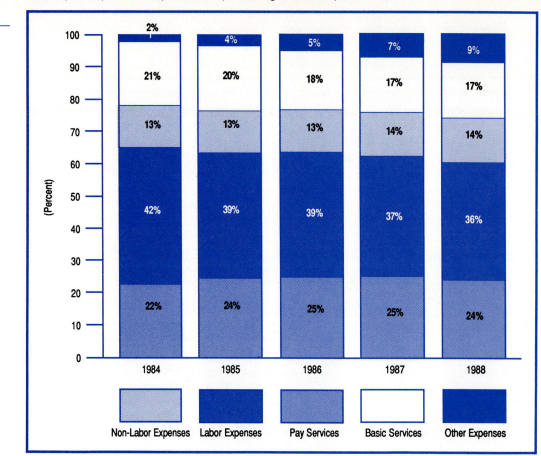

*(Source: MSO Magazine, a publication of Transmedia Partners 1, L. P.)*

reports to the program director. In music radio, particularly, news is seen today as no more than one element of the format and so must be subject to the program director's decision about how that format should best be developed. News directors may bristle at this, but the fact remains that, since FCC deregulation of radio (see Chapters 6 and 7), there are no requirements that a facility air any given amount of news—or any news at all. Generally speaking, this has meant that music-oriented stations have de-emphasized the role of news (and therefore the role of the news di-

rector) while information-based stations have expanded it. Some all-news stations, for example, have no need for a program director because their total programming comes under the news director's span of control.

As you know by this point in your reading, television stations remain more broadly targeted than do radio facilities and so most of them still try to reflect a significant news presence. One reason for this, of course, is that a local news show is about the only program matter that can be completely unique to the facility that airs it. TV stations thought to be number one in their markets are thus normally also expected to have the number one news team. Nevertheless, because news occupies a comparatively small proportion of the broadcast day, it is a rare station on which the news director carries as much clout as does the head of programming.

This should not suggest that the job of television news director is a minor one. Compared to radio, where a news director may be the only full-time journalist at the station, even an average-size TV facility employs at least twenty news staffers. The larger the station, the more likely that the news director will concentrate on such administrative matters as budgets and personnel while delegating day-to-day news judgments to other people. Sometimes an *assistant news director* post is created to carry some of the burden of either administration or news content oversight—depending on where the news director most needs assistance.

Below this level, an *executive producer* is likely to exercise responsibility for the actual content and quality of the newscasts. Sometimes, this person serves as the producer of record for the early evening newscast (which is the most important because it can generate the largest audiences). Other *producers* then serve similar functions for late night, early morning, and (if programmed) noon newscasts.

The producer works closely with an *assignment editor* in determining and gathering the stories to be featured. The assignment editor matches available resources to breaking stories by selecting and dispatching crews as events warrant. Because a great deal of news is, by its nature, unpredictable, a skillful assignment editor always makes multiple contingency plans so that reporters and videographers can be available quickly when a big story breaks. If an assignment editor is a poor planner or is slow to react to events, a producer's efforts to improve newscast quality will be largely in vain.

The smaller the station, the more these jobs are compressed. Thus, a news director might serve as producer/assignment editor for the early evening newscast with an assistant or two performing similar combination functions at other times of the day and on weekends. As in most corporate settings, the larger the operation becomes, the more its top executive must be pulled from actual production activities to concentrate on long-range administrative and planning tasks.

However large or small their market, every news director strives to make his or her unit the best news-gathering operation in town as a matter of both personal and professional pride. (A fundamental reflection of such journalistic pride is the public service announcement seen in Figure 12–4.) In pursuing success, veteran television news director turned general manager Tom Kirby of Oklahoma City's KOCO-TV maintains that there are four essential components to any TV news operation: (1) anchor persons, (2) managers, (3) reporters, and (4) videographers. Kirby found, through his experience, that any station able to be the best against competing stations in any *two* of these elements will ensure stability in the audience its newscasts draw. Any operation dominating *three* of these areas is almost certain to improve its ratings. Kirby further points out that anchors are the most critical element and get the most attention from news directors, but that few of these directors pay much attention to the quality of their videographers. This area is thus the easiest one to win if a news executive bothers to develop it.[5] (Salary requirements for various news job categories are shown in Figure 12–5.)

As in most aspects of our highly competitive industry, a successful news operation can stand out from its rivals by establishing a point of comparative superiority. Thus, news director veterans like KVBC's (Las Vegas) Rolla Cleaver always seek to establish what he refers to as "a franchise in something you can own." Being the best in business news, or local entertainment features, or city govern-

374

SECTION
THREE

Profes-
sional
Perspec-
tives

## RICK SYKES/ASSIGNMENT EDITOR
### WDIV-TV

The assignment editor serves as the heartbeat of the newsroom. This job helps shape and execute the daily plan for news coverage. The assignment editor is expected to have a grasp of the important news of the day and to be able to recommend which reporters might be best suited to cover each of the day's events. During a breaking story, the assignment editor provides the necessary information and leadership to get the story on the air accurately, completely, and, most of all, *first*—before the competition has a chance to react.

Pressure and deadlines are the constants. Deadlines for getting information to the writers for the newscasts. Deadlines for getting crews to specific locations to meet reporters and to make news conferences. An assignment editor must be able to make decisions quickly and to stay in control even when everything seems to be going to hell, while still keeping in mind that everyone must feel that they're important if you are to get the best out of them.

On any given day one or more major stories can break at the same time. A typical day starts out with the morning conference call. I have received a briefing from the morning producer and listened to the radio newscasts on the various stations while getting ready to come to work. On the way in, I've glanced through the morning newspapers. I get on the conference call and it's fairly short. The producers, news director, and myself are in agreement on the direction we should be taking today. The call does not always go this smoothly; sometimes

disagreements on direction and style develop. After I get off the phone, one of the crews calls in to say they have heard radio traffic about some accidents on one of the freeways. I call the police. The police tell me that they have a chain reaction accident. I tell the crew where it is and ask them to shoot it.

*Rule Number One: The usual can become the unusual very fast.* I get a second call from the same crew. They have heard more radio traffic about other accidents on the freeway. I ask if the rain is freezing. Meanwhile I have to update the morning news lineup and get ready for the 9:00 A.M. staff meeting. After the meeting, I am advised that the crew out on the freeway has come across at least two accidents involving fist fights. At one of them an assistant prosecuting attorney has been beaten up by another motorist. Good picture story for the noon show.

At about 11:15 we get a tip call that the FBI and a local sheriff department agency are investigating the apparent kidnapping of a General Motors executive and his wife from their home. The location is forty minutes out and we have to assume that the other stations are on to the story—which means we have to get there with a reporter fast. This will now be the lead story for the noon show.

*Rule Number Two: Once a major story breaks, the clock starts to run against you.* The best pictures and most dramatic sound usually happen at the beginning of a breaking story. The longer it takes you to get there, the greater the chance you will get beaten by another station. Luckily we were on the phones before the story hit the wires and obtained the basics. I have moved a live truck from another story to this one. But we will not get it there before the start of the noon newscast. The producer is told that we will go live as soon as possible, leading with a copy story at the top of the show. At two minutes to noon, the other assignment editor and myself gather around the TV sets to see if the other stations will beat us on the air with a live shot. Fortunately, both of the other stations also have only copy stories about the kidnapping—no live shots. Fifteen minutes into the noon newscast, still no one has a live shot. Our crew calls and says they will be ready to go shortly. The producer is alerted. Twenty minutes into the show and we go live from the scene. The

FBI and sheriff department are there. We have beaten everyone. One of the other stations goes live twenty minutes after we do. That's a long time in television news. The noon show is over now and its time to talk about what has to be done for the later shows. This is a big story and it's decided to do more than one angle on it. A night reporter is called in. We also decide to do regular cut-ins throughout the day.

*Rule Number Three: Once you have the lead on a story the competition will try everything they can to take it away from you.* This kidnapping story has now taken top priority. The personnel and crew deployment must be adjusted to deal with that reality. The sports department has their crew request killed. Two afternoon news conferences called by other groups wanting coverage are ignored.

By 4:30 in the afternoon we are still getting tape in from the various live shot locations for the kidnapping story and it's getting very intense in the newsroom. We are only 30 minutes from air. At 5:00 P.M. we hit the air and the coverage is good. Then, it's 6:30 P.M. and the night assignment editor is taking over control of the desk. The kidnapping is still the major story of the day and it will be followed throughout the evening.

I take a moment to reflect on how we did today and then remember *Rule Number Four: You are only as good as your next newscast.*

**Figure 12–4**

A nonfinancial motivation for today's news directors

"IF THE PRESS DIDN'T TELL US"     Available in :30 and :15 versions          30 SECONDS

(VO): How do you find out

when an administration is corrupt?

SUPER: Corruption.

How do you find out

when a government is hiding the truth?

SUPER: Deception.

How do you find out about those

who would like you not to find out?

SUPER: Cover-up.

To become better informed about the role of a free press,

and how it protects your rights, contact the First Amendment Center.

SUPER: 1-800-542-1600. If the press didn't tell us, who would?

**A PUBLIC SERVICE CAMPAIGN OF THE ADVERTISING COUNCIL**

Volunteer Advertising Agency: Lowe Marschalk, Inc.

CNFP -7130/7115

**Figure 12–5**
Average broadcast news salaries, 1990

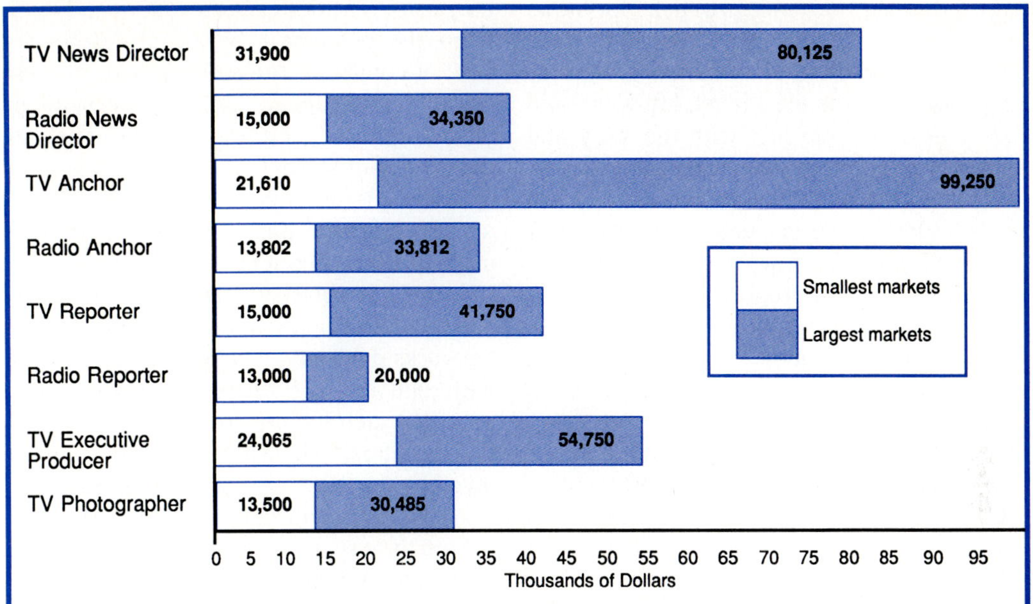

| | Smallest markets | Largest markets |
|---|---|---|
| TV News Director | 31,900 | 80,125 |
| Radio News Director | 15,000 | 34,350 |
| TV Anchor | 21,610 | 99,250 |
| Radio Anchor | 13,802 | 33,812 |
| TV Reporter | 15,000 | 41,750 |
| Radio Reporter | 13,000 | 20,000 |
| TV Executive Producer | 24,065 | 54,750 |
| TV Photographer | 13,500 | 30,485 |

0 5 10 15 20 25 30 35 40 45 50 55 60 65 70 75 80 85 90 95
Thousands of Dollars

*Source: 1990 Radio-Television News Directors Association Survey conducted by Vernon Stone, University of Missouri*

ment coverage will move a station well beyond the perception that it is just "giving the news" like everybody else.[6] News directors must also work closely with their promotion departments to make certain that this franchise is vividly communicated to the viewership at large.

Owning a news franchise is important for many radio stations too, of course. But securing that franchise is much more difficult when the news director comprises the entire department. Under such circumstances, it is usually best to program a limited number of newscasts and stack them with the information in which this particular station's listenership is most interested. This information might be agricultural news, business/financial developments, weather forecasts, street/traffic conditions, or school events. Because radio formats are targeted more and more to specific life-style audiences, news that conforms to those life-style preferences makes

good sense for both business and listener service.

A few cable systems are also establishing local news services. Sometimes this is in cooperation with a radio station, whose news director oversees the cablecasts as well. In other instances, a newspaper is a partner in the activity. In a few innovative projects, a television station programs the local cable news channel by recycling its broadcast newscasts and perhaps supplementing these newscasts with stories developed by its reporters for which it did not have space on its regular newscasts. Local cable systems seldom employ their own news directors for these enterprises but the projects do enlarge the challenges for existing news directors that the participating stations already employ.

At the opposite end of the spectrum, broadcast and certain cable *networks* (CNN is the most notable) employ scores of news executives. Even though their functions are primar-

**378**

SECTION
THREE
Profes-
sional
Perspec-
tives

ily the same, top managers in network units carry titles such titles as "president of the news division" or "vice-president for news programming" rather than news director. Producers and assignment editors are just as common as at the local level, however, and the pressures to be first with the story and first with the target audience are just as great. Whether they function at a national or local desk, today's electronic news managers must "learn trades that are not taught in a J-school, but those that the programmer knows," argues Baltimore news director Merrie Street. This means knowing the research so that you know who your audience is. "News directors cannot argue the public trust in defending their turf," Street continues. "That won't wash. You have to be in on the research, on the focus groups. Read the consultants' reports. . . . If you don't promote what you do in the newsroom, you'll lose."[7]

## Entertainment Producers

Having examined the role of news producers as well as that of the other prime executives who work within radio and television outlets, we can now look at *entertainment* producers and a number of other key directive agents who function outside the stations and networks but in closely associated enterprises.

Executives overseeing entertainment programming typically work for the large studio companies or for independent entities that frequently join with the studios to create or distribute on-air product. Some of these people, like Stephen Cannell and Hugh Wilson (see Chapter 10), are *writer-producers*. They combine directive and creative functions to place a distinctive stamp on every phase of a show's development. With more and more options now available to the viewing public, top writers who have proven that their scripts can attract an audience are in great demand.

They have now acquired the clout to insist they be true *partners* in the projects on which they work. The designation *writer-producer* is often the outcome. "'Writer-producers are now in control of the series television business,'" asserts Richard Katz, a business affairs executive for GTG Entertainment. "'They are the dominant force,'" agrees CBS vice-president for business affairs Bill Klein. "'Actors and directors are important. But there is no place to start without the writer-producer. . . . We can't go black.'" And writer-producer Hugh Wilson himself adds, "'More and more, networks don't say, 'I want to be in business with such and such studio.' They say, 'I want such and such writer.' So the studios have to give [writers] the last thing they want to give—ownership.'"[8]

A top-notch writer-producer may be able to negotiate a share of up to 50 percent of a show's net profits and so is compensated very well for fulfilling two separate functions. In addition, the exerciser of a dual role wields a good deal more creative independence than can a producer working directly for a studio. Marcy Carsey who, with partner Tom Werner, has developed such series as *The Cosby Show, A Different World,* and *Roseanne,* describes such freedom in these terms:

> "We're placing the bets we want to place in the way we want to place them. With a studio, there's a whole other voice and set of reasons for making business and creative decisions, some of which have nothing to do with the quality of the show. . . . Then there are the larger issues, like when a network is unhappy with your concept or with a cast member or with a key creative talent. The studio's more likely to go with the network's feeling for the sake of the relationship. We would hold the ground for the sake of the show."[9]

Such money and freedom do not come without a price, of course. The pressures of wearing both conceptual and directive hats have caused more than one writer-producer to suffer heart attacks, marital breakups, and stress-intensified exhaustion. Garry Marshall, whose developmental credits include *The Odd Couple, Happy Days,* and *Laverne and Shirley,* noticed this occupational hazard several years ago when he observed:

"It seems like there's an old guard of writer-producers, who have become over-worked by the networks. They are pressed by the networks to do too many shows. When they *do* too much, they become tired. They start to move out, like Larry Gelbart [M∗A∗S∗H], [Norman] Lear, and myself. During the interim, businessmen come in to run it for a while until a new guard of writer-producers rise up and kind of take over for a while, then they get tired and—"[10]

Perhaps because of these tribulations, writer-producers are still outnumbered by regular producers whose job focuses exclusively on integrating the contributions of individual writers with the other elements involved in mounting a show. Even though a producer's actual duties vary depending on whether other producer-titled jobs exist as superiors and subordinates, the essence of the job is to make certain that the project comes together on time, within budget, and in line with the agreed-on concept. The producer, in other words, is the person with the broad enough view of the show so that he or she can coordinate the production process from beginning to end without becoming buried by creative or technical details.

These executives thus direct both *above-the-line* and *below-the-line* operations. Above-the-line elements are generally considered to be the creative aspects of the project: actors, writers, directors, and the producers themselves. Below-the-line items are what we discuss in Chapter 11 as facilitative functions: camera people, designers, editors, and other craftspersons who technically execute the concept. Producers must bring integrative and cost-control skills to bear on both sides of

the line if the show is to have any hope of achieving its business and content goals.

Beyond these generalities, the producer's role can vary widely from company to company. In some series situations, different producers are assigned to monitor different episodes but with all of them reporting to the same *executive producer.* The executive producer has overall responsibility for the series and its direction and is more likely to have been involved in hiring the talent and technical expertise on which the series draws. A one-shot project, like a made-for-TV movie or a miniseries, may use the executive-producer title in a similar way, with individual producers assigned to individual segments of the projects. The project may even have *supervising producers* on the scene as intermediaries between the unit or field producers and the executive producer's office. However the workload is divided, "the producer is usually the center of the creative process," states *All in the Family* and *One Day at a Time* mastermind Norman Lear. "From working with the writers in the development of the treatment, to writing the teleplay, to casting, to rehearsal, to rewrite, to taping, to editing, to promoting the show, to the airing. . . . A producer, in my opinion, is someone who touches and effects the whole."[11]

At the top of the producer pyramid is the head of the production company or studio. In a very small organization, this executive may still function as a line producer, overseeing the actual assembly of individual projects. A corporate video unit or radio program packager is a likely environment for such a short chain of command. At the other end of the spectrum is the large studio with several series and other projects being developed simultaneously for both network and first-run syndication markets. Here, the organization's president or head is truly a chief executive officer (CEO) with several executive producers as immediate subordinates. Though this top executive may be called on to deal with major production crises (such as the threatened

**380**

SECTION
THREE

Profes-
sional
Perspec-
tives

## DANIELLE CLAMAN/MANAGER, TELEVISION SERIES DEVELOPMENT
### AARON SPELLING PRODUCTIONS

As manager of television series development for Aaron Spelling Productions, I've worked with the medium's most prolific and successful producer. Being associated with Spelling has given me a rarefied glimpse into the pantheon of producers, writers, directors, and network executives who determine and create the shows people watch each week.

Series development is creatively challenging because you are intimately involved in originating characters and their screen environment. Development demands the best of your creative and structural talents if you are to harvest successful programs. It also offers a great opportunity to launch yourself into other areas of the industry. If your ultimate goal is to produce series television yourself, development hones your people skills and calls on your ability to assemble the overall package that will make a series fly.

Staying abreast of new music, video, and artistic trends is an equally important although undervalued way to enhance the development of a project. These stylistic elements can make or break the tone of a new series. What would the now-classic *Miami Vice* pilot have been without Phil Collins's song "In the Air Tonight" underscoring the drama? Combining such elements to create a rich series franchise is essential for anyone who intends to develop or independently produce prime-time television.

As a pilot script takes shape, series developers are the liaison between agents and network executives. That script is one of *many* written during a given pilot season, so it must be designed to navigate successfully the often rough network seas. This entails staying keenly aware of the networks' needs for specific nights and time slots as well as knowing what other projects are already being generated.

As a development executive, you shepherd a show from the initial concept all the way to attaching a valuable director and star. *Agents* occupy their own special territory in the development process, trawling back and forth between the producers, network executives, and network-approved talent. Because they know the talent pool available to producers during the development season, agents comprise a unique and valuable resource. They have their own relationship with the networks. You rely on them to provide you with vital information that targets specific network needs, such as 8:00 high-concept shows or 10:00

hard-edged dramas. The development process then focuses on attaching a writer you believe will create intriguing characters and a desirable milieu. The creative crux of the development process comes into play at this juncture, as you and the writer work to bring the series to life on the page.

Even though it's an accomplishment to sell a pilot and get a series order, *keeping* the show on the air is a separate and equally difficult challenge. The network undoubtedly does some creative tinkering with the original concept to sustain an audience. Still, you can take steps to establish a beachhead for the future of the series. Staffing the show with writers capable of constructing storylines and characters that enhance the original concept will help ensure that the network executives stay true to your vision.

Series development is an absorbing and unique opportunity to interface with some of the best industry talents. This interaction with the creative community makes development a valuable learning experience and an essential component in the birth of prime-time series.

---

walk-out of a series star), for the most part, these CEOs concern themselves with setting top policy, planning goals, and determining priorities. Lower-level producers translate these decisions into completed projects. (You may wish, at this point, to review Lorimar President David Salzman's profile in Chapter 4.)

To a significant degree, network presidents and/or their programming vice-presidents are mirror images of the studio heads. These network executives are the customers whose business the studio producers are seeking. Even though their creative input is less direct, it nonetheless influences how program properties are produced—or whether a program is to be produced at all. Broadcast and cable networks have the capacity to give a show vast exposure. But a continuous pull-and-tug relationship remains between producing and network executives about the creative and scheduling decisions that determine how much positive exposure is actually achieved. In first-run syndication, program directors at key stations replace network executives in this give-and-take process, although the dynamics of the process itself remain much the same. Networks and stations are all in the business of manufacturing salable audiences, and it is the production executives who must develop and deliver the programmatic bait that lures these audiences into the appropriate media tent.

## Creative Directors

Even though the messages whose birth they oversee are much shorter, advertising agency creative directors are to commercials what producers are to programs. It is to the creative director that copywriters and art directors bring their scripts, layouts, and storyboards. Like any front-line producer, the creative director must then work with these conceptualizers to refine their message products so that they conform to the needs of the client. Here, the client is an advertiser with a certain market strategy. Commercials are expected to conform to this strategy while they

382

SECTION
THREE

Profes-
sional
Perspec-
tives

artfully and persuasively coax their target audience to watch or listen. The creative director thus must encourage art directors and copywriters to be innovative in message design while still adhering to the gameplan that an account executive (see the following section) has worked out with the client.

Creative directors almost always have been promoted to that directive post from the ranks of the copy or art departments. They thus have a certain affinity for the conceptual properties of the commercial. Nonetheless, it is their responsibility to ensure that a message always adheres to the business dictates of the client's marketing plan. Writers and artists occasionally may let an innovative idea meander off target, but a creative director is paid to nudge it back *on* target—even if that prized innovation must be reined in. Advertising executive Paul Goldsmith sketches the scene:

> When a creative person sits down to conceive an advertisement, he will often find it tempting to wander away from the agreed-upon strategy. Clearly, a desired quality is the discipline to keep the work within the confines of the product positioning. A scintillating piece of copy for a new car that highlights the fact that you need never carry a spare tire, when the strategy talks about better mileage, is a flop no matter how cleverly or brilliantly executed. "That's brilliant!" "That's funny!" "Beautifully done!" All are wasted words when the client says, "This is not the strategy we agreed upon."[12]

Creative directors, then, are selected not only for their past conceptual brilliance, but also for their demonstrated discipline in matching message execution to assignment goals.

Along the way, a creative director (like a program producer) must also keep the work flow moving so that projects are completed *on schedule*—even if a number of rewrites have had to be ordered. As one major agency's guidebook for its copywriter employees explained it, the creative director

is caught in a Quantity-Quality Squeeze. He's got to meet the quantitative demand, while satisfying the qualitative standards. So he sits in one of the hottest spots in the agency—if not *the* hottest.

He's paid to assume responsibility for copy on as many as half a dozen accounts. He's paid to supervise a number of talented people—often the hardest kind to handle—and to fit them all into the working day. He's paid to issue assignments, articulating the objectives as clearly as he can, in each and every case. He's paid to *inspire* his people to outdo themselves, and to see that they outdo themselves by the appointed hour.[13]

Pressure, as a result, is a big part of any creative director's job and the reason some writers and artists do not aspire to this position.

As with program producers, the creative director function tends to be exercised at more than one level as the size of the organization increases. A *group head,* for example, may be responsible for the work of several creative directors who all service the same large advertiser. A *creative vice-president* is the boss to whom all the group heads report. In a mid-sized agency, the group head post may be absent, with creative directors operating directly under the creative vice-president. Whatever the precise organizational chart, these executives must somehow maintain their directive perspective without losing a feel for their creative and conceptual roots. Some former creatives find this balancing act impossible to perform, especially at the larger agencies. "'There's more and more bull the higher you go,'" laments former agency creative director and president Malcolm MacDougall. "'And as agencies get bigger and bigger, you can go pretty high. You can even wind up sitting in boardrooms talking about the disaster that will befall the company should the yen fall.'"[14]

Somehow, astute creative directors manage to maintain their equilibrium. They can distance themselves from their staff's com-

**ROGER BODO**/GROUP CREATIVE DIRECTOR
INTERGROUP MARKETING AND PROMOTIONS

As a group creative director, the first thing you'll discover is that you are no longer a writer, art director, or producer trying to sell your idea or complete your task. You must now understand, assimilate, and integrate *everyone's* contributions. At every turn, it is your job to receive, translate, and transmit clear and focused communications. This will be *the* greatest challenge to your creativity because you are the person in the middle trying to keep everybody happy—including yourself.

So, what does all of this mean in terms of a typical day? First, it means you will spend a lot of time planning activities that will never happen.

Count on it. Some client or account executive will have had a bad anchovy pizza the night before and awakened with a brilliant idea for ads with paisley backgrounds. Now *you* have to make it happen. Immediately. So much for the two writers huddled over the coffee pot wringing their hands and moaning about not having any work. They are about to learn the true meaning of over-compensation.

Meanwhile, two art directors have been waiting impatiently at your door. Both are eager to air their differing points of view about the merits of nouveau art deco. Putting them back on track is a task, so both leave feeling confident in their ideas and head back to their work spaces to make those ideas even better.

What timing. Just as they leave, the phone rings with an excited client (or account executive) at the other end telling you to forget your trip to the sound studio to record that great new audio track. He wants to hear more voice auditions. Or, his legal department killed the really good stuff. Or, . . . whatever. There are as many idea killers out there as seconds on a stop watch. A quick meeting with your broadcast producer and more people than your office has square footage, and you finesse a solution. You change this word and that; play a few more voices over the phone and presto—everyone's happy. Except the writer you sacrificed and the announcer who just lost a booking. Smoothing their ruffled feathers is a job for later in the day. After all, it's still just 11:00 A.M.

Meanwhile, back in the conference room are three account executives with high anxiety and low tolerance levels who want to tell you all about the client who had the paisley dream. On the way to join them, you grab a writer and art director for support. But not before the business manager grabs you for a discussion of talent

SECTION
THREE

Profes-
sional
Perspec-
tives

payments, overages on the last commercial production, and late expense reports. After that, three account executives seem like a welcome relief; that is, *until* you hear them speak those dreaded words, "We need a full-court press here. The client expects three new ads first thing in the A.M." "Why first thing?" you ask. "Because we promised," that's why.

"Because we promised" is the number one cause of most hot deadlines and *all* cold pizzas. Neither are very appealing, and both haunt every working day. Signals change, often. Producers call with problems (sometimes solutions), and tempers flare. The air is electric. Amidst the static discharges, you create. And it's something good. The parking lot is dark and empty. Your dinner is 30 degrees beyond cold. But you created . . . and it's *good.*

Is it glamorous? Is it exciting? No. And, yes. There's nothing glamorous about working cheek to jowl with a lot of tired and sweaty people late into the night. There's nothing chic about cold pizza and midnight shadow. Or, about getting up before dawn day after day to catch first light to shoot a car. However, it is *always* exciting because it *always* challenging.

The work. The people. *The two together.* They make it worthwhile. More than that—they make it fun. They also make it possible to pack it up at the end of a day and go home, ready to come back and do it all again tomorrow—something I've been privileged to do now for almost twenty-five years.

mercials far enough to remain conceptually objective, but not so far that they can't appreciate a breakthrough execution or suggest how to attain such an execution. They can also sense "how high is too high" in terms of their own career ladders and what they most enjoy doing. Rejecting promotions to top management may be a good decision for people who want to stay involved in the idea side of the business—but there is a power price to pay. "'Being a creative person at some of these places is like being a woman at an English dinner party,'" cautions creative chief Ralph Rydholm. "'You get talked to, adored, even fawned over. But then, when the real business takes place, the men go off with their cigars and brandy.'"[15]

Some very small *boutique* agencies have been formed by disillusioned creative directors who want to own or manage their own shop while still being closely involved in the conceptual arena. Some of these boutiques have been notable successes. Some have gone bankrupt because their executives spread themselves too thin. Others have found that success only brought them full circle to the same quandary. As Grey Advertising's Chairman Ed Meyer has noticed, "'As a hot-shop boutique grows up and seeks to organize itself and its systems, as it attempts for the first time to reach the mass market instead of local markets or elite groups . . . larger clients begin to rein in the agency's high-flying impulses.'"[16]

Like writer-producers, creative directors in any setting must always play a split-personality role that encompasses both directive and creative responsibilities. Not everyone can perform such a juggling act or keep all the balls in the air for an extended period of time.

Like many jobs in our profession, creative director is a position you must grow into at your own pace but may *burn out of* much more quickly if you don't enjoy its multiple challenges.

---

## Account Executives and Managers

Account executives (AEs) perform a different kind of balancing act. While their responsibilities place them squarely on the directive (business) side of the advertising equation, they must also function as spokespersons for both the agency creative staff and the client. As the liaison between the client and the company charged with creating its advertising, the account executive must try to maintain two corporate loyalties with equal allegiance. On the one hand, the AE must try to sell the agency's creative work to the advertiser as an appropriate and effective response to that client's marketing needs. On the other hand, an account executive must convey client concerns and objections back to the creative team, even when these objections may result in scuttling advertisements of which that team is inordinately proud. Account Services Vice-President Tim Leon encapsulates AE performance this way: "As with any profession, there is a segment of our profession that aptly fits the term 'suit.' But there is a large contingent of account people who can walk the tight rope between creatives and clients and not sacrifice the integrity of good work. They can think on their feet, be the ultimate diplomats when need be and sell edgy, highly impactful advertising."[17]

Such delicate (and sometimes heated) back-and-forth negotiations are a constant test of an account executive's diplomatic and persuasive skills. The AE who slavishly panders to every client comment will lose the respect of agency creatives. They are likely to do less than their best because their work is never supported at the account level. Conversely, the account executive who presents creative work to a client on an uncompromising take-it-or-leave-it basis is likely to find the client and its business walking out the door in search of a more responsive agency.

The AE must strive to project a sense of objectivity toward both parties while keeping them both reasonably content and on the road toward a common goal. This cajoling must be done by account executives who are usually outranked by the people with whom they must communicate on both the client side and the agency side. Some senior AEs may acquire more clout, but in most cases this liaison executive must deal with creative directors at the agency and with marketing vice-presidents over at the client. Each of these forces can bring considerable muscle to bear on the less powerful account executive who is supposed to be servicing them. In a sense, the AE is like a United Nations peacekeeper. The two sometimes distrustful sides have all the weaponry, and it is your task to bring them together without getting shot in a crossfire.

In short, an account executive must perform a directive function while never actually seeming to direct anyone. Each side must perceive this executive as its loyal employee even though it is this employee who is centrally important in the clarifying and execution of advertising strategies. Along the way, the AE must acquire extensive knowledge about the client's business in order to analyze its long- and short-range sales problems. He or she must then be able to convey these problems clearly and accurately to the agency personnel whose creative output must address the issues. In dealings with the client, meanwhile, the account executive must be able to explain how the submitted advertisements meet client needs and mesh with client mar-

386

SECTION
THREE
Profes-
sional
Perspec-
tives

**ANDREW SCHMITTDIEL**/FIELD OPERATIONS DIRECTOR AND ACCOUNT EXECUTIVE
DDB NEEDHAM WORLDWIDE, ADVERTISING

The principal task for account service in general, and for account executives in particular, is to lead the account. This means possessing leadership capabilities in many business disciplines, including marketing, strategic planning, media, creative production, and budget administration.

Admittedly, the creative people create, the media people plan and negotiate, and the production people produce. But what they work on, the strategic thinking behind it, and the timeliness of the completed project are the responsibility of the account group and its executives. To achieve these ambitious tasks, you must know your client's product and competitive environment as well as, if not better than, the client or their competition themselves.

Once you have mastered the fundamental aspects of the business, you can study the human factor. This aspect of the business is the toughest part of any assignment: people management, to get the job done through other people. Motivating and managing your subordinates, your superiors, and your clients requires a personal commitment to working with people. All the business systems and personnel policies in the world are only as effective as people make them.

Perseverance is vital to the account executive's ultimate success. In today's competitive market place, there is no possibility of standing still. Either you continue to move forward or you fall behind. In spite of countless rejections and setbacks, a good account executive must continue to work for what is best for the client. As

an industry, advertising is one of the most competitive and dynamic fields in business today. Bright and talented people thrive in the challenges that face most advertisers, and advertising is one of the most visible and rewarding areas you can find. By rewarding, I speak of compensation over the long term and also of personal satisfaction. A former boss said you were underpaid your first ten years in the business and overpaid your last ten years.

An average day might include all or some of the following: 7 A.M. breakfast meeting; 8 A.M. agency staff meeting; two or three hours of telephone work and gathering field reports. Research presentations and analysis; writing call reports and endless memos; new sales presentations from media reps; and friendly and sometimes heated discussions with the creative group over the latest assignment. Reviewing production estimates, tracking budgets, forecasting agency income. Perusing the daily magazines and newspapers, tracking competitive activity and checking to see if your ad did run, as scheduled. Then you might have to catch a red-eye to the coast to sit in on a commercial production shoot or focus group. No matter what day you choose, one factor remains constant: Change. At any time, everything can and will change. So if you want a steady, orderly business environment, go into banking or insurance.

Where will you start your career? Most likely in the traffic department, or if you have spent summers in an agency intern program, maybe as an account coordinator. Smaller agencies, by necessity, combine many positions and responsibilities among a smaller group of people. Such combination jobs accelerate the learning curve, but the trade off is that you miss the benefit of getting in an agency on the ground floor and maturing through experience in consecutive rather than simultaneous positions.

The job is as fulfilling as it is challenging. We are always looking for bright, talented, and tenacious new members to join our industry. Take advantage of your school contacts to start your networking now. You will be amazed at how it will pay off down the road.

Welcome aboard and good luck!

---

keting plans. The executive must also be totally familiar with the agency's entire range of services so they can be called on as needed to help achieve client objectives.

Above all, the AE must be a *planner* so that agency output is sufficient for client marketing needs and is available at the agreed-on deadlines. An account which is marked by frantic last-minute responses to late-developing marketing plans is usually indicative of an account executive who is out of touch with the people or processes involved. Occasional problems may be someone else's fault, but they are still the AE's responsibility.

In recognition of the complexity and importance of this job, some agencies upgrade the position of account executive on larger assignments to *account manager*. This upgrade carries with it increased clout so that the manager is more a peer of counterpart creative directors and marketing vice-presidents. Junior account executives may also handle pieces of the business and report to this manager. As with the various ways the producer function can be shared, such a division of authority does not change the fundamental nature of the job, but it does better distribute the workload.

Recently, a number of stations have appropriated the title of *account executive* for their own salespersons. In so doing, they are signaling a shift in emphasis. Rather than just selling a client airtime, an account executive assists that advertiser with the production of commercials and the refinement of the marketing strategies that motivate those spots. Station account executives thus strive to provide the client with a total package of assistance that will solidify the business relationship between the advertiser and the AE's outlet. As a result, the thrust of the in-station account executive's duties is the same as that of their advertising agency namesake, but the end goal is to ensure business for a single media facility rather than for an agency, which may place client ads on several different stations.

388

SECTION
THREE
Profes-
sional
Perspec-
tives

# Media Services Executives

The placement of client advertising on various outlets is the job of media service executives. Working with the account executive and the appropriate client representatives, the media person determines which channels of communication to use and the specific vehicles to be selected within each channel. Outdoor (billboard), transit (displays on public transportation vehicles), direct mail (correspondence to individual homes), and newspaper and magazine layouts may all be used in addition to (or instead of) electronic media options. Any client, even the largest, has only so many dollars to spend on advertising placement. Thus, the media service executive's goal is to maximize the consumer impact that these dollars can buy. Saving just 2 percent on ad placements for a client like Burger King, for example, can mean that millions of dollars annually stay in BK's coffers.

Media buying services may exist as independent companies or as units within full-service advertising agencies. In independent companies, the client must derive and provide his or her own commercials and layouts. The buying service simply secures time and space and receives a commission back from the individual media vehicles it patronizes. A full-service agency, on the other hand, handles creative and other duties in exchange for the right to receive commissions from placing the client's advertising dollars. For special creative or consulting needs, the agency often charges the client a fee in addition to the media-derived commissions, but this fee is negotiated as part of a total service package.

Media planning and buying are sophisticated processes that rely on computer analysis and retrieval of a mass of cost and demographic information. The main principles of media selection would more than fill this textbook and so cannot be discussed in depth here. Fundamentally, however, any media plan must begin with decisions as to *reach*, *frequency*, and *cost* goals.

Chapter 11 discusses the cost-per-thousand (CPM) factor. An advertiser wishes to reach as many people as possible for money spent, but the types of people reached are an important consideration. That part of a station's audience not made up of potential prospects for the client's business is *waste circulation*. Thus, a station offering a low cost-per-thousand may not be a wise media buy if there is a lot of waste in its audience (such as over-thirty-five listeners on a station used by a pimple-cream manufacturer). Once these unwanted consumers are subtracted, the cost-per-thousand figure for the remaining *qualified prospects* might be unacceptably high. Media executives must decide if an outlet's audience composition merits a buy in terms of this specific client's *target universe* (desired audience).

Then there is the trade off between *reach* and *frequency*. *Reach* is how many qualified prospects will be exposed to the commercial via a certain media placement. *Frequency* is the number of times each of these prospects is likely to be exposed. Because almost all advertising depends on repetition in order to be remembered, any media buy must be calculated to deliver multiple *impressions* (contacts) with the listeners, viewers, or readers whom the advertiser is targeting.

The media services executive must manipulate these and many other specific variables to obtain the most cost-effective message circulation for any client. And with new media options and more sophisticated plans for segmenting the market appearing, the media buying job becomes more complex each day. "'In the last five years, there have been more changes in the media than there were in my first twenty years in the business,'" observes agency media department head Larry Spiegel. "'When I started in the advertising business and you wanted a packaged-goods item to reach a housewife with three kids it was

**JAY CAMPBELL**/BROADCAST SUPERVISOR
W.B. DONER & COMPANY ADVERTISING

**389**

CHAPTER 12
Directive
Functions

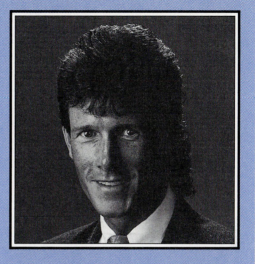

*Considering* a career in the electronic media and actually *having* one are completely different. It is essential for a student to study the development of all media prior to working in the field. Although this may seem irrelevant, you will come to appreciate your acquired knowledge throughout your career. A thorough education in your field will give you an opportunity to select from the array of positions available in the electronic media.

I held a few of these positions before becoming broadcast supervisor for W.B. Doner & Company Advertising. The experiences acquired in each job helped set the stage for my current responsibilities.

I now oversee the placement of radio and television advertising by a group of media buyers, work with a media director to establish fiscal year media plans and budgets, and coordinate computer information relating to media schedules.

One of my duties as broadcast supervisor is to ensure that each media buyer maintains a set of established guidelines as he or she places advertising time for a product or service. There may be a reason for buying spots within a specific program in one market and not in another or a rationale for including an AOR station as part of a radio buy. Knowing a media buyer's style and having a good grasp of changes in the market related not only to media but also to the overall economy aid in formulating media decisions. Working directly with the client on questions related to media execution strategies can be a bit trying, but with sound rationale and good communication abilities the experience can be enlightening for both.

In this position there are reams of information related to programming, ratings, and media vehicles that assist in the media selection. These pieces of data are essential. However, we cannot forget that we are targeting our advertising to people like ourselves and want to do so in a creative, appealing manner. This is where an open media mind will set you apart. Maintain the rules of media planning, but do it with a twist. This will keep your thinking fresh and have other people looking to you for creative media ideas.

The amount of respect you receive from professionals in your field is related directly to the amount of experience you've encountered and learned from in your career. The electronic media are constantly changing and thrive on individuals who break new ground. Don't be afraid to take risks. With a bit of research and creative thinking you'd be amazed at the possibilities; just turn on your radio or television.

390

SECTION
THREE
Profes-
sional
Perspec-
tives

easy. You used television and a few magazines. Now it's not that simple. . . . Basically, media should be as creative as creative is creative.'"[18]

To better exercise this media buying function, most agency media departments consist of multiple levels. *Assistant buyers* are entry-level persons whose main task is to execute and track the specific decisions made by their superiors. Above them, *buyers* exercise more latitude in determining which vehicles will be bought within a given medium. They may, for example, be given a radio budget of $150,000 with which to purchase a certain number of *gross rating points* (GRPs) emphasizing certain demographic groups. The buyer chooses the stations, either by working with outlet sales people themselves or with station reps. *Associate buying directors* and *buying directors* have greater responsibility and may be involved in discussions with the client about how to apportion the advertising budget among the various types of media (radio, television, outdoor, etc.) and help set campaign reach/frequency/impression goals.

At the top of the pyramid, the *head of media services* (or a similarly titled executive) oversees the media budgeting and buying activities for all of the agency's clients. This job may include combining time or space purchase orders for several separate clients or products in order to obtain a better volume discount (a cheaper rate) for all concerned. This executive may be involved in the production of barter program series created specifically to carry client advertising. Proctor & Gamble's mounting of a soap opera in conjunction with its advertising agency is one example of such activity.

As with studio producers, the smaller the shop, the shorter is the media department's hierarchy and the greater the combining of responsibilities. The essential ingredients of the media service executive's job are the same across a buying unit of any size, however. The job includes (1) helping the client set audience delivery goals, (2) determining the media apportionment best calculated to reach these goals, (3) selecting the specific media vehicles for the buy, (4) negotiating the best possible rate for time or space, (5) tracking the buy to make certain advertisements run as scheduled, and perhaps (6) cooperating in follow-up research to ascertain the effectiveness of the overall media plan. In many agencies, an associated *traffic department* may coordinate the actual distribution of message material to the media outlets and assume the auditing function entailed in task 5, tracking the buy.

Media services is neither the most glamorous part of our profession nor the most visible. For years, admits media executive Paul Benjou, "agency media departments held the tarnished reputation for breeding dull, uninteresting people and churning out dry, dusty, cookie-cutter media presentations. Finally, having come of age, media professionals are just now enjoying a spirited move to the front line."[19] Unquestionably, the decisions made by executives in this branch of our business substantially impact the financial well-being of every commercial station, cable system, and network and consequently the job security of the people who work at them. If you get along well with quantifiable data (in other words, math), are a systematic planner, and love to bargain, then there may be a satisfying future for you in a media services position.

## Owners

Speaking of future prospects, the people who seem most able to chart their own fates are the people who own outlets, agencies, and other entities associated with the electronic media. Owners, it would seem, can exercise the ultimate in directive functions and determine the entire shape of our profession.

In fact, however, most owners are just as

susceptible to continuing restrictions and un-anticipated events as are the rest of us. Competitive business pressures, changing governmental regulations, economic fluctuations, key staff turnover, and technical malfunctions/limitations are but a few of the forces that impinge on and limit an owner's options.

The discretionary power of ownership is also impacted, of course, by how the company is organized. At one end of the spectrum is the *sole owner,* who holds full title to the enterprise and is the direct beneficiary or victim of any profit or loss. Many stations, cable systems, advertising agencies, and even networks (recall Chapter 7) were created by individual entrepreneurs who built them from the ground up. Such closely held companies were a family business, and that family's fortunes rose or fell with how the business itself fared. In most instances, however, there is a limit to how far a single-owner entity can grow before it must diversify control in order to stay healthy. Ironically, the more successful a media company becomes, the more it becomes necessary to bring in outside money and partners to sustain growth and maintain its competitive position. (Review our discussion of private and publicly held companies in Chapter 3.)

In the case of stations, a single independently owned outlet may have difficulty competing with same-market rivals that are part of a multiple-outlet group. Because it owns stations in several markets, a group can negotiate first and hardest for programs because syndicators can secure carriage in several markets with a single deal. A group also has a better chance of securing lucrative regional and national advertising because its size makes it a more appealing client for the larger rep firms who, in turn, have access to the larger agencies and their media budgets. Even the day-to-day operations of the group station can be run more economically because the group can secure volume purchase discounts on everything from paper clips to transmission line. The situation, in short, is

not much different from the corner grocery store trying to compete with several chain supermarkets. It is possible to survive, but only if the independent's owner is extremely responsive to customer needs and takes special pains to deliver unique local services.

Station groups may be the possession of a sole owner, of course, but the number of individuals with the financial resources to build and maintain such an enterprise is limited. Furthermore, the FCC's liberalization of ownership rules from 7–7–7 to 12–12–12 (see Chapter 6) has meant that the more powerful, multiple-owner chains began to enlarge their holdings at the expense of smaller, less financially flexible groups. Smaller groups have thus been swallowed up by a larger entity or broken up in piecemeal sales to different companies with outlet needs in different markets.

The larger the group becomes, the more likely it will broaden its ownership base from a few individuals and their companies to a larger participation by banks and investment entities outside the broadcast industry. Ultimately, the corporation might move (as we discuss in Chapter 3) to publicly traded status, with stocks being sold on the open market and boards of directors concerned with moving as much money to the bottom line—and stockholder dividend checks—as possible. Even the networks were not immune to these forces in the 1980s. Many people now lament that the broadcasting business is no longer run by the media professionals who founded and developed it but rather by outside financiers who see broadcasting as serving no higher calling than any other goods-and-services enterprise.

Either to increase their own ownership interests or to fight off take-over attempts by outsiders, many broadcast entities were forced to borrow large sums of money from banks or through limited partnerships, stock sales, or other instruments. The monthly interest due on these borrowed funds thus increased station/network operating expenses and required leaner and meaner running in

392

SECTION
THREE

Profes-
sional
Perspec-
tives

## THOMAS ELKINS/OWNER AND GENERAL MANAGER
KNUI/KHUI

Tomorrow is payday. Had collections come in at their normal rate, you would have every right to expect that the payroll would be covered. But they didn't—and now, barring a miracle, you're going to be $20,000 overdrawn.

No sweat. You've got $150,000 worth of account receivables, (money owed to the station for advertising that has already run). But the accounts haven't paid yet. And that's what banks are for, right?

You present yourself at the bank. You are ushered into the president's office, and he says, "Now, what was that problem again?" You tell him that you are on the brink of being $20,000 overdrawn and you'd like a loan on your receivables. He frowns. This is serious business. He looks over your financial statements, obviously for the first time. Then he tells you he might let you have $10,000. You tell him that isn't enough, and point out the $150,000 in receivables. He asks what else you have.

You finally confess, "Well, I've got a house."

"How much is your first mortgage?"

"$55,000."

His eyes light up; he's got you.

"I think we can work a line of credit against that property," he says. The next problem is convincing him that he's got to cover you tomorrow. He will.

Then you head back to the station, somewhat relieved. The immediate problem is solved, but the long-range cash-flow problem remains. What's worse, you're the only one in the whole operation who can know how bad things really are. Sales people

have to stay upbeat or it'll affect their positive attitudes calling on advertisers. Your air staff can't know or they'll start thumbing through *Broadcasting* and sending out tapes.

Now you're looking at a second mortgage on your house and additional interest payments every month. But believe me, every day when people ask, "How are things going?" You really want to tell them. Instead, you smile confidently and tell them, "Great."

It takes a lot of ego to hold that position. You have to accept that on any day at least one (and probably several) of your staff thinks you are stupid. There's nothing you can do about that. It's possible that many on your staff are smarter than you in one category. But you know about the whole operation, about the community, and about the industry.

You are part programmer, journalist, salesperson, promoter, engineer, and bookkeeper. If pressed, you can do the logs and send out the bills.

You mollify the advertiser who is mad at your morning deejay. You mollify your morning deejay and convince him that we must allow advertisers their eccentricities.

You greet the man from the FCC when he comes to call and show him what he wants to see. If he finds any irregularities, you correct them and submit the necessary written response to your Notice of Violation. It's a job you can't delegate—and you wouldn't even if you could; the stakes are too high. But this morning, your news director thinks you're stupid because he's been leading with the same story—without even a rewrite—for the past 24 hours and you finally told him to kill it. Your sales manager thinks you just don't understand because you pointed out that an advertiser occupying one of the slots in "Paul Harvey" hasn't paid in four months and that slot is too valuable to waste.

I'm not suggesting that you feel sorry for the GM. He has his share of perks. He gets to play golf and call it business. He takes more trips than anyone else and nobody argues with his expense account. For the most part, it isn't a bad life. But it took some doing to reach that position.

GMs come in all shapes and sizes. I am an entrepreneurial GM. I own the business and run it. There are many more like me in broadcasting than there are of the large corporate GMs, although possibly not in major markets and certainly not in television. The GM of a large station worries a lot less about meeting the payroll than I do. He certainly doesn't have to take a second mortgage on his house. But his job is at risk if he fails too often, and it's tied directly to the bottom line.

This is an edited version of a June 1989 speech to the National Broadcast Editorial Association, when Elkins accepted the NBEA's Management Award.

order to divert more income to *debt service* (interest and principle payments). This phenomenon occurred in both radio and television, of course, but the dollar amounts were much larger in television, where both incomes and operating expenses are substantially higher. Viewing these trends, former executive director of the Television Information Office Lynne Grasz has argued:

When history looks back at television in 1989, there will surely be a footnote to the year. What history reports about television's apparently wide pendulum swing in 1989 may be characterized as the year television lost its conscience.

Television priorities did change. To some, that change was obvious and dramatic, perhaps as a reaction to the previous year's buyouts and mergers, the continuing decline of network share, the evolving technologies and the impact of cable and VCR viewing. As many in the industry have said, 1989 was the year stations paid more attention to debt service than public service.[20]

It should be noted that Ms. Grasz's comments were penned when the broadcast industry decided it could no longer financially support the thirty-year-old Television Information Office, an agency dedicated to publicizing the strengths and values of over-the-air TV. None-

394

SECTION
THREE
Profes-
sional
Perspec-
tives

theless, the thrust of her arguments have been echoed by many other veteran broadcasters who have seen the directive functions in the industry shift more and more from general managers' and group executives' offices to Wall Street and outside boards of directors.

Similar forces have been at work in the cable arena as well. Individual systems have been combined into large MSOs (*multiple-system owners*), and the MSOs themselves have diversified by obtaining financial interests in cable networks and program production houses. Furthermore, even though FCC rules prohibit single ownership of a television station and cable system in the same market, many electronic media companies now operate both stations and systems in separate locales. NBC and ABC have extensive stakes in cable networks, too, as their parent companies seek to hedge their bets and maintain audience levels via any combination of delivery systems necessary. Electronic media ownership patterns are thus more complex than before, especially in terms of the larger players, who are increasingly coming to dominate the industry. Such a vast infusion of new capital and new business interests into the electronic media has brought a wealth of new professional opportunities, but it has also made the concerns of ownership much more like that of any other commercial enterprise. The old concept of the self-contained broadcast or cable company that was thought to have a higher public service calling than other business ventures is probably gone forever.

Advertising agencies were even more subject in the eighties to consolidations, takeovers, and buy-outs. In several instances, ultimate ownership passed to overseas interests in Great Britain, France, Japan, or Australia. (This might have happened with broadcast stations, except that the Communications Act prohibits foreign ownership of stations.) As with the electronic media, their advertising agency customers are now driven by profit-and-loss concerns that transcend what is happening in the individual company itself. The fortunes of the giant parent and its partners,

investors, or stockholders have pushed final directive authority into higher, more global, and more remote board rooms. (The same condition pertains to some of the largest U.S. movie studios, which also have been purchased by overseas interests.)

Key advertising executives, who would formerly have spent most of their careers within a single shop, are now likely to jump from one agency chain to another, thereby blurring the creative distinctiveness that used to set each agency apart. As advertising industry observer Richard Morgan sees it, there is

nothing wrong with these moves, aside from their being inconceivable a few years ago, except they do transform the industry into a machine of interchangeable parts. They do move agencies closer to the category of commodities—as classically defined. (An ominous aside: commodities, as classically defined, compete only on price.)

This trend is in keeping with the rest of industry. Charles Fombrun, a professor of organizational strategy at New York University, says global and technological forces have imposed "major realignments" on many industries. When these realignments lead to takeovers, he adds, you can count on 50 percent of the team taken over being gone within three years. So much for corporate culture in the era of takeovers.[21]

If you want to run your own independent piece of "corporate culture," and you still want to do it in the electronic media, your options are limited. Perhaps you could build an LPTV station (see Chapter 2) to serve a small town or city neighborhood. Yet, even here, outlets are being consolidated into groups, and unlike conventional stations, there is no limit on the number of facilities a single group can own. A wireless cable (MMDS) operation is another possibility, but the costs and uncertainties surrounding this business have restricted it to a relatively few multisystem players. Maybe you could build an SMATV service in a posh condominium development and then hope that a cable system won't try to

**RUTH WHITMORE**/OWNER AND PRESIDENT
WHITMORE COMMUNICATIONS, INC.

Whitmore Communications is a small (fewer than twenty employees) advertising agency specializing in health care, hotel, and high-tech accounts. When you run your own agency and are competing with larger shops, there is no such thing as a typical day. What follows are segments from several days that provide an overall flavor of the challenges I face.

6:15 A.M.
Radio alarm goes off. Fax last night's updates, memos, and purchase orders to clients and suppliers.

7:30 A.M.
Breakfast meeting with a production rep concerning a client's order for oversized pocket calendars.

8:30 A.M.
Meeting at the offices of a distinguished public relations consultant who would like our two firms to joint-venture on a prospective account. Based on his telephone briefing the week before, I present the research we collected on the account and what types of advertising recommendations seem appropriate, at this early stage of the pitch. He outlines what his public relations recommendations will be, and we fine-tune our joint proposal. We also discuss our competitors for the account, analyzing what their strengths will be and how we can counter our strengths against their vulnerabilities.

9:30 A.M.
Call the office for messages and adjust my afternoon schedule to squeeze in a client request for a meeting.

10:00 A.M.
Travel to a local music production studio to review their demo, which the client selected from among four production tapes. We discuss how many usages the final music package will be required to fit, the mix of ethnic vocalists, a recommended lead singer, and adjustments to the lyrics. We agree to hold production until they can submit a price for the total, revised package.

11:00 A.M.
Back at the office, returning phone calls and reviewing materials prepared by my secretary. Most of the work I do at my desk, with lunch ordered in, involves projects that will come due in the next three days to five weeks. Today, this includes talking to a Baltimore photographer about a shoot in Chicago next week. There are also a variety of housekeeping tasks such as unsnarling a letter from the state tax department, locating insurance

396

SECTION
THREE

Profes-
sional
Perspec-
tives

forms, signing checks, reviewing invoices before they are mailed to clients, and tracking down a printing job that was delivered to the client but apparently received by the wrong department. The most important work this day focuses on a presentation I'll be making for an account with nearly $1 million in annual billings. The pitch is this afternoon, and I have to squeeze in that sudden existing-client meeting just before. I notify the art director who will be working on the new account with me—if we get it.

2:30 P.M.

After the client meeting, the art director and I leave for the new business pitch, reviewing our parts for the presentation. Their CEO is a young, highly successful entrepreneur who is impatient for results. The art director suggests a more dynamic way of presenting his work samples that will appeal more to a high-energy CEO. I agree that it's a terrific idea and we rework the order of our materials to capitalize on this angle.

3:20 P.M.

We are shown to an empty conference room, where the original interviewer, with whom I had previously talked, soon joins us. She informally reviews the presentation groundrules. We make small talk, but I can't resist asking her how many other firms they're interviewing. "You're the only *small* one," she says.

3:30 P.M.

The CEO arrives promptly and is warm in his manner and hospitality. The presentation proceeds as informal conversation (our preferred style), inviting their ques-

tions and receiving comments. Because the interviewer told us that agency smallness is a severe handicap, I address it head on. Agencies specialize in many ways, I tell the CEO. You need to find an agency that possesses (1) the special skills you require, (2) the level of taste and quality you demand, and (3) people you feel comfortable working with. I present a brief overview of types of agencies by size, specialization, focus, and service orientation. This provides the backdrop for my segue into my agency's profile as a known creative performer, detail-conscientious, service-intensive, and quick on turnaround. I also stress my seven years with ABC-owned radio and TV stations to underscore our familiarity with big league performance. The CEO is engaging, articulate, and knowledgeable. He asks very good questions.

When we wrap up, he asks, "What are your long-range plans as an agency, Ruth?"

This is usually a question I get for being a woman with a wedding ring—a question designed to elicit some assurance that I won't suddenly have babies and leave the day-to-day work to junior staffers. (One of my clients even has a clause in our contract that if my services are ever taken over by other account staff, the contract is null and void.)

But he's not asking *that* question, I surmise. He's asking the question I love to answer. I want, I tell him, to become an agency with $20 million in annual billings, representing accounts of $1 to 2 million a piece so that no one account dominates the agency; an agency delivering high-caliber creative and service with experienced, talented career professionals covering approximately eighteen full-time positions. That's good work for the client and the agency, and a good life-style. More than that is too many headaches; smaller than that inhibits the sense of challenge. He smiles. He thanks us for our time. As he's taking his leave of us, he says, "Good presentation."

4:45 P.M.
No drive back from a new business presentation is complete without overanalyzing and overkill scrutiny.

5:30 P.M.
Drop off the art director, head for 6:00 P.M. meeting with a freelance artist.

6:00 P.M.
The art work is good. I sign off on the invoices he submits and ask him to appraise the rush jobs my client gave me this afternoon. He'll call me later with cost estimate.

7:30 P.M.
Home. The answering machine has a call from my husband that he's running late, a call from the Baltimore photographer returning my call, and several follow-up messages from my secretary.

force its way onto the property. A number of small AM stations are for sale, but can you lure enough listeners to the AM band long enough to sample your signal? Maybe a boutique advertising agency that specializes in top-notch commercial creation could be your business. But what happens when your clients outgrow the services you can provide?

The point here, of course, is that certain electronic media ownership opportunities always present themselves. Many of these opportunities are comparatively small and risky ventures. Those that do succeed must usually grow in order to sustain that success, which means raising outside capital. Beyond a certain point, capital needs can be met only by sharing ownership rather than by borrowing money. The ultimate directive function of possession must therefore be shared as well.

This is why, in today's media world, many top professionals prefer to be managers with perhaps a small piece of ownership. Such an arrangement motivates them to do their best on behalf of the enterprise while preserving their personal flexibility to move on to other ventures. As we discuss in this chapter, all directive roles in our profession encompass weighty responsibilities. The roles entailing ownership involve the additional factor of significant financial risk. At some point in your career, you may have to decide how much of this risk you wish to assume.

## CHAPTER FLASHBACK

*Directive* functions are performed by executives whose decision making determines how electronic media personnel and material resources are used in serving the requirements of clients and the preferences of audiences.

*Program directors* (PDs) shape and schedule content progression in a manner calculated to attract intended listeners or viewers.

398

SECTION
THREE

Profes-
sional
Perspec-
tives

In radio, this means maintaining and refining a particular format that is most likely to appeal to an audience sliver attainable in that particular market and of interest to an identifiable group of advertisers. Television PDs, like their radio counterparts, must make decisions in light of what competing stations are airing. However, the TV program director focuses on individual and often divergent shows rather than on a single uniformly targeted format. Independent station programmers have a much greater task than do their network-affiliate counterparts because they must fill the entire schedule themselves. Cable system programmers pick and arrange complete program services to use available *shelf space* in a way that will garner the most revenue.

*Sales managers* direct the efforts of the people selling air time on their outlet. They must be skilled forecasters and motivators. Together with the facility's program director and *general manager* (GM), they must decide when *barter* and *trade-out* deals can replace cash sales. The general manager (or *system manager* in cable) has the ultimate responsibility for how the facility is run—primarily in overseeing profit and loss. Comptrollers and credit managers may help the GM keep track of cash flow and threats to it. *News directors* must make certain that money spent in news gathering can increase the outlet's visibility and demographic salability. In radio, the news director may be the only full-time journalist, but at a news-active television station, staffs of twenty or more are common. Some cable systems are also moving into local news

coverage, sometimes in cooperation with a local newspaper, radio, or television station.

*Entertainment producers* work at studios and similar enterprises to fashion program product that will be of interest to media outlets. *Writer-producers* are coming to be especially prominent in creating and packaging scripts. Their power accrues from their past successes, which enhance the prospects for their future properties. A variety of other producer titles are also used in the business to describe varying degrees of responsibility for program series and episode development.

Within advertising agencies, creative directors are to commercials what producers are to programs. Creative directors must lead copywriters and art directors in turning out on-strategy commercials within client-mandated time frames. *Account executives* serve a crucial liaison function between the creative directors and the clients, working as the guardians of each party's best interests in dealing with the other. *Media services executives* cooperate with these account executives in selecting the outlets best suited to reach target consumers in the most cost-effective manner.

The ultimate decision makers in our enterprise, as in any other, are the *owners*. Their power may be immense or diluted depending on the fiscal organization of the company. Government regulations also limit owner prerogatives, as do business conditions in general. Consequently, many top professionals prefer to retain career flexibility by remaining as full-time managers with perhaps a minority ownership share.

❑ Review Probes
_____

1. What is *waste circulation?* How might it undermine a program director's seeming success at generating substantial audience numbers?
2. Define *strip, checkerboard,* and *vertical* programming as well as *tentpoling* and *hammocking.*

3. What is the difference between delivering *share-of-market* and delivering *budget?* Who determines what standard is to be used and to which employees that standard is applied?
4. What did Edward R. Murrow call "an incompatible combination of show business, advertising and news"? What is the title of the executive responsible for each of these functions?
5. What is a *boutique* shop and why is it difficult for such an operation to remain small?
6. Why is the job of account executive sometimes referred to as "controlled schizophrenia"?

## ❏ Suggested Background Explorations

Goedkoop, Richard J. *Inside Local Television News.* Salem, WI: Sheffield Publishing Company, 1988.

Heighton, Elizabeth J., and Don R. Cunningham. *Advertising in the Broadcast and Cable Media.* 2nd ed. Belmont, CA: Wadsworth, 1984.

Hewitt, Don. *Minute by Minute.* New York: Random House, 1985.

Hilliard, Robert L., ed. *Television Station Operations and Management.* Boston: Focal Press, 1989.

Keith, Michael C. *Radio Programming: Consultancy and Formatics.* Boston: Focal Press, 1987.

Lavine, John M., and Daniel B. Wackman. *Managing Media Organizations: Effective Leadership of the Media.* New York: Longman, 1988.

Lazer, William. *Handbook of Demographics for Marketing and Advertising.* Lexington, MA: Lexington Books, 1987.

Marcus, Norman, *Broadcast and Cable Management.* Englewood Cliffs, NJ: Prentice-Hall, 1986.

Marlow, Eugene. *Managing Corporate Media.* Rev. ed. White Plains, NY: Knowledge Industry Publications, 1989.

Oringel, Robert, and Sue Buske. *The Access Manager's Handbook: A Guide for Managing Community Television.* Boston: Focal Press, 1987.

# Evaluative and Analytical Functions

❏ *Our final chapter on professional pro-spectives is distinct from the previous three in that it examines the role of professionals who function primarily outside of the electronic media's outlets, production houses, and advertising agencies. Nonetheless, these evaluators and analyzers are essential to our industry's well-being and further development. Taken together, they provide the governmental linkages, financial appraisals, training progressions, information systems, and critical commentary by which the electronic media's activities are shaped and promoted. Any profession can be only as vigorous as its support systems and the people who staff them, and so it is important to know who these staffers are.*

## Regulators

Even though there is a tendency to see them more as enforcers than as supporters, industry regulators serve a protective as well as a disciplinary function. Evenhanded rules that are impartially enforced create a stable and consistent operating environment for the players involved. As we explore in Chapter 6, broadcasting could never have emerged as a serious business in the late 1920s if the federal government had not taken steps to bring order to the airwaves. A central outcome of the 1927 Radio Act and the Communications Act that followed seven years later was the establishment of an orderly allocation of a spectrum within which legitimate interests could conduct their business. No serious investors or advertisers would have bothered with a communication enterprise made up of frequency hoppers and unpredictable reception. Once the government had cleaned up the spectrum and properly defined its uses, advertiser and audience services were free to prosper.

Subsequent regulation in other areas was not so welcomed by broadcasters, of course. Ownership restrictions on who could operate what and content strictures such as the equal time law (Section 315) and the Fairness Doctrine inhibited broadcasters in ways unexperienced by their print media competitors. The fact that all mass media are not subject to equal regulation has been a subject of more or less continuous debate for more than sixty years. Meanwhile, decrees like the Prime Time Access Rule (PTAR), multiple-ownership limits, and the network financial interest and syndication restrictions (*fin/syn*) have been hailed by some elements of the electronic media establishment and decried by others, depending on whose particular business was enhanced and whose was inhibited.

On the whole, however, the electronic media have profited more than lost from a federal regulatory system that has stabilized their operating environment and largely shielded them from potentially more quarrelsome state and local legislation. Contrary to what one would be led to believe from a few highly publicized FCC/industry clashes, the two forces have tended to work in more a consultative than a combative role. As communications law experts Erwin Krasnow and Lawrence Longley astutely point out,

At least to some degree the administrator [in this case, the FCC] can legitimately see his charge as including the preservation and encouragement of the regulated industry. The crux of this problem, then, is determining to what degree this goal should be subservient to other considerations, in particular to a larger conception of the public interest. . . . On a day-to-day basis, commissioners are forced to immerse themselves in the field they propose to regulate; however, the line between gaining a familiarity with an industry's problems and becoming biased thereby in favor of that industry is perilously thin. It is difficult for commissioners and their staff to operate closely with an industry without coming to see its problems in industry terms.[1]

Overall, then, broadcasting was helped much more than hurt by FCC oversight from the 1930s into the 1980s. This was especially true in terms of the commission's protection of free TV against competing technologies. As we have already discussed, over-the-air subscription television (STV) was delayed for some thirty years and cable was tightly controlled for more than two decades in order to preserve regular television's turf.

Many broadcasters came to appreciate this protection only after they had lost it. In the early 1980s, President Reagan's FCC chairman, Mark Fowler, announced his intention to initiate sweeping deregulation of the industry. At first welcomed by the radio/television establishment, these policies were soon shown to be a dual-edged sword. On the one hand, broadcasters were now much more free to make decisions as to program content and day-to-day operational matters. But on the other hand, they were no longer to be artificially insulated against new competition or against unfair practices by existing competitors. Fowler aides began to speak of a social Darwinism in which the marketplace should be able to decide which stations and which delivery systems would survive. "It is not the federal government's job to protect an unpopular station from bankruptcy" was a theme stressed over and over. Television, according

**401**

CHAPTER 13
Evaluative
and
Analytical
Functions

402

SECTION
THREE

Profes-
sional
Perspec-
tives

## PATRICIA DIAZ DENNIS
ATTORNEY AND FORMER FCC COMMISSIONER

It is the best of jobs; it is the worst of jobs. As an FCC commissioner, I worked on the cutting edge of the information age, helping plot this nation's communications policy and working with some of the most talented civil servants in the federal government. It was an incredible opportunity to grapple with the long-term public issues affecting our nation's competitiveness into the next century, not just the private concerns of how to make a profit tomorrow. Yet, I faced a daunting task in trying to stay abreast of developments across the entire spectrum of the communications world. Inevitably, each commissioner picks a few favorite issues or areas on which to concentrate. Of particular interest to me were the media issues of structural regulation and the promotion of diversity of viewpoint.

Spend an average week with a commissioner and at least a day is on the road. Commissioners speak at annual meetings of such organizations as the National Association of Broadcasters, the United States Telephone Association, and the Broadcast Financial Management Association. Or a commissioner can be in a foreign country, as I was, at a convening of the International Telecommunications Union to discuss the coordination and assignment of worldwide spectrum for radio and television broadcasting, or orbital slots and frequencies for satellites. I also attended meetings of the National Association of Regulatory Commissioners to discuss joint federal-state regulation of the telephone industry.

Other days, back in Washington, DC, found me meeting with a variety of communications groups, both during business hours and at evening receptions. Much of my time was spent with industry representatives, including lawyers and other advocates who walk the halls of the FCC, presenting information and arguments. I also met often with elected members of Congress or their staff. The FCC and Congress have a close and almost daily working relationship.

Wherever I was, I had to remember that I was always on stage. Industry representatives and Wall Street analysts hang on a commissioner's every word, trying to read the tea leaves and anticipate future commission decisions that can revise the ground rules for a communications business. Journalists constantly question commissioners and pour over copies of their speeches. A commissioner has to be on guard against rash comments, which could have a dramatic effect on stock prices.

**403**

CHAPTER 13
Evaluative
and
Analytical
Functions

The bulk of the commissioners' week is spent in their offices at the FCC headquarters in Washington, DC, where most of the commission's 2,000 employees work. A commissioner relies on a personal staff of three professionals who draft separate statements and memoranda for the commissioner, negotiate with the staff of other commissioners and with FCC bureau staffs, and help the commissioner make decisions. In the end, however, it is the commissioner who must read the information, listen to the arguments, and come to a conclusion on about 600 matters that come before the commission for decision each year.

Reflecting their unique backgrounds, each commissioner approaches the job differently. Because I was trained as a lawyer and served as a presidential appointee at another agency, I came to the FCC with a heightened appreciation for the importance of due process. How a regulatory agency reaches a decision is often more important than the decision itself. If affected parties believe their views were not fully considered, this can cast a cloud over the decision. The FCC must often balance conflicting interests: broadcasters versus cable operators; urban residents versus rural inhabitants; large corporations with private communications networks versus public switched network subscribers. A most difficult part of the job is guarding against the influence of personal friendships. Yet, as commissioners come to know the individuals who represent the contending interests, they learn, of necessity, to respect the assertions of some and distrust others.

Often, it seems that a commissioner can never please anyone—half hate the decision you make and the other half become ingrates who thought they deserved to win all along. I trust my three years at the FCC will be respected for my principled decision making. The tangible evidence of my legacy is the 1988 U.S. Court of Appeals decision on broadcast indecency in *Action for Children's Television* v. *F.C.C.*, which relied on my separate opinion. This was a highpoint, because rarely does a court give such credit to a commissioner. I tried to live up to the motto of North Carolina, which is "to be rather than to seem." Too often, the governing creed is the opposite.

---

to Fowler, was not much different than a "popcorn popper" or a "toaster with pictures"—the marketplace would determine which brands would succeed and which would fail without any interference from the federal government.

Suddenly, broadcasters faced unchained rivals like cable, STV, DBS, LPTV, and a reinvigorated MDS (multipoint distribution system) that would now, as MMDS, enjoy multiple channels (see Chapter 2). At the same time, with quantitative guidelines removed for nonentertainment program requirements and the number of commercials that could be aired per hour, every station was now free to go its own way. Under the old system, a broadcaster knew that the competitor down the street had to operate under the same commercial load restrictions as did his or her outlet. And everyone had to devote a certain amount of air time to those public affairs discussions that large audiences avoided.

404

SECTION
THREE
Profes-
sional
Perspec-
tives

But in a deregulated environment, this comforting predictability was gone; and competition became much more volatile.

Even more unsettling was the fact that the FCC would no longer protect a station from clearly unfair practices by its rivals. As communications attorney Arthur Goodkind prophesied in 1984,

> Broadcast deregulation has two faces. On the one hand, deregulation means that broadcasters can spend less time and effort in complying with FCC rules and regulations. Yet at the same time, deregulation also means that the FCC will be far less available than in the past to protect responsible broadcasters from illegal or unethical practices on the part of their competitors. For that protection, station operators will in the future need to look increasingly to the courts and to other methods of self-help. . . . If, for example, a radio licensee operates with excessive power or fails to do what is necessary to keep its directional antenna in correct adjustment, other stations directly or competitively affected must now assume a major new burden in detecting, recording and reporting violations of the commission's rules.[2]

This same shift in regulatory philosophy, of course, also resulted in FCC refusal to select a single standard for AM stereo, thus undercutting the viability of both that technology and the band it was intended to help.

With the help of Congress via the Cable Communications Policy Act of 1984, the FCC also lifted a number of regulatory burdens from that industry. As of this writing, in fact, many policy makers believe that these actions created a virtually unregulated monopoly, with systems able to charge whatever fee they wish for whatever service they wish to provide. The Cable Act largely put state and local cable regulatory bodies out of the picture because that federal law preempted and voided much, if not most, of the authority they had previously exercised.

In terms of today's electronic media, then, what regulation exists is first and foremost the province of the FCC and its five commissioners. The number of commissioners was reduced from seven as a government streamlining move effective June 1983. This action gave each commissioner substantially more influence in deciding or compromising on controversial matters. Each commissioner is nominated for a term of up to five years by the president, with confirmation by the Senate. No more than three commissioners may be from the same political party.

The background these persons bring to the FCC has long been the subject of debate. Should they come from the communications industries in order to offer real expertise? Or should they be experienced regulators but without prior involvement in communications matters so that their past associations do not appear to influence their decisions? In reality, according to former FCC Commissioner Glen Robinson, most members are picked on much more politically pragmatic grounds than these questions infer. Robinson argues that the selection process

is not a search for the "best candidates" if by that term is meant those qualified by experience, training or professional aptitude. . . . Appointees are not selected to represent political, social or economic interests. Nor do they represent any particular array of talents and skills that could be objectively identified as relevant to the job. . . . In a field of regulation such as communications, where there are not only one but several different industries and industry interests, the system of selecting candidates for appointments works strongly against the appointment of persons with specific views about regulatory issues because such views are likely to engender opposition from at least one major industry group sufficient to offset any support from another. . . . These factors tend to eliminate from serious contention persons with established track records in the field of communication or reg-

**405**

CHAPTER 13
Evaluative
and
Analytical
Functions

ulation—unless the record is acceptable to all of the affected interests that exercise significant political influence.[3]

Dedicated, intelligent, and effective public servants do become FCC commissioners, fortunately, but perhaps more in spite of than because of the least objectional option mode that characterizes most appointment choices.

The five commissioners are the most visible part of the FCC apparatus, but approximately two thousand other persons staff the agency and handle routine processing and decision-making duties. Actions involving individual media outlets seldom reach the commissioners themselves unless a precedent-setting or punitive issue is involved. Thus, the FCC staff, working under delegated authority from the commissioners, are the professionals who normally process the paperwork that keeps the regulatory wheels turning.

Many of these staffers are assigned to one of the FCC's four bureaus: Field Operations, Common Carrier, Private Radio, and Mass Media. The *Field Operations Bureau* is the technical inspection and enforcement arm charged with overseeing the proper use of telecommunications equipment. The *Common Carrier Bureau* is responsible for policing those open-to-all-comers delivery systems such as telephone, telegraph, and microwave companies as well as many satellite carriers. The *Private Radio Bureau* supervises point-to-point wireless communication such as amateur radio, CB (citizen's band), and local government spectrum uses. And the *Mass Media Bureau* oversees the broadcasting and cable

transmissions with which we are most concerned in this book. This bureau itself is split into four divisions (Enforcement, Policy and Rules, Audio Services, and Video Services). These divisions are charged with policing, planning/rule revision, and radio and television activities respectively.

Other than the bureau chiefs and the commissioners themselves, most FCC staff are career civil servants rather than political appointees. The president (with Senate concurrence) appoints the commissioners as their staggered terms expire and can designate who will serve as chairman. The chairman selects the bureau chiefs and a few other top managers who direct the activities of the dozens or hundreds of on-going staff members in their units. Some staff may leave for the private sector or join the commission from that sector. This revolving door has been criticized as giving unfair advantage to firms for which ex-FCC personnel now work or those whose former employees are now at the commission. Various rules, however, prohibit current staff from handling matters dealing with recent employers and former staff from immediately representing parties directly affected by their previous FCC functions. At the same time, it is argued that people moving back and forth between the FCC and the private sector ensure better lines of communication and a sharing of expertise that government otherwise might not be able to afford.

The FCC is not the only regulatory agency in town. Being a creature of the legislative branch, the commission is policed by the Congress, which must approve its annual budget

## Mass Media Bureau

Alex Felker, former chief of the FCC's Mass Media Bureau, argues that many technical regulations have stifled marketplace flexibility. Meanwhile, policing program content raises delicate First Amendment issues.

**406**

SECTION
THREE

Profes-
sional
Perspec-
tives

and creates the legal framework within which the FCC must function. As its sometimes pointless and repetitive hearings on such issues as television violence, broadcast indecency, and song-lyric labeling have shown, Congress has never been shy about intruding into FCC-delegated areas in response to constituent pressure. Not infrequently, this intrusion results in an FCC that is whipsawed between the interests of one party's Congressmen and a president from the opposing party.

For electronic media advertising, the Federal Trade Commission (FTC) is involved in the regulatory game. Even though its activities were considerably narrowed during the Reagan years, the FTC's scrutiny is still a fact of life when it comes to commercial speech. The agency has been especially committed to its advertising *substantiation* program, whereby companies and their advertising agencies must be certain they have the proper evidence in hand before disseminating product performance claims. Meanwhile, as the FTC retreated from some types of oversight, the National Association of Attorneys General moved in to fill the vacuum. Drawing its membership from the chief law enforcers in the fifty state governments, this group has exercised its influence in such areas as airline ticket and car rental price advertising. Although it has no statutory legal standing, NAAG's membership uses its collective resources to approach advertisers and their media outlets with a united voice and, implicitly, with the threat of lawsuits if its recommendations are ignored.

Other federal bureaucracies impact various aspects of electronic media operation as well. The Food and Drug Administration (FDA) may become involved in cases of pharmaceutical advertising and claims of medical endorsement. The Federal Aviation Administration (FAA) must be dealt with in terms of antenna tower placement, height, and lighting. The Bureau of Alcohol, Tobacco and Firearms scrutinizes the methods by which companies market its namesake items. The

Occupational Safety and Health Administration (OSHA) polices everything from radiation levels emitted by electronic equipment to control-room air quality. And a variety of units throughout the government monitor civil rights issues, including hiring and employment maintenance practices.

Lawsuits and similar actions also put the courts in the regulatory picture, as we discuss in Chapter 6. Unlike the FCC, the FTC, or NAAG, however, the courts become involved only when prompted by other parties in the form of cases and petitions. Because airwaves do not respect state boundaries, broadcasting (and, by extension, cable and other electronic media) have long been considered elements of interstate commerce, which thereby must be dealt with more or less exclusively at the federal level. Thus, the federal court system is the usual place where appeals from FCC or Congressional actions are taken and where complicated copyright matters are fought out. Sometimes, the threat of court action is enough to provoke out-of-court compromises in order to avoid the massive legal bills that lengthy electronic media cases have often run up.

## Communications Attorneys

The lawyers who litigate such cases (or fashion such compromises) are usually specialists in communications law. With such a large body of ever-changing regulation and policy pertaining to the electronic media, no general practitioner could hope to be conversant with even the main precedents and procedures in the field. So the comm lawyer is used by media clients, or their own in-house counsels, to represent their interests before the FCC, the courts, or other media businesses.

Over the years, the emphasis of communications law has changed depending on whether deregulatory or re-regulatory pres-

**407**

CHAPTER 13
Evaluative
and
Analytical
Functions

sures are in vogue. The attorney in this field must follow these shifts on behalf of clients in order to be the best preventer, protector, or advocate, as the situation demands. Indeed, many lawyers in the field take the position that *preventing* problems through knowledgeable anticipation is the best service a legal counsel can provide. This prevention might include, for example, reminding client stations about the types of documents they should have in their public file or advising them on what actions to take to mesh with commission shifts in its EEO (Equal Employment Opportunity) expectations. It could also involve checking the station's contracts with a syndicator or network to ensure that they conform to the client's best business and legal interests or watching FCC dockets and notices of proposed rule making that might be relevant to a given network's, station's or cable company's operations. (You may wish to reread the Alan Campbell profile in Chapter 6.)

By closely studying both business and regulatory trends, the communications counsel may, in fact, advise actions that further influence these forces. As Krasnow and Longley point out,

In the intricate and dynamic relationship between the FCC and the industry, the Washington communications lawyer plays a special role—not only in interpreting FCC policies for broadcast licensees but also in shaping the policy direction of the commission. In a study of Washington lawyers Joseph Goulden noted that while the lawyers's historic role has been to advise clients on how to comply with the law, the Washington lawyer's present role is to advise clients on how to make laws and to make the most of them. Goulden described how the Washington lawyer serves as the interface that holds together the economic partnership of business and government.[4]

Thus, again we see that, in our industry, regulation may be as much a positive as a prohibi-

tive force, depending on how it relates to the business and operational interests involved.

Through their constantly evolving familiarity with both the regulatory and business climate in our profession, skilled communications attorneys are often the essential spark plugs in driving a deal or motivating a compromise. Former FCC chairman and eminent attorney Richard Wiley once put it this way: " 'What lawyers bring to the party are a knowledge of the process and the players, and an appreciation of how best to structure arguments, based on past precedent and on what the commission is likely to do.' "[5] In an enterprise such as the electronic media, the purpose of which is the packaging and delivery of highly appealing public communication, it is vital to recognize the *private* (behind the scenes) communication expertise necessary to the entire enterprise's well-being. The best communications lawyers practice their specialty with due regard for both its private and public contexts.

*Broadcasting* magazine once compiled the following inventory of what good legal counsel must do in the service of our profession. This inventory aptly summarizes the range of evaluative and analytical functions such attorneys perform:

They shepherd applications for renewal or transfer of broadcast licenses through the labyrinths of the FCC. In the name of clients, they file tons of paper supporting or opposing (usually opposing) commission proposals. They defend clients and their interests (in the name of the public interest) before the commission and the courts, and lobby members of Congress and the commission. They are accused, sometimes with reason, of tying anchors to the ship of progress. They are credited, again sometimes with reason, with helping to pioneer new fields of telecommunications service. They are business consultants. They are, occasionally, a client's psychiatric social worker. And at times, they do public relations jobs. Probably no one lawyer pro-

**408**

SECTION
THREE

Profes-
sional
Perspec-
tives

vides all of those services, but some law firms do. . . .

Nor is that all. Given the nature of their practice before the FCC, an agency that is part judicial and part legislative, communications lawyers have an opportunity, which some have eagerly seized, to affect government policy in telecommunications.[6]

# Lobbyists and Other Influence Wielders

While actual lobbying is a single and optional facet of a communications attorney's role, for other professionals in our industry such duties are a full-time task.

All of the networks, major stations groups, and key MSOs employ lobbyists to advance the continuous stating of their case before Congressional and regulatory decision makers. In addition, every branch of the electronic media has its trade association for which lobbying is a major if not singular activity. For broadcasters, of course, it is the National Association of Broadcasters (NAB). For cable, it is the National Cable Television Association (NCTA) or the smaller operator-serving Community Antenna Television Association (CATA). Public broadcasters have the National Association of Public Television Stations (NAPTS) and the Association of Public Radio Stations (APRS). MMDS interests are pressed by the Wireless Cable Association (WCA), and those of low-power television stations are represented by the Community Broadcasters Association (CBA). Dwarfing these forces, however, are the more than 150 lobbyists working for the various telephone companies. Although the telcos are not, as of this writing, a part of the electronic mass media enterprise, their lobbyists are increasingly pushing to permit them such a role (see Chapter 4).

Lobbyists serve a positive function in bringing to the attention of government information about trends, developments, dangers, and possibilities that pertain to their industry and its contribution to the public good. There is no question that such communications are self-serving and are conducted to benefit the respective lobbyist group's cause. But if lobbyists can show that their association's interests parallel the best interests of the public in the matter under consideration, they have performed a mutually valuable service. Thus, in pushing for abolishment of the financial interest and syndication rules *(fin/syn)*, network advocates attempt to demonstrate how these rules are working against the adequate financing of high-quality free TV programming. On the other side, Motion Picture Association of America (MPAA) agents argue that lifting the rules would restore dominant power to the networks and undermine the market for a wider range of creative product. Each side assembles as much researched evidence as it can to support its assertions, thereby giving government officials and their staffs more comprehensive data than they would be able to uncover on their own.

Whether lobbying before legislators or regulatory agency personnel, professional advocates as a whole probably spend at least as much time trying to convince government *not* to do something as they do in attempting to initiate some action. Mature industries that have benefited handsomely from the status quo obviously try to maintain that status quo as long as possible. On the other hand, young upstart businesses and newly coalesced citizens groups are more likely to promote regulatory or legislative *change* that will enhance their prospects or social agendas. Nonetheless, an established entity sometimes may seek a new rule to protect its competitive position while a less-developed interest may try to block that rule to open up the game. Either way, reputable lobbyists aggressively but openly pursue their employers' objectives in whatever forums are available.

**409**

CHAPTER 13
Evaluative
and
Analytical
Functions

**GERALD UDWIN**/WASHINGTON VICE-PRESIDENT
WESTINGHOUSE BROADCASTING COMPANY, INC.

It's much easier to state my title concisely than to explain concisely what I do. Or how to prepare for a job like mine.

This is my twenty-ninth year with Group W. The first twenty-two were spent in news, as a reporter, anchor, and news director at Group W radio stations, and as correspondent and bureau chief in Washington for our radio and television stations. I moved into our governmental affairs office in 1982. Other people who do what I do for other major broadcasting companies have backgrounds as journalists, public relations professionals, or lawyers.

*Customers*—that's probably the best way to look at the people I serve and the work I do. Customers can be divided into internal and external categories.

*Internal customers* begin with my boss, the Group W chairman. But I must also respond to the needs of the presidents of our radio, television, production, and satellite communications (cable programming) divisions. These division presidents do not always share the same goals. For instance, "must carry" (the right of a local television station to be carried by the local cable systems) may be a goal for our stations but not for our cable programming division. So our first objective is to determine a Group–W-wide position on such a governmental issue. That call falls to our chairman, with input from all of us relating to the business and public policy considerations involved.

*External customers* include the Congress, the FCC, the White House, and the Washington media.

With the Congress, it is important to try to find common ground between what Group W advocates and what the other sides and the general public may be advocating. Several years ago, cable deregulation was this kind of issue. In the end, a compromise was struck—with Congressional encouragement—between the cities and the cable industry.

Meanwhile, at the FCC, Hollywood and the networks have been battling for years over whether the nets should be allowed to control the syndication of programs to individual stations after the programs have aired on the net. It is my responsibility to inform the commission of Group W's belief that the FCC should also consider how such network control of syndicated shows would affect the diversity of programming available to local stations and the general public.

In terms of the White House, Group W has long been active in producing public service programs on our radio

410

SECTION
THREE

Profes-
sional
Perspec-
tives

and television stations to help communities solve local problems. This has dove-tailed with President Bush's emphasis on volunteerism, so we've been able to arrange mutually beneficial appearances by the president in public service announcements for Group W Television's "Time to Care" campaign and our San Francisco TV station KPIX's drive to raise money for earthquake relief.

For the Washington media, we want the press to have a positive impression of our programming and our public policies. This part of my job is especially important, and spending most of my career in news has helped me understand what reporters need to know. In this connection, the single most important characteristic that any Washington representative brings to this job is a reputation for honesty. If, for example, a member of Congress believes that you will both tell the truth and disclose all points of view on an issue, you may be able to build a long-term productive relationship with the lawmaker. If you create the opposite impression, you may soon be unable to function in Washington.

There's a personal irony for me in the direction my career has taken. My father was a retailer in a small Illinois town. He would have liked to see his only child follow him into the business. But I was full of idealism about informing the public and could not picture myself in sales. Now, after spending most of my working life in broadcast news, I have gone from the journalist's observing of events to the businessperson's participation in them. I am in sales. My father would be surprised. Pleased, too, I hope.

Because of their inherently public nature and their centerpiece role in the lives of the citizenry, the electronic media are lobbied about or lobbied against to a much greater degree than are some much larger but less spotlighted industries. Citizens groups like Action for Children's Television (ACT), the Office of Communications of the United Church of Christ, Accuracy in Media (AIM), Action for Smoking and Health (ASH), and a variety of locally based organizations have, over the years, made significant impact on electronic media operations and regulations.

Virtually everyone listens to the radio and watches television—and undertakes such activities in their prized leisure moments. So a rate increase by a cable MSO is much more likely to be called by the constituency to their Congressman's attention than is a Federal Reserve Board policy that will depress the interest rates paid on their savings accounts. Very few people understand macroeconomics, despite its importance to their financial status. But everybody thinks they know all about television and how its systems should be operated. Thus, our business could not survive without a vigilant lobbying effort. When one operates in a fishbowl, it is important to keep turbulence to a minimum so nothing gets spilled.

Lobbyists work outside of government, and other important influence wielders work inside. For the electronic media, one such entity is the National Telecommunications and Information Administration (NTIA). A part of the Commerce Department (and thus of the executive branch), the NTIA has the potential to impact an administration's plans and policies as regards radio and television. Successor to the Nixon era's Office of Telecommunications Policy, the NTIA not only disburses grants to public broadcasting and assigns

**411**

CHAPTER 13
Evaluative
and
Analytical
Functions

spectrum space to federal users, but it also represents the current administration's views at the FCC and on Capitol Hill. For a president with a hands-on interest in telecommunications matters, the NTIA can play a substantial role in advocating the adding or subtracting of regulatory policies and can either accelerate or retard the application of new communications technologies.

In a similar manner, the Department of Justice can, if a president chooses, exercise considerable influence in the telecommunications arena. An activist chief executive may permit or encourage the Justice Department to pursue antitrust investigations designed to retard the formation or to initiate the breakup of consolidations in various aspects of our business. The department may also be energized to expand oversight of Equal Employment Opportunity (EEO) activities by media businesses and may push the FCC toward similar undertakings. Occasionally, the Justice Department may take the FCC to court if it disagrees with a commission action.

Many times, the department's real power comes not from bringing suit, but from behind-the-scenes influencing of involved parties through either the threat of such suits or the assurance that no legal action is contemplated. Although conducted within the fabric of government, such influencing is at least as powerful as what any concerted lobbying effort from outside interest groups can accomplish and may itself have been subtly impacted by such lobbying in other corners of the administration.

## Political and Public Relations Communicators

A special, more continuous, and more visible lobbying effort is conducted by public relations professionals who work in the field of political communications. Whether they serve as press officers on a government agency's or politician's staff, or work outside for corporate/business interests, the job of these communicators is to interact positively with the media in order to reach that media's public.

Press secretaries and holders of similar titles must be adept at making their boss or governmental agency look as good as possible but without engaging in deception when crises arise. As with lobbyists, political communicators are expected to put the best possible face on their employer's actions and positions. Journalists recognize this bias and take it into account when preparing their stories. Relations sour, however, when mutual trust is violated. A press officer who deliberately misleads a reporter or the press corps in general will have no further credibility. A reporter who betrays a confidence by publicizing an off-the-record comment or breaking a story before an agreed-on release time will be frozen out in the future. Each party is in the business of analyzing and evaluating the expected actions of the other in order to present its position or story most effectively to the mass audience. The skill by which each plays the game without breaking the rules determines the career success or failure of press officer and reporter alike.

Political communicators thus engage in a very delicate series of dances with the reporters on whom they depend for access to the public. As Professors Kathleen Jamieson and Karlyn Campbell explain,

There is a constant tension between those assigned to ferret out the news and those assigned to control press access to news sources. Press secretaries, public information officers, and public relations firms are hired to ease press access to favorable information and to minimize or block press access to unfavorable information. When negative information seeps out, it is the function of news managers to prevent or

412

SECTION
THREE

Profes-
sional
Perspec-
tives

**STEPHEN SERKAIAN**/DIRECTOR
DEMOCRATIC PRESS OFFICE, MICHIGAN HOUSE OF REPRESENTATIVES

Promoting the message of sixty-one Democrats in the Michigan House of Representatives is a world of contrasts, where substance is balanced with style, reality with perception. Trying to control the message, however, is difficult because there are more wrong ways than right ways to do it. Therein lies the challenge of practicing both media relations and politics.

As press secretary to the Speaker of the House and director of the Democratic Press Office, I am the official spokesperson for House Democrats and serve as their liaison to print and broadcast reporters. I try to balance what's best for these lawmakers with helping newspersons do their jobs.

Whether it's positive or negative news, I'm expected to be an honest broker, providing political advice to my bosses and timely and accurate information to journalists. I have to anticipate questions on hundreds of issues that reporters might ask lawmakers and must be prepared to recommend answers to them. Whether or not I personally agree with the positions I'm representing, I'm expected to support them with enthusiasm.

I also have to balance being a cheerleader for my side with being a straight shooter—always remembering that even if I can't tell reporters the truth, I must never tell a lie. If journalists ever question my credibility, my service to House Democrats instantly becomes ineffectual.

In addition, I recommend to lawmakers different ways to publicize their stories, whether it's through press releases or news conferences, or enhancing an event with camera-pleasing visuals and backdrops. Some reporters complain about being manipulated by these techniques. But the bottom line is that many issues simply receive better coverage with the added punch.

The fifteen-person press office staff I supervise promotes the legislative accomplishments of House Democrats to more than 500 newspaper and broadcasting outlets across the state, through news releases, press photographs, and radio and television reports. I make sure everyone works together as a team to communicate the same message, matching lawmakers' stories with their local media.

We try to meet the need-it-now demands that lawmakers and reporters put on us, whether it's writing a press release at the last minute to announce the introduction of a bill, or answering the constant phone calls

**413**

CHAPTER 13
Evaluative
and
Analytical
Functions

from newspersons wanting more information for their stories.

We celebrate when we place a broadcast report as the lead story on a lawmaker's hometown station. We cringe when we advise another lawmaker to hold a press conference on a slow news day and it receives no media coverage at all. And we laugh when a ceiling pipe leaks water onto the House Speaker's desk—right in the middle of a news conference.

I only wish I could take credit for creating that visual.

lessen its spread through the media and to cast it in the best possible light.[7]

For a press officer, then, it is critically important to be able to evaluate when an unfavorable story already is substantially out and proceed to disseminate whatever damage control information is necessary. Waiting too long to say anything not only loses you the chance to be heard but also is perceived by reporters as stonewalling—an action only slightly less harmful than deception to the reputation of a political spokesperson.

In the case of communicators for corporations as well as for politicians, knowing *when* is often as essential as knowing *how*. As Exxon's oil spill in Alaska demonstrated, a crisis situation involving a company (or an office holder) demands a strategic communication response within a very short time. Failure to respond expeditiously only deepens the crisis and layers a communication disaster atop the physical or economic one. "'Silence is the crime Exxon is paying for'" asserted American Association of Advertising Agencies President John O'Toole just after the accident, " 'and that's a helluva price to pay for not running an ad the very next day.'"[8] Given the near instantaneous communication that can be provided by the electronic media, a corporate foul-up or political misstep can suddenly affect the perceptions of millions of people. Thus, public communicators in a crisis situa-

tion must choose and respond wisely and quickly.

Most professionals in the field agree that the best strategy for dealing with a crisis is to anticipate it through *proactive communication*. "Before a crisis strikes, image advertising, issue advertising and PR can build a reservoir of good will," explains public relations executive Steven Fink. "'Then, when the crisis hits, the public will trust you more, forgive you faster.'"[9] Certainly, if a press secretary or corporate spokesperson has maintained positive proactive links with the media, then the task of crisis management will be easier. The topic must still be addressed directly and quickly, however; and speed must not be confused with impulsiveness. Skilled practitioners know that they must never disseminate a message that tells the truth without taking the time to cast that truth in a lucid, understandable nugget. "You can over-explain and get yourself in trouble," warns John Burke of Burson-Marsteller. "You can, for example, send a biochemist to talk about a chemical; he will tell the truth, and he'll over-tell the truth. He may create unfounded concerns about other issues."[10]

Brevity and precision are the hallmarks of most informative electronic media messages, and political/corporate conveyances are no different. Press secretaries and similar spokespersons soon learn that to serve their employers well, they must also serve the le-

**414**

SECTION
THREE

Profes-
sional
Perspec-
tives

gitimate needs of stations and networks for credible and timely information. It thus is no accident that many political and public relations communicators worked in a media outlet at some earlier point in their careers. By acquiring firsthand familiarity with how news organizations function, they can better anticipate and satisfy the requests and questions that will be directed their way. In our journalistic traditions, reporters and spokespersons may often be adversaries, but this does not mean they must be antagonists. True professionals in these endeavors know how to build mutual respect while pursuing different objectives.

## Critics and Commentators

Just as media journalists try to assess the performance of politicians and corporations, so do critics and commentators attempt to evaluate the performance of the media themselves. Because radio and television are so central to people's lives, electronic media critics and their observations are of fundamental importance in offering guidance to the public about how to use these media more enjoyably and productively. Industry-attuned critics who know how to fashion reasonable media analyses and suggestions for improvement can, in Richard Blackmur's words, "make bridges between the society and the arts."[11] By opening up lines of communication linking creator and consumer (station/network and audience), a critic makes it easier for each to comprehend the needs and limitations of the other.

Listeners and viewers, for example, can learn from the knowledgeable critic why the electronic media must take some actions and cannot take certain others. This commentator might point out that a cable system is forced

to black out a distant program because a local broadcaster is asserting rights under the syndicated exclusivity rule (see Chapter 6). Similarly, that critic might discuss economic and affiliation factors that enable one station to offer a complete noon newscast while another must make do with a sixty-second newsbreak.

Meanwhile, from the opposite perspective, a credible critic can let a cable system know that a number of subscribers are upset with its choice to move a particular program channel to an upper service tier or can alert a station that shifting a popular news anchor from the late to the early evening newscast may cost that outlet upscale viewers who aren't home to watch the five-o'clock 'cast. If the commentator passing this information along is respected by media managers as being well-versed in our industry, these executives may give that critic's bridge-building observations serious consideration for the benefit of everybody concerned.

Successful radio/television commentators thus must acquire an intimate understanding of their subject if they are to be taken seriously by both consumers and media practitioners. As former *Washington Post* columnist Lawrence Laurent once observed, "This complete critic must be something of an electronics engineer, an expert on our governmental processes, and an electrician. He must have a grasp of advertising and marketing principles. He must be able to evaluate all of the art forms; to comprehend each of the messages conveyed, on every subject under the sun, through television."[12]

Thus, an authoritative electronic media critic takes the responsibility to be broadly conversant with industry systems and issues in addition to program content. This is especially important in media criticism because radio/television consumers seldom have the contacts and the time to acquire and update a thorough knowledge of the media for themselves. According to former *New York Times*

**415**

CHAPTER 13
Evaluative
and
Analytical
Functions

writer Jack Gould, "Critics in a sense are the proxies of the viewers. This does not mean that viewers necessarily will agree with the reviewers. But it does mean that there is the common bond of an independent opinion."[13] Gould's *Chicago Tribune* counterpart, Larry Wolters, asserted at about the same time that "The critic alone can serve as a watchdog for the viewer (or listener) who cannot always speak effectively by himself."[14]

Finally, we must realize that broadcast/cable reviewers, in analyzing and evaluating an overwhelmingly entertainment-oriented industry, must be entertainers themselves if they are to maximize their exposure. The breadth and diversity of their public (as compared, say, to that of the ballet critic) requires that their output be expressed in a manner that is interesting, concise, and even fun to listen to or read. The *Minneapolis Tribune's* Will Jones candidly admitted to this aspect of his work when he wrote that his columns were supposed "to serve as an entertainment feature for the paper."[15] Nor is this a newly acquired expectation. Almost three decades ago, the trade publication *Television Age* editorialized that "the critic's function today seems to be to amuse and entertain viewers prospective and actual with wit, if not malice."[16]

Today's effective critics have learned that wit helps attract an audience, whereas malice alienates the media that critic is paid to assess objectively. Certainly, reviewers should be detached from the radio/television professionals whose programs and operations they are scrutinizing. But a detached relationship still leaves the lines of communication open so that the critic is given media access to data that are helpful in arriving at informed judgments. Once a critic assumes the role of media foe, however, these lines are shut down and neither the public nor the industry can profit from the *uninformed* pronouncements that are certain to result. If reviewers and radio/television decision makers become

enemies, the profession that both serve is the first casualty.

Rather than risk this possibility, some overzealous media protectors would prefer a situation in which there is no systematic radio/television criticism. The broadcast/cable media come directly into one's home, they argue, so there is no need for commentary to propel people to this or that concert hall, theater, gallery, movie house, or bookstore. Further, these anticritics continue, because media content is so readily and even automatically available, everybody can make unaided choices in the privacy and convenience of their own homes. All that is needed, they maintain, is a program schedule to serve as a menu from which to select. For radio, a list of stations and their formats should suffice.

There is no arguing that radio and television are popular, or that they are easily usable by virtually every inhabitant of the United States. There is also no debating that listeners and viewers each make thousands of programming choices every year and that many of these consumers and most of their choices are not motivated by a trained critic's counsel. Yet it is exactly this availability and popularity that require the attention of astute professional critics. Former FCC Commissioner Lee Loevinger once observed that "Broadcasting is popular and universal because it is elemental, responsive to popular taste, and gives the audience a sense of contact with the world around it which is greater than that provided by any other medium."[17] This sense of contact, however, can be severely warped if listeners and viewers lack the observational training and guidance necessary to (1) make their media choices wisely and then (2) evaluate the success of those choices in terms of the programmatic content to which they were, as a result, exposed.

Perceptive commentators encourage perceptive programming and media operation. They therefore help our industry improve much more than can any law or governmen-

**416**

SECTION
THREE
Profes-
sional
Perspec-
tives

tal policy. Regulators can only require or prohibit. Critics, on the other hand, can reward
and stimulate.

## Brokers and Financial Analysts

In terms of rewards, the contributions of two
groups of professionals directly relate to the
amount of monetary recognition extended to
media enterprises. Although they function
outside the public eye, these executives expe-
dite the deals that generate much of the capital flowing to and through our industry.

*Media brokers* are transactional experts
who locate buyers and sellers for radio and
television properties. In one sense, they are
station/cable system real estate specialists,
but their responsibilities go beyond the listing
and selling of physical property. A station's
physical plant is worthless without an FCC license, and a cable system cannot operate
without a local franchise. Thus, a broker also
must calculate the dollar value of these intan-
gibles in helping a facility seller set an asking
price. Using indexes such as past and antici-
pated cash flow, homes passed compared to
homes wired, income received per subscribing household, projected market advertising
growth/decline (see Figure 13–1), local media
competitors, and the calculated predictability
of license or franchise renewal, the broker
combines both tangible and intangible factors
in arriving at an appraisal. Then, the tasks of
listing and selling can begin.

The expansion of the cable business and
the associated acquisitional appetites of MSOs
together with the Reagan administration's
deregulatory initiatives have, since the 1980s,
spurred both station and system brokerage

**Figure 13–1**

Best ten markets in local TV advertising revenue per TV household, 1990

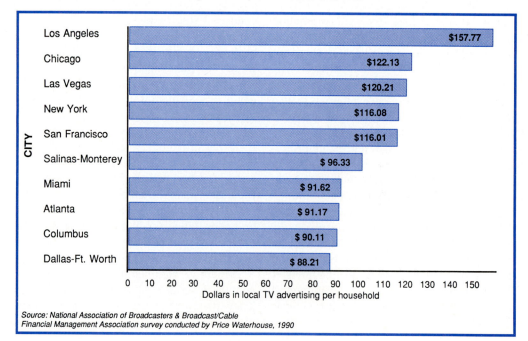

*Source: National Association of Broadcasters & Broadcast/Cable
Financial Management Association survey conducted by Price Waterhouse, 1990*

**417**

CHAPTER 13
Evaluative
and
Analytical
Functions

**JAMES GAMMON**/PRESIDENT
GAMMON MEDIA BROKERS, INC.

The principal asset a station broker deals with is the FCC license to operate a broadcast property.

For profitable radio stations, the sale price will be a multiple of cash flow (operating profit before depreciation, amortization, interest, and non-recurring expenses) for the most recent year, derived principally after analysis of:

Total market radio revenues and growth pattern
This station's ranking (audience share)
Program format and obvious format niches in the market
Historical and year-to-date operating results
Management performance
Technical facilities (ability to place a competitive signal over the market)
Amount of audience lost to out-of-town radio stations
Competition in the market and, especially, within this station's format

For profitable television stations, the cash flow multiple will result from analysis of:

Total market television revenues
This TV station's market share
This TV station's operating revenues and profit margin
The network with which it is affiliated (ABC, NBC, CBS, Fox)
If no network affiliation (if the station is an Independent), the amount, quality, and cost of syndicated product inventory under contract

(off-network sitcoms, drama, game shows, etc.)
Capital improvements needed

Regardless of network affiliation, the TV signal coverage is of paramount importance.

For unprofitable or start-up radio or TV stations, the so-called stick method is used to determine value. This method, shorn of intricacies, consists of using the foregoing variables together with sales of comparable facilities in a mock-up, showing the buyer what the station will likely achieve (and how soon) under his or her expert management.

Whether dealing with radio or television properties, the foregoing price evaluation analysis is often the simplest part of the broker's function. This, after all, only defines the object on the table. From that point forward, the broker concentrates on (a) ascer-

418

SECTION
THREE

Profes-
sional
Perspec-
tives

taining the respective emotional involvement of seller and buyer and (b)
dealing with matters of finance.

Understanding the parties' emotional involvement is critical, and the
sellers and buyers should consistently be refocused on the contemplated transaction. Nevertheless, in
the final analysis, station acquisitions are rarely emotional buys. The
parties must become aware of the
financability factors, which are paramount.

The seller must be brought to a realistic stance: "Would *you* pay your asking price for this station in this market?"

The buyer, who initially perceives
that this station will be a nice fit in his
or her overall game plan, must be
equipped to convince a banker that
the contemplated transaction makes
economic sense, both standing alone

*and* in comparison to other broadcast
stations available for purchase in this
or comparable markets.

Thus, emotion in the end gives way
to the economics (financability) of the
transaction, but the emotion that initially fired the interest must be kept
alive until closing.

In summary, the broker must perceive the real needs and desires of the
parties and diligently seek to serve
them. With this accomplished, a
transaction that makes economic
sense will fall into place. Without this,
hours will be invested, only to have
one party walk out before closing.

A final word. Brokers must be vigilant in protecting their fee position.
This requires as much skill as mas-
tery of the deal's transactional and
psychological aspects. Failure to do
this only once will be an expensive
and memorable lesson.

---

activities to unprecedented levels of intensity.
This intensity declined markedly in 1990,
however, when a recession found many outlets struggling to meet the debt servicing they
had taken on in more optimistic times. Banks
and similar financial investors consequently
became much more wary of electronic media
properties. This attitude has forced brokers to
look even harder for innovative financial
structures and sources.

As new investors have been drawn into our
industry, brokers have had to learn the more
sophisticated valuation procedures that outside financiers with no background in radio/
television understand and are used to dealing
with. In earlier times, when broadcasting and
cable were more isolated businesses still in
the hands of their founders, a broker could
rely on old-boy relationships and common un-

derstandings to bring buyer and seller together. Today, however, as veteran broker of
thirty years Dick Blackburn points out, the
enterprise has turned into a "'science. . . . I
think that anyone in the last five years who
has relied on the 'old boy network' type thing
has found themselves out in left field. . . . If
you're up to meeting the demands you'll do
fine, you have a place. If you're going to
cruise, people will blow by you.'"[18]

Before the recessionary downturn, station
brokering alone was estimated to be a $50
million business in 1989, with brokers, like
conventional real estate agents, usually paid
through commissions based on property selling prices. Because of the vast sums often associated with a media outlet, however, the
percentage of this commission usually de-
creases as the sale price gets larger. Thus, a

common pattern is the "5–4–3–2–1" commission, through which the broker receives 5 percent of the first million dollars, 4 percent on the second, and so on. For very large deals, other patterns operate to keep the broker's fee from eclipsing the seller's profit margin.

An additional variable, and one that makes a broker's life more complicated, is the perceived value of the on-site management at the facility for sale. How much have these executives contributed to the success or failure of the property? If they have been successful, are they likely to remain in place after the sale if the buyer so wishes? More than one station's profits have plummeted when a locally well connected general manager or sales manager has left in the wake of an ownership change. As we have seen again and again in our discussions, talented *people* remain our profession's most important resource despite the preoccupation with hardware and technological developments.

To make some deals work, a media broker must also be able to locate sources of capital and financing for the prospective buyer. A good residential real estate agent has the same responsibility, of course, but few home sales are multi-million-dollar deals. Knowing which banks, other investment houses, and individual companies are interested in media propositions and the financial instruments they are willing to use can be the crucial ingredient in a broker's ability to consummate the sale.

*Financial analysts* who work for securities brokerage firms and investment banking houses can thus be key factors in whether capital is made available to a prospective buyer or to the industry as a whole. In fact, as we mention in Chapter 3, the evaluations of such analysts are tremendously influential not only in facility sales but also to the viable operation and growth of our entire electronic media system. Radio/television enterprises must often raise capital to expand or sustain their competitive position in a constantly changing marketplace. A good financial report card from key media analysts can affect a company's ability to secure funding and also the advantageous or disadvantageous way their debt service (interest payments) will be structured.

Consequently, the publicly held media companies especially make frequent and carefully packaged presentations to the financial analysts who head the media investment divisions at major banks and other investment firms. These analysts take this information, combine it with their own data, and then issue evaluative guidelines to their own bosses and investor-clients.

Each financial analyst's determination will, of course, be shaped by the overall business strategies and philosophies of the institution for which they work. Some investment houses are more conservative than others. Some stress short-term dividend potential more than long-term growth. But taken together, these analysts' pronouncements constitute a decisive diagnosis of the fiscal health or infirmity of the largest players in our industry. If the networks, station groups, and large MSOs are judged by the analysts to be risky or poor-return ventures, such judgment can adversely impact the fund-raising ability of

**419**

CHAPTER 13
Evaluative
and
Analytical
Functions

CNN **Media Stock Market**

Careful analysis and lively stock speculation were preludes to the ultimate merger of Time-Life with Warner Communications.

SECTION
THREE

Profes-
sional
Perspec-
tives

## MARY KUKOWSKI/MEDIA SECURITIES ANALYST
### BEAR, STEARNS & CO.

As a media securities analyst, my job is to offer investment advice about the stocks of various media companies. In other words, I tell people whether they ought to buy, sell, or hold specific media stocks. My primary clients are professional portfolio managers who manage very large pools of institutional money, such as pensions, trusts, and mutual funds. What my job entails, in general terms, is highly skilled observation of trends in the media business and then analysis of how those trends will translate into future stock price movements.

How does one go about this? About 40 percent of my time is spent on research—keeping abreast of and analyzing industry news and trends, becoming extremely familiar with the specific media companies I follow, and translating all of this knowledge into the earnings and cash flow models that will form the basis of my decision on whether the stock is a good value for investors. The other 60 percent of my time is spent imparting this information and my conclusions to our clients. This takes on many forms—frequent written reports, visiting with and telephoning clients, and conveying information to my firm's institutional salespeople, who also interact with our clients on my behalf.

A typical day for me starts very early, about 5:30 A.M. By 7:00, I have skimmed the *Wall Street Journal,* the *New York Times,* and *Investors' Daily* to see if there is any breaking news that I'll need to address at our daily morning call. This meeting starts at 8:00 AM, before the U.S. markets open and is teleconferenced to all our branches worldwide. It serves as a forum for analysts such as myself to discuss news, events, and issues of importance to the financial markets. After addressing the morning meeting, if the news is very important, I'll spend the better part of the day on the telephone discussing its impact with clients.

If there are no major news events, a typical day might see me visiting with the management of one of my companies to discuss both industry issues in general and their company specifically. I might return from such a visit, update my financial model on that company, perhaps change my opinion on the stock, and spend the next several days crafting a report to communicate this information to clients. Another day might find me visiting with clients on an individual basis or giving a speech at a luncheon gathering of clients organized for me by one of our institutional salespeople.

**421**

CHAPTER 13
Evaluative
and
Analytical
Functions

In my view, one needs several important attributes in order to be happy and successful as a securities analyst. Foremost are keen intelligence and a real enjoyment of the intellectual pursuit of analysis. One should also be comfortable with and genuinely enjoy interacting with large numbers of people. Being able to write and speak well helps, too, because this business is largely one of communicating information. As to formal education, securities analysts come from a variety of backgrounds, but an M.B.A. or some kind of financial training is increasingly important.

A background coupling financial and investment skills with some exposure to the media industry is probably ideal. Last and probably most important, high levels of energy and discipline are needed in my business. Wall Street has become highly competitive, and this profession is very demanding of both time and energy.

The rewards, though, are many. Media security analysis is often tremendously stimulating and enjoyable, and I urge anyone with a strong interest in both the media and the financial markets to consider it seriously.

smaller companies throughout their respective branches of our business as well. In many ways, the one or two dozen media analysts at the top investment firms may be the most powerful people in our profession in charting its directions and anointing its victors.

## Business Development Executives

One of the best ways for a company to improve its fiscal attractiveness to analysts, investors, and other loaners of capital is to show that it is in a growth mode. The best way to grow, of course, is to attract new business. Certain elements of our profession have been much more active than others in this area, but virtually every electronic media sector is now taking a serious look at new business development. If your enterprise is to grow faster than the market, then new clients must fuel such growth.

Advertising agencies are paying special attention to such missionary or "rain making" work, with most shops employing a high-level executive as a vice-president or senior vice-president for business development. "Once a dead-end job where old account people went to die, the rainmaker now holds a prestigious and powerful position in most agencies," writes industry observer Robyn Griggs.[19] This person also is an analyst who takes the pulse of potential clients and evaluates the chances of converting them to *actual* clients. Because agencies service only one company in a given product category, the development officer isolates areas in which his or her shop has, as yet, no substantial business and then prospects for clients within the most promising of those areas.

Despite continuous attempts to quantify it, advertising remains an intensely subjective and image-oriented business. Thus, new business professionals must move beyond media budget figures and expenditure patterns and attempt to assess whether the personality of the agency will match the peculiar character

422

SECTION
THREE

Profes-
sional
Perspec-
tives

of the company being studied. Many client/agency affiliations that looked wonderful from a purely financial perspective have quickly degenerated when their corporate cultures failed to mesh. The development executive is paid to be sensitive to such matters before hasty marriages result in equally hasty and financially damaging divorces. The signing of a big, new account can mean a rapid expansion in billings and the addition of new staff. It might even result in the opening of a new branch office to better service that client in their headquarters city. The quick loss of that same client, however, will mean terminations, career dislocations, and professional embarrassment that more than offsets any temporary increase in the agency's profits.

After the analytical work has been done, and if the opportunity to pitch that prospect business can be secured, it frequently falls to the development executive to be the lead presenter in making such a pitch. At this point, presentational and persuasive skills take over from purely analytical ones. Clearly, professionals in this field must be multitalented if they are successfully to meet the consecutive challenges that pursuit of a new account entails. People who are only number crunchers or hospitable glad-handers need not apply. New-business head-hunting is a difficult, expensive endeavor that must be led by individuals who know how to isolate and capture an objective. "'It's analogous to detective work,'" observes NW Ayer's director of worldwide business development Charlie Decker. "'Ninety percent is drudgery and shoe leather.'"[20]

Business development personnel are also increasingly found in larger stations, though with different job titles. Usually located in the sales department, they may be known as co-op or local sales specialists. Co-op staffers analyze reams of market data to find out which manufacturers have programs that split the cost of radio/television advertising with local dealers. Using this information, the co-op executive isolates relevant retailers in the market and helps them obtain co-op funds. These manufacturer dollars are available only if the retailer uses them to purchase airtime, of course, so the station has thus hooked a new advertiser. McCann-Erickson Advertising estimates that in 1990, more than $7.3 billion will have been spent in local *radio* co-op alone—triple the level of the ten previous years. The agency also pegs local television station co-op at $8.7 billion for the same period, with an additional $425 million estimated for cable system advertising.[21] In radio especially, it appears that co-op development professionals have been doing their jobs.

*Local sales* developers may also use co-op in their efforts, but they are more broadly concerned with stimulating new business from any retail or service enterprise regardless of co-op availability or of whether they have previously advertised over radio and television. Sometimes this task is foisted off on the station's newest salesperson, who must build his or her commissioned account list from scratch. At more entrepreneurial stations, however, a more experienced staffer is paid a firm salary to conduct these analytical explorations—thereby upgrading the activity and increasing its chance for success. To this point in history, most cable system sales staff are new business developers by definition because local cable advertising activities are still in their infancy, at least when compared to the broadcast competition. (Review Wayne Hindmarsh's comments in his profile in Chapter 3.)

There is also another side to cable development, of course. This involves signing new subscribers to the basic service and upgrading basic customers to purchasing of pay channels. It costs little more for a cable company to wire forty homes on a street than it does to wire two homes at either end. But the *income* differential between serving two and serving forty is obviously vast. The customer service or development staffer thus tries to keep the ratio of homes-passed-to-homes-served as low as possible in order to maximize system reve-

**423**

CHAPTER 13
Evaluative
and
Analytical
Functions

**DON PEPPERS**/EXECUTIVE VICE-PRESIDENT,
BUSINESS DEVELOPMENT
LINTAS:USA

The 1980s saw advertising agencies, large and small, paying serious attention to the problem of winning new clients. This was a result, at least in part, of a decade-long slowdown in the growth of ad spending. Nevertheless, until fairly recently, the coordination of new business development as a discipline at most agencies was a function usually handled by the chief executive officer (CEO) directly.

At Lintas:USA, one of the country's top ten advertising agencies, I am the senior business development official—reporting to Lintas's CEO. In the United States, we have two large offices (New York and Detroit), two smaller offices (Los Angeles and Washington, DC), and ten other offices or subsidiary organizations around the country. Outside the United States we have more than 100 offices in more than 50 countries.

A lot of my time is spent studying individual companies and their various marketing divisions. We sift through hundreds of companies and advertising budgets, looking for those particular ones that would be attractive as clients for Lintas. With each company we make sure, first, that we don't already have a client that would pose a conflict. For instance, because we do the advertising for Chevrolet ("Heartbeat of America"), we would not be permitted to handle Ford's account—Chevrolet wouldn't let us, and even if they did, Ford wouldn't want us.

Determining when and how a conflict exists is not always so easy, however. We advertise diet Coke—but would Coca Cola find it a conflict for us to handle Ocean Spray fruit juices? Or what about a mineral water? We are the agency for Bayer Aspirin, which is produced by Sterling Drug, which is a subsidiary of Kodak. Would Kodak object if we did advertising for Fuji Films? Every client company has its own policy on ad agency conflicts.

In addition to clearing the companies on our list of prospects, which involves quite a bit of internal and external homework, I try to piece together the various contacts the people at Lintas have had with the people at key prospects. Just keeping track of these contacts is a full-time job for several of our people, using a computer data base.

McDonald's, for instance, might make a good client for Lintas:USA someday. One of our subsidiaries already does a substantial amount of business with a number of McDonald's local co-op organizations (franchisees in a local area who band together to run areawide advertising

424

SECTION
THREE
Profes-
sional
Perspec-
tives

programs or promotions). We have no client conflicts with McDonald's, our cultures are compatible, and we do advertising work similar to what they ask of their current agency. So, as the business development manager, it's my job first to inventory all the McDonald's contacts within the various Lintas offices. Then, we put together a plan to create a continuing dialogue with senior officials in the McDonald's organization. This dialogue must cover topics that are informative and interesting to McDonald's as well as nonthreatening to their current agency relationships or else McDonald's will not participate. The objective of our dialogue is to assure that the people within the McDonald's marketing organization are given opportunities over a period of time to become personally familiar with Lintas —our work, our culture, and our people. Naturally, while we may have spent a lot of time and energy studying *them,* they will not have spent the same kind of effort studying *us.* So, we create dialogue opportunities to expose our thinking and our people to McDonald's.

Now suppose that in a few years McDonald's decides to take a look at Lintas for a potentially large piece of its advertising budget. At that time, it will be my job to organize Lintas's pitch. McDonald's would probably look not just at Lintas, but at several other large, compatible agencies. Our goal would be to differentiate our own firm in a way that McDonald's people would find relevant to their needs. Obviously, the more we actually *know* about their needs, the better prepared we will be to do this. So, during the years of dialogue and courtship preceding a formal pitch opportunity, my staff and I constantly document and organize what we find out about the company and how they view their marketing situation.

Naturally, once any pitch is concluded, we will either have a new client or we will not. Unfortunately, it is not possible to win all the pitches. In fact, it is unusual to win more than 10 to 20 percent of them. Obviously, this means we end up losing a lot. So, one of the most important personal traits that any good business development manager must have is resilience. And, of course, the more prospects you are following, the more pitches you'll be invited into, and thus the more new business you'll win, in the long run.

nues. In preparation for this selling job, the advantages of various cable channel packages *(tiers)* must be carefully evaluated and matched with the likely viewing preferences of the neighborhoods in question. At the same time, continuous analysis of the *churn rate* (new connects compared to disconnects) is carried out to see if certain new business pitches are giving customers inaccurate expectations. High churn rates quickly drain a system's bottom line. Obviously, overblown promises to new subscribers do more financial harm than good.

Finally, development officers are also active at public broadcasting outlets and systems. In such noncommercial settings, their duties are twofold. First, they devise campaign strategies to encourage contributions from individual viewers and listeners. These strategies may take the form of auctions, pledge drives, and the extension of membership opportunities to people who donate. Second, public broadcasting developers structure underwriting plans through which local businesses can support the cost of prestige programming in exchange for on-air credits *(donor spots)* and carefully explained tax deductions. As we learn in Chapter 9, such new revenues are essential because federal dollars for public broadcasting have become more and more scarce.

Agency or station, broadcast or cable, commercial or noncommercial, off-air or on-air (as in Figure 13–2), development is a grueling, unending process that is usually removed from the glamour portions of our industry. Yet, this ongoing evaluative and analytical task is often responsible for unearthing the money that pays for the sparkle and sheen our audiences have come to expect in commercials and programs.

## Consultants and Standards Officials

Other unobtrusive evaluators at work in our industry also deserve mention here. We discuss these two categories of professionals together because each is the mirror image of the other. Generally speaking, consultants are *outside evaluators* brought in to advise a media business on what it should do. Standards (also known as standards and practices) officials, conversely, are *inside evaluators,* who provide guidelines for what should *not* be done.

Consultants offer a wide range of expertise to their clients; expertise that would be too expensive or specialized to *have on the payroll full-time.* Some consultants work with the station's on-air product. Often referred to as program or news doctors, these professionals formulate suggestions about how an outlet can make its service more attractive to its target audiences. It is often said that "much of

what a consultant sells to a client is his own success story."[22] Thus, most programming consultants have proven track records in improving the performance of stations for which they previously worked. Operating from their own reservoir of experience, these visitors offer program and news directors shortcuts to success by articulating what has and has not worked in similar situations elsewhere. Rather than re-inventing the wheel, in-station managers get a refined view of options much more quickly and efficiently than by their own trial-and-error experimentation.

Sales consultants perform a similar function by providing suggestions about how a station can improve its billings. Some of these tips may be technical in nature, such as redesigning the outlet's rate card or advocating a different system for dividing account lists and responsibilities among the existing sales staff. Other advice might be more motivational, such as offering techniques and philosophies to boost sales success by restructuring how the account executives make their client pitches or changing the method and type of system management uses to reward the selling staff.

Other consultants may be called in to assist a media business with engineering, accounting, data management, or bill collection problems. Whatever the subject, a skilled consultant will first analyze the existing situation and then lay out options. He or she will never come to town with a predetermined answer nor attempt to jam any single solution down the local manager's throat. In our industry, as in most others, prized consultants are careful analyzers and evaluators rather than off-the-cuff dictators. What award-winning radio consultant Donna Halper said of her branch of the business should be equally true of other types of electronic media consultants as well:

"Everything we do is based, at least in part, on research findings. We are anything but rash in our judgments. Suggestions and recommendations are invariably inspired by

**425**

CHAPTER 13
Evaluative
and
Analytical
Functions

**426**

SECTION
THREE
Profes-
sional
Perspec-
tives

**Figure 13–2**

Some broad-scope business development efforts are designed for on-air exposure, as in these five ten-second spots

# Virginia Department of Economic Development
:10 TV

## BUTTONS

MUSIC UP, AS KEYS MOVE AND LIGHTS FLASH.

ANNCR: Our AAA bond rating

is drawing lots of buttoned-up

companies to Virginia.

## BRITISH AEROSPACE

MUSIC: BRITISH THEME. ANNCR: British Aerospace came to Virginia to be closer to our nation's capital...

SOUND EFFECTS: CONCORDE TAKING OFF. And theirs.

## PENTAGON

MUSIC: MILITARY DRUMS. ANNCR: Virginia has what every high-tech company needs.

A customer.

## GOODYEAR

SOUND EFFECTS: TIRE INFLATING, WITH MUSIC. ANNCR: Goodyear has performed so well in Virginia, they've

expanded their tire plant 12 times.

## NAUTILUS

MUSIC: WORKOUT THEME. ANNCR: Nautilus moved to Virginia

on the strength of our work force.

PRODUCED BY SIDDALL, MATUS & COUGHTER INC.

**427**

CHAPTER 13
Evaluative
and
Analytical
Functions

**RUSSELL MOURITSEN**/MEDIA CONSULTANT

Observers often look on consultants as generalists and all-purpose fix-it people with a bag of tricks they can apply to any problem. Nothing could be further from the truth. Media communications is a broad and dynamic arena ranging from highly technical satellite communications, fiber optics, interactive computer technology, and intelligent television, to human relations and management issues relative to radio, TV, cable, and other electronic media. Because the media environment covers such a broad spectrum, successful media consultants typically specialize in facets of the industry in which they have experience and credibility.

The media include a variety of disciplines often quite disparate, yet all have in common the purpose of communicating ideas through channels we refer to as the *media*. These channels of communication range from traditional print and broadcast media to newer technologies.

Media consultants have two things in common: good academic backgrounds and diverse media experience; these credentials are important for the consultant. Consultants often get involved in their work indirectly. A TV station manager, for example, might run a very successful operation and be asked to share his expertise with another station in another city; thus, the genesis for a consultant is born. University professors often become involved in consulting through expertise they have acquired in academic circles. Experience is a requirement, and thus it is prudent for recent graduates to become seasoned be-

fore they attempt to promote their consulting skills.

Media consultants typically focus on problems related either to people or technology. In a TV station, for example, we find that departments needing consultants are either technically oriented or human relations oriented. The departments that focus on technology include production, research, and engineering; management, sales, personnel, programming, and community relations are concerned more with human relations approaches. Typically, a media problem is not just a vertical problem. It tends to cross over into several departments. Therefore, a media consultant must have access to many resources in order to do the job.

Knowledge of your specific field, credibility, good contacts, an ability to write proposals, good organizational skills, and, of course, computer skills (which include a thorough knowledge of spreadsheet and graph-

428

SECTION
THREE

Profes-
sional
Perspec-
tives

ics programs) are all essential attributes of a good media consultant. This may mean bringing in outside help from a good base of contacts in the media field. Access to a good library is important, because staying current is critical.

Many media consultants are independent, although a few large consulting organizations do exist. The latter typically specialize in such areas as programming and management. Independent consultants often find it more comfortable and prudent to have a base of employment in media and consult from that base. This is smart for two reasons: first, your salary is secure; and second, you have access to resources and contacts you otherwise would not have. There are many advantages to combining an academic career with consulting. Consultants are able to apply their practical applications to classroom theory and likewise to draw on that theory as they apply solutions to consulting problems. A good foundation of theory is an essential basis for consulting.

Remuneration for consultants is paid primarily in one of two ways. Consultants can agree to a specific monthly salary, called a retainer. They thus become available to work on specific projects as requested and are on call for information and advice. The next most common method of remuneration is by contract for a set-dollar amount for specific jobs. Consultants on retainer with a company are not permitted to work with competing organizations, for obvious ethical reasons.

The future for media consultants is very bright. Because the media marketplace is dynamic and sophisticated, organizations typically will be unable to afford in-house problem-solving resources and thus will have to look outside for solutions.

---

some type of on-the-scene or nationally conducted research. Instincts are important in this business, and I pride myself on having some of the best, but I am also long enough on experience to know the value of careful, methodical study."[23]

*Standards and practices officials,* the in-house evaluators mentioned earlier, may also rely on research to help justify their findings, and good instincts are a valuable quality for them as well. But standards officials (disparagingly referred to as *censors*) have to apply their research and instincts to the difficult task of deciding what is and what is not appropriate for a given outlet's airwaves. Rather than offering a consultant's detached, objective, and outside view of what the station should be doing to improve performance in some area, the standards or continuity acceptance person brings an intimate and continuous analysis to bear in a more preventative manner. As an in-house employee, the standards executive's job is to protect the operation from legal or public relations trouble through careful and tactful scrutiny of commercial and show content. Thus, their work has been dubbed *prophylactic programming*—taking action now that will prevent unfortunate consequences for the radio or television facility later.

Standards divisions exist at most networks and in the headquarters of the major broadcast group owners. Larger stations may also

**429**

CHAPTER 13
Evaluative
and
Analytical
Functions

employ such a person, but at the local level these duties usually are the responsibility of the program director, with the advice of legal counsel sought as needed.

There is no question that the role and scope of standards activities has changed at both the network and station level over the years. Until 1982, the NAB Radio and Television Codes served as virtually industrywide guidelines for both programming and advertising content. When these were withdrawn in deference to antitrust concerns (see Chapter 6), each broadcast operation was left to its own devices. Some formulated or expanded the policies they already had in place. Others simply continued independently to follow the last version of the NAB documents under the reasonable assumption that the Codes' utility had been proven over the years. Some others ignored the situation entirely—at least until they ran into trouble for something they aired.

At the same time, the fragmentation of the radio audience and the explosion of new cable services pushed back the boundaries of acceptable on-air program content—most noticeably for certain format radio outlets and limited-access pay cable offerings. Meanwhile, the Reagan administration's narrowing of Federal Trade Commission activities left stations and systems to police the advertising that they aired without much help from the federal government.

The result of all these conflicting trends was a predictably mixed one. All three major television networks greatly reduced their standards offices—and then found they had to rescind these cuts partially in order to maintain credibility and consistency. Stations found themselves hurriedly authoring new policies to provide a rationale for turning down undesirable product advertisers now seeking radio/television exposure. And cable operations discovered that acceptance standards were critical if they were to project an image attractive to reputable, mainstream advertisers. Then, at the end of 1989, a Con-gress-pressured FCC began a crusade against aired indecency that raised even more standards questions.

Where the pendulum will swing from here is difficult to predict. But it is probably a fair assumption that standards or continuity acceptance staff will be an important factor in at least the major electronic media enterprises for the foreseeable future. With larger-market licenses and franchises worth millions of dollars, a competent and pragmatic standards executive can detect content situations likely to put those investments in danger and then take preventative action. Civil lawsuits arising from allegedly deceptive commercials and listener/viewer protests about tawdry or disparaging programming are both threats to the bottom line. The skilled standards executive is paid to protect the station or network from such eventualities without inhibiting an expressiveness that keeps the interest of both audiences and advertisers. Even coming close to walking that line (see Figure 13–3) demonstrates analytical and evaluative skills of the highest calibre.

It must be made clear that in respected media companies, standards and practices staff do *not* oversee news operations. A hallmark of electronic journalism is that it should be discrete from advertising and entertainment functions—and this includes freedom from content oversight. Thus, news directors must be their own standards officer, calling on the additional evaluative skills of their communications attorneys as circumstances warrant.

As long as they occupy the public airwaves and flow unfettered into every functioning radio and television set, broadcasters will have to contend with content concerns beyond those faced by their print and even their cable colleagues. The content of a book or magazine can be scanned by a consumer prior to bringing it into the house. And cable service, whether pay or basic, can be refused simply by not hooking up. But broadcast material cannot be scanned in advance, and of-

**430**

SECTION
THREE

Profes-
sional
Perspec-
tives

**Figure 13-3**
Daring program concepts can test the boundaries and clarity of broadcast
standards decision making

fensive stations cannot be clipped from a receiving set's tuner. Especially given its non-previewable access to children, broadcasting thereby is afflicted with special standards responsibilities. The presence in-house of intelligent standards executives is a preferable way of addressing these responsibilities than are capricious outside censors' alternatives.

## Librarians and Teachers

We have just specified intelligence as the key characteristic for an industry standards official. In fact, any of us working in a profession that possesses the capacity to touch the lives and minds of millions of people immediately had better exhibit this characteristic, too. Though they can't *give* us intelligence, our final pair of analyst/evaluators are the most directly involved in directing the intelligence we do possess toward the attainment of our professional goals.

The electronic media collectively constitute a vast information industry and one that consumers preeminently rely on for concise and immediate enlightenment. However, we cannot convey information efficiently to other people if we cannot keep track of it ourselves. Working in a variety of electronic media settings, *librarians* arrange and locate the data on which so many other radio/television professionals rely to accomplish their own jobs.

**431**

CHAPTER 13
Evaluative
and
Analytical
Functions

**SUSAN HILL**/VICE-PRESIDENT, LIBRARY AND INFORMATION CENTER
NATIONAL ASSOCIATION OF BROADCASTERS

At the NAB Library, we begin the day by clipping seven daily newspapers and routing industry-related stories to each of the association's departments. We scan trade and business press every day as well, sending copies of articles to staff working on those issues and clipping stories for our subject files. There is a lot of scanning in this job, but not much reading of entire books and journals. Contrary to popular belief, we librarians rarely get to read many of the books in our collections from cover to cover. We do make it a point to check the books, however, for indexes, glossaries, and chronologies, all of which help us find answers quickly.

Incoming telephone calls help shape the day. A member station asks for the number of television stations broadcasting in stereo. Another wants to know about broadcasting in South Africa. A public-relations firm asks for the names of persons able to speak about the future of television. A reporter needs the names of weather-service providers.

The mail brings requests for literature on improving AM reception, industrywide practices concerning vacation policies, material for a speech on media ethics, and articles on using 900 telephone numbers in advertising. A staff member preparing testimony for a Congressional hearing needs statistics on sports programming costs. Another one asks us to search a data-base service for an article on children's television.

The reference desk is our equivalent of a news bureau's assignment desk. Our reference editor assigns each question to an information specialist. Assignments are made on the basis of interest, knowledge, and expertise. All of us are responsible for knowing how to find everything, but with experience we develop specialties. One librarian usually handles the NAB history-related questions. Another knows a lot about radio station management practices. And another does most of the data-base searching.

We work as a team. If one of us is stuck on a query, we ask the others for ideas. If we get a rush request, we work together to get the information. We keep each other informed about the status of our requests. And when we find a long-sought-after piece of information, we share the triumph with our colleagues, should the same question occur again.

What does it take to be an electronic media librarian besides an interest in media and a knowledge of library science techniques? An ability

**432**

SECTION
THREE
___
Profes-
sional
Perspec-
tives

to work well under pressure is an absolute must, as is a knack for juggling
several tasks at one time. A persever-
ing drive is another plus. No shrinking
violets need apply, as daily give-and-
take exchanges are crucial to successful information searches. Marketing skills are useful, too, as we look
for ways to attract new clients and to
promote our services to established
clients.

Some librarians are employed by industry trade associations. This is a very efficient deployment because individual or corporate members from around the country thereby have a common resource on which they can draw and a much more comprehensive resource than any single company could construct on its own. Trade association librarians concentrate on compiling and accessing the kinds of materials that people in their particular branch of the industry are more likely to need. Because the scope of their subject is relatively limited, they acquire in-depth expertise in it and can identify and assemble materials of greatest importance to their memberships.

Other librarians work for governmental agencies or communications law firms. In these instances, of course, the focus is on collecting and retrieving legal documents and public filings. Ideally, the information they uncover helps a citizen or client deal more efficiently and responsibly with government so that both parties' interests are served. The administrative or legal librarian may also be asked to provide documents that will help a party defend itself in a government adjudicatory proceeding (like an FCC license-renewal hearing) or better prepare its case in a civil or criminal trial. Even the brightest communications attorney can do a client little good without swift access to the materials and case studies that bear on the filing or proceeding being undertaken. A skilled legal librarian helps ensure such access.

Large news gathering operations, particularly at the network level, also use librarian expertise, of course, in order to maintain that wealth of background material necessary to round out news coverage and provide the source for interesting background or sidebar pieces on a breaking story. Much of this material may be audio/visual in nature (photographs, audio recordings, film and video footage), which can mirror that sense of actuality audiences have come to expect from electronic journalism.

When library professionals move beyond print matter or data-base collections into these other realms they are usually referred to as *media librarians*. In addition to news organizations, media librarians are found at industry archives such as the Museum of Radio and Television in New York; within college, university, and school district libraries and resource centers; and at companies that specialize in the rental of large collections of recorded material. A notable aspect of this last enterprise is the *stock photography* business, which accumulates and cross-indexes vast quantities of still photos and motion picture footage. News departments, studio and independent producers, as well as advertising agencies use the services of a stock house to obtain photos, slides, or rushes (motion picture/video segments) to be used as elements within their various projects. If the needed item can be located by a knowledgeable stock librarian, obtaining the rights for its use is much more cost-efficient than sending a crew or photographer to shoot it fresh. And in the case of historical pictures or rushes, of course, the stock archive becomes irreplaceable.

Finally, large advertising agencies also employ in-house librarians. In most instances, their collections include both print and audio/visual matter that account, media, and creative departments can consult in helping with client research, audience and marketing studies, and campaign development. Those other in-house analyzers, the new business development executives, especially may rely on their agency libraries to pull together the product category and company profiles necessary to targeting the best prospective clients.

If you previously thought of librarians only in conjunction with municipal and school facilities, the variety of situations we have just cited demonstrate the spectrum of other library-related prospects. Schools do provide the environment within which our final category of evaluator/analyzers—electronic media *teachers*—perform their instructive functions.

Broadly speaking, media teachers are divided into two groups: (1) those who teach *via* radio/television and (2) those who teach about radio/television *itself*. The former group trace their heritage at least as far back as 1930, with the Ohio School of the Air and similar enterprises (see Chapter 9). During the last sixty years, and with varying degrees of success and public acceptance, instructors from a variety of disciplines have been put on the air in an attempt to share their expertise with larger or more dispersed student bodies. But as we also discuss in Chapter 9, the surge of interest over in-school instructional television (ITV) during the late 1950s and 1960s gradually ebbed as the concept of *educational* broadcasting gave way to that of *public* broadcasting. Because ITV had previously deflected attention from instructional radio, this meant that in-school broadcasting as a whole became significantly diminished.

However, even though over-the-air uses declined markedly, the availability of low-cost, reliable video equipment provided, by the 1980s, a number of off-air options for teaching by television. National, regional, and local programs can be put on cassette and distributed for playback on the VCRs that are present in virtually every school. Larger school districts can, with minimal expenditure, put their own master teachers on tape as supplementary resources for classrooms throughout their communities. Particularly when combined with an educational access channel provided by the local cable system as part of its franchise agreement, these lessons can even be fed to the community at large and to home-bound students as well. Increasingly, adjacent school districts are combining forces to provide so-called *interactive* services for sharing specialized classes that no single district could afford to offer. Some of these services *are,* in fact, interactive, providing audio talkback circuits through which participating students in other school buildings can converse with the presenting teacher in his or her own classroom.

Through the use of now-abundant satellite capacity, video teleconferencing is another teaching tool. Especially as used at the college level, it can deliver instructional experiences that are even international in nature with students, faculty, and other experts joining together for global lessons and seminars. Finally, with the support of the Annenberg Foundation and other agencies, certain college-level coursework has been presented as public broadcasting series programming, with students able to secure credit through a participating campus in their area.

The essential ingredient in all of these projects is the articulate faculty member. Beyond being masters of their own subject area, these teachers must be able to structure and deliver this material clearly and do so in a way that projects well through the television screen. Thus, they must carefully analyze their own field to isolate the topics most essential to the course at hand and then evaluate which particular lessons and materials would be most

**433**

CHAPTER 13
Evaluative
and
Analytical
Functions

434

SECTION
THREE

Profes-
sional
Perspec-
tives

**JAY ROUMAN**
HIGH SCHOOL MEDIA PRODUCTION TEACHER

Teaching audio and video production at a vocational secondary education program combines the excitement of the broadcast industry with the energy and enthusiasm of teenagers. It also provides the challenge of working within a skills-based environment that is rapidly changing in a desperate attempt to keep pace with the industry. Adding this to a traditional high school program, which sometimes seems to have been cast in stone in 1900, produces a combination that can charitably be described as "interesting." Fortunately, the synergism between the two programs makes up for many of the problems.

Perhaps the most useful skill a person in my position can possess is the ability to deal with a wide variety of people who have different and often conflicting ideas about how you can best serve them. Students, other teachers, administrators, and the public outside the school system all represent varying needs and expectations that sometimes seem to require attention simultaneously. The trick is to satisfy at least some of the demands while keeping some semblance of sanity. The neatest trick of all is having fun while you're doing it.

Our vocational program features a heavy emphasis on building skills through hands-on experience. Although there is a certain amount of unavoidable lecture time, the great bulk of the class periods are devoted to the production of a wide variety of programs and segments. Students are encouraged to try anything that does not conflict with safety considerations and the laws of the land.

Our primary goal is producing people who have the skills and attitudes necessary to work in a typical production environment, be it broadcast, cable, or industrial. It is strongly suggested that students pursue training beyond the secondary level, although many secure jobs directly out of high school, and some use their entry-level jobs as a source of income during their college years.

I always tell students that the broadcasting and production industry will probably remain a tough job market. It would be totally dishonest even to suggest that employers are going to be waiting with open arms on graduation day. Even so, most of our students who have a serious interest in the field have found employment—literally from coast to coast.

Because I operate a one-person department and take care of the engineering and equipment maintenance as well as teaching and general organizing, my days are seldom boring or routine. Each group of new students, each piece of new equipment, and each new production provides its own challenge and fascination.

effective in the tele-viewing setting. Poor teaching will never make good television, and ill-conceived television will not successfully convey great teaching. Instructors who appear on the tube must be intimately aware of the interdependency of content and electronic delivery.

Sometimes outside subject matter specialists are assisted and tutored by other instructors whose discipline *is* the electronic media itself. Radio/television faculty, our second category of media teachers, strive to increase understanding of the role, content, and techniques of audio and video communication and mass communication. Although primarily found at the post-secondary level, media studies teachers are becoming increasingly prevalent in certain high school settings as more districts recognize the importance of the electronic media in the present and future lives of their students.

Still, such recognition has been slow in coming. Our educational system prides itself on its ability to turn out productive citizens who have learned how to earn a wage, evaluate a purchase, balance a checkbook, and make some sense out of the printed word. Yet, the purchase of electronic media content through the prioritized expenditure of one's own time and the analysis and evaluation of that content via one's own intellect are subjects that are still too rare in the standard school curriculum.

How many book reports, for example, were you called on to complete before leaving high school? On the other hand, how many electronic media listening or viewing reports were assigned? That there were probably many times more of the former than the latter directly contradicts the media use pattern that dominates most people's lives. Unfortunately, a significant number of graduates seldom read more than a book or two a year, but all absorb the collective equivalent of thousands of book-length narratives through continuous consumption of radio and television content.

This immense divergency between classroom training and real-world behavior exists in the college as well as the secondary school. "To say that the communications media are central to the functioning of our society is to state the obvious," observes Professor Everette Dennis. "However, American undergraduate education almost completely ignores the study of mass communication. Unless students major in communications, journalism, or media studies, they can go through college without acquiring more than fragmentary knowledge about mass communication."[24] Recently, print literacy has grudgingly had to share the spotlight with computer literacy, but *media literacy* remains a largely unmet need.

One important task for electronic media educators, then, is to convince curricular authorities of the importance of their discipline so that they can proceed to educate a generation of discerning listeners and viewers. The second key task for these faculty members is to train skilled and dedicated media *practitioners* who will use our high-tech tools to their full potential. If, as we contend throughout this book, electronic media personnel constitute a *profession,* then these personnel must be thoroughly and authoritatively educated. This is the ultimate analytical and evaluative duty because it will shape the people who themselves will shape the destiny of the entire radio/television enterprise.

"Broadcasting," "telecommunications," or "media studies" instructors as they are variously known are found in college/university, trade/technical school, and, less often, in secondary school settings. The high school teacher's task may involve classes in media appreciation for the student body as a whole as well as preprofessional training for students interested in pursuing media careers. Trade and technical school faculty take the process one step further by offering detailed postsecondary instruction designed to qualify graduates for entry-level jobs somewhere in our industry. The limitation of some trade

**435**

CHAPTER 13
Evaluative
and
Analytical
Functions

436

SECTION
THREE

Profes-
sional
Perspec-
tives

**LOUIS DAY**/MEDIA PROFESSOR
LOUISIANA STATE UNIVERSITY

In this information age, broadcast journalists sit at the vortex of our pluralistic society and provide the most dramatic and powerful vicarious link between many citizens and their environment. Thus, the necessity for educated and knowledgeable electronic journalists is more acute today than at any period in the history of mass communication. Most stations now recognize this imperative and demand college-trained journalists. Therefore, my job as a broadcast educator is to provide the technical skills and professional competence and knowledge expected of today's graduates.

With this in mind, my faculty colleagues and I serve two masters: the practical side of our curriculum designed to prepare students for their first jobs and the more academic side that broadens and enriches the student's educational perspective on the electronic media. Most of us bring to the university some combination of professional experience and advanced study in the form of at least a master's degree and in many cases a Ph.D. in journalism or mass communication.

The skills component of our curriculum consists of twelve semester hours of intensive instruction in writing, reporting, and electronic news gathering. One goal is to sensitize students to the realities of the newsroom, as our faculty critique story assignments and as deadline pressures disturb the traditional atmosphere of academic tranquility.

But not all of the student's time is spent learning the hands-on aspects of broadcast journalism. As a member of a university faculty committed to a broad liberal arts education, I believe that journalism students should understand the history, economics, legal constraints, and ethical responsibilities of their profession. Much of my time, therefore, is spent supplementing their practical training with academic instruction and discussion in these areas.

One theme that underlies all of my teaching is that the standards of performance and conduct expected within our curriculum should exceed those of the industry. This statement might appear to reflect overtones of elitism, but I believe it is the university's obligation to contribute to the professionalization of the electronic media industries.

In addition to my instructional responsibilities, much of my time is devoted to advising and career counseling. The academic advising is concerned primarily with course selec-

**437**

CHAPTER 13
Evaluative
and
Analytical
Functions

tion and fulfillment of degree requirements. In career counseling, I assess the student's strengths and weaknesses and describe the career opportunities available within the electronic media industries.

Perhaps the most satisfying aspect of my position on a university faculty is to watch my four years of instruction and counseling bear fruit as my students land their first jobs and begin what (hopefully!) will be successful careers in the electronic media. However, this enthusiasm is tempered by the knowledge that they are joining an industry in which professionalism is often elusive and the financial rewards are rather meager for beginning reporters. This is the most frustrating part of the job. Students come to me full of idealism and energy. The quandary confronting me, as a media teacher, is whether to quell this enthusiasm with brutal candor early in the student's program or to temper my criticisms and allow students to make their own judgments once they have joined the ranks of media practitioners.

---

school curricula, however, is that their narrowness and brevity prepare students only for their *first* job. No real attention is given to the broader educational prospectives that a person needs in order to move to higher and more managerial roles.

For their part, four-year college and university media professors seek to integrate profession-specific insights with the more comprehensive instruction from other academic departments. The goal is to fashion bachelor's and graduate degree programs that can underpin a person's entire career. Most faculty strive, therefore, for a curricular balance between technical training and theoretical education. In this way, both short- and long-term career and life considerations can be raised. As with law, medicine, or any other endeavor, the profession that trains its members only in its own aspects does not prepare them to function successfully in the larger society.

Astute electronic media faculty at all levels realize the value of instruction in specific skills. But they also perceive the broader picture. In his book *Technology and the Academics,* Sir Eric Ashby wrote that one of the strongest desires of human beings seems to involve learning to perform at least one thing thoroughly and with a high degree of expertise. In a highly technological age, the close co-operation of applied arts such as media studies with the more traditional liberal arts perspectives can construct curricula in which specialist training provides the viable and valuable core for a modern liberal education. As the role of the electronic media becomes more prominent in interconnecting our life experiences, and as concern about the content and responsibilities of these media becomes more central to the concerns of society as a whole, media studies themselves can constitute the nucleus of instruction for the educated person of the nineties and beyond.

Electronic media teachers whose backgrounds reflect a blend of industry and academic experience are maximally qualified to serve the immediate and long-range preparatory needs of their students. Graduates of such faculty's curricula learn to manipulate the devices and procedures common to radio/television. But these students also acquire perspectives on the analytical and evaluative processes needed in *any* field in which the abilities to formulate and to communicate

**438**

SECTION
THREE
Profes-
sional
Perspec-
tives

policy action are at a premium. The out-of-work aerospace expert and the unemployed liberal arts student are practical illustrations of the human fallout that occurs when either a person's wish to do one thing well or his or her eventual need to adapt to new conditions is ignored by the people who design instruction.

In the past four chapters, we explore at least the major careers that the electronic media encompass. Whether you find yourself in any of these, or in one of the myriad of other positions that exist today or will exist tomorrow, try to develop and maintain the broadest professional perspective possible. This perspective will help you to detect the full range of your own potentialities, and it will also optimize your value to our industry. Because of their power, cost, and complexity, the electronic media will always be group endeavors. Individuals who possess the widest view of where the group needs to be headed are most likely to avoid disasters and amplify opportunities.

## Chapter Flashback

Evaluator/analysts primarily function outside core electronic media businesses to provide the liaisons, systems, and development essential to our profession's well-being. Although they are most often perceived as enforcers, *regulators* also serve a protective role in creating a stable operating environment. The FCC is the most obvious regulator of much of our industry; the Congress, courts, and a variety of other federal agencies such as the FDA and FAA also exercise authority, as do state and local units like attorneys general and cable franchise awarders.

*Communications attorneys* are specialists in electronic media law and regulation; they seek to prevent problems before they are required to litigate them. The most successful

lawyers practice with a keen appreciation of communications law's private and public interests. *Lobbyists* keep government informed about trends and needs in their employer's branch of the media and strive to demonstrate that their positions parallel the best interests of society. Many lobbyists work for industry companies; other influence wielders represent citizen's groups like ACT or governmental agencies like the NTIA. *Political and public relations communicators* are more visible lobbyists who strive to represent their boss's or company's positions to and through the media as a means of positively influencing the general public.

*Critics* and *commentators* evaluate the performance of the electronic media itself and offer guidance to the public on media use and interpretation. The respected critic thus stimulates both industry improvements and increased public enjoyment of the products of that industry. *Brokers* and *financial analysts* can be thought of as specialized financial commentators. Brokers use their knowledge of media properties and financing mechanisms to facilitate the sale of radio and television outlets. Financial analysts evaluate the fiscal health of media businesses and advise potential investors and lenders on which enterprises constitute the best investment choice.

*Business development executives* seek to identify and attract new corporate customers to their firms. In this process, both fiscal and corporate culture compatibility needs to be considered. Other business developers such as cable customer representatives and noncommercial station membership coordinators focus their efforts directly on the public. *Consultants* are outside specialists called in by a media company to improve its performance or operation in any of a variety of internal or external functions. *Standards officials,* on the other hand, are regular employees of a radio/television outlet who strive to ensure that what is aired is responsible and in the best interests of the facility.

**439**

CHAPTER 13
Evaluative
and
Analytical
Functions

*Librarians* preserve, organize, and retrieve the data and program content elements on which other media professionals rely to accomplish their own tasks. When librarian responsibilities move beyond print matter or data-base collections into pictorial or audio holdings, they are often more precisely titled *media librarians*. Finally, *electronic media teachers* perform one of two roles in the service of education. Some use radio/television as tools to extend their own academic discipline (English, mathematics, etc.); others teach actual media techniques and issues. These latter educators strive to enhance media literacy among the general student body and/or to prepare future professionals for media employment.

## ❑ Review Probes

1. List three examples of regulators performing a media *protective* function.
2. What are the titles and responsibilities of each of the FCC's four bureaus?
3. How does the Department of Justice sometimes serve as a lobbyist on media-related issues?
4. What is meant by *proactive* communication?
5. State an example of a financial analyst's pronouncements having a direct impact on a broker's ability to consummate the sale of a media property.
6. What is the more official term for in-house censor and why is this job more prominent in *broadcast* as opposed to *cable* operations?

## ❑ Suggested Background Explorations

Allen, Robert C., ed. *Channels of Discourse: Television and Contemporary Criticism.* Chapel Hill: University of North Carolina Press, 1987.

Cartwright, Steve R. *Training with Video.* White Plains, NY: Knowledge Industry Publications, 1986.

Day, Louis. *Ethics in Media Communications: Cases and Controversies.* Belmont, CA: Wadsworth, 1991.

Diamond, Edwin, and Stephen Bates. *The Spot: The Rise of Political Advertising on Television.* Rev. ed. Cambridge, MA: MIT Press, 1988.

Kern, Montague. *30-Second Politics: Political Advertising in the Eighties.* New York: Praeger, 1989.

Lichter, Linda S., and S. Robert Lichter. *Prime Time Crime: Criminals and Law Enforcers in TV Entertainment.* Washington, DC: Media Institute, 1983.

Liebert, Robert M., and Joyce Sprafkin. *The Early Window: Effects of Television on Children and Youth.* 3rd ed. New York: Pergamon, 1988.

Mickelson, Sig. *From Whistle Stop to Sound Bite: Four Decades of Politics and Television.* New York: Praeger, 1989.

Plevan, Kenneth, and Miriam Siroky. *Advertising Compliance Handbook.* New York: Practicing Law Institute, 1988.

C H A P T E R   **1 4**

# Toward the New Millennium

❑ *This textbook, like any print media vehicle, is frozen in time. Whatever has been said in the previous chapters about the current state of our industry is, at best, a series of status quo snapshots. Therefore, because no book in our fast-changing field can be fully up-to-date by the time it is published, we take a few moments here to isolate a select few of our industry's volatile aspects. These aspects are likely to have evolved further by the time this text is in your hands.*

## Video Thrusts

Because so much of our profession is characterized by the pictorial hardware on which it is built, it is appropriate to begin our conjecture with some equipment-based projections.

### High Definition Television (HDTV)

Once it actually enters the marketplace, *high-definition television* (HDTV) literally will bring a new dimension to the video scene. As we discuss in Chapter 11, this dimension will be *16 by 9*—HDTV's screen width-to-height *aspect ratio* as contrasted with the *4 by 3* ratio of standard television set screens. What is even more striking is the panorama that appears within HDTV's parameters. The picture is made up of at least twice the number of lines as our current 525-line NTSC system. (See Figure 14–1.) This gives the HDTV picture a resolution that comes close to that of 35-mm film, at least to the eye of the casual viewer.

As a technology, HDTV has been around for some time. A joint consortium of Japanese manufacturers conducted experiments with it throughout the 1970s, and a public display of their system was mounted at the 1981 meeting of the Society of Motion Picture and Television Engineers. A group of European interests also became involved in HDTV, although their "Eureka 95" is not compatible with what the Japanese have created. (See Figure 14–2.) Meanwhile, the United States remains a secondary force. With only one domestic set manufacturer remaining (Zenith), the United States is having to make HDTV decisions without, as yet, being a primary player in the development process.

To buy time and avoid the rapid obsolescence of U.S. transmission and reception equipment, the FCC ruled in 1988 that any approved HDTV system must be compatible with existing U.S. standards. At about the same time, and sensing a threat to U.S. security, the Department of Defense pledged $30 million to spur U.S. research efforts in both military and civilian applications of HDTV. Several U.S. interests, including the David Sarnoff Research Center (a private contract facility), have become involved in the effort to develop an acceptable HDTV system for the United States. U.S. subsidiaries of foreign companies are also active in this area.

A first step was the Sarnoff Center's 1987 demonstration in Ottawa of ACTV, or Advanced Compatible Television. Even though it contained only 1,050 scanning lines (versus the Japanese system's 1,125 and the latest European 1,250-line proposal), ACTV's lower picture quality was compensated for by the fact that it was compatible with existing U.S. receivers. In other words, an ACTV signal would appear as a viewable regular picture when picked up by conventional 525-line sets. Three years later, in 1990, ACTV's proponents (NBC, the Sarnoff Research Center,

**Figure 14–1**

Some reasons that HDTV offers more realistic viewing

| | HDTV | Conventional TV Systems (NTSC) |
|---|---|---|
| Number of scanning lines | 1125 lines or more | 525 lines |
| Screen size ratio | 9 : 16 (3 : 5.33) | 3 : 4 |
| Optimum viewing distance | 3 times screen height | 7 times screen height |
| Angle of vision | 30 degrees | 10 degrees |
| Audio system | Digital | Analog |

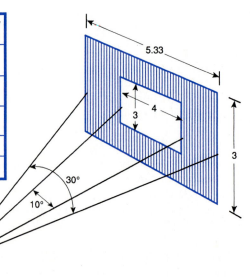

**Figure 14–2**

**443**

CHAPTER 14
Toward
the New
Millennium

A frame from a Eureka 95-system production. Note the 16 X 9 aspect ratio.

and Thomson Consumer Electronics) joined with North American Philips to promote a slightly improved standard known as ACTV–2 (see Figure 14–3).

The industry-backed Advanced Television Systems Committee (ATSC) and the FCC advisory committee on advanced television service (known as the ATS committee) are look-ing long and hard at their options. Under Chairman Richard Wiley (a former FCC chairman), the ATS committee established and operates the Advanced Television Test Center to evaluate the various HDTV or near-HDTV options and attempt to make a standards recommendation to the FCC sometime in 1993. The stakes are obviously high. One wrong de-

**CNN HDTV**

U.S. production companies are already involved in high definition television (HDTV)—even before standards have been set. Producers praise the flexibility of the technology, which one says "is like looking through a clean window."

**Figure 14–3**

Photo of an ACTV-2 image on a TV screen

cision could mean massive retooling expenses for U.S. broadcasters. Such expenses would undercut their ability to compete with alternative pay-TV services.

Part of the problem is that the true HDTV picture still requires a channel that is at least 9 MHz wide in order to carry all its electronic information properly. But as we learn in Chapter 2, a *broadcast* (over-the-air) television channel is only 6 MHz wide. Thus, the transmission of HDTV by television stations would require additional (and scarce) spectrum space. This would not pose a problem for cable or DBS (direct broadcast satellite) operations, who could simply reapportion their lines or transponder capabilities respectively to accommodate fewer but wider channels. Similarly, because it does not involve

any real signal transmission beyond its connector cable, an HDTV VCR requires no spectrum space to deliver its programming to a companion monitor.

How, then, will HDTV be introduced into the U.S. market? Do we adopt a compromise ACTV signal to give broadcasters time to retool or to find a way to *compress* true HDTV successfully into 6 MHz (assuming such compression systems are feasible)? Or, do we endorse true HDTV for technologies that can already implement it so as not to deprive interested U.S. consumers of this appealing picture quality?

Such *compression* technologies are looming as a fundamentally important subject in their own right. Through sophisticated digital sampling, compression devices may be able to offer broadcasters an HDTV avenue that fits within existing spectrum space. The lower power required by digital transmission also brings with it the potential to place stations closer together on the spectrum and to use channel assignments that heretofore have had to be kept vacant to avoid signal interference. Thus, it would be easier for the FCC to find extra channels for broadcasters to simulcast HDTV with their existing NTSC service. Compression also means that broadcast and cable networks could place four or more signals on a satellite transponder that previously carried only one. Digital compression even could create enough channel capacity to make Direct Broadcast Satellite (DBS) operations true multichannel competitors with cable. Although compression ratios of 4 or 5 to 1 are seen as the most economical for the immediate future, several companies are hard at work on devices that offer 8 to 1 or even 10 to 1 capability.

HDTV's economic, political, and (given military applications) national security aspects are both substantial and multifaceted. As we have seen time and time again, electronic media technologies have always been far ahead of our ability to use them equitably. HDTV is certainly no exception. It is clear that we *will* have it, just as it was clear by the late 1930s that we would have FM radio. But the political, financial, and international trade ramifications of HDTV must first be sorted out and dealt with.

The ultimate danger to U.S. interests that is posed by HDTV and by other cutting-edge electronic systems is that the United States may lose any vestige of technological dominance in the field. In more and more instances it seems that Japanese and/or European interests (both often supported by governmental structures) are dictating the technical standards to which U.S. media industries must conform. With most of our professional and consumer electronics industry already dominated by foreign brands, HDTV development may be this country's last

chance to avoid permanent status as a passive consumer rather than as an active inventor of telecommunication systems and equipment.

HDTV (even in its ACTV simulation) will let you see a movie as you saw it in the theatre—without its left and right wings chopped off. The 16-by-9 ratio will also reveal more of the stadium, arena, or race track. And even with the compromise ACTV, the picture you see will be sharper and much more detailed than before. Still, questions remain: To what degree are we willing to dislocate our industry and our bank accounts to achieve this? And how long can we wait before outside events make the choices for us?

## Video Compact Discs (VCD)

Also contributing to improved picture quality is the *video compact disc* (VCD). As with audiotape and CDs, video compact discs enjoy significant quality advantages over their tape counterparts because the recorded information is read by a highly efficient laser rather than being the result of tape stock mechanically dragged across a magnetic head. The laser can also jump instantaneously from one section of the recording to a later or earlier segment without the time-wasting rewinding or fastforwarding required with tape.

Video discs themselves are not new, of course. RCA introduced a needle-in-a-groove model more than a decade ago—at the same time IBM and MCA were jointly developing a laser-read system. Unfortunately for both ventures, the home VCR came to the fore at the same time and offered consumers the ability to make their own recordings rather than being forced exclusively to buy or rent software from other sources. Soon, high demand for VCRs lowered their prices to the point at which they were competitive with the play-only discs. RCA dropped out of the market, and the laser-driven models migrated to corporate/industrial applications, where they could be used for training and other informational programming that benefited from their large storage and random-access capabilities.

Now, with the compact audio disc having helped pave the way, VCDs seem ready to re-enter the consumer market. This will most likely occur via the new combination audio-video disc players (*combiplayers* for short) that can use both kinds of discs to feed stereo systems and television monitors. Movie and other program producers are especially in favor of this technology, of course, because it is playback-only. Consumers must *buy* the disc rather than merely record the show off-air or off-cable.

The preprogrammed access and storage advantages of the video disc also offer special potential for computer-linked uses. The result can be time-efficient *interactive* programs that lead a student or a customer through a series of optional lessons or product-line displays at the perceiver's own pace and in line with each individual's own needs or interests. As with HDTV, however, the lack of industry-wide standards has, to this point, inhibited the acceptance of this technology and therefore has kept equipment prices high. Simple VCD applications, like movie playbacks with flawless sound and picture quality, are well within reach. But the true *interactive* potential of the VCD—where each viewer instantaneously controls which segments of the disc will be accessed—has yet to be fully exploited.

Certainly, as VCD appeal illustrates, consumers are taking greater control of their electronic media environment. The VCR and the take-out stores that service it, the event selectivity of pay-per-view, the home production capability of the camcorder, the rise of special-purpose PC (personal computer) networks, and the amalgamation of all of these devices into increasingly sophisticated home entertainment/information centers give households who can afford it tremendous flexibility (see Figure 14–4).

Little more than a decade ago, most U.S. consumers could select only from what three

**Figure 14–4**

U.S. household media penetration, mid-1990

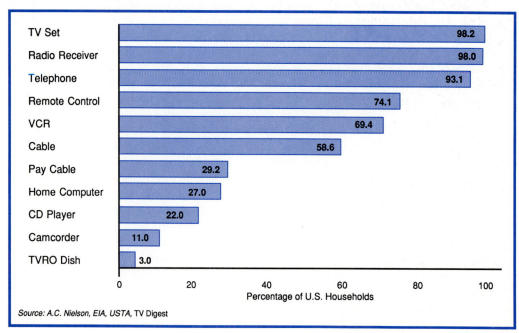

*Source: A.C. Nielson, EIA, USTA, TV Digest*

or four television networks (counting PBS) and perhaps an independent station had to offer. Now, many upscale homes have the ability to interact with several hardware and software systems to create custom video schedules and even custom programs. All of this, of course, is based on ability to pay. The old broadcast democracy, where everyone had access to the same choices (or lack of them), is being supplanted by a new pecking order that mirrors social and economic class distinctions. In other words, your range of media use options, like options in many other phases of life, is being determined more and more by your income level and the tools it puts in reach.

## Teletext and Videotext

*Teletext* possesses the capability to accelerate this consumer differentiation trend even more. With this system, even hundreds of pages of printed and graphic material can be sent via a broadcast station or cable channel. In all but the most primitive applications, the viewer can select individual pages or sections to appear on the screen. This material is encoded on an unused portion of the television signal cluster known as the *vertical blanking interval*. Through use of a decoder, the consumer can call up this information on the screen.

Perhaps the best known offshoot of this technology in the United States is the closed-captioning system through which hearing-impaired individuals receive subtitles that reproduce the main sense of the TV presentation's soundtrack. Since 1980, the nonprofit National Captioning Institute (NCI) has prepared the captions for network and certain other widely distributed programs. These captions are transmitted as part of the total video information. The hearing-impaired person (as well as persons trying to improve their English reading ability) has then had to obtain a decoder for about $180. This device, the Tele-Caption 4000, automatically pulls up the captioning data for on-screen display.

In the case of prerecorded programs, NCI captioner staff work from scripts or videotapes. Live show subtitling is more difficult, of course. Here, the captioner watches a monitor while operating a computer-assisted stenographic machine that can function at a rate of up to 300 words per minute before beaming to the transmission source. The caption then appears on the screen with no more than a four- or five-second delay. (The 1990 Decoder Circuitry Act requires that most television sets sold after mid-1993 have closed-caption capability built in. This should prove a significant boost to the NCI and to the consumers it was set up to serve.)

The British were the first to introduce teletext operations as far back as 1974 via the British Broadcasting Corporation's *Ceefax* service. The technology was quickly given a further lift when the competing IBA (the country's commercial television system) brought out its ORACLE (Optional Reception of Announcements by Coded Line Electronics). ORACLE became the world's first advertiser-supported teletext project and proved the commercial viability of such a system. Several other countries now engage in similar teletext activity in both public and for-profit applications. Up to now, however, virtually all of these operations have been aimed at corporate/institutional markets.

Unsure of whether the future of U.S. teletext lies in the business or mass consumer sector, the FCC has yet to specify a single standard for the system (although the implementation of the Decoder Circuity Act at least partially fills this void). In comparison to what has happened in other countries, the U.S. response to teletext remains fragmentary. CBS tested teletext over its then-owned KMOX–TV (St. Louis) as long ago as 1979, with similar trials undertaken at the same time by Salt Lake City's KSL–TV. Yet, without the strong national push of a government service, such as occurred in Europe, these isolated projects did not catch fire.

Teletext to this day remains essentially

one-way. *Videotext,* on the other hand, is more sophisticated. Sent via telephone or cable lines and linked to a computer, videotext operation permits two-way (interactive) communication between the viewer and a data bank. France's *Minitel* system is generally conceded to be the world's videotext leader. Begun in 1981 by the French telecommunications ministry, subscribers can use *Minitel* for shopping, banking, electronic message-sending, and access to constantly updated news. The project was successfully launched with the ministry's free distribution of basic decoders and the immediate on-line offering of an easy-access electronic business directory. Newspapers were allowed to participate in the operation and so became a source of classified advertising use and support. Thousands of business interests have purchased so-called pages on *Minitel,* thereby entrenching the system in the mainstream of French telecommunications activity.

Like teletext, videotext has met with a generally cold reception in the U.S. market. The contrasting success of both technologies in Europe may have been attributable to the centralized, government-operated telecommunications entities then in place. These integrated structures were able automatically to tap a wide institutional market with fully developed service. Even though there is now an increasing proliferation of private telecommunications enterprises on the European continent, teletext/videotext were introduced when the old centralized systems were still dominant.

## Direct Broadcast Satellite (DBS) Horizons

The United States has also lagged behind Europe (as well as Japan) in the building of a DBS service (see Chapter 2). During the early 1980s, COMSAT, United Satellite Communications, Inc. (chiefly financed by Prudential Insurance), Rupert Murdoch's Skyband, and Crimson Satellite Associates (Home Box Office and GE Americom) collectively lost more than $100 million in abortive attempts to establish a U.S. low-power DBS industry. USCI actually launched a service in November 1983 via a Canadian satellite and signed up several thousand East Coast subscribers, but the project closed with severe operating losses in April 1985. The causes of these failures were many. Chief among them were the large and comparatively expensive receive dishes that were required, limited program service, and the fact that many potential subscribers were just then being approached by new and expanding cable television operations.

In 1990, however, encouraged by more compact antenna availability and a global programming marketplace, some major players announced plans to try for DBS launch once more. Rather than relying on an unsightly dish 40 inches or more in width, high-power DBS would be receivable via a 12-inch by 18-inch rectangular panel that can sit on a windowsill and costs less than $300. By 1993, the Sky Cable project (promoted chiefly by General Motors's Hughes Communications) claims it will be offering subscribers a 108-channel true DBS service with HDTV potential.

Sky Cable plans to rely on a compression ratio of at least 4 to 1. Hughes forsees building a trio of 9-transponder satellites (see Figure 14–5) for the project, with 108 channels deriving from the 4 compressed channels per each of the 9 transponders (4 × 9 transponders on each of 3 satellites = 108).

By mid-1991, at least two competing DBS projects were actively being pursued. Prime-Star Partners (a consortium of nine major MSOs plus GE Americom) launched a 10-channel service on November 5, 1990. Using immediately available technology, this effort was not true DBS because it relied on medium rather than high-power satellites and thus required receiving dishes of at least one meter (40 inches). PrimeStar hoped later to expand into true DBS service with the high-power satellite deployment that makes 12-by-18-inch

**Figure 14–5**

**449**

CHAPTER 14
Toward
the New
Millennium

An artist's rendition of the Hughes HS601 high-power DBS satellite slated to relay Sky Cable Ku-band transmissions beginning in 1993

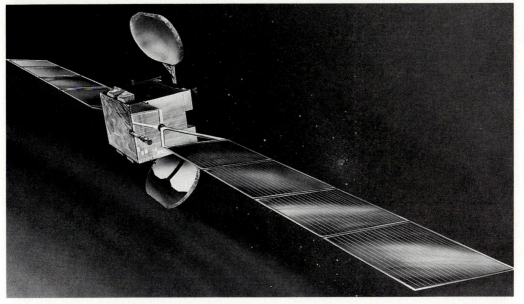

dishes feasible. Another midpower enterprise, SkyPix, joined with the Home Shopping Network to launch an 80-channel service via eight transponders and a prototype 10-to-1 compression device. Fifty of these channels were initially to be devoted to pay-per-view (PPV) movies, with SkyPix also making the service and its compression technology available to cooperating cable systems.

The SkyPix agreement with cable notwithstanding, the primary market for all of these DBS ventures is the millions of households not passed by conventional cable lines. PrimeStar gambled that by being first in the field, it would establish a critical foothold before Sky Cable's entry—even though its medium-power delivery meant that PrimeStar customers would have to purchase bigger and more expensive reception equipment. SkyPix had a similar strategy. Sky Cable, which joined with Hubbard Broadcasting in mid-1991, on the other hand, took the position that being first with true (high-power) DBS

was much more important to financial success than was being first with a potentially obsolete semi-service. The stakes here are high, of course, with additional DBS ventures waiting in the wings to see what happens. At this time, it appears that the convergence of DBS, compression, and HDTV technologies is the key to success—but such convergence is itself dependent on how long it takes the FCC to settle on an HDTV standard.

## Fiber Optics

Prophesy is further complicated by the emergence of *fiber optics* as a state-of-the-art replacement for conventional telephone and cable television lines. Fiber optic cable directs light waves through ultrathin strands of glass. The flexibility and small diameter of the fiber optic lines, together with the purity of the glass transmission environment, provide a vehicle that is interference-free, easy to install, and possesses a much greater signal capacity than traditional copper cable. Furthermore, the laser light pulses that in fiber optics re-place electrical signals are able to travel much farther before they must be ream-plified. Fiber optics are already being intro-duced into long-distance telephone transmis-sions, and the telephone industry as a whole is gradually replacing its old copper wires with low-maintenance fiber.

Given all of these advantages, the applica-tion of fiber to cable television is an obvious extension. Once installed, a fiber optic system significantly lowers maintenance costs while providing a greatly expanded channel capac-ity. The introduction of HDTV programs and a wealth of interactive services as part of the cable system's (or telco's) offerings would be no problem with high-capacity fiber, thereby providing more sources of revenue and en-hanced customer appeal. The major diffi-culty, in fact, may be the mundane and time-consuming task of replacing the copper wire plant in each home and business once the fiber optic line gets there.

On the other hand, cautions international marketing executive David Rosen, "the rapid maturation of DBS could have a profound im-pact on the rapidity of fiber deployment. Con-gress regulates the satellite industry, and its decisions to either foster media competition or protect under-served rural constituencies could shape the future of DBS. If successful, DBS, and particularly Sky Cable, could retard fiber deployment. By increasing program-ming supply, it could siphon off significant consumer demand for more conventional ser-vices, undercutting one of fiber's chief bene-fits."[1]

If they are fully deployed, fiber optic lines may have the advantage of lessening that pre-viously discussed trend toward media access based on ability to pay. Since most house-holds can now afford a copper-wire telephone line, and a basic cable drop as well, it is to be presumed they could still afford these ameni-ties if they were delivered via multiple-capac-ity fiber optics. Certainly some interactive services provided on these lines would incur additional charges. But the broadband car-riage of this new avenue also would be cer-tain to offer many enhanced elements as part of the fundamental service, and without the need for DBS-related equipment expenses. If the company owning the fiber optic plant would not agree to offer these no-additional-charge elements on its own, it is probable that government would require them in exchange for use of the public right-of-way.

## Audio Thrusts

Video advances tend to command the most attention. However, we should not neglect the audio side of our profession. Here, three new potentialities (DAT, DAB, and RSS) are expected to reshape radio in the new millen-nium. Beyond the year 2000, audio improve-ments are likely to be as dramatic, and as commonly taken for granted, as are the tele-vision breakthroughs we have just discussed.

### Digital Audiotape (DAT)

*Digital audiotape* equipment has been in evi-dence in major sound studios for years. Like any digital process (such as computer data), a digital tape system translates its information into a *binary code*. Simply put, this means that each element of the signal is converted into a two-value designation, with *1* being *on* or *closed* and *0* being *off* or *open*. Each sound sample (or, in the case of television, each pic-torial element) becomes a sequence of binary numbers, such as 110 or 010, with the se-quences taken together constituting the whole. Whereas the older *analog* system changes energy into continuous voltage fluc-tuations, the digital process converts voltage into a finite number of variations or values. Digitalization of a message thus involves three operations:

1. *Sampling* of analog voltages/readings over time.
2. *Quantification,* or the assigning of a discrete number of levels to each of the values within the range sampled.
3. *Coding* in order to assign a specific number (binary set) to each of these levels.

Because compact discs have accustomed U.S. consumers to the superiority of digital sound, it is natural that these same consumers would want to bring this sound quality to recordings they make themselves—hence the DAT (digital audiotape) recorder. For several years, however, record companies have fought the introduction of consumer DAT machines. They reason that because a DAT recording of a CD would produce sound just as good as the original, the market for CDs would be undercut. As was (and is) the case with analog recordings, people would simply borrow originals from friends and make copies. In 1989, an agreement was reached that permits the sale of consumer DAT equipment in the United States, and this should cause this technology to proliferate in the decade ahead. Using a tape cassette only half the size of conventional analog audiocassettes, DAT's sound reproduction and size advantages are likely to constitute the next home audio revolution—if a way can't be found for consumers to record directly on CDs.

Even more innovative are digital-audio options that spring from computer-based workstations. These stations record digital audio programming directly onto floppy or hard discs. Using a technique called *bit-rate reduction,* a 40-megabyte hard disc drive, for example, can have its stereophonic audio recording storage capacity increased from four to about thirty minutes. Bit-rate reduction capitalizes on the acoustic principle that the human ear "is unable to perceive quiet sounds when they are accompanied by other louder sounds composed of similar frequencies. Simply put, the digital audio data need only contain those parts of the original sound which can really be heard by the listener. Several systems have been developed to remove this 'redundancy and irrelevance.'"[2]

## Digital Audio Broadcasting (DAB)

Even though digital gear has established itself in recording studios and is gaining a substantial foothold in home stereo systems, the actual transmission of a signal by a radio station remains an analog function. In 1990, however, a European system for digital audio broadcasting (DAB) was demonstrated to U.S. broadcasters. Developed as Eureka (a partnership of several European governments and private manufacturers) the DAB procedure delivers a sound fidelity equal to that provided by a CD player right in the home. DAB is also four times more spectrum efficient than FM so that twelve to sixteen stereo channels could fit into between four and six MHz of space. What is more, the frequency response of a DAB receiver is seven kHz greater than that of FM (twenty-two kHz to only fifteen kHz).[3]

Early in 1991, the National Association of

## CNN  Digital Audiotape

The introduction into the U.S. market of DAT recorders was delayed due to recording industry concern about unauthorized copying. DAT dubs of an original track are so digitally accurate that they are considered clones rather than mere copies.

Broadcasters endorsed the Eureka 147 system and took steps to become the U.S. licensing agent for it. In taking this action, the NAB was attempting to advance the cause of terrestrial (land-station based) DAB implementation in lieu of satellite-delivered DAB that could drive existing broadcasters out of business. The NAB also intended that every existing AM and FM broadcaster would be first in line for a DAB license. Once all stations had taken up residency on the new (and higher) DAB portion of the spectrum, transmissions on the old AM and FM bands could gradually be phased out. The technical disadvantages under which AM operators have long labored would thus be abolished, with all radio broadcasters now at parity on the DAB band.

Worried about the economic implications of this parity, a number of large FM station group owners began lobbying for Acorn, a competing DAB protocol developed by Gannett Radio and SRI International. Acorn (also known as USA Digital) makes possible DAB transmissions on the existing FM band—thus upgrading current FM operations while leaving AM broadcasters to their own devices. Some experts claim that such an in-band option is also possible for AM, but this contention has yet to be tested beyond the theoretical stages.

Clearly, significant obstacles to U.S. implementation of DAB must be overcome. If the Eureka 147 approach is adopted, earmarked spectrum space must be found for it. Portions of the UHF band might be available, but those allocations are being frozen pending resolution of the HDTV situation. In addition, no DAB transmissions could be received on existing consumer radios. Like the early days of FM, the new enterprise must depend on the willingness of listeners to purchase new equipment. Finally, because of the nature of DAB technology, the number of DAB stations assigned to each market must be decided in advance and allocated in blocks. "In the digital audio broadcasting system," explains NAB vice-president for science and technology, Michael Rau, "there is only one 'splotch' of RF

[radio frequency] energy on the band and all the stereo channels are within that splotch of RF energy."[4] Thus, individual station power upgrades or other facility changes would not be possible because they would automatically interfere with every other DAB outlet in the cluster.

When DAB service will come to the United States is open to a great deal of speculation. Most experts believe that the technology could be fully developed by the middle of the 1990s. But the legal, economic, and political decisions that would have to be made are likely to push any activation of DAB much closer to the new millennium's beginning.

## Radio Satellite Service (RSS)

The future of DAB is further clouded by the shadow of another potential competitor that also is fully digital. At the 1992 World Administrative Radio Conference (WARC), it is expected that the nations of the globe will agree to assign spectrum space to a new enterprise known as RSS (*radio satellite service*). In essence, RSS is the audio equivalent of DBS but with the added potential of being truly global in its coverage pattern. Through the use of only three satellites, an RSS signal could be receivable on a worldwide basis. With only one satellite, the signal could still cover most of the North and South American continents.

Because of its wide footprint (the planet surface covered by its signal), RSS could thus reach every U.S. home and car no matter how remote its location. And in contrast to the poor signal quality and unpredictable reception of shortwave or nighttime AM transmissions, RSS would offer virtually interference-free and digitally perfect fidelity. Approximately twenty RSS channels, located somewhere between 500 and 3000 MHz on the spectrum, are expected to be allocated by WARC for use in the United States. This opens up the possibility for a number of new radio network services. Some of these services may be presented by the existing network companies, but many will probably be programmed by new players.

Just as broadcast television faces new or renewed competition from DBS, cable, and related technologies, broadcast radio (including terrestrial DAB) is likely to have to contend with RSS. Still, as a national, if not a worldwide, service, RSS will not be in a position to offer highly localized content. Thus, its introduction and expansion would probably be accompanied by even greater attempts at localization on the part of conventional stations. How many local stations will still be needed, and whether some networks will still need local affiliates, are open-ended questions that will no doubt prove unsettling to radio broadcasters as we move closer to the year 2000. New receivers will have to be built and sold in order for RSS signals to reach consumers, of course. But there is nothing about the technology that would make these receivers significantly more expensive or any larger than the transistor and car radios we purchase today.

Certainly, auto radios were AM-only for years before FM came to the fore. It is likely, however, that RSS will penetrate the in-car market much more rapidly because it provides high-quality digital sound even when driving 100 miles or more from the nearest town or conventional station. The global radio show may not be far away.

## Pending Legal Issues

Beyond the technical standards and spectrum allocation decisions facing the federal government in general (and the FCC in particular), several other regulatory controversies remain at center stage as this page is being written.

### Fin/Syn Implications

In April 1991, the FCC relaxed barriers to the so-called big three networks' ownership and syndication of the programming they carry. Under the new rules, the networks are permitted to syndicate and acquire all rights in all of the shows they run in dayparts other than prime-time. The networks can also acquire most rights to prime-time shows produced by others but only through negotiations taking place at least 30 days after the network had agreed to license the show for its initial on-net run. The nets cannot syndicate these programs in the United States, however, and are also barred from engaging in first-run syndication activities. The networks also were granted the right to produce up to 40 percent of their prime-time shows themselves.

Because the FCC action also defined a network as an entity providing more than 15 hours per week of prime-time programming to affiliates, the fledgling Fox operation was not subject to these modified fin/syn rules, thereby continuing its advantageous flexibility in intermixing its network and studio (Twentieth Television) activities. Should the FCC rules stand legal challenges, the Fox advantage may spur ABC, CBS, or NBC to reduce their own prime-time offerings in order to fall below the 15-hour threshold.

At the crux of the matter is the continuing debate over the remaining power of the big three. These networks have argued that in an era when cable is a maturing industry and other delivery technologies are proliferating, they no longer enjoy the dominance they once had when they were virtually the only major buyers of the television community's production wares. In fact, claim the nets, even the relaxed fin/syn rules left them at a disadvantage with the newer industries who can share in the profits from every stage of program development and exhibition. The producers, syndicators, and other interests claim, however, that these three broadcasting companies still control the majority of over-the-air viewing. The new rules are far too liberal, the producers charge, and will once again allow the networks to dictate terms to the studios that depend on these nets for a significant portion of their business.

As is often the case with compromise regulations, neither side is happy with the FCC ruling. A number of legal challenges to it are being contemplated at this writing. What will survive, however, is the continuing policy quandary over how active the federal government should be in dealing with matters of program diversity and the related business practices of the broadcast industry. Because their influence is so pervasive, should the electronic media's enterprises be more closely regulated than is most other commercial activity? And, because it uses the public spectrum, must broadcasting's operations be subject to more governmental oversight than are the non-over-the-air delivery systems with which it increasingly must compete? These questions transcend fin/syn, of course, and pertain to the much larger issue of how new technologies impact government's old regulatory assumptions.

## FTC Reawakening

Certainly, the Federal Trade Commission (FTC) is now showing signs of stirring from its Reagan-era slumber. New FTC Chair Janet Steiger is making it clear that perceived monopolistic and anticompetitive trends in the media industries will be closely monitored. "We do intend to be very vigilant and vigorous wherever we find anti-competitive behavior," Steiger recently warned. She seems especially interested in the increasing consolidation occurring in the cable industry:

> In particular . . . the questions of mergers in this industry—whether horizontal or vertical—with programers, such mergers are bound to come to our attention. We have more and more Americans choosing cable, wanting to take advantage of a panoply of broadcast options, and it has become a national issue. . . . We are looking at allegations that acquisitions in the cable industry could eliminate competition between cable systems. We are also looking into allegations that such acquisitions may set up entry barriers into the programing systems which support the cable programing networks.[5]

*Horizontal* mergers occur when one aspect of a business is consolidated into a comparatively few hands, such as a small number of MSOs owning a substantial majority of the nation's cable systems. *Vertical* mergers occur when a single company comes to control the production, distribution, and sale/exhibition of its product. Thus, when a giant cable enterprise commissions and owns part of the program content it distributes via its own cable network that is picked up by local systems it also owns, a vertical integration has taken place.

The multiple ownership (12–12–12) rules, fin/syn, and the Prime Time Access Rule (PTAR) all inhibit horizontal and vertical integration in the broadcasting sector, as we have seen. But as Steiger's comments suggest, the cable industry may have grown to the point at which similar restrictions must be placed on its competitive practices. This will likely be an increasingly volatile issue in the years immediately ahead, especially if broadcasters feel more threatened by cable and DBS expansionism.

## On Fairness and Indecency

In the area of program content, the questions of the Fairness Doctrine and indecency remain hot topics. As you recall from Chapter 6, the FCC abolished the Fairness Doctrine in August 1987. Congressional attempts to reinstate it have, to this point, been blocked by presidential vetoes, but the skirmishing continues. Not repealed were two corollaries to the Doctrine. The *personal attack rule* requires stations to give time to individuals or groups that are attacked on the air. The *political editorializing rule* mandates that stations who editorialize in favor of a political candidate must give reply time to opposing candidates. Broadcasters and journalists are asserting that the preservation of the corollaries in the absence of the overall Doctrine is, in the words of the Radio Television News Directors Association, "arbitrary and capricious and in violation of the First Amendment." In a contrary position, many members of Congress argue that the restoration of the full Fairness Doctrine is the only way to ensure that all sides of important controversies are given adequate exposure over the air.

Meanwhile, the Congress is also sparring with the FCC over if and when *indecent* program matter may be broadcast. Indecency is currently defined by the FCC as "language or material that, in context, depicts or describes, in terms patently offensive as measured by contemporary community standards for the broadcast medium, sexual or excretory activities or organs." Up until 1988, court decisions established the premise that indecency could be aired if channeled to a time of day when unsupervised children were unlikely to be in the audience (see the 1978 *Pacifica* case discussed in Chapter 6). But in 1988, Congress passed legislation requiring the FCC to ban indecent speech *entirely*. As of this moment, the matter is being constitutionally challenged in the courts, and the commission is enforcing the ban for broadcasters only between the hours of 6 A.M. and 8 P.M. Under Chairman Alfred Sikes, fines have been levied against stations that appear to have aired indecent content outside the "safe harbor" time frame, and powerful forces are lining up on both sides of the issue.

Even more unclear is how indecency regulation might relate to other nonbroadcast delivery systems. Should basic cable, given its wide access, be subject to the same restrictions as broadcasters while pay services, due to their separate and voluntary purchase, re-main exempt? What about DBS and MMDS (wireless cable) transmissions? More fundamentally, does Congress or the FCC have the constitutional right to regulate the content of nonbroadcast signals? If not, then why should the federal government continue to restrict content aired on the broadcast stations that must compete with these other services? As communications attorney J. Brian DeBoice sees it:

> Broadcast programming has been singled out for examination concerning possible indecency, because broadcasting today is still the most pervasive, the most powerful, and at the same time the most uniquely vulnerable of the communications media. Broadcasters are federally licensed as public trustees, and the licensing process provides a convenient, available legal framework within which to impose content restrictions. . . . If efforts to rein in broadcasters prove successful, cable television, videocassettes and other media are the next logical objects of more stringent program content restrictions.
>
> In the broadcast indecency dispute, broadcasters stand guard at a first breach in the wall of First Amendment freedoms. While acting in defense of their own liberty of speech, broadcasters defend also the liberties of those who stand behind them—including cable television, other marketplace competitors and ultimately, the public at large.[6]

### Telco Participation

Speaking of other delivery systems and the

---

**CNN   Indecency Revisited**

Congressional pressure to ban indecency from the airwaves completely has embroiled the FCC, the courts, and broadcasters in a complicated First Amendment controversy. Parental supervision is seen as being insufficient to protect children from indecent programming.

laws that regulate them leads us unavoidably to the subject of the telephone establishment. As we discuss in Chapter 4, the telcos are poised to assume the role of electronic mass media. Armed with their fiber optic technology and eager to put it to full revenue-producing use, the phone companies are seriously exploring the options that might exist beyond their traditional common-carrier voice/data delivery system.

The broadband linkage that fiber optics provide can carry hundreds of times more data than that capable of carriage by the traditional copper phone line. As phone companies replace their old wire infrastructure with fiber, new services will be offered to make use of this new capacity. So the twin questions likely to command attention for much of this decade are (1) exactly *which* new services will the phone company deliver, and (2) who will own the *content* of those services?

If permitted by the federal government, the telco of the twenty-first century could provide meter reading, home security, and automatic thermostat (heating/air conditioning) remote control. It could deliver a much wider selection of computer-generated data than is now possible, including teletext and videotext material. And, it could carry television information and entertainment programming in true HDTV format. The phone company could own any or all of the content (software) involved in these various applications—or it could remain a passive conduit for programming owned and booked by other organizations. This passive role is sometimes referred to as a *video dialtone* service. Under one scenario, the telco might compete with or even replace the conventional cable television company as a passive carrier of others' content. Under another scenario, the phone industry might supplant broadcast stations with that spectrum being converted to other uses, and the former broadcaster would then be no more than a software packager. Still a third and even more extreme prediction puts the telco in the position of actually commission-

ing program creation just as a conventional broadcast network has done for more than half a century.

The one certainty is that the telephone companies will expand their sphere of operation. The 1984 breakup of the monolithic AT&T empire into the seven baby Bells (regional companies, also referred to as BOCs) created smaller, hungrier corporations that can't afford to let new technological potentials pass them by. It would be bad business to allow the great majority of fiber optic capacity to lie fallow; and phone executives are not known for being bad businesspersons. Whether they originate video programming of their own or are content to be permitted a greater role in carrying the video programming of others, the telcos will be mass media players in the new millennium—and perhaps before.

If current Congressional disenchantment with the cable industry continues to fester, the phone companies may have legislative barriers to their television entry lifted sooner rather than later. Some members of Congress, such as Representative Rick Boucher, perceive cable to be an unregulated and unresponsive monopoly that should best be checked by allowing phone companies into the same business. As of this writing, Boucher is advocating a removal of telco-cable cross-ownership prohibitions. In support of his bill, he wrote the following statement that cogently summarizes contemporary pro-telco-entry arguments:

Telephone companies operate in every market that cable systems do and their fiber systems will not be encumbered by any radio reception problems that would interfere with over-the-air video transmission. Moreover, unlike cable, telephone companies would have incentive to deploy new technologies and to develop new services in addition to their existing voice and data service offerings and could bring video services to rural consumers currently unserved by cable. Telephone companies also have a long track record of providing reliable quality service.[7]

Although this is a decision fueled by technological change, the redefinition of telephone companies (and therefore the redefinition of the entire electronic media landscape) will ultimately be decided by legislators rather than technologists. And this decision will undoubtedly be formulated well in advance of the next century's arrival—if it has not been made already.

## Operational Outlooks

Not all unresolved electronic media questions are awaiting technological or regulatory change. Some are evolving within already-established legal and technical procedures.

### The Cable Station

In Rochester, New York, for example, the local cable system is programming its Channel 5 as though it were an independent television station. Using the call letters WGRC-TV, this channel is competing with regular TV outlets for programming, viewers, and advertising sales. A disadvantage to the scheme is that the cable station can be received only by households who subscribe to the system. But the outweighing advantage is that the costs of operation are much less than for a conventional television facility. Rochester Cablevision already has its lines in place. It does not need an expensive television transmitter or FCC license nor a dedicated studio building. The sole additional costs of WGRC are programming product and personnel. Even sales can be handled by the existing staff, which was already selling *avails packages* (see Chapter 11) on the system's basic cable channels.

From a signal delivery standpoint, cable station WGRC is thus much more cost-effi-cient than are the conventional over-the-air stations that must compete with it. It can therefore turn a profit with much lower advertising revenues while potentially draining profitability from some of its conventional competitors. WGRC has, of this writing, already attracted a top-rated newscaster from one of the local stations and has also hired away a chief engineer, a production manager, and two sales executives from other outlets. Should this kind of operation catch on in heavily cabled markets (Cox Cable has initiated one such cable station in Eureka, California), the economic implications for all but the most powerful over-the-air stations could be severe.

### Pay-per-View (PPV) Options

Another variable in the television world is *pay-per-view* (PPV). As we mention in Chapter 3, PPV operations pioneered by companies like *Request* (see Figure 14–6) allow viewers to choose and be billed for individual programs. This, of course, has been possible within the easily wired confines of hotels for some time, but extensive home PPV still lacks widespread availability. Before long, however, new computer technology combined with the massive two-way capacity of fiber optic lines could make PPV as commonplace as basic cable. Compression devices offer another possibility for literally hundreds of PPV channels via DBS or cable delivery. Outstanding concerts, movies, and sporting events will be able to assemble substantial PPV audiences because a large critical mass of homes will be able instantaneously to subscribe to a PPV offering. No human operator need intercede, and the consumer won't even have to make a telephone call. With the simple press of a button or two on a keypad the event can be ordered and, in some cases, delivered immediately. As more and more cable and satellite dish homes become PPV-addressable, that industry will acquire the financial clout to outbid conventional broadcast and cable networks for prestige programs. Without prohibitive Congressional action, it appears that sports classics like the Super Bowl and the World Series will one day migrate to a PPV environment.

A fundamental shift in the character of radio and television in the United States is thus likely to become even more profound. Broadcasting, as we have seen, began in this country as a highly democratic medium. Anyone who could afford a receiver was able to access the same programming as anyone else in the same locale—regardless of income or neighborhood. Once urban cable entrepreneurs began to focus on more affluent suburbs and ignore inner cities, this condition began to change. Change accelerated, of course, as pay cable and the short-lived STV offerings (see Chapter 8) were made available based on ability to pay. PPV simply extends the practice to its logical conclusion. Top properties will command top dollar from those upscale consumers able to afford them, and television product will be functionally divided into price categories, as are real estate, clothing, and automobiles.

### The Camcorder Community

Yet, while PPV threatens to create a viewer aristocracy, the *camcorder* seems to be making video content production a much more democratic enterprise. By 1990, camcorders were well established as the playthings of mil-

lions of U.S. families. (Refer again to Figure 14–4.) Steve Ridge, an executive with news consultant firm Magid Associates, estimated at that time that approximately 20 percent of network-affiliate station news departments encouraged viewers to call if they had captured a newsworthy event on tape.[8] Despite the lower resolution of camcorder pictures, even the networks resort to such footage in order to illustrate visually otherwise copyonly stories. In fact, at least one network equipped Palestinians with camcorders and trained them in their use in order to obtain visuals from riot-torn enclaves that the Israelis had sealed off from foreign journalists. Closer to home, a civilian's 1991 camcorder footage of a brutal motorist beating by Los Angeles police was distributed around the world. It raised a storm of controversy not only in Southern California, but in foreign capitals as well.

Less dramatically, entire entertainment series like *America's Funniest Home Videos* are now being harvested from the sometimes outlandish submissions of amateur videographers. With camcorder prices continuing to decline, and new digital chip cameras weighing less than one pound hitting the market, it is likely that even more citizen-generated video will be seen on U.S. television screens. Whether the bulk of this footage will be newsworthy or merely goofy, its dissemi-

**Figure 14–6**
Logo of REQUEST TELEVISION, one of the oldest and most successful PPV enterprises

## The Best in Movies, Sports and Specials

nation could have the positive effect of casting the electronic media as more of a democratic "us" than a distant, autocratic "them."

## Our Global Profession

While on the subject of democracy, the rapid changes in Eastern Europe that marked the end of the 1980s had significant electronic media ramifications. The availability of VCRs and small, less obtrusive personal satellite dishes in Poland and other countries shattered the video monopoly of government-mouthpiece television stations. Slow change in Poland was visually witnessed by dissidents in other Eastern European countries and helped propel much more rapid change in their own nations. It is perhaps indicative of the importance of television in this process that in Romania, where violent revolution was waged, the capital's television station became a main battleground and the symbol of reformation.

The implications of these changes for U.S. electronic media enterprises are enormous. In 1990, Chase Cable of West Hartford, Connecticut, announced plans to begin building cable systems in a number of Polish cities. The Polish government also decreed that two of its over-the-air television channels would be converted to commercial use, with contracts for airing of *The Wonder Years* and the *Santa Barbara* soap opera among the first to be signed.[9] In Hungary, meanwhile, VOA Europe assisted in the operation of a commercial FM station known as Radio Bridge, which was selling airtime from a sophisticated grid rate card only weeks after its 1990 initiation.[10] Programming *glasnost* even flowered in the Soviet Union when the talk show *Geraldo* became the first U.S. series to be scheduled there on a daily basis. Premiering in March 1991, with a segment on Elvis Presley's death,

the advertiser-supported *Geraldo* reached some 30 million Soviets over Moscow Channel 2x2.

The 1991 Persian Gulf War proved a boon to the global market for hard news as well. CNN's worldwide reach and already-established linkages with governments and media systems made it the conduit through which information and arguments instantaneously passed back and forth between allied and hostile bureaucracies. Diplomatic and military maneuverings ebbed and flowed as private citizens watched and public opinions were shaped.

These and other developments likely to follow will further expand the global program marketplace and its importance to the U.S. media as we move toward the year 2000. We should not attempt to shape these new outlets and systems into occupied dependencies for U.S. producers. The number of nations that already compete with us on the international program market would make such media imperialism impossible, even if we sought it. Rather, the richer and more multifaceted the world electronic media environment becomes, the greater will be the opportunities for joint ventures, program exchanges, and the diversification of radio and television product available to U.S. consumers as well.

As other areas of U.S. industry are learning, we can no more expect other countries to buy our products blindly than we can expect U.S. consumers to ignore appealing products from other lands. The global marketplace that the electronic media are helping to fashion will be a highly competitive arena in which product quality becomes much more important than national origin. As media professionals, the stakes for us are very high. We can either seize the opportunity to expand our industry into new technologies and locales or devote most of our energies to protecting what we inherited (see Figure 14–7) from the radio/television entrepreneurs who preceded us. Choosing the latter course can be the road to stagnation, with Hollywood and our entire

**Figure 14–7**

The boundaries of our profession not so many years ago. A farmer tunes into 1920s radio

program production infrastructure in danger of becoming the next Detroit.

Truly international production/distribution and consumption of radio/television content will inevitably broaden U.S. programming tastes just as German and then Japanese engineering and marketing triumphs established new preferences in the cars we drive. Virtually every major U.S. studio and network is now actively pursuing foreign coproduction deals and other joint ventures. We do not yet know whether such trends will diversify or homogenize electronic media content. But we do know that most successful members of our profession will, in the new millennium, be part of truly international enterprises. As Mel Harris, president of Paramount Pictures television group, observes, "'It's a natural result of the expanding global market and desire to tap into new creative forces. You're just not going to meet the needs of the European market by producing in Hollywood. We've been an international distributor. The next step for us is becoming a worldwide producer.'"[11]

"A ship in a harbor is safe," U.S. philosopher John Augustus Shedd once wrote, "but that is not what ships are built for."[12] In times of major turbulence, however, the open sea is often safer because the vessel will not be buffeted and broken on the shores of a too-confining anchorage. As you begin a career in the tumultuous *global* media environment, give some thought to how your own professional ship should most prudently be navigated.

## CHAPTER FLASHBACK

Several emerging areas and issues are in the spotlight as this book goes to press. These areas and issues can be divided into technical, legal, operational, and global trends. In the technical arena, *HDTV* promises a striking improvement in television picture quality at the same time it poses major questions as to how it will be delivered and via what specific set of electronic standards. A wrong or too-long-delayed decision on the part of the United States could have disastrous economic and political consequences for our electronic media and what remains of our electronic equipment industry.

The *video compact disc* constitutes a storage medium that, like HDTV, possesses substantial pictorial quality advantages. VCDs also have significant *interactive* potential, as does *videotext*. The two-way videotext and one-way *teletext* electronic print systems are sent, respectively, by wire or over the air. Both have proven much more popular in Europe, where centralized, government-run telecommunications structures facilitated their introduction. Direct broadcast satellite (DBS) activity has also been slow to develop in the United States, but some major companies have plans to exploit the medium in the nineties. Fiber optic replacement of conventional copper telephone and cable lines is likely to broaden the number of telecommunications services entering the home and also to increase chances that the telephone companies will become more active mass media players.

On the exclusively audio side, *digital audiotape* (DAT) promises all the fidelity advantages of the compact disc plus the ability for consumers to make their own recordings in the format. *Digital audio broadcasting* (DAB), as its name implies, also uses digital technology to deliver CD-quality radio signals at four times the spectrum efficiency of conventional FM broadcasting. DAB may constitute a new radio service that, due to its technology, would require the assignment of stations in blocks rather than as mutually exclusive channels. Another new possibility is *RSS* (radio satellite service). Operating somewhere between 500 and 3000 MHz, an RSS signal on three satellites could deliver virtually interference-free and digitally perfect fidelity service to the entire globe.

Pending legal issues include the continuing controversy over the power and competitive position of the broadcast networks. This controversy is most graphically encapsulated in the debate over the *fin/syn* (financial interest and syndication) rules. Fin/syn is a part of a larger issue of how new technologies are challenging old regulatory assumptions. A re-energized Federal Trade Commission is facing this same question. The subjects of fairness and indecency constitute more specific flashpoints, with substantial differences of opinion about how they should be treated and about whether broadcasting's responsibilities are greater in these two areas than are the responsibilities of newer delivery systems.

New operational possibilities and quandaries are posed by cable stations, pay-per-view (PPV) competition for programming, the use and solicitation of private camcorder footage, and the dimensions of the telephone company's role in the electronic mass media of the twenty-first century. However these elements evolve, it is certain that the radio/television industry of the future will be much more global in its outlook, business relationships, and product development.

❑ Review Probes

1. Why are the cable and DBS industries much more excited about HDTV than are television *station* interests?
2. Define and isolate the differences between *ORACLE* and *Minitel*.
3. What are the fundamental differences in technological and marketing philosophy between the Sky Cable and PrimeStar projects?
4. What are two reasons for and two reasons against dropping the financial interest and syndication rules?

5. Distinguish between *horizontal* and *vertical* mergers and give a specific electronic media example of each.
6. What advantages and disadvantages does a cable station possess as compared to a conventional television station?

❑ Suggested Background Exploration

Alber, Antone. *Videotext/Teletext: Principles and Practice.* New York: McGraw-Hill, 1985.

Becker, Lee B., and Klaus Schoenbach. *Audience Responses to Media Diversification: Coping with Plenty.* Hillsdale, NJ: Lawrence Erlbaum Associates, 1989.

Dizard, Wilson, Jr. *The Coming Information Age: An Overview of Technology, Economics, and Politics.* 3rd ed. New York: Longman, 1989.

Gross, Lynne Schafer. *The New Television Technologies.* 3rd ed. Dubuque, IA: Wm. C. Brown Co., 1990.

Meyrowitz, Joshua. *No Sense of Place: The Impact of Electronic Media on Social Behavior.* New York: Oxford University Press, 1985.

Mowlana, Hamid, and Laurie J. Wilson. *Communication Technology and Development.* Lanham, MD: Unipub, 1988.

Palais, Joseph C. *Fiber Optic Communications.* Englewood Cliffs, NJ: Prentice-Hall, 1988.

Prentiss, Stan. *HDTV: High Definition Television.* Blue Ridge Summit, PA: Tab Books, 1990.

Williams, Frederick. *The New Communications.* 2nd ed. Belmont, CA: Wadsworth, 1989.

## CHAPTER 15

# Cueing Up
# Your Career

❏ *The following insights are an edited version of an address delivered by Fred Jacobs, founder and president of the* Media Strategies *research firm, to the 1990 Great Lakes Radio Conference. Even though the speech focused on radio, most of his comments apply equally to our profession as a whole and also provide an articulate summation of many of the themes that interlace the previous fourteen chapters.*

## Back to the Basics
## by Frederick Jacobs

Let me ask some basic questions to those of you already in the industry—the veterans and the newcomers. And to those of you who are students dreaming about how you're going to get in.

Why are you here?

Why did you pick the radio business?

What is it you want to achieve in your careers?

Is this industry the one you want to be in for a major chunk of your working life?

**Figure 15–1**
Frederick Jacobs, chapter author

I told you they'd be very basic questions. They're also intensely difficult ones. Most of us are busy wrestling with more immediate concerns. The industry folks are focused on getting ratings, selling spots, and making profits for their parent companies. You students are deeply concerned about passing exams, getting that degree, and nailing down that first job. But we all often lose sight of the more basic issues. I spent eight years of my life on college campuses, getting degrees and teaching. But it's been fourteen years since I've been involved with the academic community. I've spent this intervening time carv-ing out my career in radio. I'd like to give you a little of my perspective.

**This business used to be a lot more fun than it is today.**

I didn't make that statement to bring you down or to gloom-and-doom you . But I think that anyone who's been in radio for at least ten years was probably nodding his or her head when I said it. What's happened? What's changed? Simply stated, it's gotten tougher, more competitive, and it's a much bigger business than ever before. Many people who originally got in because it seemed like radio would be a lot of fun have either rearranged their goals or are now doing something else. Most of us have simply bought in. Like the fliers in the book *Catch 22,* we basically accept our marching orders, carry out our missions, and as our corporate lords or our bankers raise the bar and heighten the goals, we generally keep our heads down and set our sights on the new tasks at hand.

As a result, we get caught up in the math. The math of achieving higher ratings goals, higher sales goals, higher profit goals. Most of the time, we spend our waking hours worrying and sweating out how we're going to squeeze out more ratings points, sell more spots, and write snappier liners that promise "the most music, the most variety, with the least repetition."

Perhaps you've read about Sony executive Akio Morita who feels that U.S. business is so caught up in achieving monthly sales goals that it's completely lost sight of long-term planning and strategy. That philosophy very much describes the radio business these days. We don't think five years down the road or even about next year at this time. It's much more popular to worry about the next monthly Arbitrend or this week's sales figures. In fact, many radio stations knowingly damage or mortgage their futures by being so fixated on today.

Sometimes we get so blinded by the science and the math that we lose sight of the fact that this still is a fun business and that radio stations are fascinating places to work. In spite of the bankers who now dominate our business and the brokers who buy it, sell it, and leverage it, *and* the consultants who homogenize it, we're still talking about an industry that is based on very subjective qualities—fun, entertainment, excitement. You can't research these things or computerize them or even steal them from the station across the street. And in spite of the fact that it's the nineties and everyone wants to be able to punch up the winning formula on their PCs, the central core of what works in radio is unquantifiable. There's a certain magic to radio when it's done right. You can't explain it, but you know it when you hear it. Like any other form of pop culture and entertainment, great radio is unscientific, unpredictable, and great fun to be a part of.

I've walked in and out of literally hundreds of radio stations during the past fourteen years, and I can tell you that you can pick out the fun ones and the ones that you'd want to work at in thirty seconds. You can feel it in the hallways, see it in the eyes of the people who work there, and sense it when you talk to the programming people. There's a saying in this business that a radio station takes on the personality of its program director. There are exceptions to that, of course, but in many cases, show me a dull PD and you'll probably hear a rather lethargic radio station. Show me a mover and a shaker PD, and the odds are you've got a hot, happening station that's on the street and plugged into the local community. Those are the stations you want to work for and be a part of.

The same holds true for the people on the air. There's a certain quality that you can hear from morning shows and, clearly put, you can hear when they're having fun. Many shows go through the motions, do the hot bits that Z100 is doing, and use all the latest jingles—but you can clearly hear when the players really aren't having fun.

Even the personalities in the other dayparts are often dead giveaways. If you listen carefully, you can get a sense of whether a jock has those studio monitors cranked up and is really getting into the music—or when a jock is on the phone ordering vertical blinds for his den with the monitors turned down, watching the VU meters.

As a consultant, I can tell you that as an industry, we've done a very poor job of teaching and training air personalities. We teach them how to run the board and follow a log, but we often fail to enlighten them about their basic goals—to entertain and service the audience. If you're beginning to disagree with me right now, consider the following:

Have you ever watched how many jocks answer the request lines and how they treat their customers? God forbid, a poor listener calls and asks for something that's out of the format—could you imagine walking into a Kentucky Fried Chicken, ordering a burger, and have the person behind the counter yell at you or humiliate you for ordering the wrong thing? But it happens everyday on the phones.

Or, how many times have you gone to a station event and seen a jock mistreat or snub a listener? It happens all the time. And yet, the basic truth is that given our thoroughly professional way of gathering ratings, it doesn't take too many Arbitron diaries to make you really smart or really stupid. The listeners are our lifeblood; we need them, and as a guy who's conducted hundreds of focus

groups with the listening public, I can tell you that many stations aren't excelling at the basics.

Here's a real-life horror story. I was in Laurel, Maryland, conducting an Arbitron diary review with one of my clients. We were reading the comments and happened across a diary with this notation: "I usually listen to WAAA all day, but I called their morning man Joe Blow to request a song and he was rude to me. Since then, I have stopped listening to his show." Sure enough, we opened the diary to the individual days segment and saw the reality. In the morning hours, the listener went to a competitor and didn't turn on WAAA until after 10 A.M.

Our lack of training in the basics for air personalities runs deep. We've allowed jocks to get bored with their jobs, and the result is often a mechanical approach. *They* don't view themselves as professional entertainers, so how can we expect anything more than a mundane job? The very fact that we use the

**Figure 15–2**
Weekly reach of radio by band, 1990

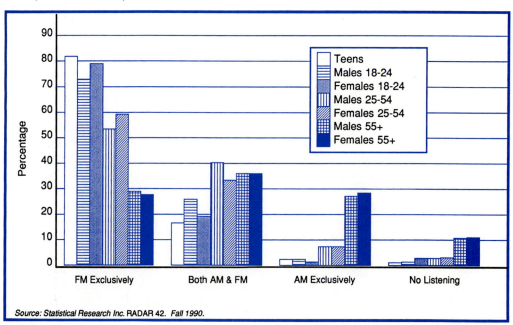

*Source: Statistical Research Inc. RADAR 42. Fall 1990.*

term *shift* like a factory should tell us a lot about how we're failing at the basics. People who work shifts are building Tauruses and Accords. That's a punch-in—punch-out job that doesn't demand creativity, warmth, and excitement. Our personalities *should* view each day as a performance, a show, another chance to win over and enthuse an audience. (A breakdown of that audience by band preference appears in Figure 15–2.)

Jocks often complain that the music becomes repetitive and that it's hard to get excited when everyday is programmed to sound pretty much the same. That's when I think about a different medium—Broadway. One day, I'll be lucky enough to see the "Phantom of the Opera." It may be 1992, 1993, or even later, but the odds are good that it'll still be on Broadway because it's a wonderful show. Even though I'll probably see performance #4312, there's no doubt in my mind that it will be a great experience and an electric show. Why? The lines are the same every night. The songs don't change. It's the *exact same* show, night in and night out. But the actors, the stagehands, the directors, the special effects people all understand the basics. It's a show, it's a performance, and if some guy from Detroit is going to plunk down his $50 to get in, he's going to see a professional, thoroughly entertaining production.

I'm often asked by students the exciting question, "How do you get that first job?" Radio executives are looking for what you can bring to the party, what type of person you are, your attitude and energy. I would venture to say that every professional attending this conference first got in the business because they thought it would be a fun career. For some of us, that's likely changed somewhat over the years, but fun and enjoyment were the primary considerations.

If you're going into radio because of the money—I'd urge you to rethink your decision. That's not to say that a lot of money cannot be made, because many people in this business have done very well for themselves. But if money is your prime motivator, other businesses are much easier and offer greater opportunity.

Maybe the word to think about is *passion*—without it, radio can be a very tough place to carve out a successful career. And how do you measure passion? Do you have it? Many things can and will go wrong in this business. Radio can produce some incredibly great highs, *but* it also can crash down on you with some major-league lows. Your passion for radio will get you through.

I ask myself two questions on a very regular basis—interestingly, they're both related to the bedroom.

1. *How am I sleeping at night?* If the answer is "not very well," then I have to do a little follow-up interview with myself to find out why. What kind of job or career is worth losing significant amounts of sleep or peace of mind over?

2. *Do I still jump out of bed when that alarm goes off?* Do I even get up before it chirps? Now, we all have bad days; we all have mornings when we've got to face a tough meeting, an unrealistic deadline, an uncomfortable confrontation, or whatever. But overall, do you look forward to the coming day? Do you get psyched to go to your radio job and get things done?

These are basic questions that we all have to ask ourselves on a periodic basis.

As I said at the outset, this is still a fun business, and radio stations can and should be incredibly magnetic places in which to spend large chunks of your life. But as the old Excedrin commercials remind us, "Life Got Tougher," and it'll take more passion, more tolerance, and more dedication on all of our parts to keep it that way.

# Appendix

Alpha Epsilon Rho (AERHO): National Broadcasting Society composed of electronic media professionals and students preparing to enter the profession.

American Association of Advertising Agencies (AAAA): Key trade and lobbying organization for agencies and their top executives.

American Society of Composers, Authors and Publishers (ASCAP): Oldest of the three music licensing organizations. (See also BMI and SESAC)

American Women in Radio and Television, Inc. (AWRT): Professional society for persons throughout the electronic media; offers special services, seminars, and scholarships for students.

Association for Education in Journalism and Mass Communication (AEJMC): Academic organization of journalism, advertising, and public relations faculty; also serves as the accrediting body for college/university programs in these areas.

Association of Independent Television Stations, Inc. (INTV): Trade and lobbying group for television stations that are not affiliated with a major network.

Association of Public Radio Stations (APRS): Spokes-organization for noncommercial radio stations and their executives.

Audio Engineers Society (AES): Main organization for audio recording technologists and developers.

Broadcast/Cable Financial Management Association (BCFM): Organization for electronic media business officers and comptrollers; aids in improving and standardizing financial procedures and reporting mechanisms.

Broadcast Designers Association, Inc. (BDA): Professional society for artists, art directors, and designers who work in the electronic media.

Broadcast Education Association (BEA): Academic organization for college and university radio/television faculty; affiliated with the NAB.

Broadcast Music, Inc. (BMI): Music licensing organization set up by broadcasters as an alternative to ASCAP. (See also ASCAP and SESAC)

Broadcast Pioneers: Association of veteran broadcasters who promote a number of industry-benefiting causes, including library services and student scholarships.

Broadcast Promotion and Marketing Executives, Inc. (BPME): Key association for radio/television promotion and creative services personnel.

Community Antenna Television Association (CATA): Trade and lobbying group for smaller cable system operators.

Community Broadcasters Association (CBA): Trade organization for low-power (LPTV) outlets and executives.

Federal Communications Bar Association (FCBA): Professional organization for communications attornies, particularly those eligible to represent clients before the FCC.

International Radio and Television Society, Inc. (IRTS): Electronic media forum and development organization supported by top companies and executives in the industry. Hosts key conferences and faculty and student seminars and internships.

International Television Association (ITVA): Key organization for the advancement of video applications in the corporate/industrial sector.

Motion Picture Association of America (MPAA): Trade and lobbying group for the major film production studios.

National Academy of Television Arts and Sciences (NATAS): Association to support and recognize creative achievement in television program content and technique; bestower of the Emmys.

National Association of Broadcasters (NAB): Chief trade and lobbying organization for the commercial broadcasting industry.

National Association of College Broadcasters (NACB): Cooperative organization of student-operated media facilities and their staffers designed to improve student outlets and enhance career preparation.

National Association of Public Television Stations (NAPTS): Spokes-organization for non-commercial television outlets and their executives.

National Association of Television Program Executives (NATPE): Trade organization that brings together program creators, syndicators, and station program directors.

National Cable Television Association (NCTA): Chief trade and lobbying association for the cable industry.

National Religious Broadcasters (NRB): Lobbying and trade association for the operators of religious program outlets; administers a code of ethics pertaining to fundraising and related monetary activities.

Network Television Association (NTA): Trade association designed to promote the so-called big three broadcast networks to the advertising industry and its clients.

Public Relations Society of America, Inc. (PRSA): Key organization to advance the standards and practice of public relations as a profession; also supports student chapters.

Radio Advertising Bureau (RAB): Industry organization designed to promote radio as an advertising vehicle; hosts frequent seminars to improve time-selling and copy technique.

Radio Television News Directors Association (RTNDA): Main organization and sounding board for electronic journalism executives; also maintains student chapters.

Recording Industry Association of America (RIAA): Chief trade group for the producers and distributors of music and other recorded product for the consumer market.

SESAC, Inc. (SESAC): Smallest of the three music licensing organizations. (See also ASCAP and BMI)

Society of Broadcast Engineers, Inc. (SBE): Organization representing the interests and certification of technical staff working in the broadcast industry.

Society of Motion Picture and Television Engineers (SMPTE): Influential forum for leading film and television recording technologists; often aids in refinement and specification setting for new devices and procedures.

Society of Professional Journalists, Sigma Delta Chi (SPJ, SDX): Prime organization for the advancement and protection of the practice of journalism; facilitates involvement by students as well as by working professionals.

Society of Professional Videographers (SPV): Enrichment association for people making a career of shooting event-type video.

Station Representatives Association, Inc. (SRA): Trade organization of rep firms and their executives.

Television Bureau of Advertising (TvB): Industry office for the promotion and expansion of broadcast television time sales and monitoring of advertising trends.

Television Critics Association (TCA): Alliance of writers who regularly prepare television critiques for media outlets.

Wireless Cable Association (WCA): Trade group for MMDS and related television delivery systems.

❏ Major Unions Active in the Electronic Media

American Federation of Musicians (AFM): Musical performers working in both media and live venues.

American Federation of Television and Radio Artists (AFTRA): On-air talent, including entertainers, commercial actors, announcers, and newscasters. (See also SAG)

Directors Guild of America, Inc. (DGA): Directors working in all phases of film and the electronic media.

International Alliance of Theatrical Stage Employees & Moving Picture Operators of the United States and Canada (IATSE): Stage hands, lighting personnel, and other technical trades in film, video, and stage.

International Brotherhood of Electrical Workers (IBEW): Engineers and technicians; affiliated with the AFL–CIO.

National Association of Broadcast Employees and Technicians (NABET): Engineers and technicians plus other support personnel; affiliated with the AFL–CIO.

Screen Actors Guild (SAG): Performers appearing in motion picture and television entertainment programming and commercials; affiliated with the AFL–CIO. (See also AFTRA)

Writers Guild of America (WGA): Writers of radio/television entertainment programming and motion pictures; divided into East (New York) and West (Los Angeles) offices.

# Endnotes

## ☐ Chapter 1

[1]Harold Lasswell, "The Structure and Function of Communication in Society," in Lyman Bryson (ed.), *The Communication of Ideas* (New York: Harper & Brothers, 1948), 38.
[2]Arnold Hauser, *The Social History of Art,* vol. I (New York: Vintage Books, 1951), 63.
[3]A concise discussion of the evolution of communications vehicles is provided in Maurice Fabre, *A History of Communications* (New York: Hawthorn Books, 1963).
[4]Edwin Emery, Phillip Ault, and Warren Agee, *Introduction to Mass Communications,* 4th ed. (New York: Dodd, Mead & Company, 1974), 4.
[5]Walter Emery, *National and International Systems of Broadcasting* (East Lansing: Michigan State University Press, 1969), 458–459.
[6]Kwentin Keenan, circulation manager, *Broadcasting.* Telephone conversation with the author, April 23, 1991.
[7]Siegfried Kracauer, *Theory of Film* (New York: Oxford/Galaxy, 1965), 167.
[8]Roger Wimmer, Susan Eastman, and Timothy Meyer, "Program and Audience Research," in Susan Eastman, Sydney Head, and Lewis Klein, *Broadcast/Cable Programming,* 3rd ed. (Belmont, CA: Wadsworth, 1989), 79.
[9]S. J. Ball-Rokeach and Melvin DeFleur, "The Interdependence of the Media and Other Social Systems," in Gary Gumpert and Robert Cathcart (eds.), *Inter/Media: Interpersonal Communication in a Media World,* 3rd ed. (New York: Oxford University Press, 1986), 81.
[10]Letter to the author from Bruce Fohr, June 27, 1990.
[11]Alan Fletcher and Thomas Bowers, *Fundamentals of Advertising Research,* 3rd ed. (Belmont, CA: Wadsworth, 1988), 7.

## ☐ Chapter 2

[1]Ronald Seidle, *Air Time* (Boston: Holbrook Press, 1977), 179.
[2]For a detailed comparison of AM and FM audiences at the end of the 1980s, see "AM Radio: Survival of the Fittest," *Broadcasting* (August 14, 1989): 54–57.
[3]Stephen Battaglio, "Radio Marches to a Business Beat," *Adweek* (May 22, 1989): B.M. 40–41.
[4]"Expanded AM Band: Problem or Solution?" *Broadcasting* (August 28, 1989): 48.
[5]*Ibid.*
[6]"FCC Comes Up Short on Shortwave," *Broadcasting* (June 5, 1989): 72.
[7]Sydney Head, *World Broadcasting Systems* (Belmont, CA: Wadsworth, 1985), 136.
[8]John Hasling, *Fundamentals of Radio Broadcasting* (New York: McGraw-Hill, 1980), 45.

[9]Christopher Sterling and John Kittross, *Stay Tuned: A Concise History of American Broadcasting,* 2nd ed. (Belmont, CA: Wadsworth, 1990), 295.

[10]Thomas Baldwin and D. Steven McVoy, *Cable Communication,* 2nd ed. (Englewood Cliffs, NJ: Prentice-Hall, 1988), 9.

[11]A concise overview of the state of MMDS in early 1990 is presented in "Wireless Cable: Bloodied but Unbowed," *Broadcasting* (January 15, 1990): 122–123.

[12]"Bob Schmidt: Champion with a New Cause," *Broadcasting* (October 17, 1988): 73.

## ❏ Chapter 3

[1]Remarks by Wayne Coy to the Yale Law School, January 22, 1949.

[2]See, for example, Communications Act of 1934, Sections 303, 307, and 309.

[3]For a concise discussion of the legal evolution of MMDS, see Michael Drayer, "MMDS: New Opportunities for Fifth Estate Entrepreneurs," *Broadcasting* (March 30, 1987): 26.

[4]NAB's *TV Today* (July 24, 1989): 1.

[5]"Free Association," *Broadcasting,* (July 17, 1989): 8.

[6]Evolving marketing strategies for PPV are compared in "CTAM Presents the PPV Point of View," *Broadcasting* (April 30, 1990): 47–49.

[7]"Summary of Broadcasting & Cable," *Broadcasting* (April 1, 1991): 73.

[8]The legal boundaries of enhanced underwriting are probed in "FCC Rescinds Its Under-writing Admonition of Cincinnati FM," *Broadcasting* (April 9, 1990): 65–66.

[9]C-SPAN's development and early impact are detailed in "Free(r) at Last," *Broadcasting* (August 11, 1986): 41–46.

[10]Charles Warner, *Broadcast and Cable Selling* (Belmont, CA: Wadsworth, 1986), 309.

## ❏ Chapter 4

[1]Moves toward combining or replacing the commission system with plans based on sub-sequent product sales are chronicled in Cathy Madison, "Agencies 'Scared to Death' of Plans to Link Profits to Performance," *ADWEEK* (April 23, 1990): 1; and also in Robyn Griggs, "The Needham Plan: So What's New?," *ADWEEK* (May 14, 1990): 1.

[2]A more complete breakdown of radio and television advertising by type can be found in "A Short Course in Broadcasting, 1990," *Broadcasting Cable Yearbook 1990,* (Washington, DC: Broadcasting Publications, 1990) A–3. Subsequent years of this an-nual publication will also provide updated figures, on a two-year delayed basis.

[3]Doug Newsom and Bob Carrell, *Public Relations Writing: Form & Style,* 3rd ed. (Bel-mont, CA: Wadsworth, 1991), 3.

[4]Susan Eastman and Robert Klein, *Promotion & Marketing for Broadcasting & Cable,* 2nd ed. (Prospect Heights, IL: Waveland, 1991), 4.

[5]David Dachs, *Anything Goes: The World of Popular Music* (Indianapolis: Bobbs-Merrill, 1964), 12.

[6]Edd Routt, James McGrath, and Frederic Weiss, *The Radio Format Conundrum* (New York: Hastings House, 1978), 19.

[7]Charles Turner, "Music Videos and the Iconic Data Base," in Gary Gumpert and Robert Cathcart (eds.), *Inter/Media,* 3rd ed. (New York: Oxford University, 1986), 382.

[8]"Don't Touch That Dial," *CBS Reports* television presentation, December 23, 1982.

[9]"State of the Art: Journalism," *Broadcasting* (September 11, 1989): 45.

[10]Jhan Hiber, *Hibernetics: A Guide to Radio Ratings and Research* (Los Angeles: R&R Books, 1984), 5.

[11]Herbert Howard and Michael Kievman, *Radio and TV Programming* (Columbus, OH: Grid Publishing, 1983), 157.

[12]Frank Lloyd, writing in "Monday Memo," *Broadcasting* (April 30, 1990): 30.

[13]A breakout of the various advanced television options is provided in "Refined HDTV Cost Estimates Less Daunting," *Broadcasting* (April 9, 1990): 40–41.

## ❑ Chapter 5

[1]Thomas Hoffer, "Nathan B. Stubblefield and His Wireless Telephone," *Journal of Broadcasting* (Summer 1971): 318.

[2]Helen Fessenden, *Fessenden: Builder of Tomorrows.* (New York: Coward-McCann, 1940), 153.

[3]Gordon Greb, "The Golden Anniversary of Broadcasting," in Lawrence Lichty and Malachi Topping (eds.), *American Broadcasting: A Sourcebook on the History of Radio and Television* (New York: Hastings House, 1975), 98.

[4]*Events in Telephone History* (New York: American Telephone and Telegraph Co., 1957), 21.

[5]Advertisement in *Pittsburgh Sun,* September 29, 1920.

[6]J. H. Morecroft, "1923 Passes in Review," *Radio Broadcast* (March, 1924): 390.

[7]*Ibid.,* 391.

[8]"Year of Progress," *Radio Broadcasting* (February 3, 1924): 26.

[9]"Two Plans Left to Clear Radio of Howls and Whistles," *New York Times* (December 4, 1927): 14.

[10]Joe Alex Morris, *What a Year* (New York: Harper Brothers, 1956), 166.

[11]Erik Barnouw, *Mass Communication* (New York: Rinehart & Company, 1956), 34.

[12]Raymond Yates, *ABC of Television* (New York: Norman W. Henley Publishing, 1929), 66, 142.

[13]*Ibid.,* 4–5.

[14]Editorial, *Scientific American* (June 1929): 493.

[15]"Television and Radio Today," *Etude* (September 1931): 616.

[16]A. Dinsdale, "De-Bunking Television," *Radio News* (January 1931): 592.

[17]"Television—by Telephone," *Keesing's Contemporary Archives* (June 2, 1932): 334.

[18]Wilson Dizard, *Television: A World View* (Syracuse: Syracuse University Press, 1966), 22–23.

[19]Llewellyn White, *The American Radio* (Chicago: The University of Chicago Press, 1947), 24.

[20]"Philco's Television," *Business Week* (August 15, 1936): 16.

[21]Don Rushin, "Five Decades of Magnetic Tape in Broadcasting," *College Broadcaster* (April–May 1990): 32.

[22]Peter Witkin, "Live Images Transmitted across Ocean for First Time," *New York Times* (July 11, 1962): 16.

[23]"Cable—A Cure for the Population Explosion?" *Broadcast Management Engineering* (April 1969): 76.

[24]"Biography of John Walson, Service Electric, and the Genesis of Cable Television," press release from Service Electric Cable TV, Inc., September 14, 1989.

[25]Mary Phillips, *CATV: A History of Community Antenna Television* (Evanston, IL: Northwestern University Press, 1972), 13–14.

[26]"Cable: The First Forty Years," *Broadcasting* (November 21, 1988): 38.

[27]Eddie Fritz, Keynote speech at the 1991 National Association of Broadcasters Convention, Las Vegas, April 15, 1991.

[1]J. M. Stark, "Lots Sold over Airwaves," *Editor and Publisher* (August 3, 1922): 87.

[2]Erik Barnouw, *A Tower in Babel* (New York: Oxford University Press, 1966), 120.

[3]"Broadcasters to Press Fight to Send Out Copyright Music," *New York Times* (April 26, 1923): 1.

[4]Herbert Hoover, *The Memoirs of Herbert Hoover: The Cabinet and the Presidency, 1920–1933* (New York: Macmillan, 1952), 140.

[5]"Second National Conference," *New York Times* (March 7, 1923): 18.

[6]"FTC Takes Control over Radio Advertising," *Broadcasting and Broadcast Advertising* (September 1, 1935): 5.

[7]"Philco's Television," *Business Week* (August 15, 1936): 16.

[8]George Waller, *Kidnap: The Story of the Lindbergh Trial* (New York: Dial Press, 1961), 302.

[9]"Broadcasting Code Cuts Controversy," *New York Times* (July 12, 1939): 1.

[10]*Four Decades of Service: The BMI Story* (New York: Broadcast Music, Inc., 1985), 2.

[11]"Music Licensing," remarks by Charles Halteman (BMI field representative), Wayne State University, Detroit, June 4, 1969.

[12]Robert Landry, *This Fascinating Radio Business* (Indianapolis: Bobbs-Merrill, 1946), 225–226.

[13]*In the Matter of Editorializing by Broadcast Licensees,* 13 FCC 1246 (June 1, 1949).

[14]Merle Miller, *The Judges and the Judged* (Garden City, NY: Doubleday, 1952), 174.

[15]"Slipped Disc: Payola," *Reporter* (December 10, 1959): 4.

[16]Charles Van Doren, "I Was Involved in a Deception," *Time* (November 16, 1959): 73.

[17]"Tarnished Image," *Time* (November 16, 1959): 72–74.

[18]"FCC Flicks Its Whip at Telecasters," *Business Week* (May 20, 1961): 34.

[19]Douglas Ginsburg, *Regulation of Broadcasting* (St. Paul: West Publishing, 1979), 581.

[20]*Notice of Inquiry and Proposed Rulemaking in the Matter of Deregulation of Radio* 73 FCC 2d 457, September 27, 1979.

## ❑ Chapter 7

[1]Frederick Lewis Allen, *Only Yesterday* (New York: Bantam Books, 1959), 55.

[2]"College Lectures by Radio," *The Literary Digest* (May 13, 1922): 28.

[3]"Stations That Entertain You," *Radio Broadcast* (December 1922): 138.

[4]"Radio's Increasing Value to Public," *Editor and Publisher* (November 20, 1922): 143.

[5]"Radio Cutting Down Church Attendance by Broadcasting Services, Says Bishop," *New York Times* (May 27, 1923): II/1.

[6]"Review of the Year 1923," *Scientific American* (January, 1924): 14.

[7]David Sarnoff, "Two Schools of Thought," *The Nation* (August, 1924): 12.

[8]O. E. Dunlap, "Shall Advertising Be Given the Air?" *Outlook* (November 11, 1925): 387–388.

[9]"Radio Conference Ends," *New York Times* (December 20, 1925): 8/13.

[10]Robert Landry, *This Fascinating Radio Business* (Indianapolis: Bobbs-Merrill, 1946), 63.

[11]Joe Alex Morris, *What a Year* (New York: Harper Brothers, 1956), 162.

[12]Harrison Summers (ed.), *A Thirty-Year History of Programs Carried on National Radio Networks in the United States, 1926–1956* (Columbus: Ohio State University, 1958), 21.

[13]George Manning, "Average Radio Cost is $310 per Hour," *Editor and Publisher,* (November 15, 1930): 13.

[14]Robert Mann, "Radio 'Spotlight' Copy Is Increasing," *Editor and Publisher* (June 14, 1930): 9.

[15]"Yardstick to Radio," *Time* (September 9, 1935): 41.

[16]Gilbert Gant, "Publishers Liberalize Press-Radio Plan," *Broadcasting and Broadcast Advertising* (May 1, 1935): 7.

[17]"Blurbs in the Breaks," *Business Week* (January 16, 1937): 35.

[18]Donald O'Toole, "Remarks in the House of Representatives," *Congressional Record* (December, 1937), 23891.

[19]Editorial, *Broadcasting and Broadcast Advertising* (July 1, 1938).

[20]Llewellyn White, *The American Radio* (Chicago: University of Chicago Press, 1947), 76–78.

[21]Recorded transcript of an April 1937 Father Coughlin transmission in author's private collection.

[22]*Ibid.*

[23]White, *American Radio,* 75.

[24]"1941," *Broadcasting* (December 22, 1980): 101.

[25]"Outspoken Broadcast," *Time* (August 9, 1943): 62.

[26]William Robson's comments on a CBS commemorative recording of *Open Letter on Race Hatred.* n.d.

[27]*Open Letter on Race Hatred* commemorative recording. n.d.

[28]"The Revolt against Radio," *Fortune* (March 1947): 101.

[29]"Tubeless Radio," *Time* (October 25, 1954): 71.

[30]"Radio—A New Era?" *Time* (June 27, 1955): 82.

[31]Dick Osgood, *WYXIE Wonderland* (Bowling Green, OH: Bowling Green University Popular Press, 1981), 370.

[32]Robert Lewis Shayon, "Disc Jockeys Top Senators," *Saturday Review* (November 26, 1960): 30.

[33]"FM-Stereo Programs Reach 70 Million Listeners," *Electronics World* (August, 1962), 75.

[34]"1961," *Broadcasting* (May 18, 1981): 87.

[35]Michael Keith, *Radio Programming: Consultancy and Formatics* (Boston: Focal Press, 1987), 89.

[36]Osgood, *WYXIE Wonderland,* 485.

[37]Joel Lind, remarks to the Great Lakes Radio Conference, April 6, 1991, Mt. Pleasant, MI.

[38]Keith, *Radio Programming,* xiii.

## ❏ Chapter 8

[1]"What's Television Doing Now?," *Business Week* (August 12, 1939): 24.

[2]Robert Conly, "The Promise of Television," *American Mercury* (July, 1944): 63.

[3]"What Happened to the Dream World?" *Fortune* (February 1947): 93.

[4]*The Story of Television,* promotional film issued by DuMont Television, ca. 1950.

[5]Dick Osgood, *WYXIE Wonderland* (Bowling Green, OH: Bowling Green University Popular Press, 1981), 267.

[6]Alexander Klein, "The Challenge of the Mass Media," *Yale Review* (June 1950): 684.

[7]Leo Sards, "The Microwave Era Begins," *Radio and T.V. News* (October 1950): 35–38.

[8]Fred Friendly, *Due to Circumstances beyond Our Control* (New York: Random House, 1967), 55.

[9]"Film for Television," *Business Week* (March 3, 1956): 109, 115.

[10]John Crosby, "Radio and TV Programming," *Time* (August 20, 1956): 71.

[11]*Americana Annual, 1958* (New York: Americana Corporation, 1958), 505.

[12]Paul Witty, "Some Results of Eight Yearly Studies on TV," *School and Society* (June 21, 1958): 288.

[13]Allen Widem, "Pay-TV: An Interim Report," *Motion Picture Herald* (April 17, 1963): 11.

[14]"1968," *Broadcasting* (July 8, 1981): 73.

[15]"White on Black," *Newsweek* (March 11, 1968): 87.

[16]Excerpts from the released text of Vice-President Spiro T. Agnew's speech to the Midwest Regional Republican Committee, at Des Moines, Iowa, November 13, 1969.

[17]"How They Do It," *Newsweek* (December 1, 1969): 56.

[18]Herbert Gans, "How Well *Does* T.V. Present the News?" *New York Times* (January 11, 1970): 31.

[19]"Life without the Tube," *Time* (April 10, 1972): 47.

[20]Author conversation with Robert Pierpoint, at Mt. Pleasant, Michigan, November 18, 1980.

[21]Author's notes taken at Richard Nixon's Press Conference, NAB Convention, Houston, Texas, March 18, 1974.

[22]Thomas Girard, "Branching Out on Broadcast Row," *WATCH Magazine* (December 1979): 54–56.

[23]Andrew Fox, "Toe to Toe: STV Versus Cable," *WATCH Magazine* (August 1980): 37–38.

## ❑ Chapter 9

[1]Ben Darrow, *Radio: The Assistant Teacher* (Columbus, OH: R. G. Adams & Company, 1932), 54.

[2]*Ibid.*, 55.

[3]"FM Stations Encouraged," *School Life* (December 1941): 68.

[4]Vernon McKown, "Students Run WNAS," *Senior Scholastic* (April 4, 1951): 25T.

[5]"A-V Newsnotes," *Educational Screen* (May 1954): 204.

[6]"Is the Network Dead?" *Newsweek* (August 20, 1956): 62.

[7]"Educational TV," *New York Times* (April 14, 1956): 2.

[8]"Airborne TV Revives," *Business Week* (January 28, 1961): 110.

[9]James Mead, *A Study of a Low-Power School Radio Station: WOAK.*" Ed.D. diss., Wayne State University, 1965, p. 6.

[10]Betty McKenzie (ed.), *The Feasibility and Role of State and Regional Networks in Educational Broadcasting* (Washington, DC: National Association of Educational Broadcasters, 1961), 55.

[11]Peter Orlik, *A Survey of Public School Radio in the United States* (Detroit: Wayne State University Mass Communications Center, 1966).

[12]Clay Whitehead, "Local Autonomy and the Fourth Network: Striking a Balance," *Educational Broadcasting Review* (December 1971): 6.

[13]John Weisman, "Public TV in Crisis," *TV Guide* (August 1, 1987): 7.

[14]*Ibid.*, (August 8, 1987), p. 27.

[15]"FCC Permits Short Wave to Carry Commercials," *New York Times* (June 4, 1939): 8.

[16]Giraud Chester, Garnet Garrison, and Edgar Willis, *Television and Radio,* 3rd ed. (New York: Appleton-Century-Crofts, 1963), 184.

[17]Erik Barnouw, *The Golden Web* (New York: Oxford University Press, 1968), 128.

[18]Earl Sparling, "Uncle Sam at the Microphone," *American Mercury* (February 1940): 225–227.

[19]Barnouw, *Golden Web,* 129.

[20]Sydney Head, *World Broadcasting Systems* (Belmont, CA: Wadsworth, 1985), 373.

[21]" 'Monitior' Reaching around the World with Radio," *Broadcasting* (March 27, 1989): 54.

[22]"Radio Opelika," *Broadcasting* (December 9, 1985): 86.

[23]Leonard Carlton, "Voice of America: The Overseas Radio Bureau," *Public Opinion Quarterly* (Spring 1943): 47.

[24]"Report from the East," *Time* (December 13, 1943): 58.

[25]Walter Emery, *National and International Systems of Broadcasting* (East Lansing: Michigan State University Press, 1969): 538.

[26]Chester, Garrison and Willis, *Television and Radio,* 188.

[27]*The Voice of America,* undated VOA leaflet, circa 1969.

[28]*Facts about the USIA* (Washington, DC: U.S. Government Printing Office, 1964), 7.

[29]*Facts about VOA* (Washington, DC: USIA, February 1983), 1.

[30]Neil Hickey, "Worldnet Fires Away in the 'Star Wars' of Ideas," *TV Guide* (May 2, 1987): 12–13.

[31]Emery, *National and International Systems* 545.

[32]Victor Marchetti and John Marks, *The CIA and the Cult of Intelligence* (New York: Knopf, 1974), 169.

[33]"Burnishing the Reputation of RFE/RL," *Broadcasting* (January 19, 1987): 200.

[34]Head, *World Broadcasting Systems,* 341.

[35]*Ibid.*, 37.

[36]Sig Michelson, "The First Eight Years," *Saturday Review* (October 24, 1970): 22.

[37]Sydney Head, *World Broadcasting Systems Update Notes* (Miami: Author published, 1987), 5.

[38]Don Flournoy, writing in "Monday Memo," *Broadcasting* (November 20, 1989): 25.

[39]Telephone interview with Steve Haworth, CNN Director of Public Relations, July 27, 1990.

[40]Isaac Asimov, "The Fourth Revolution," *Saturday Review* (October 24, 1970): 18–19.

## ❏ Chapter 10

[1]Tim Moore, "Producing the Image," Speech to the Great Lakes Radio Conference, Mt. Pleasant, Michigan, April 25, 1981.

[2]Tyree Ford, writing in "Monday Memo," *Broadcasting* (May 11, 1987): 18.

[3]*Ibid.*

[4]"Morning Drive Radio: Looking for New Animal," *Broadcasting* (June 12, 1989): 37.

[5]*Ibid.*

[6]*Ibid.*

[7]*Ibid.*

[8]Susan Eastman, Sydney Head, and Lewis Klein, *Broadcast/Cable Programming,* 3rd ed. (Belmont, CA: Wadsworth, 1989), 446.

[9]"Radio DJ's Crank Up Public Protest over Hill Pay Hike," *Broadcasting* (November 20, 1989): 33–34.

[10]Frank Thayer, *Legal Control of the Press,* 4th ed. (Brooklyn, NY: The Foundation Press, 1962), 23.

[11]Walter Lippmann, *Public Opinion* (New York: Free Press, 1967), 25.

[12]Peter Orlik, "Systemic Limitations to Irish Broadcast Journalism," *Journal of Broadcasting* (Fall 1976): 473.

[13]Shirley Biagi (ed.), *Newstalk II* (Belmont, CA: Wadsworth, 1987), 116.

[14]*Ibid.*, 9–10.

[15]"The Marriage of Radio Advertising and New Product Lines," *Broadcasting* (June 22, 1987): 43.

[16]"Stakelin Accentuates the Positive of Radio," *Broadcasting* (May 20, 1985): 85.

[17]"Testifying to Radio's Powers," *Broadcasting* (June 24, 1985): 51.

[18]Jim Dale, "Budget TV," *ADS Magazine* (June 1985): 96.

[19]Charles Kuralt, speaking on a panel at the Center for Communications, Inc., Writing for Television Seminar, New York, November 12, 1985.

[20]"Storyboards That Really Control Production and Save Money Too," *ASAP* (May/June 1988): 12.

[21]"The Write Stuff," *Broadcasting* (December 9, 1985): 119.

[22]"Hugh Wilson: On Top of the World," *Broadcasting* (November 27, 1989): 95.

[23]John Houseman, "Is TV-Acting Inferior?" *TV Guide* (September 1, 1979): 25.

[24]Horace Newcomb, *TV: The Most Popular Art* (Garden City, NY: Anchor Books, 1974), 249.

[25]George Schaefer, comments in *Television Makers,* Newton E. Meltzer-produced tele-vised PBS documentary, 1986.

[26]Ken Howard, "Why I Left Prime-Time TV for Harvard," *TV Guide* (February 21, 1987): 6.

[27]"Celebrity Q's Say Who's Who," *ASAP etc.* (July, 1989): 1–2.

[28]*Ibid.,* 2.

[29]Merrill Panitt, "Wheel of Fortune," *TV Guide* (October 5, 1985): 1.

[30]Fred Cohn, "Actors Strut Their Stuff on the Corporate Stage," *Corporate Video Decisions* (November, 1989): 32.

[31]*Ibid.,* 33.

[32]*Ibid.,* 29.

[33]John Morley, "Working with Scriptwriters," *Audio-Visual Communications* (December 1986): 45.

[34]Carl DeSantis and Phyllis Camesano "The Professional Draft," *Audio-Visual Communications* (March 1979): 24.

[35]Robert Emmett Dolan, *Music in Modern Media* (New York: G. Schirmer, Inc., 1967), xi.

[36]Robert MacKenzie, "Highway to Heaven," *TV Guide* (December 29, 1984): 40.

## ❑ Chapter 11

[1]"Robotic Cameras: Cutting out the Middlemen," *Broadcasting* (December 7, 1987): 96.

[2]Peter Caranicas, "The Cost Cutting Edge," *Channels Field Guide 1991,* 34.

[3]"Endangered Species," *Broadcasting* (January 15, 1990): 146.

[4]William Moylan, "Employment Trends," *Recording Engineer/Producer* (December 1988): 38.

[5]*Ibid.*

[6]Herbert Zettl, *Sight, Sound, Motion: Applied Media Aesthetics* (Belmont, CA: Wadsworth, 1973), 44.

[7]*Ibid.,* 38.

[8]Joseph Tawil, "Lighting with Pencil and Paper—The Light Plot," *Educational & Industrial Television* (April 1975): 22.

[9]Jac Holzman, writing in "Monday Memo," *Broadcasting* (July 19, 1989): 24.

[10]"The Role of Film in TV Programming," *Broadcast Engineering* (May, 1979), 77.

[11]Holzman, "Monday Memo."

[12]"SMPTE '89: HDTV and Beyond," *Broadcasting* (October 30, 1989): 49.

[13]"John Finger Talks about the Challenges of Filming 'Cheers,' " *NATPE Programmer* (January 1986): 152.

[14]Neal Koch, "TV's New Ruling Class," *Channels* (May 1989): 31.

[15]Mill Roseman, "Joy Radio," *Communication Arts* (January/February 1989): 66.

[16]A. William Bluem and Roger Manwell (eds.), *Television: The Creative Experience* (New York: Hastings House, 1967), 48.

[17]*Ibid.,* 42.

[18]Stephen Barr, "Directing: Auteurs Need Not Apply," *Corporate Video Decisions* (April 1990): 40.

[19]"Networks and TV's Significant Others Line Up for Fall," *Broadcasting* (September 4, 1989): 27.

[20]Walt Wurfel, "How Some of America's Successful Salespeople Operate," *NAB Radio Week* (January 15, 1990): 4.

[21]Sondra Michaelson, "Empathy vs. Sympathy as a Radio Sales Approach," *Broadcasting* (February 8, 1988): 42.

[22]Vince Manzi, "Servicing What You Sell," panel presentation to National Association of Television Program Executives at New Orleans, January 17, 1990.

[1]Bill Hennes, "Fighting Copycat Syndromes among Radio Stations," *Broadcasting* (April 14, 1986): 22.

[2]Clark Smidt, writing in "Monday Memo," *Broadcasting* (May 8, 1989): 22

[3]Martin Antonelli, writing in "Monday Memo," *Broadcasting* (January 16, 1989): 38.

[4]William McCavitt and Peter Pringle, *Electronic Media Management* (Boston: Focal Press, 1986), 58.

[5]Tom Kirby, comments on "Number One in News" panel, National Association of Broadcasters Convention, at Las Vegas, April 12, 1988.

[6]Rolla Cleaver, comments on "Number One in News" panel, April 12, 1988.

[7]Merrie Street, comments on "Radio News: It Ain't What It Used to Be" panel, Radio Television News Director's Association Convention, at Kansas City, September 16, 1989.

[8]Neal Koch, "TV's New Ruling Class," *Channels* (May, 1989): 30–31.

[9]Kathy Brown, "The King and Queen of Comedy" *ADWEEK* (June 19, 1989): B.T. 52–53.

[10]Horace Newcomb and Robert Alley, *The Producer's Medium* (New York: Oxford University Press, 1983), 239.

[11]*Ibid.*, 183–184.

[12]Paul Goldsmith, writing in "Monday Memo," *Broadcasting* (September 22, 1980): 12.

[13]Donald David, *I Wish Somebody Had Told Me That the Day I Started* (Campbell-Ewald Advertising corporate publication, 1965), 8.

[14]Richard Morgan, "Peter Principle: Should a CD's Desire to Make Ads Be a Fireable Offense?" *ADWEEK* (June 19, 1989): 2.

[15]*Ibid.*

[16]Richard Morgan, "Commerce, Creativity Collide in Minneapolis," *ADWEEK/Midwest* (December 19, 1988): 52.

[17]Tim Leon, Letter to the Editor, *ADWEEK* (December 3, 1990): 8.

[18]Nancy Bishop, "A New Channel for Dallas' Media Mover," *ADWEEK* (July 24, 1989): 25.

[19]Paul Benjou, writing in "Monday Memo," *Broadcasting* (March 12, 1990): 25.

[20]Lynne Grasz, writing in "Monday Memo," *Broadcasting* (November 6, 1989): 33.

[21]Richard Morgan, "As Ad Biz Is Overrun with Free Agents, the Personality of the Players Is Lost," *ADWEEK* (July 24, 1989): 2.

## ❑ Chapter 13

[1]Erwin Krasnow and Lawrence Longley, *The Politics of Broadcast Regulation,* 2nd ed. (New York: St. Martin's Press, 1978), 38–39.

[2]Arthur Goodkind, "Broadcast De-Regulation and Self-Defense," *Broadcasting* (February 13, 1984): 36.

[3]Glen Robinson, *Communications for Tomorrow: Policy Perspectives for the 1980s* (New York: Praeger, 1978), 384–385.

[4]Krasnow and Longley, *Politics of Broadcast Regulation,* 39–40.

[5]"The Washington Lawyer: Power behind the Powers That Be," *Broadcasting* (June 16, 1980): 57.

[6]*Ibid.*, "Washington Lawyer," 32.

[7]Kathleen Jamieson and Karlyn Campbell, *The Interplay of Influence* (Belmont, CA: Wadsworth, 1983), p. 81.

[8]Richard Morgan, "Exxon Learns the Hard Way," *ADWEEK* (April 24, 1989): 3.

[9]Teresa Tritch, "Crisis Ads: When All Hell Breaks Loose," *ADWEEK/Midwest* (October 17, 1988): 48.

[10]John Burke, "Crisis Public Relations: Tylenol and Other Headaches," presented at the Center for Communication Seminar, at New York, November 13, 1986.

[11]Richard Blackmur, "A Burden for Critics," in *The Lion and the Honeycomb*, ed. Richard Blackmur. (New York: Harcourt Brace, 1955), 206.

[12]Lawrence Laurent, "Wanted: The Complete Television Critic," in *The Eighth Art* (New York: Holt, Rinehart and Winston, 1962), 156.

[13]Jack Gould, "A Critical Reply," *New York Times*, (May 26, 1957) n.p.

[14]George Brandenburg, "TV Critic's Role is Middleman—Wolters," *Editor and Publisher* (December 23, 196): 39.

[15]George Condon, "Critic's Choice," *Television Quarterly* (November 1962): 27.

[16]"But Who Listens?," *Television Age* (September 27, 1965): 19.

[17]Lee Loevinger, "The Ambiguous Mirror: The Reflective-Projective Theory of Broadcasting and Mass Communications," *Journal of Broadcasting* (Spring 1968): 110–111.

[18]"The Business of Brokering/89," *Broadcasting* (August 7, 1989): 37.

[19]Robyn Griggs, "Weathering Tough Times in the Agency Business," *ADWEEK* (July 2, 1990): 18.

[20]Debra Goldman, "Glitz Is Gone for New-Business Gurus," *ADWEEK* (January 7, 1991): 2.

[21]"Co-Op: Covering the Basics," *ASAP* (November/December 1988): 17.

[22]Karrie Jacobs, "Watching a Radio Consultant Consult," *ADWEEK'S Radio 1985 Issue* (July 1985): 8.

[23]Michael Keith, *Radio Programming: Consultancy and Formatics* (Boston: Focal Press, 1987), 8–9.

[24]Everette Dennis, "Undergraduate Education Should Stop Ignoring the Importance of the Media," *The Chronicle of Higher Education* (February 4, 1987): 36.

## ❏ Chapter 14

[1]David Rosen, "Fiber Optics & the Future of Television," *NVR Reports* (Winter 1991): 5–6.

[2]Stan Salek, "Expanding Digital Audio Storage," *NAB RadioWeek* (April 23, 1990): 7.

[3]"On the Road to NAB: Radio and Audio Processing," *Broadcasting* (February 5, 1990): 66

[4]*Ibid.*

[5]"Janet Steiger: The FTC's Vigilant Enforcer," *Broadcasting* (February 5, 1990): 76.

[6]J. Brian DeBoice, writing in "Monday Memo," *Broadcasting* (August 28, 1989): 25.

[7]Hon. Richard Boucher, *Cable Competition vs. Cable Regulation: White Paper on Telecommunications Policy* (February 22, 1990): ii.

[8]Joanna Elm, "Tonight's Hot Story Is Brought to You—by You!" *TV Guide* (February 24, 1990): 25

[9]"USIA Publishers Guide to TV in Eastern Europe," *Broadcasting* (March 5, 1990): 58–59

[10]Author interview with Frank Scott, director, VOA-Europe. Atlanta, Georgia, March 31, 1990.

[11]"MIP Market Abounds with Co-Production Deals," *Broadcasting* (April 30, 1990), p. 38.

[12]John Augustus Shedd, *Salt from My Attic* (Portland, ME: Mosher Press, 1928), 20.

# Index

Aaron Spelling Productions, 380–381
A/B switch, 232
ABC, 18, 58, 141–142, 145–146, 153, 159, 186, 188, 194, 198, 205–206, 211, 214, 217, 221, 225–226, 230–232, 343, 394, 396, 453
Above-the-line elements, 379
Abrams, Lee, 196
ABSIE (Armed Forces American Broadcasting System in Europe), 258
Academy of Television Arts and Sciences, 207
Account executives, 70–71, 296, 338, 382–388, 421
Account manager, 387
Accuracy in Media (AIM), 410
Acorn (DAB system), 452
ACT, 222, 403, 410
Action for Children's Television. See ACT
Action for Children's Television v. Federal Communications Commission, 403
Actors, 84, 289, 304–306, 308–309, 311, 327, 330, 336–337, 378–381, 383–384, 467
ACTV (Advanced Compatible Television), 442–445
Addressable pay systems, 51, 233. See also PPV
Adult contemporary format (AC), 279–280
Advanced Television Systems Committee (ATSC), 443
Advanced Television Test Center, 443
Advertising, 12–18, 52–54, 61, 68–76, 121, 134–136, 141–142, 151–153, 155, 157–158, 171–178, 183, 186–189, 193–195, 198, 203–205, 207, 209, 214, 217, 225, 228–229, 254, 256–258, 262, 269, 279, 289, 291–302, 335, 338–341, 344, 350, 359, 361, 365, 368, 385–397, 401, 406, 414, 416, 421–424, 429, 447. See also Advertising agencies; Commercials
Advertising agencies, 68–71, 88, 90, 289, 291–293, 296–297, 300–304, 306, 312, 314, 327, 333–334, 341, 343, 345, 350, 354, 370, 381–391, 394–397, 400, 421–426, 432–433
Affiliates (network), 33, 179, 188–189, 198, 345, 363–364, 417, 453, 458
AFRTS (Armed Forces Radio and Television Service), 183, 257, 266–267
Agents, talent, 83, 172, 303, 380

Agnew, Spiro, 220–223, 283
Album-oriented rock. See AOR
Alexanderson, F. W., 102
"All-Channel" requirement, 120
All In the Family, 223
All-news radio, 194–195, 340, 344, 372
Allen, Frederick Lewis, 170
Allen, Steve, 212
AM (amplitude modulation), defined, 21–24, 102
AM stations, 23–30, 94, 112–113, 150, 158–159, 177, 185, 187, 190, 193–198, 242, 246, 260, 264, 266, 319, 397, 452, 466
Amateur radio, 48, 405
American Bar Association (ABA), 136
American Broadcasting Company. See ABC
American Newspaper Publisher's Association (ANPA), 174–175, 178
American Public Radio Network (APR), 254
American School of the Air, 178
American Society of Advertising and Promotion, 306
American Telephone and Telegraph. See AT&T
American Top 40, 336
America's Funniest Home Videos, 458
Amos 'n' Andy, 173–174, 187
Ampex Corporation, 120–121
Analog process, defined, 450
Anchor (news), 284–287, 308, 373, 377, 409, 414
Anderson, Michael, 314–315
Andy Griffith Show, The, 350
Animation, 332, 354
Annenberg Foundation, 433
Announcer/presenter, 284–287, 383. See also Disc jockey; Video jockey
Antennas, station, 27, 30–32, 34–35, 227, 404
Anti-trafficking rule, 156
Anti-trust issues, 134, 140, 145, 157, 159, 211, 213, 411, 454, 456
Antonelli, Martin, 365, 367
AOR (Album-oriented rock), 193, 196, 280, 389
Arbitron, 89–90, 92, 198, 234, 359–361, 465–466
Armed Forces Radio and Television Service. See AFRTS
Armstrong, Edwin, 110–112, 196
Army Hour, The, 183
Army-McCarthy Hearings, 211–213, 223. See also McCarthy, Joseph
Art directors, 70, 295–297, 300–302,

312, 327, 334–335, 353–354, 364, 379, 381–383, 396–397
Arts & Entertainment Network (A & E), 15, 230, 255, 341, 343
ASCAP, 130–131, 137–139, 187–188, 191, 313
Ascertainment, 155–156
Ashby, Eric, 437
Asimov, Isaac, 269
Assertion, defined, 3–4, 7
Assignment editors, 373–375, 378, 431
Assistant director, 333
Assistant news director, 373
Associated Press (AP), 86–87, 172, 175, 178, 182, 196
Association of Public Radio Stations (APRS), 408
Associations, electronic media, 468–469
AT&T, 104, 108–109, 114–115, 119–120, 129–130, 132, 171–172, 203, 205, 209, 211, 232, 256, 456
Attitude, defined, 3–4, 7
Audience flow, 363
Audience measurement, 87–92, 178, 207, 216, 231, 234, 263, 279, 282, 339–340, 350. See also Ratings
Audimeter, 89, 178, 234
Audio engineers, 319–322
Audion tube, 103–104, 111
Audiotape, 80, 184, 185–186, 445
Audit Bureau of Circulation (ABC), 87, 178
Auditorium test, 18
Australian Broadcasting Corporation, 18
Avails, 53–54, 338, 345, 363, 367, 371, 457
Axis Sally, 183

Backhaul feeds, 62
Baird, John, 114–115
Bardeen, John, 189
Barnouw, Erik, 109
Barr, Stephen, 337
Barrow, Roscoe, 146–147
Barrow Report, 146–147
Barter advertising, 348, 350, 367–368, 390
Beat the Clock, 209
Beaudin, Ralph, 194
Bell, Alexander Graham, 99, 113, 124
Bell regional companies (BOCs), 456
Bell System. See AT&T
Below-the-line elements, 379
Benjou, Paul, 390
Bergen, Edgar, 179–180, 187
Berle, Milton, 207

Bernays, Edward, 73, 76
Bernstein, Leonard, 145
*Big Show, The,* 188
*Billboard,* 362
Birch radio ratings, 89–90
Bit-rate reduction, 451
Blackburn, Dick, 418
Blackmur, Richard, 414
"Blue Book," 142–143, 187
Blue network, 139–141, 172, 174–175, 179
BMI, 138–139, 187–188, 191, 313
Board of International Broadcasting, 265
Bodo, Roger, 383–384
*Bonanza,* 350
Book publishing, 14, 429, 435, 441
Boscarino, Paul, 366–367
Boucher, Rick, 456–457
Boutique agencies, 384, 397
Bradsell, Robert, 74–76
*Brady Bunch, The,* 350
Braun, Carl Ferdinand, 115
Braunlich, Cynthia, 346–347
*Break the Bank,* 184
British Broadcasting Corporation (BBC), 115, 142–143, 447
Broadband communications, 92–94. *See also* Fiber optics
Broadcast Programming, Inc., 362
Broadcast Rating Council. *See* Electronic Media Rating Council
Broadcasting, defined, 15, 106, 122, 172
*Broadcasting* magazine, 8–9, 303, 392, 407–408
Broadway (shows), 467
Brokers, media, 59, 416–419, 465
Brown, Himan, 196
Bureau of Alcohol, Tobacco and Firearms, 406
Bureau of Broadcasting, 263
Burke, John, 413
Burkhart, Kent, 280
*Burns and Allen,* 174–175
Bush, George, 410
Business development executives. *See* New business activities

Cable Communications Policy Act, 48, 158, 404
Cable stations, 457
Cable television:
  access channels, 158, 365, 433
  basic, 53, 62–63, 158, 338, 341, 365, 371, 422, 429, 455, 457
  beginnings, 122–124, 213–214, 222
  conflicts, 40–41, 49, 91, 93–94, 124, 158–159
  defined, 122, 124, 127
  fiber optic use, 450
  franchise, 13, 40, 48, 60, 158, 365, 371, 416, 429, 433
  managers. *See* System manager

networks, 15–16, 34, 53–54, 57, 61–62, 80, 82, 225, 228–229, 255, 394
  pay. *See* Pay cable
  penetration, 12–13, 225
  regulation, 48, 151–154, 157–159, 232, 401, 404, 454. *See also* Syndex
  system defined, 48
  system news, 377
  system operation, 33–34, 36, 41, 50–51, 53–55, 57, 60–61, 121–125, 364–365, 371–372, 422, 424
Caesar, Sid, 207, 209
Caldwell, O. H., 109
Call signs, 106–107, 173
Camcorder, 123, 234, 446, 458–459
*Camel News Caravan,* 206
Camera operators, 323, 325, 333, 379. *See also* Cinematographers; Videographers
Campbell, Alan, 155–156, 407
Campbell, Jay, 389
Campbell, Kevin, 310–311
Cannell, Stephen, 303, 378
Canon 35. *See* Code of Judicial Conduct
CapCities/ABC. *See* ABC
*Capital Broadcasting Co.* v. *Mitchell,* 153
Capital Cities Communications, 231–232
Carlin, George, 154
Carnegie Commissions, 250–251, 253
Carnegie Corporation, 242, 250–251, 254
Carrier wave, 21–22, 24–25
Carsey, Marcy, 378
Caruso, Enrico, 103
Casady, Chris, 308–309
Castro, Fidel, 264
Cathode ray tube, 115–116, 118, 201–202, 206–207, 209
CATV. *See* Cable television
C-band frequencies, 35
CBS, 18, 58, 107, 115, 118–120, 140–141, 145, 153, 159, 172, 175–180, 182–184, 187–188, 191, 194, 196–197, 203, 205–206, 209, 211–214, 217, 221, 223, 230, 232, 242, 245, 256–259, 294, 301, 304, 308, 319, 343, 346, 378, 447, 453
*CBS Radio Mystery Theatre,* 196
CD (audio compact disc), 123, 445–446, 451
*Ceefax,* 447
Censors, network. *See* Standards officials
Censorship. *See* First Amendment issues; Prior restraint
Central Intelligence Agency (CIA), 265
Chain broadcasting. *See* Network development
*Chandler* v. *Florida,* 151
Channel 1, 32, 119

*Chase and Sanborn Hour,* 179
Checkerboarding, 364
*Cheers,* 307, 336, 364
Cherry, Don, 277
Chiaroscuro lighting, 322–324
Children's programming, 159, 179, 181, 214, 222–223, 251, 255, 430, 455
Children's Television Act, 159, 255
Children's Television Workshop (CTW), 251
CHR (Contemporary hit radio), 261, 279–280, 344
Christian Science Publishing Society, 28, 257
Churn rate, 371, 424
Cigarette advertising, 151–153, 206
Cinematographers, 323, 325, 327–329, 334
Claman, Danielle, 380–381
Claymation, 354
Clear channel stations, 109
Clearance, program, 363
Cleaver, Rolla, 373, 377
Closed-captioning, 56, 447
Closed-circuit television, 247
CNN, 54, 87, 225, 230, 234, 255, 263, 267–269, 290–291, 318, 341, 377, 459. *See also* Turner Communications
*CNN World Report,* 268–269
Coaxial cable, 15, 119, 122, 203, 205–206, 209, 211
Coca, Imogene, 207, 209
Code of Judicial Conduct, 136, 159
Cohn, Fred, 309
*Colgate Comedy Hour, The,* 211
Color television development, 115, 118–121, 203–204, 209, 211, 214, 217, 220, 222
Columbia Broadcasting System. *See* CBS
Columbia Phonograph Company, 172
*Columbia Workshop,* 178
*Command Performance,* 183, 257
Commercial medium, defined, 53
Commercials, 54, 61, 69–71, 73–76, 171–172, 179, 181, 194, 205, 216, 231, 254, 266, 292–302, 308–309, 312–314, 321, 323–325, 328, 333–339, 343, 345, 348, 351, 355, 358–359, 361–363, 366–367, 381–384, 387–388, 397, 403, 426, 429. *See also* Advertising
Commission (compensation), 69, 345, 367, 388, 418–419, 422
Common Carrier Bureau (FCC), 405
Common carriers, defined, 48–49, 94, 135
Communication, defined, 1–5
Communications, defined, 5–6
Communications Act of 1934, 47–48, 135–136, 141, 143, 145, 147–148, 151–153, 191, 394, 401

Communications attorneys, 155–156, 402–409, 429, 432, 455
Communist scare, 144–145, 188, 211–212
Community Antenna Television Association (CATA), 408
Community Broadcasters Association (CBA), 38, 408
Compact disc. *See* CD
*Companionate Radio,* 189
Competing applications (license), 143
Compression (video), 124, 444–445, 448–449, 457
Comptroller, 370–371
Compulsory license (cable), 154, 158, 225
Computers, 290, 297, 310, 319, 331–332, 353–354, 362–363, 388–389, 427–428, 446, 448, 451, 456–457, 465
COMSAT, 230, 267, 448
Conglomerates, 80
Conly, Robert, 203
Conrad, Frank, 105–106, 170
Consultants, 38, 195–196, 198, 346, 361, 364–365, 378, 407, 425, 427–428, 458, 465
Continental Radio News Service, 176
Controversial issues, 181–184. *See also* Fairness Doctrine
Conus Communications, 87
Cook, Fred, 152
Cook, Jay, 279
Coolidge, Calvin, 109, 133
Cooney, Joan Ganz, 251
Co-op advertising, 422
Copland, Aaron, 145
Coproduction, 84, 460
Copyright issues, 130, 137–138, 151, 154, 231, 313, 406, 451
Copyright Royalty Tribunal, 154, 371
Copywriters, 70, 289, 291–297, 303, 327, 335, 337, 381–383
Corporate video, 308–314, 321, 325, 328, 337, 354–355, 379, 445
Corporation for Public Broadcasting (CPB), 56, 251–255
Corporation for Public Television, (CPT), 250–251
*Cosby Show, The,* 364, 378
Cost-per-thousand (CPM), 339–340, 345, 359, 388
Coughlin, Charles, 181–182, 184
Counterprogramming, 214, 225, 363–364
Courtroom access, 136, 150–151, 159
Coy, Wayne, 47
CPB. *See* Corporation for Public Broadcasting
CPM. *See* Cost-per-thousand
Cream-skimming, 41
Creative directors, 70–71, 296, 381–385, 387

Creative services. *See* Promotions people
Creative vice-president, 382
Credit manager, 371
Creel, George, 76
Crenshaw, Mills, 283
Critics, 414–416
Cronkite, Walter, 49, 206
Crookes, William, 115
Crosby, Bing, 185–186, 188
Crosby, John, 213
Crosley Radio Corporation, 107, 243, 256
Crossley Reports, 87, 178
Crystal receiver, 108–109
C-SPAN, 49, 57, 225–226, 255
Cuba, 262–264
Cycles, defined, 29

DAB (Digital Audio Broadcasting), 124, 451, 453
Dachs, David, 79
Dailies (visual footage), 330
Dale, Jim, 293
Daley, Richard, 220
Daly, Lar, 149
Damrosch, Walter, 243
DAT (Digital audiotape), 123, 450–451
David Sarnoff Research Center, 442–443
Davis, Elmer, 141, 183
Davis, Harry, 105–106
Day, Louis, 436–437
DBS, 13, 15–16, 41–42, 48, 53, 60–61, 96, 127, 230, 233, 403, 444–445, 448–450, 452–455, 457
DeBoice, J. Brian, 455
Debt-servicing, 368, 393, 418
Decker, Charlie, 422
Decoder Circuitry Act, 56, 447
Dees, Rick, 282
DeForest, Lee, 102–105, 109–111, 169–170, 187
Dennis, Everette, 435
Dennis, Patricia Diaz, 402–403
Deregulation, 157, 159, 197, 372, 401, 403–404, 409, 416
Designer. *See* Art directors
*Detroit News,* 107, 170
Dewey, Thomas, 184
Dews, Peter, 337
Diaries (Audience measurement), 90, 234, 466
*Different World, A,* 364, 378
Digital Audio Broadcasting. *See* DAB
Digital audiotape. *See* DAT
Digital process, defined, 450–451
Dill-White Radio Act. *See* Radio Act of 1927
Dimling, John, 88–89
Direct Broadcast Satellite. *See* DBS
Direct mail, 388
Direct waves, 27–28

Directors, 304–305, 325, 327, 330, 332–337, 378–380
Directors Guild of America, 223, 335
Disc jockey, 10, 59–60, 80, 187–188, 190–193, 277–281, 358–359, 368, 392–393, 465–466
Discovery Channel, The, 228–230, 255, 343
Disney Channel, 230
Distribution network (cable), 34
Distributors, record, 81–82
Dolan, Robert Emmett, 312
Donahue, Phil, 268
*Douglas Edwards with the News,* 120, 206
Downey, Gerald, 70–71
Drake, Bill, 195
Drive-in theaters, 213
Drucker, Peter, 368
DuMont, Allen, 206–207
DuMont Television, 119, 143, 188, 203, 205–206, 209, 211–212
*DuMont v. Carroll,* 143
Dunbar, Al, 318
Durr, Clifford, 141

Early Bird, 12, 220, 267
EARS (Electronic Attitude Research System), 18
Eastman, Susan, 76
Eastman Kodak, 328
*Eddie Cantor,* 174
Edison, Thomas, 77
Editorializing, 139, 143. *See also* Fairness Doctrine
Editors (film/video), 305, 326, 328–332, 334, 336, 354, 379
EDTV (Enhanced Definition Television), 96
Educational broadcasting, defined, 242
Educational radio, 242, 245, 249, 253. *See also* Instructional radio
Educational television, 246–251. *See also* Instructional television
Educational Television and Radio Center, 247
Educational TV Facilities Act, 249
Effective radiated power (ERP), 32
EFP (Electronic field production), 325
8MK, 107, 170. *See also* WWJ
8XK, 105. *See also* KDKA
Eisenhower, Dwight, 212, 216
Electronic Media Rating Council, 216
Electronic television. *See* Television, electronic
Elkins, Thomas, 392–393
Emmys, 207
ENG (Electronic newsgathering), 325, 327–328
Engineers, 95, 121, 171, 203, 317–322, 325, 332–333, 353, 367, 392, 414, 425, 427, 434

Equal Employment Opportunity pro-
grams (EEO), 151, 406–407, 411
"Equal Time" (for political candidates),
133, 135, 143, 148–150, 401
Equipment manufacturers, 94–96, 105,
120, 123, 130, 186, 196, 204–
207, 256
*Ernie Kovacs Show, The,* 209–210
Ertel, Henner, 222
ESPN, 54, 225, 230, 343
*Estes* v. *Texas,* 150
Eureka 95 (HDTV system), 442–443
Eureka 147 (DAB system), 451–452
European media, 52–53, 60–61, 261–
262, 267, 348, 442–443, 445,
447–448, 451, 459–460
EUTELSAT, 267
Evergreens (TV program series), 350
Executive producer, 373, 377, 379

*Face the Nation,* 213
Fairness Doctrine, 143, 151–152, 158,
401, 454–455
Family Network, The, 225
"Family Viewing," 222–223
Farnsworth, Philo, 116
FCC:
   commissioners, 401–405, 415
   creation, 135
   definitional actions, 36–38, 40, 49,
      122, 155–157, 230, 453
   network regulation. *See* Network reg-
      ulation
   noncommercial decisions, 243, 245–
      247, 254
   ownership regulations, 92, 94, 141,
      158, 198, 211, 391, 394, 401
   procedures and organization, 145,
      155–156, 204, 227, 230, 393,
      401, 403, 405–407
   program content regulation, 56, 112–
      113, 135, 139, 141, 143, 152–
      154, 157–158, 179, 193, 196–
      197, 222–223, 225–226, 230,
      256, 363, 403, 454–455
   regulatory rationale, 47–48, 60, 214
   scope of authority, 136–137, 139,
      145–146, 151, 216, 408, 416, 455
   technical decisions, 23–24, 32, 38,
      56, 94, 111–112, 118–120, 136,
      143, 150, 184, 189, 198, 203,
      205, 209–210, 245, 249, 257,
      329, 404–405, 442–443, 447, 449
Federal Aviation Administration (FAA),
406
Federal Communications Commission.
*See* FCC
*Federal Communications Commission*
v. *Pacifica Foundation,* 154, 179
*Federal Communications Commission*
v. *WNCN Listeners Guild,* 157
Federal Election Campaign Act, 153

Federal Radio Commission, 109, 133–
135, 172–173, 242, 256
Federal Radio Education Committee,
245
Federal Trade Commission. *See* FTC
Feedback, 2, 16–19
Felker, Alex, 24, 405
Ferrer, José, 145
Ferris, Charles, 157
Fessenden, Reginald, 102–105, 111,
169–170
Fiber optics, 15, 93, 124, 427, 449–450,
456–457
Field Operations Bureau (FCC), 405
*Fighting Men,* 183
Film, defined, 114, 304, 325, 328–329,
442
Financial analysts, 58–60, 402, 419–421
Financial interest and syndication
rules. *See* Fin/syn
Financial officer. *See* Comptroller
Finger, John, 336
Fink, Steven, 413
Fin/syn, 153, 159, 225, 348, 401, 408–
409, 453–454
First Amendment issues, 141, 143, 150,
152–154, 179, 223, 405, 454–455
First-run syndication, 348, 350, 381,
453. *See also* Syndication, televi-
sion
Flaherty, Joseph, 319
Fleming, J. Ambrose, 103
Floor manager, 333
Flournoy, Dan, 269
Fly, James Lawrence, 140–141
FM (frequency modulation), defined,
23–25, 32, 110–111
FM stations, 23–25, 27–28, 56, 86, 112–
113, 150, 158–159, 185–191,
193–198, 245–246, 257, 260–
262, 452, 466
Focus groups, 18–19, 278, 362, 378,
387, 466
Food and Drug Administration (FDA),
406
Ford, Tyree, 278–279
Ford Foundation, 245, 247–249, 251,
254
Format changes, 157
Formats. *See* Radio formats
*Fortnightly* v. *United Artists Television,*
151
Fowler, Mark, 401, 403
Fox Network, 232, 363, 453
France, 448
FRC. *See* Federal Radio Commission
Freberg, Stan, 291
Freed, Alan, 188, 191
Freelancers, 289, 303, 309, 333
"Freeze." *See* Television "Freeze"
Frequencies, defined, 29–35
Frequency (message repetition), 339–
340, 367, 388, 390

Friendly, Fred, 212, 221–222
Fritz, Eddie, 124
FTC, 135–136, 147, 216, 406, 429, 454
Fuhr, Brad, 358–359
Futures (program sales device), 348

Gabel, Martin, 188
Gallant, Denise, 95
Game shows. *See* Quiz shows
Gammon, James, 417–418
Gans, Herbert, 222
Garroway, Dave, 211
Gartner, James, 334–335
*Gary Moore Show, The,* 209
Gelb, Bruce, 263
Gelbart, Larry, 379
General Electric, 112, 116, 129–130,
132, 134, 172, 191, 232, 256, 448
General managers, 222, 359, 363, 366–
371, 392–394, 419, 427
Generics (promos), 352
Geosynchronous/geostationery orbit,
27, 267
*Geraldo,* 459
Gigahertz, defined, 31, 34–35
Global Village, 266–269
Goetz, Peter Michael, 305–306
Goich, Lisa, 292–293
*Goldbergs, The,* 188
Golden, Joy, 337
Goldenson, Leonard, 145–146, 211
Goldsmith, Paul, 382
Goldwater, Barry, 217–219
Goodkind, Arthur, 404
Gould, Jack, 414–415
Graphic artist. *See* Art director
Grasz, Lynne, 393–394
Grauer, Ben, 145
"Great Debates," 149–150, 215–216
Green, John, 294–295
Grid card, 341–342, 365, 459
Griggs, Robyn, 421
Gross rating points (GRP), 339–341, 390
Ground waves, 26–27, 30
Group head, 383–384
Group (station) 60, 80, 85, 232, 391,
394, 408–410, 419, 428
GTE, 125
Gunnison, Royal, 258

Halper, Donna, 425, 428
Hammocking, 364
*Happy Days,* 379
Harding, Warren, 114, 130
Harris, Byron, 287
Harris, Mel, 460
Hauptmann, Bruno, 136–137, 150
Hauser, Arnold, 5
HBO, 10, 53, 124, 222, 225, 448
HDTV, 94, 96, 121, 123–124, 328–329,
441–446, 449–450, 452, 456
Head, Sydney, 28
Headend (cable), 34, 41

Hellman, Lillian, 145
Hennes, Bill, 361
Hennock, Frieda, 246
Herman, Ron, 43–44
Herrold, Charles, 103–104, 170
Hertz, Heinrich, 29, 100–102
Hiber, Jhan, 89
High Definition Television. *See* HDTV
Hill, Susan, 431–432
Hindmarsh, Wayne, 54
Hitchcock, Alfred, 334
Holzman, Jac, 328–329
Home Box Office. *See* HBO
Home Shopping Network (HSN), 55,
    232, 449
Home video, 63–65, 96, 231
"Hook" commercial, 205
Hooperatings, 87, 89, 178, 207
Hoover, Herbert, 130–132
*Hoover* v. *Intercity Radio Company,*
    *Inc.,* 132
"Hot clock," 362
Houseman, John, 304
Houston, University of, 247
Howard, Ken, 304
*Howdy Doody,* 207
Hubbard Broadcasting, 449
Hughes Communications, 41–42, 448–
    449
Hungary, 261, 269, 459
*Huntley-Brinkley Report, The,* 206
HUT (Homes using television), 340
Hyde, Rosel, 247

*I Love Lucy,* 209, 350
Iconoscope, 116
Image advertising, 73, 327, 350–352
Image orthicon, 118, 207
Impressions, 388, 390
Indecency, 154, 156, 179, 403, 406,
    429, 454–455
Independent (nonnetwork) stations, 33,
    80, 225, 232, 345, 363–364, 417,
    457
Independents:
    film/video, 82, 85
    recording companies, 80–82
India, 8
Industrial television. *See* Corporate
    video
Information, defined, 3–4, 7
Instructional broadcasting, defined,
    242–243
Instructional radio, 243–245, 249, 433
Instructional television, 36, 38, 203,
    245, 247–251, 255, 433
INTELSAT, 267
Interactive television, 263, 268, 433,
    446, 448, 450
Interconnects, cable, 61
International Telecommunications
    Union (ITU), 28, 31, 402
International TV set penetration, 52

*Intersputnik,* 267
Ionosphere, 25–28, 31
Ireland, 285, 287
Isacsson, Paul, 343
Issue advertising, 73
ITFS (Instructional Television Fixed Ser-
    vice), 36, 38, 56, 249

*Jack Benny Show, The,* 187, 209
*Jackie Gleason Show, The,* 209
Jackson, Michael, 193
Jacobs, Frederick, 463–466
Japan, 442, 445, 448, 460
Jargon, industry, 278
Jefferson, Thomas, 283–284
Jenkins, Charles, 114–115
Johnson, Lyndon, 217–220, 250
Joint Committee for Educational Televi-
    sion (JCET), 245–246
Jones, Will, 415
Journalists. *See* News directors; Report-
    ers
Joyner, Tom, 279
*Judy Splinters Show, The,* 207
Jukebox, 78–80
*Just Plain Bill,* 175

Kaltenborn, H. V., 180
*Kate Smith Hour,* 209
Katz, Richard, 378
KBSC, 226
KDKA, 106, 173. *See also* 8XK
KDYL, 171
Kefauver, Estes, 210
Kelly, Kris, 351
Kennedy, John, 149–150, 215–216, 259
Kennedy, Robert, 220
Kernen, Dick, 195
KGF, 369–370
Kierker, William, 182
Killian, James, 250
Kilohertz, defined, 29–31
Kinescope recordings, 120, 207, 209,
    247
King, Martin Luther, 220
Kirby, Tom, 373
Kirkpatrick, Theodore, 145
Klein, Bill, 378
KMOX, 447
KNET, 300
KNUI, 392–393
KNX, 174
KOA, 173
Koch, Neal, 336
KOCO, 373
Kompas, John, 37–38
KPIX, 410
Kracauer, Siegfried, 11
Krushchev, Nikita, 213
KSD, 171
KSL, 447
Ku-band frequencies, 35, 449
KUHT, 247

*Kukla, Fran and Ollie,* 207
Kukowski, Mary, 420–421
Kuralt, Charles, 294
KUSW, 257
KVBC, 373
KXAS, 326–327
KYOI, 257

Land mobile services, 32, 119
Lani Bird, 220
*Lassie,* 350
Lasswell, Harold, 3, 5
Laurent, Lawrence, 414
Lear, Norman, 223, 379
Lehmann, Arlene, 353–354
Leon, Tim, 385
Lewis, Fulton, 180
Lexicon, 332
Libel, 143–144
Librarians, 430–433
License fees, receiver, 52–53
Licensing, station, 128, 132–134, 139–
    141, 143, 145–146, 157, 416–
    417, 429, 457. *See also* Renewal,
    license
Lico, Gary, 349
*Life of Riley, The,* 188
Lighting directors, 322–324, 333, 336
Lighting plot, 323
Limited partnerships, 58, 391
Lind, Joel, 196
Lindbergh case, 136–137
Lintas: USA, 423–424
Lippmann, Walter, 284
Listener-supported radio, 51, 194
*Little Orphan Annie,* 175, 183
*Live Aid,* 268
Lloyd, Frank, 94
Lobbyists, 408–411
Local origination (LO) channels, 33
Localism, 37–38, 60–61, 87, 192–193,
    197–198, 252, 279–280, 361,
    363, 465
Loevinger, Lee, 415
Loews Corporation, 232
Logo(type), 297, 300
Lois, George, 301–302
*Lone Ranger, The,* 169, 176–177, 188
Lorimar, 83–85, 381
Low power television. *See* LPTV
LPTV, 36–38, 227, 230, 319, 365, 394,
    403, 408

*Ma Perkins,* 191
MacArthur, Douglas, 188
McCabe, Ed, 291
McCarthy, Joseph, 144–145, 211–213.
    *See also* Army-McCarthy Hear-
    ings
MacDougall, Malcolm, 382
McFarland Bill, 145
McKenzie, Robert, 312
MacLeish, Archibald, 178

McLendon, Gordon, 188, 194
McLuhan, Marshall, 268
Magazines, 8–12, 14, 37, 43, 65, 69, 87, 171, 178, 183, 186, 217, 222, 224, 341, 362, 387–388, 390, 429, 431
Magid Associates, 458
Makeup artist, 297, 300
Mallary, Richard, 87
*Man behind the Gun,* 183–184
Mansen, R. H., 115
Manzi, Vince, 352
Mapes, Pier, 49–50
Marconi, Guglielmo, 100–101, 129
Marconi Wireless Telegraph Company, 100–101, 104, 107, 115, 129
Marr, Bruce, 281
*Married—With Children,* 430
Marshall, Gary, 379
Marx, Groucho, 209
*M*A*S*H*,* 379
Mass communication, defined, 6–9
Mass communications, defined, 6
Mass Media Bureau (FCC), 405
Maxwell, James Clerk, 100
Mayflower Case, 139, 143. *See also* Fairness Doctrine
MDS, 36, 62, 403
Mead, James, 249
Mechanical (recording) rights, 313
Mechanical television. *See* Television, mechanical
Media buying, 69, 343, 345, 388–390. *See also* Media director
Media director, 296, 343, 388–390
Media librarian, 432–433
Media literacy, 269, 435
Megahertz, defined, 29–32
Megastations, 159
*Men O' War,* 183
Mencken, H. L., 334
Merchandising, 84
Meteorologists, 290–291
Metromedia, 232
Meyer, Ed, 384
*Miami Vice,* 364, 380
Mica, Dan, 263
Michaelson, Sondra, 343
Microwave relay operations, 48, 119, 124, 151, 206, 209, 211, 249, 327–328, 405
Microwaves, defined, 33–35
Midband converter, 33
Miller, Arthur, 145
Mini-series, 225–226, 379
*Minitel,* 448
Minow, Newton, 150, 191–192
MMDS. *See* Wireless cable
Molinello, Alexander, 297
*Monitor,* 189
Monroe, Robert, 189
Moore, Tim, 278
Morgan, Henry, 188

Morgan, Richard, 394
Morita, Akio, 465
Morley, John, 309
Morning drive, 279
Morse, Samuel, 99
Motion Picture Association of America (MPAA), 408
Mouritsen, Russell, 427–428
Movie industry, 10–13, 82, 143, 145–146, 172, 209, 213–214, 217, 231–232, 320–321, 378–381, 408–409, 446, 459–460
Moylan, William, 319, 321
MPATI (Midwest Program for Airborne Television Instruction), 248–249
MSOs (Multiple system operators), 60, 123, 365, 394, 408, 410, 416, 419, 448, 454,
MTV, 80, 230
Muggs, J. Fred, 211
Multiple ownership rules, 141, 146, 198, 401, 454
Multiplex. *See* SCA
Murdoch, Rupert, 232, 448
Murray, A. F., 117
Murrow, Edward R., 180, 182, 211–213, 259, 371
Museum of Radio and Television, 432
Music director, 80, 361–362
Music libraries, 313–315
Music suppliers, 312–315, 395
Must-carry rule, 158, 232, 409
Mutual Broadcasting System (MBS), 140, 176–177, 179, 180, 183–184, 188–189, 198, 258
Muzak, 25, 51–52, 189


NAB. *See* National Association of Broadcasters
NAB Codes, 134, 137, 139, 148, 157, 181–182, 209–210, 223, 429
Nadell, Carol, 309
Nader, Ralph, 281
Nairn, Charles, 320–321
Nashville Network, 230
Nathan, Sydney, 147
National Advisory Commission on Civil Disorders, 220
National Advisory Council on Education by Radio, 242
National Association of Attorneys General (NAAG), 406
National Association of Broadcasters (NAB), 49, 103, 120, 124, 130, 134, 137–142, 148, 150, 157, 172, 181, 187, 209–210, 216, 223–224, 246, 261, 402, 408, 431–432, 451–452
National Association of Educational Broadcasters (NAEB), 251–252
National Association of Public Television Stations (NAPTS), 254, 408

National Broadcasting Company. *See* NBC
*National Broadcasting Company, Inc. et al.* v. *United States et al.,* 141
National Cable Television Association (NCTA), 408
National Captioning Institute (NCI), 447
National Committee on Education by Radio, 242–243
National Programming Service (NPS), 255
National Public Affairs Center for Television (NPACT), 252
National Public Radio (NPR), 251, 253–254
National Telecommunications and Information Administration (NTIA), 410–411
National Television System Committee (NTSC), 118–119, 442, 445
NBC, 58, 118–120, 129, 139–142, 145, 148, 153, 159, 171–176, 178–180, 182, 187–189, 194, 197–198, 202–207, 209, 211, 214, 216–217, 220–221, 226, 230, 232, 242–243, 245, 256–258, 312, 318, 343, 364, 394, 442–443, 453
NDXE, 257–258
NERN (National Educational Radio Network), 249
NET (National Educational Television), 247, 249, 251–252
Net comp(ensation), 363
Networks (broadcast):
  affiliates. *See* Affiliates
  defined, 60–61, 252–253
  evolution, 109, 171–173, 176–177, 188–189, 191, 194, 196–198, 205–207, 209, 211, 251–254
  program executives, 378, 380–381
  regulation, 136–137, 139–141, 146, 153, 159, 194, 348, 363, 453–454
New Business activities/executives, 43, 54, 352–354, 395–397, 421–426, 432–433
*New Leave It to Beaver, The,* 350
Newcomb, Horace, 304
News director, 328, 371–374, 376–378, 393, 409, 425, 429
News services, 85–87, 172, 175–178, 196
Newscasts, 149, 152–153, 173–176, 179–180, 182–184, 188–189, 192, 196, 206, 211, 216, 220–224, 255, 257, 259–260, 264–266, 268, 284–290, 308, 318, 325, 327, 332–333, 335–336, 346, 374–375, 377, 414, 458
Newspapers, 7, 9–13, 69, 87, 139, 143, 171–172, 174–175, 177–178, 183–184, 186, 205, 217, 224, 284, 286, 288, 338, 341, 374, 377, 387–388, 431, 448

Niche programming, 364
Nickelodeon, 230, 341
Nielsen Media Research, 88–91, 178, 189–190, 216, 234
9XM, 107. *See also* WHA
Nipkow, Paul, 114
Nixon, Richard, 149, 215, 220–221, 223–224, 251–252
"No censorship" provision (of Communications Act), 135, 143
Noble, Edward, 58, 141–142
Noncommercial media, 53, 55–57, 241–257, 371. *See also* Public broadcasting
Nonduplication rule, 112–113, 150, 193, 196, 198
Nonmass media, 13–14
North American Philips, 443
Notan lighting, 322
NPR. *See* National Public Radio
NTIA. *See* National Telecommunications and Information Administration
NTSC. *See* National Television System Committee

Obscenity, 156
Occupational Safety and Health Administration (OSHA), 406
*Odd Couple, The,* 379
Off-network programs, 348, 350
Office of Censorship, 141
Office of Telecommunications Policy (OTP), 251–252, 410
Office of War Information (OWI), 141, 183, 257–258
Ohio School of the Air, 243–244, 433
Ohio State University, 243
*Open Letter on Race Hatred,* 184
Operations manager. *See* Production manager
Option time, 140
ORACLE (Optional Reception of Announcements by Coded Line Electronics), 447
Order No. 37, 136
Oscillator, 104
Osgood, Dick, 191
O'Toole, Donald, 179
O'Toole, John, 413
Otte, Ruth, 228–229
Outdoor advertising, 388, 390
Owners, 301–302, 359, 378, 390–397, 417–419
*Ozzie and Harriet,* 187

Pacifica Foundation, 154, 156, 241, 249, 455
Paley, William, 58, 172, 188, 257
Panitt, Merrill, 308
*Pantomine Quiz,* 209
Paramount Pictures, 172, 460
Parikhal, John, 359
Parsons, Ed, 122

Passion, professional, 467
*Pat 'n' Johnny Show,* 207–208
Pay cable, 10, 51–53, 62–63, 71, 82, 123–124, 213–214, 222, 225, 232–233, 365, 371, 422, 429, 446, 455, 457. *See also* Pay television
Pay-per-view. *See* PPV
Pay television, 62, 205, 209, 211, 213, 216, 222, 226, 230, 232. *See also* Pay cable
Payne, Allison, 286–287
Payne, Virginia, 191
Payola, 147, 190–191, 362
PBS. *See* Public Broadcasting Service
PCNs (Personal communications networks), 158–159
Pell, Eugene, 265
Peoplemeters, 88–90, 234, 339
Peppers, Don, 423–424
Performance rights, 313
Persian Gulf War, 234, 263, 285, 459
Personal attack rule, 152, 454
Petry Television, 346–347
*Philadelphia Daily News,* 174
Philco Radio and Television Corporation, 117–119, 203
Phonevision, 205, 209
Phonograph, 77–80, 105
Pierpoint, Robert, 223
Pilot program, 85, 380–381
Pirating, 64
Playlists, 188, 193, 196, 361–362
Poland, 269, 459
Pole attachment fees, 91, 158–159
Political candidates, access regulations, 133, 135, 143, 145, 148–150, 153, 454
Political commercials/communications, 217–219, 411–414
Political editorializing rule, 454
Poole, Don, 294
*Port Huron* decision, 143
Portable radio, 111, 189, 193–195
Porter, Paul, 141
Positioning, 278, 364, 382
PPV, 51, 55, 232–233, 449, 457–458
Preece, William Henry, 100
Press-Radio Bureau, 175–176, 178, 183
Price, Byron, 141
Prime time access, 364
Prime Time Access Rule (PTAR), 153, 225, 348, 401, 454
PrimeStar, 448–449
Print media, 7–14, 68–69, 87, 145, 150, 152, 183, 186, 287–288, 291, 293, 311, 338, 401, 427, 429, 435, 441. *See also* Magazines; Newspapers
Prior restraint, 134, 141–143, 152–153, 183–184, 188, 223
*Private Eye,* 364
Private Radio Bureau (FCC), 405

Privatization, 348
Proactive communication, 413
Proctor and Gamble, 390
Producers, 82–85, 222, 286, 305, 313–315, 326–327, 330–331, 350, 373–375, 378–384, 390, 432, 443
Production heads (studio), 83–85, 379–381
Production house marketers, 43–44, 352–355
Production manager, 361, 364
Program directors and strategies, 80, 277, 357–359, 361–365, 367–368, 371–372, 381, 425, 429, 465
Program salespersons, 347–350, 391, 407, 453. *See also* Syndication
Progressive radio format, 193, 195–196
Promise vs. performance, 141–143
Promos (promotional messages), 289, 300, 313, 326–327, 350–352, 361–362, 465
Promotions people, 350–352, 367, 371, 392
Prophylactic programming, 428
Public broadcasting, 7–8, 15, 51, 242, 250–255, 352, 408, 410, 424–425, 433
Public Broadcasting Act, 250–251, 254
Public Broadcasting Laboratory (PBL), 251
Public Broadcasting Service (PBS), 7–8, 242, 251–255
Public domain, 138–139
Public interest/public trustee concepts, 47, 133–135, 141, 152, 156, 246, 401, 407, 429, 455
Public Law 238, 128
Public relations, 71–77, 289, 309, 327, 346, 353–354, 395, 409–414, 428, 431
Public service announcements (PSAs), 373, 376, 409–410
*Public Service Responsibility of Broadcast Licensees. See* "Blue Book"
Publicists, 76
Publicly held companies, 58, 60, 391
PUR (Persons using radio), 340
Purdue University, 248–249

Q Ratings, 306–308
Quiz show host, 308
Quiz shows, 17, 147–148, 178, 184–185, 209, 214, 308, 335, 364

Rack jobber, 81–82
RADAR (Radio All Dimension Audience Research), 90, 279
Radio Act of 1912, 128, 131–133
Radio Act of 1927, 47, 133, 135, 143, 242, 401
Radio Advertising Bureau (RAB), 71, 191, 291
*Radio and Records,* 362

Radio Bridge, 261, 459
Radio Code. *See* NAB Codes
Radio Corporation of America. *See* RCA
Radio formats, 23–25, 86, 188–198,
    261–262, 277–282, 340, 344,
    347–348, 357–364, 372, 377,
    417, 466
Radio Free Europe/Radio Liberty
    (RFE/RL), 28, 264–266
Radio Group, 172
Radio Marti, 262–264
Radio News Association, 176
Radio Satellite Service (RSS), 452–453
Radio-Television News Directors Associ-
    ation (RTNDA), 454
RadioRadio, 197
*Rags to Riches,* 364
Rate card, 340–342, 353, 365, 425
Rather, Dan, 223
Ratings, 339–341, 347, 351, 358, 364,
    368, 370, 373, 389, 464–465. *See
    also* Audience Measurement
Rau, Michael, 452
RCA, 107–108, 110–111, 115–121, 129–
    130, 132, 134, 136, 139–140,
    172, 201–203, 209, 211, 213,
    230, 232, 256, 445. *See also* NBC
RCA Records, 79–80, 147
Reach (audience), 388, 390
Reagan, Ronald, 157, 254, 260, 264,
    267, 401, 406, 416, 429
Reality programs, 84
Record rotation, 361–362
Recording industry, 13–14, 77–82, 85–
    86, 187, 362, 451
*Red Channels,* 145
*Red Lion Broadcasting Co., Inc. et al.* v.
    *Federal Communications Com-
    mission et al.,* 152
Red network, 139, 171–172, 174, 179
*Red Skelton Show, The,* 187
Reference desk, 431
Religious broadcasting, 134, 181–182,
    184, 225, 241, 249, 257
Renewal, license, 141, 143, 150–151,
    153, 155–156, 159, 197
Rep firms. *See* Station representatives
*Report on Chain Broadcasting,* 139–140
Reporters, 222, 284–290, 294, 308, 325–
    326, 373–375, 377, 409–414,
    431–432, 436
Request Television, 233, 457–458
Reruns, 202–203
Researcher manager, 346–347
Reuters, 178
Rhapsodes, 5
Richards, George, 184
Ridge, Steve, 458
*Right to Happiness,* 191
RKO, 216
RKO Radio Networks, 197
Robertson, Pat, 225
Robinson, Edward G., 145

Robinson, Glen, 404–405
Robotic cameras, 318, 325
Robson, William, 183–184
Rock and roll, 80, 139, 188–189, 191
Rockefeller Foundation, 242
Romania, 459
Roosevelt, Franklin Delano, 118, 135,
    141, 174, 176, 181, 183–184,
    202, 215–216, 256–257
*Roots,* 225–226
*Roseanne,* 378
Rosen, David, 450
Rosing, Boris, 115
Rouman, Jay, 434
Royal, John, 256
Rushes (visual footage), 329
Rydholm, Ralph, 384

Sajak, Pat, 308
Salaries, 280, 296, 308, 349, 354, 367,
    377–378, 386, 393, 422, 428, 467
Sales (time), 37, 54, 61, 172, 187, 228–
    229, 338–347, 350, 358, 365–
    367, 369, 387, 392–393, 422,
    425, 457, 459, 464–465
Sales manager, 228, 344–345, 365–368,
    371, 393, 419
Salzman, David, 83–85, 381
*San Francisco Chronicle,* 288
*San Francisco Examiner,* 287–288
*Santa Barbara,* 459
Sarnoff, David, 58, 104, 117–118, 172,
    202, 213
Satellite NewsChannel, 230
Satellites, 13, 16, 27, 34–35, 40–42, 87,
    120–121, 124–125, 197–198,
    220, 225, 230, 233, 248, 253–
    254, 260–263, 266–269, 325,
    371, 402, 405, 427, 433, 444–
    445, 448–450, 452. *See also* DBS
Scanning disc. *See* Television, mechani-
    cal
SCAs (Subsidiary Communications Au-
    thorizations), 24–25, 51–53, 55,
    112, 189
Scatter market, 343
Scenic designer, 297, 300
Schaefer, George, 304
Schaffner, Franklin, 337
Schmidt, Robert, 40
Schmittdiel, Andrew, 386–387
Schuler, Robert, 134
Scott, Frank, 261–262
Scrambling (signal), 13, 41, 51, 62–64,
    216–217, 230, 232
Screen Actor's Guild, 223, 308
Scriptwriters. *See* Writers, feature
*Second Mrs. Burton, The,* 191
Section 315. *See* "Equal Time"
Securities analysts. *See* Financial ana-
    lysts
*See It Now,* 211, 213. *See also* Murrow,
    Edward R.

Selenium, 113–114
Series development executives, 380–
    381
Serkaian, Stephen, 412–413
SESAC, 313
*Sesame Street,* 251
Sevareid, Eric, 85
Sgriccia, Philip, 330–331
Shane, Ed, 279
Share (of audience), 339–341, 417
Shearer, William, 369–370
Shedd, John Augustus, 460
Shelf space, 61
Shirer, William, 180, 182
Shockley, William, 189
Shortwave stations, 25–28, 30–31, 61,
    141, 183, 256–258, 264–266
Shortwaves, defined, 25–26
Shot transitions, defined, 331–332
Showtime, 225
Siano, Jerry, 291
Siepmann, Charles, 142–143
Sikes, Alfred, 455
Silverman, Fred, 226
Simplex, 189
Simulcasting, 112
Situation comedies, 17, 302–304, 307,
    335–336, 364
Sixth Report and Order, 119, 145
Skiatron Corporation, 209, 211
Sky Cable, 448–450
Sky waves, 26–27, 30
SkyPix, 449
SMATV (Satellite Master Antenna Tele-
    vision), 40–41, 53, 61, 263, 394
Smidt, Clark, 364
Smith, Willoughby, 113
SMPTE time code, 331
Snyder, Jim, 87
Soap operas, 183, 189, 191, 302, 335,
    346, 390, 459
Social heritage, 5
Social process, 3, 5
Society for Motion Picture and Televi-
    sion Engineers (SMPTE), 331,
    442
Sound engineers. *See* Audio engineers
Soviet Union, 264–268, 459
Space brokerage, 69
Spark discharge coherer, 100, 115
Spectrum allocations, 108–109, 111,
    118–119, 131–134, 172–173,
    184, 205, 210, 242–243, 245–
    246, 401, 410–411, 444–445,
    451–452. *See also* Frequencies,
    defined
Spectrum scarcity tenet, 133, 139, 152
Spencer, Susan, 289
Spiegel, Larry, 388, 390
Sports coverage, 61–62, 87, 91, 170,
    175, 203, 205, 225, 230, 233,
    249, 266, 277, 325, 332, 343,
    346, 363, 445, 457–458

Spots. *See* Commercials
Squelch button, 281
Stakelin, Bill, 291
Standards officials, 425, 428–430
Station managers. *See* General managers
Station Program Cooperative (SPC), 252, 255
Station representatives (Reps), 343, 345–347, 386, 391
Steiger, Janet, 454
Stereo broadcasting:
   AM, 23, 94, 96, 198, 404
   FM, 24, 112, 191, 261, 451
Stevens, Gary, 59
"Stick method" (station evaluation), 417
Stiehl, John, 249
Stock analyst. *See* Financial analyst
Stock photography, 432–433
Stokey, Mike, 209
*Stop the Music,* 188
Storyboard, 296–299, 333–334, 353, 381
Storz, Todd, 188
Street, Merrie, 378
Strip programming, 364
Stubblefield, Nathan, 101–103, 111, 170
STV, 62, 209, 216–217, 222, 226, 230, 232, 401, 403, 458
Subscriber drop (cable), 34
Subscription television. *See* STV
Sullivan, Ed, 145. *See also Toast of the Town*
Superstation, 33, 62, 82, 225, 365
Surrogate services, 263–266
Sustaining programs, 176, 178, 243
Swayze, John Cameron, 206
Swing music, 79–80
Sykes, Rick, 374–375
Synchronization rights, 313
Syndex rules, 151, 157, 414
Syndication:
   radio, 10, 173, 197–198, 261, 266, 336–337, 348, 361–362
   television, 82–85, 302, 304, 347–350, 379, 381, 409, 417. *See also* Fin/syn
System manager (cable), 365, 371

Talk show hosts, 281–284, 308
Talk show:
   radio, 13–14, 17, 23, 87, 193, 281–283
   television, 17, 281, 308, 335, 346
Target universe, 388
Tarleton, Robert, 122
Tawail, Joseph, 323
Teachers, 314, 346, 427–428, 433, 438, 464–466
Technical directors, 332–333
Technicians. *See* Engineers
Teleconferencing, 433
Telegraph, 99–100, 171, 405

Telephone, 99–100, 130, 158, 193, 232, 281, 314–315, 346, 375, 405, 446, 448, 449–450, 457
Telephone coincidental, 89–90, 178, 362
Telephone industry, 13, 48–49, 72, 91–94, 96, 108, 130, 159, 402, 408, 450, 456–457
Teletext, 11–12, 447–448, 456
Television:
   electronic, 113, 115–118
   mechanical, 113–117, 119, 122
Television addiction, 222
Television Bureau of Advertising (TvB), 71
Television Code. *See* NAB Codes
Television Decoder Circuitry Act. *See* Decoder Circuitry Act
Television "Freeze," 119, 145, 205, 209–210, 245
Television Information Office (TIO), 214, 393
Telstar, 120
Tentpoling, 364
*Texaco Star Theater,* 207
The Source, 197
Thomson Consumer Electronics, 443
Tiering, 365, 414, 424
Time-shifting, 230–231
Tisch, Laurence, 232
*Titanic,* 104, 128, 160
Tito, Josip, 213
*Toast of the Town,* 211. *See also* Sullivan, Ed
*Today,* 148, 211, 263
Tokyo Rose, 183
Toll broadcasting, 129–130, 172
*Tonight Show,* 212, 339
"Top 40" format, 188, 190, 193
Topicals (promos), 352
Toscanini, Arturo, 178
Tower, Phil, 282–283
Trade-outs, 367–368, 371
Traffic director, 362–365
Traffic function, 228–229, 387, 390
Transatlantic cable, 113
Transistors, 121, 189, 193
Transit advertising, 388
Transit radio, 188–189
Translators (television), 36, 230
Transradio Press Service, 176–178
*Trinity Methodist Church, South* v. *Federal Radio Commission,* 134
Triode, 103, 109. *See also* Audion
Truman, Harry, 209, 258
Turner, Charles, 80
Turner (Ted) Communications, 16, 225, 232, 268. *See also* CNN; WTBS
Tuttle, Valerie, 344–345
*TV Guide,* 308, 312, 367
TV Marti, 263–264
TVRO (Television receive-only dish), 16, 40–41, 62, 233, 263, 446, 457, 459

Twentieth Century Fox Film Corporation, 232, 453
*Twenty-One,* 148

Udwin, Gerald, 409–410
UHF stations, 32–33, 36, 42, 56, 119–120, 158, 211–213, 363, 452
UHF (ultra high frequency) waves, 30–33
Underground radio, 195
Underwriting, 56–57, 254, 425
Unions, electronic media, 470
United Church of Christ Case, 151
United Fruit Company, 102
United Independent Broadcasters, 172. *See also* CBS
United Paramount Theaters, 145–146, 211
United Press International (UPI), 86–87, 174, 178, 196
United Satellite Communications, Inc., 448
United States Department of Commerce, 106–109, 128, 130–133, 173, 410
United States Department of Defense, 442
United States Department of Justice, 411. *See also* Anti-trust issues
United States Department of State, 258–259, 262
*United States et al.* v. *Southwestern Cable Co. et al.,* 152
United States Information Agency (USIA), 259, 262–264, 267
United States Information and Education Exchange Act, 258–259
United States Navy, 104–105, 129
United States Office of Education, 248, 251
*United States* v. *Zenith Radio Corporation et al.,* 132–133
*Universal City Studios, Inc.* v. *Sony Corporation of America,* 231
*University of the Air,* 178–179
Unwired networks, 61, 345
Upfront market, 343
USA network, 15, 225, 341, 343

*Vallee Varieties,* 174
Value-added advertising, 352, 368
Van Doren, Charles, 148
VCR, 63, 121, 123, 230–231, 234, 269, 335, 393, 433, 444–446, 459
Vertical blanking interval (VBI), 55–56, 447
Vertical programming, 364
VH-1, 230
VHF stations, 32–33, 36, 56, 119–120, 213, 363
VHF (very high frequency) waves, 30–32
Viacom, 225

Video cassette recorder. *See* VCR
Video compact disc (VCD), 445–446
Video dialtone service, 456
Video jockey, 280–281
Video store, 10, 12, 64–65, 231, 446
Video switcher, 332
Videographers, 286, 323, 325–328, 373, 377, 458
Videotape, 10, 120–121, 214, 216–217, 247, 281, 323, 328–329, 335–336, 445, 447
Videotext, 448, 456
Vietnam coverage, 220
Viewer's Choice, 233
Violence, in programming, 159, 222–223, 226–227, 406
Visnews, 87
VOA, 28, 31, 141, 257–265, 459
Voice of America. *See* VOA
Voss, Valerie, 290–291

WAAB, 139
WABC, 191
Wagner, Richard, 313
Wallop, Malcolm, 74–76
Walson, John, 122–123
"War of the Worlds," 180–181
Wardrobe artists, 297, 300, 334, 336
Warner, Charles, 61
Washington Radio Conferences, 130–132
Wasilewski, Vincent, 224
Waste circulation, 8, 359, 361, 388
Watergate coverage, 223
Wavelengths, defined, 29–30, 34–35
Wayne, Patti, 326–327
WBZ, 107
WCAU, 174
WCBG, 226–227
WCCO, 26, 193
WDIV, 374–375
WEAF, 108–109, 129–130, 171
WEAO, 243
Weaver, Sylvester ("Pat"), 189, 216–217

Welch, Joseph, 212
Welles, Orson, 145, 180–181
West, Mae, 179–180
Western Union, 119
Westinghouse, 105–108, 116, 129–130, 132, 134, 172, 194, 230, 256, 409–410
Westwood One, 198
WGN, 171, 173, 176, 225, 286–287
WGRC, 457
WHA, 107. *See also* 9XM
*What's My Line?,* 209
WHAZ, 171
WHCT, 216
*Wheel of Fortune,* 308
Wheeler, Burton, 136, 178
Wheeler-Lea Act, 136
Whitehead, Clay, 251–252
Whitmore, Ruth, 395–397
Whittle Communications, 255
Wick, Charles, 263
Wierznski, Gregory, 265–266
Wiley, Richard, 223, 407, 443
Wilson, Hugh, 303–304, 378
Wilson, Woodrow, 128–129
Wire recordings, 184–185
Wire services. *See* News services
Wireless Cable (MMDS), 36, 38–40, 48–49, 51, 53, 56, 61, 127, 230, 233, 249, 365, 394, 403, 408, 455
Wireless Cable Association (WCA), 408
Wireless Ship Act, 127–128, 160
Wireless telegraphy, 100, 104–105, 108–109, 115, 129
Wireless telephony, 103–107, 169–170
Wisconsin, University of, 107, 170, 249
WJAR, 171
WJR, 26, 173, 193
WJZ, 107, 171
WKBD, 351
*WKRP in Cincinnati,* 303–304, 350
WLBT, 151
WLTO, 358–359
WLW, 176, 243

WMAF, 171
WMAQ, 173
WNAS, 245
WNBC, 118. *See also* W2XBS
WNET, 251
Wolters, Larry, 415
Wolzien, Tom, 318
*Wonder Years, The,* 331, 459
WOO, 171
WOOD, 282–283, 342, 366–367
WOR, 130, 176, 193, 209
World Administrative Radio Conference (WARC), 452
Worldnet, 262–263, 267
WPVI, 300
WQED, 247
WRAL, 318
Writer-producers, 303–304, 378–379, 384
Writers, feature, 302–304, 309, 311, 336, 379–381
Writers Guild of America (WGA), 223, 303
WRNO, 257
WTBS, 16, 55, 225. *See also* Turner Communications
W2XBS, 118. *See also* WNBC
W2XMN, 111
WWJ, 107, 344–345. *See also* 8MK
WXYZ, 176–177, 192, 207–208

XTRA, 194

*You Bet Your Life,* 209
Young, Owen, 129
*Young Dr. Malone,* 191
*Your Hit Parade,* 209
*Your Show of Shows,* 207, 209

Zenith Radio Corporation, 112, 118, 132, 191, 205, 209, 211, 442
Zettl, Herbert, 322–323
Zworykin, Vladimir, 115–116, 118

Security Administration photo by John Collin. From Library of Congress; p. 86: The Associated Press; p. 91: John Dimling, Nielsen Media Research; p. 92: Tom Mocarsky, The Arbitron Company; p. 99: Clarke Historical Library, Central Michigan University; p. 101: Professors Ray Mofield and L. J. Hortin; p. 103: Susan Hill, NAB Library; p. 106: Westinghouse and Susan Hill, NAB Library; p. 107: *The Detroit News*, A Gannett Newspaper; p. 108: Susan Hill, NAB Library; p. 111: The Bettmann Archive; p. 113: Siemens Corporation; pp. 116, 117: AT&T Archives; p. 121: Clarke Historical Library, Central Michigan University; p. 123: Hoyt D. Walter, Service Electric Cable TV, Inc.; p. 125: GTE Spacenet Corporation; p. 127: Neil J. Kirby; p. 128: The Bettmann Archive; p. 131: Jim Steinblatt, ASCAP; p. 137: National Archives photo no. 306–NT–313 A–18; p. 138: Burt Korall, BMI; p. 140: *Broadcasting* Magazine; p. 144: CBS, Inc.; p. 147: University of Cincinnati Information Services; pp. 148, 149: *Broadcasting* Magazine; p. 169: Peter B. Orlik; p. 170: *The Detroit News*, A Gannett Newspaper; p. 173: Susan Hill, NAB Library; p. 176: The Bettmann Archive; p. 177: "WYXIE Wonderland" by Dick Osgood; p. 180: *Broadcasting* Magazine; p. 181: CBS, Inc.; p. 182: WJR and Clarke Historical Library, Central Michigan University; p. 186: 3M Corporation; p. 192: "WYXIE Wonderland" by Dick Osgood; p. 195: Dick Kernen; p. 201: Clarke Historical Library, Central Michigan University; p. 202: The National Broadcasting Company, Inc.; p. 204: Susan Hill, NAB Library; p. 206: *Broadcasting* Magazine; p. 208: Detroit Free Press photo 12–11–52; p. 210: The National Broadcasting Company, Inc.; p. 212: Susan Hill, NAB Library; p. 215: *Broadcasting* Magazine; pp. 218–219: Len Sternbach, Levine, Huntley, Schmidt and Beaver, Inc. Advertising, Art Director/Copywriter Team: Ernest Neira and Ryan Ng; p. 221: *Broadcasting* Magazine; p. 224 top: Susan Hill, NAB Library; p. 226: C-SPAN; p. 227: Neil Evans, Lindsay Specialty Products; p. 233: Copyright 1988 United Artists Cablesystems Corporation. United Artists Cable; p. 241: Steve Haworth, CNN; pp. 243, 244: State of Ohio Department of Education; p. 246: *Broadcasting* Magazine; p. 248: Reprinted with permission of the Purdue University Libraries, Special Collections, West Lafayette, Indiana 47907; p. 250: Clarke Historical Library, Central Michigan University; p. 256: The National Broadcasting Company, Inc.; p. 259: Frank Cummins, VOA; p. 260: John Stevens, VOA; p. 268: Steve Haworth, CNN; p. 277: Fred Phipps, Canadian Broadcasting Corporation; p. 285: Neil J. Kirby; pp. 298–299: David Wozniak, NW Ayer Inc.; p. 300 top: Austin Hale, KYYK/KNET; p. 300 bottom: James Denney, WPVI-TV; pp. 306, 307: Carol Heller, Marketing Evaluations, Inc.; p. 311: Used by permission. Concept: Larry Hover. Copyright 1990 Sony Video Institute; p. 317: © Alan Carey/The Image Works; pp. 318, 322: Neil J. Kirby; p. 324: Thomas F. Steiner, Wesley-Jessen Corporation; p. 328: Ted Kendrick, ENG Mobile Systems, Inc.; p. 342: Paul Boscarino, WOOD Radio; p. 357: Robert Barclay, Central Michigan University; p. 360: Tom Mocarsky, The Arbitron Company; p. 376: Public service announcement created by Lowe Marschalk, Inc., on behalf of the Society of Professional Journalists/Sigma Delta Chi, working with the Ad Council. Writer: Pat Sutula; Art Director: Barbara Simon; p. 400: Federal Communications Commission; p. 426: Roberta Drummond, Siddall Matus & Coughter Inc.; p. 430: Gary Lico, Columbia Pictures Television; p. 441: © Ulrike Welsch/Photo Edit; p. 443: Reproduced by permission of Thames PLC (U.K.); p. 444: David Sarnoff Research Center; p. 449: Hughes Communications, Inc.; p. 458: Barbara Piscitelli, Group W Satellite Communications; p. 460: Library of Congress; p. 463: Neil J. Kirby; p. 464: Fred Jacobs.